Economic Report
of the President

Transmitted to the Congress
February 1995

TOGETHER WITH
THE ANNUAL REPORT
OF THE
COUNCIL OF ECONOMIC ADVISERS

UNITED STATES GOVERNMENT PRINTING OFFICE

WASHINGTON : 1995

For sale by the U.S. Government Printing Office
Superintendent of Documents, Mail Stop: SSOP, Washington, DC 20402-9328
ISBN 0-16-045414-X

CONTENTS

*For a detailed table of contents of the Council's Report, see page 13.

(iii)

ECONOMIC REPORT
OF THE PRESIDENT

ECONOMIC REPORT OF THE PRESIDENT

To the Congress of the United States:

Two years ago I took office determined to improve the lives of average American families. I proposed, and the Congress enacted, a new economic strategy to restore the American dream. Two years later, that strategy has begun to pay off.

Together we have created an environment in which America's private sector has been able to produce more than 5 million new jobs. Manufacturing employment grew during each month of 1994—the first time that has happened since 1978. We have cut the deficit in the Federal budget for 3 years running, we have kept inflation in check, and, based on actions I have already taken, the Federal bureaucracy will soon be the smallest it has been in more than 3 decades. We have opened up more new trade opportunities in just 2 years than in any similar period in a generation. And we have embarked on a new partnership with American industry to prepare the American people to compete and win in the new global economy.

In short, America's economic prospects have improved considerably in the last 2 years. And the economy will continue to move forward in 1995, with rising output, falling deficits, and increasing employment. Today there is no country in the world with an economy as strong as ours, as full of opportunity, as full of hope.

Still, living standards for many Americans have not improved as the economy has expanded. For the last 15 years, those Americans with the most education and the greatest flexibility to seek new opportunities have seen their incomes grow. But the rest of our work force have seen their incomes either stagnate or fall. An America that, in our finest moments, has always grown together, now grows apart.

I am resolved to keep the American dream alive in this new economy. We must make it possible for the American people to invest in the education of their children and in their own training and skills. This is the essence of the New Covenant I have called for—economic opportunity provided in return for people assuming personal responsibility. This is the commitment my Administration made to the American people 2 years ago, and it remains our commitment to them today.

The Administration's Economic Strategy

Our economic strategy has been straightforward. First, we have pursued deficit reduction to increase the share of the Nation's economic resources available for private investment. At the same time we have reoriented the government's public investment portfolio with an eye toward preparing our people and our economy for the 21st century. We have cut yesterday's government to help solve tomorrow's problems, shrinking departments, cutting unnecessary regulations, and ending programs that have outlived their usefulness. We have also worked to expand trade and to boost American sales to foreign markets, so that the American people can enjoy the better jobs and higher wages that should result from their own high-quality, high-productivity labor. Having fixed the fundamentals, we are now proposing what I call the Middle Class Bill of Rights, an effort to build on the progress we have made in controlling the deficit while providing tax relief that is focused on the people who need it most.

Putting Our Own House in Order

The first task my Administration faced upon taking office in January 1993 was to put our own economic house in order. For more than a decade, the Federal Government had spent much more than it took in, borrowing the difference. As a consequence, by 1992 the Federal deficit had increased to 4.9 percent of gross domestic product—and our country had gone from being the world's largest creditor Nation to being its largest debtor.

As a result of my Administration's deficit reduction package, passed and signed into law in August 1993, the deficit in fiscal 1994 was $50 billion lower than it had been the previous year. In fact, it was about $100 billion lower than had been forecast before our budget plan was enacted. Between fiscal 1993 and fiscal 1998, our budget plan will reduce the deficit by $616 billion. Our fiscal 1996 budget proposal includes an additional $81 billion in deficit reduction through fiscal 2000.

Preparing the American People to Compete and Win

As we were taking the necessary steps to restore fiscal discipline to the Federal Government, we were also working to reorient the government's investment portfolio to prepare our people and our economy for 21st-century competition.

Training and Education. In our new information-age economy, learning must become a way of life. Learning begins in childhood, and the opportunity to learn must be available to every American child—that is why we have worked hard to expand Head Start.

With the enactment of Goals 2000 we have established world-class standards for our Nation's schools. Through the School-to-

4

Work Opportunities Act we have created new partnerships with schools and businesses to make sure that young people make a successful transition to the world of work. We have also dramatically reformed the college loan program. Americans who aspire to a college degree need no longer fear that taking out a student loan will one day leave them overburdened by debt.

Finally, we are proposing to take the billions of dollars that the government now spends on dozens of training programs and make that money directly available to working Americans. We want to leave it up to *them* to decide what new skills they need to learn— and when—to get a new or better job.

New Technology. Technological innovation is the engine driving the new global economy. This Administration is committed to fostering innovation in the private sector. We have reoriented the Federal Government's investment portfolio to support fundamental science and industry-led technology partnerships, the rapid deployment and commercialization of civilian technologies, and funding for technology infrastructure in transportation, communications, and manufacturing.

A Middle Class Bill of Rights. Fifty years ago the GI Bill of Rights helped transform an economy geared for war into one of the most successful peacetime economies in history. Today, after a peaceful resolution of the cold war, middle-class Americans have a right to move into the 21st century with the same opportunity to achieve the American dream.

People ought to be able to deduct the cost of education and training after high school from their taxable incomes. If a family makes less than $120,000 a year, the tuition that family pays for college, community college, graduate school, professional school, vocational education, or worker training should be fully deductible, up to $10,000 a year. If a family makes $75,000 a year or less, that family should receive a tax cut, up to $500, for every child under the age of 13. If a family makes less than $100,000 a year, that family should be able to put $2,000 a year, tax free, into an individual retirement account from which it can withdraw, tax free, money to pay for education, health care, a first home, or the care of an elderly parent.

Expanding Opportunity at Home Through Free and Fair Trade

Our efforts to prepare the American people to compete and win in the new global economy cannot succeed unless we succeed in expanding trade and boosting exports of American products and services to the rest of the world. That is why we have worked so hard to create the global opportunities that will lead to more and better jobs at home. We won the fight for the North American Free Trade Agreement (NAFTA) and the Uruguay Round of the General Agreement on Tariffs and Trade (GATT).

5

Our commitment to free and fair trade goes beyond NAFTA and the GATT. Last December's Summit of the Americas set the stage for open markets throughout the Western Hemisphere. The Asia-Pacific Economic Cooperation (APEC) group is working to expand investment and sales opportunities in the Far East. We firmly believe that economic expansion and a rising standard of living will result in both regions, and the United States is well positioned both economically and geographically to participate in those benefits.

This Administration has also worked to promote American products and services to overseas customers. When foreign government contracts have been at stake, we have made sure that our exporters had an equal chance. Billions of dollars in new export sales have been the result, from Latin America to Asia. And these sales have created and safeguarded tens of thousands of American jobs.

Health Care and Welfare Reform: The Unfinished Agenda

In this era of rapid change, Americans must be able to embrace new economic opportunities without sacrificing their personal economic security. My Administration remains committed to providing health insurance coverage for every American and containing health care costs for families, businesses, and governments. The Congress can and should take the first steps toward achieving these goals. I have asked the Congress to work with me to reform the health insurance market, to make coverage affordable for and available to children, to help workers who lose their jobs keep their health insurance, to level the playing field for the self-employed by giving them the same tax treatment as other businesses, and to help families provide long-term care for a sick parent or a disabled child. We simply must make health care coverage more secure and more affordable for America's working families and their children.

This should also be the year that we work together to end welfare as we know it. We have already helped to boost the earning power of 15 million low-income families who work by expanding the earned income tax credit. With a more robust economy, many more American families should also be able to escape dependence on welfare. Indeed, we want to make sure that people can move from welfare to work by giving them the tools they need to return to the economic mainstream. Reform must include steps to prevent the conditions that lead to welfare dependency, such as teen pregnancy and poor education, while also helping low-income parents find jobs with wages high enough to lift their families out of poverty. At the same time, we must ensure that welfare reform does not increase the Federal deficit, and that the States retain the flexibility they need to experiment with innovative programs that aim to increase self-sufficiency. But we must also ensure that our reform does not

6

punish people for being poor and does not punish children for the mistakes of their parents.

Reinventing Government

Taking power away from Federal bureaucracies and giving it back to communities and individuals is something everyone should be able to support. We need to get government closer to the people it is meant to serve. But as we continue to reinvent the Federal Government by cutting regulations and departments, and moving programs to the States and communities where citizens in the private sector can do a better job, let us not overlook the benefits that have come from national action in the national interest: safer foods for our families, safer toys for our children, safer nursing homes for our elderly parents, safer cars and highways, and safer workplaces, cleaner air and cleaner water. We can provide more flexibility to the States while continuing to protect the national interest and to give relief where it is needed.

The New Covenant approach to governing unites us behind a common vision of what is best for our country. It seeks to shift resources and decisionmaking from bureaucrats to citizens, injecting choice and competition and individual responsibility into national policy. In the second round of reinventing government, we propose to cut $130 billion in spending by streamlining departments, extending our freeze on domestic spending, cutting 60 public housing programs down to 3, and getting rid of over 100 programs we do not need. Our job here is to expand opportunity, not bureaucracy— to empower people to make the most of their own lives. Government should be leaner, not meaner.

The Economic Outlook

As 1995 begins, our economy is in many ways as strong as it has ever been. Growth in 1994 was robust, powered by strong investment spending, and the unemployment rate fell by more than a full percentage point. Exports soared, consumer confidence rebounded, and Federal discretionary spending as a percentage of gross domestic product hit a 30-year low. Consumer spending should remain healthy and investment spending will remain strong through 1995. The Administration forecasts that the economy will continue to grow in 1995 and that we will remain on track to create 8 million jobs over 4 years.

We know, nevertheless, that there is a lot more to be done. More than half the adult work force in America is working harder today for lower wages than they were making 10 years ago. Millions of Americans worry about their health insurance and whether their retirement is still secure. While maintaining our momentum toward deficit reduction, increased exports, essential public investments, and a government that works better and costs less, we are

7

committed to providing tax relief for the middle-class Americans who need it the most, for the investments they most need to make.

We live in an increasingly global economy in which people, products, ideas, and money travel across national borders at lightning speed. During the last 2 years, we have worked hard to help our workers take advantage of this new economy. We have worked to put our own economic house in order, to expand opportunities for education and training, and to expand the frontiers of free and fair trade. Our goal is to create an economy in which all Americans have a chance to develop their talents, have access to better jobs and higher incomes, and have the capacity to build the kind of life for themselves and their children that is the heart of the American dream.

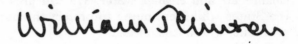

THE WHITE HOUSE
    FEBRUARY 13, 1995

THE ANNUAL REPORT
OF THE
COUNCIL OF ECONOMIC ADVISERS

LETTER OF TRANSMITTAL

COUNCIL OF ECONOMIC ADVISERS,
Washington, D.C., February 3, 1995.

MR. PRESIDENT:

The Council of Economic Advisers herewith submits its 1994 Annual Report in accordance with the provisions of the Employment Act of 1946 as amended by the Full Employment and Balanced Growth Act of 1978.

Sincerely,

Laura D'Andrea Tyson
Chair

Joseph E. Stiglitz
Member

Martin N. Baily
Member-Nominee

CONTENTS

LIST OF BOXES

CHAPTER 1

Implementing a National Economic Strategy

BY MOST STANDARD MACROECONOMIC INDICATORS, the performance of the U.S. economy in 1994 was, in a word, outstanding. The economy has not enjoyed such a healthy expansion of strong growth and modest inflation in more than a generation.

Growth in 1994 was robust, fueled by strong investment spending. Nonfarm payroll employment grew by 3.5 million jobs, the largest annual increase in a decade, and the unemployment rate fell by more than a full percentage point, to 5.4 percent. Buoyed by improving job prospects and growing incomes, consumer sentiment hit a 5-year high, and retail sales expanded at their fastest pace in a decade. Yet despite growing demand both at home and abroad, inflation remained modest and stable. The core rate of consumer price inflation (which removes the effects of volatile food and energy prices) registered its smallest increase in 28 years. And the Federal deficit declined by more than $50 billion, as the ratio of Federal discretionary spending to gross domestic product (GDP) fell to its lowest level in 30 years.

The economy's performance in 1994 is even more remarkable when viewed against the backdrop of the economic challenges confronting the Nation around the time this Administration took office. Then the economy seemed mired in a slow and erratic recovery from the 1990–91 recession, business and consumer confidence was low, and the unemployment rate was over 7 percent. Between 1989 and 1992 the Federal deficit had jumped by $137.9 billion, to 4.9 percent of GDP, and even larger deficits were looming on the horizon. To make matters worse, the problems of anemic recovery and mounting deficits were superimposed on some disturbing long-term trends: a 20-year slowdown in productivity growth, a 20-year stagnation in real median family incomes, and a 20-year decline in real compensation levels for many American workers. For an increasing number of these workers and their families, the dream of rising incomes and prosperity appeared to be fading away under the pressures of rapid technological shifts and a changing global economy.

This Administration moved quickly and decisively to improve the economic situation, and the turnaround in macroeconomic performance has been dramatic. The deficit has declined sharply, the economy has grown at a more rapid and even pace, and more and more Americans are participating in the Nation's economic expansion. At the same time, the Administration has acted to help reverse the long-term trends that continue to depress the incomes of many Americans. That, however, will take time: problems that were 20 years in the making cannot be solved in the course of 2 years. But the Administration's economic policies have begun to move the Nation in the direction necessary to again place the American dream within the grasp of all Americans.

This chapter describes the Administration's strategy for reviving economic growth and job creation, preparing American workers for the challenges and opportunities of changing technology and a global economy, opening foreign markets, and restructuring the Federal Government for greater efficiency and effectiveness. The chapter also provides an overview of three major policy initiatives—middle-class tax relief, welfare reform, and health care reform—that the Administration plans for the coming year. The remaining chapters of this *Report* examine both the accomplishments of the past year and the outlook for the future in greater detail.

THE ADMINISTRATION'S ECONOMIC STRATEGY: A MIDTERM REPORT

This Administration entered office at a time of sluggish economic recovery, mounting fiscal deficits, disappointing income growth, and growing income inequality and poverty. The first challenge was to get the Nation's fiscal house in order after more than a decade of fiscal profligacy. One of the most fundamental lessons of economic history is that sustained economic expansion depends on sound fiscal foundations. Therefore the linchpin of the Administration's economic strategy was and remains a deficit reduction plan that is balanced and gradual, yet large enough to be credible and to have a significant and sustained effect on the course of the deficit over time.

A second defining component of the strategy is a set of policies to help American workers and businesses realize the opportunities that flow from rapid changes in technology and an increasingly global economy. The common theme of these policies is investment, public and private: on the public side, a shift in government spending away from current consumption and toward investment in children, education and training, science and technology, and infrastructure; on the private side, tax incentives to encourage investment by businesses and individuals in physical, scientific, and human resources. A logical implication of these policies is that government must not only spend less—it must also spend better, by focusing more of its resources on the Nation's future.

A third component of the Administration's economic strategy is tax relief for working families who have seen their incomes stagnate or decline over the past 15 to 20 years. The dimensions of the family income problem are compelling. The real median family income in 1993, the last year for which complete data are available, was virtually unchanged from what it had been in 1973, despite the fact that during the intervening 20 years real output had increased by 57 percent.

The stagnation of real median family income has been accompanied by an equally disturbing trend of increasing income inequality. In contrast to the years from 1950 to 1973, when average real family incomes increased across the entire income distribution, between 1973 and 1993 the share of total family income declined for the lower 80 percent of the income distribution (Chart 1-1). Meanwhile, at the bottom of the income distribution, the number of Americans living in poverty hit a 30-year high in 1993 of 39.3 million, 40 percent of them children.

Chart 1-1 **Share of Aggregate Family Income by Quintile**
Between 1973 and 1993, the share of money income received by the 20 percent of families with the highest incomes rose substantially. The shares for all other quintiles fell.

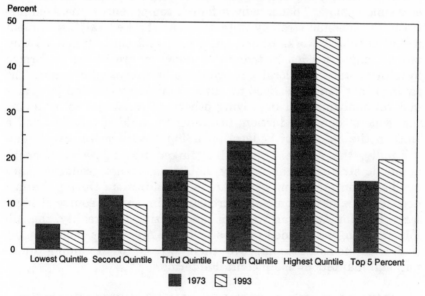

Source: Department of Commerce.

Although not all of the forces behind the rise in income inequality are understood, most economists agree that changes in technology that have reduced the demand for workers with relatively low levels of skill and education have played a major role. This insight lies behind the Administration's efforts to help Americans attain the skills and training they need for today's high-paying jobs through changes in both government spending priorities and tax policies.

The Administration's first response to the dwindling income prospects of many working Americans took the form of a substantial expansion of the earned income tax credit (EITC). The EITC expansion, included in the Omnibus Budget Reconciliation Act of 1993 (OBRA93), increased the after-tax incomes of over 15 million American workers and their families. The EITC is a refundable tax credit that provides a bonus to eligible low-income workers—a bonus that can amount to over $3,000 a year for a family with two children. Through the EITC these workers may realize after-tax incomes well in excess of their wages.

At the end of 1994 the President proposed a package of additional tax cuts that will extend tax relief to middle-class American families, to help them meet the costs of raising their children, acquire more education and training, and save for a variety of purposes. These proposed tax cuts reflect the much-improved outlook for the fiscal deficit, which allows the President to deliver on his campaign promise of tax relief for the middle class.

The Federal Government, too, must respond to the demands of economic change. That is why a fourth component of the Administration's economic strategy is to reinvent the Federal Government itself, so that it works better, costs less, and sheds functions that are no longer needed in today's economy or are better performed by either State and local governments or the private sector. The savings that can be realized by eliminating some existing programs and rationalizing and improving others are essential to achieving the goals of deficit reduction, tax relief to working families, and a shift in the balance of Federal spending toward more investment.

Finally, the Administration has linked its ambitious domestic economic strategy to an equally ambitious foreign economic strategy based on promoting global trade liberalization. During the last decade trade has become an increasingly important source of high-wage jobs for American workers. Recognizing this reality, the Administration has wedded policies to make Americans more productive with policies to improve their access to expanding international markets on more equitable terms.

TOWARD FULL EMPLOYMENT WITH FISCAL RESPONSIBILITY

In early 1993, the Administration faced the challenge of ensuring that the economic recovery from the 1990–91 recession would gain strength and return the economy to full utilization of its resources. At the same time it was vital that this be accomplished in a sound and balanced way, to avoid an acceleration of inflationary pressures. As the preceding discussion indicates and as Chapter 2 delineates in greater detail, this challenge was met in 1994.

In part as a result of the Administration's 1993 budget package, the Nation's fiscal environment today is sounder than it was during the preceding 14 years. Federal Government purchases of goods and services declined in real terms, and the Federal deficit in fiscal 1994 was more than $50 billion lower than in fiscal 1993 and about $100 billion lower than what had been forecast before the enactment of OBRA93. Excluding interest payments on the debt incurred by previous Administrations, the Federal budget in fiscal 1994 was essentially balanced, and the Federal debt outstanding, which had nearly quadrupled between 1981 and 1992, had begun to stabilize relative to the size of the economy. Moreover, as Charts 1–2 and 1–3 indicate, the Administration's deficit reduction measures—along with welcome slowdowns in projected medicare and medicaid spending—have significantly improved the long-run deficit and debt outlook.

Chart 1–2 shows the Federal deficit as a percentage of GDP for fiscal 1993–98 as projected in April 1993, prior to the passage of OBRA93. The deficit was then expected to be around 5.0 percent of GDP in 1993, falling to a low of 4.1 percent in 1996 before rising again to 4.9 percent of GDP by 1998. The chart contrasts these gloomy predictions with the actual deficits for 1993 and 1994 and the projected deficits for 1995–2000 based on OBRA93, the Administration's fiscal 1996 budget proposal, and its current economic forecast. The actual deficit in 1993 was only 4.1 percent of GDP, thanks to the stronger than expected economic recovery and lower than expected interest rates. In 1994 the deficit fell to $203.2 billion, or 3.1 percent of GDP, and in 1998 it is slated to fall to 2.4 percent of GDP, the lowest level since 1979. Over the entire 1994–2000 period the deficit is forecast to average about 2.5 percent of GDP, well below the levels that would have been reached in the absence of OBRA93 and nearly 2 percentage points less than the 1982–93 average of 4.4 percent. Chart 1–3 shows that the debt-GDP ratio is also expected to be stable through the end of the decade.

The effects of the Administration's budget plan on economic performance were in line with its predictions—and completely at odds with the gloomy prognostications of its critics. A dramatic decline in long-term interest rates in 1993, occasioned in part by market expectations of a significant long-term reduction in government borrowing needs, fostered strong growth in interest-sensitive investment and consumption spending. As business expectations improved, new job creation picked up pace, and the growth in incomes in turn reinforced consumer spending, creating the kind of virtuous

23

Chart 1-2 Federal Budget Deficits With and Without Deficit Reduction
Budget deficits would have remained quite large relative to the size of the economy without
deficit reduction initiatives. Instead, deficits have fallen sharply.

Percent of GDP

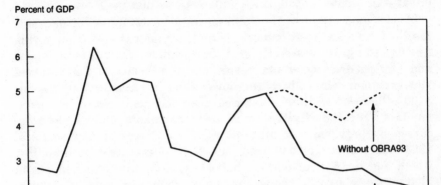

Source: Office of Management and Budget.

Chart 1-3 Publicly Held Federal Debt With and Without Deficit Reduction
Federal indebtedness as a percent of GDP is expected to remain approximately constant
through 2000 under OBRA93 and the Administration's 1996 budget proposal.

Percent of GDP

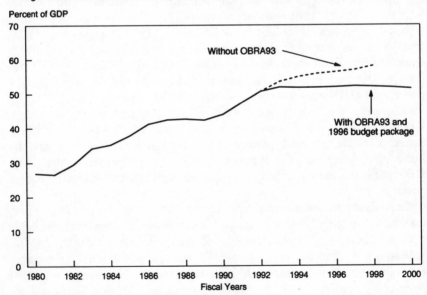

Source: Office of Management and Budget.

24

cycle of employment, income, and spending growth that is the hall-mark of periods of robust expansion. The acceleration of growth around the world, coupled with the Administration's strong leadership in expanding world trade, added to the momentum by encouraging American companies to invest in greater capacity to serve growing global markets.

As the economy expanded, the Federal Reserve raised interest rates several times, tightening the stance of monetary policy in an effort to prevent inflation from accelerating. The increase in short-term interest rates resulting from Federal Reserve actions was substantial. Long-term rates also increased significantly during the year, and the flattening of the yield curve (which plots rates of interest for debt of all maturities prevailing at a given time) that most economic forecasters had predicted failed to materialize. Although the causes of the rise in long-term rates continue to be debated, the analysis in Chapter 2 suggests that it was largely the result of a strong economy and reflected an increase in the demand for capital, as businesses and households increased their borrowing to invest in durable goods and structures both at home and around the world. Despite this increase, however, long-term interest rates remained lower than they would have been if the government's voracious borrowing needs had not been curbed by the enactment of the Administration's deficit reduction program.

ENHANCING THE ECONOMY'S LONG-RUN GROWTH POTENTIAL

Chapter 3 analyzes the sources of long-term growth in the economy and confirms a simple but powerful proposition: the rate of growth of productivity is the most important determinant of how fast the economy can grow and how much living standards can rise over time. What happens when productivity growth slows? Chart 1–4 shows that growth in both real compensation per hour and real median family income slowed markedly in the early 1970s. This is precisely the period when productivity growth also slowed, from an annual average rate of 3.1 percent between 1947 and 1973 to an average of just 1.1 percent in the two decades since. This slowdown shows up not only in the economic statistics, but also in the lives of many Americans who know that they are working harder for less. (Productivity growth is measured here using fixed-weight data. An alternative measure using chain-weighted data is presented in Chapter 3. See Box 3–1 for a more detailed discussion. Although the two measures differ somewhat, both show a similar post-1972 slowdown in productivity growth.)

Although economists do not completely understand all the determinants of productivity growth, it is known that increases in physical, human, and technological capital play a key role. This insight

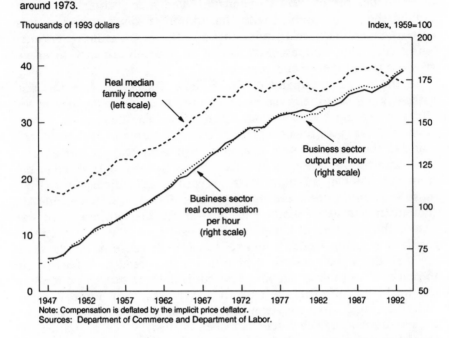

Thousands of 1993 dollars
Index, 1959=100

Note: Compensation is deflated by the implicit price deflator.
Sources: Department of Commerce and Department of Labor.

has shaped the Administration's economic strategy from the beginning. The link between real productivity growth and the rate of investment in the Nation's capital stock is straightforward: investment in physical capital and new technology equips workers with more and better capital; workers so equipped are more productive. Investment in skills and training also adds to productivity by allowing workers to utilize physical capital more effectively. And more-productive workers tend to earn higher real wages. Few propositions in economics are as well documented as these or command as much support among professional economists, whatever their political persuasion.

DEFICIT REDUCTION AND INVESTMENT

A primary economic reason for reducing the Federal deficit is to increase national saving, in the expectation that increased saving will in turn increase national investment in physical capital (Box 1–1). As Chart 1–5 shows, investment rates and productivity growth rates correlate highly across countries. National saving rates and national investment rates also correlate highly across countries, despite the increasing globalization of world financial markets. The implication is that increased national saving should be associated with increased productivity.

Box 1–1.—The Economic Rationales for Deficit Reduction

Perhaps the most important reason for reducing the Federal budget deficit is to increase national saving. A higher rate of saving cuts the cost and increases the availability of capital for private borrowers and reduces the need for the United States to borrow from the rest of the world. The personal saving rate in the United States has been too low to cover both private investment needs and the combined borrowing needs of all levels of government. As a result, the Nation has borrowed massively from the rest of the world, running a persistent surplus in its international capital account. Since the capital and current accounts must balance under floating exchange rates, the mirror image of this capital account surplus has been an equally large current account deficit.

Demographics are likely to exacerbate the problem of insufficient national saving in the first half of the next century. As the U.S. population ages, the payment of federally sponsored retirement and health benefits will place increasing burdens on the budget. Absent an increase in private saving, larger government deficits will mean diminished resources for private investment and a further increase in borrowing from the rest of the world. However, since many countries will be facing similar demographic pressures, the United States is likely to find itself competing with them for worldwide saving to cover its borrowing needs.

A second reason for reducing the deficit is to reduce the debt burden that the present generation will bequeath to future generations. Gross Federal debt per capita—a debt that every American is saddled with at birth—is approaching $20,000. This legacy of debt is a real concern, yet it is important not to overstate the problem or to use it as an excuse to skimp on public investment. We also bequeath to future generations a stock of physical capital—highways, airports, and the like—as well as a stock of human capital and technological knowledge. Because these add importantly to future generations' productivity and well-being, these assets will somewhat reduce their debt burden.

A third reason is that a large deficit hamstrings discretionary fiscal policy as a tool of macroeconomic stabilization. In the presence of a looming deficit, it is difficult for the Federal Government to respond to cyclical slowdowns by cutting taxes or increasing spending. A gradual policy of reducing deficits can build a cushion in case the Federal Government needs to engage in countercyclical fiscal policy sometime in the future.

Chart 1-5 · **Investment and Productivity**
There is a close correlation between investment rates and productivity growth
rates across industrialized countries.

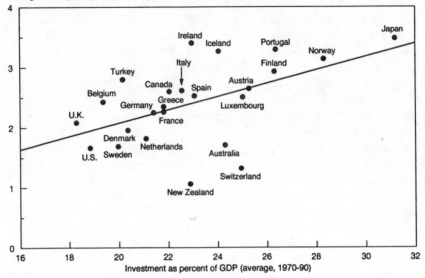

Average annual per capita real GDP growth rate, 1970-90 (percent)

Investment as percent of GDP (average, 1970-90)

Source: International Monetary Fund.

According to this reasoning, deficit reduction is not an end in itself but a means to the end of greater national investment and higher living standards. This logic has three important corollaries.

First, bringing the Federal deficit down is only one step toward a more productive and prosperous future. That is why, in addition to measures to reduce the deficit, the Administration's 1993 budget package contained several new proposals to encourage private investment, including an increase in the amount of equipment that small businesses may deduct immediately in computing their income tax liability, a targeted reduction in capital gains tax rates on long-term equity investments in certain small businesses, and needed public investments. The President's 1996 budget plan builds on these priorities, holding the line on the deficit, cutting outdated government programs while investing in new and existing ones, and offering a package of new middle-class tax incentives.

Second, squeezing worthwhile public investments out of the budget is the wrong way to reduce the deficit. America needs more of both public and private investment, not a swap of one for the other. That is why the Administration seeks not only to constrain total government spending but also to reorient it more toward the future. Between fiscal 1993 and fiscal 1996, overall discretionary government spending is expected to remain nearly unchanged in nominal terms (and fall by more than 6 percent in real terms). At the same time, discretionary spending on the Administration's public investment programs in such vital areas as education and training, technology support, public health, and infrastructure increases by over $24 billion. Over this short time period, investment programs will increase from 11.5 percent to 15.5 percent of total discretionary spending.

Third, because deficit reduction—whether accomplished through increases in revenues or decreases in spending—has a direct contractionary effect on aggregate spending, there are limits to the amount of deficit reduction the economy can be expected to withstand within a short period without endangering economic growth. Over the long run, deficit reduction makes room for additional private investment, but in the short run it depresses aggregate demand and as a result can actually depress private investment. If long-term interest rates do not decline sufficiently fast and far to replace the aggregate demand lost through deficit reduction, economic growth will slow, and this will discourage private investment. The policy challenge is to bring the deficit down gradually and credibly, so as to increase national saving and investment, but not so rapidly as to threaten continued economic expansion. This challenge was met in 1994, and the Administration's economic forecast indicates that it will continue to be met through the remainder of this decade. The success to date in meeting this challenge is one reason why the Administration opposes a balanced budget amendment to the Constitution (Box 1-2).

INVESTING IN SKILLS AND EDUCATION

Education and training—investments in human capital—are a wellspring of human progress, a basic foundation of the country's long-run growth potential and its long-run viability as a democracy, and the ladder of opportunity for all of its citizens (Box 1-3). As already noted and as analyzed in considerable detail in Chapter 5, today's high-paying job opportunities demand increasing levels of education and training. In part as a result of rapid changes in technology and the global economy, the real average annual earnings of male high school graduates declined by 15 percent between 1979 and 1992. In 1992 the annual average earnings of a male college graduate were 64 percent higher than the average annual earnings of a male high school graduate; in 1979 the difference had been only 43 percent (Chart 1-6).

The Administration is embarked on an ambitious agenda to improve the education and training prospects for all Americans, and with support in the Congress it has achieved considerable success on this agenda during the last 2 years. The Administration is committed to ensuring that at every stage of life—preschool, elementary school, secondary school, college, and in the work force—all

29

Box 1-2.—The Shortcomings of a Balanced Budget Amendment

Continued progress on reducing the Federal budget deficit is sound economics; a constitutional amendment requiring annual balance of the Federal budget is not.

The fallacy in the logic of the balanced budget amendment lies in the premise that the size of the Federal deficit is purely the result of deliberate policy decisions. In reality, the pace of economic activity also plays an important role. An economic slowdown automatically depresses tax revenues and increases government spending on such cyclically sensitive programs as unemployment compensation and food stamps. As a result, the deficit automatically worsens when the economy goes into recessions, and these temporary increases in the deficit act as "automatic stabilizers," quickly offsetting some of the reduction in the purchasing power of the private sector.

A balanced budget amendment would throw the automatic stabilizers into reverse. The Congress would be required to raise taxes or cut spending programs in the face of a recession, to counteract temporary increases in the deficit. Rather than moderate the normal ups and downs of the business cycle, fiscal policy would be forced to aggravate them.

Under a balanced budget amendment, monetary policy would become the only tool available to stabilize the economy. But there are several reasons why the Federal Reserve on its own would not be able to moderate the business cycle as well as it can in concert with the automatic fiscal stabilizers. First, monetary policy affects the economy only indirectly and with long lags, making it difficult to time the desired effects with precision. Second, the Fed could become handcuffed in the event of a major recession, its scope for action limited by the fact that it can push short-term interest rates no lower than zero, and probably not even that low in practice. Third, the more aggressive interest rate movements required to limit the cyclical variability of output and employment could actually increase the volatility of financial markets—something the Fed would probably try to avoid.

The role that fiscal policy can play in smoothing fluctuations in the business cycle is one of the great discoveries of modern economics. Unfortunately, the huge deficits inherited from the last decade have made discretionary changes in fiscal policy in response to the business cycle all but impossible. A balanced budget amendment would eliminate the automatic stabilizers as well, thus completely removing fiscal policy from the macroeconomic policy arsenal.

Box 1–3.—The Relationship Between Poverty, Education, and Earnings

Our core democratic values affirm that each individual should have the opportunity to reach his or her full potential, regardless of race or the income or educational attainment of his or her parents. Yet numerous studies confirm that our Nation today is far from reaching this ideal. That shortfall imposes great costs both on individual Americans and on the country as a whole.

A recent study by a group of economists chaired by a Nobel laureate and commissioned by the Children's Defense Fund examined the effects of childhood poverty on an individual's future living standards. The study concluded that childhood poverty itself, as distinct from such factors as family structure, race, and parental education, has a significant adverse effect on both the educational attainment and the future wages of the Nation's poor children. The study found that children who experience poverty between the ages of 6 and 15 years are two to three times more likely than those who are never poor to become high school dropouts. Using years of schooling as a predictor of future hourly wages, the study concluded that just 1 year of poverty for the 14.6 million children and their families in poverty in 1992 costs the economy somewhere between $36 billion and $177 billion in reduced future productivity and employment.

Significantly, one of the studies that the group examined concluded that each $1 reduction in monthly assistance through the aid to families with dependent children (AFDC) program may reduce future output by between $0.92 and $1.51 (in present value terms) solely by reducing the educational attainment and future productivity of the children who are AFDC's beneficiaries.

Americans have the opportunity to acquire the skills they need to participate fully in today's economy. Chapter 5 of this *Report* describes the major components of the Administration's lifelong learning approach; we summarize them here.

Expanded support for Head Start—funding for which increased by 45 percent between the fiscal 1993 and fiscal 1995 budgets—has ensured that fewer disadvantaged children will have their opportunities shut off even before they reach kindergarten. Goals 2000 has put in place a national framework for school assessments to help citizens throughout the country evaluate how well their local schools are achieving basic educational goals. The School-to-Work

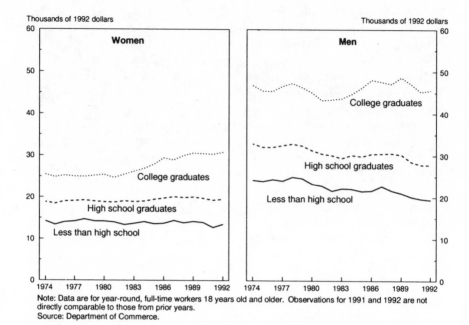

Chart 1-6 **Average Annual Earnings by Educational Attainment**
The gap in earnings between college graduates and workers with less education has widened among both men and women.

Note: Data are for year-round, full-time workers 18 years old and older. Observations for 1991 and 1992 are not directly comparable to those from prior years.
Source: Department of Commerce.

transition program has provided support to States to develop partnerships between schools and businesses, to facilitate the process of moving high school graduates into promising job opportunities or further training and education.

Two innovative education programs developed by the Administration during its first 2 years are AmeriCorps (the national service program) and the income contingent student loan program. The former provides Americans with the opportunity to participate in community service projects while earning funds that can be used to pay for college or other postsecondary education. The income contingent student loan program both reduces the cost of student loans, by making them directly available from the Federal Government at more attractive rates than those offered by private sector lenders, and makes loan repayment after college less burdensome by allowing repayments to vary with the borrower's postcollege income. This program addresses one of the major capital market imperfections that discourages many Americans from attending college at a time when the returns to higher education have increased dramatically.

INVESTING IN SCIENCE AND TECHNOLOGY

As the analysis in Chapter 3 indicates, advances in scientific and technological knowledge are another important determinant of long-run productivity growth. Moreover, as the history of this and other nations demonstrates, public investment has long played a vital role in promoting scientific discovery and technological change. At the heart of the dramatic improvements in agricultural productivity in the United States over the last century have been the research efforts conducted at federally supported land-grant colleges and the rapid dissemination of their results to millions of American farmers through the agricultural extension services supported by the Department of Agriculture. Similarly, Federal investments to promote research in public health, primarily through the National Institutes of Health, have produced many commercially successful new drugs, new treatment regimes, and innovative medical equipment, which are the foundations of America's premier position in the global biotechnology and medical equipment industries.

Federally supported research during World War II and the cold war promoted or accelerated the development of many new technologies for defense purposes—such as jet engines, computers, and advanced materials—that eventually found widespread success in commercial markets. One of the most successful computer-based innovations created by the Defense Department and adopted by the private sector is the Internet, which began life as ARPANET, a geographically distributed computer communications system designed to link researchers located at universities around the country. Today tens of millions of people around the world are communicating via the Internet for business, educational, and recreational purposes.

Most Federal investments in science and technology support the realization of a particular national mission—for example, increasing national security or enhancing public health. But economists have long recognized that there is a powerful rationale for Federal support to increase the general level of scientific investigation and technological innovation. Markets shape the behavior of private participants through incentives, but individuals and companies may invest too little in research and development (R&D), because market incentives do not reflect the full value to society of such investment. Significant economic gains from scientific discovery and technological innovation may remain unexploited because markets alone cannot guarantee that the innovator will capture all or even most of the economic returns to innovation. This is particularly true of basic research, which increases the store of fundamental knowledge that underlies most technological innovation. But it is also true of many generic technologies, the benefits of which flow quickly and in some cases automatically beyond the laboratory or the factory floor where they were invented.

Empirical research tends to support these analytical arguments. As Chapter 3 documents, the estimated annual social rate of return to R&D spending can be as high as 50 percent, much higher than the average estimated private rate of return of 20 to 30 percent.

This Administration has built on the strong bipartisan tradition of Federal support for basic research and technological innovation. Even as overall discretionary spending has remained approximately constant in nominal terms, Federal spending on science and technology in this Administration has edged upward. Moreover, as Chapter 4 discusses in greater detail, the Administration has introduced several policy innovations to enhance the efficiency of Federal R&D support and to refocus it in ways that reflect tighter budgetary constraints, the new national security environment, and changing market conditions in high-technology industries.

REINVENTING GOVERNMENT

Through the Vice President's National Performance Review (NPR), the Administration has, from its inception, taken on the difficult but critical task of reinventing government.

When an organization in the private sector becomes unresponsive to customers, encumbered by inflexible internal rules, saddled with ineffective management, or unwilling to buy inputs or produce goods and services at lowest cost, it will lose customers to rivals offering lower prices, superior products, or better service. If the firm's customers do not force an improvement in organizational behavior, its shareholders may replace senior management directly or do so indirectly by selling the company, or the company may simply go out of business.

Public sector organizations, on the other hand, often lack a clear and indisputable bottom line for their performance and are not subject to the same remorseless pressures that force private firms to function efficiently. The Office of Management and Budget, along with relevant congressional committees, attempts to monitor organizational performance within the Federal Government. But systematic and thoroughgoing organizational improvement of how the government functions requires strong leadership and the commitment of the most senior executive branch officials—as has been provided in this Administration through the NPR.

The NPR analyzed the characteristics of successful organizations in both the public and the private sector. Four principles emerged from this analysis as key to success: cutting red tape, putting customers first, empowering employees to get results, and getting back to basics, which in the context of the Federal Government means producing a government that "works better and costs less." To implement these principles throughout the Federal Government, the NPR has sought ways to decentralize decisionmaking power within agencies, to give Federal workers the tools they need to do their jobs and hold them accountable for results, to replace regulation with incentives and market solutions, to expose Federal operations to competition, to eliminate unnecessary or duplicative government functions and rules, and to establish concrete measures of success, one of which is customer satisfaction with government services.

Through the end of 1994 the Administration's reinventing government reforms had reduced the Federal work force by about 100,000 employees, out of a total reduction of 272,000 planned by 1999, and essentially shredded the 10,000-page Federal personnel manual. Other NPR initiatives—including procurement reform, one of its notable successes, and the proposal to restructure the organization controlling the Nation's air traffic control system—are discussed in Chapter 4.

At the end of 1994 the Administration announced a second round of NPR reforms, beginning with the restructuring of three cabinet departments and two major government agencies. The reform plan proposes to consolidate 60 existing programs in the Department of Housing and Urban Development (HUD) into three performance-based funds. This will enable HUD to focus its mission more sharply on promoting economic development for communities and facilitating transitions to economic independence for needy families. The Department of Transportation will collapse its 10 operating agencies into 3 and consolidate over 30 separate grant programs to States and cities into one flexible transportation infrastructure program, emphasizing capital investment assistance. And the Department of Energy will privatize some of its oil and gas reserves, sell its excess uranium, reduce costs in its research programs and laboratories, and substantially reorganize its nuclear waste cleanup program.

Taken together, the NPR reforms announced at the end of 1994 will cut $26 billion from government spending over 5 years. Yet another phase of the NPR will propose additional agency restructuring in the coming months. The savings from these and other reforms will be used to finance the President's proposed middle-class tax cuts and to continue progress on reducing the Federal deficit. With these additional cuts, discretionary government spending as a share of GDP is slated to fall below 6 percent by the year 2000, less than half the share in 1970, and the Federal work force is slated to fall to its lowest level in the decades.

OPENING FOREIGN MARKETS

The expansion of international trade is integral to raising American incomes, and exports play an increasingly important role in providing a livelihood for American workers. Between 1986 and 1993 increased exports were responsible for 37 percent of U.S. output growth. The jobs of more than 10 million American workers now depend on exports, and export-related jobs pay wages significantly above the average. In addition, the reduction of barriers to trade raises standards of living by providing a wider variety of goods at lower prices. And foreign competition leads to greater efficiency and higher quality in U.S. production, spurring the productivity growth that is essential for real income growth.

This Administration came to office committed to opening foreign markets to U.S. exports and bringing down barriers to trade, and it has achieved remarkable success. As detailed in Chapter 6, the Uruguay Round agreement of the General Agreement on Tariffs and Trade (GATT) will bring down foreign tariffs facing U.S. exporters by about a third on average, open foreign markets in agricultural products and services for the first time, and do much to establish a single rulebook for all trading countries. The North American Free Trade Agreement (NAFTA) with Mexico and Canada is a pathbreaking accord with two of our three largest trading partners, achieving a degree of liberalization well beyond that of similar international agreements. In its bilateral negotiations, the Administration has been forceful in seeking market-opening measures in Japan, China, and other countries and in advancing the interests of U.S. exports through its National Export Strategy. Finally, during the second half of 1994 the Administration helped launch negotiations that will lead to the creation of open and free trade areas among the countries of the Western Hemisphere by 2005 and among the countries of the Asia-Pacific Economic Cooperation forum by 2020.

The Administration's efforts come at a moment of historic opportunity in the global trading system. Less developed countries and the economies in transition from central planning, having recognized the importance of international trade in fostering economic growth, are now willing to lower their barriers to imports. The Administration's efforts in NAFTA and in encouraging movement toward free trade areas in the Western Hemisphere and the Asia-Pacific region have established an environment in which countries feel they must participate in meaningful trade liberalization efforts or be left out.

In a dynamic world economy, trade means challenge and adjustment as well as opportunity. The Administration's domestic economic policy is a necessary complement to its trade policy. By encouraging investment and research and development to maintain

36

and increase U.S. competitiveness, and by investing in people—maximizing their ability to acquire skills and move to higher paying jobs in newly emerging occupations—the Administration seeks to ensure that Americans gain all the benefits possible from competing in world markets.

THE ADMINISTRATION'S ECONOMIC STRATEGY: THE UNFINISHED AGENDA

For all of its remarkable accomplishments, the American economy continued to suffer from some persistent long-term difficulties in 1994. Although improvement was seen in the quality of new jobs created, the real earnings of American workers continued to stagnate. Long-term unemployment rates remained stubbornly high, especially when viewed against the backdrop of more than 3 years of economic recovery. The unemployment rates of black Americans remained more than double that for whites. More children lived in poverty in 1993 than in any year since 1965, despite the doubling of real GDP over the same period.

In light of such disturbing trends, it is not surprising that so many Americans feel increasingly cut off from the prosperity of an expanding economy. The experience of 1994 confirms that even though a strong and sustainable economic expansion is a necessary condition for improving the living standards of all Americans, it is not sufficient. Still other policies are required to help Americans obtain the skills and the education demanded by today's technologies and international markets, and to cope with the often significant dislocations that are a natural feature of today's economy.

Over the next 2 years the Administration plans several major policy initiatives, including tax relief for middle-class families, welfare reform, health care reform, and continued restructuring or reinvention of the Federal Government. In addition, the President recently announced a proposal to increase the minimum wage from its current level of $4.25 per hour. This proposal reflects a determination to ensure that working families can lift themselves out of poverty, as well as a recognition that inflation has reduced substantially the real value of the minimum wage (see Chapter 5 for further discussion of the minimum wage). Every one of these policy initiatives is designed to keep the economic expansion and deficit reduction on track while enabling all Americans to enjoy the benefits of a healthy American economy.

MIDDLE-CLASS TAX RELIEF

A little over 50 years ago the GI Bill of Rights, designed to help average Americans purchase homes, improve their educations, and raise their families was signed into law. The GI bill helped trans-

form a wartime economy into an extraordinarily successful peacetime economy and in the process helped build the great American
middle class. At the end of 1994 the President announced a new
Middle Class Bill of Rights, which like the GI Bill of Rights from
which it draws its inspiration, is designed to help average Americans cope with the demands of today's economy.

The Middle Class Bill of Rights includes a three-part tax package: a $500 per-child tax credit, a tax deduction for up to $10,000
for annual expenses on postsecondary training and education, and
an expansion of individual retirement accounts (IRAs) to all middle-class families. An estimated 87 percent of the benefits of the
proposed tax cuts would go to families with annual incomes under
$100,000. In addition, the Middle Class Bill of Rights contains a
plan to consolidate over 50 government training programs into a
single training voucher system that would allow eligible workers to
finance the training they need to obtain employment. What ties the
package together is the belief that appropriately structured tax relief and support for training can help middle-class Americans invest in their own future earning power and that of their children.

The Administration proposes a $500 nonrefundable tax credit for
children under 13 in middle-class families. The credit would be
phased out between $60,000 and $75,000 of annual adjusted gross
income (AGI). This measure would increase the income tax threshold (below which no income tax is paid) for a married couple in the
15-percent tax bracket with two eligible children by $6,667 (about
a 30-percent increase over the current threshold). The child-based
tax credit complements other parts of the Administration's
profamily policy agenda, including the earned income tax credit expansion and welfare reform.

The proposed credit reflects the fact that the existing tax allow-
ance for children—the dependent exemption—has not kept pace
with inflation and income growth. In 1948 the real value of each
child's personal exemption—$3,700 as measured in 1994 dollars—
was nearly half again as large as today's $2,500 exemption. Mean-
while many of the costs of raising children—especially medical care
and education—have increased far more rapidly than the overall
price level. And child-rearing costs are often more burdensome for
younger families, who are generally at a stage in their lives when
incomes are relatively low. For all these reasons, taxpayers with
children may have a substantially reduced ability to pay income
taxes.

In addition to the child-based tax credit, the Administration has
proposed a tax deduction for postsecondary education and training
expenses (Box 1–4). Each year of postsecondary education or training has been shown to boost future earnings between 6 and 10 percent on average. Meanwhile the costs of a college education have

increased much faster than the overall consumer price index. Middle-class families have become less able to afford higher education just at the time when it is becoming an increasingly critical determinant of future earnings.

Box 1–4.—The Proposed Tax Deduction for Postsecondary Education and Training

The Administration's tax proposal would allow a deduction of up to $10,000 for amounts spent by a taxpayer on postsecondary education and training expenses for the taxpayer and his or her spouse and dependents. This deduction would be used in determining the taxpayer's adjusted gross income. The maximum allowable deduction would be phased out for taxpayers filing a joint return with AGIs (before the proposed deduction) between $100,000 and $120,000. For a taxpayer filing as head of household or single, the maximum allowable deduction would be phased out for AGIs between $70,000 and $90,000. Qualifying educational expenses are those related to postsecondary education paid to institutions and programs eligible for Federal assistance. This includes most public and nonprofit universities and colleges and certain vocational schools.

Over 90 percent of families could potentially benefit from the proposed deduction.

Businesses have long been allowed to deduct the costs of providing education and training for their employees. Yet despite the high returns and the high costs of postsecondary training and education, the current tax code provides only limited preferences to individual taxpayers making such investments. The Administration's proposal will help ensure that the income tax deductibility of training and education expenses does not depend on one's employer paying for it. But more important, it will provide a financial incentive for Americans to get the education and training necessary to thrive in a changing economy. The Administration's proposed deduction recognizes that investment in human capital, like investment in physical capital, is a major determinant of growth in productivity and living standards.

The third component of the Administration's proposed tax package is an expansion of individual retirement accounts, aimed at encouraging households to save more and increase the Nation's worrisomely low private saving rate. Under current law, for taxpayers with employer-provided pension coverage, eligibility for deductible IRAs is phased out for AGIs between $40,000 and $50,000 (for married couples filing joint returns; a lower threshold applies to taxpayers filing as single or head of household). Neither the maximum

mum annual deductible contribution per worker ($2,000) nor the income thresholds are indexed for inflation. The proposal doubles the existing thresholds, making IRAs completely deductible for married couples filing joint returns with incomes below $80,000, regardless of pension coverage, and allowing partial deductions for those with incomes up to $100,000. In addition, the income thresholds and the $2,000 contribution limit (both set in 1986) would be indexed for inflation. Finally, withdrawals from IRAs would be allowed without penalty to buy a first home, to pay for postsecondary education, to defray large medical expenses, or to cover long-term unemployment expenses. As already noted, faster wage and income growth is possible only by boosting investment and saving in America. The Administration's proposed IRA expansion is a way to promote greater awareness of personal responsibility for saving.

WELFARE REFORM

The President entered office with a promise to reform the welfare system so that it would function as an effective safety net promoting work and family, rather than as a snare enmeshing poor families in long-term dependence. Under the current system some people have become long-term welfare recipients—although more than one-third of all women who ever receive AFDC do so for less than 2 years, almost one-fourth end up receiving AFDC for over 10 years during their lifetime. And, as currently structured, the welfare system in effect imposes a high marginal tax rate on paid employment, because low-income mothers lose their AFDC and food stamp benefits and eventually their medicaid health insurance for themselves and their children when they take a job. In short, for many the current system contains powerful disincentives against work and in favor of continued welfare.

The fundamental goal of all of the Administration's policies aimed at those at the lower end of the income distribution is to increase the rewards and hence the incentives to work. These policies are also designed to ensure that those willing to work will be able to live above the poverty level (see Box 1–5 for a discussion of how housing reforms relate to welfare reform).

The Administration's proposed welfare reform legislation, the Work and Responsibility Act, will help make work pay, by ensuring that welfare recipients obtain the skills they need to find employment, and by eliminating long-term welfare dependency as an option for those able to work. Under the Administration's plan, welfare recipients who are job-ready will begin a job search immediately, and anyone offered a job will be required to take it. Support for child care will be provided to help people move from dependence to independence. For those not ready for work, the Administration's proposed reforms will provide support, job training,

Box 1–5.—HUD Reforms and Welfare Reform

The Administration has proposed major reforms aimed at reinventing the Federal Government's housing programs. These reforms will focus the efforts of the Department of Housing and Urban Development on two major tasks: empowering individuals and empowering communities.

The Administration's proposals for empowering individuals in the housing market bear a close connection to its proposals to reform welfare. The HUD reforms will gradually end public housing as we know it, moving from support of public housing *projects* to support of individuals who need housing. The current system impedes the job mobility of public housing recipients. In order to accept a job in another community, a recipient may have to give up the subsidized public housing he or she has and sign up at the bottom of a waiting list for housing assistance in the new location. In addition, public housing often concentrates the poor in areas where few jobs are available close at hand. Under the reinvention proposal, instead of being tied to a particular unit in a public housing project, households would be given portable rental housing certificates, which could be used to obtain housing in the private market. This reform would encourage mobility between jobs, impose market discipline on public housing authorities, help break up the dysfunctional concentration of the poor, and enable individuals to make housing choices best suited to their needs. In all these ways the HUD reform effort complements welfare reform by removing barriers to participation in the paid labor force.

and assistance in finding a job when they are ready. Each adult recipient of AFDC will be required to create an employability plan, to ensure that he or she will move into the work force as quickly as possible. Time limits on receipt of welfare benefits will require that anyone who can work, must work—in the private sector if possible, in a temporary, subsidized job if necessary.

The proposed program will strongly discourage children from bearing children. Parents under the age of 18, if they apply for welfare payments, generally will not be allowed to set up independent households; instead they will receive assistance to stay in school. The Administration's proposal also includes funding for grants to schools and communities to prevent teen pregnancy, and it toughens efforts to collect child support from all absent fathers—a provision that is expected to double Federal collections of child support payments, from $9 billion to an estimated $20 billion by 2000. These proposals to discourage teen pregnancy and to foster parental responsibility will help prevent the need for welfare in the first place.

In welfare as in other areas of joint Federal and State responsibility to help the poor, such as medicaid, the Administration is committed to working with the States to enhance the flexibility and efficiency of programs. For this reason the Administration has been an active proponent of granting waivers from various regulatory constraints, to allow States to experiment with new ways of designing welfare strategies and find the ones that best suit their particular needs and characteristics. During its first 2 years in office, this Administration granted waivers to enable 24 States to undertake welfare reform—more than all previous Administrations combined.

Partnerships with State and local governments take many forms. Box 1-6 describes one of the Administration's initiatives for working with State and local governments to encourage community-based solutions to economic development problems in poverty-stricken areas.

HEALTH CARE REFORM

The President entered office with a pledge to reform the Nation's health care system, and he will continue to work with the Congress to realize this objective during the coming year. Reform is essential to address four separate but interrelated problems of the current system, which if left unsolved will result in an increasingly heavy financial burden on governments and individuals (Box 1-7).

First, millions of Americans, both insured and uninsured, do not have health security. Those who are insured face the risk of losing their coverage, at least temporarily, if they lose or change their jobs. Meanwhile the number of uninsured Americans continues to grow at an alarming rate.

Second, the current health insurance system has a number of shortcomings. One is that insurers know that a small proportion of the population incurs the bulk of medical expenditures, making it profitable to screen prospective purchasers to determine their risk characteristics; those who are sick—who have so-called pre-existing conditions—may be unable to purchase insurance altogether, or may only be able to purchase it at exorbitant prices. Another shortcoming is that people unable to obtain health insurance through their employers may be offered coverage only at prices unaffordable for many Americans. Still another is that many insurance policies do not cover a variety of large financial risks (e.g., high-cost illnesses), although these are exactly the kinds of risks for which insurance is most needed.

Third, the current health care system imposes a large and unsustainable burden on public sector budgets. Governments account for nearly half of all health care spending in the United

Box 1–6.—Empowerment Zones and Enterprise Communities

OBRA93 contained a provision to create 9 empowerment zones and 95 enterprise communities in selected localities across the Nation. The designated zones and communities will receive significant tax benefits and new Federal resources totaling an estimated $3.8 billion over the next 5 years, to support economic revitalization and community development. In December 1994 the President announced the areas selected to participate. Selections were based primarily on the strength of the applicants' proposed strategies for community-based development. Cities receiving urban empowerment zones are Atlanta, Baltimore, Chicago, Detroit, New York, and Philadelphia/Camden. Rural empowerment zones designated are the Kentucky Highlands region of Kentucky, the Mid-Delta region of Mississippi, and the Rio Grande Valley in Texas.

The empowerment zone/enterprise community program is based on the notion that development efforts can be targeted to areas that have been economically left behind. Besides receiving monetary awards totalling $1.3 billion in financial assistance and $2.5 billion in tax benefits over the next 5 years, the selected zones and communities (as well as nonselected applicants) may request waivers from many Federal regulations, and their requests will be processed on an expedited basis. To date over 1,200 such requests have been received. Perhaps more important, the areas selected generally are those that have effectively mobilized local private and public sector resources to leverage the potential Federal commitments. The application process encouraged localities to harness their own creative talents and financial resources to frame a comprehensive response to the problems of local economic development.

In a sense, the zones and communities selected are laboratories for experiments in local economic development. The Federal Government realizes that it does not have all the answers to the economic development conundrum; instead it has enlisted institutions at the State and the local level (including the private and nonprofit sectors) to help design possible solutions.

For the program to work, however, successful areas and the reasons for their success must be identified. Therefore a comprehensive evaluation process will follow the progress of the selected zones and communities and report periodically on them. The evaluation will largely determine whether the program should be replicated elsewhere.

Box 1–7.—The Cost of Doing Nothing About Health Care

If no steps are taken to reform the Nation's health care system, existing trends will result in increased health care costs and reduced health insurance coverage. Neither of these outcomes is desirable. Without reform:

- Per capita health care costs will rise from about $3,300 in 1993 to about $5,200 in 2000.
- Aggregate health care costs, currently running at around 14 percent of GDP, will increase to an estimated 18 percent of GDP by 2005.
- Health care expenditures by the Federal Government will increase from 21 percent of total expenditures in 1994 to 26 percent by 2000.
- Medicare and medicaid expenditures will grow at 9.1 percent and 9.2 percent per year, respectively, over the foreseeable future, nearly three times as fast as overall consumer prices.
- More Americans will lose health insurance coverage, adding to the nearly 40 million without health insurance in 1993.
- Wages will continue to be held down, as an ever-greater proportion of total compensation is paid in the form of health benefits. In the past 5 years, health care benefit costs per employee rose at about twice the overall rate of inflation.

States, primarily in the form of payments for medicaid and medicare. Since 1980 the share of health care spending in the Federal budget has doubled; the budgets of State and local governments also saw larger shares going toward health expenditures.

Fourth, the current health care system suffers from numerous structural features that may keep costs high. For instance, fee-for-service providers may have an incentive to overprovide care, and provide some care that is inappropriate or of equivocal value, because they are generally reimbursed for each additional test or procedure they perform. For their part, consumers often do not have the information they need to evaluate the differences among providers or to determine whether or not the care prescribed for them is necessary. Moreover, in a system dominated by third-party payers (insurers), consumers seldom have a strong reason to be directly concerned about the cost-effectiveness of their care. Third-party payers have responded by establishing programs to review diagnoses and suggested treatments. Competition among insurers may help offset some of the effects of informational asymmetries.

Over the past few years, under the pressure of rapidly escalating costs, the private health care system has begun a process of dramatic structural change. In 1988, for example, only about 29 percent of health insurance enrollees were in some form of managed care plan, in most cases either a health maintenance organization (HMO) or a preferred provider organization (PPO). By 1993 this figure had increased to 51 percent. Much of this migration toward managed care has occurred in larger firms, where nearly 60 percent of covered employees are now in managed care plans. Many analysts credit managed care with keeping health care costs down. In the Far West, where HMO penetration is higher than elsewhere in the country, real spending on health care grew more slowly over the 1980–91 period than in any other region in the country (3.4 percent per year versus a national average of more than 4.5 percent). In part as a result of these changes, there is some promising evidence that growth in health care costs in the private sector may be slowing somewhat. For instance, medical price inflation slowed to a 5.4 percent annual rate in 1993 and slowed still further to 4.9 percent in 1994. Even the 1994 rate, however, was still well above the overall rate of inflation.

For a variety of reasons discussed in Chapter 2, the increases in medicare and medicaid spending projected for the coming years have been revised downward significantly. For instance, in January 1993 medicaid expenditures were projected to increase at an annual rate of nearly 15 percent through 1997. Yet actual medicaid expenditures grew by only 11.8 percent in fiscal 1993 and 8.2 percent in fiscal 1994. Accordingly, the 1996 budget projects slower growth in medicaid than did prior budgets, averaging slightly over 9 percent for 1996–2000. The situation for medicare is similar. Even with these changes, however, health care spending is slated to remain the most rapidly growing component of the Federal budget during the rest of this century, and to escalate during the first decade of the next century, partly in response to the aging of the American population.

This Administration remains firmly committed to reforming the current health care system in order to expand coverage, contain costs, and curb public sector deficits. Last year's debate on health care reform produced a consensus on several key points. Many of the alternative proposals included insurance market reforms, such as provisions to prevent insurers from denying coverage to those who have been ill. A number of bills recognized the importance of providing health care coverage to low- and middle-income Americans, especially children. It is possible to build on this consensus and achieve real reform.

The Administration believes that any successful reform must ultimately be comprehensive in scope, even if it proceeds step by step. This belief rests on the reality that none of the four major problems of the current health care system identified above can be solved in isolation. For example, any attempt to impose arbitrary caps on Federal health care spending without more-fundamental reforms would simply shift more government program costs onto either State and local governments or the private sector. According to one recent estimate, uncompensated care and government programs that reimbursed hospitals below market prices shifted about $26 billion in costs onto the private sector in 1991. Similarly, any attempt to provide universal coverage without complementary measures to improve competition and sharpen the incentives for more cost-conscious decisions by both providers and consumers would mean even more dramatic increases in systemwide costs. Limited reforms designed to eliminate the most glaring shortcomings of private insurance markets, although desirable, would not solve either the problem of providing health security for all Americans or the problem of escalating public health care bills. Finally, efforts by the private sector to control costs might well increase the number of Americans without health insurance, especially children and those most in need of medical attention.

Ultimately, meaningful reform of the Nation's health care system will do more than just unburden public sector budgets and provide health security. It will also improve living standards. For years, the rising cost of health care has forced a shift in the composition of the typical compensation package away from take-home wages and salaries and toward fringe benefits, especially health insurance. Between 1966 and 1994 the share of health benefits in total labor compensation increased from 2.0 percent to 7.2 percent, while the share of cash compensation correspondingly fell. In absolute terms average real take-home pay barely increased: most of the gains in total compensation were realized as fringe benefits. In short, working men and women, for the most part, paid for escalating health costs by taking home lower pay than they would have otherwise. On the assumption that the future will look much like the past, the Administration expects that any benefits of a reduction in health care costs resulting from meaningful reforms will show up in higher take-home pay for working Americans.

CONCLUSION

Nineteen ninety-four was a very good year for the American economy. Indeed, robust growth, a dramatic decline in the unemployment rate, low inflation, and a much improved outlook for the Federal budget combined to yield the best overall economic performance in at least a generation. In addition, last year's economic performance ranks as the best among the advanced industrial countries with which the United States is usually compared.

But the economic successes of the past year must not obscure the long-term economic challenges facing the Nation. Some of these, like the dramatic growth in entitlement spending projected for the first few decades of the next century, or the disturbing increase in the number of Americans without health insurance, result in large part from the interaction of national economic policy choices with the changing demographics of the American population. Others, such as the persistent decline in real compensation for many groups and overall increasing income inequality, may in large part result from worldwide changes in technology and other areas. These changes are creating a new world economy and a new American economy, which hold both the promise of a more prosperous future and the threat of more dislocation and adjustment for many American workers and their families.

As the Nation enters the last half-decade of this century, this Administration has already put in place some important foundations for greater prosperity. Over the coming year we look forward to working with the Congress, with the States, and, most important, with the American people, to address the Nation's long-term economic challenges and to make the most of the Nation's long-term economic opportunities.

CHAPTER 2

The Macroeconomy in 1994 and Beyond

IN 1994 THE AMERICAN ECONOMY enjoyed a balanced and broad-based expansion, marked by rising real output, declining unemployment, and modest and stable inflation. Over the year, real gross domestic product (GDP) advanced 4.0 percent and real disposable income rose 4.3 percent. Between January and December 1994 the unemployment rate declined 1.3 percentage points, and 3.5 million more payroll jobs existed in December 1994 than in December 1993. The consumer price index (CPI) rose by 2.7 percent, essentially the same rate recorded over the past 3 years. The economy's performance in 1994 was a dramatic improvement over its performance at the beginning of the recovery from the 1990–91 recession, when output growth was fitful and anemic, and over its performance in 1992, when despite a strong gain in output, employment growth remained lackluster. Indeed, the combination of rapid job growth and low inflation gives 1994 one of the best macroeconomic performances on record (Chart 2–1).

Initially, recovery from the 1990–91 recession was hampered by several special factors including large household and business debt burdens, high vacancy rates in commercial real estate, tight credit practices by many lenders, stagnant growth in much of the rest of the world, and declining Federal purchases, especially of military goods and services. As the recovery progressed, all but the last of these impediments diminished in importance, providing a more favorable environment for a pickup in economic growth and job creation. As described in last year's *Report,* the pace of expansion also improved as a result of a substantial decline in long-term interest rates in 1993 that accompanied first the anticipation and then the passage of the Administration's deficit reduction package in August of that year. Lower interest rates strengthened the interest-sensitive components of private spending, which in turn bolstered the rest of the economy.

The expansion of output and jobs that characterized the second half of 1993 persisted and strengthened in 1994, despite a shift toward tighter monetary and fiscal policies. In February 1994 the Federal Reserve began reducing the degree of monetary accommodation, and by the end of the year the resulting increase in interest

Chart 2-1   **Job Creation and Inflation**
Compared with the experience of the 1980s and early 1990s, the economy in 1994
produced a large number of jobs with low inflation.

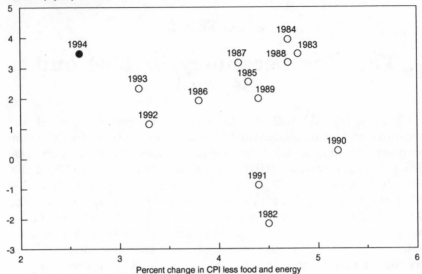

Millions of payroll jobs created

Note: Data represent changes from December to December.
Source: Department of Labor.

rates was substantial. Continued fiscal restraint was also significant, as evidenced by a decline of $20 billion in the structural
budget deficit ($40 billion excluding special factors like deposit in-
surance) during fiscal 1994. Nevertheless, investment and consumption spending remained strong. High rates of inventory accumulation through most of the year signaled business confidence
about future demand for output, as did business investment in
equipment and structures, which rose 12.9 percent over the year.
Households, too, showed substantial optimism about their income
and employment prospects, as purchases of motor vehicles and existing homes as well as residential construction were at high levels
despite rising interest rates. Overall, the economy grew at a faster
rate than virtually all forecasters had projected at the start of
1994, and it did so despite interest rates that were much higher
than forecast at that time.

   The performance of inflation in 1994 was equally impressive,
with most price measures near forecasts made at the beginning of
the year, despite much stronger than expected levels of output and
employment. These price developments reflected continued growth
above trend in labor productivity and a surprisingly modest increase in hourly compensation. As discussed below, compensation
increased less than would have been expected based on historical

experience, indicating possible changes in the dynamics of the labor market.

CLOSING IN ON POTENTIAL OUTPUT

Over the last 2 years the economy has grown at an average annual rate of 3.6 percent, as aggregate demand rebounded from the 1990–91 recession and the sluggish growth that initially followed it. In part the economy's expansion was accomplished through an increase in the quantity and quality of the labor force and through net additions to the capital stock, the latter financed by both domestic saving and foreign borrowing. In part average labor productivity increased as a result of efficiency-enhancing technologies embedded in the capital stock. But to a significant extent, output was able to satisfy the strong growth of aggregate demand in 1994, because workers who had been unemployed were reemployed, and because capital that had been idle or underutilized was brought back on line or utilized more intensively. By the end of 1994, however, both labor and capital utilization rates were in ranges that suggested little remaining slack.

As the margin of underutilized capital and labor reserves diminishes, the economy's growth rate becomes increasingly constrained by the rates of growth of new entrants into the labor force, net additions to the capital stock, and the productivity of labor and capital owing to technological progress and to improvements in the quality of the labor force. Over the long run these factors determine the economy's growth rate of *potential output*. If, in the absence of slack in labor or product markets, growth in aggregate demand outstrips growth of the economy's potential output, pressures to increase wages and prices are likely to mount, increasing the probability of a rise in inflation. In turn, the buildup of wage and price pressures is likely to cause interest rates to rise, dampening aggregate demand growth and bringing it back in line with the growth of potential output.

The preponderance of the available empirical evidence suggests that the growth rate of potential output is currently around 2.5 percent. But the economy's strong performance in 1994 has caused some observers to speculate that the growth rate of potential output is now, or soon will be, higher. This hypothesis is examined in Chapter 3, which analyzes the major factors behind the economy's long-run growth potential. The remainder of this chapter analyzes the economy's macroeconomic performance in 1994, a year during which the margins of slack were sharply reduced. This chapter also examines the course of fiscal and monetary policy in 1994, looks at the surprising rise in long-term interest rates, and presents the Administration's economic forecast for the 1995–2000 period.

OVERVIEW OF THE ECONOMY IN 1994

A sector-by-sector look at economic performance provides a clearer picture of the factors contributing to the continued strong expansion in 1994.

BUSINESS FIXED INVESTMENT

A key factor driving the current expansion has been the rapid growth of business fixed investment, particularly spending on capital equipment (Chart 2–2). Between the trough of the 1990–91 recession and the end of 1994, investment in producers' durable equipment (PDE) increased at an average annual rate of 12.8 percent, while real GDP rose at an annual rate of 3.1 percent. (Table 2–1 summarizes the growth of GDP by component.)

Chart 2-2 **Growth in Real Nonresidential Investment**
Investment in business equipment has surged during the current expansion, but investment in nonresidential structures has just begun to increase.

Percent change from four quarters earlier

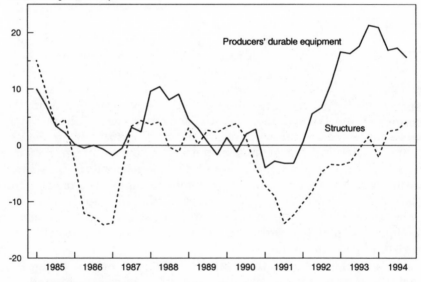

Source: Department of Commerce.

The extraordinary growth in PDE reflects the strong growth posted by spending on both computers and noncomputer equipment. Since the current expansion began, real investment in computers and peripheral equipment has increased at an average annual rate of 33.9 percent, while real spending on equipment other than computers has increased at an annual rate of about 8 percent. As a share of real GDP, noncomputer investment during 1994 was higher than at any time since separate records were first kept for computer and noncomputer investment spending. Over 1994, PDE

TABLE 2–1.— *GDP Scorecard for 1994*

[Real growth fourth quarter to fourth quarter]

Component	Percent change, except as noted	Comments
Consumer expenditures	3.4	Strong gains in employment as well as in households' willingness to increase levels of indebtedness accounted for broad–based increases in consumer spending.
Producers' durable equipment	15.6	The real success story underlying the strength of the current expansion.
Housing	1.9	Residential investment showed remarkable resilience in the face of rising interest rates throughout 1994, partly due to adjustable–rate mortgages.
Nonresidential structures	4.2	This sector rebounded after a surplus of commercial and industrial real estate led to no growth during the early part of the expansion.
Change in inventory investment [1] (billions of 1987 dollars)	$37.1	A key to maintaining momentum in the economy during 1994.
Federal Government purchases	–6.2	Corporations were not the only organizations downsizing in the current expansion. Federal spending was a net drag on economic growth in 1994.
Exports of goods and services	10.2	A marked increase in exports reflected the pace of economic recoveries abroad.
Imports of goods and services	14.9	Strong consumption and investment demand showed up in imports during 1994. Computers and computer components accounted for much of the runup.

[1] Change between 1993 and 1994 in annual inventory investment.
Note.—Data are preliminary.
Source: Department of Commerce.

spending reflected especially robust investment in cars and trucks, total sales of which to business and households rose to 15 million units.

Whereas *gross* investment in PDE has been on a fairly steady upward trend for most of the postwar period, the trend in *net* investment (that is, net of depreciation) is less pronounced. Because the composition of PDE investment has shifted toward short-lived equipment, such as computers, a growing proportion of gross investment each year represents replacement of existing capital stock rather than a net increase in its overall level. The growing wedge between gross and net real PDE investment is illustrated by the fact that depreciation of PDE, relative to GDP, rose to roughly 6.5 percent in 1994 from about 5.8 percent a decade earlier. Gross investment has beneficial effects on the economy, contributing to income growth and facilitating the introduction of new technologies into the production process. But net investment is even more important to the Nation's economic well-being, because by adding to the amount of capital per worker, it raises labor productivity and the long-run earning potential of workers.

The other major component of business investment is spending on nonresidential structures, including office buildings, shopping malls, and retail stores. During 1994 the shadow cast over this sector of the economy by overbuilding during the 1980s began to fade, and nonresidential investment in structures increased 4.2 percent. The supply of bank credit for new construction appeared to be plentiful, and increased demand for office and industrial space was reflected in a fall in vacancy rates in some parts of the country. Contract awards for commercial and industrial construction increased during the second half of 1994, and sales prices for office, industrial, and other commercial structures posted solid increases during the year.

CONSUMER SPENDING

A favorable environment for consumer credit and strong gains in employment contributed to healthy increases in consumer spending and sentiment during 1994. Personal consumption spending advanced at a 3.4-percent pace during the year, led by an 8.1-percent rise in purchases of consumer durables. In turn, durable goods purchases were buoyed by double-digit growth in consumer expenditure on furniture and household equipment, especially video, audio, and computer equipment. Consumer sentiment returned to pre-recession levels early in the year and surged to a 5-year high at the end.

Households increased their indebtedness in 1994, as the ratio of debt to disposable personal income reached a record 81 percent (Chart 2–3). Undoubtedly, households were reacting in part to the fact that the cost of borrowing had declined dramatically during 1993 and remained low throughout much of 1994. Growth of consumer credit may also have been spurred by the proliferation of credit card programs that offer rewards to cardholders—such as direct rebates on purchases or frequent-flyer miles—based on amounts charged. Nonetheless, as in 1993, Americans devoted the smallest fraction of their disposable income to scheduled payments on principal and interest since 1984. The decline represented a substantial windfall for debtor households: had the debt-service burden remained at its 1989 peak, the average American household would have paid about $965 more in principal and interest during 1994. The reduction in the debt-service burden, which primarily reflected lower financing costs on mortgages, freed up income, fueling part of the increase in household discretionary spending.

An increase in the personal saving rate occurred toward the end of the year, with the rate rising to 4.6 percent in the fourth quarter from 3.6 percent in the first quarter. In part this rise reflected a likely worsening in the ratio of net worth to income, as household debt burdens rose relative to income, while household assets—such as corporate equity—declined slightly relative to income.

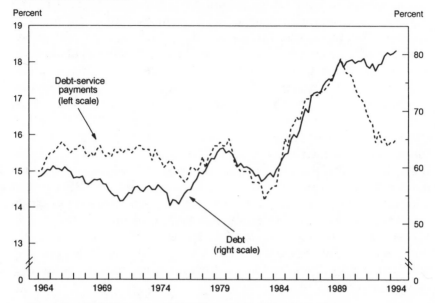

Chart 2-3 **Consumer Debt and Debt-Service Payments**
Despite an increase in the ratio of debt to disposable income, debt-service payments declined relative to income.

Sources: Department of Commerce and Board of Governors of the Federal Reserve System.

INVENTORIES

The sustained pace of inventory accumulation during 1994 was in marked contrast to the early stages of the recovery, when businesses refrained from rebuilding inventories out of concern that the recovery might lose steam. A hefty accumulation of inventory stocks occurred in the second, third, and fourth quarters, particularly in the wholesale and retail trade sectors. Although it is impossible to know with certainty to what extent the accumulation was intended, sales and shipments were also robust, so that there was little evidence of an inventory overhang that would warrant significant production cutbacks over the near term. Instead, the pace of inventory accumulation in the trade sector suggests that business expected continued growth in demand for its production. Inventory accumulation was modest in the manufacturing sector, and movement in the manufacturing inventory-to-sales ratio was dominated by the strong downward trend seen the past several years.

RESIDENTIAL INVESTMENT

Residential fixed investment was buoyed throughout 1994 by growth in incomes and employment. This traditionally interest-sensitive sector of the economy showed remarkable resilience in the face of rising interest rates. Housing starts totaled 1.5 million units, their highest level since 1988, with single-family home starts posting their highest annual total since 1978. Although a slowdown in residential investment took hold during the second half of the year as real investment dropped at an annual rate of 4.3 percent, average 1994 residential investment was still over 8 percent greater than the average for 1993. Sales of existing single-family homes, at just under 4 million, posted the highest resale total since 1978.

One factor that sustained the strength in housing in 1994 was the increased reliance on adjustable-rate mortgages (ARMs) in financing home purchases. During the summer of 1993 the ARM share of mortgage originations was only about 17 percent—near the historic low for this series. By November 1994, however, more than half of all mortgage originations were ARMs—the highest proportion in more than 5 years. Not only were many ARMs priced with a first-year discount, but they also allowed borrowers to structure their payments in a variety of ways; for example, some ARMs offered fixed rates for the first 7 or 10 years. The pricing of ARMs mitigated the initial cash crunch facing many home buyers and meant that fewer families were priced out of the market as interest rates rose (Chart 2–4).

Chart 2-4 **Fixed-Rate Mortgage Interest Rates and the Share of ARMs**
Over the past year, more home buyers turned to adjustable-rate mortgages (ARMs) as rates on fixed-rate mortgages rose.

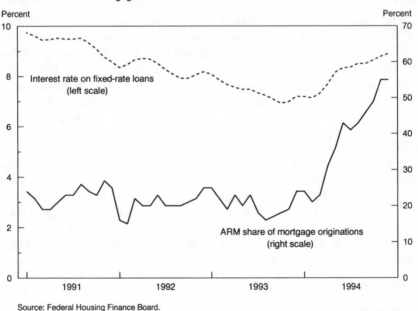

Source: Federal Housing Finance Board.

Construction of multifamily units gradually picked up following the overbuilding of the 1980s. The willingness to build new units was boosted by the increased availability of credit for such construction over the course of the year. During 1994, multifamily housing starts rose by 59 percent relative to 1993.

EMPLOYMENT AND PRODUCTIVITY

The strength of the expansion in 1994 was accompanied by a rapid pace of job creation. According to current estimates the economy generated an average of 290,000 new payroll jobs per month, for a total of 3.5 million jobs, more than 90 percent of which were in the private sector. An early analysis of forthcoming revisions to estimates of payroll employment indicates that the job gains in 1993 and 1994 may prove to have been even stronger. For the 12 months ending in March 1994, the Bureau of Labor Statistics (BLS) estimates that as many as 760,000 additional jobs may have been created. When the revised data are released next summer, it is expected that the job gains since the Administration took office will have exceeded 6 million.

The employment gains of 1994 were spread widely throughout the economy (Table 2–2). Among goods-producing industries, construction employment posted its largest annual gain in a decade, while manufacturing employment recorded its largest increase since 1987. However, almost 85 percent of the advance in payroll employment was concentrated in the services sector, with 20.3 percent originating in the business services category (temporary agencies, building maintenance, and the like) and another 7.3 percent in the health services industry. Employment of Federal workers declined by 46,000.

TABLE 2–2.— *Growth in Nonagricultural Payroll Employment*

Sector	Employment in December 1994 [1] (thousands of persons)	Change since December 1993 [1]	
		Thousands of persons	As percent of total change
Total nonagricultural employment	115,864	3,490	100.0
Goods–producing industries [2]	23,779	553	15.8
Construction	4,956	298	8.5
Manufacturing	18,226	277	7.9
Durable goods	10,419	250	7.2
Services-producing industries [2]	92,085	2,937	84.2
Retail trade	21,297	811	23.2
Business services	6,817	710	20.3
Health services	9,153	256	7.3
Government	19,491	252	7.2
Federal	2,872	−46	−1.3
State and local	16,619	298	8.5

[1] Preliminary.
[2] Includes industries not shown separately.
Note.—Data are not seasonally adjusted.
Source: Department of Labor.

Although job creation has been exceedingly strong during the past 2 years, some analysts have expressed concern about the quality of the jobs created. In particular, it has been noted that, during the late 1980s and the early part of this decade, job growth in the traditionally high-wage manufacturing sector lagged increasingly behind gains in the relatively low-paying services sector. Less frequently cited, however, is the fact that recent gains in employment, although concentrated in relatively low-wage industries, have at the same time favored high-wage occupations.

For example, according to BLS, managerial and professional occupations represented 26.5 percent of total employment in 1992. In 1993 this share rose to 27.1 percent. Although the data for 1994 are not directly comparable because of the introduction of a new survey of household unemployment, the share of total employment accounted for by managerial and professional occupations last year rose to 27.5 percent. Managerial and professional jobs paid a median wage for full-time employees of $680 per week—some 47 percent above the median wage of all full-time workers.

One characteristic of recent job growth that warrants concern has been the increase in the share of new jobs accounted for by temporary jobs. Employment at so-called help supply services (the best available measure of temporary employment) has accounted for 13.8 percent of all new jobs created during the current expansion. By comparison, over the 1982–90 period, only 4.4 percent of total growth in employment was in the help supply services category.

With the sharp job gains in 1994, the civilian unemployment rate fell by more than 1 percentage point, from 6.7 percent in January to 5.4 percent in December. Despite the fact that the new survey method is likely to have raised the measured unemployment rate, December's rate was the lowest since 1990 (Box 2–1). Nevertheless, over the current expansion, the average duration of unemployment has increased, and the share of unemployed workers reporting permanent job losses has risen.

Not only were more people working in 1994, but they were working longer hours. In the manufacturing sector, employment posted its first annual increase since 1988, and both the factory workweek and manufacturing overtime hours increased to postwar records. Labor productivity in the nonfarm business sector has also been strong: since the trough of the recession in 1991, output per hour in the nonfarm business sector has risen at an annual rate of 2.1 percent, well above most estimates of its long-run trend. Because productivity generally grows at above-trend rates during a cyclical rebound, it would be premature to conclude that there has been an increase in the long-run trend in productivity growth. Chapter 3 provides a more detailed discussion of the factors affecting long-run productivity growth.

INCOMES AND PROFITS

The gains in employment during 1994 were reflected in strong aggregate income growth. Real disposable income increased 4.3 percent over the year. Nonetheless, the gain in real compensation per hour remained modest. Hourly compensation, as measured by the employment cost index, increased 3.0 percent, barely outpacing the 2.7-percent increase in CPI inflation.

Based on a statistical relationship between the unemployment rate and the growth rate of hourly compensation, actual growth in compensation (with the compensation measure taken from the national income and product accounts, or NIPA) was lower than would have been expected. The same was true in 1993. Statistical relationships are meant to explain only average historical experience, and their predictions can err substantially on a year-by-year basis. Nevertheless, the shortfall in actual relative to predicted growth in hourly compensation averaged 1.4 percent in the 2 years—a shortfall that by its size and persistence could suggest some substantial changes in the dynamic behavior of the labor market.

The increase in corporate profits in 1994 was impressive. Although the January 1994 earthquake in Northridge, California, depressed profits (so that first-quarter profits fell by 18 percent at an annual rate), they rebounded quickly. Despite the earthquake-related drop, corporate profits increased at an annual rate of 5.6 percent over the first three quarters of 1994.

INFLATION

Some observers expressed concerns during 1994 that the strong gains in employment would translate into upward pressure on labor costs and prices by the end of the year. Indeed, the prices of some highly visible commodities, including coffee, cotton, and basic metals, did rise by significant amounts during the year. In addition, surveys of industrial prices by the National Association of Purchasing Managers and the Federal Reserve Bank of Philadelphia indicated that prices in the industrial sector were accelerating. Although increases in commodity prices, particularly among industrial goods, made for some disturbing headlines, rising commodity prices are a normal phenomenon during a cyclical rebound in the economy and do not typically lead to a noticeable increase in broader measures of inflation. However, with capacity tight in many industries, there was concern that commodity price increases would spill over into increases in other goods. Moreover, for the first time in 4 years, import prices began edging up more rapidly than overall inflation.

Despite the episodes of price acceleration for some commodities, and despite real GDP growth that sharply reduced slack in labor and capital markets, broad measures of inflation remained stable throughout the year (Table 2–3). Inflation ended the year about in line with the consensus forecast made at the beginning of the year. Core CPI and PPI inflation rates (measures that exclude volatile food and energy components) were lower during the second half of 1994 than during the first half of the year. Core CPI inflation was just 2.6 percent last year—the lowest rate since 1965 (Chart 2–5). (Box 2–2 Contains a discussion of problems in the CPI as a measure of changes in the cost of living.) A major source of the restraint in inflation was modest growth in employee compensation accompanied by strong growth in labor productivity.

REGIONAL DEVELOPMENTS

The ongoing effects of the national economic expansion were felt in all major regions of the country during 1994. Although the pace of the expansion was uneven across the country, all major regions (that is, all nine Census divisions) enjoyed stable employment or outright employment growth, steady or declining unemployment rates, and real growth in income and retail sales.

In 1994 the Midwest and South continued along the moderate-to-strong growth path established over the preceding 2 years, with payroll employment rising 2 to 3 percent, unemployment rates falling steadily, and income rising more than 6 percent. In the Northern Plains States the unemployment rate fell below 4 percent—its lowest level in 15 years. Parts of the Northeast also grew strongly. In New England, employment rose nearly 2 percent in 1994, and the unemployment rate dropped to below the national average. The Middle Atlantic region displayed somewhat weaker growth but nevertheless generated increased employment, with the region's unemployment rate falling to 5.4 percent in December (Chart 2–6).

TABLE 2–3.— *Measures of Inflation*

Measure	1993	1994	1994 IV (annual rate)
	Percent change		
GDP fixed–weight price index	2.8	[1]2.9	[1]2.6
Non-oil import prices	1.5	3.9	4.6
CPI–U:			
All items	2.7	2.7	2.2
All items less food and energy	3.2	2.6	2.0
Medical care	5.4	4.9	6.1
PPI:			
Finished goods	.2	1.7	1.0
Finished goods less food and energy	.4	1.6	–.6
Intermediate materials less food and energy	1.6	5.1	9.0
Crude materials	.1	–1.1	2.8
Employment cost index: [2]			
Total compensation	3.5	3.0	2.6
Wages and salaries	3.1	2.8	2.4
Benefits	4.6	3.4	2.8

[1] Preliminary.

[2] For civilian workers.

Note.—Inflation as measured by the GDP price index is computed from fourth-quarter to fourth-quarter for 1993 and 1994, and from 1994 III to 1994 IV. All other measures are calculated from December to December for 1993 and 1994, and from September to December for 1994 IV.

Sources: Department of Commerce and Department of Labor.

Chart 2-5 Consumer Prices Less Food and Energy

In 1994 consumer prices less food and energy increased at the lowest annual rate since 1965.

Percent change, December to December

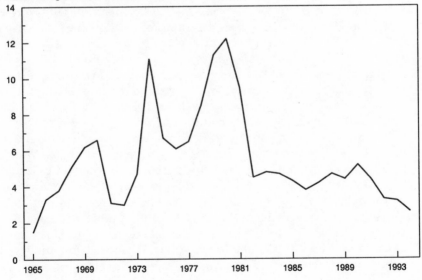

Source: Department of Labor.

61

Box 2-2.—Problems in Measuring Cost-of-Living Increases

It is impossible in practice to calculate an index number that accurately reflects changes in the cost of living for American families, because no two families are alike and because the quality and the availability of goods and services change. Private companies and public policymakers, needing an objective measure of consumer inflation but aware of the limitations to which all are subject, have used what is widely regarded as the best available index, the consumer price index (CPI).

Researchers at the Bureau of Labor Statistics, which prepares the CPI, have identified several problems with the index, and the agency has moved, where possible, to address them. The most important technical problems remaining are *substitution bias* and the treatment of *quality changes and new products*. The net effect of these and other problems is probably to make the CPI overstate actual cost-of-living increases, but this is controversial and estimates vary widely.

Substitution bias arises because consumers regularly shift the composition of their purchases, substituting goods that have become relatively cheaper for goods that have become relatively more expensive. The CPI, which measures the price changes of a mostly fixed basket of goods, fails to capture such shifts. This is inherent in the nature of the CPI, which was designed originally to measure the average price increase for a fixed basket of goods and services, not to capture changing consumption patterns. Whenever the market basket used to calculate the CPI is updated (usually every 10 years), substitution bias is mitigated, only to worsen again over time as consumer choices diverge from the new market basket. More frequent changes in the market basket would reduce the bias but would require additional resources as well as research to determine how frequently the updates should occur.

The quality of the goods and services purchased by consumers also changes over time. In principle, a change in price that reflects a change in quality is not a change in the cost of living. The CPI cannot, however, adjust the prices of all the products in its market basket for changes in their quality: it is simply impossible to measure the extent of ongoing quality changes in the myriad products consumers purchase. Experts disagree about how well the CPI in practice has accounted for quality changes and how this accounting might best be improved.

Chart 2-6 **Unemployment Rates by State, December 1994**
Though gains in employment were spread widely across the Nation during 1994,
state unemployment rates still vary greatly.

(U.S. average = 5.4 percent)

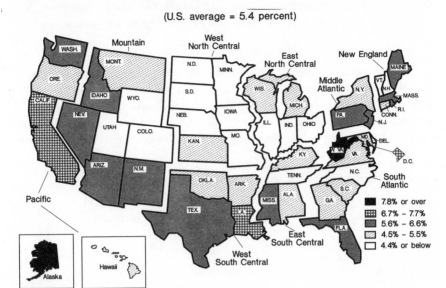

Source: Department of Labor.

The West was a region of sharp contrasts. The Rocky Mountain region was the star performer of 1994. Payroll employment rose more than 4 percent and personal income jumped more than 8 percent. Similarly, the Mountain region led the Nation in retail sales growth. Although the unemployment rate fell less sharply there than in other regions in 1994, by September the rate was less than 5 percent.

In contrast, the Pacific region's performance continued to lag well behind its strong growth of the 1980s, largely reflecting the subpar performance of California. Payroll employment growth in the Pacific region, although positive, trailed that of other regions; even by the end of the year the level of employment had not yet regained its prerecession peak. California's unemployment rate remained far above the national average throughout the year, and the pace of job creation there was much slower than in the rest of the country.

Much of the softness of the California economy reflected weakness in the southern part of the State. The loss of jobs associated with defense downsizing and the collapse of the Los Angeles area real estate market over the past few years has been well documented. Although the number of jobs in the aerospace industry continued to decline, there is now evidence that other sectors of Southern California's economy are picking up and that the real es-

63

tate market has finally stabilized. Moreover, California should benefit from the growth in incomes elsewhere in the Nation as it translates into increasing orders for California producers who "export" their goods and services to the rest of the country.

INTERNATIONAL DEVELOPMENTS

During 1994, America's merchandise trade deficit (the excess of merchandise imports over exports) increased to 2.7 percent of GDP, reaching a total deficit of $169 billion (Chart 2–7). More rapid growth at home than in the rest of the world was a major factor responsible for the deterioration in the Nation's external position.

Chart 2-7 **Merchandise Exports and Imports**
Since 1991 the deficit on merchandise trade has been widening.

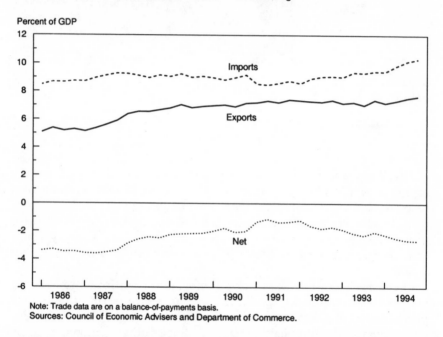

Percent of GDP

Note: Trade data are on a balance-of-payments basis.
Sources: Council of Economic Advisers and Department of Commerce.

Real exports of goods and services expanded briskly, rising 10.2 percent in 1994, and the United States maintained its position as the world's largest exporter. The strengthening recovery in foreign industrial countries, continued robust growth in developing countries, the decline in the dollar's exchange value, the implementation of the North American Free Trade Agreement, and the ongoing improvement in America's underlying competitiveness all helped to boost export sales to record highs. But the rise in exports was outstripped by the increase in imports that accompanied strong domestic investment and consumption demand. The performance of the trade deficit in 1994 was consistent with estimates indicating that, for the United States, the response of imports to a change in domestic income is generally greater than the response of exports to a similar change in foreign income.

America as an International Debtor

The United States remains critically dependent on foreign capital inflows to finance its sizable external deficit. Since the early 1980s, when America's claims on foreigners exceeded foreigners' claims on the United States, persistent current account deficits and the counterpart foreign acquisition of U.S. assets have led to a buildup of U.S. international indebtedness. By the late 1980s the value of U.S. assets owned by foreigners was larger than the value of foreign assets owned by American residents, and the gap has continued to grow since then (Table 2–4). Total net U.S. international debt exceeded $500 billion in 1993; the figure is $556 billion if direct investment holdings are valued at current cost, and $508 billion if those holdings are evaluated at market value. As a share of nominal income, the burden of net international debt has risen to between 8 and 9 percent of GDP. Regardless of whether it is measured in billions of dollars or as a share of income, however, the debt owed to foreigners remains high.

TABLE 2–4.— *U.S. Net International Investment Position*

End of year	Billions of dollars		Percent of GDP	
	At current cost	At market value	At current cost	At market value
1982	379	265	11.9	8.3
1987	−23	58	−.5	1.2
1990	−251	−224	−4.5	−4.0
1993	−556	−508	−8.6	−7.8

Source: Department of Commerce.

Yet despite its position as an international debtor, the United States until very recently registered a positive balance on net investment income. Higher rates of return on U.S. holdings abroad than on foreign holdings of U.S. assets reflected in part low rates of return on foreign holdings, most notably on investments in real estate. During 1993, however, the balance on investment income switched from positive to negative. Net investment payments now add to our current account deficit, increasing our financing needs and our dependence on foreign capital. Without a sizable reduction in the net debt owed to foreigners, either through an increase in U.S. holdings of foreign assets or through a reduction in U.S. liabilities to foreigners, net investment income payments are likely to remain in deficit through the end of the decade and beyond. Over time, net investment income payments to foreigners will constitute a larger and larger share of our current account position.

65

Exchange Rates

The value of the dollar declined about 8 percent last year when measured on a trade-weighted basis against the currencies of the nine major foreign industrial countries. However, the nominal value of the trade-weighted dollar has been broadly trendless since early 1987, following the Louvre Accord among the six major industrialized countries to stabilize exchange rates.

The dollar moved more substantially against some individual currencies than is reflected in the weighted-average rate (Chart 2–8). Between the end of 1993 and July 1994, the dollar declined some 12 percent against the Japanese yen, bringing the cumulative decline vis-a-vis the yen since the end of 1992 to 21 percent. After midsummer the dollar's value in terms of the yen was more stable, and the dollar ended the year trading at 99.6 yen. Movements in the dollar-yen rate reflected to some extent trade tensions between Japan and the United States (see Chapter 6). In addition, the rising current account deficit in the United States and surplus in Japan may have increased downward pressure on the dollar and upward pressure on the yen. Although both the American and the Japanese current account imbalances have been rising in recent years, external imbalance is not new for either country; thus it remains a question how much this factor influenced the behavior of financial markets in 1994.

Chart 2-8 **Measures of the Dollar's Value**
The dollar fell against the currencies of Japan and Germany in 1994 but appreciated against the Canadian dollar.

Index, January 1987=100

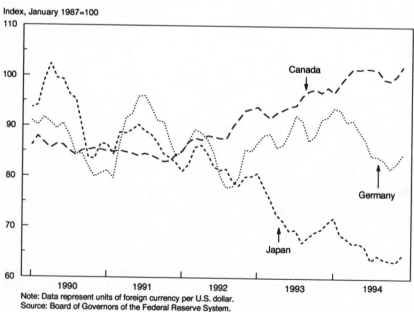

Note: Data represent units of foreign currency per U.S. dollar.
Source: Board of Governors of the Federal Reserve System.

66

The dollar also weakened significantly against some European currencies, most notably vis-a-vis the German mark and the currencies that are closely tied to it through the European Exchange Rate Mechanism, such as the French franc, the Belgian franc, and the Dutch guilder. Over the course of the year the dollar fell 11 percent against the mark. At the beginning of 1994 market participants expected some rise in the dollar's value relative to the mark, as monetary policy in the United States was widely expected to grow tighter and that in Germany to become easier over the year. The strength of the German recovery relative to expectations may have accounted for some of the appreciation of the mark against the dollar.

Against the currency of our largest export market—the Canadian dollar—the U.S. dollar appreciated 5 percent last year. Since mid-1991 the Canadian dollar has lost 19 percent of its value relative to the U.S. dollar. Major contributors to the slide in the Canadian dollar have been rising government debt and political uncertainty: the ratio of Canadian Government debt to GDP hit 95 percent in 1994 (up from less than 70 percent in 1989), and the increasing strength of the Quebec separatist movement has gained widespread attention.

At the end of 1994 the Mexican peso declined sharply—by some 31 percent—vis-a-vis the U.S. dollar. Details of the peso's fall and efforts by the Administration to address Mexico's resulting liquidity crisis are discussed in Chapter 6.

Other factors are likely to have influenced the overall depreciation of the dollar as well. First, the perception by at least some market participants that the Federal Reserve was slow to tighten the stance of monetary policy may have led investors to sell dollar assets. In addition, the widely discussed move by institutional investors out of dollar assets and into emerging-market funds in order to diversify portfolios no doubt contributed to the dollar's weakness.

FISCAL POLICY IN 1994 AND BEYOND

As noted in Chapter 1, the Administration's 1994–98 budget package, embodied in the Omnibus Budget Reconciliation Act of 1993 (OBRA93), resulted in a dramatic reduction in the Federal deficit in 1994 and markedly improved the deficit outlook for the remainder of this decade. The fiscal 1994 deficit was $52 billion lower than the fiscal 1993 deficit, and $72 billion lower if special factors, such as net receipts from sales of assets acquired from failed savings and loans, are excluded. Over the entire 1994–98 period, the Administration estimates that accumulated deficits will fall by some $616 billion relative to the pre-OBRA93 baseline—

roughly $500 billion from OBRA93's spending cuts and revenue increases, and the remainder from technical revisions as well as improved economic conditions, the latter in part due to the budget package. The Administration's 1996 budget package preserves OBRA93's deficit reduction measures and adds another $81 billion in budgetary savings through 2000, even as it provides full funding for the Administration's proposed middle-class tax cuts, which will total $63 billion between 1996 and 2000.

As a result of the Administration's deficit reduction measures, along with projected slowdowns in medicare and medicaid spending, the Federal deficit will continue to decline as a share of GDP, averaging about 2.5 percent during the 1994-2000 period, nearly 2 percentage points less than the 4.4-percent average for the 1982–93 period.

Because the size of the budget deficit depends not just on policy decisions but also on the state of the economy, economists prefer to use the so-called structural or cyclically corrected deficit to assess the stance and direction of fiscal policy. The structural deficit, defined as the deficit that would result if the economy were operating at or near its potential output level, is designed to capture the effects of policy and exclude the effects of the business cycle on the size of the deficit.

Chart 2–9 shows the Administration's estimates of the structural deficit relative to the economy's potential output. The chart reveals that this ratio rose dramatically during the 1980s, reaching a peak of 5 percent in 1986 and averaging 3.9 percent between 1982 and 1993. Between 1993 and 1994 the stance of fiscal policy became contractionary in response to OBRA93's implementation, and this ratio fell from 3.3 percent to 2.8 percent. The decline in the ratio of the structural deficit to potential GDP is even more impressive when special factors such as deposit insurance are excluded: from 3.7 percent in 1993 to 2.9 percent in 1994. Moreover, based on the Administration's current economic forecast, projected slowdowns in the growth of medicare and medicaid spending, and the Administration's deficit reduction policies, the structural deficit is projected to decline throughout the remainder of the decade as a share of potential GDP and to average 2.5 percent for the entire 1994–2000 period.

THE BUDGET OUTLOOK OVER THE LONGER RUN

Current long-run projections suggest that if the Administration's current policy proposals are enacted and the anticipated slowdowns in medicare and medicaid spending persist, the improvement in the deficit should be preserved for at least the next 10 years. Beyond 2000 the deficit is anticipated to remain roughly constant. Relative to GDP, however, the deficit is likely to continue its gradual de-

Chart 2-9 **Structural Budget Deficits**

Policy changes enacted in 1993 arrested the upward trend of the deficit, and the President's proposed budget for fiscal 1996 will achieve even more deficit reduction.

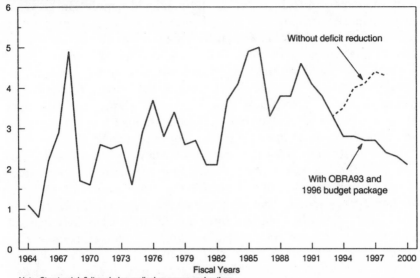

Percent of potential GDP

Without deficit reduction

With OBRA93 and
1996 budget package

Fiscal Years

Note: Structural deficit excludes cyclical revenues and outlays.
Sources: Council of Economic Advisers and Office of Management and Budget.

cline, falling below 2 percent early in the next century. Over the longer run, changing demographics will put upward pressure on the deficit as the baby-boom generation, born during the first two decades after World War II, begins to retire. The aging of the population will contribute to rising expenditures for both Social Security and Federal medical programs, because medicare is primarily a program for those over the age of 65, and medicaid is increasingly a program for elderly people needing nursing home care.

During the 1996–2000 period, spending for both medicare and medicaid is projected to increase at a slower rate than in recent years. This projected slowdown is the result of several factors including lower projected medical cost inflation, slower projected growth of the medicaid beneficiary population, and increased scrutiny of State claims for certain Federal medicaid matching payments. Despite these changes, however, the projected growth rates for both medicare and medicaid remain very high. Medicare benefits are projected to grow at an average annual rate of 9.1 percent, and medicaid benefits at an average annual rate of 9.3 percent. Both of these growth rates are nearly three times the projected general inflation rate of 3.2 percent, and at these rates both medicare and medicaid spending will double every 8 years. As a result, by 2000 spending on these programs will account for one-fifth of total Federal outlays, rising from 3.4 percent of GDP in fiscal 1994 to 4.1 percent by 2000. By 2005 these health care programs will amount to 4.9 percent of GDP.

The number of people participating in the Federal health programs is expected to increase as the medicaid population grows at an anticipated 3.8-percent annual rate on average between now and 2000. However, this expansion makes up a relatively small part of the increase in total Federal spending for medicare and medicaid—it could be accommodated without undue pressure on the deficit. The main reason why the fiscal impact of these programs is such a problem is that health care spending per beneficiary keeps rising faster than inflation—indeed faster than inflation plus the general increase in real per capita GDP.

Chart 2–10 illustrates the impact of rising medicaid and medicare spending on the deficit. If spending on these programs grew at the rate of increase of the beneficiary population, but spending per beneficiary rose in line with per capita nominal GDP, the Federal budget would be balanced by the year 2003. Obviously it is unrealistic to anticipate such a sharp change in health care spending trends given the long history of rapid growth, but this fact helps pinpoint the real problem behind the continuing large Federal deficit and confirms the need for genuine health care reform.

Chart 2-10 **Health Care Inflation and the Federal Deficit**
If per beneficiary costs of medicare and medicaid rose only at the rate of growth of nominal per capita output, the Federal deficit would vanish by the year 2003.

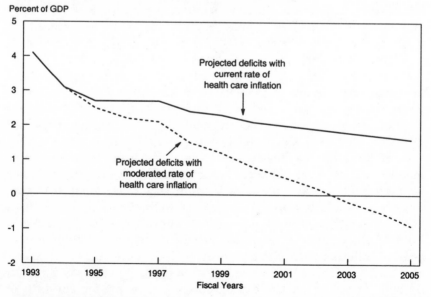

Source: Office of Management and Budget.

As noted in Chapter 1, the Administration remains committed to such reform, to provide health security to all Americans and contain health care costs for families, businesses, and Federal, State, and local governments. Because of the linkages and interactions between public health care programs and the private health care market, attempts to stem the growth of Federal programs by such mechanisms as spending caps will not solve the underlying problem of costs. Instead, the imposition of caps will shift costs to the private sector and threaten the availability and quality of services for the medicare and medicaid populations.

THE CHANGING COMPOSITION OF FEDERAL SPENDING

One of the underappreciated aspects of fiscal policy is the change in fiscal spending priorities that has emerged during the last three decades. Chart 2–11 presents the major categories of Federal spending over this period. The chart indicates that—contrary to conventional belief—the long-run growth of nondefense discretionary spending has been considerably slower than GDP growth for much of this period, and the ratio of nondefense discretionary spending to GDP is projected to remain well below the peak realized in 1980.

Chart 2-11 **Composition of Federal Spending**
Relative to GDP, discretionary spending has fallen during the past two decades, while entitlement spending and interest on the debt have grown.

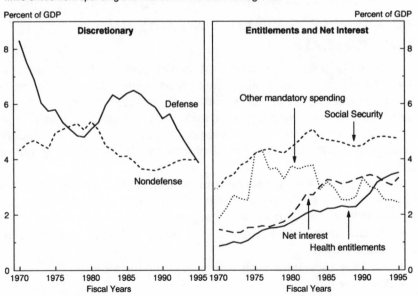

Source: Office of Management and Budget.

71

To some extent, the diminishing claim on economic output of nondefense discretionary spending reflects competition between defense and nondefense spending. But to a larger extent the contraction of nondefense discretionary spending relative to GDP reflects the pressure on the budget of rapid growth in both net interest payments on the debt and entitlement spending. Over the early 1980s the buildup in Federal debt was particularly large. As a result, 1994 interest payments on the debt constituted 3.1 percent of GDP, compared with an average of 1.6 percent between 1970 and 1981.

The most dramatic feature in the changing expenditure mix is the growth of spending on entitlement programs, especially health care programs. Federal health care spending grew from an average of 1.3 percent of GDP over the 1970–81 period to close to 3.4 percent of GDP by 1993–94. Between 1970 and 1994, average annual growth in health care spending was about 1¾ times average annual growth in nominal GDP.

Chart 2–12 provides detail on the projected composition of Federal spending for fiscal 1995. The four largest components of Federal spending are Social Security, national defense, interest on the debt, and medicare, in that order. Together these categories account for about 65 percent of total Federal spending. Expenditures for medicare, the smallest of these four components, are over five times spending on food stamps, over eight times spending on international affairs, and over nine times spending on aid to families with dependent children.

PRINCIPLES FOR EVALUATING ALTERNATE TAX PROPOSALS

As already noted and described in Chapter 1, the Administration's 1996 budget proposal contains a package of tax cuts for middle-class Americans. These include a child-based tax credit, a tax deduction for postsecondary education and training expenses, and expanded availability of individual retirement accounts (IRAs). These initiatives are paid for primarily by discretionary spending cuts.

In its assessment of various tax proposals that are likely to be considered by the Congress during the coming year, the Administration will rely on four basic principles:

- Do the proposed changes in tax policy enhance long-run economic growth?
- Are they consistent with norms of economic efficiency?
- Are they fair?
- Are they fiscally responsible?

Chart 2-12   **Federal Outlays by Function, Fiscal 1995**
Social Security, defense, medicare, and net interest on the debt comprise 65 percent of
Federal spending, dwarfing outlays on international affairs and social insurance programs.

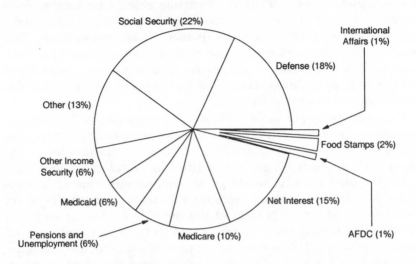

Note: AFDC is aid to families with dependent children.
Source: Office of Management and Budget.

Although each of these principles is important in its own right, any set of tax proposals should be evaluated in terms of how it measures up against all four.

The first of these principles focuses on the incentive properties of tax measures and takes a long-run view of their likely results. The Administration's proposed tax deduction for postsecondary education and training expenses, for example, is · designed to strengthen individual incentives to invest in these activities, both of which have been demonstrated to offer good rates of return on average. Similarly, the Administration's proposed IRA expansion is intended to focus more attention on household saving. The goal of these tax proposals is to increase the economy's aggregate amounts of human and physical capital, thereby increasing incomes in the long run.

The second principle concentrates on economic efficiency by examining the distortions that proposed taxes might create in basic economic choices. In the early 1980s, for example, changes in tax policy produced a proliferation of tax shelter activity, with adverse consequences for both investors and the tax system. Another example of a proposal that is deeply flawed from an efficiency point of view is the "neutral cost recovery system" proposed in the House Republican Contract with America. This system offers, for certain types of assets, depreciation allowances that are indexed for inflation and then increased by a factor of 3.5 percent per year. However, it does not index debt, so that businesses can deduct all of their interest expense rather than only that portion associated with the real interest rate. Thus it effectively shields businesses from taxation on many of their investments while permitting them to deduct fully the costs of debt to finance those investments. This would create a large economic distortion in investment choices both because it would result in a negative income tax on a significant fraction of total business investment and because it would treat different types of capital differently.

The third principle for evaluating tax proposals is fairness, an important dimension of which is vertical equity, or the distribution of the tax burden among families at different income levels. As noted earlier, about 87 percent of the benefits of the Administration's proposed tax cuts would go to families with annual incomes under $100,000. In contrast, according to analyses by the Treasury Department, about 50 percent of the benefits of the tax cuts proposed in the Republican Contract would go to families with annual incomes over $100,000—only 10 percent of all American families. The overall effect of the Contract's tax package would be to reduce substantially the progressivity of the Federal tax system. A second important dimension of fairness is horizontal equity—that is, providing similar treatment to taxpayers in similar economic situations. By further increasing the gap between the tax burdens on labor income and capital income, the capital gains rate reductions proposed in the Republican Contract fall short on this score as well.

Finally, whether a proposed tax reduction is desirable economic policy depends on whether it provides social benefits greater than its revenue cost. As already noted, the revenue losses resulting from the Administration's tax proposal are fully offset by specific spending cuts, allowing continued progress on deficit reduction through the end of the decade. Specific revenue offsets have not been offered for the substantial costs of the tax proposals in the Republican Contract; those costs have been estimated by the Treasury Department at $205 billion between fiscal 1995 and fiscal 2000, and $725 billion between fiscal 1995 and fiscal 2005.

Moreover, the Administration uses conventional accounting methods to "score" the impact of its tax proposals. In contrast, some members of the Congress have proposed using so-called dynamic scoring methods to evaluate the budgetary impact of their proposed tax reductions. For the reasons noted in Box 2–3, although such methods sound reasonable in theory, in practice they would pose grave risks, because they could easily be used to rationalize tax reductions that would sharply increase the deficit over time.

Box 2-3.—Scoring the Revenue Consequences of Tax and Expenditure Changes

Current "static" budgeting techniques recognize and incorporate many kinds of behavioral responses to proposed changes in government policies. For example, if an increase in the tax on gasoline is being considered, budget analysts will estimate the likely reduction in gasoline purchases and adjust their revenue estimates. But current techniques also assume that these behavioral responses are not large enough to significantly affect the level of total output or its growth rate within the 5-year budget window.

Nearly all economists would agree that in principle policymakers should consider the effects of policy changes on the aggregate economy. But the consensus quickly falls apart when it comes to the details of how such "dynamic" scoring should be conducted. The lack of consensus reflects the fact that models of the macroeconomy are very complex, embodying myriad assumptions about the behavior of individuals and businesses. Even small differences in these assumptions can lead to different conclusions.

For example, different assumptions about the sensitivity of labor supply decisions to changes in income tax rates, and about the sensitivity of saving to changes in the after-tax rate of return, can lead to very different conclusions about the extent of revenue loss resulting from a reduction in the income tax rate or the capital gains tax rate. Unfortunately, existing empirical techniques make it impossible to determine which estimates are the best predictions of behavioral responses to tax rate changes with the degree of precision necessary for reliable dynamic analysis.

Although static scoring techniques rest on simplifying assumptions, budget decisions involving tens of billions of dollars are too important to leave to dynamic scoring techniques which are fraught with uncertainties and easily manipulated. It is not hard to imagine how dynamic scoring techniques could be used to justify generous tax cuts on the grounds that they would pay for themselves, when it is all too likely that they would cause a large increase in the deficit.

The Debate over Further Reduction in the Capital Gains Tax Rate

One of the fiscal initiatives that is likely to be proposed and debated during the coming fiscal year is a further reduction in the tax rate on capital gains. Under current law, capital gains income already receives a tax preference relative to other forms of income. This preference arises from several provisions. First, the statutory rate on capital gains is capped at 28 percent, compared with a 39.6-percent marginal rate on other forms of income for upper income households. Second, capital gains are taxed only when an asset is sold, not as the gain accrues. Third, the tax liability against an appreciated asset is forgiven when the owner of the asset dies. Fourth, the tax liability on the sale of a principal residence is deferred provided the seller purchases another house at least as expensive within 2 years. Finally, taxation on up to $125,000 of the capital gain on the sale of a principal residence is forgiven if the owner is over the age of 55 (this exclusion may be taken only once in a taxpayer's lifetime). OBRA93 further expanded the tax preference for capital gains by exempting from tax one-half of all capital gains generated by equity investments held for at least 5 years in certain small businesses.

Arguments in favor of yet more generous treatment of capital gains are based largely on claims that a cut in the tax rate would spur saving and investment and would raise, rather than lower, government tax revenues, especially capital gains tax receipts. Although a reduction in capital gains tax rates would increase the after-tax rate of return on savings (for a given before-tax rate of return), the preponderance of the available empirical evidence suggests that private saving is not likely to increase much in response. Indeed, private saving (both from domestic sources and from an inflow of foreign capital) has historically been fairly insensitive to changes in the rate of return. In addition, as discussed below, government revenues from capital gains are likely to fall with a cut in the tax rate, unless there are feedback effects on the growth of the economy (for instance from channeling more, or redirecting existing, resources into new ventures) that are implausibly large. If total saving—the sum of private saving and government saving—did not increase, neither investment spending nor aggregate output would increase.

Can lower capital gains tax rates raise capital gains revenues even if they do not induce an increase in the economy's growth rate? In the short run, revenues could increase as lower tax rates caused asset holders to accelerate the sale of their assets. Especially if the tax cut is thought to be temporary, the incentive could be strong to realize the gain and pay the tax sooner rather than later. But such a shift in the timing of the tax would probably mean a reduction in total capital gains taxes paid on a given asset over the long run. Indeed, the acceleration in payment would occur precisely because asset owners view this as a tax-minimizing strategy.

In the long run, without an induced increase in economic growth, a cut in the capital gains tax rate could raise capital gains revenues only under the following circumstances. First, an increase in the differential between the tax rate on capital gains income and that on ordinary income might lead taxpayers to transform ordinary income into tax-preferred capital gains income, hence generating more capital gains revenue. Of course, aggregate income taxes inclusive of capital gains taxes would fall. Second, a reduction in the capital gains tax rate could induce a shift in investors' portfolios away from tax-exempt bonds or even housing into assets subject to capital gains taxes. Third, and most important, a reduction in the tax rate could encourage a decrease in the value of assets that are held until death in order to escape taxation. Whether the increase in the realization of capital gains that would otherwise escape taxation would be large enough to offset the decline in tax revenues from assets whose gains are generally taxed is an empirical question.

Although studies have found a wide range of responses, recent research suggests that capital gains realizations would rise over the long haul if tax rates were reduced, but not by enough to keep capital gains revenues from falling. In any case, eliminating the capital gains tax preference given to inherited assets is a more straightforward and certain way of eliminating the lock-in effect, and thus raising capital gains tax revenues, than a reduction in the capital gains tax rate itself.

Finally, income tax revenues other than on capital gains could increase if a reduction in the capital gains tax rate raised the turnover rate of assets subject to sales commissions that are either fixed or based on gross value rather than capital gain.

When judged by the four principles of long-run growth, economic efficiency, fairness, and likely effects on revenues and the deficit, the reduction in the capital gains tax rate proposed by the House Republican Contract with America—which calls for a 50-percent tax exclusion for all capital gains and, for certain assets, the taxation of only *real* capital gains (through the indexation for tax purposes of capital gains for inflation)—is problematic and ultimately ill-advised. For the reasons already noted, the direct effects of additional capital gains tax relief on private saving and investment—perhaps its only valid rationale—are likely to be small. The creation of a larger wedge between the rate of capital gains taxation and the rate of income taxation for higher income taxpayers is likely to encourage more-aggressive tax-sheltering activities. And a reduction in the capital gains tax rate that applied both retrospectively and prospectively would provide a substantial windfall to investments undertaken before the change in the tax code, which does not serve the purpose of encouraging *new* saving and investment.

An across-the-board reduction in the capital gains tax rate also violates the principle of tax fairness. By providing different tax treatment to different classes of assets, the proposal would create an uneven playing field for investors. Moreover, according to available estimates, about 50 percent of the benefits of a uniform capital gains rate cut would go to the 1 percent of the population with the highest incomes, and over 75 percent of the benefits would accrue to the top 10 percent of the income distribution. Such a skewed distribution of benefits follows directly from the current distribution of wealth in the United States. According to the Survey of Consumer Finances, Americans in the top ½ percent of the net worth distribution owned 29.1 percent of aggregate net worth in 1989, while the bottom 90 percent owned only 30.7 percent. The share of the wealthiest ½ percent increased by 5 percentage points and that of the bottom 90 percent fell by 2.6 percentage points between 1983 and 1989.

Finally, a uniform and generous reduction in the capital gains tax rate is likely to be expensive in terms of forgone revenues. The Treasury estimates that the capital gains tax reduction currently proposed in the Contract with America would reduce tax receipts by about $60 billion between fiscal 1995 and fiscal 2000 and by about $183 billion between fiscal 1995 and fiscal 2005. These lost revenues would have to be offset by an equivalent amount of spending cuts (or increases in other revenues) to make the overall proposal deficit-neutral.

MONETARY POLICY IN 1994

At the beginning of 1994 a growing number of observers began to express concern that continued economic growth at the pace experienced over the second half of 1993 would soon close the gap between actual and potential output, precipitating increases in wage and price inflation. This concern was heightened both by a jump in GDP growth at the end of 1993, to a rate in excess of 6 percent, and by the degree of underlying momentum the economy carried into 1994.

Acting to forestall inflation, the Federal Reserve raised the Federal funds rate (the rate on overnight interbank loans) by one quarter percentage point in early February 1994. Monetary policy was tightened further in five subsequent Fed policy actions over the course of the year, and by December 1994 the Federal funds rate stood 2.5 percentage points higher than in January 1994. Although the year-end Federal funds rate was still considerably lower both in nominal and in real terms than it had been in 1989 and early

1990 (Chart 2–13), when the gap between actual and potential output was roughly comparable to where it was at the end of 1994, the cumulative rise in the rate was substantial when measured against changes in the first year of earlier episodes of tightening.

Chart 2-13 **Nominal and Real Federal Funds Rates**
The rising Federal funds rate in 1994 reflected the Federal Reserve's shift toward tighter monetary policy.

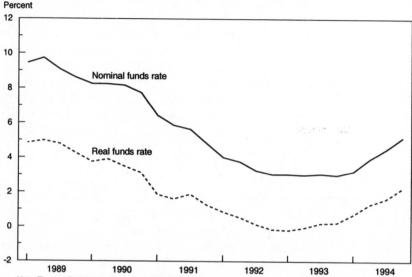

Percent

Note: The real Federal funds rate is the nominal rate less the rate of inflation, measured by the change in the GDP fixed-weight price index over the past year.
Sources: Department of Commerce and Board of Governors of the Federal Reserve System.

The Fed's action in February, in advance of any apparent increase in inflation, reflected its view that economic activity responds with a lag and then only gradually to changes in interest rates. In the belief that the risks on inflation had shifted to the upside, the Federal Reserve reduced the degree of monetary accommodation slowly but substantially. In the Fed's view, the risk of increased inflation was augmented by the actual and expected strength of real activity, and by the absence of any appreciable slack in labor markets. Additional factors that influenced the Fed included a significant pickup in inflation at the early stages of processing, and an acceleration in nonoil import prices. The Fed also saw signs that inflationary expectations had risen in the behavior of foreign exchange and long-term debt markets: bond prices rallied initially with many of the rate hikes, but retreated subsequently with the release of additional news confirming the persistent strength of the economy. Finally, the Fed believed that various practices of banks during 1994—lowering standards for business loans and passing through to consumer loans an unusually small portion of the rise in market interest rates—were offsetting some of the effects of higher interest rates and thus warranted somewhat larger interest rate hikes.

By the end of 1994 the effects of higher interest rates on real activity had shown up clearly only in the most interest-sensitive sectors, such as housing. Still, the expectation was that the bulk of the restraint imposed by higher rates in 1994 would materialize over the coming months, moderating the pace of economic activity in 1995. Although it is expected that the economy will slow just enough to bring it to its long-run sustainable path, neither the timing nor the ultimate size of interest rate effects is known with certainty. Thus, it is possible that the Fed will decide that another rise in interest rates will be required to slow the economy sufficiently, or that the Fed's monetary tightness will cause economic growth to slow more than anticipated by the Administration's forecast.

RISING INTEREST RATES

An element of considerable surprise in financial markets over the past year was the sharp increase in yields on long-term bonds in most industrial countries. Although bond yields might have been expected to rise somewhat with the increase in short-term rates engineered by the Fed, the yield curve (the rates of interest across all maturities that prevail at a given time) nevertheless would have been expected to flatten significantly. Instead, from a low of 5.78 percent on October 15, 1993, the yield on 30-year U.S. Government bonds rose markedly during 1994, peaking at 8.16 percent in early November and ending the year at 7.89 percent. Thus, even before the first Fed action in February, yields across the maturity spectrum had risen fairly uniformly relative to the yield on 3-month Treasury bills, and the spread vis-a-vis the 3-month bill rate continued to rise through early April. Over the remainder of the year, spreads between the 3-month bill rate and yields on 1- to 3-year notes were roughly constant, while the spread between the bill rate and yields on longer term debt narrowed somewhat, especially after the Fed's tightening in November (Chart 2–14).

All told, the increase in bond yields was unusually large when judged by the historical relationship between year-to-year movements in short- and long-term interest rates. Chart 2–15 plots the actual yields on U.S. long-term corporate bonds and the yields that would be predicted from historical experience. The chart shows the uncharacteristic size of the 1994 prediction error, with actual long-term rates much higher than expected. The prediction is based on a relatively standard equation that explains the relationship be-

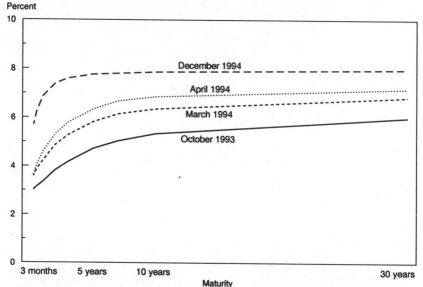

Chart 2-14 **Term Structure of Interest Rates on Government Debt**
Contrary to most expectations, long-term interest rates rose by almost as much as short-term rates over the course of 1994.

Percent

December 1994

April 1994

March 1994

October 1993

3 months   5 years   10 years   30 years

Maturity

Note: Based on 3-, 6-, and 12-month Treasury bills, 2-, 3-, 5-, and 7-year notes, and 10- and 30-year bonds.
Source: Department of the Treasury.

tween short-term and long-term yields—the term structure of interest rates.

The rise in long-term interest rates in the United States was fully matched by increases in the weighted average of interest rates in Japan, Germany, France, Italy, the United Kingdom, and Canada (Chart 2–16). Since the end of 1993, the weighted average of 10-year interest rates in the foreign G–7 countries moved up 2.1 percentage points over the year. However, this average movement disguises experiences that differed markedly across individual countries—for example, long-term interest rates rose 1.3 percentage points in Japan and 3.6 percentage points in Italy.

What explains the unusual rise in long-term rates both in the United States and in other industrial countries? To sort out the alternative explanations one must first determine the extent to which the increase in yields constituted a rise in *real* rates of interest, and the extent to which it reflected heightened expectations of inflation. If real rates have risen, the cause could be either stronger than expected aggregate demand or an increase in the risk premium (or some combination of the two). Only limited evidence exists to help make these distinctions. The relative importance of each factor is likely to have differed—perhaps significantly—across countries. The next section sets out a framework for examining the rise in interest rates and applies it to the U.S. experience.

81

Chart 2-15 Actual and Predicted Long-Term Interest Rates

The increase in long-term interest rates during 1994 is at odds with standard models of interest rate determination.

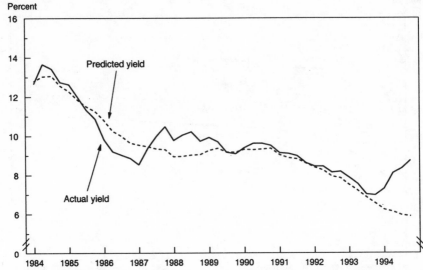

Percent

Predicted yield

Actual yield

1984 1985 1986 1987 1988 1989 1990 1991 1992 1993 1994

Note: Yields are for Moody's seasoned Aaa bonds and are reported as effective yields. The predicted yields are based on the term structure equation of the MPS model, estimated over 1957-1983.
Sources: Board of Governors of the Federal Reserve System and Moody's Investors Service.

Chart 2-16 U.S. and Foreign Long-Term Interest Rates

The rise in interest rates in the United States in 1994 corresponded to similar increases in foreign industrialized countries.

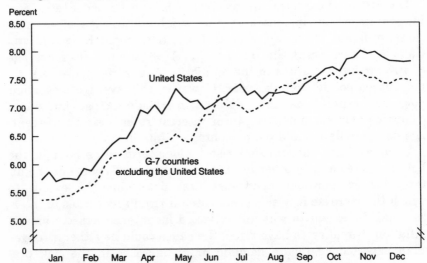

Percent

United States

G-7 countries excluding the United States

Jan Feb Mar Apr May Jun Jul Aug Sep Oct Nov Dec

Note: Foreign rate computed as weighted average using shares in 1991 GDP, converted at purchasing-power-parity exchange rates. Interest rates are for 10-year bonds. G-7 (Group of Seven) countries excluding the United States are Canada, France, Germany, Italy, Japan, and the United Kingdom.
Sources: Board of Governors of the Federal Reserve System and Organization for Economic Cooperation and Development.

82

EXPLAINING THE RISE IN LONG-TERM RATES

Theories of the relationship between the yields on assets of different maturities generally argue that the yield on a 30-year bond should equal the average of expected yields on 1-year bonds over the next 30 years, plus some premium to compensate the bondholder for a loss of liquidity or other sources of long-term risk. Under the assumption that there was no change in the risk premium, the term structure theory suggests that the average expected 1-year rate over the next 30 years rose by 2.1 percentage points in the United States between October 1993 and the end of 1994, 0.4 percentage point less than the increase in the Federal funds rate during 1994. Moreover, because the rise in rates was roughly uniform for 1- to 30-year debt through most of the year, financial market participants acted as if the higher level of short-term rates would persist *indefinitely*. Thus, the market seemed to be saying that short-term rates would remain high for many years.

Based on historical experience—experience that is captured in equations used to model the term structure of interest rates—expectations about future short-term rates are not based solely on the value of the current short-term rate but also on values of past short-term rates. The almost contemporaneous increase in short- and long-term rates over 1994 thus signaled a fundamental change in the outlook for future rates. This change in interest rate expectations coincided with a growing consensus that the underlying strength of the U.S. economy was greater than first thought.

To see how the increased strength of the economy could raise rates, consider two alternative scenarios. Each scenario highlights one extreme on the spectrum of interpretations of the increase in interest rates. Both scenarios assume that the economy is operating close to its level of potential output and that something happens to raise the outlook for aggregate demand. For instance, foreign GDP growth could strengthen relative to prior expectations, thus enhancing the prospects for U.S. exports. Alternatively, housing starts or other elements of domestic demand could appear to be unusually immune to high interest rates.

In the first scenario, in order to prevent the economy from operating above its potential level following the increase in aggregate demand, the real interest rate would have to rise. Moreover, if the upward shift in aggregate demand is expected to be sustained for some years, the rise in the real interest rate must also be sustained. This scenario attributes the rise in expected short-term rates implicit in the rise in long-term interest rates to an expected and sustained increase in *real* short-term rates. This scenario is consistent with a view that the Federal Reserve's commitment to a goal of price stability will lead it to raise real rates when an increase in demand would otherwise result in the economy operating above its potential.

The second scenario attributes the rise in long-term rates to an increase in the long-term forecast for *inflation*. It is based on a view that, although aggregate demand has shifted upward, the Federal Reserve either does not fully recognize the increased strength of demand or reacts only after some time has elapsed, during which price pressures build. In this scenario, in which the Fed is seen as tolerating an economy operating above its potential, the rate of inflation increases until either aggregate demand shifts back to its original level or the Fed steps in and raises real interest rates by the amount necessary to dampen the level of demand. Thereafter the inflation rate stabilizes, but at a higher level—the longer the economy is allowed to operate above potential, the larger is the sustained increase in the inflation rate.

Both of these scenarios assume that the impetus to the runup in long-term yields in 1994 was a reassessment of the fundamental strength of demand in the U.S. economy. How large would that upward revision have to have been to justify a sustained increase in expected real rates of 2.1 percentage points or an increase in the inflation premium of the same magnitude? And how plausible is such an upward revision in view of the behavior of the U.S. economy over 1994? In short, is either of the two scenarios plausible?

Rules of thumb derived from U.S. macroeconomic data can be used to quantify, albeit very crudely, the size of the perceived shock to aggregate demand under these two alternative scenarios. In the first scenario, the size of the upward shift to aggregate demand that can be offset by a given increase in real rates depends on the sensitivity of aggregate demand to changes in such rates. The more interest-sensitive is demand, the larger is the shift in aggregate demand associated with the observed increase in the real rate. Based on estimated statistical relationships, an increase in real interest rates of 2.1 percentage points would offset a permanent upward shift in aggregate demand of about 1.9 percent of GDP. That is, to keep the level of output unchanged—despite an increase of about 1.9 percent in the level of demand associated with any given real interest rate—real rates would have to rise by about 2.1 percentage points.

In the second scenario, where the entire rise in rates reflects an increase in the long-term inflation forecast, the cumulative output gap—defined as the excess of actual output relative to potential output over the period when the economy is operating above potential—is roughly 10.5 percentage points (Box 2–4 describes this calculation). A cumulative gap of this magnitude can arise either quickly or over a longer period of time. For instance, the anticipated shift in aggregate demand could be a near-term phenomenon, with the level of output exceeding potential by 5.3 percent over each of the next 2 years. Alternatively, investors may think that the additional strength in the economy is likely to last about 5 years and be worth a little more than 2 percent on the output gap each year.

Box 2–4.—Calculating the Cumulative Output Gap

The output gap associated with a permanent increase in the inflation rate of 2.1 percentage points can be calculated by using Okun's rule and an estimate of the sacrifice ratio (defined as the percentage-point decline in the unemployment rate required to raise the long-term rate of inflation by 1 percentage point). From Okun's rule, every percentage-point increase in the gap between actual and potential output reduces the unemployment rate by 0.4 percentage point. Then, using a mean estimate of 2 for the sacrifice ratio, each percentage-point decrease in the unemployment rate that is sustained for 1 year adds 0.5 percentage point to the permanent rate of inflation.

EVIDENCE FROM THE UNITED STATES

Is there evidence to discriminate between these hypotheses—an expected permanent increase in the real interest rate or an expected increase in the long-term inflation rate? What evidence is there for some middle ground—a combination of an expected increase in both the real interest rate and the inflation rate? And is the magnitude of the implied shift in aggregate demand reasonable under either of these scenarios, or is it so implausibly large that alternative explanations of the rise in long rates must be sought?

Monthly Blue Chip forecasts help to shed some light on these questions (the Blue Chip forecast is a consensus forecast of some 50 private sector economists). Beginning with the Blue Chip forecast of real GDP growth made in October 1993 (the recent low point for long-term yields) and continuing through the forecast made early in January 1995, upward revisions were made to the level of real GDP projected to prevail in the fourth quarter of 1994. By January 1995 the forecast of the *level* of real GDP for the final quarter of 1994 was 2 percent higher than the forecast made in October 1993. Forecasts of 1995 growth (on a fourth-quarter-over-fourth-quarter basis) were essentially unchanged over this period, indicating that the upward shift in the level of demand was expected to be sustained at least through 1995. These forecast revisions underestimate—possibly significantly—the perceived upward shift in aggregate demand because they occurred at the same time that actual interest rates and projected interest rates were increasing (and thus do not reflect the increase in demand that would have been consistent with unchanged yields).

Blue Chip projections for the U.S. economy over the next decade are broadly consistent with the notion that the upward shift in the underlying strength of the economy in 1994 was expected to be sustained for a period of years. In October 1993 the unemployment rate was projected to average 6.0 percent and the yield on corporate Aaa bonds was expected to average 7.4 percent between 1995 and 2004. By October 1994 the average unemployment rate projected to prevail between 1996 and 2005 had risen only to 6.1 percent (roughly 5.9 percent after correcting for the difference in the new and old unemployment rate survey) despite the sizable increases in interest rates that had already occurred and an upward revision of about 0.5 percentage point to 10-year forecasts of both nominal and real interest rates (as discussed below). Thus, sustained higher interest rates were expected to be necessary to restore the level of output approximately to where it would have been in the absence of the upward shift in demand.

The Blue Chip forecasts also offer some evidence on the decomposition of the rise in interest rates into real and inflation components. Between October 1993 and January 1995, forecasts of consumer price inflation over the year ending in the fourth quarter of 1994 were revised downward slightly—from 3.2 percent to 2.8 percent. Similarly, projections of inflation over the year ending in the fourth quarter of 1995 were revised upward modestly—from 3.3 percent to 3.5 percent. In addition, forecasts of the average annual increase in the CPI over the next 10 years were revised down between October 1993 and October 1994 by 0.1 percentage point. Taken as a whole, these revisions offer no evidence for an increase in the inflation premium and thus lend support to the hypothesis that the rise in long-term rates was largely due to an increase in the real component.

Clearly, revisions to Blue Chip forecasts of output growth and inflation provide at best imperfect evidence on long-run expectations, and even then are limited by their 10-year horizon. Moreover, there is some evidence to suggest that financial market participants saw a very different story. For instance, the dividend-price ratio of the stocks in the Standard & Poor's 500 index—a reasonable proxy for the expected real rate of return on equity—showed no significant sustained increase over the course of 1994. So, from the behavior of equity markets, the rise in long-term interest rates either was due to heightened expectations of inflation or represented some shift in the preference for equity over bonds. A popular view in the financial press was that, for much of the year, the Fed was "behind the curve"; in that case, some fraction of the rise in long-term rates would have reflected market fears of increased inflation. In fact, the flattening of the yield curve that followed the Fed's November tightening is consistent with the view that the Fed had only then assumed the appropriately aggressive stance.

An increase in the market's required compensation for risk could also be an important factor in the rise in long-term yields. The risk premium is difficult to measure and can vary over time as perceptions change. The events in financial markets in 1994 no doubt heightened market participants' assessments of risk, as is evidenced by a rise in expected volatilities inferred from options prices. But expected volatilities remained well below levels recorded through much of the 1980s, and thus this measure of riskiness, by itself, does not support the hypothesis that higher risk premia accounted for a significant portion of the runup in U.S. long-term interest rates.

On balance, therefore, the evidence from the United States is mixed. The consensus of forecasts sees no major increase in inflation. But there are indications that financial markets did see inflation and that the increase in long-term rates was therefore not entirely due to an increase in its real component.

More direct and reliable readings of inflation expectations would be provided if one could compare rates of return on bonds whose yields are invariant to inflation with yields on conventional bonds (Box 2–5). Such inflation-indexed bonds have been issued in other countries, but not in the United States, and valuable information about inflation expectations has been obtained from their yields.

EVIDENCE FROM FOREIGN COUNTRIES

A number of factors appear to have contributed to the rise in long-term interest rates in foreign countries during 1994. Probably the most important development—virtually identical to the evolution of forecasts for the U.S. economy—was the better than expected recovery in real economic activity in the foreign G–7 countries. At the beginning of 1994, market forecasters expected real GDP growth to average 1.1 percent in the major foreign countries in 1994 and 2 percent in 1995. By the end of last year those expectations had been revised upward to 2.1 percent and 2.6 percent, respectively. As in the case of the United States, there is some limited evidence available to decompose the rise in nominal yields into real, inflation, and risk components.

Evidence from the United Kingdom's well-established market for indexed bonds suggests that only about one-half of the rise in nominal interest rates in that country has shown up in real rates. The remaining increase in nominal interest rates during 1994 is viewed as compensation for inflation, a measure that includes the expectation of inflation as well as any premium for inflation risk. That the United Kingdom would have experienced such a large in-

Box 2-5.—Indexed Bonds

Although the inflation-indexed bonds that various countries have issued differ somewhat in their design, their terms generally guarantee that the principal and coupon payments are adjusted to reflect the cumulative change in a specified price index since a base period. For instance, consider an indexed bond that is issued with 2 years to maturity, a maturity value of $100 in real terms, and an annual coupon rate of 5.0 percent. One way of structuring the payments stream is as follows. If prices rise by 3 percent in the first year, the first-year coupon payment would be $5.15 (0.05 times $100 times 1.03). If prices rise by 4 percent in the second year, the second-year coupon payment would be $5.36 ($5.15 times 1.04). The maturity value at the end of the second year would be $107.12 ($100 times 1.03 times 1.04). If this bond sells for $100, its real yield is 5 percent.

For this indexed bond, the real yield to maturity is set once the purchase price of the bond is determined. The real yield does not vary with the rate of inflation, although the realized nominal yield to maturity does. By contrast, with a conventional bond the nominal yield to maturity is known given the purchase price, and the realized real yield to maturity will depend on the actual course of inflation.

An estimate of the expected rate of inflation can be derived by comparing the real yield on an indexed bond with the nominal yield on a conventional bond. For example, if the average annual nominal yield on a conventional bond is 9 percent and the average annual real yield on an indexed bond is 5 percent, then the average annual expected rate of inflation is approximately 4 percent, assuming that, except for the indexation, the bonds are perfect substitutes for each other in investors' portfolios. Differences between the bonds' maturity, coupon payments, tax treatment, and other features could affect the preference for one type of bond relative to the other, in which case the difference in yields would not correspond exactly to the expected rate of inflation. For example, investor preferences for certainty about the real rate of return are likely to cause the spread between yields on conventional and indexed bonds to overestimate the expected rate of inflation, because investors would be willing to pay a premium on indexed bonds (or would require additional compensation on conventional bonds). Similarly, if investors preferred certainty about nominal returns, the yield spread would be likely to understate the expected inflation rate.

crease in compensation for inflation over 1994 should come as no surprise, given that inflation there in recent years has been somewhat volatile. Moreover, the withdrawal of the pound sterling from the Exchange Rate Mechanism of the European Monetary System in September 1992 may have increased the risk premium attached to British assets. Notwithstanding this evidence of a greater likelihood of inflation, or increased uncertainty about inflation prospects, forecasts of U.K. retail price inflation for 1994 and 1995 were actually revised *downward* over the year.

With the exception of Italy, inflation forecasts for 1994 and 1995 remained unchanged or declined between January and December 1994 in the foreign G–7 countries. This evidence, by itself, would suggest that in most countries the rise in yields was due to higher real rates or increased premia for risk. However, some analysts have suggested that the rise in long-term bond yields across countries in 1994 should be viewed in the context of each country's inflation history. Chart 2–17 demonstrates that the rise in long-term interest rates last year was smaller in countries with a history of lower inflation (such as Japan and Germany) than in countries with a history of higher inflation.

Others have suggested that the size of fiscal deficits may have played a role. But the evidence on the link between government spending and increases in long-term yields is more mixed. The total stock of government debt is a far better indicator of a nation's fiscal position than is the size of the deficit in a single year. Whereas in Italy and Sweden increases in long-term yields of 3.6 and 3.7 percentage points, respectively, seemed to be related to government debt levels around 100 percent of GDP, rates rose in Belgium by a smaller 1.9 percentage points, despite government debt near 150 percent of GDP. There was considerable discussion among analysts about the determinants of the rise in long-term yields, but past price and fiscal developments were not "news" in 1994, and therefore it is difficult to understand why financial market participants had not already incorporated such developments into their expectations. In some cases these variables, when coupled with an uncertain political environment, may have increased the market's required compensation for risk.

FISCAL DEFICITS, DEMOGRAPHICS, AND EMERGING MARKETS

Some analysts have pointed to other factors as possible contributors to increased capital demands and last year's global rise in long-term interest rates. One factor frequently mentioned is government deficits in industrial countries, which are sizable but generally did not increase appreciably last year. Another factor mentioned is demographic shifts that will begin in some countries by

89

Change in rates on 10-year bonds during 1994 (percentage points)

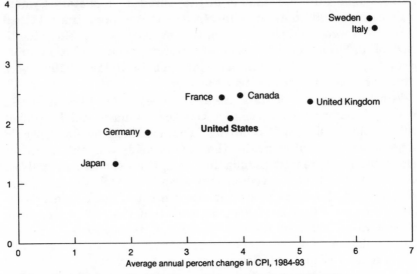

Average annual percent change in CPI, 1984-93

Sources: Board of Governors of the Federal Reserve System and Organization for Economic
Cooperation and Development.

the end of this century and are expected to bring with them increased health care costs and rising pension liabilities. Ultimately, fiscal deficits may grow significantly larger, as countries face the expenses associated with aging populations. Finally, increased investment opportunities in developing countries and transition economies are often viewed as having added to global demands for capital in 1994. Many commentators have pointed to the rise in stock market capitalizations in emerging economies and the increased flow of capital into those markets from U.S. institutional investors seeking portfolio diversification.

None of these factors was new last year, however, and it is difficult to see what would make them suddenly become important in 1994. Although the factors just enumerated may be important in assessing the expected competition in world capital markets over the longer term or the generalized rise in the level of real interest rates since the 1960s and 1970s, it seems improbable that they contributed substantively to increases in long-term interest rates during 1994.

THE ADMINISTRATION FORECAST

The Administration expects the economic expansion to moderate in 1995 as the effects of increases in interest rates to date spread more broadly through the economy. The actual growth rate is forecast to approach the growth rate of potential output, with the economy achieving a so-called soft landing. Over the longer run, output is forecast to grow in line with potential output, and the rate of inflation to remain roughly constant at 3 percent (Table 2–5).

TABLE 2–5.— *Administration Forecast*

item	1994 (actual)[1]	1995	1996	1997	1998	1999	2000
	Percent change fourth quarter to fourth quarter						
Real GDP	4.0	2.4	2.5	2.5	2.5	2.5	2.5
GDP implicit deflator	2.3	2.9	2.9	3.0	3.0	3.0	3.0
Consumer price index (CPI-U)	2.6	3.2	3.2	3.2	3.2	3.1	3.1
	Calendar year average						
Unemployment rate (percent)	6.1	5.5–5.8	5.5–5.8	5.5–5.8	5.5–5.8	5.5–5.8	5.5–5.8
Interest rate, 91–day Treasury bills (percent)	4.3	5.9	5.5	5.5	5.5	5.5	5.5
Interest rate, 10–year Treasury notes (percent)	7.1	7.9	7.2	7.0	7.0	7.0	7.0
Nonfarm payroll employment (millions)	113.4	116.7	118.3	120.1	121.7	123.4	125.1

[1] Preliminary.

Sources: Council of Economic Advisers, Department of the Treasury, and Office of Management and Budget.

By early 1996 the forecast predicts an easing in short-term interest rates. Over the forecast horizon, long-term interest rates also are projected to decline, and the spread between long- and short-term rates is projected to narrow, as the near-term slowing of growth dispels any fears on the part of financial market participants of an overheated economy. The decline in nominal long-term rates reflects a decline in real long-term rates and, in turn, is a consequence of the growing restraint implied by the stance of fiscal policy. Absent the decline in the real rate, output growth would be likely to slow with the slowing in Federal Government spending. Thus the Administration's longer term outlook is consistent with a growing share of private sector spending (especially of its interest-sensitive components) and a declining share of Federal spending in GDP.

The unemployment rate is forecast to be between 5.5 and 5.8 percent. A range, rather than a single figure, is projected both because the relatively short experience with the new unemployment rate survey increases the uncertainty associated with its forecast, and because, as indicated earlier, some structural change could be under way in labor markets. Nevertheless, the Administration expects that economic growth over the next several years will be strong enough to absorb all new entrants into the labor force. For budget purposes, the more conservative projection of a 5.8 percent unemployment rate was used.

As always, there are risks to the forecast. In assessing the near-term risks, some possibility exists that the interest rate increases to date will not succeed in dampening growth as quickly as anticipated and that the pace of the expansion could overshoot the projected growth rate of 2.4 percent for 1995. Were this to happen, interest rates would be likely to rise further, slowing the economy thereafter more than expected.

On the downside, there remains the possibility that interest rate increases already in the pipeline will moderate the expansion sooner and by more than anticipated. Compounding this risk is the risk that foreign economic growth may stall, reducing foreign demand for U.S. exports. The sharp decline in the Mexican peso and the ensuing slowdown in the Mexican economy will also cut into U.S. export growth. In addition, the substantial inventory accumulation over the past year may not be entirely intentional. If this is the case, production could be scaled back more than anticipated in order to reduce the degree of inventory overhang.

Finally, the course of the economy depends as always on budgetary and other policy decisions of the Congress. Perhaps more than usual in recent years, there is substantial uncertainty about future congressional action in matters that can influence the paths of output, deficits, and interest rates over the medium run.

CONCLUSION

Strong, investment-led growth with rapid job creation and low inflation is a winning combination, and this is what the U.S. macroeconomy has achieved over the past 2 years. In part, the robust pace of growth in GDP in 1993 and 1994 was possible because considerable slack existed in the economy in January 1993. Because most of that slack had disappeared by the end of 1994, it is unlikely that the economy will realize the same rate of growth over the next few years. That is why the Administration—and most private forecasters—predict a soft landing in which GDP growth moves to what is widely viewed to be its long-run potential rate of about 2.5 percent a year.

Despite the likely slowing of growth, the macroeconomic outlook remains very favorable. Continued increases in employment and incomes are expected. Job creation should be sufficient to keep the unemployment rate down, and sustained economic expansion with moderate inflation should allow more Americans to increase their real earnings and their family incomes over the next 2 years and beyond.

As always, there are risks in the economic outlook. The Federal Reserve has increased short-term interest rates, and long-term rates have risen almost in parallel. Indeed, long-term rates have risen around the world. The rise that has already taken place could slow growth more than expected. However, the Council of Economic Advisers views this as an unlikely outcome.

In the 1980s the U.S. economy collided with exploding budget deficits. That situation has changed. The deficit reduction measures already enacted have paid off, leading to an improved deficit outlook for the remainder of the decade. The President's 1996 budget proposal includes additional deficit reduction, as well as a middle-class tax cut. The Administration's progress on reducing the deficit has provided the basis for a stable and balanced long-term growth path.

One weak spot in the macroeconomic picture for 1994 has been the current account deficit, which widened significantly over the year as the strong U.S. expansion, combined with less robust growth overseas, resulted in stronger growth in imports than in exports. An improvement in the current account is anticipated for 1995, as growth overseas strengthens and U.S. import growth slows. Over the longer run, reductions in the budget deficit will aid in reducing the current account deficit.

With a budget deficit that is under control, strong growth of jobs and GDP, and continued low inflation, the macroeconomy has changed vastly for the better over the past 2 years, and the U.S. economy looks forward to continued growth with rising incomes in 1995.

Vigorous growth in 1993 and 1994, an expected soft landing in 1995, large increases in employment, and modest rates of inflation—these are noteworthy achievements for any economy. But the unemployment rate remains high—especially for teenagers, blacks, and Hispanics—despite a significant decline over the past 2 years, and the real incomes of many Americans have shown only meager growth. Chapter 5 discusses the Administration's proposals for life-long learning, which have the potential to greatly improve the earning prospects of those Americans who have not participated fully in the economy's expansion. First, however, Chapter 3 discusses policies to enhance the economy's long-run growth.

93

CHAPTER 3

Expanding the Nation's Productive Capacity

HOW FAST CAN THE ECONOMY grow on a sustainable basis? Most mainstream analysts currently believe that aggregate output can grow about 2½ percent per year. Recently, however, some analysts—perhaps inspired by the outstanding performance of the economy in 1994—have asserted that much more rapid growth, possibly as fast as 5 percent per year, may be sustainable.

The answer to this question has profound implications for the future well-being of the American people. If the mainstream view is correct, aggregate output will double only every 28 years or so, and per capita output only about every 56 years (assuming population growth of 1 percent per year). But if the alternative view is correct, aggregate output could double every 14 years, and per capita output every 18 years.

The answer also has important implications for the conduct of government policy. Sensible Federal budget planning can proceed only in the context of a realistic assessment of the long-term outlook for the economy. If the outlook is robust, then a more expansionary fiscal policy may well be consistent with a responsible outcome on the deficit. If, on the other hand, the outlook is more subdued, a greater degree of fiscal restraint may be required.

Chart 3–1 illustrates one simple method for assessing the sustainable rate of growth of gross domestic product (GDP). (The estimates of GDP used in this chapter are based on so-called chain-type annual weighted data, which are discussed in Box 3–1.) The chart focuses on the growth of real GDP between the first quarter of 1988 and the fourth quarter of 1994. The reason for focusing on these two quarters is that the unemployment rate was very similar in both: 5.7 percent and 5.6 percent, respectively. This suggests that a similar fraction of the economy's overall productive capacity was being utilized in both quarters. Thus the average rate of growth of output in the interval between them should give a good indication of the average rate of growth of the economy's productive capacity during that period.

As the chart shows, real GDP increased at an average annual rate of 2.1 percent between the first quarter of 1988 and the fourth quarter of 1994. This suggests that the economy's productive capac-

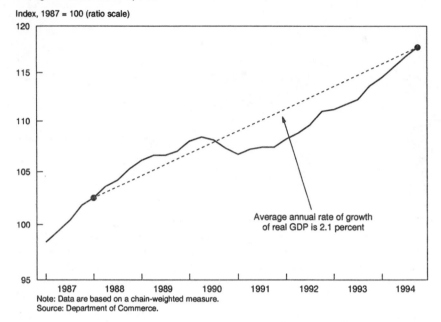

Chart 3-1 **Real Gross Domestic Product**
Between the beginning of 1988 and the end of 1994, real GDP increased at an average annual rate of 2.1 percent.

Index, 1987 = 100 (ratio scale)

Average annual rate of growth
of real GDP is 2.1 percent

Note: Data are based on a chain-weighted measure.
Source: Department of Commerce.

ity—potential GDP—also grew at about that rate. Over the same period, real GDP measured on the more conventional basis (1987 dollars) increased at an average annual rate of 2.3 percent. Therefore, this simple method suggests that the consensus view that the sustainable rate of growth is about 2½ percent per year is slightly more optimistic than a purely mechanical reading of recent experience would warrant.

But does the simple graphical method, based only on historical experience, provide an accurate signal about the future growth of the economy's capacity? Historical experience does not yield certain knowledge of future trends. In particular, it does not take into account the influence of policies adopted by this Administration with the goal of enhancing the productive capacity of the economy. This chapter undertakes a systematic analysis of the factors contributing to the growth of the economy's potential, mainly for the purpose of assessing future growth prospects. The chapter begins by reviewing trends in the growth of GDP since the early 1960s. Next it analyzes improvements in the productivity of American workers and increases in their hours of work—the two major sources of growth in the economy's productive capacity. This discussion also examines the shortcomings of existing measures of productivity growth and concludes that the economy's actual performance may be stronger than current estimates indicate. The chapter then

Box 3–1.—Chain-Weighted Measures of Output and Productivity Growth

Any index of aggregate output is constructed as the weighted sum of the output of the myriad types of goods and services produced in the economy. But what weights does one use? From an economic standpoint, it makes sense to use relative prices as weights. In the United States, government statisticians traditionally have used *fixed* weights, namely, the relative prices that prevailed in a particular recent year (currently 1987). The resulting index is appropriate for assessing economic performance in years when the relative price structure was similar to that in the base year.

Over time, however, relative prices can change greatly, making a fixed-weight index less useful for gauging long-term trends in output. Computers serve as a good example. The rapid increase in the quantity of computers produced over the past 30 years has been accompanied by a sharp decline in their relative price. Because the price of a computer in 1987 was far lower than it was in, say, 1963, the fixed-weight index understates the sector's share in total output in 1963, and hence understates total output growth between 1963 and 1987. After 1987, the effects are reversed: the price of computers has continued to decline, so use of 1987 weights for 1994 computer output causes an overstatement of the contribution of computers to 1994 output. Because the output of the computer sector has continued to grow faster than the economy as a whole, this overweighting causes the fixed-weight index to overstate the growth in output between 1987 and 1994.

Fortunately, the Department of Commerce, which prepares the traditional fixed-weight measures of GDP, also now publishes alternative GDP measures that eliminate this bias. One such alternative is the so-called chain-type annual weighted measure. The Department of Labor uses a similar chain-weighted measure (for the private nonfarm business sector) to construct the productivity measures cited in this chapter. According to the chain-type output measure, between 1963 and 1987 real GDP increased by an average of 3.3 percent per year, or 0.3 percentage point faster than the fixed-weight measure. Between 1987 and 1993, output as measured by the alternative index grew an average of 1.9 percent annually, or about 0.2 percentage point less than the official fixed-weight figures. Thus, correcting for fixed-weight bias makes the post-1987 performance of output (and therefore also of productivity) look somewhat less encouraging relative to its pre-1987 performance.

turns to an examination of the appropriate role of government policy in enhancing the economy's sustainable long-run growth rate. The chapter concludes with a brief assessment of the outlook for trend productivity growth and for the growth of the economy's potential.

FACTORS GENERATING GROWTH
OF POTENTIAL GDP

Between 1963 and 1994 real U.S. GDP increased at an average annual rate of 3.1 percent per year. Because the economy appears to have been operating about at its potential in both those years, the average rate of growth of *actual* output between those dates should provide a relatively accurate estimate of the average rate of growth of *potential* output during the same period.

Growth of real GDP can be decomposed into two main components: growth of output per hour worked (or productivity) and growth of hours worked. As Chart 3–2 illustrates, these two components each contributed 1.7 percentage points to the growth of GDP between 1963 and 1994. (Strictly speaking, the data on productivity and hours worked pertain only to the private nonfarm business sector, whereas the data on output pertain to the total economy. As a result, and because the output of the private nonfarm business sector was increasing slightly more rapidly than the output of the total economy, the growth of output per hour and the growth of hours worked add up to slightly more than the growth of GDP).

Chart 3–2 also shows that the average experience since 1963 subsumes two very different episodes. Between 1963 and 1972 real GDP increased at an average annual rate of 4.2 percent. By contrast, since 1972 real GDP has increased only about 2.6 percent per year. (The economy appears to have been operating at about its potential in 1972; as a result, that year should also serve as a useful benchmark for purposes of estimating potential GDP growth rates.) The slower rate of growth of GDP since 1972 can be attributed to a slowdown in the rate of growth of productivity, since the growth of hours worked was about as rapid after 1972 as before.

Chart 3–3 examines the slowdown in the growth of productivity in more detail. The chart illustrates one of the most significant economic developments of the postwar period. Whereas productivity in the private nonfarm business sector increased at an average annual rate of 2.8 percent between 1963 and 1972, it increased only 1.7 percent per year between 1972 and 1978, and only 1.0 percent after 1978 (yet another year in which the economy was operating close to potential).

By contrast, productivity growth in the manufacturing sector seems to have slowed much less during the past four decades. As

98

Chart 3-2 Factors Generating Growth of Gross Domestic Product
Since 1972, real GDP has increased more slowly than before, owing to a reduction
in the rate of growth of output per hour worked.

Average annual percent change

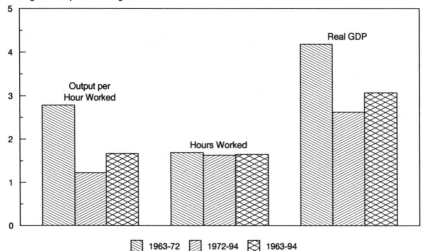

☒ 1963-72   ☒ 1972-94   ☒ 1963-94

Note: Estimates of growth in output and output per hour are based on chain-weighted measures.
Data on output per hour and hours worked pertain to the private nonfarm business sector, whereas the data
on GDP pertain to the whole economy.
Sources: Council of Economic Advisers, Department of Commerce, and Department of Labor.

Chart 3-3 Output per Hour in the Private Nonfarm Business Sector
Productivity growth in the private nonfarm business sector seems to have slowed
markedly sometime in the early 1970s.

Index, 1987 = 100 (ratio scale)

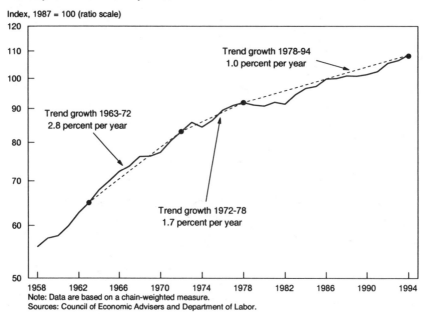

Note: Data are based on a chain-weighted measure.
Sources: Council of Economic Advisers and Department of Labor.

Chart 3–4 shows, output per hour in the manufacturing sector is estimated to have increased on average about 3.3 percent per year between 1963 and 1972, 2.6 percent between 1972 and 1978, and 2.6 percent again between 1978 and 1987. (The chain-weighted data used in Chart 3-4 were only available through 1991. Growth in manufacturing productivity between 1987 and 1991 was quite weak, but this is not surprising given that the economy was still in recession in early 1991. Assessment of the more recent trend in manufacturing productivity will have to await publication of data for subsequent years, when the economy was once again operating closer to potential.)

Chart 3-4 **Output per Hour in the Manufacturing Sector**
Productivity growth in the manufacturing sector appears to have slowed only a little since the 1960s and early 1970s.

Index, 1987 = 100 (ratio scale)

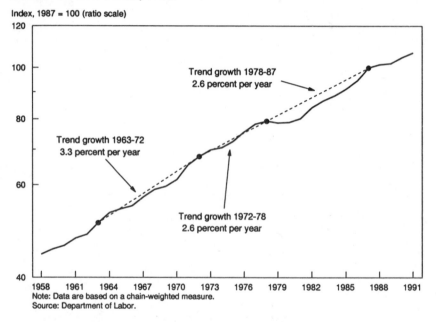

Note: Data are based on a chain-weighted measure.
Source: Department of Labor.

Taken together, Charts 3–3 and 3–4 suggest that the slowdown in the growth of productivity after 1972 was concentrated outside the manufacturing sector. It has been argued that these and similar data exaggerate that concentration, because they do not control for the fact that the manufacturing sector may have increasingly "outsourced" some low-productivity activities. For example, if factories contract with security firms to do work formerly done by their own security guards, that activity will be counted in the services rather than the manufacturing sector, and if security guards' productivity is less than that of the factories' assembly-line workers, official statistics may report an increase in overall manufacturing productivity that does not reflect an increase in the productivity of any individual worker. What this argument ignores, however, is that *high*-productivity jobs may also have been outsourced, in which case the direction of bias in the official estimates would be ambiguous. On balance, the evidence suggests that the apparent strength of productivity growth in manufacturing is not a figment of job migration.

Much of the discussion in this chapter focuses on the slow rate of growth of productivity in the United States since the early 1970s, relative to earlier U.S. experience and the experience of other countries. But it is worth noting that U.S. workers remain among the most productive in the world. This suggests that the productivity "problem" in the United States has much more to do with the rate of growth of productivity than with its level. Box 3–2 discusses one possible explanation for the coincidence of a high level and slow growth of productivity in the United States compared with other countries.

FACTORS GENERATING GROWTH OF PRODUCTIVITY

Productivity can be raised by improving the quality of the work force (adding human capital per worker in the form of education or training); by increasing the quantity of capital (investing in new private equipment and structures and in public infrastructure); and by improving the efficiency with which these factors of production are used. Improvements in efficiency can come from advances in technology (due to basic research or applied research and development, or R&D), but they can also come from other sources, such as process innovation, that are not conventionally thought of as technology. Chart 3–5 summarizes the behavior of the main factors contributing to the growth of productivity since 1963. (Box 3–3 discusses whether an increase in productivity comes at the expense of a reduction in jobs.)

THE QUALITY OF THE WORK FORCE

One important determinant of worker productivity is the workers themselves and the skills and abilities they bring to the workplace. Increases in the hourly output of the average worker can reflect an improvement in the characteristics that allow workers to accomplish the same tasks in less time, to adapt to changing situations with greater flexibility, and to become the engineers of change themselves.

Two rough indicators of work force quality are average educational attainment (average years of schooling per worker) and average experience. Since 1963 the average educational attainment of

101

Box 3–2.—Technological Catch-up and International Differences in Productivity Growth

How could it be that the United States, with one of the highest *levels* of productivity in the world, is not also among the countries where productivity is growing most rapidly? Some economists have suggested that, far from being a paradox, this circumstance is to be expected. The slow-growing leader, fast-growing follower pattern may simply reflect the dynamics of technological "catch-up."

Standard models of economic growth assume that richer and poorer countries have the same production technologies at their disposal (even if they choose to implement them with different mixes of capital and labor). Recently, however, growth economists have begun to question the realism of this assumption. In practice, technological diffusion—the spread of ideas—from leader to follower is far from automatic. Firms in follower countries may lack the skilled workers (engineers, managers) needed to exploit technologies used in leader countries efficiently. In addition, firms in leader countries may attempt to guard their core technologies to prevent or delay their spread to potential competitors abroad. Technological diffusion may be particularly slow in the case of "soft" technologies (process technologies and work organization), which cannot be imported and reverse-engineered as new products can.

For follower countries a gap in technology creates an opportunity. Leader countries (such as the United States) will find their productivity growth limited by the rate of creation of new knowledge. But followers can grow more quickly by closing a portion of the technology gap. It appears that success in closing this gap helped spur the postwar growth of Japan and the East Asian newly industrializing countries, which invested heavily in technology acquisition and human resources and created business environments conducive to technological growth. Not every country succeeds, however, in closing the technology gap. Indeed, some followers have fallen farther behind, and follower countries as a group have not become richer faster than leader countries. Nevertheless, the evidence suggests strongly that, for followers, the upper limit on growth in per capita income and productivity exceeds that for technological leaders.

the work force has increased by about 2 years. The Bureau of Labor Statistics (BLS) of the Department of Labor estimates that investment in education boosted productivity about 0.3 percentage point per year, on average, between 1963 and 1992. In contrast, the average experience level declined slightly between 1963 and 1992,

Chart 3-5 **Factors Generating Growth of Output per Hour**
Most of the slowdown in productivity growth after 1972 reflects a deceleration
of the so-called residual factor.

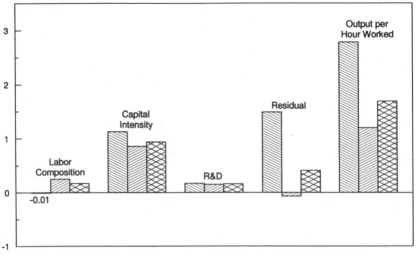

Average annual percent change

Note: Data are based on chain-weighted measures and pertain to the private nonfarm business sector.
Source: Department of Labor.

knocking about 0.1 percentage point off productivity growth each
year. On net, therefore, measured changes in worker quality have
added an estimated 0.2 percentage point per year to productivity
growth since 1963. Interestingly, worker quality appears to bear
none of the responsibility for the post–1972 slowdown in productivity growth. In fact, the estimated contribution of improvements in
worker quality to productivity growth *increased,* from essentially
nothing before 1972 to about 0.3 percentage point per year between
1972 and 1992 (Chart 3–5).

One caveat is in order here. Although the BLS education measure captures changes in the average number of years of schooling,
it does not capture changes in its quality. Clearly, quality matters:
a worker who spent 12 years marking time in poorly taught classes
is likely to be less productive than one who spent the same number
of years actively learning from skilled teachers. Unfortunately, the
evidence on whether any such decline in the quality of schooling
could help explain the productivity slowdown is too scanty to support any firm conclusions.

Training workers on the job is another way of increasing their
human capital and contributing to aggregate productivity growth.
Solid quantitative estimates have not been made of the contribution of training to aggregate productivity growth because there are
no reliable data on the aggregate amount of training taking place.

103

Box 3–3.—Productivity and the Growth of Jobs

A persistent concern, voiced by many workers and business owners as well as some economic analysts, is that rapid growth of productivity may cause job losses. This concern seemed validated early in the current expansion, when strong growth of productivity seemed to be standing in the way of a vigorous pickup in the pace of hiring. Does this concern have any analytical basis?

At the macroeconomic level, a pickup in the rate of productivity growth need not be associated with any reduction in the aggregate number of jobs available in the economy—at least not once fiscal and monetary policy have been adjusted to reflect the favorable change in productivity growth. An increase in productivity growth allows GDP to grow more rapidly without generating inflationary pressures. Over the long term, macroeconomic policies can bring the growth of aggregate demand in line with the improved rate of expansion of the economy's productive capacity, and thus sustain the growth of employment.

At the microeconomic level, productivity growth may change the composition of available jobs, and thus may be associated with significant dislocation as workers are forced into new jobs, possibly requiring different skills and perhaps even relocation. In this context, the role of government is to facilitate the transition of workers and capital to their most productive uses, while setting fiscal and monetary policies to keep the economy on a sustainable trajectory of high employment with low inflation.

Nevertheless, available microeconomic evidence suggests that training matters. Studies of the wages of individual workers indicate that the payoff to formal training (including apprenticeships) can be quite substantial: a year of training typically provides returns of a similar magnitude to those offered by a year of formal schooling (an increase in wages of about 6 to 10 percent on average). Other research has found that companies offering more training enjoy higher rates of productivity growth. (Chapter 5 discusses the importance of worker training in greater detail.)

THE SIZE OF THE PRIVATE CAPITAL STOCK

Increasing capital intensity—roughly speaking, the amount of capital per worker—has been a key source of productivity improvement over the postwar period. When new investment has been undertaken to support an improved technology, the gains have sometimes been especially impressive. For example, output per hour in the telecommunications industry increased an average of 5.5 percent per year between 1969 and 1989, as the industry invested heavily in new satellite, cellular, and fiber optic technologies.

Productivity increases through capital investment have often involved exploiting economies of large-scale production. Industries such as food processing, beverages, and electricity generation are cases in point. In the beverage industry, for example, high-speed canning lines have raised productivity, but their contribution has been made possible in part by the development of large markets. To operate efficiently, these lines must produce nearly 500 million cans per year!

Data from the BLS indicate that increases in capital intensity—also known as capital deepening—added about 0.9 percentage point per year to the growth of U.S. productivity between 1963 and 1992. As Chart 3–5 shows, a reduction in the pace of capital deepening explains only a small portion of the post–1972 slowdown in productivity growth.

INFRASTRUCTURE

Historically, investment in public capital such as roads, bridges, airports, and utilities has made a significant contribution to the Nation's productivity growth. Yet the net public capital stock in the United States has declined relative to GDP, from 50 percent of GDP in 1970 to only a bit more than 40 percent recently. The net public capital stock has also declined relative to the net private nonresidential capital stock. These declining trends in public capital suggest that infrastructure investment has been a net drag on the growth of productivity since 1970, but there is no consensus as to the quantitative importance of this effect.

RESEARCH AND DEVELOPMENT

Total Federal and private spending for research and development has averaged about 2½ percent of GDP since 1960 (Chart 3–6). In dollar terms, American investment in R&D in 1992 was greater than the R&D investment of Japan, Germany, and France combined. Even relative to national income, the United States was roughly tied with Japan for first place among major industrialized countries.

As Chart 3–6 shows, a much larger share of total R&D spending in the United States is privately financed now than used to be the case. Relative to GDP, Federal spending for R&D was at a high level in the early 1960s, after the Sputnik launch provoked a wave of concern that the United States was lagging behind the Soviet Union technologically. But that ratio trended down during most of the 1960s and 1970s and has been more or less flat since the late

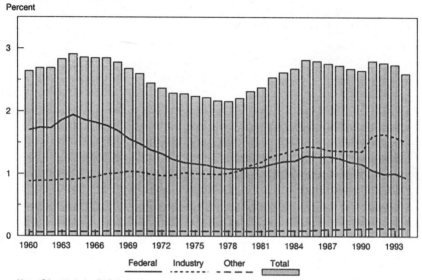

Chart 3-6 **Expenditures for Research and Development Relative to GDP**
Total R&D expenditures have been fairly steady over the past three decades, but the share financed by private industry has risen since 1980.

Percent

Federal   Industry   Other   Total

Note: "Other" includes R&D funded by universities and other nonprofit organizations. Observations after 1990 are not strictly comparable with those of earlier years, due to a change in the survey methodology.
Sources: Council of Economic Advisers and the National Science Foundation.

1970s. In contrast, industry-funded R&D investment has been noticeably greater relative to GDP during the 1980s and early 1990s than during the 1960s and 1970s. Indeed, since 1980 the private sector has sponsored more R&D than has the Federal Government.

According to BLS estimates, investment in R&D contributed about 0.2 percentage point to the growth of productivity between 1963 and 1992, with essentially no difference before and after 1972 (Chart 3–5). In all likelihood, however, R&D has played a more important role than these estimates would indicate, for a number of reasons. First, given the difficulties involved in measuring the return to investment in R&D, part of it probably shows up in the unexplained residual (see below). Second, because it is very difficult for anyone investing in R&D to capture all of the benefits of that investment, part of the return to American investment in R&D probably is captured by foreign producers. (Similarly, American producers probably capture some of the benefits of R&D investment undertaken by foreign firms.) Finally, some investment in R&D has had important benefits in addition to whatever improvement in the measured growth of productivity it may have yielded. For example, medical research (which claims 18 percent of total U.S. R&D) has substantial payoffs, but it is highly unlikely that these payoffs are fully reflected in the statistics on output per hour.

THE RESIDUAL

Over the postwar period, increases in human and physical capital and investment in R&D fail to account for all of the measured growth in productivity. The remainder generally is presumed to reflect unmeasured improvements in the quality of the capital stock and the work force, as well as more efficient utilization of capital and labor in the production process. Available data suggest that this unexplained residual contributed about 0.5 percentage point per year to the growth of productivity between 1963 and 1992.

The nature of this residual has puzzled economists for 40 years and has stimulated a vast literature seeking to explain it and to understand the dramatic difference in its behavior before and after 1972. Between 1963 and 1972 the residual contributed about 1.5 percentage points per year to the growth of productivity. Between 1972 and 1992, however, the residual made no contribution at all (Chart 3–5).

Two possible explanations as to the source of the residual follow from the previous discussion. The data from the BLS do not quantify the effect of either on-the-job training or investment in infrastructure, so any contributions of those two factors end up in the residual. In addition, industries evolve in ways that increase productivity, and the contributions of these evolutions are not captured in existing measures of capital, labor, or R&D investment. For example, the shift from small food stores to supermarkets gave a substantial boost to productivity in food retailing in the United States in the 1950s and 1960s. Similarly, many American companies have improved their business systems, and the contributions of these improvements are likewise not captured in the official statistics except, by default, in the residual. For example, the redesign of production processes within the manufacturing sector (such as lean manufacturing of automobiles) and the redesign of products to make them easier to assemble have been sources of productivity growth.

Some observers have argued that an increasing burden of government regulation may account for part of the reduction in the contribution of the residual during the 1970s. Since the late 1970s, however, a number of important industries—including trucking, airlines, and rail—have been deregulated. In addition, competition has been introduced into the market for long-distance telephone services. These factors suggest that any role of regulatory burden in the post–1972 productivity slowdown probably has not been large.

Another commonly mentioned explanation for the reduction in the contribution of the residual to productivity growth is the rise in energy prices during the 1970s. According to this logic, efforts to reduce energy consumption reduced measured productivity growth. This explanation is not very convincing, however, because energy costs do not bulk large in total costs, and because productivity growth has not revived despite the reversal of most of the 1970s runup in real oil prices.

Finally, it is possible that part of the slowdown in *measured* productivity growth is not real but reflects measurement error. This could be the case if, for example, measurement error has caused the official statistics to understate productivity growth by more since 1972 than before. Even if measurement error does not help explain why productivity growth has been slower since 1972 than before, it may help explain why it has been so slow in absolute terms. A later section of this chapter examines the extent to which the productivity problem might reflect faulty measurement.

HAS THE TREND IN PRODUCTIVITY GROWTH IMPROVED RECENTLY?

Since 1987, according to current estimates, productivity growth in the private nonfarm business sector has averaged 1.2 percent per year, somewhat faster than the average during the previous decade. And since 1991, productivity growth has averaged about 2.0 percent per year—more than twice the 1978–87 average. Are recent claims of a pickup in trend productivity growth justified? (Provided there has been no offsetting reduction in the growth of hours, such a pickup would translate into an increase in the economy's potential growth rate.) This question is not easily resolved because the recent behavior of productivity has been heavily influenced (for the better) by the faster pace of economic activity during the last 2 years. A proper assessment of the trend in productivity growth can be made only by abstracting from cyclical influences.

Chart 3–7 focuses on the behavior of productivity since 1976. Between 1978 and 1982—a period that included the deepest recession of the postwar period—productivity actually declined slightly according to official estimates. Then, as recovery took hold, productivity rebounded. By 1987 the economy once again was operating in the neighborhood of its full potential. Between 1978 and 1987 the growth of productivity averaged about 0.9 percent per year.

Since 1987 this chain of events has essentially repeated itself: a period of slow growth in productivity as the economy endured a recession, followed by a period of rebound as the recovery gathered strength. Today, well into the expansion, the economy once again appears to be operating in the neighborhood of its potential. Between 1987 and 1994—as was noted above—productivity growth averaged about 1.2 percent per year. Thus, currently available data do seem to hint that the trend in productivity growth has picked up in the last few years. However, the magnitude of that pickup

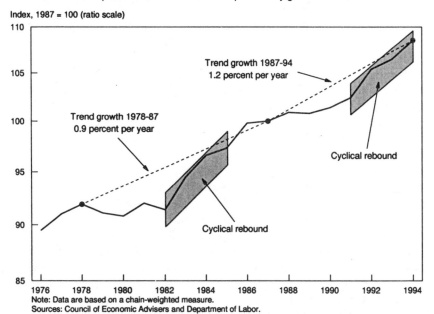

Chart 3-7 **Output per Hour in the Private Nonfarm Business Sector**
Productivity has increased rapidly since 1991. Nonetheless, it is still difficult to know whether there has been an improvement in the trend rate of productivity growth.

Index, 1987 = 100 (ratio scale)

Trend growth 1987-94
1.2 percent per year

Trend growth 1978-87
0.9 percent per year

Cyclical rebound

Cyclical rebound

Note: Data are based on a chain-weighted measure.
Sources: Council of Economic Advisers and Department of Labor.

pales in comparison to the decline that occurred earlier in the postwar period. Moreover, the evidence in support of a pickup is still inconclusive. For example, if trends are computed for the periods 1978–86 and 1986–94 rather than 1978–87 and 1987–94, the suggestion of a pickup is much weaker: productivity growth averaged 1.0 percent per year in the earlier alternative subperiod and 1.1 percent in the later one. On the other hand, if the breakpoint chosen is 1988 or, especially, 1989, the evidence in favor of a pickup appears stronger. However, the averages over these later periods, especially the one since 1989, are dominated by the cyclical recovery and so may create a false impression of an improvement in the trend.

Furthermore, the Labor Department released data in 1994 suggesting that the growth of hours worked between 1993 and 1994 may be revised upward by enough to shave 0.1 percentage point off the average rate of productivity increase for the period 1987–94. Thus, while the evidence in favor of a slight improvement in the productivity growth trend is encouraging, it is not yet decisive. The experience of the next few years will be quite telling for this issue.

ISSUES RELATED TO THE MEASUREMENT OF PRODUCTIVITY

To many in the business community, the idea that there has been a slowdown in the rate of improvement of business efficiency would simply be implausible. International comparisons based on detailed case studies suggest that the level of productivity is higher in the United States than in Germany or Japan and that many important innovations—especially in the services sector—have originated in the United States.

Examples of such innovations abound. Retailers have invested heavily in information technology to improve efficiency and the quality of service. New specialty formats provide customers with a wider array of choices. Financial institutions have simultaneously improved their efficiency and expanded their product lines dramatically. Mortgages are now processed much more quickly and in much greater volume. Customer service has been enhanced by the widespread introduction of automatic teller machines as well as automatic deposit and withdrawal services. The mutual fund industry now provides individual investors with diversification possibilities that would have been barely conceivable 30 years ago. In the field of medicine, with the introduction of microsurgical techniques, a cataract operation performed today is faster and safer than one performed even a decade ago. And with the advent of arthroscopic surgery, repair of a torn knee ligament involves a shorter stay in the hospital, less chance of collateral damage during surgery, and a faster recovery time. Telecommunications companies have introduced many new services, including high-speed data transfer and mobile cellular telephone service.

To some extent, these dramatic changes in service industries are not reflected in the productivity data presented in this chapter. Either they do not enter the standard productivity calculations at all, or their contribution to growth is understated. For example, within the financial services area, productivity growth in the banking industry has averaged more than 2 percent per year in recent years, according to BLS estimates. However, these estimates are not used in the construction of aggregate measures of output and productivity. Instead, for these measures, growth of real output in banking and other financial services is assumed equal to the increase in hours worked in the industry, so that growth in labor productivity is roughly zero by assumption.

Measurement issues are particularly important in the area of health care, both because that sector now accounts for 14 percent of GDP and because the conceptual difficulties there are so great. For example, current productivity measures would not reflect the influence of a technological advance that allowed a gallbladder patient to be treated and to recover in a much shorter time than before. As for telecommunications, productivity data understate the benefit to consumers of newly available services.

These examples reflect underlying problems in productivity measurement associated with the changing character of the economy. But there are also other general problems in measuring productivity. Roughly speaking, official measures of average labor productivity are calculated by dividing the nominal output of a given sector (e.g., the private nonfarm business sector or the manufacturing sector) by an estimated price index and a measure of hours worked. The trends in all three of these variables are subject to measurement error.

In concept, the task of measuring nominal output is straightforward: one need only calculate the current dollar value of total production of "final" goods and services—that is, goods and services that are used for either consumption or investment at home or abroad, by either individuals, businesses, or governments. In practice, however, the task is challenging. One important set of difficulties involves the definition of investment goods. Traditionally, investment goods have been defined as tangible assets, such as factories or drill presses, that have a useful lifetime of more than 1 year. As a result, intangibles such as computer software and research and development have for the most part been treated as intermediate goods and services—that is, as inputs into the production process—and therefore not as part of final demand.

Recently, however, a number of observers have suggested that the traditional definition of an investment good should be expanded to include business expenditures for computer software. A move in this direction would raise the measured level of GDP and hence would also raise the measured level of productivity. Moreover, to the extent that business expenditures for computer software have been growing more rapidly than the economy as a whole, such a redefinition would also raise the *rate of growth* of both output and productivity. Finally, such a redefinition would temper the apparent slowdown in productivity growth since 1972, assuming that, as seems likely, the growth of software production has been more rapid since 1972 than before. Box 3–4 discusses issues related to treatment of software as an investment good in the national income and product accounts (NIPAs).

Measurement of prices is *the* critical problem in the measurement of productivity. The output of the economy increasingly is shifting away from standardized commodities with easily definable characteristics that change little over time, toward goods and services for which issues of quality and even definition are of primary importance. And if the trend in prices is mismeasured, so will be the trend in output and hence productivity. As an illustration of

111

Box 3–4.—Business Expenditures for Computer Software in the National Income and Product Accounts

Much of computer software is treated as an intermediate good in the national income and product accounts rather than as an investment good. (Software that is sold with computer hardware as part of a package is, however, included in the current NIPA measure of investment if the machine itself is so treated.) In part, the current treatment of software reflects a presumption that much computer software has a useful lifetime of less than 1 year, and thus does not qualify as an investment good under current definitions. In part, however, it also reflects a lack of information; many companies probably do not themselves know how much they spend on computer software, and the Department of Commerce certainly does not know, because none of its ongoing surveys requests this information.

If computer software were to be included in the national income accounts as an investment good, estimates would have to be developed not only of nominal outlays for computer software, but also of a quality-adjusted price of software. To estimate such prices, analysts would have to determine, for example, how much more "word processing power" was provided in a new release of a word processing package than in the one it superseded.

It is difficult to know how much the treatment of computer software as an intermediate good affects the overall productivity picture. But because the volume of software purchases is vastly greater today than it was three decades ago, it may help explain part of the productivity puzzle. The case of computer software also illustrates some of the serious conceptual difficulties involved in improving current measures of productivity.

the difficulties involved in measuring prices, consider the increased prominence of discount outlets in the retail sector. In constructing the consumer price index, government statisticians treat goods sold at discount retailers as distinct from similar or identical goods sold through traditional outlets. When a discount retailer adds to its product line an item already being sold by traditional retailers, but offers it at a lower price, the difference between the discounter's and the full-service merchant's price is treated as signaling a difference in the quality of a total package: item for sale, service provided, and possibly other consumer amenities. Hence, the lower price suddenly available at the discounter is considered not to imply a reduction in the cost of living, and it is not allowed to drive the index down. But while it may be true that discounters provide less attentive or complete service and a less enjoyable overall shopping experience than their full-price counterparts, it is also plausible that part of the difference in initial price reflects operating efficiencies and hence does represent a true reduction in the cost of living; if so, it would argue for taking at least partial account of the discounter's initial prices in computing the index.

Even measurement of hours worked is more difficult than one might imagine. Estimates based on surveys of employers and households show different trends. In part this divergence may indicate that employers have a relatively poor idea of how many unpaid overtime hours their employees are working at home. For their part, workers have been shown to overstate hours worked on average.

It is easy to point to deficiencies of existing elements of the measurement system—deficiencies that could be alleviated by a reallocation of resources for data collection and analysis—but it is much harder to pinpoint the quantitative significance of such deficiencies. The Bureau of Labor Statistics has been in the forefront of research into methodological improvements in both price and productivity data and, indeed, has implemented many improvements in both types of data in recent years.

What are the implications of possible measurement errors? First, they are likely to provide at least a partial explanation for why the measured growth of productivity has been slow in recent years. Second, as was noted earlier, they help explain the post–1972 slowdown in productivity growth to the extent that they have been more severe since 1972 than before. Although the magnitudes involved are not known with any precision, it is likely that error-contaminated data understate the economy's productivity growth rate and hence its capacity growth rate.

FACTORS GENERATING GROWTH OF HOURS WORKED

In addition to increases in output per hour worked, the other source of growth in the productive capacity of the economy is increases in the total number of hours worked. Of course, the implications of increases in work hours for the economic well-being of the American people are not the same as the implications of increases in productivity, because increases in hours worked impose some cost in terms of time no longer available for other activities.

Growth in hours worked can come from four main sources: growth in the number of hours worked each week by the average employed worker; growth in the fraction of the labor force that is employed; growth in the fraction of the working-age population that is in the labor force; and growth in the size of the working-

113

age population. Chart 3–8 summarizes the behavior of each of these factors since 1963.

According to the Department of Labor, the number of hours worked per week on the average job in the nonfarm business sector declined from just over 38 hours per week in the mid-1960s to about 34 hours in the early 1980s. Since then it has been about flat (Chart 3–9). (The nonfarm business sector differs from the *private* nonfarm business sector in that it includes government enterprises such as the U.S. Postal Service.) On net, the decline in the average workweek has taken about 0.4 percentage point off the growth of aggregate hours worked since 1963—a bit more between 1963 and 1972, and a bit less since 1972 (Chart 3–8).

Changes in the employment rate have contributed essentially nothing to the trend growth in hours over any of the periods shown in Chart 3–8. This outcome reflects two facts. First, the years 1963, 1972, and 1994 were chosen as endpoints precisely because the employment rate was near its so-called full-employment level in those years. Second, the full-employment level of the employment rate has not changed greatly over the periods examined here.

One of the most striking macroeconomic developments of the postwar period has been the convergence in the labor force participation rates of men and women (Chart 3–10). Thirty years ago fewer than 40 percent of working-age women were in the labor force; today that fraction stands at nearly 60 percent. The largest increases in labor force activity took place among younger women, but substantial gains were also registered by women in their forties and fifties. The trend among men has been in the opposite direction. In 1960 more than 83 percent of working-age men were in the labor force, but by the early 1990s that fraction had dropped below 76 percent. The reduction in the labor force participation of men was particularly pronounced among older workers.

On balance, the influx of women into the labor force was the more important of the two gender-related trends, and the aggregate participation rate displayed a marked upward drift over the last 35 years, contributing about 0.4 percentage point per year to the growth of hours. The contribution of the participation rate to the growth of hours has been a shade greater since 1972 than before.

Since 1989, however, the growth in labor force participation has been unusually slow. In fact, the average participation rate in 1993 was below the average rate in 1989. The average rate did move up noticeably in 1994, but it is still too early to know whether the upward trend in this variable has resumed. Moreover, the interpretation of the participation data for 1994 has been made more problematic by the introduction in January 1994 of the redesigned Current Population Survey (the Labor Department survey that is one of the key sources of monthly data on the labor market). Data col-

114

Chart 3-8 Factors Generating Growth of Hours Worked
Overwhelmingly, the increase in aggregate hours worked since 1963 reflects the
increase in the working-age population.

Average annual percent change

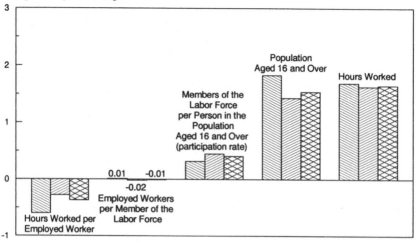

Note: Data on hours worked, total and per worker, pertain to the private nonfarm business sector, whereas data
on the employment rate, participation rate, and population pertain to the whole economy.
Sources: Council of Economic Advisers and Department of Labor.

Chart 3-9 Average Weekly Hours in the Nonfarm Business Sector
The length of the average workweek trended downward from the early 1960s until
the early 1980s. Since then it has been about flat.

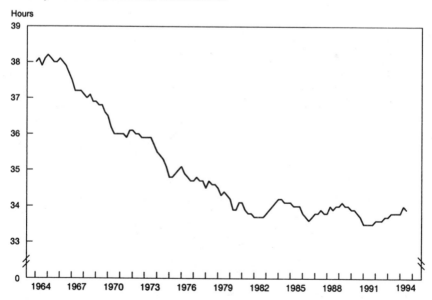

Source: Department of Labor, unpublished data.

115

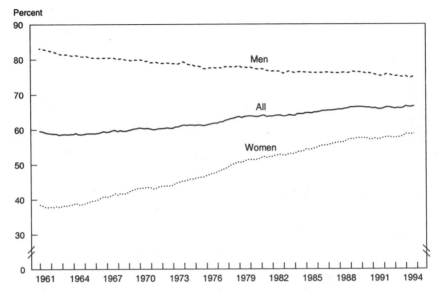

Chart 3-10   Civilian Labor Force Participation Rates for Men and Women
The participation rates of men and women have converged over the past three decades.

Note: Data for 1994 come from the redesigned Current Population Survey.
Source: Department of Labor.

lected over the next few years should help resolve whether the pause in the increase in the participation rate between 1989 and 1993 was a temporary aberration or a signal of a new, permanent state of affairs.

Between 1963 and 1972 growth of the working-age population averaged nearly 1.8 percent per year. By contrast, since 1972 this growth has averaged 1.4 percent per year, and since 1982 only about 1.1 percent per year.

Since 1963, aggregate hours worked in the private nonfarm business sector have increased at an average pace of about 1¾ percent per year, with little difference in the growth rate before and after 1972. By happenstance, the slower rate of decline in the workweek after 1972 and the slight step-up in the rate of change of the participation rate (both pluses for the growth of hours) were about offset by the slower growth in the working-age population.

WHAT CAN THE GOVERNMENT DO TO IMPROVE THE ECONOMY'S LONG-RUN GROWTH POTENTIAL?

Without a doubt, the future rate of increase in the economy's productive capacity will be largely determined by the decisions of the millions of individual businesses and households in the private economy. The role of the government is, and will continue to be, a limited one: to foster an open and competitive market environment, and to help the market work better when it would otherwise generate an inefficient result.

Government policies to advance these objectives generally fall into two broad categories. First, government must address the question of national saving. Historically, nations that have saved the most have also invested the most, and investment has been strongly correlated with productivity. Therefore, it is a matter of considerable concern that the national saving rate in the United States is low by international standards and has declined in the last 20 years. Second, government must address market failures. Depending on the context, pursuit of the second objective may require the government to strengthen market forces already in place (as, for example, when it subsidizes student loans or provides support for worker training and skill acquisition); to impose regulation (as, for example, when it takes actions to curb excessive market power or to protect the environment); to enhance competition (as, for example, when it reduces barriers to international trade); or to provide public goods (as, for example, when it funds R&D). The need for public goods arises especially in situations in which private market incentives on their own would result in less than the optimal amount of investment being undertaken because the returns from that investment are not fully appropriable by the private investor. Investment in basic research is a case in point. It should go without saying that government policies to address market failures should be designed to achieve their objective while imposing the lightest possible burden on the economy. (Chapter 4 discusses this point further.)

BOOSTING PRODUCTIVITY BY INCREASING DOMESTIC SAVING

During the 1960s and 1970s gross saving in the United States averaged about 17 percent of GDP. As Chart 3–11 shows, gross saving declined markedly thereafter, averaging roughly 15½ percent during the 1980s and only about 12½ percent between 1990 and 1993 (fiscal-year basis). In part this decline reflected the deteriorating fiscal position of the government sector (defined to include all levels of government—Federal, State, and local). Measured on a national income accounts basis and averaged over fiscal years, the deficit of the government sector was only 0.2 percent of GDP during the 1960s and about 1 percent during the 1970s. But during the 1980s the average deficit widened to 2½ percent of GDP, owing entirely to a dramatic increase in the Federal deficit. And the average between 1990 and 1993 was even a bit worse because of a decline in the surplus of State and local governments.

117

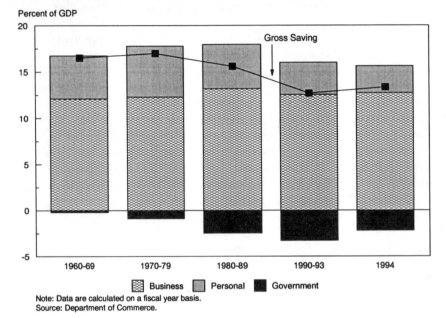

Chart 3-11 **Components of Gross Saving**
Gross saving has declined since the 1970s, partly because the personal saving rate has
declined and partly because the public sector has run much larger deficits.

Percent of GDP

Gross Saving

| | Business | Personal | Government |

Note: Data are calculated on a fiscal year basis.
Source: Department of Commerce.

Personal saving has also declined, from about 4½ percent of
GDP during the 1960s and 5½ percent in the 1970s to only 3½
percent during the early 1990s. Meanwhile, the trend in business
saving—which accounts for the bulk of gross saving—has been re-
markably flat since the 1960s.

In fiscal 1994, gross saving, private and public, reversed course
and edged up to nearly 13½ percent. The main cause of this development was a considerable reduction in the deficit of the consoli-
dated government sector, almost exclusively the result of a sharp
improvement at the Federal level: measured on a national income
accounts basis, the Federal deficit in fiscal 1994 (the first year in
which this Administration's budget plan was in effect) declined to
2.6 percent of GDP, a full 1.5-percentage-point reduction from the
preceding year.

Gross saving serves as a good measure of the Nation's saving effort, but saving net of depreciation may be a more meaningful
measure of the domestic resources available for increasing the capital stock. Unfortunately, the trend in net saving has been even
more disturbing. As Chart 3–12 reveals, the decline in net saving—
from an average of 8 percent of GDP in the 1960s to an average
of 2 percent of GDP between 1990 and 1993—has been even steeper than the decline in gross saving. Net saving increased in 1994,
and it is in this light that the reduction in the Federal deficit is

especially significant: the fiscal consolidation at the Federal level accounts for *all* of the improvement in the Nation's net saving rate in 1994 over the average for the early 1990s.

Chart 3-12   **Gross Saving, Depreciation, and Net Saving**
Since the 1960s, net saving has fallen more sharply than gross saving, in part because of a shift in investment toward more rapidly depreciating equipment.

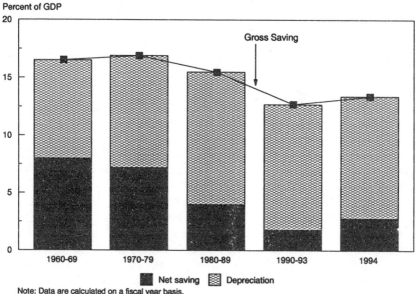

Percent of GDP

Note: Data are calculated on a fiscal year basis.
Source: Department of Commerce.

In theory, domestic investment need not be tightly linked to domestic saving, and a country that succeeds in boosting domestic saving may not be rewarded with an increase in domestic investment. In that event, however, it would be rewarded with a reduction in its current account deficit (roughly speaking, its balance of trade in goods and services with other countries). In the case of the United States, either outcome—an increase in investment or a reduction in the current account deficit—would be a desirable result of an increase in the domestic saving rate.

In this light it is relevant to ask what the government can do to stimulate the rate of gross saving. Fundamentally, two approaches are possible: one is to boost public saving (that is, cut the deficit of the government sector), and the other is to stimulate private saving.

Increasing Public Saving

As has been documented in Chapters 1 and 2, this Administration has made a very substantial contribution toward the reduction of the Federal deficit (Chart 2–9 in Chapter 2). Even so, the longer term outlook for the deficit remains troublesome, owing in part to the projected shift in demographics, as the baby-boom generation moves into retirement and begins collecting Social Security and medicare benefits. This aspect of the long-term outlook suggests that, despite the progress achieved under the Omnibus Budget Reconciliation Act of 1993 and the additional deficit reduction proposed in the Administration's 1996 budget package, more work remains to be done to put the budget on a secure footing for the long term and hence to ensure a healthy national saving rate.

Increasing Private Saving

The Federal Government has often sought to increase national saving by inducing the private sector to save more. The evidence on the effectiveness of such efforts is mixed.

Many of these attempts have focused on increasing the after-tax rate of return to the owner of a particular type of asset. For example, individual retirement accounts (IRAs) increase the rate of return on saving by allowing tax-free accumulation of funds held in qualified accounts, from which the funds cannot be withdrawn without penalty until the owner reaches the age of 59½. The Administration has proposed an expansion of IRAs, to allow tax-deductible contributions by all couples with incomes below $100,000 (and individuals with incomes below $70,000), and to allow penalty-free withdrawals before age 59½ for the purpose of purchasing a first home, paying for postsecondary education, defraying large medical expenses, and covering long-term unemployment expenses. Chapter 1 discusses this initiative in greater detail.

BOOSTING PRODUCTIVITY BY HELPING MARKETS WORK BETTER

Aside from increasing domestic saving, a government can increase the productivity of its citizens by improving the quality of the labor force, increasing the quantity and improving the quality of the available capital stock, promoting the development of new technology, and fostering a free market characterized by vigorous competition.

Improving the Skills of the Work Force

The Federal Government has an important role to play in improving the quality of labor. Individual workers have an incentive to acquire productive skills on their own, without government involvement, if for no other reason than that better skills usually mean higher earnings. As is discussed in Chapter 5, however, individuals and organizations left to themselves are likely to underinvest in skill acquisition. To help overcome this problem, the Administration has devised a comprehensive set of education policies centered on the theme of lifelong learning. Together these policies are aimed at ensuring that students enter school ready to learn (thanks to Head Start and other programs); that schools work as effectively as possible in helping students to live up to their potential (through the Goals 2000 program); that students make a smooth and well-planned transition from high school to a job or further training (through the School-to-Work program); and that workers are given an opportunity to upgrade their skills (for example, with the help of a tax deduction for postsecondary training or through a grant for retraining in the event of unemployment). Each of these initiatives is described in detail in Chapter 5.

Increasing Investment in Technology

Firms that invest in technology often are unable to capture all of the benefits of their investment. That is, there appear to be important spillovers or "positive externalities" from such investment, in the form of benefits captured by other firms without compensation to the firm making the investment. These externalities imply that the social return to investment in R&D is higher than the private return, and that a private market left to its own devices would invest too little. As a result, government has an important complementary role to play, either in sponsoring research itself or in subsidizing private-sector research, or both.

Increasing investment in research and development is one way to promote technological innovation and productivity growth, because well-directed R&D spending has a very high growth payoff per dollar. Indeed, estimated social rates of return to R&D average around 50 percent—much higher than the average estimated private rate of return of 20 to 30 percent. (Box 3–5 discusses empirical evidence on average rates of return on R&D investment.)

For this reason the Administration has supported extending the research and experimentation (R&E) tax credit. (Box 3–6 examines the R&E tax credit in more detail.) The Administration is also increasing funding for government-industry research partnerships and is working to restore a 50–50 balance between the military and civilian components of its technology investment. (The defense share of Federal R&D spending has already fallen from 69 percent in the government's fiscal year 1986 to a projected 55 percent in fiscal 1995.) In addition, the Administration is working to focus a larger portion of the Federal R&D effort on so-called dual-use technologies (those with both military and civilian applications). Other Administration research initiatives reflect a strong continuing commitment to basic science, to the creation of improved information and transportation infrastructure, and to the development of technology in pursuit of other national goals, such as environmental protection and world-class manufacturing. These initiatives and others are designed to speed the pace at which new technological ideas are discovered and disseminated in the private sector. Chap-

121

Box 3-5.—Research and Development Pays Off

Investment in R&D appears on average to have an impressive payoff. One recent study concluded that the private rate of return—that is, the return to the firm performing the R&D—averages perhaps 20 to 30 percent. For comparison, the average rate of return to investment in the business sector as a whole is thought to be in the neighborhood of 10 percent.

Estimated rates of return in R&D to society as a whole are even higher, thanks to the spillovers described in the text. For specific innovations, estimates of the returns have ranged as high as 423 percent in the admittedly atypical case of optical fiber. In a wide range of areas, however, case study evidence points to rates of return of between 30 percent and 80 percent.

By choosing particular technologies for study, case study research runs the risk of choosing only "winners" (that is, R&D investments that have paid off handsomely), thus biasing the results upward. But the case study evidence has been widely corroborated by industry-level studies. By estimating the industry-wide returns to R&D carried out within the industry itself and within related industries, these studies have provided additional evidence that social rates of return greatly exceed private returns. On the basis of such evidence, a recent survey concluded that, with spillovers taken into account, the returns to R&D average perhaps 50 percent.

Typically, we might expect such high returns to encourage firms to spend more on R&D, driving down the rate of return until it equals the return to other activities. Why have returns remained so high? In the case of private returns, one probable explanation is that investing in R&D is risky. For every idea that yields a high payoff there may be dozens of "losers" into which a firm sinks resources in vain. If the firm were unconcerned about risk—for example, if it were able to farm out its risk by selling shares of its R&D activities to mutual funds—the variability of returns would not matter. But in practice, because of the problems of communicating the quality of a potential innovation to investors, the firm is likely to have to shoulder some of the risk itself. As a result, unless it is large enough to withstand the resulting variability of returns without difficulty, the firm will probably require a higher return as compensation for the greater risk.

ter 4 provides more details on the Administration's reorientation of Federal R&D policy in light of the end of the cold war.

Box 3–6.—The Research and Experimentation Tax Credit

The research and experimentation tax credit is a Federal tax subsidy available to firms engaging in certain research activities. To address concerns that the subsidy be focused as narrowly as possible on research that otherwise would not have taken place, the credit is made available only on the increment of domestic research expenditures over a threshold amount.

The incremental nature of the credit means that some taxpaying firms (those with total research spending below the threshold) will not receive a subsidy for their research activities, worthwhile though they may be. The Congress recognized this concern but believed that an incremental credit was a more efficient subsidy mechanism than one that subsidized all research spending—in other words, that an incremental credit could achieve most of the benefit provided by a flat (nonincremental) credit at a lower budgetary cost.

Empirical research on the effectiveness of the R&E credit has yielded mixed results. Many of the early studies found that the credit was not very effective: an additional dollar of Federal tax subsidy was estimated to generate less than a dollar of additional research. However, the credit was substantially restructured in 1989, and more recent studies have indicated that the R&E credit is more cost-effective than previously thought.

The spillovers from both basic research and more applications-oriented activities cross national boundaries. In recent decades such transnational spillovers have probably been magnified by the revolution in communications, which allows news about innovations to be transmitted instantaneously around the world. Importantly, the existence of these spillovers suggests that the *global* return on R&D investment exceeds the *national* return. As a result, even national governments, acting on their own, will tend to sponsor too little basic research and applied R&D. If this analysis is correct, there may be a role for international coordination in support of such research. By instituting a formal mechanism for sharing research costs, such coordination could reduce the incentive of each country to free-ride on innovations financed by others.

Working to Reduce Trade Barriers

Barriers to international trade inhibit the efficient allocation of production across industries and countries and lower the real purchasing power of consumers. Trade barriers at home permit inefficient industries to continue using labor and capital resources that could be used more productively in other sectors. And trade barriers abroad limit the access of our efficient industries to foreign markets. One of the most beneficial aspects of an open world trading environment is that it exposes businesses all over the globe to greater competition, and forces firms and industries either to improve their efficiency or to free up their productive resources (labor and capital) for use elsewhere in the economy. Box 3–7 describes a recently developed theory suggesting that traditional analyses have been far too *conservative* in their conclusions regarding the costs of protectionism.

Box 3–7.—A New Analysis of the Costs of Protectionism

Traditionally, in extolling the virtues of free trade and warning against excessive tariff protection, economists have focused on trade-induced efficiency gains of the type discussed in the text. But estimates of the costs of protectionism obtained from traditional economic models have typically turned out to be quite small. The inefficiencies caused by a 20-percent tariff, in one such analysis, turn out to cost the economy perhaps 4 percent of national income—hardly trivial, but far too little to explain why highly protected developing economies have often remained very poor. This finding has become more puzzling over the past decade or two, as mainstream opinion in development economics has swung firmly toward the view that integration in the world trading system has been critical to the success of the fastest growing developing nations.

Recent research has suggested one possible solution to this puzzle. If international trade barriers prevent new goods and technologies from being introduced into an economy, rather than simply raising the cost of goods that are currently available, then the cost of protection may be much higher. In one simple new-goods model, for example, a 20-percent tariff exacts costs equal to an astounding 39 percent of income—nearly 10 times as much as in the standard model. No highly abstract model is likely to give definitive estimates of the costs of protectionism, of course, and models with different assumptions yield very different results. Nevertheless, the new research does suggest a way to bring theory more closely into line with experience.

In light of the significant long-run benefits accruing to the economy from the pursuit of open markets, the Administration strongly supports the creation of a world trade and investment environment free of international barriers and has made historic progress toward that objective. After securing the ratification of the North American Free Trade Agreement (NAFTA) in 1993, the Administration scored several major achievements on the trade front in 1994. Most important was the signing of the Uruguay Round agreement of the General Agreement on Tariffs and Trade and its subsequent congressional approval. The Administration also made strides toward achieving freer trade and investment flows within Asia and Latin America. Chapter 6 describes at greater length the accomplishments of the Administration on the trade front.

Although removal of trade barriers leads in the long run to an improvement in the standard of living in all countries that participate, it can involve significant costs in the short run for some industries and some workers. For example, the transition to a new job from one lost because of trade liberalization can be difficult and may require significant retraining for the new job and even relocation. However, part of society's overall income gain from the move to freer trade can be used to reduce the cost of dislocation borne by individual workers. To ease the transition of workers affected by the implementation of NAFTA, as well as of other displaced workers, the Administration has introduced a number of innovative programs focusing on worker retraining. These programs are described in Chapters 5 and 6.

Improving the Efficiency of Regulation

Government regulation plays a central role in shaping the competitive environment in which firms operate. In many cases an improvement in regulation can simultaneously promote the more effective attainment of policy objectives and increase the efficiency of the economy. For example, a traditional approach to the problem of reducing emissions of sulfur dioxide (a major cause of acid rain) might have entailed mandatory investment in costly new pollution reduction equipment by all emitters. Instead, a market-oriented system, based on tradable emissions allowances, is achieving the same results while allowing the efficient allocation of the task of reducing pollution across emitters. Chapter 4 addresses in much greater detail the important contribution of efficient regulation to overall productivity.

CONCLUSION: PROSPECTS FOR GROWTH

In sum, the preponderance of the available empirical evidence supports the conventional wisdom that the economy's productive capacity is expanding at roughly a 2½-percent annual rate. Growth in the productivity of American workers appears to have picked up slightly in recent years, to about 1¼ percent per year, measured on a chain-weighted basis (this is roughly equivalent to 1½ percent

125

on the more usual fixed-weight basis). However, trend growth in the aggregate number of hours worked in the economy probably will be somewhat slower than it has been during the past decade or two, owing largely to a decline in the rate of growth of the working-age population. On balance, the sustainable rate of growth of the economy's potential appears to be nearly the same as it has been over the past two decades, with the increase in the trend growth of productivity offsetting part of the decline in the population growth rate.

The Administration's economic projection for the next 5 years reflects this analysis. Thus, among other factors, the projection reflects a cautious assessment of the beneficial effects of Administration policies to enhance the Nation's productive capacity and to foster more rapid growth of productivity. The projection also places the Administration squarely within a broader consensus about the longer term outlook for the economy. The Administration has attempted to adopt a balanced assessment of the outlook, grounded in rigorous analysis and consistent with recent experience. Although some observers maintain that the economy can grow much more rapidly on a sustained basis, currently there is no convincing empirical evidence to support such claims.

To illustrate the difficulty of improving the trend in the growth of the Nation's productive capacity, consider the following example. Suppose that a particular set of policies were to result in an immediate and permanent increase in the investment rate of 1 percentage point of GDP. Given that investment now constitutes about 14 percent of GDP, this would be an impressive accomplishment indeed. Under plausible assumptions, a standard approach to modeling the long-term growth of the economy suggests that such an increase in investment would boost the average annual *rate of growth* of potential GDP only by about 0.2 percentage point per year for the first 10 years. Thereafter the growth effects would diminish, fading eventually to nothing—but leaving the *level* of potential GDP an estimated 3½ percent higher than it would have been without the investment push.

The analysis in this chapter also indicates that currently available official statistics probably understate the true rate of growth of productivity, and hence the rate of expansion of the Nation's productive capacity. Furthermore, to the extent that problems of measurement have become more acute during the last two decades (as might be suggested by the shift in the economy toward the services sector, where measurement is particularly difficult), the slowdown in the trend rate of productivity growth during the mid-1970s apparent in the official data is probably overstated.

Clearly, a full understanding of the scope and magnitude of measurement error is important for the proper design and conduct of economic policy. In particular, measurement error may cause official statistics to understate the performance of the American business sector, both relative to its international competitors and relative to its earlier performance. At the same time, measurement error does not provide a basis for adjusting one's view of the appropriate stance of monetary and fiscal policy. An upward revision in the estimated pace of innovation and growth in the economy would have similar implications for estimates of both actual and potential output, and thus would result in no revision in the estimated gap between the two.

The improvement in the trend rate of growth of productivity that is embedded in the Administration's economic forecast has important implications for the wealth and welfare of the Nation. If policies to boost the annual growth of productive capacity by 0.2 percentage point had been implemented a decade ago, the American economy would now have the capacity to generate an additional $150 billion in goods and services every year. Fortunately it is not too late to lay the foundations for comparable gains in productivity and incomes 10 years hence. The disappointing growth record of the last 20 years, and the anxieties that so many Americans have about their own and their children's economic prospects, demand that every effort be made today to expand the economy's capacity in the future.

CHAPTER 4

Public and Private Sector Initiatives to Promote Economic Efficiency and Growth

FROM THE DAYS OF ADAM SMITH, economists have recognized that a system of perfectly competitive markets enhances economic well-being in several ways: by permitting resources, products, and services to go to those who value them most; by providing incentives for cost savings and innovation in the production and distribution of goods and services; and by fostering low prices. Yet like Adam Smith, today's economists also recognize that under some limited but important circumstances markets do not always achieve these desirable ends. When they do not, appropriate government action can improve markets' functioning and so increase economic well-being—for example, by enhancing health and safety, protecting the environment, maintaining competition, and helping develop the intellectual and physical infrastructure that undergirds economic progress.

Markets may fall short in several ways. Markets in some sectors of the economy are imperfectly competitive because a few suppliers exercise market power, keeping prices high and discouraging innovation. Markets may also be subject to externalities, in which private actors, responding to market incentives in their own self-interest, impose costs on others (for example by polluting the environment) without compensating them for their loss. Finally, markets by themselves are not likely to provide appropriate amounts of some goods and services—like national security, education, and research and development—because these "public goods" have value to society far in excess of their value to any individual buyer.

Governments, like markets, may fall short of perfection. Government operations are not always as efficient as they could be, and government regulations, however well intentioned, may sometimes themselves distort economic activities so that markets function less than perfectly. Accordingly, the Administration has taken on the challenge of creating a government that, in the words of the National Performance Review (NPR), "works better and costs less."

This chapter begins by describing the results so far of the Administration's effort to reinvent government. The remainder of the chapter examines some of the Administration's policy initiatives toward making markets work better. These initiatives reflect the positive role of government, long recognized by economists, in promoting competition in particular markets, remedying harmful externalities, and providing public goods.

IMPROVING HOW THE GOVERNMENT FUNCTIONS

For Americans used to hollow rhetoric about efforts to change the culture of government, the first fruits of the National Performance Review, directed by the Vice President, come as a welcome surprise. In its first report, in September 1993, the NPR identified 384 separate actions that the Federal Government could take to save money while preserving or even improving the level of service. One year later, more than 90 percent of the NPR's recommendations were being implemented. Actions already taken are expected to achieve more than half of the $108 billion in savings the NPR forecast achieving over 5 years. Thirty bills covering one-fifth of the NPR's legislative recommendations have been signed into law, including the Procurement Reform Act, the Customs Service Modernization Act, the Federal Employee Buyout Bill, Financial Management Reform, and the Department of Agriculture Reorganization Act. The Federal Government is buying fewer custom-designed products and becoming a more sensible shopper of merchandise off the rack. Agencies are saving taxpayers millions of dollars by slashing red tape. Federal employees have contributed hundreds of promising practices to share with other Federal agencies. Across the country, 135 "reinvention labs" are fostering innovation by Federal employees.

The Administration's efforts to improve government functioning and government regulation seek to replace administrative controls with market constraints and market-like incentives where feasible. For example, Federal agencies have long been in the habit of providing certain financial and administrative services for themselves. The NPR directs Federal agencies to open up these internal monopolies by exposing their operations to competition. Agencies can now purchase over 100 financial, administrative, and other services from competitive suppliers in other agencies. Similarly, the General Services Administration has begun a pilot initiative to reduce its monopoly on government real estate services and instead give its agency customers a choice of service providers. This initiative involves the creation of competitive enterprises to provide real property services on a fee basis, with benchmarks for performance.

The NPR also challenges Federal agencies themselves to search for market, not administrative, solutions to agency needs and missions. Agencies can now make small purchases with an ordinary, commercially issued credit card; this move saved $50 million in

1994 alone. At the Defense Department a new travel process is expected to save $1 billion over 5 years. And as discussed below, the Federal Communications Commission has begun to auction the rights to portions of the radio spectrum that previously were allocated in a cumbersome administrative hearings process or by lottery. These auctions have already raised hundreds of millions of dollars.

The NPR encourages government agencies to replace regulations with incentives. For example, the Environmental Protection Agency (EPA) is shifting its emphasis from regulation-based pollution control to providing incentives for pollution prevention. The EPA's Common Sense Initiative involves six major U.S. industries in creating more cost-effective pollution control and prevention strategies, such as allowing companies to trade pollution credits (the advantages of tradable credits are explored later in this chapter). The Occupational Safety and Health Administration has restructured its approach to workplace safety, empowering OSHA inspectors to identify better ways to protect American workers.

PROCUREMENT REFORM

For decades, changes in government purchasing rules were more often proposed than enacted. But with the support of the Administration a bipartisan coalition in the Congress passed the Federal Acquisition Streamlining Act of 1994. The act changes the way the Federal Government buys $200 billion worth of goods and services each year—everything from paper clips to jet aircraft. Two hundred and twenty-five major provisions of law are either repealed or reformed, resulting in a purchasing system that will increase competition and lower costs.

To most Americans government procurement has become almost synonymous with "waste, fraud, and abuse." This is understandable, given the many well-publicized anecdotes over the years suggesting a regulatory bureaucracy gone out of control. Yet, ironically, the web of laws and regulations that gave rise to such horror stories as the Defense Department's $600 toilet seat actually evolved out of laudable efforts to *protect* the taxpayer from waste, fraud, and abuse.

Since the Civil War, Federal authorities have sought ways to ensure fair competition for government contracts. By 1994 no fewer than 889 oversight laws and regulations were on the books. Oversight activities employed thousands of procurement officials and added billions of dollars each year to the cost of running the Defense Department. Today the Congress and the Administration believe the public interest can be better served by a procurement system that is less regulated, more flexible, and much more compatible with commercial practices.

131

The inherited procurement system raises costs and impedes innovation by discouraging commercial firms from doing business with the government, and especially with the Defense Department, which accounts for well over half of all Federal procurement. Particularly cumbersome are the provisions of the Truth in Negotiations Act of 1962 (TINA), which among other things generally require companies with government contracts worth over $100,000 to account for every 6 minutes of each of their employees' time. One leading defense contractor, a manufacturer of aircraft engines for commercial as well as military customers, has to employ 52 extra people, at a cost to taxpayers of $13 million a year, just to comply with TINA and other government procurement regulations. The high overhead costs of dealing with the purchasing bureaucracy have led at least one other large corporation, faced with declining sales due to military downsizing, to sell its defense division to a defense contracting specialist, which could afford the cost of doing business with the public sector because it could spread the overhead costs over a greater sales base.

The procurement barriers that prevent the Defense Department from buying commercial items off the shelf do not merely raise costs to the taxpayer; they also impede the Pentagon's access to commercial technology, which in many critical areas is now more advanced than military technology. Because of specialized cost accounting practices and other demands unique to the government, leading-edge commercial producers of advanced technology sometimes refuse to become partners with military contractors. The result is to choke off the flow of technology from the civilian to the defense sector.

An incident during the Persian Gulf crisis offers probably the best-known recent example of how procurement regulations can prevent the Defense Department from taking full advantage of the inventiveness and efficiency of commercial producers. The Pentagon placed an emergency order with a leading U.S. telecommunications equipment supplier for 6,000 commercial radio receivers. The Pentagon waived all military-unique specifications, but procurement officials were still legally bound to ensure that the government was getting the lowest available price. Unfortunately, the company's commercial unit lacked the specialized recordkeeping systems required to demonstrate that the quoted price was indeed the lowest for that radio available anywhere. And since any misstatement regarding the price might constitute a felony, no company official would risk making the certification. The impasse was resolved only when the Japanese Government, unencumbered by such rules, agreed to purchase and "donate" the radios as part of its promised contribution to the allied war effort.

Past efforts to fine-tune the procurement system have not solved its problems. The entire system has to be fundamentally redesigned. The Federal Acquisition Streamlining Act of 1994 begins this process by making three key statutory changes.

First, the new law simplifies government contracting for commercial purchases. Agencies acquiring goods shall give preference to commercially available versions rather than ones specifically designed for the government. The law waives many laws that required supplier companies to provide the government with data they did not already routinely collect or that their commercial customers did not also require. Second, the law authorizes the Defense Department to undertake pilot projects to test innovative approaches to acquiring military equipment derived from commercial products.

Third, the law authorizes greatly simplified contracting procedures for small purchases while also encouraging electronic commerce—in effect, Federal contracting by electronic mail. The new law waives the paperwork and recordkeeping requirements of numerous existing laws for purchases of less than $100,000 (the previous threshold was $25,000). The increase will make an additional 45,000 procurement actions annually—valued at about $3 billion each year—eligible for simplified acquisition procedures. Federal agencies also are given greater flexibility to make "micro purchases" of $2,500 or less. For example, a Federal office manager can now buy pencils at a local discount store without having to fill out a stack of government purchasing forms.

The new law facilitates electronic commerce by encouraging Federal agencies to plug into a publicly accessible Federal Acquisition Computer Network. The President has also ordered all Federal purchasing agencies to utilize electronic commerce to the extent possible; as a result, nearly 250 Defense Department offices, which account for 80 percent of small defense purchases, plan to be online within 2 years.

Building upon these legislative reforms, the Pentagon is redesigning its buying practices to reduce significantly its reliance on so-called milspecs, the 31,000 military specifications that describe down to the minutest detail how items ordered by the military are to be made—everything from shotgun ammunition to macaroons for the mess hall. Another case from the Persian Gulf conflict highlights the urgent need for change. The U.S. Army had placed an emergency order with a large defense contractor for 12,000 handheld navigation devices. The devices would receive signals from the Global Positioning Satellite (GPS) System, thus enabling soldiers to know their precise position on the desert battlefield. The contractor responded that, to comply with milspecs, each receiver would cost $34,000 and weigh 17 pounds, and the order would take at least

18 months to fill. The Army obtained an exemption from the milspecs and found two commercial firms that could fill the order quickly with GPS receivers that weighed only 3 pounds and cost only $1,300 apiece.

Milspecs may have made more sense in the past, for sophisticated weapons systems at least, when the Pentagon and the defense industry dominated advanced technology. But for the fields of technology most important to the Defense Department today—semiconductors, computers, software, telecommunications—technical leadership now generally resides with commercial industry. By adopting commercial standards, the Defense Department expects to pay less to provide the armed forces with the latest generation of equipment than if it attempted to design and maintain its own unique standards. Under the new procurement system, to be fully implemented in 3 or more years' time, the Defense Department will no longer tell contractors how most of the products it buys must be made. Milspecs will be the exception, not the rule.

The complete restructuring of the government's procurement system will take time. Some analysts believe that nothing less than a cultural revolution is needed to make the shift to a system that supports innovation and rewards market-driven, entrepreneurial management. That may be so, but in the meantime the Federal Acquisition Streamlining Act, together with other reforms being actively implemented by the Defense Department, will produce—indeed, are producing—positive results.

REFORMING THE FEDERAL AVIATION ADMINISTRATION

The National Performance Review also called for reform of the way the Federal Aviation Administration (FAA) operates the Nation's air traffic control system. Emerging, satellite-based technologies of air navigation and air traffic control promise to reduce routine air travel times and congestion-related delays by freeing aircraft from having to travel in designated airways. But, the NPR argued, existing budgeting, personnel, and procurement rules so hobble the agency as to impede its ability to adopt this cutting-edge technology quickly. To create an organization that would be up to the challenge of building and running a state-of-the-art air traffic control system, the NPR proposed transferring that responsibility from the FAA to a public corporation set up for that purpose. The National Commission to Ensure a Strong Competitive Airline Industry contemporaneously made a similar recommendation.

In May 1994 the Administration announced a plan to implement these recommendations. The new government corporation would be funded in part from fees paid by the commercial aviation firms using the new system. It would also be permitted to borrow from the Treasury and from private capital markets, so that the substantial capital investment needed to complete an advanced air traffic control system would not be limited by the flow of user fees. Accelerating the full deployment of the new system in this way will, it is hoped, speed complementary investments by the airlines in aircraft equipment needed to use the system.

The Administration's proposal assigns the users of the air traffic control system a significant role in its corporate governance: aviation company executives would be not merely advisers to the corporation but its directors as well. In part because of the fees they would pay, users would have a direct and substantial financial stake in ensuring that air traffic control services promote safe and rapid air travel, that those services are provided at low cost, and that beneficial investments are not delayed. Strong user representation on the board of directors would therefore encourage sensible and cost-effective corporate decisionmaking.

Regulatory oversight remains important to ensure safety in air travel, to prevent monopoly abuses in the setting of user fees, and to ensure that the corporation does not abuse its ability to borrow. In the Administration's plan, these functions would be performed outside the corporation by the Department of Transportation. Safety regulation would remain in the hands of a slimmed-down FAA, which would oversee the new air traffic control corporation in much the same way it now oversees air carriers and manufacturers. The Secretary of Transportation would have the power to disapprove user fees that harm new entrants, diminish competition, or lead to excessive fees for air service, and the power to disapprove borrowing in excess of the corporation's ability to repay or borrowing intended for inappropriate, wasteful, or unreasonably speculative activities.

PROMOTING EFFICIENCY IN THE MARKET ECONOMY

Government can promote efficiency in the market economy in many ways, including these three: restraining anticompetitive practices, ensuring that the costs of externalities are taken into account by those who create them, and undergirding markets with research and information that would be undersupplied—or not supplied at all—by private markets. This Administration is committed to making the Federal Government perform these and other important functions efficiently so that markets perform better, and is working on many fronts to do so. Notable examples are initiatives in antitrust enforcement and interstate banking legislation. Other challenges—and opportunities—for improving the performance of the market economy lie ahead, for example in the areas of agricultural policy and ground transportation regulation.

ANTITRUST ENFORCEMENT

The Nation's antitrust laws, effectively enforced, preserve competition and the economic benefits it yields. This Administration is committed to maintaining antitrust protections. In 1994 the Justice Department filed three complaints challenging firms for monopolizing markets, including a widely publicized settlement involving the largest firm in the computer software industry. In contrast, the Justice Department had filed only four other such complaints since the successful conclusion, in 1982, of the prolonged government lawsuit to break up what was then the nationwide telephone monopoly. Other important antitrust initiatives of the past year included a renewed campaign against foreign anticompetitive conduct that harms U.S. interests, the settlement of the Justice Department's price-fixing case against the major airlines (Box 4–1), new efforts in reviewing proposed mergers and acquisitions to harmonize the need to protect competition with industry trends toward rationalization, and efforts to protect incentives for firms in competition to innovate. This last initiative is discussed later in this chapter (in the section on "Intellectual Property"); the other three are considered here.

Anticompetitive Foreign Practices

For 50 years the antitrust laws have been interpreted as forbidding anticompetitive foreign practices that harm U.S. interests, whether by raising the prices of imports to American consumers or by closing markets to American exporters. In the past, for example, the antitrust laws have been employed against foreign buying cartels using monopsony power—the market power of a single buyer—to lower the price received by U.S. exporters. Such enforcement not only protects specific U.S. interests directly, but also advances U.S. interests more broadly by promoting a global regime of competitive open markets.

In 1988 the Justice Department chose to disavow the use of these laws to protect U.S. export trade. That policy was renounced in 1992, but no new case was filed until 1994, when the department reached a settlement with a large British producer of float glass (the type of glass used in automobiles and buildings). The Justice Department charged that the company used exclusive territories and other restrictions in licensing its technology in an attempt to monopolize this $15-billion-a-year global industry. The licensing restrictions discouraged U.S. firms from designing, building, or opening float glass plants abroad. Because much of the technology being licensed is now in the public domain, and thus could not claim intellectual property protection as trade secrets, the Justice Depart-

Box 4–1.—Airline Price Fixing

In 1994 the Justice Department settled a case involving price-fixing charges against eight major airlines. What was new about the case was the way in which new forms of information exchange made possible by advances in telecommunications and computerization were allegedly used to facilitate illegal conduct.

The major airlines are connected through a computerized system, set up by the airlines themselves through a joint venture, that collects fare information from each of them and transmits it to the various computer reservation systems used by travel agents. Through the joint venture, the air carriers process and sort fare change information to produce detailed daily reports displaying relationships among fares. The Justice Department emphasized that much of this information is unavailable in practice to travel agents and other users of the reservation systems.

According to the Justice Department, the carriers' joint venture was used in a novel and anticompetitive way to coordinate fare decisions over a 5-year period. Using certain features of the fare records (first and last ticket dates and footnote designators) and often employing prospective fares never offered to the public, the carriers created a detailed language for striking complex bargains across fares and routes. For example, one carrier might agree to raise its fares for a certain city-pair market in which a rival carrier would prefer a higher fare than the first carrier desired, in exchange for the rival carrier agreeing to raise its fares in a second market in which the preferences were reversed. The rapid information exchange made possible by the computerized network aided the carriers in enforcing such bargains: an airline could usually detect and respond to a rival's deviation from such a deal within a day.

The Justice Department claimed to have identified over 50 such collusive agreements between carriers using the computerized joint venture for negotiations, and challenged as unreasonable the features of the fare records that made these conversations possible. If such coordination had raised fares by as little as 5 percent for 5 years on 300 routes, the cost to consumers would have been nearly $2 billion, according to the Justice Department. The price-fixing charges were settled by an agreement approved by a Federal court which forbids the carriers from using the features of the fare records that facilitate bargaining.

ment concluded that the licensing provisions were not legitimate business practices but were instead being used to close off foreign markets to U.S. competitors. The settlement eliminates the British company's territorial restrictions, allowing U.S. firms to manufacture float glass abroad. This case also illustrates the Justice Department's renewed focus on anticompetitive distribution practices and the anticompetitive potential of sham intellectual property licensing arrangements.

The ability of Federal antitrust enforcers to challenge international cartels and other anticompetitive foreign practices that harm U.S. consumers and exporters was enhanced by legislation enacted in 1994. The new act allows the Justice Department and the Federal Trade Commission to enter into reciprocal agreements with foreign antitrust agencies, under which the U.S. and the foreign agencies will assist each other's investigations by obtaining antitrust evidence from firms and persons within their own jurisdictions. Safeguards in the legislation ensure that confidential business information supplied to foreign antitrust authorities will not be improperly used or disclosed.

Antitrust Review of Mergers and Acquisitions

Mergers and acquisitions are on the upswing: both their number and the value of the assets transferred have increased every year since 1991. But half of all mergers and acquisitions in 2 recent years, as measured by asset value, have occurred in four industries: telecommunications, health care, financial services, and defense and technology (Table 4–1). These are all industries in which technology or the government's role has been changing dramatically, leading firms to alter their business strategies through restructuring.

TABLE 4–1.—*Announced Mergers and Acquisitions Transactions in 1992 and 1993*

Industry	Transactions		Asset value	
	Number	Percent of total	Millions of dollars	Percent of total
All industries	5,237	100.0	273,088	100.0
Finance	900	17.2	65,030	23.8
Telecommunications	249	4.8	62,615	22.9
Health care	598	11.4	18,503	6.8
Defense and technology	226	4.3	8,913	3.3

Source: Merrill Lynch, *Mergerstat Review 1993.* Reprinted with permission.

Mergers and acquisitions may be attractive to the parties involved for a number of reasons. They may allow the merging firms to lower costs, improve management, stimulate innovation, or reduce taxes. But they may also—and this is the concern of antitrust enforcers—enable the expanded company to exercise market power.

Acquisitions in industries undergoing widespread restructuring are more likely than most to raise conflicts between the business trends that encourage consolidation and the need to preserve and promote competition. Such conflicts have arisen in the hospital industry, where a consolidation has been under way for some time. Nationwide, almost 100 hospitals merge or close in a typical year, and consolidation is occurring in all regions of the country. Because many hospitals serve highly localized geographic markets, where few alternative providers exist or could enter the market, the loss of a single hospital through merger or closure can often sharply reduce competition in its locality. In part the trend toward industry concentration reflects, ironically, the efforts of health insurers and managed care providers to lower the prices they pay by encouraging competition among neighboring hospitals and the rationalization of duplicative facilities. Hospitals also face increasing competition from surgical and outpatient clinics, which can offer at lower cost some health care services that formerly only hospitals provided.

Cost-saving consolidations can lower the price of hospital services and improve health care delivery—so long as they do not undermine competition. Competition ensures that hospital cost reductions will benefit consumers. Antitrust enforcers have not challenged the more than 95 percent of all proposed hospital mergers, and the even greater fraction of proposed joint ventures, that they did not find threatening to competition. But a few proposed consolidations do raise conflicts between the trend toward rationalization and the need to promote competition.

During 1994 the Department of Justice, in partnership with the Florida Attorney General's office, responded innovatively to one such conflict. Under the terms of a consent settlement of an antitrust case, the two largest general acute care hospitals in northern Pinellas County, Florida, were permitted to collaborate in providing those services in which they compete with nonhospital or distant hospital providers, including many outpatient services and tertiary care services. The hospitals were also allowed to consolidate billing, procurement, and other administrative functions. But the settlement requires them to market their collaborative services independently and to continue to compete in offering those inpatient services for which there may be no practical alternative supplier for most patients in their region.

In recognition of the restructuring under way in the health care industry, the Justice Department and the Federal Trade Commission have jointly issued several antitrust guidelines for the health care industry as a whole. The agencies' joint statement on hospital mergers declares that the government will not normally issue a challenge if either of the merging hospitals averages fewer than

100 beds and fewer than 40 patients per day over a 3-year period—regardless of concentration in their geographic market. Guidelines such as these should encourage needed investment and reorganization in this industry by lessening uncertainty about the antitrust consequences of proposed restructurings.

INTERSTATE BANKING

Legislation enacted in 1994 takes a giant step toward interstate banking and bank branching in the United States. The new law removes Federal barriers to geographic expansion and authorizes the States to remove the rest. Lowering the hurdles to interstate banking and branching improves the efficiency of the banking system in three ways. First, banks can increasingly consolidate branches across State lines into one network and accept interstate deposits without restrictions. This will lower costs for banks operating in more than one State.

Second, increased interstate banking reduces the likelihood of bank failures by facilitating greater diversity in bank loan portfolios. Banks can more easily avoid tying their profitability and solvency to the health of a single region. This will make it easier to diversify against regional risks such as weather- or disease-related crop failure, earthquake, or energy price fluctuations.

Finally, banks' increased ability to enter new markets across State lines will boost competition. To further promote competition, the legislation limits mergers and acquisitions that would cause a bank holding company to control more than 30 percent of the bank deposits in a State, unless the State waives this limit.

INTRASTATE TRUCKING

The trucking industry was partially deregulated in 1980, with the enactment of legislation significantly reducing Federal control over entry, pricing, and operations of interstate trucking. Scholars estimate that this legislation has generated annual savings in the tens of billions of dollars. Legislation enacted in 1994 removes the most burdensome remaining governmental constraints: regulation by more than 40 States of the rates, entry, and routes of motor carriers.

The end of intrastate trucking regulation in 1995 promises to lower the prices of trucking services. For example, under current State regulation, one consumer products distributor pays $560 to ship products the 422 miles between Dallas and Laredo, Texas, but only $410 to ship the same goods the 480 miles between Dallas and Topeka, Kansas, in largely unregulated interstate commerce. The new legislation discourages inefficient business practices predicated on State regulation. For example, cargo carriers will no longer have an incentive to ship to inconvenient out-of-State airports in order to avoid regulated intrastate trucking rates. Competition among truckers and multimodal cargo carriers implies that much of the savings from deregulation will be passed through to consumers.

FARM POLICY REFORM

The drafting of a new farm bill in 1995 will give the Federal Government an opportunity to reassess and redesign its role in the agricultural economy. A more efficient farm policy would reflect contemporary economic conditions, environmental needs, and public values. As described below, efficiency requires that farmers be given greater opportunity to respond to market incentives, and that cost-effective public policies be used to correct market failures in agriculture. Revising government policy to meet better these objectives will help unleash more of the innovative energy that has long characterized American agriculture.

Changing Conditions in the Agricultural Economy

Today's agricultural commodity support programs are rooted in landmark New Deal legislation that followed the agricultural depression of the 1920s and 1930s. These programs were designed to sustain prices and incomes for producers of cotton, milk, wheat, rice, corn, sugar, tobacco, peanuts, and other crops. However, changing economic conditions and trends in agriculture over the past half-century suggest that many of the original motivations for farm programs no longer apply.

The farm sector no longer looms large in the macroeconomy. Commodity programs were originally instruments of macroeconomic policy as well as a means of sustaining farm families' incomes. In the 1930s farm households accounted for 25 percent of the U.S. population and generated over 10 percent of gross domestic product (GDP). Today they comprise less than 2 percent of the population. Although the U.S. food and fiber system as a whole (including food processing and marketing) provides an estimated 18 percent of U.S. jobs and contributes over 15 percent of GDP, farming alone now generates only 9 percent of rural employment and less than 2 percent of GDP. Technological progress and growth in farm productivity permit a smaller labor force to supply the agricultural needs of the entire country. As a result, government farm programs play a reduced role in the U.S. macroeconomy.

International trade in agricultural products has grown. Productivity gains in agriculture have helped fuel growth in agricultural exports. For example, wheat exports have grown from 8 percent of U.S. wheat production in the 1930s to over 50 percent today, while corn exports have grown from less than 2 percent of production to about one-quarter. Such growth has helped convert agriculture from a trade deficit sector to an important trade surplus sector, contributing over $19 billion to the U.S. balance of trade in 1993.

141

The average farm payment recipient is no longer poor. In the 1930s per capita farm income was only one-third the per capita income of the remaining population. Commodity programs were intended to reduce this disparity. Today, however, recipients of farm program payments (about one-third of all farm operators) tend to be better off than the average American. Overall, farm households have about the same average income and quadruple the net worth of the average U.S. household. Moreover, two-thirds of program payments go to the largest 18 percent of farms—even though the average income of these recipients is triple that of the average U.S. household.

Agricultural production is increasingly concentrated. The number of farms has fallen by more than 60 percent since 1950, while the size of the average farm has doubled. Moreover, 92 percent of what the Bureau of the Census terms farm households operate small farms but receive almost all their income from off-farm sources; they have about the same average income as the typical nonfarm household and receive only a small share of government farm program payments.

Demographic data indicate that these trends will continue, in part because the young increasingly choose nonfarm occupations. During the 1980s, entry rates into farming fell by 50 percent among those under 25 years of age and by 35 percent among those aged 25 to 34. Low rates of young farmer entry have persisted since 1987. By 1990, as a result, 22 percent of farm operators were 65 or older, compared with only 3 percent of the U.S. work force as a whole.

Farmers now can insure themselves against price declines. In the early 1930s farm incomes were at the mercy of year-to-year fluctuations in farm prices. Commodity programs provided price floors for agricultural producers, insuring them against adverse price swings. The growth of futures and options markets now lets farmers protect against short-term price declines without the need for a government program.

The potential environmental costs of farming have increased. Modern agricultural practices can sometimes lead to substantial runoff of nutrients and chemicals, which pollute downstream water resources. The use of both pesticides and fertilizers has doubled since the 1960s, and agriculture is now considered a contributor to water quality problems in approximately 60 percent of river and lake areas that are impaired. An increasing rural population has raised the potential public health costs of environmental damage from agricultural activities. Agriculture has also been a major source of wetlands losses, which can diminish floodwater storage capacity and harm water quality and wildlife. The upper Midwest, for example, once had an estimated 53 million acres of wetlands;

today only about 23 million acres remain, 29 million acres having been converted to cropland. (Wetlands policy is discussed further below.)

New Foundations of Agricultural Policy

Both changing economic conditions and the quest for efficiency in government motivate a new set of objectives for agricultural policy.

Market incentives at home and abroad. With the increasing importance of international markets to U.S. agriculture, free trade between nations has also become increasingly important to this sector. As discussed in Chapter 6, the Administration has achieved historic agreements that will lower international trade barriers around the world, including some prominent barriers to agricultural trade. These agreements will yield large dividends to the farm sector and the U.S. economy at large.

At home, farmers must be given appropriate market signals so that their decisions will help maximize aggregate economic welfare. Unfortunately, some government farm programs impede market processes and efficient choices. In some agricultural markets, the Federal Government operates programs that do not involve taxpayer subsidies, but that nonetheless reduce economic efficiency. For example, in markets for sugar, peanuts, and tobacco, above-market prices are supported by cartel-like supply restrictions that are enforced by the Federal Government. The sugar and peanut programs also impose marketing restrictions in ways that inhibit shifts of production from more costly to less costly producers.

Farm commodity programs currently come in two main forms. Income support is provided by *deficiency payment programs,* which make payments that depend on a commodity's statutory target price, the actual market price, and the number of acres a farmer has accredited to the commodity program. To maintain their benefits, farmers have an incentive to plant the same crops year after year. Deficiency payments are sometimes tied to a requirement that farmers idle a portion of their land. Farmers that are eligible for deficiency payments also benefit from *price support programs* that pay them the difference between a commodity's support price and its international price on each unit of a program crop that they produce.

Both programs affect economic behavior in ways that may prove costly. By encouraging overinvestment and overproduction in agriculture, the programs affect the allocation of resources in the economy and thereby reduce overall productivity. The programs also reduce the productivity of agriculture itself because they subsidize different crops to different extents. Indeed, almost half of agricultural production is not covered by either price support or deficiency payment programs. In addition, farm programs may have long-run costs: by raising agricultural land values, crop subsidies may raise

143

the financial barriers to entry into farming, deterring some entry and increasing the financial vulnerability of new farmers.

The programs may also discourage environmentally beneficial practices. By favoring program crops over nonprogram rotation crops, both programs discourage crop rotations that break pest cycles and promote soil conservation. Price support programs can encourage the use of pesticides, herbicides, and fertilizers, which may raise yields but contribute to off-site environmental damage. By increasing the returns to crop cultivation, both programs may encourage the farming of marginal lands, which for environmental reasons may be better left fallow. And both programs may skew the composition of farm output toward program crops, some of which are particularly intensive in environmentally harmful inputs. For example, a 17-State Department of Agriculture survey found that farms growing cotton, a program crop, use almost twice as much pesticide per acre as the average farm.

Some economists argue that current farm programs can be reformed to increase economic efficiency, better serve environmental objectives, and still provide government support to the agricultural sector. For example, one approach would sever the link between commodity program payments and farmers' crop choices by fixing farmers' commodity program acreages, allowing farmers complete planting flexibility on these acreages, terminating acreage control requirements, and rolling price support programs for the income-supported commodities into deficiency payments (thus curtailing overproduction incentives implicit in price supports).

Farm survival. Farmers are subject to daunting risks from both nature and markets. For a variety of economic reasons, including incentive considerations, these risks are mostly borne by farmers themselves. Investment in farmland and farm capital generally requires a combination of a farmer's own funds and bank loans. When the agricultural economy suffers a downturn, farmers' debts can threaten their financial stability and indeed the survival of their enterprises, as was witnessed most recently in the agricultural recession of the early 1980s. For would-be farmers with limited capital, such prospects can limit the availability of bank funds and deter entry, even if that entry appears profitable, on average, in prospect. Government support of farm credit and crop insurance is intended to counter these effects.

Risks to farm revenues come from two sources: prices and yields. When both prices and yields are insured, so is the product of the two, farm revenues. Price insurance is now available on private markets in the form of futures and options contracts. Yield insurance, on the other hand, is offered by the Federal Government in the form of subsidized crop insurance.

In principle, private insurance markets can mitigate risks to farm revenue when an individual farm's revenues are closely tied to observable regional measures of crop revenue. Regional revenue insurance can offer farmers compensation when revenues are low, without creating problems of adverse selection and moral hazard (Box 4–2). In practice, however, the Federal Government has deterred the development of a private insurance market by offering subsidized crop insurance of its own and by standing ready to underwrite many farm losses in the event of natural disasters.

Even if regional revenue insurance were available, some risks specific to individual farms may remain uninsurable in private markets because of adverse selection and moral hazard. Farm disaster insurance responds to this market failure. The Administration has moved swiftly to address the need for farm disaster insurance that both protects farmers from large crop losses on their individual farms and clarifies the government's role in disaster relief. The Federal Crop Insurance Reform initiative, signed into law in the fall of 1994, provides for minimal disaster insurance coverage for all farmers that participate in government farm programs and any others that choose to purchase this coverage; the insurance protects farmers from yield losses above 50 percent of their historical average yields, with payments for such losses at a rate of 60 percent of the expected crop price. This reform provides farmers with disaster protection that is statutory and hence dependable. With this basic protection in place, the stage is set for advancing market alternatives to conventional government crop insurance, in order to insure against low, but noncatastrophic, revenues. Regional revenue insurance represents one possible private market insurance alternative.

Environmental stewardship and efficient land use. The choice of farm practices can have a wide range of environmental effects, positive and negative. Negative effects include off-site costs of soil erosion and agricultural runoff; positive effects include wildlife preservation benefits from hedgerows and windbreaks, and reduced greenhouse gas emissions due to improved fertilizer management and processing of confined livestock waste. Over the past two decades, farm conservation practices have improved dramatically. Nonetheless, farmers should be given incentives to consider the environmental costs and benefits of their actions. Federal policy can incorporate environmental and public health values into farmers' decisionmaking through an incentives-based approach that leaves management decisions in farmers' qualified hands while turning collective environmental objectives into individual financial ones. For example, the environmental costs of agricultural erosion and runoff stem from both the application of fertilizers and pesticides and a variety of other farm practice decisions, including tillage

Box 4-2.—Adverse Selection and Moral Hazard in Crop Insurance

When some farmers face a higher risk of crop shortfalls than others, but potential insurers cannot identify which farmers are high-risk, insurance premiums must be set to reflect the *average* risk of insured farmers. However, for low-risk farmers, such premiums will be higher than their average revenue losses, and these farmers may therefore decide not to buy the insurance. As a result, only the high-risk farmers may choose to purchase private crop insurance, leaving all other farmers to face the full range of revenue risk, and leading insurers to raise their premiums on the now-riskier pool of customers. The problem that arises when individual farmers know their own vulnerability to specific hazards better than do insurers is called *adverse selection.*

Crop insurance can also fall victim to what economists call *moral hazard*, the problem that arises because a farmer who is insured against crop loss has less of an incentive to avoid the loss. Moral hazard in this setting occurs when insured farmers adjust their production practices to increase the likelihood of receiving an insurance payment. This can be done, for example, by producing a small crop and a large crop in alternating years. The large crops keep the insured revenue level up, while the small crops permit the farmer to collect on the insurance contract.

Both adverse selection and moral hazard problems could be avoided with *regional revenue insurance* that compensates each farmer only for shortfalls in regional revenue, not the farmer's own revenue. For example, a regional insurance contract could be tied to average corn revenue in a given county, defined as the product of the county-wide average yield on corn acreage and a corn price index. An insured farmer would receive a payment when average corn revenue falls below a given level; the size of the payment would depend upon the amount of insurance the farmer has purchased. To the extent the farmer's own corn yields match those of the region, regional insurance would provide financial relief in times of low revenue, without tying insurance payments to outcomes that depend upon the farmer's own planting decisions or risk attributes.

practices, crop rotation decisions, and the use of filter strips that absorb runoff in the boundaries of croplands. When the application of fertilizers and pesticides imposes off-site costs, farmers can only be expected to make efficient decisions if they are themselves confronted with these costs. One possibility by which policy could use markets to do this is to levy fees on the use of these inputs that reflect the environmental cost of their application in different geographical areas. Another option is to use positive financial incentives to encourage the adoption of conservation practices that reduce erosion and runoff or provide wildlife habitat.

Federal policy also needs to be concerned with agricultural land use. In some cases the public benefits from preserving uncultivated land or returning cultivated land to its native form may exceed the potential private benefits of cultivation. This is likely to be the case with some highly erodible land and many wetlands. About 120 million acres of cropland, representing over 25 percent of all U.S. cropland, is considered highly erodible. These lands are estimated to erode at least eight times as fast as their soil can be naturally regenerated, leading to high off-site costs of sediment and chemical runoff. Such lands have been among the most important targets of the Agriculture Department's principal land retirement program, the Conservation Reserve Program, which has succeeded in reducing the overall national soil erosion rate by an estimated 20 percent. Federal policy should continue to target such sensitive lands and do so in a way that yields the greatest environmental benefit per tax dollar.

How wetlands are used affects a wide variety of public resources, including water quality, groundwater supplies, floodwater storage, and wildlife. To protect these resources, Federal wetlands policy should address both wetlands *restoration* and wetlands *conversion*. The Administration has sought to accelerate wetlands restoration through the Wetlands Reserve Program. To date, this program has permanently restored 125,000 acres of critical wetlands from cropland at a cost of less than $1,000 per acre.

The conversion of natural wetlands to cropland has been regulated by the Federal Government under both Section 404 of the Clean Water Act and a provision of the farm bill called "Swampbuster." Under Section 404, permits are often required for the conversion of wetlands; the Army Corps of Engineers and the Environmental Protection Agency share responsibility for granting the permits. Under the Swampbuster provision, agricultural producers can sometimes be denied farm program benefits if they cultivate a native wetland.

The Administration has worked to resolve a variety of wetlands policy issues by streamlining administrative procedures for issuing wetland conversion permits, clarifying the delineation of wetlands that are subject to regulation, promoting flexibility in wetlands regulation so as to achieve wetlands preservation at a lower cost, and providing incentives for States and localities to engage in watershed planning and thus reduce conflicts arising from permit-by-permit decisionmaking. For example, to reduce regulatory duplication

147

and delays, the Administration has designated the Natural Resources Conservation Service (formerly the Soil Conservation Service) as the lead Federal agency for wetlands delineation on agricultural lands under both the farm bill and the Clean Water Act. The Administration has also exempted 53 million acres of converted agricultural wetlands from regulation and endorsed the use of mitigation banking. Mitigation banking allows environmental damages from a given wetland conversion to be offset by the prior creation or restoration of other wetlands. It thus allows valuable development to proceed while protecting wetlands and making the permitting process more flexible and cost-effective.

Critics of Federal wetlands regulation have argued that restrictions on private wetlands conversion constitute a government "taking" for which private landowners should be compensated. Such claims are part of a broad and important public debate on the appropriate scope of the takings doctrine (Box 4–3).

Food safety. When consumers cannot easily determine for themselves the healthfulness and safety of the foods they buy, they cannot appropriately reward producers for providing these attributes even though they value them. Government can enhance social welfare in these circumstances by undergirding markets with food safety protection. This undergirding of markets takes four forms: inspection of meats and other foods for contaminants, standards for pesticide residues on food, regulation of the pesticides themselves and their availability to farmers, and consumer information through education and labeling.

Food safety policy has evolved to address public demands for protection, but not always in cost-effective ways. Inspection programs need to provide food producers with appropriate incentives to prevent contamination, while at the same time keeping regulatory design standards to a minimum. Overproliferation of prescriptive standards can prevent firms from developing the protection systems best suited to their facilities. Appropriate incentives can be provided through effective Federal contaminant detection programs, combined with penalties and remedies for contamination.

The Administration's pathogen reduction initiative is an important step in this direction. This initiative provides for the recall of meat and poultry products that pose a threat to public health, the assessment of penalties when health standards or inspection procedures are violated, and the introduction of the latest pathogen detection technology in a meat inspection system that has become outmoded. The Administration is moving toward a system based on detecting the microbial contaminants that are the sources of foodborne illness rather than relying on visual inspection alone. This reform should permit the cost-effective achievement of public

Box 4–3.—The Takings Debate

Federal, State, and local governments regulate land use in a variety of ways, to protect their citizens from harmful externalities and to preserve public resources, including wildlife, water quality, and open space. State and local authorities, for example, routinely make decisions about zoning and permits that constrain the uses of private lands and the buildings allowed on them. Such constraints protect residential and other property from harm by noxious development on neighboring property. Federal land use regulations include wetlands protection and endangered species preservation.

Compensation for some regulatory actions affecting property values is required by the Fifth Amendment to the Constitution, which forbids the government to take private property for public use without just compensation. This provision establishes and protects the institution of private property, thus laying the foundation for economic growth financed largely by private investment.

Recent legislative debate has centered on the extent to which landowners should be compensated for regulatory actions affecting the value of their property in situations in which compensation is not constitutionally mandated. Under many proposals for expanded compensation, the government would thus be required to provide compensation when zoning, environmental, or other regulations prevent landowners from using their property in ways that harm other property owners or the public.

An expanded compensation requirement could harm the economy in at least two ways. First, it would tend to discourage Federal, State and local governments from a critical task of microeconomic policy: that of addressing market failures, such as externalities or the underprovision of public goods, in order to protect health, safety, and the environment. For example, enactment of some proposals to expand compensation could discourage environmental regulations that prevent landowners from storing barrels of toxic waste near a neighborhood or school. Second, an expanded compensation requirement might give landowners an incentive to alter the use of their land in order to increase the likelihood or amount of compensation. If environmental resources could be protected only by paying off those who would benefit from damaging them, then landowners, for example, would have an incentive to seek compensation by proposing environmentally damaging projects that they might never have otherwise considered.

health goals, the importance of which has been highlighted by recent episodes of contamination by the intestinal bacterium *E. coli.*

The Federal Government determines pesticide residue standards according to criteria laid out in the Federal Food, Drug, and Cosmetic Act (FFDCA). The so-called Delaney clause in this act requires that processed foods contain no additives that, in any quantity, could potentially cause cancer. For residues on raw agricultural commodities, in contrast, the FFDCA gives regulators greater flexibility in determining the amounts of chemical residues allowed. The zero-risk standard implicit in the Delaney clause requires that even safe amounts of pesticide residues not be allowed in processed foods, no matter how much the application of pesticide might reduce the cost of producing food.

The government's pesticide registration process has been criticized for costly delays and a statutory apparatus that can sometimes prevent the substitution of less toxic new pesticides for more toxic older ones. To address these problems, the Administration has proposed a periodic review of all registered pesticides and an expedited registration process for those pesticides that present reduced risk and for minor use pesticides. Beyond these administrative reforms, efficiency dictates that pesticide registration decisions be guided by benefit-cost criteria. If regulation is imposed even though the benefits of reduced risk do not justify the costs, the Nation loses an opportunity to redirect resources toward more effective risk-reduction activities.

Finally, government policy can be used to help consumers become better informed about the foods they purchase. To promote this end, Federal grading and labeling standards should focus on providing the information about nutrition, food safety, and other health concerns that consumers may lack, and not on cosmetic attributes (such as fruit size and external blemishes) that consumers can readily observe for themselves. Beyond grading and labeling, the government can usefully promote access to additional information about food product attributes, whether it concerns the use of additives, irradiation, or other food production processes that consumers may care about.

Research and development. The U.S. Government has a long and distinguished history of sustaining research that advances agricultural production capabilities. Today agricultural research confronts new challenges as the farm economy strives to sustain its high productivity, meet a growing concern with the environmental effects of agricultural practices, and find new uses for farm products. Research and development on bioenergy is a prime example of Federal Government efforts to respond to these new challenges.

Biomass from tree and grass crops may become an important new fuel source for electricity generation in future decades. To foster this emerging technology, the Administration is pursuing a collaborative interagency effort to promote research, development, and demonstration of new bioenergy-generating technologies and feedstock crop systems. Studies using economic and technological models of biomass production have produced preliminary estimates indicating that a commercially viable biomass industry could represent a significant share of new U.S. electric generating capacity within a couple of decades. Commercial viability is judged in these studies without incorporating any environmental benefits of biomass generation, even though two such potential benefits are foreseen. First, fuel crops are suitable for production on highly erodible land, giving farmers a potentially profitable alternative crop that also promotes erosion control and water quality improvement. Second, biomass power can help to reduce net greenhouse gas emissions to the extent they supplant fossil fuels: both types of fuel release carbon dioxide when combusted, but growing biomass crops reabsorb it from the atmosphere—fossil fuels do not.

Bioenergy crops could also provide an important new source of agricultural income in future decades. Some forecasts suggest that as many as 50 million cropland acres could, under favorable conditions, be devoted to feedstock production. New agricultural activities of this kind, together with rural bioenergy generation, may help reinvigorate America's rural economy.

The Federal Government has an important economic role to play in promoting biomass power generation for two reasons. First, private markets are likely to fail to capture the promised environmental benefits. Second, research and development in this infant technology is likely to be a public good that merits government support, because its benefits are difficult to appropriate.

POLICIES FOR MORE EFFICIENT TRANSPORTATION

About 12 percent of national income is spent on transportation services, including efforts to reduce the environmental impacts of transportation. However, several types of external costs of motor vehicle usage are not reflected in prices. As a result, excessive driving-related social harms are likely to occur.

For example, traffic congestion and wear on roads will be excessive when individuals' driving and road use decisions do not take these costs fully into account. Similarly, the tax deductibility of businesses' expenses for employee parking constitutes a subsidy, which artificially encourages driving. The environmental costs of motor vehicle fuel use are also important externalities. Although new-car tailpipe emissions per mile traveled have decreased at least 76 percent and possibly as much as 96 percent since the late 1960s, total travel has increased by two-thirds, consumers have shifted vehicle purchases toward light trucks with lower fuel economy and higher emissions, and older, more polluting vehicles remain on the road longer than before. Vehicle traffic is responsible for roughly 40 percent of emissions of ozone precursors and is an important source of toxic air pollutants, as well as a source of polluting runoff into waterways. The transportation sector is also a significant contributor to greenhouse gas emissions.

When externalities are significant, government policy can promote economic efficiency by seeking to ensure that private agents pay the full costs of their transportation decisions. Many of these costs are interrelated and therefore demand integrated regulatory approaches. Such approaches are consistent with the Administration's commitment to exploring more effective regulation by exploiting synergies between achieving economic and environmental goals. For example, policies to reduce peak traffic congestion, if carefully designed, can also reduce some pollution problems, and conversely, policies that increase the total cost of driving by making drivers pay the environmental costs of vehicle usage also will limit road congestion.

The challenge is to design a menu of policies that achieves objectives set for pollution and congestion reduction at minimum cost. Needlessly rigid emissions and fuel economy standards can raise the cost of regulatory compliance, by limiting flexibility and incentives to innovate.

Overly prescriptive vehicle inspection and maintenance programs have been criticized as costly and ineffective at emission reduction. Finally, vehicle environmental standards that are not well integrated with approaches to emissions reductions from other sources lead to economic waste when the marginal cost of emissions reduction varies across sources. Social science research can suggest new tools for addressing those regulatory problems (Box 4–4).

Greater regulatory flexibility and reliance on economic incentives would provide opportunities for vehicle users, manufacturers, fuel suppliers, and local regulators to develop innovative, cost-effective solutions. This would tend to alleviate congestion and pollution, and encourage the development of environmentally beneficial changes in technology. One step forward would involve making current vehicle emission standards more flexible by allowing automakers to trade vehicle emission credits. Companies that can cheaply overcomply with average per mile emission standards could sell excess credits to those facing higher compliance costs. Such policies are similar in spirit to tradable emissions allowances for sulfur dioxide (Box 4–5).

Economic efficiency may also be increased through greater flexibility in the control of mobile and other pollution sources, although more experimentation is needed to determine the size of the likely social benefits. For example, "cash for clunkers" programs, which

152

Social science provides an important link between science and technology investments and the Nation's social concerns, including economic development, health, and environmental quality. In particular, social and economic research helps to develop knowledge that decisionmakers can use in formulating cost-effective, incentive-based environmental policy instruments.

The further development of policies establishing tradable rights or allowances for pollutant emissions or the use of natural resources provides an example. Such policies have emerged from over a quarter-century of social science research and are now in active use in the United States and other countries to regulate a variety of activities, including local and regional air pollution emissions and catches from open-access fisheries. Current support for social science research should allow the expansion of similar trading systems to cover other problems such as vehicle emissions and water pollution, generating important resource savings for the Nation as a whole.

Beyond contributing to policy design, social science research undergirds efforts to better understand the benefits to society of public resource preservation and environmental protection. This information is important for setting rational standards for resource protection. Important examples of research issues now under study include tradeoffs between environmental and other risks and the valuation of nonmarket environmental attributes. The techniques developed for environmental resource valuation and policy design should find applications in numerous other areas, including worker safety, health, and investment in human capital.

purchase and remove from service older, high-emissions vehicles, may be a cost-effective way of reducing emissions quickly, and industrial emitters may be willing to pay the costs as an alternative to tighter controls on their own sources. In addition, automobile sellers may be able cost-effectively to reduce total emissions in an airshed by, for example, subsidizing the purchase of low-emission lawn mowers.

GLOBAL CLIMATE CHANGE

The external costs of environmental pollution and degradation are often local or regional in nature—this is true, for example, of the costs associated with certain farming practices, such as pesticide use, discussed earlier in this chapter. But scientists and economists also recognize the possibility of environmental externalities on a global scale. A potentially important example is the accumulation of greenhouse gases in the earth's atmosphere. This buildup, which derives from a variety of human activities, including those that use fossil fuels, agriculture, and deforestation, poses an uncertain but potentially great long-term danger to the global biosphere and human well-being. The best scientific evidence indicates that the release of carbon dioxide, methane, and other gases that trap heat in the Earth's atmosphere has already reached levels well above those of preindustrial times. At current rates of growth in emissions worldwide, the concentration of carbon dioxide in the atmosphere by the middle of the next century will be equivalent to twice its current atmospheric concentration. Because these gases linger for a long time in the atmosphere, the effects of past emissions would persist even with significant reductions in current emissions.

The effects of greenhouse gas accumulation on ecosystems and human well-being have received extensive international scrutiny in an effort to develop a range of agreement on the impacts and to identify the limits of current knowledge. A number of analysts believe that significant negative impacts could result. Possible effects include a rise in sea levels, inundating some island nations as well as some inhabited coastal areas; shifts in optimal growing regions for crops, due to changes in temperature and moisture patterns that hamper agricultural productivity in some regions (even while increasing it in others); threats to human health from greater heat exposure and changes in the incidence of disease; and threats to "unmanaged" ecosystems, with adverse effects on biodiversity. The possibility that the global climate changes discontinuously—that significant effects do not occur until greenhouse gases accumulate beyond a certain threshold—must also be considered.

The potential for harmful climate change, combined with uncertainty about the likelihood and magnitude of adverse effects, suggests the value of taking action to reduce these risks and their impacts. This action can take a variety of forms, including a slowing of emissions, investment in greater adaptation capacity, and accumulation of additional knowledge about the threats and possible technological responses.

Climate change is inherently a long-term issue. The effects of any actions taken today will benefit the current generation's children and grandchildren. Reducing greenhouse gas emissions is also inescapably a global problem: no country acting alone can, as a practical matter, reduce the total flow of emissions, or reverse their effects. To date, the vast bulk of greenhouse gas emissions has come from activities in the advanced industrialized countries. In the absence of significant technical change, however, economic progress and increased energy use in what are now the lower and middle-income countries will cause an enormous swelling of emissions. Moreover, the effects of climate change and efforts to mitigate them will differ in different countries. For example, low-lying island nations will be affected more severely than the United States. These differences in vulnerability and the debate over the apportionment of responsibility for greenhouse gas control complicate the effort to achieve and implement international agreements to deal with the problem.

Despite these complications, the United States and most members of the world community have signed the Framework Convention on Climate Change, which was announced during the Earth

155

Summit in Rio de Janeiro in 1992. This convention sets out a long-term objective of limiting greenhouse gas concentrations and a commitment to negotiate interim steps to attain that long-term goal. An interim aim of the more industrialized countries of the world is to reduce their rates of greenhouse gas emissions to 1990 levels by the year 2000. Beyond this initial step, the Administration currently is developing a decision framework to guide U.S. climate policy in the 21st century, and to support the next round of international negotiations on climate measures.

In devising strategies to curtail greenhouse gas emissions, several objectives are important.

Cost-effectiveness. Cost-effective greenhouse gas control policies must rely as much as possible on economic incentives, to motivate the responses of the literally billions of people responsible for greenhouse gas-emitting activities.

Concern for the future. Cost-effective policies also need to provide appropriate insurance against the threat of climate change to future generations. The concept of "sustainability" may provide relevant insights (Box 4–6).

Flexibility. Because the potential damages from climate change are related directly to the long-term accumulation of greenhouse gases, and not just to the annual rate of emissions, it is important to address long-term greenhouse gas concentrations while providing flexibility in the timing of emissions reductions. Such flexibility would allow emitters and national policymakers to benefit from new information about climate change hazards and technologies, and to adjust behavior and policies to differing near-term economic development objectives. Flexibility also is needed in the pursuit of measures aimed at mitigation, adaptation, and technology development.

Comprehensiveness. Given the global scope of the issue, it will become increasingly important to coordinate national responses in order to avoid excessively costly or perverse outcomes. For example, focusing only on emissions in today's advanced industrialized countries would do little to prevent the "leakage" of emissions to other countries that are expanding their industrial bases.

Compatibility with diverse international interests. In the short run it is unlikely that developing countries will make substantial efforts to curb their greenhouse gas emissions without technical and financial assistance from the more developed countries, which are likely to take the lead in developing low-carbon energy and other technologies. This observation suggests that there are benefits to be had from helping developing countries improve their capacity to monitor their emissions and analyze policy options; from supporting measures in those countries that will both lower emissions and improve economic growth; and from assisting in developing a technological capacity in developing countries for reducing emissions in the future.

To translate these principles into practice, the Administration has initiated a Climate Change Action Plan to lower the rate of greenhouse gas emissions in 2000 to 1990 levels, through largely voluntary measures that focus on education and expanding the use of cost-effective technologies with lower greenhouse gas emissions. Examples include Green Lights, an initiative to promote the use of energy-efficient lighting; Natural Gas Star, promoting efforts to reduce methane leaks; and the Motor Challenge, designed to assist in the promulgation of high-efficiency motor systems. However, the difficulty of achieving the targeted emissions reductions even with this program underscores the challenge that the climate change issue presents. The Administration is considering other potentially cost-effective measures for slowing U.S. emissions after 2000, including emissions reductions in the transportation sector and encouraging greater use of biomass fuels.

To support international progress in addressing climate change, the Federal Government has invested in a "country studies" program that provides technical and financial support for developing and transitional countries to understand better their own greenhouse gas emissions sources, vulnerabilities to climate change, and options for cost-effective mitigation. Ultimately over 50 countries are expected to develop joint programs with the United States as a result of the country studies. Such assessments of international circumstances provide a foundation for the diffusion of cost-effective emissions reduction strategies to other countries, and for the "joint implementation" pilot program initiated by the Administration. Joint implementation permits U.S. emitters of greenhouse gases to achieve emissions reduction goals by undertaking mitigation activities in and with other countries, where the costs of greenhouse gas control may be much lower than in the United States. Joint implementation is thus an important example of the use of flexible, cost-effective policies to meet the divergent interests of the world's nations.

ENCOURAGING ECONOMIC GROWTH

As the analysis in Chapter 3 indicates, technological change is an important determinant of the economy's potential growth rate. Recognizing this, the Administration has worked to support technological innovation by the private sector and to improve the effectiveness of Federal spending on science and technology. This section provides an overview of the Administration's science and technology policy, focusing on efforts to facilitate the telecommuni-

161–672 – 95 – 6

Box 4-6.—"Sustainability" and Economic Analysis

The concept of sustainability, commonly invoked in debates about environmental, economic, and social values and policies, involves a number of important economic issues. One of these is *intergenerational equity.* The growing scale of human impact on the planet's ecosystems creates concern about the kind of environment we will leave to future generations. The economic methodology used in policy evaluation can in principle incorporate distributional effects across generations. Doing so requires attention to ethical concerns in setting the social discount rate, and to the collective bequest values experienced by the current generation in providing for our descendants.

A second fundamental concern involves the *substitutability* of other forms of wealth—physical capital and knowledge—for the services of the natural environment that are lost as natural systems are degraded. If substitution is relatively easy, as often assumed in economic analysis, then concern for the future largely reduces concern about the overall level of savings across generations, without regard to whether the saving takes the form of preserved ecological assets or other forms of wealth. But if substitution possibilities are more limited when human impacts are large, then greater concern for natural preservation is warranted.

Several other economic ideas also are relevant to discussions about sustainability. The concept of fully valuing all the consequences of pressures on the environment, including irreversible losses and the value of preserving options, is an economic approach for setting priorities in the use of scarce resources for environmental protection. The concept of cost-effectiveness—meeting environmental and other policy targets at minimum cost, typically by employing economic incentives and by allowing flexibility in the means for attaining goals—also is important.

The criticisms of economic analysis in the sustainability debate point to important directions for further study. For instance, equity concerns may receive inadequate consideration in standard benefit-cost analyses. This omission is especially important to overcome for issues that have substantial distributional impacts over time. Similarly, information provided by ecologists about the complex and interdependent functioning of natural systems should be considered in economic policy analyses.

cations revolution, and on efforts to restructure Federal research and development programs.

TELECOMMUNICATIONS

The telecommunications industry plays a crucial role in our economy. Like the railroad and highway infrastructures built by earlier generations, the telecommunications infrastructure brings people together and helps firms reach their customers and suppliers quickly and cheaply. As a result, our lives are enriched and our firms and workers are more productive.

The vast opportunities created by recent advances in communications and information services will likely transform the economy and the way we live and work. Innovation in this sector is continuing at a rapid rate. Within just the past decade, the facsimile (fax) machine and the cellular telephone have ceased to be curiosities and are now commonplace. Television news is now transmitted instantaneously from the field to the studio by satellite. Access to the Internet computer network is spreading beyond the government and academic researchers that were its original users, to involve private individuals, businesses, and other government functions as well. The number and variety of cable television channels continue to grow. More and more, people work from home or on the road by computer and modem, far from their offices. The power and sophistication of personal computers in homes and offices have grown by leaps and bounds.

Even more important advances in technology are on the horizon. Technical change will permit private industry to make new products and services available. Two-way, interactive, broadband service will someday be the norm, although it is not yet clear whether the emerging broadband network will be formed from wires, fiber optic lines, wireless technologies, or hybrids thereof. The computing power available to consumers of multimedia services provided by the emerging information infrastructure will undoubtedly rise, though it remains to be seen whether that power will be lodged in a server outside the house or office, or within the home or office through a personal computer or a set-top box connected to a television.

Legislative Proposals and the Prospects for Growth

The Administration seeks Federal legislation to accelerate the progress of the telecommunications and information services revolution. The Vice President has articulated five principles on which legislative and administrative reform of telecommunications policy should be based: policy should encourage private investment in the national information infrastructure, should promote and protect competition, should provide open access to the infrastructure for consumers and service providers, should preserve and advance uni-

159

versal service to avoid creating a society of information "haves" and "have-nots," and should ensure flexibility so that the newly adopted regulatory framework can keep pace with rapid technological and market changes.

New Federal legislation consistent with these principles can be expected to accelerate the development of the national information infrastructure in three ways: by reducing uncertainty about the course of national and State regulation, by promoting competition throughout the telecommunications and information services industries, and by providing a mechanism for removing existing regulatory restrictions as the development of competition makes them unnecessary. Private industry will thereby be encouraged to invest more aggressively in information infrastructure and to develop new services more rapidly. The new legislation sought would also reduce the likelihood that regulation will distort the choice of technology or other investment decisions. It would allow beneficial regulatory changes to occur more quickly, more consistently, and with greater certainty than would be achieved through market-by-market regulatory reforms in the States and by the Federal Communications Commission (FCC).

According to a study by the Council of Economic Advisers, reform of the Nation's regulatory framework could add over $100 billion (in discounted present value) to GDP over the next decade by encouraging greater private investment to develop and deploy new telecommunications services, and by spurring new entry and greater competition throughout the telecommunications and information sector. An acceleration of private investment and of the pace at which new services become available could increase GDP through three transmission mechanisms.

First, each new job in the telecommunications and information sector should produce greater output per hour worked than the average new job in the economy. Hence, when the economy shifts inputs, especially workers, into this high-value-added sector, national wealth will increase even at full employment. This process is impeded today because existing regulations restrict entry and otherwise create distortions that limit the sector's output. Many of these regulations have been necessary in the past to prevent even worse distortions resulting from the exercise of market power by monopolists. But as developments in technology shrink the potential scope of this monopoly power, and as regulatory reforms encourage competition, the economy can shift resources into this more productive sector, and so increase social wealth. As this happens, however, the sector's marginal productivity advantage over other sectors should eventually diminish.

Second, the new information infrastructure will boost productivity throughout the economy. Geographically distant firms will be able to behave more like neighbors, and new ways of working will produce changes in the innovation process, increasing the likelihood of future discoveries. If new legislation can accelerate the investments needed to develop the national information infrastructure, so that new services come on line more quickly than they would have otherwise, these productivity gains will be realized more quickly.

Third, appropriate legislation is likely to encourage industry to invest in the new technologies sooner than it otherwise would. Should the economy exhibit a tendency to operate at less than full employment at any time during the next decade, the resulting higher level of overall domestic investment would tend to offset the loss of potential GDP.

Reinventing Spectrum Allocations

The FCC allocates portions of the electromagnetic spectrum for each communications service—radio and television broadcasting, cellular telephone, and so on—and issues licenses to would-be service providers. For many years the FCC selected for licenses those applicants that it believed would best serve the public interest. It made this determination by holding hearings to compare applicants' business plans, experience, and backgrounds. Because the number of competing licensees allowed in a given geographic market is limited, successful applicants have frequently earned substantial profits.

Critics of the elaborate comparative hearing process argue that its length, administrative burden, and cost to applicants outweigh any benefit to the public. The reason for choosing the one winning candidate over the many losers, all of which may be basically qualified, is often obscure. Often the successful applicant earns profits not shared by the public, thus appropriating much of the value of the public resource.

About a decade ago, the Congress authorized the FCC to use lotteries to choose among competing applicants in licensing some services. Lotteries took much less time than comparative hearings. They were criticized, however, because often the lucky winner, having paid the government nothing for the license, would turn around and sell it for a high price. This process merely delayed getting licenses into the hands of the firms that would eventually build the communications facilities and operate the services. And, like the comparative hearings, the lotteries failed to compensate the public for the private use of the resource. To address these problems, the spectrum allocation process is being reinvented to substitute public auctions for lotteries in some cases.

Economists have long recognized the advantages of auctioning spectrum licenses. An auction puts the license directly in the hands of the applicant who values it most, and is thus likely to provide the most aggregate value to the public. An auction also allows the public to share in the financial benefits that accrue from the use of the resource. Auctions are compatible with the pursuit of other societal goals: applicants can continue to be screened for basic qualifications, and license uses can be regulated as necessary to protect the public interest. Even with these restrictions, using auctions to license spectrum is more efficient and less costly than lotteries and comparative hearings.

In 1993 the Congress authorized the FCC to invite competitive bids for initial licenses for spectrum dedicated to commercial subscription uses. The first auctions, for spectrum devoted primarily to advanced and two-way paging, took place in 1994 and yielded substantially more revenue to the government than some industry forecasters had predicted. Auctions for spectrum devoted to personal communications services (PCS) are anticipated to generate billions of dollars over the next several years.

SCIENCE AND TECHNOLOGY

Scientific discovery and technological innovation play central roles in increasing productivity and economic growth. In the long run, it is the discovery of new ideas—better "recipes," as distinct from merely more cooking in the traditional way with more of the same limited supply of ingredients—that reduces the cost to society of producing any given amount of goods. Ultimately these cost reductions will translate into some combination of lower prices for consumers, higher wages for workers, and higher profits for investors. Over time these changes can lead to significant, cumulative increases in living standards. Today the pace of scientific and technological progress is accelerating in tandem with the pace of the product cycle in international markets. These twin accelerations blur the lines and shrink the intervals that formerly separated basic from applied research, fundamental science from engineering and technical progress, and technological innovations from their initial commercial applications.

Wherever they originate, in the laboratory or on the factory floor, new scientific and technological ideas are often expensive to discover, yet cheap to replicate. It still costs something to draft the blueprint that captures the new idea, and something to make each unit of the product that embodies it, but once created, the idea itself is easily and often beneficially copied. Thus the economic returns to one company's investment in innovation can pass quickly to others. Economists have estimated that, because of this tendency of new ideas to become rapidly diffused, innovators typically capture less than half the total social returns to their investments in research and development (R&D). In short, the difficulty of establishing and enforcing property rights to new ideas reduces the economic incentive for private companies to invest in a socially and economically optimal level of R&D. Bolstering that incentive is therefore an important efficiency-enhancing function of government. Government can do so through enhanced patent protection—while bearing in mind the potential inefficiencies in production and innovation that can occur with even temporary market power—and through public support for R&D.

Even before this Administration came into office, historic changes in the global distribution of wealth and power had sparked a public reexamination of the nature and extent of Federal support for the Nation's science and technology enterprise. Much of this attention focused on the implications for Federal R&D spending of the end of the cold war and the growing technical competence of foreign-based firms in areas where U.S.-based industry had traditionally been the world leader. To respond to these changes, this Administration has reoriented the Federal R&D effort from primarily defense-related investments toward investments in a broader set of national goals, including health, prosperity, environmental responsibility, and improved quality of life, in addition to national security. Although the United States is still in the midst of a major transition in the way both the public and the private sector manage the development and commercialization of science and technology, recent changes are beginning to show positive results.

Trends in National R&D

Together industry, government, and universities in the United States have typically spent more money on R&D activities than their counterparts in any other country—an estimated $176 billion in 1994, or 2.6 percent of GDP. Indeed, in 1992, the most recent year for which comparative data are available, the United States spent 28 percent more on R&D than did Japan, Germany, and France *combined*. However, these countries collectively spent nearly as much as the United States on nondefense R&D. As a percentage of GDP, U.S. spending for civilian R&D stood at 2.1 percent in 1992, compared with 2.4 percent in Germany and 2.8 percent in Japan.

Long-term real growth in U.S. R&D has also been slow: just 0.9 percent per year on average between 1985 and 1993, compared with 5.3 percent per year between 1975 and 1985. This slowdown of total R&D growth has been paralleled by slower growth in private R&D. In 1994 R&D spending by U.S. industry decreased by 0.5 percent in real terms; this followed an average annual real growth rate of only 1.2 percent between 1986 and 1993, compared with a robust real annual growth rate of 6.7 percent between 1976 and 1985.

Some of the slowdown in R&D spending may reflect the recent recession. The slowdown may also reflect recent corporate cost-cutting drives that have shifted R&D spending toward in-house development of technologies closer to commercialization and that have prompted collaborative research, which is less costly to individual firms. (More than 350 multifirm collaborative research ventures, among them many R&D consortia, have been created in the United States since 1985, as well as more than 1,000 university-industry research centers, 72 percent of which were established with State or Federal support.) Finally, the slowdown in R&D spending reflects the end of the cold war. R&D spending by industry is highly concentrated in the United States—eight industries account for more than 80 percent of the total—and the top two, aircraft and communications equipment, are closely related to defense.

The deceleration of growth in spending for R&D has been accompanied by a shift in the sources of R&D funds and a shift in where the R&D is actually performed. Nongovernmental sources of funding have become increasingly important. Universities' share of R&D performance rose to 12 percent by 1993 from just 9 percent in 1985. Although Federal spending on all university research has risen, the share of university research funding that comes from the government has declined and recent financial problems of some universities may jeopardize their direct expenditures on research. Meanwhile industrial support for academic research has grown dramatically, from 3.9 percent of the total in 1980 to 7.3 percent in 1993. Industrial firms are still responsible for performing most of the Nation's R&D—$125 billion worth, or 71 percent in 1994— but even if their increased support for academic research is included, their share of the total national R&D effort has fallen since 1985.

Recent trends in U.S. R&D investment leave some analysts concerned that the Nation is spending too little on the *basic* research that will drive tomorrow's revolutionary breakthroughs. This concern is supported by empirical evidence that suggests there are large unexploited economic gains to be realized from raising our society's level of scientific activity and technological research and development; in the past, the social rate of return on such investments has been high. As a central component and stimulus of U.S. innovation, Federal R&D investment can lead technological innovation nationwide and affect the Nation's military posture, a variety of important social objectives, and the competitive performance of U.S.-based firms in domestic and foreign markets.

Confronting the Cold War Legacy

This Administration has realigned Federal spending for R&D so that it more equally balances civilian and military priorities. The purpose of this shift is not only to strengthen civilian industry, but also to promote the cost-effective development of new technologies for national defense and stimulate the creation of an integrated civilian-military industrial base. The Administration is also reorienting the Federal Government's R&D portfolio toward the achievement of important social objectives that would otherwise be inadequately addressed. These include the development of cleaner and more efficient transportation systems, more rapid and widespread diffusion of technological and managerial innovations to small and medium-sized manufacturers, environmental remediation, and pollution prevention.

The Administration's R&D strategy relies on a combination of grant programs in which industry and government share the costs; national initiatives in areas such as manufacturing, transportation, high-speed computing and telecommunications, and environmental technology; defense reinvestment efforts; and enhanced technology-transfer mechanisms (for example, the increased use of cooperative research and development agreements, or CRADAs, which ease private companies' access to the scientific and technological resources in U.S. Government laboratories). These programs require Federal agencies to work more closely with commercial industry to strengthen the technological underpinnings of the entire economy.

Reflecting cold war concerns, national security long commanded the largest share of Federal R&D funds. Spending priorities shifted even further—dramatically so—toward defense programs in the 1980s. The defense share of Federal R&D spending reached its most recent peak in 1987, when it accounted for 69 percent of the total. The defense share declined from 59 percent to 56 percent between 1992 and 1994, indicating progress toward the Administration's goal of restoring a 50–50 split by 1998.

The national security focus of U.S. R&D spending during the cold war has also affected the agenda for government support of much industrial and university-based science. During the late 1980s, for example, the Defense Department provided 32 percent of all funds for academic engineering research. While Federal funds account for just one-fourth of the money private industry spends to support R&D, 76 percent of that Federal support goes to aerospace and communications equipment firms, primarily for development of weapons and related systems of military application. The cold war emphasis on defense also affected the structure and objectives of the Nation's Federal laboratory system.

In an era of increasing budget pressure—an era, too, in which commercial technology development defines the leading edge in key strategic areas—the maintenance of a defense industrial base separate from commercially oriented industry is in many areas economically inefficient. Recognizing this, the Defense Department is now working more closely with firms engaged in commercial and dual-use production than in the past (dual-use goods are those with both military and commercial uses). Dual-use R&D programs, including the Administration's Technology Reinvestment Project (TRP), are a different—and more economically efficient—way of carrying out the Defense Department's traditional R&D activities. The TRP has played a role in facilitating new partnerships between defense and commercial industry. Combined with the procurement reforms discussed earlier, the program is expected to make the Defense Department a more attractive customer for civilian producers. It is also exposing traditional defense contractors to innovative management and production techniques that can lower their costs and encourage more rapid technology transfer from the commercial sector.

Other important examples of Defense Department dual-use R&D initiatives include the development of flat panel display technology (Box 4–7) and microwave and millimeter wave monolithic integrated circuit technology (MIMIC). Commercial applications for MIMIC devices include their use in collision avoidance systems for automobiles, satellite communications, and portable telephones. The development of dual-use components that can be built on the same production line as the military-only versions has resulted in lower cost devices for the military and new, commercially marketable products for U.S. firms. Commercial technology cannot supply defense needs in all instances—tanks and nuclear attack submarines, for example, require technology that is defense-unique. But a great many defense needs can be served more efficiently— and less expensively—by commercial firms and facilities. Indeed, as flexible manufacturing systems are developed and more widely adopted, it will be increasingly possible to produce in a single plant both low-volume military equipment and high-volume commercial equipment.

Private Innovation and Public Goods

Beyond reorienting the government's own R&D portfolio, this Administration has worked on many fronts to increase the level of private innovation—by supporting public-private partnerships for the provision of industry-specific public goods, by supporting the extension of the R&D tax credit (discussed in Chapter 3), and by proposing changes in intellectual property law that will increase the incentives for efficient creation and use of private inventions.

Industry-specific public goods. It has already been noted that individual firms typically have too little incentive to invest in R&D, because an innovation and its payoffs may pass quickly to other firms and to consumers, who paid little or nothing to create the innovation in the first place. The constant creation and rapid diffusion of scientific discovery and technological innovation are good for the economy as a whole, but investment in innovation may not appear to be a prudent move for any individual firm.

Box 4–7.—The National Flat Panel Display Initiative

Today's computers display information in one of two ways: on cathode ray tubes, the bulky devices now used in television sets and most desktop computers; or on flat panel displays, the thin, light, rugged screens used in laptop computers. Flat panel displays are already key components in many consumer products: facsimile machines, portable telephones, compact disc players, and videocassette recorders, as well as laptops. They will also transform future battlefields, where they will be used to satisfy the huge demand for information from myriad sensors, providing real-time intelligence to combatants in aircraft, ships, tanks, and the infantry.

A recently completed interagency study of flat panel displays shows them to be increasingly important in military applications. But with 95 percent of supply controlled by foreign producers, whose willingness to work with the Defense Department cannot be taken for granted, access to the latest flat panel display technologies for timely incorporation into defense systems is not assured. The Department of Defense requires early, certain, and affordable access in order to integrate displays into systems and to work out tactics for their use in military situations.

To answer these national security concerns, the Defense Department is implementing the National Flat Panel Display Initiative, a 5-year, $587 million program of support for research and development into flat panel displays, including research on their manufacture. Part of this precompetitive R&D funding is focused on ensuring that the research leads to actual products that will be used in important military applications. A portion will go to an innovative program in which firms with a demonstrated commitment to build current-generation displays share with the Pentagon the burden of developing dual-use technology for next-generation products and manufacturing processes. Matching funds will be awarded in competitions open to a variety of flat panel display technologies.

A similar logic is at work with regard to investments in industry-specific public goods. Investments in a particular technological breakthrough may create large economic benefits for the industry as a whole, from which no single producer or subset of producers can be excluded, even though the breakthrough was financed and achieved by others.

The Commerce Department's Advanced Technology Program (ATP) is a policy experiment to test whether government-industry

167

partnerships can overcome market barriers to the provision of industry-specific public goods. Take, for example, the barriers that have impeded some potentially lucrative technical improvements in the materials and manufacturing processes for printed-wiring boards (PWBs). PWBs comprise the backbone and much of the nervous system of virtually every modern electronic product. Each increase in the speed and complexity of electronic devices has increased the density of the PWB's lacework of copper lines, which must be embroidered to tiny plated holes. By the early 1990s, PWBs were beginning to reach the fundamental physical limits imposed by both materials and manufacturing processes. PWB market analysts understood that relatively minor material or process improvements could result in sizable cost savings for the entire industry, yet no single company or group of companies was willing to risk a large-scale investment.

The ATP stepped into the breach, agreeing to help finance a 5-year research plan developed by an industry consortium, as long as the consortium's members were themselves willing to put up at least half of the money. The $28 million effort began in 1991. A study conducted in 1993 found that after 2 years the project had already saved the participants about $13.5 million simply by helping them to avoid redundant research, to share results more rapidly, and to access each other's specialized know-how and facilities.

The ATP itself is only 4 years old, and the Administration is creating long-term and intermediate performance measures in order to rigorously evaluate its economic impact. This effort to promote innovation in the private sector is itself an innovation in the relationship between industry and the government, one that was begun during the previous Administration.

Intellectual property. Incentives for technological innovation are affected by the regime of intellectual property rights, including patents and copyrights. Absent well-defined and effectively enforced intellectual property rights, rivals could readily duplicate new inventions or writings without offering compensation; this reduces the innovator's likely profit and mutes the incentive to develop and market his or her creations in the first place.

The economics of patent protection have long been understood as posing the following policy tradeoff: patent protection encourages innovation, but that social benefit comes at the cost of allowing some successful innovators to price the resulting products well above marginal cost. In recognition of this tradeoff, patent protection is granted for a limited term of years. Yet appropriate public policy toward innovation must also recognize a second tradeoff, involving the scope rather than the term of patents.

The scope or breadth of patents refers to the extent to which a new innovation must differ from an existing one in order to avoid infringing on the latter's patent rights. Under some circumstances, narrowing the scope of patent rights would increase aggregate innovation rates. When an inventor's patent rights are broad in scope, extending to a relatively wide range of similar innovations, later inventors will not be permitted to use their own innovations that fall within that broad penumbra of similarity, without the first inventor's permission. Recognizing that such permission will frequently involve negotiating a payment to the first inventor (a negotiation in which the second inventor will sometimes have little bargaining leverage), the second inventor may be discouraged from exploring his or her new ideas to begin with. Or, if the second innovation is produced but the first and second innovators dispute its value, and in consequence are unable to reach a bargain, the second innovation may not be used until the patent expires. Giving broad scope to patent rights may thus discourage potential innovators from undertaking R&D effort in areas likely to produce follow-on inventions. Yet in other cases, narrowing the scope of intellectual property rights would reduce aggregate innovation rates by lowering the value of initial innovations, thus reducing the incentive for initial innovation.

In part to promote innovation, the U.S. Patent and Trademark Office has proposed legislation to permit greater third-party participation in patent reexamination proceedings. Under this proposal, industry experts and rivals would have a greater opportunity to present information about novelty or obviousness to the patent examiner after a patent is issued. In addition, the Department of Justice has drafted proposed new antitrust guidelines for the licensing and acquisition of intellectual property. By clarifying the conditions under which trade restraints involving intellectual property, like those involving other forms of property, can harm competition and run afoul of the antitrust laws, the Justice Department seeks to explain how antitrust law and intellectual property protections can be harmonized to encourage innovation and efficiency, and so benefit consumers.

CONCLUSION

Adam Smith published *The Wealth of Nations* in 1776, the same year Thomas Jefferson wrote the Declaration of Independence. Since that time the United States has become a vastly larger and more prosperous Nation. One reason is that, throughout our history, government has worked in partnership with the private sector to promote competition, discourage externalities, and provide public goods. The policy challenges that face us vary from generation to generation, and government institutions appropriate for addressing one era's problems must be reinvented for the next. But in every era, the role of government in helping remedy market failures remains central for enhancing the Nation's well-being.

CHAPTER 5

Improving Skills and Incomes

BETWEEN 1973 AND 1994 the U.S. economy created 37 million additional jobs. This growth in employment absorbed an unprecedented number of new entrants, including millions of baby-boomers and women, into the work force and surpassed the record of the other large industrial nations. During this same period, however, slow productivity growth in the United States was reflected in slow growth in average real compensation. Indeed, real compensation per employed person increased more slowly in the United States than in the other large industrial countries (Chart 5–1). Even worse, income growth stagnated in the middle of the income distribution and declined sharply for those at the low end, causing insecurity and falling living standards for many Americans. The large declines in the real wages of less educated and lower paid workers were associated with increased inequality in family incomes and with growing rates of poverty among working families. For a growing number of workers without college degrees or significant on-the-job training, the American dream faded.

This chapter examines the factors that underlie the disappointing growth in the incomes of most American workers over the past 20 years and describes this Administration's policy responses.

The sluggish growth of incomes is due to dramatic changes in technology and in global competition that have affected industrialized economies around the world, reducing the relative demand for workers with less education and training. Industrialized nations have differed in their response to these common changes. Since 1973, the U.S. economy has created more jobs than all of the European Community. But at the same time the other industrialized economies have experienced more rapid growth in wages and productivity and slower growth in inequality.

Although these differing patterns appear to suggest a trade-off between rapid job growth and high wage and productivity growth, this Administration believes that such a trade-off is not inevitable. To sustain rapid job growth while increasing growth in wages and productivity, the Administration has undertaken an ambitious agenda of lifelong learning to help American workers respond to the challenges and grasp the opportunities afforded by the new economic realities.

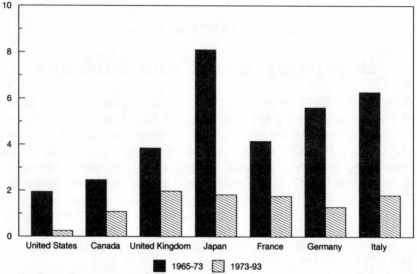

Chart 5-1 **Growth in Real Compensation per Person Employed**
Real compensation has grown more slowly in the United States than in the other major industrialized countries.

Average annual percent change

Legend: ■ 1965-73 ▨ 1973-93

Note: Data for Canada begin with 1966.
Source: Organization for Economic Cooperation and Development.

WHAT HAS HAPPENED TO WAGES AND INCOMES

Compared with the preceding decades, family incomes over the last 20 years have either grown more slowly or actually declined at all income levels. This discouraging picture emerges no matter what statistical measure of compensation or inflation one chooses (Box 5–1).

SLOW GROWTH IN PRODUCTIVITY AND AVERAGE WAGES

Growth in average real compensation declined from 3.0 percent a year between 1948 and 1973 to 0.7 percent a year between 1973 and 1993. This decline parallels a similar drop in worker productivity growth, from 2.5 percent per year to only 0.9 percent. If real compensation had continued to grow at the same rate after 1973 as it had in the previous 25 years, the average compensation of a full-time worker in the United States in 1993 would have been $62,400 instead of $40,000.

The slowdown in wage growth can be seen within the span of a single individual's career. Sixty-two percent of men aged 22 to 26 in 1967 enjoyed earnings growth of over 40 percent by 1979; only 9 percent suffered earnings declines. In contrast, only 42 percent of young men in the 1980s enjoyed wage gains over 40 percent, while the proportion of those with wage declines tripled to 26 percent.

Box 5-1.—Measuring Trends in Pay and Inequality

Measures of changes in real pay differ across a number of dimensions: how inflation is adjusted for; whether pay is measured as wages per hour or earnings per year; whether it is limited to cash wages or includes benefits (the latter is referred to as total compensation); and whether the mean or the median is chosen as the measure of central tendency. All standard measures of pay show both a slowing of overall growth and a concentration of the bad news among those with less than a college degree; nevertheless, different measures show somewhat different patterns over the last few decades (Chart 5-2).

Mean and median wages differ. The mean is the average of all wages earned, whereas the median is the wage of the worker who falls precisely at the middle of the distribution, with half of all workers earning more and half less. Because wages at the high end of the distribution have risen much more rapidly since 1973 than those in the middle, the mean wage has risen more rapidly than the median.

Wages differ from total compensation. Total compensation includes such benefits as health insurance and employers' contributions to pensions in addition to wages. Expenditures on these benefits, led by rising prices for health care, have grown rapidly since 1973. Thus, hourly compensation continues to grow more rapidly than wages, although both have slowed in the last 2 decades.

Hourly wages differ from annual earnings because the number of hours worked per year is not constant. The trend in overall hours is not clear, with employers, but not employees, reporting declining hours. This divergence may be due to an increase in unpaid overtime or work at home, but it remains an area of active research.

The method of adjusting for inflation makes a difference. As noted in Chapter 2, it is possible that actual increases in workers' cost of living have been smaller than trends in the consumer price index (CPI) would suggest. Consequently, standard measures that rely on the CPI may understate the growth in real pay. But the basic finding of slower wage growth since 1973 holds for all standard measures of inflation (although all suffer from possible mismeasurement of quality changes). In any case, the finding that wage dispersion has grown holds regardless of how inflation is measured.

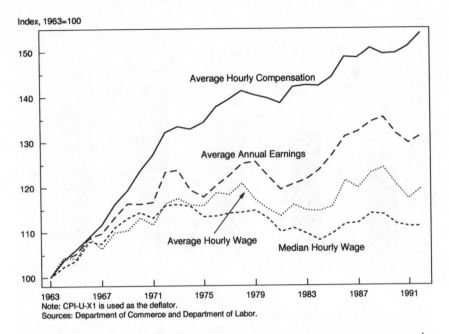

Index, 1963=100

Note: CPI-U-X1 is used as the deflator.
Sources: Department of Commerce and Department of Labor.

SLOWDOWN FOR MOST, STAGNATION FOR MANY

What growth there has been has not been shared by all Americans. The median real hourly wage fell by 6 percent from 1973 to 1993. The middle of the income distribution was hurt more by the slowdown than the top, largely reflecting a dramatic shift in the rewards offered in the labor market against those without a college degree or a high level of skill (Chart 5–3). For example, the average real wage of male high school graduates fell 20 percent, from $14.02 per hour in 1973 (measured in 1993 dollars) to $11.19 per hour in 1993. The decline was even steeper for male high school dropouts, whose average wage fell 27 percent over the same period, from $11.85 to $8.64 per hour. At the same time, the average hourly wage for males with a college degree but no further education fell by 9 percent, from $19.41 to $17.62. Hourly wages of those with a college degree and 2 or more years of additional education fell by only 2 percent, from $22.20 to $21.71. Trends for women show a similar though less extreme widening in the wage differential between those who went to college and those who did not (Chart 5–4). Wage dispersion also increased within demographic and skill groups. The wages of individuals of the same age, education, and sex, working in the same industry and occupation, were more unequal in the early 1990s than 20 years earlier.

174

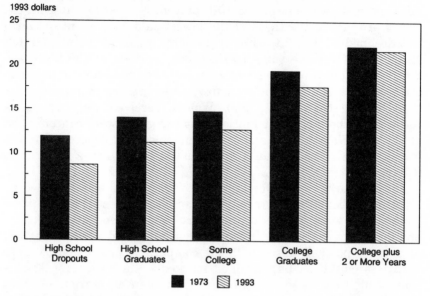

Chart 5-3 **Real Hourly Wages for Men by Level of Education**
Real wages have fallen for men of all education levels, but those with the least
education have been hurt the most.

1993 dollars

Source: Economic Policy Institute.

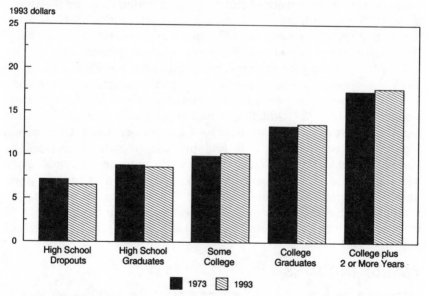

Chart 5-4 **Real Hourly Wages for Women by Level of Education**
Women with at least some college education have seen modest wage gains, while
wages have fallen for those without.

1993 dollars

Source: Economic Policy Institute.

175

Another perspective on the decline in real wages can be seen by examining trends at points in the wage distribution other than the median (Chart 5–5). Between 1973 and 1993 real hourly wages of full-time male workers at the 10th percentile (that is, those whose wages are just above those of the lowest-paid 10 percent of workers) declined 16 percent, while real hourly wages at the median fell 12 percent. Over the same two decades, workers at the 90th percentile eked out a wage *gain* of 2 percent. The net effect is that levels of wage inequality for men have been greater in recent years than at any time since 1940. Women received wage increases throughout the wage distribution, but the gains were concentrated at the top. Women at the 10th percentile earned 6 percent higher wages, while those at the 90th percentile had gains of 24 percent (Chart 5–6).

The decline in wages for high school graduates was matched by a decline in benefits coverage. For example, whereas the proportion of the work force with education past college who have company- or union-provided health insurance has remained almost constant at over 75 percent since 1979, the comparable proportion of those with less education has declined markedly. In 1992, only 60 percent of high school graduates and fewer than 40 percent of those who did not graduate from high school had company- or union-provided health insurance.

As already noted, women were an important exception to the broad pattern of wage declines. Overall, the median real hourly wage of women who worked full time, year round, rose by 9 percent from 1973 to 1993, and rose as a proportion of the median wage for men from 63 percent in 1973 to 78 percent in 1993. Much of the improvement in women's earnings relative to those of men was due to the growing labor market experience of working women. In 1975 the average working woman had put in not much more than half (57 percent) the years of full-time work that the average male worker had; by 1987 that figure had risen to 73 percent. A second important factor was that women increasingly went to work in higher paid occupations that had previously been dominated by males. Statistics from several traditionally male professions reveal the size of the shift: from 1970–92 the proportion of female graduates from medical schools rose from 8 percent to 36 percent; the proportion graduating from law schools rose from 5 percent to 43 percent; and the proportion from dental schools from less than 0.1 percent to 32 percent.

FAMILY INCOMES

Incomes have stagnated for many American families as well as for individual workers. Family income as reported in U.S. statistics differs from annual earnings per worker both because there can be

Chart 5-5 Real Hourly Wages for Men by Wage Percentile
Real wages have declined for all but the highest-paid male workers.

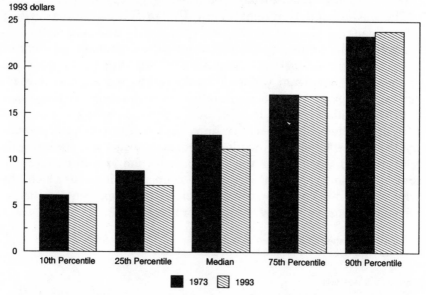

Source: Department of Labor.

Chart 5-6 Real Hourly Wages for Women by Wage Percentile
Women at all wage levels received increases in pay, but those at the top gained the most.

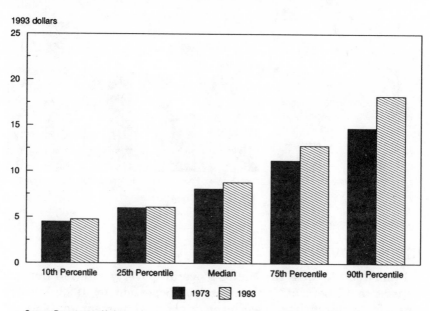

Source: Department of Labor.

more (or fewer) than one wage earner in a family and because family income includes nonwage income such as interest, dividends, profits, and government transfer payments.

The median family income in the United States grew a meager 0.2 percent in the entire 20 years between 1973 and 1993—although hardly impressive, this performance at least was better than the outright decline in median hourly wages. In addition, there was a significant widening in the family income distribution. Average incomes rose 25 percent for those families in the upper fifth of the distribution, but fell by 15 percent among the poorest fifth of families (Chart 5–7). An important reason why median family incomes rose slightly while the median wage was declining is that married women now work more hours for pay. Between 1973 and 1992 the proportion of married couple families in which the wife worked for pay grew from 42 percent to 59 percent and those wives who worked for pay worked more hours.

Chart 5-7 **Average Family Income by Quintile**
Incomes have fallen for the poorest forty percent of families.

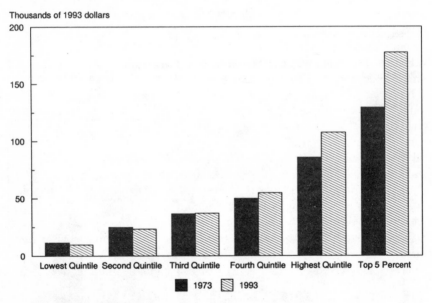

Thousands of 1993 dollars

Source: Department of Commerce.

RISING POVERTY

From 1960 to 1973 the Nation's overall poverty rate fell from 22 percent to 11 percent; it then rose to 15 percent by 1993. Poverty rates for children have been even higher: 27 percent in 1960, 14 percent in 1973, and 23 percent in 1993. The observed rise in poverty remains even after taxes and transfers are accounted for: pov-

178

erty rates by this measure rose from 9 percent in 1979 to 12 percent in 1993 (comparable figures are not available prior to 1979). The increase in poverty has occurred in spite of slow growth in average income over the last 20 years.

A large portion of the rise in poverty is due both to the increase in wage inequality discussed above and to a rise in the proportion of female-headed households. The proportion of children under 18 who live with one parent has nearly tripled, from 9 percent in 1960 to almost 27 percent in 1992. More than half of the children born in America today will spend time living in a single-parent home, either because of divorce or because the parents were never married. Because the poverty rate in female-headed families with children is higher, at 46 percent, than in other families, increases in the proportion of families headed by a single parent increase the poverty rate.

Many explanations for the increase in single parenthood have been proposed, ranging from the rise in women's labor force participation (which has increased women's ability to live without a husband), to the falling wages and employment of the men they might marry, to cultural changes reducing the stigma of divorce and unwed motherhood.

Some have blamed the rise in female-headed households on the welfare system. Although the current system has a number of problems (discussed in Chapter 1), careful studies have concluded that it has not played a major role in the increase in female-headed households. Nationwide, average benefits under the aid to families with dependent children (AFDC) and food stamp programs rose from 1964 to 1972, and during those years single-parenthood rates did rise; however, those rates continued to rise over the next 14 years even as the level of benefits fell by 20 percent in inflation-adjusted terms. In addition, States with more generous AFDC benefits do not have a higher proportion of children in single-parent households. Although welfare has not caused most of the changes in family structure, the welfare system does have aspects that discourage marriage—elements of the Administration's welfare reform proposal, discussed in Chapter 1, address these problems.

THE DECLINING FORTUNES OF BLACK AMERICANS

Black workers have been particularly harmed by recent earnings trends. After a decade of progress following the Civil Rights Act of 1964, the trend in the relative earnings of blacks to whites reversed. In the early 1960s, the wage gap between black and white men of similar age and with similar education was over 20 percent. This gap closed to less than 10 percent in the mid-1970s, but a significant proportion of this gain has since eroded. In addition, the employment-to-population ratio for black men over 20 years old has declined, from about 6 percentage points less than the rate for whites to about 9 percentage points, over the last 20 years. The drop in employment is due to a decline in black labor force participation as well as increases in black unemployment. In some inner-city neighborhoods as few as 40 percent of black men are employed—that is less than three-fifths the male employment rate for the Nation as a whole.

In contrast to the decline in relative earnings, years of school completed and test scores among blacks have risen relative to whites. The difference in high school dropout rates between blacks and whites has narrowed sharply. From 1973 to 1992, dropout rates for blacks fell from 12.3 percentage points more than for whites to only 4.1 percentage points more. Black educational attainment (as measured by the National Assessment for Educational Progress) generally increased significantly from 1978 to 1992, while white test scores rose only slightly. But in many inner-city districts the dropout rate remains above 50 percent, and Hispanic dropout rates remain very high.

Inner cities have experienced poor job opportunities, more concentrated poverty, and low-quality schools. At the same time a majority of young black male high school dropouts have turned to illegal activities for income. Surveys indicate that young black men are more likely now than a decade ago to perceive greater rewards from crime than from regular employment. Young persons' participation in crime has adverse effects on their likelihood of future employment, especially if their activities lead to incarceration. These problems feed on each other: a child's chances of attending a low-quality school, becoming a teen parent, dropping out of school, living with only one parent, and having parents who do not work for pay are all associated with living in a poor neighborhood.

Racial and ethnic discrimination remains a significant barrier for minorities in the job market. Direct measures of discrimination in employment are available from experiments in which similarly qualified white and black candidates, or Anglo and Hispanic candidates, applied for the same job. In one such experiment, white applicants were found to be 24 percent more likely to receive significantly better treatment than black applicants, and Anglo applicants were 22 percent more likely to receive significantly better treatment than Hispanic applicants. In addition, among applicants who reached the interview stage, whites were over four times more likely to be offered a job than were blacks with similar qualifications.

Government antidiscrimination efforts became less aggressive in the 1980s, and this may account for some of the persistence of discrimination. An analysis of data collected by the Office of Federal Contract Compliance Programs (OFCCP) shows that enforcement of affirmative action rules between 1974 and 1980 improved the job opportunities of black men and women as well as white women with Federal contractors. In the 1980–84 period the activities of the OFCCP were not as spirited as previously, and coverage by Federal affirmative action policies was no longer associated with gains in black and female employment.

CHANGES IN THE ECONOMY

Although a complete explanation of the declining economic fortunes of so many American workers and families is lacking, most economists believe that a shift in the demand for labor in favor of more highly skilled, more highly educated workers has played a key role. Such a shift is consistent with the fact that even though the percentage of the labor force with a college degree increased from 16.4 percent in 1973 to 27 percent in 1993, the same period saw a pronounced increase in the relative wages of college graduates (Charts 5–3 and 5–4).

In part, the shift in demand in favor of more educated workers reflects a shift in employment away from those goods-producing sectors that have disproportionately provided high-wage opportunities for blue-collar men, toward medical, business, and other services that disproportionately employ college graduates and women. In addition, employment has grown in such low-wage sectors as retail trade. These interindustry shifts appear to explain some of the decline in the wages of high school graduates over the last 20 years.

Intensifying global competition is also cited as a factor in putting downward pressure on the wages of less educated workers. However, a number of studies have found that the easily measured direct effects of trade on the wage distribution were small, implying that the vast majority of the demand shift originated domestically.

These effects of trade may be larger if the internationalization of the U.S. economy also affects wages indirectly—for example, if the threat of increased import competition or of the relocation of a factory to another country undermines workers' bargaining power. It is not known how important such effects have been. Trade may also become a more important factor in the future, as international commerce continues to expand.

Immigration has increased the relative supply of less skilled labor in the United States and has contributed to the increasing inequality of income, but the effect has been small. One study found that immigration explained less than 1 percent of the change in the college-high school wage differential between 1980 and 1988. Although immigration flows were considerably larger in the late 1980s than the early 1980s, this study makes it seem unlikely that

181

the recent contribution of immigration could be more than a few percent of the total change.

Within-industry shifts in labor demand away from less educated workers are the most important factor behind their eroding wages, not the shift out of manufacturing. On the basis of current research—much of which remains anecdotal or indirect in nature—most economists believe that such shifts in turn are primarily the result of economy-wide technological and organizational changes in how work is performed. The computerization of work appears important. Recent empirical evidence indicates that workers who use computers are paid on average 15 percent higher wages than those who do not. And the use of computers in the workplace has increased significantly in recent years: between 1984 and 1993 the share of the labor force using computers on the job increased from 25 percent to 47 percent.

In addition to shifts in labor demand, two institutional factors appear to have contributed to the increase in earnings inequality over the last 20 years. One of these is the decline in the proportion of workers belonging to unions. Empirical evidence suggests that unions tend to raise wages for workers who would otherwise be in the bottom half of the wage distribution. The share of the labor force belonging to unions fell from 26 percent in 1973 to 16 percent (and only 11 percent of the private sector labor force) today. According to recent studies, the precipitous decline in unionization explains a modest but significant portion of the increase in wage inequality during the last 15 years, especially among men.

The decline in the real value of the minimum wage has further contributed to greater wage dispersion. Adjusted for inflation, by 1995 the minimum wage has fallen by about 50 cents since 1991 and is 29 percent below its 1979 level, leaving it at its second-lowest level since the 1950s. Because women are almost twice as likely as men to work at minimum-wage jobs, the erosion of its value has had its largest effect at the lower end of the female wage distribution. Recent empirical research finds that modest increases in the minimum wage from historically low levels in the late 1980s were associated with reductions in both wage and income inequality without significant adverse effects on employment.

Of workers affected by the most recent (April 1990) increase in the minimum wage, 36 percent were the only wage earner in the family, and the average minimum-wage worker contributed about half of his or her family's total earnings. Contrary to some press reports emphasizing the youth of minimum-wage recipients, 70 percent were aged 20 and over. In part because of the changes in the wage structure discussed above, workers affected by this change in the minimum wage were more likely to be poor than in the past. About 20 percent of minimum-wage earners were poor, and another 13 percent were near poor (earning between 100 and 150 percent of the poverty line).

IMPROVING EDUCATION AND TRAINING

It is becoming increasingly difficult for those without higher education to earn enough to support a traditional middle-class standard of living. Increasingly, however, a high school education is not enough. Fewer high-wage jobs remain for high school graduates, and even many workers with college educations face the prospect of stagnant wages. This is a fundamental change in the economy. Although government is not the cause, it has the ability and the responsibility to improve the way Americans are educated and trained so as to mitigate this adverse trend.

This Administration views education as, ideally, a lifelong process for all workers, particularly in the changing economic environment of today. Improved education and training opportunities not only should have a direct effect in increasing the incomes of those who take advantage of them, but may as a side effect improve the incomes of unskilled workers as well, as their relative supply is decreased.

In designing programs to promote lifelong learning, Federal policies operate in an environment where education is primarily the province of States and localities, and training is provided primarily by employers. Thus, the Federal Government's most effective role is often to serve as a catalyst for change.

Evaluations of many of the Federal Government's education and training programs have questioned their efficacy, although careful studies have found some programs to be highly successful. In designing new programs, the Administration has attempted to learn from these experiences, to imitate the successes and avoid the failures. In predicting future performance, it would be excessively pessimistic simply to extrapolate from the past failures; on the other hand, it would perhaps be overly optimistic to believe that we can bring all programs up to the level of the most successful just by replicating their best features. Yet there are certain features that many successful programs have in common—such as integrating different services to address problems with multiple aspects, and providing incentives that reward success—whose scope for broader application is far from exhausted.

THE QUALITY OF AMERICAN EDUCATION

By many measures, the quality of education in the United States has improved in recent years. Test scores in reading, writing, mathematics, and science have generally risen over the past decade for almost all ages and racial and ethnic groups. As noted above, dropout rates have fallen, declining most sharply for black students. Enrollments in both preschool and postsecondary school have increased. Preschool enrollment rates have risen since 1970 from 14 percent of children aged 3 to 4 years to one-third. The percentage of high school graduates who enrolled in college following graduation increased from 49 percent in 1980 to 62 percent in 1992. Few other countries have postsecondary enrollment rates as high as those in the United States.

The United States still has far to go, however, to ensure that all its young people are acquiring the knowledge and skills they need to obtain high-paying jobs and adapt to future changes in the economy. High school dropout rates, for example, are still high, nearly 13 percent overall, and the dropout rate for Hispanics is over twice as high. Comparisons of U.S. and foreign test scores give additional cause for concern. Although test scores are imperfect measures of school quality, scores of U.S. students have generally risen. However, in the math portion of the International Assessment of Educational Progress in recent years, the United States remains among the industrialized world's laggards. U.S. students at both the 9-year-old and 13-year-old levels not only trail their Taiwanese and Korean counterparts—the world leaders in this area—but also lag behind students in every other major nation participating in the test.

THE IMPLICATIONS OF RISING RETURNS TO EDUCATION

Numerous studies have established that workers with more education earn substantially higher wages than workers with similar characteristics, such as age, experience, race, and sex, but with less education. However, this relation does not necessarily imply that raising the educational level of those who are now undereducated will lift their earnings substantially. It may be that those students who obtain the most schooling are those who start out with greater ability. Nevertheless, a number of innovative studies that address this problem still support the conclusion that, on average, students at all skill levels gain substantially from additional education. These results are consistent with the thesis that for many students growing up in low-income households, limitations on access to information and to funds for paying for education, not lack of payoff from further schooling, are major causes of their lower educational attainment.

POLICIES TO PROMOTE A LIFETIME OF LEARNING

The Goals 2000: Educate America Act, enacted last year, sets eight ambitious national education goals to be achieved by the end of the decade:

- *School readiness.* All children will start school ready to learn.
- *Improved student achievement.* All students will demonstrate competence in challenging subject matter in core academic subjects.
- *Best in math and science.* U.S. students will be first in the world in mathematics and science achievement.
- *Safe, disciplined, and drug-free schools.* Every school will be free from violence, disruptive behavior, and illegal drugs.
- *Increased graduation rate.* The high school graduation rate will improve to at least 90 percent.
- *Teacher education and professional development.* All teachers will have the opportunity to acquire the knowledge and skills needed to prepare their students for the next century.
- *Parental involvement.* Every school will promote parent-teacher partnerships that will increase parents' involvement in the social and academic enrichment of their children.
- *Adult literacy and lifelong learning.* Every adult will be literate and possess the skills necessary to compete in a global economy.

These goals establish a framework for a lifetime of continuous learning, starting before kindergarten and continuing throughout adulthood. New opportunities for all Americans to engage in lifelong learning should help rebuild the American dream that working hard and playing by the rules will lead to a higher standard of living.

Readiness to Learn

The first national goal is to ensure that all children start school ready to learn. Even good schools will have trouble educating children who come to school unprepared to learn because of poor nutrition or for other reasons. Some of these children will always find themselves struggling to catch up. The Administration is committed to expanding two programs that promote early cognitive and physical development and help prepare children for school. The first is the Special Supplemental Food Program for Women, Infants, and Children (WIC), which provides food supplements and health education to 6 million low-income pregnant women, new mothers, and their children up to age 5 annually. Funding for WIC increased from $2.6 billion in 1992 to $3.5 billion in 1995, with $3.8 billion proposed for 1996. The WIC program has been shown to save the government money as well as increase children's health (Box 5–2). The second program, Head Start, also has a proven track record. Head Start is an intensive preschool program designed to improve the cognitive and social functioning, health status, and school readiness of low-income youth. Head Start funding has increased from $2.2 billion in fiscal 1992 to $3.5 billion in fiscal 1995, with $3.9 billion proposed for 1996. The new funding has been focused on improving program quality for children already in the program and in expanding the new "Early Head Start" program for children in the first 3 years of life.

Box 5–2.—What Works: Preparing Students to Learn

WIC has been shown by many studies to be highly effective in improving the health status of infants. In addition, WIC appears to be a money *saver*: for every dollar spent on the prenatal WIC program, approximately $3.50 is saved in medicaid and other costs due to lower incidence of low-birthweight births and improved health. To the extent that poor prenatal care and infant health are associated with future behavioral and academic problems, the benefits of WIC are even greater.

Head Start and other preschool programs have also demonstrated their ability to improve preparedness for school. Numerous studies have found that participation in Head Start produces immediate gains in health and in scores on tests of intellectual ability, emotional maturity, and school readiness. They also find, however, that these gains in test scores decline over time. Nevertheless, some Head Start and other similar programs that have been evaluated over many years have found that participants are less likely to be assigned to special education classes, and are less likely to be held back a grade.

Improving Student Achievement

The Goals 2000 act provides a framework for comprehensive State and local efforts to improve both teaching and learning, based on clear and challenging academic standards for all students. The framework of Goals 2000 is meant to encourage the alignment of various aspects of the educational system including curriculum design, student assessments, teachers' professional development, and instructional materials. These systemic reforms are voluntary, and their design in each State will be a group effort including parents, business people, educators, and others.

The 1991 reforms adopted in Kentucky are an example of the type of alignment Goals 2000 is intended to promote in other States. Kentucky adopted six broad goals and further refined these in 62 specific academic expectations. One of the goals, for example, is that students should be able to apply principles from mathematics, science, social studies, and other disciplines to real-life situations. In science, this goal translates into such concrete expectations as that students should be able to recognize and use patterns such as cycles and trends to understand past events and make predictions. The State's major employers have been involved throughout the reforms, helping to ensure that the schools' expectations match the needs of employers and future graduates.

The State's new goals are accompanied by new assessment procedures that combine traditional multiple-choice questions with tests requiring students to solve practical problems, and with evaluations of each student's best classroom work collected throughout the year. This new assessment better measures the full range of each student's progress. The assessment also is used to evaluate schools' success in improving student performance; schools that do well will receive monetary rewards, while unsuccessful schools will be required to develop plans for improvement. Coupled with the increased accountability, Kentucky is decentralizing decision making to school-based councils of teachers, parents, and principals on matters such as curriculum and assignment of staff. In addition, resources for professional development have been increased and family and youth service centers have been established at low income schools to provide and coordinate services for families such as child care, family counseling, and referrals to service agencies.

Results in Kentucky are preliminary so far, but encouraging. After 2 years, average test scores in core academic subjects increased markedly at all grade levels tested. Time will tell if these results are sustained and translate into better careers for Kentucky's graduates.

The reforms embedded in Goals 2000 and its companion legislation, the Improving America's Schools Act, are part of the Administration's effort to move away from rigid rules to a new model where the Federal Government provides seed money and technical assistance for States and local school districts to engage in their own reform efforts, keyed to high standards. The acts enhance local flexibility by providing States and local school districts the opportunity to better coordinate the activities of federally funded programs in their areas. Both acts allow States and school districts to apply for waivers of Federal rules that impede their plans for school improvement. The objective is to create a system in which highly skilled teachers can focus on achieving clear, widely agreed-on goals, assisted by parents and the community, who in turn can look to a set of well-defined standards by which to hold educators and school systems accountable.

Increasing Graduation Rates

Goals 2000 also focuses on reducing dropout rates. In addition, the Improving America's Schools Act ensures that Federal funds will be available to middle and high schools with very high poverty rates—schools that also have a high proportion of students at risk of dropping out.

This goal is important both to students at risk of dropping out and to society as a whole. On average high school dropouts earn

35 percent less per year than high school graduates with no additional education, and 70 percent less than college graduates, leading the average high school dropout to pay far less in taxes over the course of his or her working life than the average high school graduate. Dropouts are also more likely than graduates to end up on welfare or in prison. For example, on any given day in 1992 almost one-quarter of all males between 18 and 34 who had not received a conventional high school diploma—but less than 4 percent of those who had—were either in prison, on probation, or on parole. According to preliminary Department of Labor estimates, the typical young female high school dropout receives on average more than twice as much in food stamps and public assistance payments as high school graduates and almost five times as much as those with at least some college.

The present value of total welfare, prison, and parole costs averages about $69,000 over the course of an adult lifetime for each individual who does not graduate from high school, but only about $32,000 for each high school graduate who does not attend college, and only $15,000 for those who attend college. (These figures are calculated as the net present value at age 18 of the costs of criminal justice and welfare incurred between the ages of 18 to 54, using 1992 data. Costs are discounted at a 4-percent annual rate.) Thus, ignoring differences in taxes paid, a program capable of influencing young people who would otherwise drop out of high school to graduate and behave like other high school graduates would reduce spending on welfare and the criminal justice system by about $37,000 in present value terms for each youth induced to graduate. These figures are almost the reverse of public spending on education and training: on average, the typical college graduate is the beneficiary of over $29,300 in public spending between the ages of 16 and 24, while the typical high school graduate receives about $13,900 and the typical high school dropout less than $6,500.

However, because high school dropouts differ from graduates along many dimensions other than the fact of dropping out, these calculations do not necessarily translate into potential gains for society whenever a student is kept in school to graduation. Furthermore, many dropout prevention programs are too new to have accumulated a substantial record of long-term results, and the current, incomplete state of research makes conclusions somewhat premature. Nevertheless, a number of programs for at-risk youth have been reliably evaluated and found to dramatically reduce dropout rates over several years of operation; in addition, the best of these programs appear to save the government money.

The evidence suggests that many students at risk of dropping out are helped by guidance, academic assistance, career information, and general support in order to stay in school and succeed. After-school and summer programs and linkages to postgraduation jobs and schooling can be effective in keeping children in school and in improving academic achievement and other outcomes. The difficulty in improving the poor labor market prospects of youth once they have dropped out underscores the importance of efforts to reduce the number of dropouts. Although the current, incomplete state of research makes conclusions somewhat premature, two general observations may be hazarded.

First, it is possible to prevent students from dropping out, but it is difficult. A number of programs for at-risk youth have been reliably evaluated and found to reduce dropout rates substantially; many others, however, have not been so successful. Second, it is difficult to make initial gains last. Several programs have shown a pattern of marked improvement in attendance and academic achievement during their first year, but these initial gains often disappear over the next few years. Fortunately, there are models of integrated programs that have been effective in dramatically reducing dropout rates over several years of operation (Box 5–3).

From School to Work

The School-to-Work Opportunities Act, proposed by the Administration and passed by the Congress in 1994, addresses the increasingly poor job prospects of high school graduates by providing States and localities with venture capital to build systems that prepare young people to pursue a variety of options after completing high school: a good first job, career-oriented training, or college. The School-to-Work initiative funds partnerships among businesses, labor representatives, and educators to offer young people learning experiences in both school-based and work-based settings that will help provide them the knowledge and skills they will need to make a smooth transition into the world of work.

The School-to-Work initiative creates the opportunity for students to learn in a setting that connects academics with problems in a real workplace. The program integrates classroom instruction with work experience, structured training, mentoring at job sites, and matching of students with participating employers. Whenever possible, students are paid for their work. School-to-Work opportunities bring the workplace into the classroom, combining quality coursework at school with hands-on learning and training in a work environment. By the end of a course of study, students will have received a high school diploma, an industry-recognized skill certificate, and, for some, a diploma for completion of 1 or 2 years of postsecondary education.

In 1994 all 50 States received Federal funding to plan and develop School-to-Work Opportunities systems, and 8 States were already implementing comprehensive systems. In almost all cases, employers are directly contributing to the development of industry-

161–672 – 95 – 7

Box 5–3.—What Works: The QUOP Experiment

The Quantum Opportunities Program (QUOP) is an experiment in the use of community-based organizations to improve the academic and social competencies of disadvantaged students by providing continuing adult support throughout their high school years. In each of several cities, QUOP programs offer tutoring, adult mentoring, career and college planning, and other services and activities to children from families receiving AFDC, starting in the ninth grade. There is also a financial incentive: participating students receive small stipends and bonuses for completing segments of program activities, as well as payments into a trust fund for their eventual postsecondary education. Because participants were randomly chosen, the program provides a test of whether the combination of a rich array of services and tangible financial rewards for success, sustained over the whole of a high school career, can induce students to stay in school and out of trouble, and go on to college.

Over 4 years the average QUOP student participated in 1,286 hours of educational activities beyond regular school hours and accumulated $2,300 in his or her postsecondary account. Overall 4-year costs of the program were $10,600 per enrollee. At the end of the program's demonstration period an evaluation comparing randomly selected participants and nonparticipants (controls) found that 63 percent of QUOP students, but only 42 percent of controls, had graduated from high school. Only 23 percent of QUOP students had dropped out, versus 50 percent of the controls. And 42 percent of QUOP students, compared with 16 percent of controls, were enrolled in postsecondary education. Participants were also half as likely to report engaging in criminal activity and one-third less likely to have had children. The experiment was small, following only 100 students at four of the sites, and results varied widely across sites, yet for the experiment as a whole all these differences in outcomes were statistically significant.

The results of integrated programs such as QUOP defy the common presupposition that disadvantaged youth will not take advantage of, or cannot benefit from, enhanced educational offerings. Rather they support the notion that many students need both academic help such as tutoring and the incentive of being assured that academic success has a payoff, in the form of better prospects for employment or college.

190

based standards in broad clusters of occupations. By 2000 almost half a million young Americans are expected to have entered School-to-Work programs during their last 2 years of high school. To the extent School-to-Work programs are successful, they should benefit many students by connecting academic learning with problem solving in an actual workplace, thus making learning more relevant; they should also provide valuable labor market experience and connections. These programs should also benefit businesses by increasing the number of trained workers with experience in specific fields.

Better Access to Education After High School

Creating a system of lifelong learning for adults is another essential part of Goals 2000. The Administration is creating a system with a number of components, each applying not just to the traditional path of college education immediately following high school, but also to continuing education and training for those who have jobs or are between jobs.

Reformed student loans will reduce the burden of borrowing for college and for continuing education. Under the new Federal Direct Loan Program, individuals can borrow money for college directly from the Federal Government and can tailor their repayments to suit their financial circumstances. Borrowers will be able to choose from among four repayment plans—standard, extended, graduated, and income contingent—and to switch plans as their needs change. The standard plan, the one most widely used today, will continue to allow students to repay their loans in fixed monthly payments over 10 years. The extended plan provides for a smaller fixed payment but a longer term, from 12 to 30 years. Under the graduated plan, also with a 12- to 30-year term, the size of the monthly payment starts smaller than in the first two plans and increases over time according to a predetermined schedule; this should reduce the repayment burden in the early years when incomes are likely to be modest. Finally, the income contingent (or "pay-as-you-can") plan takes the notion of graduated payment a step further: monthly payments are determined by the borrower's actual income. This choice of plans makes it easier for graduates to start businesses, work in their communities, or meet other family responsibilities by better matching their loan service to their varying incomes.

In addition to lightening the burden of loan repayment, the Student Loan Reform Act restructures the Federal student loan program itself, phasing in direct lending to students over the next few years. Direct lending will significantly reduce the costs of the loan program by eliminating middlemen, thus streamlining the system. The savings are estimated at approximately $6.8 billion over a 5-year period.

AmeriCorps, the national service program, lets Americans earn money for education while gaining practical experience as they serve American communities. Twenty thousand participants entered the program in 1994. By 1996 an estimated 100,000 AmeriCorps members will have served American communities. AmeriCorps participants will devote themselves to community service projects, chosen by local nonprofit organizations, such as teaching in urban school districts, wildlife habitat restoration, immunization of children, crime deterrence, and low-income housing restoration. In 1994 participants earned a $7,640 yearly stipend for living expenses and a $4,725 yearly grant for college or graduate school.

Additional initiatives to make continuing education affordable include the proposed income tax deduction and expanded use of individual retirement accounts for educational expenses, as discussed in Chapter 1. Both of these proposed changes in the tax code are intended to further lower the financial burden of pursuing postsecondary education.

FACILITATING LIFELONG LEARNING AND CAREER-LONG JOB MOBILITY

Training on the job or in a work-related setting tends to be especially well tailored to the requirements of the workplace. One study of work-related training, while not fully capturing the vital but hard-to-measure effect of informal on-the-job training, showed that the impact of such training on wages is of similar magnitude to that of more traditional schooling. (As with measures of the returns to education, these measures of the returns to training may be over- or understated if there are other, unobserved differences between those who do and do not receive training.)

Provision of on-the-job training is skewed in favor of those already relatively well educated. Among young college graduates 35 percent received training from their employers between 1986 and 1991, whereas only 19 percent of high school graduates and 9 percent of high school dropouts received any training during that time period.

Formal on-the-job training is considerably less common in the United States than in other industrialized nations such as Germany and Japan. Large Japanese companies train their workers far more than do their U.S. counterparts, partly because employees there are much less likely to switch employers. In Germany, high levels of training take place in formal apprenticeship systems that are supported by the government as well as by powerful industry and union federations.

Skill Standards

Skill standards can play an important role in increasing the supply of highly skilled workers and smoothing their transitions between jobs. The United States is unique among its major competitors in lacking formal mechanisms for national certification of most worker skills. This lack diminishes the portability of training and reduces the incentives for employees to invest in increasing their skills.

The National Skills Standards Act creates a framework for voluntary development of work force skills standards in broad clusters of occupations. The law promotes standards that include both the skills needed in the high-performance workplace (such as problem solving and teamwork) and industry-specific skills. Many industry groups are already at work designing their standards for occupations in their industries. A blue-ribbon National Skill Standards Board is being established to stimulate the development and adoption of the new voluntary skill standards.

Skill standards can also help alleviate imperfections in the market for training. Often training provided by one employer is useful to another. Thus, when trained workers change employers, the benefits to the first employer of its investments in training may be captured by the second. This reduces employers' incentives to train. Skill certificates developed in cooperation with industry leaders should reduce this market imperfection, since employees would be more willing to pay for training if it leads to a certificate that another company recognizes and will pay a premium for. These payments to employers for training may take the implicit form of lower wages during the training period, just as they do for traditional union apprentices or medical residents. Because of this implicit or explicit payment, employers would take less of a risk when they provide training. Some economic theory predicts that making general training more visible to the market will increase turnover, but in fact turnover is *lower* at many companies that pay for publicly certified training. The reason for the divergence of theory and evidence is unclear, although it may be that company-sponsored education increases worker loyalty, or there may be a selection effect, whereby hard-working employees are both less likely to quit and more likely to take advantage of company-sponsored education.

Building a Reemployment System

Each year more than 2 million U.S. workers permanently lose their jobs through no fault of their own, when plants close or there are mass layoffs. Although most dislocated workers find new jobs within 15 weeks of their job loss, it is estimated that 15 percent of all workers who were displaced between 1987 and 1991 remained unemployed for over 6 months. Older workers and those with less education were the least likely to find a new job after dis-

193

placement. Of those involuntarily displaced workers fortunate enough to find new employment, 47 percent suffered a decrease in their wages.

Just as the Administration's education policies focus on smoothing the transition from school to work, its labor policies focus on smoothing the transition from work to work and on increasing skills to avoid job loss. Workers often find the path from one job to the next beset with hurdles. Many do not know what other jobs are available, and having found out, discover they lack the skills to fit into any of them. And some who clear both those obstacles find that their new jobs do not work out, because for one reason or another employee and employer do not fit together well. These bad matches can increase turnover and reduce satisfaction and productivity.

To address these problems, the Nation's unemployment system is undertaking a transition of its own—to a reemployment system. A key element of the new system is one-stop career centers for all workers. The Administration is working with the States to create a nationwide network of local centers, offering job counseling and allowing workers to apply for jobless benefits and sign up for training programs all in one place.

An important element of the reemployment system is an easily accessible store of labor market information. The one-stop centers will build a data base of training providers. The data base could include such information as records of training providers' completion and placement rates and the average starting wages of their graduates. The centers will also provide information on job openings; on local employment trends, including the wages and skill requirements of occupations in demand; and on relevant Federal, State, and local programs.

The Extended Unemployment Compensation Act, passed in 1993, requires that all States establish and utilize a system for profiling all new unemployment insurance claimants to identify, and refer to job search assistance, those who are likely to exhaust their regular unemployment benefits and are at risk of experiencing long-term unemployment. In 1995 this program, similar to successful programs implemented in several States (Box 5-4), is expected to help an additional 150,000 Americans who have lost their jobs.

As one-stop centers, improved training and assistance between jobs, and improved labor market information come together to create a national reemployment system, movement between jobs should become smoother, and the economy should be able to operate at a lower rate of unemployment without the risk of pushing up inflation.

During the 1980s five States experimented with programs to change the focus of their unemployment insurance systems from passive provision of income support to active efforts at re-employment. The programs profiled unemployment insurance applicants and targeted those most at risk for long spells of unemployment for participation in intensive job search assistance and counseling. All of the experimental initiatives realized cost savings, the key to which proved to be finding new jobs for most newly unemployed workers quickly. The results demonstrated that it is cost-effective to focus job search assistance on those most at risk for long spells of unemployment.

The programs were rigorously evaluated through random assignment of clients to either an experimental group which participated in the program, or a control group which did not. On average, those receiving job search assistance found new employment from half a week to 4 weeks sooner than similar individuals in the control group. This reduction in unemployment not only benefited the workers themselves, but also saved the government between $1.80 and $4.80 for each dollar invested in profiling and job search assistance.

Facilitating Retraining

Needs for increased training are not well matched with the current complicated system of dozens of government-assisted training programs, each with its own rules, regulations, and restrictions. Therefore, the Administration has proposed replacing this complex system with a single coherent, choice-based system for adults. This proposal will consolidate nearly 70 current training or related programs. Dislocated or low-income workers would be eligible for "skill grants" of up to $2,620 per year for 2 years, enough to cover tuition, supplies, and fees at a typical community college. Unlike the current system, in which government agencies often choose what training workers will receive and who will provide it, the new skill grants could be used at any eligible training provider, including community colleges and private technical schools.

An important element of this new system will be the labor market information system described above, in which users have access to the track records of local education, training, and job placement providers. With this information available, the power of the market and of informed consumer choice should work to weed out ineffective programs and reward those that help workers get the skills they need.

POLICIES TO IMPROVE WORKPLACES

Policies to increase the supply of skilled workers are important but may not be sufficient unless jobs are available that utilize the enhanced skills. Skills alone may not lead to high wages, high productivity, or even interesting work. This Administration is pursuing a number of policies to enhance the trend toward workplaces that rely on high levels of skill, lifelong learning, and continuous skill improvement.

High-performance workplaces typically are quite different from traditional ones. They have been transformed so as to give employees greater ability and the incentive to improve their workplaces. Workers' ability to generate good ideas is often strengthened by high levels of training and of information sharing. Forms of worker empowerment vary widely but often include work teams and forms of representative participation such as elected committees of workers or union representatives. Incentive schemes vary as well but typically reward individuals for learning new skills, reward groups of workers for their collective success, and build cohesiveness and solidarity more than individualistic competition. Motivation is also supported when companies ensure that the efficiency gains achieved by implementing workers' suggestions do not end up costing them their jobs.

Although it is difficult to obtain reliable nationwide data on the extent of employee involvement in decisionmaking, the evidence is that employee involvement and other plans spread rapidly during the 1980s. By the early 1990s the vast majority of very large U.S. companies had experimented with at least a small amount of employee involvement in at least a portion of their organizations, and many smaller companies were experimenting as well. At the same time, however, only a minority of companies reported widespread implementation of an integrated set of high-performance workplace practices.

The effects of the high-performance workplace can be impressive. The Department of Labor recently reviewed a host of studies on the effects of high-performance work practices on organizational performance. The result is a collage of evidence that a coordinated change in work organization can pay handsome rewards. For example, a multiyear study of steel finishing lines identified four distinct human resource management systems. The more innovative production lines had introduced problem-solving teams, higher levels of training, innovative incentive compensation systems, and higher levels of employment security, while the most traditional lines had few or none of these practices. The more innovative lines enjoyed significantly higher productivity. The most innovative lines ran 98 percent of the scheduled time, while the untransformed plants ran only 88 percent of the scheduled time; plants intermediate in their introduction of innovative human resource policies were also intermediate in productivity. Plants with more innovative practices also produced higher quality steel. A separate study of steel mini-mills found that high-involvement plants not only excelled in quality and productivity, but also enjoyed lower turnover. These results have been replicated in a number of other industries, as well as in multi-industry studies. Several studies find that these innovative workplace practices are associated with financial gains, such as higher cash flow and stock market value.

MARKETS AND THE HIGH-PERFORMANCE WORKPLACE

If high-performance workplaces are so productive, why do they remain relatively rare in the United States? A number of factors can inhibit their spread, even when they hold the promise of improved outcomes for both workers and employers.

One problem is imperfect information in financial markets. Relative to other companies, high-performance workplaces usually invest heavily in employees' skills and in the company's reputation as a trustworthy employer and business partner. These investments frequently take years to pay off. Managers are able to inform investors about their investments through many avenues. Yet investors will almost always have better information on, and thus likely pay more attention to, investments that are reported in publicly available financial statements, comparable across time and between companies. Informing investors about investments in human resources is more difficult because no common language exists to describe them in a way that allows outsiders to assess their value. Partly because of these communication problems, corporate managers in a recent survey rated employee satisfaction, turnover, and training expenditures the 3 least important out of 19 measures of financial and nonfinancial performance to report to outside investors. These measures not only lagged earnings (ranked first) and capital expenditures (14th), but even lost out to corporate ethics statements (16th).

Because human resource investments are so hard to monitor, they may be especially sensitive to cutbacks during downturns in a corporation's cash flow. These information problems, plus the general difficulty that investors have in knowing whether managers are investing for the long run, can lead to inefficiently few high-performance workplaces.

The long-term commitment of high-performance organizations to their work forces can have favorable macroeconomic effects. Under reasonable assumptions, each firm that avoids layoffs helps stabilize demand for other firms' products, which the original firm's workers, by keeping their jobs, are able to continue purchasing. High-performance organizations usually try to build trust and protect their investments in workers by minimizing layoffs. Thus, when an economy has many high-performance workplaces it may well find that its recessions become less severe.

The present system of unemployment insurance may well *encourage* layoffs. Employers in most States pay unemployment insurance premiums that are not closely related to their record of past layoffs. As a result, companies that avoid layoffs implicitly subsidize those that frequently lay off workers.

Another set of problems centers around deficiencies in the incentive system facing American managers. Many American managers have spent years in workplaces designed for top-down control, not for encouraging initiative from low-level workers. In addition, new work practices diffuse slowly partly for the same reason management initiatives often diffuse slowly—learning takes time. A number of innovations ranging from hybrid corn varieties to the divisional corporate structure have taken a generation or longer to spread to half the companies that would eventually adopt them, and employee involvement appears to be no exception.

A legal difficulty augments these problems: some high-performance work practices have been subject to challenge under U.S. labor law, which has developed within a decades-long adversarial system of worker-management relations. Some forms of substantive employee involvement have been found to be in violation of the National Labor Relations Act, because they are deemed the equivalent of "company-dominated unions" or blur the legal line between workers and managers.

The policy response of the Administration to the problems facing high-performance workplaces is to remove obstacles and to improve the quality and delivery of information that can facilitate private-sector initiatives. The Department of Labor has created a new Office of the American Workplace to reduce barriers that impede organizations from adopting high-performance work structures. Its initiatives include creating a clearinghouse of information on high-performance workplaces, creating educational programs for unions and for CEOs to learn how to work better together, and working with institutional investors such as pension funds to better measure which companies are investing in their people for the long run. To examine a broad range of workplace issues, including the legal difficulties mentioned above, the Administration appointed a Commission on the Future of Worker-Management Relations (Box 5–5).

The Administration is expanding the National Institute of Standards and Technology's (NIST) Manufacturing Extension Partnership (MEP). MEP centers provide small- and medium-sized manufacturers with access to public and private resources, information,

198

Box 5–5: Reforming Workplace Regulation

In March 1993 the secretaries of Labor and Commerce announced the formation of the Commission on the Future of Worker-Management Relations to study what, if any, changes should be made in U.S. workplace laws and regulations to facilitate employee participation and reduce labor-management conflict. In January 1995 the Commission released a number of recommendations. These recommendations, and the reasoning behind them, included the following:

- In the 1920s and early 1930s many companies created company-dominated unions, largely in an effort to keep out independent unions. In response, the 1935 National Labor Relations Act banned company unions. Its definition of illegal company unions is very broad, however, and encompasses many legitimate employee involvement groups.

  Recommendation: Continue to ban company unions, but amend the act to permit employee involvement groups that improve productivity and safety and only incidentally discuss employment terms and conditions.

- A company must hold an election on union representation if 30 percent of its workers sign a petition calling for such an election. But often the election is delayed for months by legal challenges such as disputes about the size of the bargaining unit. In addition, in about one out of four companies holding elections, a worker is dismissed for being pro-union; companies face no threat of punitive fines or sanctions for these illegal acts.

  Recommendation: Elections should generally take place within 2 weeks of the request, with disputes settled afterward. Speedy elections should reduce the number of labor law violations, hence reducing concerns about the lack of penalties.

- Millions of American workers are injured and thousands killed on the job each year, yet safety regulations are often burdensome and ineffective and do not permit companies and workers to tailor their decisions to local conditions.

  Recommendation: Require all but the smallest workplaces to have a formal safety program, meeting minimum standards such as regular safety training and investigation of all serious accidents. In workplaces with high-quality safety programs, regulators should reduce penalties and the frequency of inspections.

and services designed to increase firms' use of appropriate technologies and modern manufacturing practices. Building work force skill and a work environment that fosters a culture of continuous improvement is a major factor in companies' ability to benefit from these technologies. Thus, the Administration's MEP program is helping U.S. industry to move toward adoption of the high-performance workplace model. NIST is working with the Department of Labor's Office of the American Workplace and its Employment and Training Administration to create linkages between the extension centers and training and modernization services. In the future, small manufacturers will be able to work with a local MEP center for needs ranging from new technology to redesigning the entire workplace.

One means of promoting high-performance workplaces is through recognition programs, most notably the Malcolm Baldrige National Quality Award (Box 5–6). Because of its past success in encouraging quality performance, the award program is being expanded to make schools and health care enterprises eligible.

Box 5–6.—What Works: The Baldrige Award

The Malcolm Baldrige National Quality Award measures companies' progress on a number of quality goals. The company (or division) must provide evidence that it incorporates a focus on quality into management practices, works closely with suppliers, trains workers in quality techniques, and meets customers' desires. The completed application must be less than 70 pages. The examination process begins with a board of examiners scoring the written application. The examiners are recognized quality practitioners themselves, whose feedback the contestants value. High scorers then have site visits led by a senior examiner, and winners are selected by a panel of judges.

The Baldrige Award has been an effective catalyst for managerial change. More than 1 million copies of the award criteria have been distributed, and the award serves as the model in many companies' internal evaluations of their move to high performance.

Although few companies have won the coveted award, its effects are more broadly felt. For example, one truck engine manufacturer that was having serious quality problems applied for the Baldrige Award as a way of "turning a harsh spotlight on itself." Although the company did not come close to winning, the feedback it received led to valuable new practices concerning worker training and listening to truckers' complaints. Defect rates plunged from 10 percent to below 1 percent in only 2 years.

REINVENTING GOVERNMENT AS A HIGH-PERFORMANCE WORKPLACE

Reinventing government, as noted in Chapter 1, is crucial for creating a government that works better and costs less. One key element of this reinvention is to turn the Federal Government itself into a high-performance employer, one that relies on the skills and motivates the creativity of its employees (Box 5–7).

Box 5–7.—What Works: Empowering Civil Servants to Better Serve Citizens

One goal of the Vice President's reinventing government initiative is to empower Federal employees. Simply by listening to their good suggestions, the government can become a better provider of services. An example of empowered civil servants making good policy at the front line involves the restoration of the Santa Monica Freeway after California's Northridge earthquake of January 1994.

The Santa Monica Freeway is one of the most important transportation corridors in the United States, and for each day that it was shut down the local economy suffered about $1 million in lost output. However, the highway administration often takes over a year just to develop a plan, solicit bids, review proposals, and award funding for a major project such as rebuilding the Santa Monica. Fortunately, the Chief of District Operations for the Federal Highway Administration in Sacramento had some ideas for improving the process.

The main ideas were to speed up the bidding process and to award large bonuses to contractors who finished ahead of the date proposed in their bid (and impose equally large penalties on contractors who missed deadlines). By accelerating the competitive bidding process and rewarding speedy completion, the Chief of District Operations and other empowered Federal employees helped finish in 84 days projects that would normally have taken 2 years. In addition, thanks to cooperation between groups ranging from Amtrak and the Army Corps of Engineers to the city's transportation department, traffic patterns were quickly rerouted, averting gridlock.

Reinventing procurement, as described in Chapter 4, is another key aspect of reinventing government. Part of reinventing procurement involves purchasing more goods and services on the basis of expected quality as well as low price. In the private sector many large customers have increasingly relied on certifications of the quality processes of their suppliers, often using certifications very similar—or even identical—to those of the Baldrige Award.

The Administration, drawing on successful private sector experience, is also beginning to use existing supplier certifications and awards to improve procurement. These efforts to promote purchasing from high-quality suppliers should not only save the government money but also increase the quality of U.S. jobs, because high-quality suppliers tend to rely on their workers for help in improving quality.

CONCLUSION

The U.S. labor market is a leader among the industrialized nations in job creation. At the same time, however, wages have stagnated for many Americans and declined markedly for those at the bottom of the income ladder.

No single policy will reverse this disappointing performance, but taken together, the policies described in this chapter can enhance the chances of all Americans to live prosperous, middle-class lives. These policies will increase the likelihood that children will be born healthy, enter school ready to learn, and stay there long enough to learn the skills they will need in the workplace of the future. Policy innovations in the labor market promise new entrants better prospects for finding a satisfying first job, and all workers a greater likelihood of smoother transitions between jobs and of continued learning on their jobs and throughout their careers. If successful, these policies will promote higher productivity and rising living standards, as well as make work more interesting for all.

CHAPTER 6

Liberalizing International Trade

SINCE THE SECOND WORLD WAR the United States has taken the lead in championing liberalized trade and open markets. A series of trade negotiations at a variety of levels has produced a world economy that is far more open, integrated, and efficient than that of the 1950s. For the global economy this has meant an extraordinary expansion of income, not only in the industrialized world but shared by those developing countries that were willing to promote international trade. For producers, trade liberalization has meant access to lower cost supplies and the ability to reap returns on investment over a much larger market. For consumers it has meant wider choices, higher quality, lower prices, and higher real incomes.

In the 1950s almost all trade was in commodities or manufactured goods, transported by sea, and trade barriers consisted of tariffs and quotas. Levels of trade protection were high, and negotiating reductions was relatively easy. Trade negotiations today are severalfold more difficult. Tariffs, which are easily observed and compared, are now much less important. Tighter integration among economies has shifted the emphasis of negotiations to domestic practices that inhibit trade, while new, nontariff trade barriers have been devised to take the place of those reduced through negotiation. Trade in intellectual property, technology-intensive goods, and a wide array of services has changed the product landscape, and trade now takes place among a much wider group of countries. In the 1990s, firms regularly operate subsidiaries in their major overseas markets, blurring the definition of what is a national firm. Their foreign direct investment has both pushed the expansion of trade and, in many industries, been pulled by the necessity to be in close touch with customers, so that rules governing foreign investment now have a direct effect on trade. All of these changes have made the pursuit of effective trade liberalization more challenging.

This Administration, like its predecessors, has responded to these changes by pursuing liberalization and the promotion of exports at a variety of negotiating levels. The American approach has been that of nondiscrimination: negotiated reductions in trade barriers should apply to all trading nations; individual nations should not cut deals that benefit themselves at the expense of others. This principle of U.S. diplomacy goes back to the Nation's early history as a new entrant in the trading world, but it has roots in both fairness and economic efficiency. Nondiscrimination as a goal received powerful support from the disastrous experience of discriminatory trade and payment regimes during the Great Depression. Often called the most-favored-nation (MFN) principle, since each participant receives the same treatment accorded the "most-favored nation," nondiscrimination formed the basis of the postwar trade order.

Even though nations will seek concessions by others in areas of most immediate interest to themselves, nondiscrimination makes trade liberalization a public good—what is produced by one country in negotiation with another is available to all. This gives rise to the coordination problem shared by all public goods, that of getting each party to participate rather than sit back and let others do the liberalizing, free-riding on their efforts. The solution to this dilemma requires commitment on the part of the major trading nations, coupled with ingenuity and the artful use of the fear of exclusion. Thus, while the United States has continued to support multilateral liberalization efforts, it has been forceful in bilateral negotiations as well, and has also pursued liberalization on a regional basis, both as a way of extending market opening and as a way of pressing for greater liberalization in the full multilateral arena.

This Administration has achieved remarkable success at each of these three levels of trade negotiations. After 7 years of negotiating and two missed final deadlines, the Administration brought the most ambitious of postwar multilateral negotiations, the Uruguay Round, to a successful conclusion. At the regional level the Administration brought about the enactment of the North American Free Trade Agreement (NAFTA) with Canada and Mexico, and has reached agreements to move toward free trade in the entire Western Hemisphere and in the Asia-Pacific region. At the bilateral level the Administration has concluded a number of agreements, the most important of them within the Framework for a New Economic Partnership with Japan.

In its first 2 years in office the Administration has achieved more in international trade policy than any other postwar administration. The agreements it has reached and implemented change the landscape of future trade issues. This chapter reviews those agreements and their consequences for the United States and the world trading order, and then explores the issues that will govern future trade relations.

MULTILATERAL INITIATIVES: THE URUGUAY ROUND AND THE WORLD TRADE ORGANIZATION

The Uruguay Round took a full 7 years (1986–93) to complete, and the resulting agreement is by far the most extensive and comprehensive yet concluded under the General Agreement on Tariffs and Trade, or GATT (Table 6–1). It goes beyond all previous GATT agreements in three respects (Box 6–1). First, it deals more directly and extensively with nontariff barriers to trade than any past agreement. Second, it brings several major product sectors under international trade rules for the first time. Finally, the agreement goes a long way toward establishing a single set of trade rules applicable to all member countries, limiting the ability of countries to pick and choose what trade obligations they will accept. The Uruguay Round agreement offers huge benefits for the United States and for the other signatories and will shape the future of multilateral trade negotiations.

TABLE 6–1.—*GATT Negotiating Rounds*

Negotiating round	Dates	Number of participants	Tariff cut achieved (percent)	Comments
Geneva	1947	23		
Annecy	1949	13		
Torquay	1951	38	73	
Geneva	1956	26		
Dillon Round	1960–61	26		
Kennedy Round	1964–67	62	35	Antidumping agreement signed
Tokyo Round	1973–79	99	33	Addressed nontariff as well as tariff barriers; codes (optional) on government procurement, dumping, subsidies, standards, and customs valuation
Uruguay Round	1986–93	125	40	Addressed nontariff as well as tariff barriers; covered new areas of agriculture, services, intellectual property; strengthened dispute settlement

Note.—Tariff cuts achieved are those agreed to by the major industrial countries on industrial products. The tariff cut achieved in the first five negotiations is an estimate. Tariffs fell from an average of about 40 percent at the time of GATT's founding to 7 percent by the beginning of the Tokyo Round.

Source: General Agreement on Tariffs and Trade.

TARIFF AND NONTARIFF MEASURES

Even in the traditional areas of trade negotiation the Uruguay Round marks a significant achievement. The agreement reduces average industrial product tariffs by 34 percent overall, and by 40 percent for industrial countries. Tariffs were eliminated entirely in "zero-for-zero" agreements in several sectors, including pharmaceuticals, steel, construction equipment, medical equipment, and paper. Overall, the Round is estimated to result in a $744 billion cut in world tariffs over the next 10 years. In addition, many countries agreed for the first time to bind (cap) a significant portion of their tariffs, giving up the possibility of future rate increases above the bound levels. The increase in tariff bindings among less devel-

205

Box 6-1.—Uruguay Round Highlights

Tariffs. The Uruguay Round agreement achieved a 34-percent average reduction of industrial product tariffs. Most of these tariffs are now bound (capped).

Agriculture. The agreement converts quotas and other trade restraints to bound tariffs. It requires cuts in export and domestic subsidies and minimum market access commitments.

Textiles and clothing. The agreement eliminates quotas on textile and clothing imports over a 10-year period.

Services. The agreement extends MFN treatment, national treatment, and other principles to service sectors in which countries make specific market-opening commitments. Specific sectoral commitments were negotiated or are being negotiated.

Intellectual property. Patent, trademark, and copyright protections are recognized as trade obligations and strengthened.

Rules governing trade. So-called voluntary export restraints are forbidden, and country-specific import safeguard measures are allowed only in limited circumstances. Antidumping procedures become subject to limited duration ('sunset') provisions and improved standards of transparency and procedural fairness. Subsidies are divided into categories: those prohibited outright, those subject to countervailing duties if they cause injury to producers in other countries, and those explicitly declared exempt from such duties.

Trade-related investment measures. Measures requiring foreign subsidiaries to achieve a specified minimum level of domestic content in their production or requiring that imports be balanced by equivalent exports, as well as certain other measures, are to be eliminated within 2 years for developed countries, and within 5 years for less developed countries.

"Single undertaking." With the exception of a few sectoral agreements, a single set of trade rules applicable to all signatories is established.

World Trade Organization (WTO). The agreement ends the ambiguous foundation for world trade that the GATT had provided, regularizing and creating a legal basis for previous GATT practice. The WTO provides a single umbrella for trade agreements in goods, services, intellectual property, and other areas.

Dispute settlement. Disputes involving all WTO matters are subject to a single dispute settlement process. Losers in a panel decision may take the matter to a new Appellate Body but no longer have the ability to block panel decisions. Retaliation is authorized in the absence of a settlement.

oped countries was striking: by the end of the Round 73 percent of their industrial product tariffs, covering over 60 percent of total imports, were bound.

The Round made significant progress in reducing or eliminating nontariff barriers. The government procurement agreement strengthens the provisions of the earlier Tokyo Round code, opening a wider range of markets for signatory countries. In addition, the Round made extensive efforts to eliminate quantity restraints on trade and require countries to rely instead on price (tariff) measures. In the textile and apparel sector, the various bilateral quotas that have arisen to control international trade are to be raised, and phased out entirely by 2005. In agriculture, quantitative restraints and other nontariff barriers to trade are to be replaced by tariffs of equivalent restrictiveness. Finally, the safeguards agreement prohibits the use of voluntary export restraints.

The elimination of quantity restraints on trade, even when replaced by tariffs that reduce trade by the same amount, is an important liberalizing step. With a quota, when imports reach the quota limit, the domestic market is completely insulated from foreign competition. Quotas effectively carve up the market, whereas tariffs maintain competition. The anticompetitive effect is most striking if domestic producers collude to raise prices. Under a quota, imports cannot respond and thus provide no brake on domestic price increases, whereas under a tariff, imports increase at the tariff-inclusive price, limiting the ability of producers to raise prices.

NEW SECTORS

The Uruguay Round achieved significant liberalizations in the traditional areas of trade negotiations, but what made it a breakthrough agreement was its extension of trade disciplines to three new areas: agriculture, services, and intellectual property.

Agriculture

The Uruguay Round for the first time brings agriculture, a sector that accounts for 13 percent of world trade, under international trade rules. Measures to support farm incomes in the industrial countries have led to a variety of trade-restraining measures, excess production, and an expensive system of export subsidization that has done little to increase world demand for agricultural products but has greatly depressed world agricultural prices.

The agriculture agreement requires that nontariff barriers to agricultural trade be converted to their tariff equivalents, and that the resulting tariffs be reduced by a minimum of 15 percent in each tariff line and by an average of 36 percent overall. Countries are also required to grant minimum market access in products where there has been little or no trade. This means the end of the bans

207

on rice imports in Japan and the Republic of Korea, and commitments by all countries to increase wheat, corn, rice, and barley imports by a total of 3.5 million metric tons.

The agreement also contains first steps to reduce agricultural subsidies. Export subsidies must be reduced by 36 percent in value from 1986–90 levels over 6 years, and the volume of subsidized exports by 21 percent. Since current U.S. and European subsidy levels exceed this base, the actual reduction will be considerably higher. Domestic subsidies that increase output must be reduced by 20 percent from their 1986–90 levels.

Since the United States has a strong underlying comparative advantage in agriculture, the mutual reduction in trade barriers and subsidization will be to the distinct advantage of U.S. producers. Because European export subsidization in the base period used for calculating reductions was 14 times that of the United States, and domestic support 4 times as great, the European Union's subsidy reductions will dwarf those of the United States. As a result of world income gains and the realignment of world sales due to the Uruguay Round agreement, annual U.S. agricultural exports are expected to increase by somewhere between $4.7 billion and $8.7 billion by 2005.

Services

The second new area opened by the Uruguay Round is international trade in services. This trade has grown to $1 trillion per year and now accounts for over a fifth of all international trade. Services trade liberalization is of major concern to the United States, the world's largest services exporter, with annual exports of over $170 billion and a surplus of $59 billion in 1993.

The General Agreement on Trade in Services (GATS) is the first multilateral agreement covering services trade issues. The GATS has two distinct components. The first is a general statement of principles, such as national treatment and MFN treatment, that cover trade in services, along with descriptions of how these are to be interpreted in individual sectors (Box 6–2). Recognizing the differing ways in which services trade can take place, the GATS covers cross-border trade, movement of persons, and investment issues. The agreement creates a general obligation to offer MFN treatment to signatories, requires transparency in regulation of services, and brings services trade disputes under the general dispute settlement mechanism of the WTO.

The first component of the services agreement does not in itself create any liberalization of services trade. Liberalization is provided in the second component, where each country lists the sectors to which it will apply GATS obligations, as well as any exceptions to those obligations that it will maintain in each sector. Once a sector and its exceptions are listed, those commitments are bound,

Box 6–2.—National Treatment, MFN, and Market Access Under the GATT and the GATS

The fundamental principles on which the GATS is based mirror in many ways those applied to goods within the GATT, but there are some important differences.

Most-Favored-Nation Treatment

GATT: A country agrees to treat goods from other GATT members no less favorably than it treats those from any other foreign supplier, on tariffs and other measures that affect the import or export of goods.

GATS: Identical, except that there is a one-time opportunity to exempt specific service sectors from MFN obligations, for a period of up to 10 years.

National Treatment

GATT: Once foreign goods have entered a country and paid any tariffs or other customs duties, they must be treated no less favorably than domestically produced goods, and subject to no taxes or charges that are not also levied on domestically produced goods.

GATS: The same, but only for sectors listed by countries in their sectoral commitments, and subject to any exceptions listed in those commitments.

Market Access

GATT: No obligation.

GATS: No explicit definition. However, countries agree *not* to impose various limitations (on total value or quantity, extent of foreign investment or ownership, or number of persons employed) in sectors in which they make commitments.

and no further limitations on trade may be applied. The sectoral commitments, although neither as extensive as originally sought by the United States nor as far-reaching as those under NAFTA, do contain important liberalizations. Most country commitments include a standstill on new barriers, which is significant in many countries where services sector regulation is just beginning to develop. Countries made broad commitments in trade in professional services and tourism and agreed not to restrict access to telecommunications services to resident foreign-owned service providers. Negotiations on specific commitments in financial services, basic telecommunications, and maritime transport services were not completed by the end of the Round and are to continue. Despite the negotiations that remain, the GATS is a breakthrough, not only for the specific liberalizations that it contains but also because it establishes the framework for further liberalization of trade in services, just as the GATT did for goods in 1947.

Intellectual Property Protection

The extension of multilateral trade rules to intellectual property protection is a further area where the Uruguay Round broke new ground. The Agreement on Trade-Related Aspects of Intellectual Property Rights (TRIPs) adopts and strengthens existing conventions on intellectual property, adds protection for several new areas including integrated circuits and computer software, and provides a mechanism to enforce intellectual property rights. It also extends national and MFN treatment to intellectual property holders. The agreement, with just a few exceptions, eliminates the ability of countries to deny patentability to certain categories of inventions such as pharmaceuticals and restricts forced licensing of technology.

Enforceability was a major concern in the negotiation. Principles of intellectual property law are set out in the agreement, along with requirements for transparency in application procedures, and disputes are covered in the general WTO dispute settlement mechanism. In return for substantial concessions on protection and enforceability, less developed countries received a lengthy transition period: 5 years for most of these countries and 11 years for the least developed ones.

WIDENING PARTICIPATION

A failing of past trade negotiations was the limited number of countries that were active negotiating participants—many countries remained on the sidelines as free riders on others' liberalizations. Moreover, by the time the Uruguay Round was launched, GATT obligations had become a kind of a la carte system, where countries were free to subscribe to the agreements they chose and abstain from others. The Uruguay Round reversed this trend, both increasing the number of countries making concessions and achieving a much greater uniformity in the rights and obligations of GATT (now WTO) members.

The increased participation of countries in the negotiations was in large part due to a sea change in ideology in developing countries in favor of privatization, economic liberalization, and competition, as described in more detail below. But it also had much to do with the fact that the Uruguay Round was a "grand bargain," linking concessions by less developed countries on tariffs, services, and intellectual property with liberalization of trade in textiles, apparel, and agriculture.

The Uruguay Round has also done much to establish a single rulebook for international trade competition. In contrast to previous negotiations the outcome of the Uruguay Round, and WTO membership, is a single undertaking. With few exceptions (notably the agreement on government procurement), countries joining the WTO agree to all of its obligations—the GATT itself, the GATS, the TRIPs agreement, dispute settlement procedures, and others. Finally, the increasing perceived value of trade liberalization in many market economies and the breakdown of central planning in the economies in transition have resulted in a large number of new applicants for WTO membership, including China and Russia. Their accession negotiations require both adoption of WTO obligations and initial liberalization of trade, expanding the number of countries trading by a single set of rules.

DISPUTE SETTLEMENT

Strengthening the GATT dispute settlement mechanism has been a longstanding goal of the United States; indeed, it was listed first among the principal U.S. negotiating objectives in the Omnibus Trade and Competitiveness Act of 1988. The previous GATT dispute mechanism suffered from long delays, the ability of accused parties to block decisions of GATT panels that went against them, and inadequate enforcement. The dispute settlement agreement addresses each of these issues. It guarantees the formation of a dispute panel once a case is brought and sets time limits for each stage of the process. The decision of the panel may be taken to a newly created Appellate Body, but the accused party can no longer block the final decision. A country that loses a dispute must either bring the offending practice into conformity, offer suitable compensation to the aggrieved parties, or face retaliation, which is now authorized under the agreement. Furthermore, this strengthened mechanism now becomes the single dispute settlement mechanism for the WTO, covering the GATT, the GATS, the agreement on intellectual property, and other agreements.

The dispute settlement issue has been important to the United States because this country has been the most frequent user of the GATT dispute mechanism. Frustration with the old mechanism was one of the factors behind the development and use of Section 301 of the Trade Act of 1974, which allows the United States to retaliate against "unjustifiable" or "unreasonable" foreign practices that hinder U.S. commerce. The new dispute settlement mechanism changes the sequence in which Section 301 is used but does little else to limit its use. Section 301 requires that, if a case involves an existing trade agreement, the United States must use the dispute settlement provisions of that agreement. If the United States wins a WTO case, and if the losing party does not then change its practice or offer suitable compensation, Section 301 retaliation is authorized by the WTO.

Perhaps the most important use of Section 301 has been in the promotion of U.S. interests in cases not covered by multilateral trade rules, such as services and intellectual property in the past. Here Section 301 can be used as before both to promote U.S. interests and to prompt multilateral negotiations on new liberalization. Even with modifications in the use of the legislation, the *package* of the new dispute settlement mechanism plus Section 301 is a far stronger vehicle for defending U.S. interests. A strengthened dispute settlement mechanism and multilateral backing for retaliation greatly increase the leverage the United States will have in protecting its trading rights.

THE WORLD TRADE ORGANIZATION AND U.S. SOVEREIGNTY

The GATT of 1947 was unusual in that it started out as a trade agreement, not an organization. Through improvisation and experience its small secretariat became an effective coordinating body for multilateral trade negotiations. The Uruguay Round establishes a World Trade Organization to bring under a single umbrella a variety of trade agreements negotiated under GATT auspices along with the single dispute settlement mechanism, and to regularize and clarify the practice that had been built up under the GATT. Although both the single undertaking and strengthened dispute settlement were U.S. objectives in the Round from the beginning, their achievement and the creation of the WTO have raised fears in some quarters that the United States might be surrendering sovereignty to an international organization over which it would have little control.

These fears are unwarranted. The WTO is an administrative body, designed to facilitate trade negotiations and dispute settlement among its members, not a legislature for creating obligations. Its charter explicitly links it to the decisions and customary practice under the GATT, including the dependence on consensus in reaching decisions. Although the principle of one country, one vote has always characterized the GATT, in fact GATT votes were almost never taken; decisions were reached on the basis of consensus among members. In practice, the United States has always had a major influence over the course of GATT policy, not because it has had a larger formal vote but, in baldest terms, because it brought the largest market to the table. The WTO does not change this. What the WTO does is to define fallback requirements if consensus is not reached. These are both limited in scope and stringent. Interpretations of agreements and waivers of obligations require a three-fourths majority of the entire membership (not just of those voting), and the creation of a new obligation on a country is possible only if that country accepts it. In any case, each member has the ability to leave the WTO with 6 months' notice.

The most fundamental reason why U.S. sovereignty is not diminished by the WTO is that WTO agreements and dispute panel decisions do not have legal force in the United States (or in other member countries)—they are not "self-actuating." In situations where existing U.S. legislation is contravened or new legislation required, it is up to the Congress whether to take that action. If the United States were to lose a dispute panel decision on a matter of fundamental national interest, it need not bring U.S. law or practice into conformity. The United States could instead offer compensation through liberalization in other areas, or accept equivalent foreign retaliation through increased barriers to U.S. exports. Panels rule on disputes that arise on rules and disciplines that WTO members have agreed to; they do not create new obligations. Furthermore, U.S. negotiators were particularly careful to limit the scope of panel review in cases involving national health and safety standards.

To allay concerns about the operation of the WTO, the Administration supports the establishment of a WTO Dispute Settlement Review Commission. The commission, which will consist of five Federal appellate judges, will review all final WTO dispute settlement reports adverse to the United States to determine whether the panel has exceeded its authority or acted outside the scope of the agreement. Following three determinations by the commission in any 5-year period that panels have so exceeded their brief, any member of the Congress may introduce a joint resolution to disapprove U.S. participation in the WTO. If the resolution is enacted by the Congress and signed by the President, the United States would withdraw from the WTO. By focusing informed, high-level attention on the operation of the WTO, the review commission should help develop a fair, effective, and widely accepted dispute settlement system within the organization.

Of course, the Uruguay Round agreement and the WTO do place obligations on the United States, but the balance of obligations in this accord is favorable, both because the United States had considerable influence on the Uruguay Round outcome, and because this country has a transparent, rules-based system and the WTO represents a convergence toward a system of this type. This point is important to consider when weighing the strengthened dispute settlement apparatus of the WTO. As with any legal institution, the force of dispute settlement will be established through use and experience. The U.S. interest in strengthening a rules-based international trading system implies that the United States should actively bring cases to dispute settlement and, in general, abide by the results. This is not to say that the United States should ignore fundamental national interests in deciding whether to implement a WTO panel decision, but simply that our willingness to be bound by international trade disciplines will in large part determine whether those disciplines will be observed by others.

FUTURE MULTILATERAL NEGOTIATIONS

The Uruguay Round of multilateral trade negotiations was such an ambitious and far-reaching undertaking that much of the multilateral trade agenda for the next few years will consist of developing experience with the agreement. Nonetheless, there are a few sectors where negotiations still need to be completed, new areas opened up by the agreement that need to be fleshed out, and areas that were not covered in the Round that will clearly form the basis of the future multilateral trade agenda.

Four sectoral negotiations in services were incomplete at the end of 1993 when the Round was drawn to a close: financial services, basic telecommunications, audiovisual services, and maritime transport services. In both financial services and basic telecommunications, a U.S. commitment to national treatment under the services agreement and a standstill on new measures would commit our vast and generally unrestricted markets to foreign competition. Therefore, in exchange, the United States has insisted on a relatively high level of liberalizing commitments by its trading partners as part of any agreement.

Although agreements were reached in other service sectors, liberalization in services generally is still in its infancy. Further bargaining on specific service sector liberalizations will take up much of the trade agenda for the next several years. The Uruguay Round agreement also sets the stage for continued negotiations on agriculture, covering further reductions in subsidies and tariff rates, and expansion of the volume of imports subject to lower duties under tariff-rate quotas.

The trading world rarely stands still for a negotiation to conclude, and certainly not for one that lasted as long as the Uruguay Round. New trade issues have arisen in the interim that will occupy trade negotiators. The most prominent of these—trade and the environment, competition policy, investment rules, and labor standards—are described in more detail below. In many cases these issues arose in regional and bilateral negotiations, to which this discussion now turns.

PLURILATERAL INITIATIVES

Possibly the most distinctive legacy of this Administration in international trade is the foundation it has laid for the development of open, overlapping plurilateral trade agreements as stepping stones to global free trade. The Administration's plurilateral initiatives in North America, the rest of the Western Hemisphere, and Asia embody principles of openness and inclusion consistent with the GATT. They will serve as vehicles for improving access to foreign markets and easing trade tensions, and as models for future multilateral liberalization through the WTO in areas such as intellectual property rights, services, investment, and environmental and labor standards.

DYNAMIC EMERGING MARKETS

The recent U.S. emphasis on regional agreements responds to a massive shift taking place in the global economy. The economies of the world have long been categorized as either industrialized or less developed economies. Today, however, these distinctions are becoming obsolete as emerging economies in Asia, Latin America, and elsewhere are quickly approaching the ranks of the rich, industrialized countries. In the future these emerging economies are expected to grow rapidly and generate a larger share of world output and trade. The World Bank forecasts that developing economies will grow by 60 percent over the next decade, double the growth forecast for the industrialized countries. The share of gross world product produced in developing countries is expected to reach one-quarter by 2002, up from roughly one-fifth in 1972 (Chart 6-1). And purchasing-power-parity estimates, a more accurate method of making comparisons across countries, would attribute an even greater share of world output to developing countries.

Export and investment opportunities in emerging markets in Latin America and Asia will be a key engine of growth for the U.S. economy over the next decade. Exports are projected to grow far faster than other components of U.S. national income over that period. And this trend is already apparent. Over the last 7 years, U.S. exports of goods and services accounted for over one-third of economic growth, and export-related jobs grew over five times faster than total employment.

Much of this dynamism is driven by demand from newly industrializing and developing countries. Exports to emerging markets in Latin America and Asia are growing much faster than those to our traditional export markets. Already, U.S. exports to developing countries exceed exports to our traditional customers, Europe and Japan. This trend will continue, since emerging Asian and Latin American economies are expected to grow more than twice as fast as Europe and Japan.

Both Latin America and Asia are seeing a virtual explosion in the number of households with middle-class incomes and consumption patterns. By one estimate, China, India, and Indonesia will to-

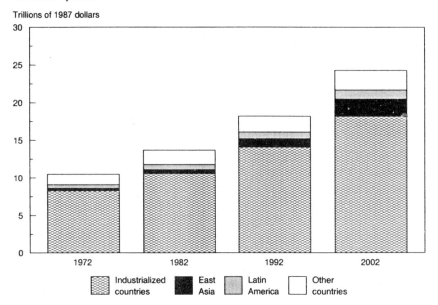

Chart 6-1 **Income Growth in Industrialized and Developing Countries**
The share of world income received by developing countries is expected to reach one-fourth by 2002.

Trillions of 1987 dollars

| | Industrialized countries | East Asia | Latin America | Other countries |

Source: International Bank for Reconstruction and Development.

gether have over 700 million middle-class consumers by the year 2010. That is roughly the current population of the United States, Europe, and Japan combined. As consumers in emerging markets join the middle class, their demand for household goods will soar, whereas in the United States and Europe most households already own such goods.

The rapid growth rates of emerging economies reflect a combination of factors, including technological catch-up to the most industrialized countries and, in many Latin American countries, recovery from the recessions associated with overindebtedness in the first half of the 1980s. More generally, economic theory predicts that lower income countries will grow faster than those with higher incomes, provided they are following sound economic policies. Because lower income countries have less infrastructure and plant and equipment, additional investments will be particularly productive. Less developed countries can also adopt and adapt technology that has already been discovered and developed in the rich countries. But there are prerequisites to taking advantage of additional capital and technology, among them stable political systems and sound economic policies. Broad access to primary education, an open economy, and sound macroeconomic policies all contribute to strong growth.

The most dynamic emerging economies have generally embraced market-oriented economic policies and opened themselves to the world economy. Not only have they lowered barriers to trade and investment, but they have adopted stable fiscal and monetary policies and transparent regulations. Many have also succeeded in improving the educational attainment of their work forces and have benefited from high rates of saving and accompanying high rates of investment. Sound economic policies will enable these countries to continue to take advantage of world capital flows and technological advances from abroad.

This rapid economic growth creates a number of opportunities for the United States. First, demand for U.S. products rises as the worldwide market grows. Many of these emerging economies will have particularly large demands for investment goods, transportation systems and products, infrastructure, environmental technologies, information systems, energy technologies, and financial services. These are all sectors in which the United States is particularly competitive.

In addition, countries that are growing rapidly are likely to invest more than they save. As long as they enjoy high growth rates and pursue sound economic policies, foreign capital will be readily available to finance this excess of investment over saving. Greater capital inflows in turn will permit greater imports from strong exporting countries such as the United States. Larger markets will also allow firms both in the United States and abroad to exploit greater economies of scale, as their fixed costs are spread across greater sales.

The Administration's regional initiatives in the Americas and in the Asia-Pacific community are critical for placing the United States squarely at the fulcrum of two of the most dynamic regions in the world.

REGIONAL BLOCS AS BUILDING BLOCKS

From a purely economic point of view, the effects of increased regional integration are well understood. The establishment of principles and dispute resolution procedures governing international transactions regularizes and improves the environment for intraregional flows of goods, services, and investment. A plurilateral trade agreement generates an increase in trade among member countries, due to reductions in the cost of importing from each other that are associated with lower tariffs and enhanced market access. Thus, for example, in 1993, 55 percent of the trade flows of countries that belong to the European Union (EU) involved other EU member markets. In general, cheaper imports and more efficient production patterns should improve the well-being of the participating countries. But plurilateral liberalization may also re-

217

duce trade with countries that are not members, since imports from nonmember countries do not benefit from the reduction of trade barriers. Trade diversion arises when members of a plurilateral trade arrangement switch from importing goods from the lowest-cost nonmember market to importing from members, even though the tariff-free cost of the goods in nonmember countries is lower than that in member countries. The beneficial trade creation effects are more likely to outweigh the harmful trade diversion effects if barriers to imports from nonmember countries are not allowed to rise—a condition that is codified in Article XXIV of the GATT.

Trade creation is also more likely to outweigh trade diversion when the "natural" costs of trade such as freight and insurance are low among members, because of geographical proximity or shared borders, and high between members and nonmembers. In general, countries trade the most with countries that are geographically close: proximity and shared borders lower transportation costs and thereby lower the total cost of imports. It is for this reason that plurilateral agreements are so often regional in nature.

Plurilateral trade initiatives generally take one of two forms. Customs unions, like the European Union, require members to remove all barriers to trade with other member countries and to maintain a common external tariff toward nonmember countries. As a member of a customs union, when Germany wants to change its tariffs on imports from nonmembers, it must first persuade France, Spain, and all the other EU members to do the same. In contrast, free trade areas such as NAFTA liberalize internally but do not impose any restrictions on members' external trade policies.

Stumbling Blocks

Traditionally, economists have voiced concerns that an increased emphasis on plurilateralism might divert attention and energy away from multilateralism and result in harmful trade diversion. And indeed, certain types of preferential trade agreements can undermine the multilateral system.

In general, preferential trade agreements that reduce the discretion of member countries to pursue trade liberalization with nonmembers are more likely to become stumbling blocks. Thus, for instance, members of customs unions are unable either to negotiate tariff reductions with nonmembers individually or to reduce external tariffs unilaterally. In contrast, NAFTA allows its members to enter into trade agreements with outsiders, and indeed Mexico has negotiated separate free trade agreements with several other Latin American countries since signing NAFTA.

In addition, as a bloc expands, its bargaining power in international negotiations and its market power in international commerce grow, especially if it imposes a common external tariff. This may have the undesirable effect that the bloc finds it advantageous to increase barriers to outsiders. These harmful effects are unlikely to arise in a free trade area as opposed to a customs union, and when external barriers are constrained by WTO disciplines.

Building Blocks

When structured according to principles of openness and inclusiveness, regional blocs can be building blocks rather than stumbling blocks for global free trade and investment. Seen in this light, carefully structured plurilateralism is a complement rather than an alternative to U.S. multilateral efforts.

There are a variety of ways in which plurilateral agreements can serve as building blocks for multilateral market opening. First, plurilateral accords may achieve deeper economic integration among members than do multilateral accords because the commonality of interests is greater and the negotiating process simpler. The multilateral framework of the WTO achieves liberalization by requiring each member to extend any new trade preferences to all trade partners on a nondiscriminatory basis. Although this principle is intended to generate broad liberalization across countries, it may have the unintended effect that countries are less willing to offer concessions to certain of their trade partners because they must then offer the same concessions to over 100 other countries. Plurilateral agreements, by achieving both greater depth and breadth in their disciplines, can support the multilateral system by forging ahead on issues that are likely to be incorporated in future multilateral negotiating rounds.

Second, a self-reinforcing process is set in place by the creation of a free trade area. As the market encompassed by a free trade area expands, it becomes increasingly attractive for outsiders to join in order to receive the same trade preferences as member countries. Companies from nonmember countries find themselves at an increasing competitive disadvantage as the free trade area expands, and they petition their national governments to apply for membership.

Third, plurilateral liberalization encourages partial adjustment of workers out of the import-competing industries in which the country's comparative advantage is weak, and into exporting industries in which its comparative advantage is strong. As adjustment proceeds, the portion of the work force that benefits from trade expansion and liberalization rises, and the portion that loses out declines, which in turn builds political support for liberalization in a self-reinforcing process.

For all of these reasons, when plurilateral agreements are structured according to principles of openness, they tend to overlap and expand, building toward global free trade from the bottom up.

Open Regionalism

Open regionalism refers to plurilateral agreements that are nonexclusive and open to new members to join. It requires first that plurilateral initiatives be fully consistent with Article XXIV of the GATT, which prohibits an increase in average external barriers. Beyond that, it requires that plurilateral agreements not constrain members from pursuing additional liberalization either with nonmembers on a reciprocal basis or unilaterally. Because member countries are able to choose their external tariffs unilaterally, open agreements are less likely to develop into competing bargaining blocs. Finally, open regionalism implies that plurilateral agreements both allow and encourage nonmembers to join. This facilitates the beneficial domino effect described above.

To ensure that its plurilateral initiatives strengthen the multilateral trading system and enhance market opening globally, the United States is pursuing a policy of open regionalism. The Administration is working to lay the foundations for a world with several overlapping, open plurilateral arrangements, with the United States playing a leadership role in North America, Asia, and Latin America, rather than two or three competing blocs.

THE NORTH AMERICAN FREE TRADE AGREEMENT

On January 1, 1994, a historic trade agreement between the United States, Canada, and Mexico went into force. In both the level and the scope of the disciplines covered, NAFTA is the most far-reaching and forward-looking trade agreement ever adopted by these three countries. NAFTA provides for phased elimination of tariff and most nontariff barriers for both industrial and agricultural products, protection of intellectual property rights, investment rules, liberalization of services trade, and an innovative dispute settlement mechanism (Box 6–3).

The Economic Effects of NAFTA

It is far too early to evaluate the full economic impact of NAFTA, since the provisions have been in place for only 1 year and many of the measures are being phased in over 10 to 15 years. There is a widespread consensus that NAFTA's overall net impact will be positive. But it is important to keep in mind that Mexico's GDP is only about 4 percent that of the United States, and that the United States had a preexisting free trade agreement with Canada when NAFTA was signed.

There are a number of reasons why NAFTA will benefit the United States. First, prior to NAFTA, Mexico had trade barriers that were 2.5 times higher on average than those in the United States. Thus it is Mexico that will undertake the greater reduction in trade barriers. Second, although investment barriers in Mexico have been

220

Box 6–3.—NAFTA Highlights

- Phaseout of most tariffs and nontariff barriers in industrial products over 10 years, including for all textiles and apparel that have substantial regional content
- Phaseout of tariffs and most nontariff barriers in agricultural products over 15 years
- Investment rules ensuring national treatment, eliminating most performance requirements in all sectors, and reduced barriers to investment in the Mexican petrochemicals and financial services sectors
- Liberalization of financial, land transportation, and telecommunications services markets
- Mechanisms for enforcement of national labor and environmental laws
- A dispute resolution mechanism
- Protection of intellectual property rights
- Funds for environmental cleanup and community adjustment along the border

lowered, making it easier to establish operations there, the fact that trade barriers are also being reduced makes investment in Mexico less necessary. Evidence suggests that most U.S. direct investment abroad is intended to gain market access, not to exploit low-wage workers or lax regulations. And indeed, some U.S. investments in Mexico have already increased U.S. exports dramatically. For instance, one major U.S. discount store chain has opened 9 stores in Mexico. The chain's Mexico City store alone sells $1 million worth of merchandise on an average weekend, most of which is imported directly from the United States.

Third, although wages are lower in Mexico than in the United States, the productivity of Mexican workers is also lower than that of U.S. workers. Moreover, companies make plant location decisions based on a variety of factors in addition to wages, including telecommunications and transportation infrastructure and business services, all of which are more sophisticated in the United States.

Perhaps most important is the simple fact that trade liberalization encourages specialization that benefits both countries. Thus, while NAFTA is expected to raise production in Mexico of goods that require a lot of low-skilled labor hours, there should be a concomitant increase of production in the United States of goods that require highly skilled labor. Specialization allows both types of goods to be produced more cheaply, lowering the cost of living for the population on both sides of the border. Moreover, increased trade and investment associated with NAFTA should result in higher income in Mexico, which in turn will translate into greater

221

demand for U.S. exports, and increased investment and employment in export industries in the United States.

Although the beneficial effects will take years to manifest themselves fully, the results to date confirm the view that NAFTA is good for the United States, Mexico, and Canada. So far there is little evidence of the sucking sound that critics had alleged would accompany NAFTA. Indeed, the sounds most associated with NAFTA are those of trains, trucks, and ships loading cargo bound for destinations across the border. Overall, U.S. exports to Mexico grew by 21.7 percent in the first three quarters of last year over the same period in 1993—more than twice the growth rate of U.S. exports overall. Imports from Mexico have also increased by 22.8 percent, but much of this import growth is associated with the strength of the economic recovery in the United States during the period, and would most likely have taken place in the absence of NAFTA, since U.S. barriers on many Mexican imports were already low.

While the rapid growth in trade between the United States and Mexico testifies to the opportunities created by NAFTA, it is important to emphasize that the bilateral balance of trade is not a scorecard by which to judge the success or failure of the agreement. The United States gains from its imports from as well as its exports to Mexico, from the ability to specialize and compete more effectively in world markets, and from the opportunities opened up to U.S. firms in Mexico as it develops. Trade between the two countries will grow rapidly, but the trade balance will fluctuate, depending on macroeconomic conditions in the two countries, just as the rapid growth in the U.S. economy boosted U.S. imports during the past year.

The NAFTA also benefits the United States through the more prosperous and stable Mexico that it fosters. This is particularly important, since the United States and Mexico are so closely linked by geography as well as economy. As Mexican wealth and political stability increase, the result is not only a larger market for U.S. exporters, but also higher environmental standards and reduced illegal immigration.

NAFTA and the Peso

On December 22, 1994, the Mexican Government decided to abandon the fixed exchange rate between the Mexican peso and the dollar, allowing the peso to float. The decision came after intense pressure on the peso in foreign exchange markets had severely depleted Mexico's international reserves. The pressure resulted from Mexico's inability to finance its large current account deficit, which reached almost $30 billion in 1994, or about 7.6 percent of GDP.

Following Mexico's debt repayment problems in the early 1980s, its government pursued a course of macroeconomic stabilization that included fiscal restraint, wage and price restraints, and a target range for the dollar value of the peso. As part of its inflation-fighting measures, starting in the late 1980s, the government adjusted the target range for the peso more slowly than the rate of inflation. By 1994 the peso had appreciated significantly in real terms, making foreign goods cheaper for Mexican consumers. Real appreciation was accompanied by increasing trade and current account deficits, which were financed by borrowing from foreign investors, a large portion of which took the form of short-term portfolio investment. As the Mexican presidential election approached in 1994, an uprising in the State of Chiapas and the subsequent assassination of the ruling party's candidate contributed to investor uncertainty. As investors lost confidence and the inflow of portfolio capital dried up, the government found it increasingly difficult to maintain its exchange-rate policy, and eventually it decided to let the market determine the value of the peso.

Shortly afterward, the Mexican Government announced a comprehensive economic plan to restore confidence and stabilize the economy. At the request of the Mexican Government, the United States organized a financial stabilization package of $18 billion designed to restore investor confidence and give the Mexican Government breathing room to implement its economic package. The package included multilateral and private sector participation.

However, despite the decision to float the peso and the announcement of the international support package, pressures on the peso continued. Investors became increasingly reluctant to roll over maturing short-term obligations of the Mexican Government and, in some cases, of Mexican banks. The flight from Mexican assets also showed signs of spreading to other emerging markets.

In order to restore confidence in emerging financial markets, the President decided to expand U.S. financial support for Mexico to $20 billion. The U.S. support includes short- and medium-term swaps (an exchange of dollars for pesos for a specified period of time) and longer term loan guarantees. The Treasury's Exchange Stabilization Fund is providing a substantial portion of this support. In addition, the Federal Reserve is providing a part of the support, in the form of short-term swaps. These guarantees and swaps are structured to provide maximum protection for U.S. assets and to encourage the Mexican Government to return to private sector financing as soon as possible. In order to make use of the guarantees, the Mexican Government will be required to pay large up-front insurance fees. All drawings will be backed by claims on the proceeds from oil exports. The swap facility must be fully repaid; it is not a grant. The United States has had a swap line with Mexico for over 50 years, and Mexico has repaid all of its drawings.

Additional financial support will come from a variety of sources. The International Monetary Fund (IMF) made a commitment to

223

provide a total of $17.8 billion, from a combination of its own resources and contributions from member countries. The Bank for International Settlements committed $10 billion in short-term financing, Canada committed itself to provide a $1 billion swap facility, and Argentina and Brazil committed themselves to arrange $1 billion in financial assistance to Mexico.

Together, these resources will enable the government of Mexico to refinance its debt and shift to longer term maturities, thereby easing the current liquidity squeeze. The support package imposes stringent financial conditions. Mexico must implement an economic plan that includes reductions in government spending, an incomes policy to reduce inflation, and tight control of credit. Mexico has also pledged to accelerate the privatization of key industries and increase access for U.S. and other foreign investors. These measures are designed to ensure that Mexico will be able to restructure and service its debt and to restore economic stability and growth.

It is also important to understand that NAFTA neither contributed to the peso devaluation nor in any way affected the U.S. Government's response. Indeed, the NAFTA measures adopted by Mexico to lock in market reforms and provide safeguards for foreign investors have, if anything, shored up investor confidence and mitigated the peso depreciation. The United States is providing support to Mexico because we have a stake in the stability of a country with whom we share a 2,000-mile border and important commercial ties. There is no commitment under NAFTA to do so.

NAFTA Side Agreements

NAFTA includes three innovative side agreements that reflect the Administration's commitment to ensure that expanded trade does not result in deterioration of environmental or labor standards on either side of the border or in damaging import surges. The labor and environmental side agreements define guiding principles and create institutions to ensure that each member country enforces its own laws protecting labor and the environment. They are described in detail below. The side agreement on import surges creates an early warning mechanism to identify sectors where rapid growth of imports is likely to generate significant dislocation of domestic workers. If a domestic industry is threatened by serious injury from an import surge during the NAFTA transition period, a temporary snapback to pre-NAFTA duties is permitted as a safeguard. However, if exports from a NAFTA member do not account for a substantial share of total imports or do not contribute significantly to the threat of injury, the member country's exports must be excluded from safeguard actions.

Adjustment

Although the United States chose to join NAFTA because it will benefit U.S. consumers, shareholders, farmers, and workers generally, it was also recognized that some jobs in some industries would be threatened by increased imports from Mexico. NAFTA contains a number of provisions intended to mitigate these adjustment costs. First, the elimination of trade barriers is phased in over 10- to 15-year horizons in industries where liberalization is expected to require significant adjustment. Second, there are safeguard provisions (described above) permitting the temporary imposition of trade restrictions when surges in imports cause serious injury to a domestic industry. Third, the U.S. implementing legislation established a Transitional Adjustment Assistance (TAA) program for workers who experience or are threatened with job loss or reduction to part-time status as a direct result of either increased imports from or a shift of production to Mexico or Canada, to help them retool and reengage. There is no requirement that the dislocation be directly related to NAFTA, although it must have occurred after NAFTA went into effect. Assistance includes employment services, training, income support following exhaustion of unemployment insurance, job search allowances, and relocation allowances.

As of November 1, 1994, the NAFTA-TAA program had approved assistance for over 12,000 workers. In two-thirds of these cases, the dislocation was associated with either a shift of U.S. production to or increased imports from Mexico. Eighty-eight percent of the NAFTA-TAA-certified layoffs were in manufacturing firms, 9 percent were in agriculture, and 3 percent were in services industries. Within manufacturing, the apparel, industrial machinery and equipment, electronic and other electric equipment, and instruments and related products industries accounted for 72 percent of the certified layoffs. Most of the firms that have qualified for NAFTA-TAA so far are smaller manufacturers producing apparel or parts and components with either less skilled workers or less sophisticated factory equipment.

The NAFTA-TAA program indicates that increased trade with Mexico and Canada has had an adverse effect on some workers, although the number of job losses has been small relative to the 100,000 jobs estimated to have been created through expanded exports to Mexico. Reemployment data on NAFTA-TAA-certified workers are not yet available, so it is too early to tell how long-lived the job displacement effects will be. However, it is important to recognize that layoffs and other displacements are a constant feature of the U.S. economy, and that relative to overall annual job losses for workers with over 3 or more years on the job (1.5 million per year on average between 1991 and 1993), the displacement associated with NAFTA is very small.

NAFTA and Open Regionalism

NAFTA is both the United States' most significant plurilateral initiative to date and a likely model for such initiatives in the future. As such, it is worth noting that NAFTA is consistent with open regionalism along all the dimensions discussed above. First, it explicitly prohibits any increase in external barriers, and indeed external barriers in all three of the member countries are scheduled to fall as part of the Uruguay Round agreement. Second, it imposes no constraints on the ability of member countries to lower their barriers to nonmember countries, and indeed Mexico has granted trade preferences to several nonmember countries since the agreement was signed. And third, NAFTA contains a provision specifying that the members can choose to admit additional members. Indeed, the President, together with the Prime Minister of Canada and the President of Mexico, announced the start of accession negotiations with Chile in December 1994.

SUMMIT OF THE AMERICAS

On December 9, 1994, the President convened the first-ever hemispheric summit held in the United States—and the first to be attended solely by democratically elected leaders. The summit celebrated an unprecedented conjuncture in the hemisphere's history. For the first time, all 34 leaders share a common commitment to democracy and open markets. Many of the Latin American leaders have put their countries on a course of stable, sustainable economic growth by taking difficult steps to address the indebtedness, rampant inflation, and high unemployment that robbed this region of a decade of growth.

The cornerstone of the summit was the call by all leaders for the creation of a Free Trade Area of the Americas (FTAA) by 2005. This will create a market of over 850 million consumers with a combined income of roughly $13 trillion. It will also level the playing field for U.S. exporters, who currently face Latin American trade barriers over three and one-half times those in the United States. It is critical to secure a commitment to work toward a hemispheric free trade area now, even though it will take years to achieve, in order to set the standard in the region and ensure that subregional integration initiatives are consistent with the goal of creating the FTAA and with the multilateral system.

The President tangibly demonstrated his commitment to this goal by announcing that the United States along with our NAFTA partners Mexico and Canada will initiate negotiations with Chile on accession to NAFTA. The inclusion of Chile would expand the total population of NAFTA to 381 million and its combined income to 30 percent of the world's total. The United States is an important trade partner for Chile; U.S. exports already account for over 20 percent of Chile's total imports.

The decision to start accession discussions with Chile reflects the enormous progress that country has made in achieving macroeconomic stability, liberalization of trade and investment policy, convertibility of the currency, improvement of living standards, and alleviation of poverty. Through a combination of stabilization and liberalization measures, Chile has achieved sustained real growth of 7 percent on average over the past 8 years. It has brought its external tariffs down by 79 percent since 1975. These measures have led to significant inflows of foreign capital, and the ratio of foreign debt to GDP has been reduced by nearly 60 percent since 1985. At the same time, inflation has fallen to 10 percent per year and unemployment is a low 4.5 percent.

At the Summit of the Americas the leaders set in place a process for achieving free trade in the hemisphere. Over the next several months members of existing subregional trade groups such as NAFTA will hold consultations on achieving regional trade liberalization. The United States will initiate discussions to determine interim steps with each of the countries in the region through previously established Trade and Investment Councils. The Administration will hold discussions with the Congress and with the United States' NAFTA partners on NAFTA expansion. In addition, the Organization of American States' Special Committee on Trade will develop a compendium of all existing trade agreements within the hemisphere to increase transparency and identify areas of potential trade facilitation, such as customs harmonization. Meetings of the countries' ministers are scheduled for June 1995 and March 1996 to review progress and further define the work program.

Economic Impact

The southern Americas (here defined to include Central America, the Caribbean except for Cuba, and South America) make up one of the most economically dynamic regions in the world. Sustained income growth in the region reflects in part a robust recovery from the recessions associated with the debt crisis of the early 1980s, and in part significant structural reforms on the domestic front and in trade policy. Many of the countries in the region are expected to continue to experience high growth rates due to the reduction of both debt levels and inflation through macroeconomic stabilization measures. The southern Americas account for about 6.5 percent of world population and 3.5 percent of world income. Brazil is by far the largest country in this region, with over 40 percent of the region's income and population.

As income in this region grows, its imports from the United States will grow even faster. Over the past 5 years, exports from the United States to the southern Americas have grown almost 10 percent per year—far faster than the region's income growth. By far the greatest share of the region's imports—29 percent—come from the United States. This reflects in many cases geographical proximity, as well as historical and cultural ties. Interestingly, however, Brazil's largest trade partner is not the United States but the European Union, which accounts for 25 percent of Brazil's trade compared with 22 percent for the United States. Overall, the southern Americas currently account for nearly 8 percent of U.S. exports, as shown in Chart 6–2.

Chart 6-2 **U.S. Merchandise Exports by Region in 1993**
By far the majority of U.S. exports go to our NAFTA partners, Western Europe, and the APEC countries. The southern Americas take nearly half of the remainder.

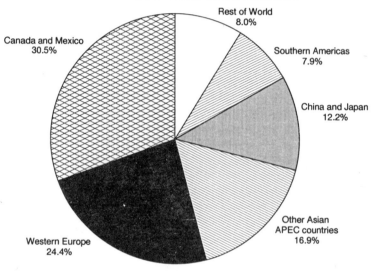

Note: The southern Americas include Central America, the Caribbean except for Cuba, and South America. Percents do not add to 100 because of rounding.
Source: Department of Commerce.

As noted above, Latin American tariffs are over three and one-half times those in the United States on average. Thus, trade liberalization is likely to result in increased market opportunities for U.S. products and associated export and job growth. A variety of studies have analyzed the impact of a possible hemispheric trade agreement on the U.S. economy. Most of these studies find that the effects of expanding NAFTA southward will be beneficial for both the U.S. economy and our regional trade partners.

In addition to the direct beneficial effect of cheaper imports from the United States and expanded export opportunities, countries in the southern Americas would benefit from the enhanced credibility of their market reforms that a trade liberalization agreement with the United States or NAFTA would bring. This commitment to a liberal trade regime should increase investment by both domestic and foreign investors and contribute to long-term growth. This is good for the United States both because it will improve the prospects for peace and political stability in the region and because it will further raise the purchasing power of southern American consumers, increasing their spending on U.S. goods.

If instead the United States should fail to recognize the historic opportunity that this conjuncture represents, and if we do not work to improve access to southern American markets for both trade and investment, U.S. companies and workers will lose out to foreign competitors. Most countries in the southern Americas have already joined one of four preferential subregional trading blocs. Most of these subregional blocs have plans to adopt a common external tariff (CET). This will make it more difficult for countries to liberalize individually and will result in diversion of imports in favor of member-country products and away from U.S. products. In the case of Mercosur—the largest group, whose membership includes Argentina and Brazil—a CET was scheduled to go into effect in January 1995 on products accounting for roughly half of imports from nonmember countries. Coverage will be expanded to all products by early in the next century. Led by Brazil, Mercosur is also working to conclude agreements with Chile and Bolivia, as well as with the European Union, and has plans to create a South American Free Trade Area. Unless we move soon, U.S. exporters will be at a disadvantage relative to their competitors inside these blocs.

ASIA-PACIFIC ECONOMIC COOPERATION

Asia-Pacific Economic Cooperation (APEC) was first established in 1989 as a regional forum for economic cooperation. APEC has since expanded to include 18 members: Australia, Brunei, Canada, Chile, China, Hong Kong, Indonesia, Japan, Malaysia, Mexico, New Zealand, Papua New Guinea, the Philippines, Singapore, South Korea, Taiwan, Thailand, and the United States.

At the President's invitation, the leaders of the APEC countries met in 1993 in Seattle. There they put forth their vision of an Asia-Pacific economic community. Last November in Bogor, Indonesia, the APEC leaders established a common frame of reference for achieving that vision. They made a political commitment to eliminate barriers to trade and investment in the region by the year 2020. All countries will begin to liberalize at a common date, but the pace of implementation will take into account the differing levels of economic development among APEC economies: the industrialized countries will achieve free and open trade and investment no later than 2010, and the developing economies no later than 2020. The leaders also reaffirmed their support for the multilateral trading system and APEC's continued commitment to global trade liberalization and to the WTO-consistency of any APEC trade and investment initiatives. The APEC leaders instructed their ministers to work together to develop a detailed blueprint, laying out an action plan and timetable to achieve progressive liberalization in the region. The leaders will review this blueprint at their meeting in Japan in 1995.

Over the next year the Administration will work to ensure that the action plan describes comprehensively and in detail the process by which Asia-Pacific free trade and investment will be achieved. The Administration will consult closely with the Congress and the U.S. business community as it works with our APEC partners to develop a plan that addresses the widest possible range of barriers to the free flow of goods, services, and capital. APEC may focus initially on trade facilitation issues, such as standards conformance and customs simplification. The liberalization process will build on the Uruguay Round's achievements, possibly accelerating the implementation of commitments in the early stages of APEC liberalization, and also on the work program undertaken by APEC's Committee on Trade and Investment. Negotiators may work on issues not covered adequately in the WTO and issues of particular importance to APEC members—including investment, intellectual property, rules of origin, some service sectors, government procurement, competition policy, and infrastructure, as well as elimination of tariffs and nontariff barriers.

The Economic Importance of the Asia-Pacific Region to the United States

APEC's markets are critical to U.S. exporters, both for their size and because of their dynamism. The 14 Asian APEC economies already account for $135 billion, or nearly 30 percent of U.S. exports in 1994 (Chart 6–2). By comparison, Western Europe accounts for less than one-quarter. The Asian APEC economies are among our fastest-growing export markets: U.S. exports to Asian APEC members grew 9.9 percent per year on average over the past decade, compared with 8.3-percent growth in U.S. exports to the rest of the world. Their aggregate income of nearly $6 trillion accounted for one-quarter of world income in 1992 and is projected to grow 4.4 percent per year in real terms over the next decade. U.S. exports to the region are projected to grow even faster than income, at a rate of 6.4 percent per year.

Although the opportunities for U.S. businesses are tremendous, the obstacles are often very large. Between 1989 and 1992, automobile sales in Malaysia, the Philippines, and Thailand doubled, but tariffs on automobile imports into these countries remain high at between 17 and 57 percent. Studies estimate that Asian APEC members will invest $1.1 trillion in infrastructure projects over the next 6 years. China, which alone accounts for nearly half of this planned investment, has tariffs of 38 percent on machinery and equipment and 15 percent on steel. Overall, manufactured imports into Asian APEC markets face tariffs much higher than the average tariff on imports into the United States. Market-opening initiatives through APEC will help reduce these barriers, creating tremendous opportunities for U.S. companies and workers.

U.S. companies must remain actively engaged in the region or risk losing out to Asian competitors. Currently 58 percent of total imports by Asian APEC economies are from other Asian APEC economies—over three times the share from the United States. And this intra-Asian share is growing rapidly. The liberalization measures that APEC members will undertake will be critical in ensuring that U.S. firms are able to compete on equal terms in this large, booming market.

BILATERAL NEGOTIATIONS

At any time the United States is engaged in several negotiations with individual countries on trade issues or disputes. These bilateral negotiations are less glamorous than multilateral or plurilateral trade initiatives, but they are extremely important in opening up markets, settling disputes, and protecting U.S. trading rights. In addition, these negotiations are often where new trade issues are first discussed or tested. Although the United States has bilateral negotiations at one time or another with almost every country with which we trade, we focus here on two bilateral relationships of particular importance, those with Japan and China, and on the Administration's broader export strategy.

JAPAN

One of the most prominent of our bilateral trade relations, and the one that generates the most negotiating activity, is that with Japan. This is to be expected given the size of the trade involved ($155 billion in total trade in 1993, the second largest among our trading partners), the size of the bilateral trade imbalance (a U.S. deficit of $60 billion, our largest with any country), and the character of the barriers to foreign goods within Japan.

Last year's *Report* examined the character of the Japanese economy and Japanese trade in detail. Japan has relatively low formal trade barriers outside the agricultural sector. Yet at the same time Japan has strikingly low levels of import penetration in many sectors in which there is very large mutual trade among most industrialized countries. Japanese domestic prices for traded goods are often significantly above world market prices, even after accounting for taxes, tariffs, and higher distribution charges.

Although there are examples of foreign firms that have done very well in the Japanese market, there are also widespread complaints, and not just from American firms, that the Japanese market is closed to outsiders. The barriers are often subtle and take a variety of forms. Government licensing, regulation, and administrative guidance, restrictions on product specifications or pricing, and procurement practices all can be difficult for foreign firms to satisfy, and often difficult even to discover. In other cases private practices, such as control over distribution channels, group affiliations, or share crossholdings, make it difficult for foreign firms to sell or invest in Japan. The fact that the barriers vary from industry to industry, and are often opaque, means that negotiations are extremely detailed, sector-specific, and time-consuming. The Market Oriented Sector Specific (MOSS) negotiations of 1985–86 were the first of a series of targeted attempts to open individual markets. The Semiconductor Trade Agreement in 1986 also focused on the effective opening of a single sector. The Structural Impediments Initiative (SII) of 1989–90 took a somewhat different approach, focusing on the macroeconomic balance between national saving and investment that lies behind both Japan's large global current account surplus and the large deficit in the United States, while at the same time tackling a series of regulatory and competition issues that stood in the way of increased foreign sales in Japan.

The President and the Japanese Prime Minister announced their Framework for a New Economic Partnership at the July 1993 economic summit in Tokyo. The Framework contained macroeconomic goals and five sectoral and structural "baskets" for talks between the two nations. The macroeconomic goals included a shift to domestic demand-led growth in Japan to reduce its current account surplus, and a reduction in the U.S. fiscal deficit and an increase in the U.S. saving rate. The baskets were government procurement, regulatory reform and competitiveness, major sectors (most prominently, automobiles and parts), economic harmonization, and follow-up on the implementation of existing agreements.

Negotiations were complicated by two major changes in Japan's government, and in addition, talks broke down temporarily in February 1994. Despite their rocky path, a series of results and agreements were reached in the fall of 1994. Both sides made progress in macroeconomic policy that should narrow the overall deficit in each country. The Congress passed the Administration's deficit reduction program in August 1993, and the Japanese Diet voted to increase government spending and cut income taxes, while postponing a planned increase in consumption taxes. Japan's fiscal measures have contributed to its emergence from recession, and its current account surplus has fallen as a percentage of GDP and should fall further in the near term.

In the economic harmonization basket, the United States reached an agreement on intellectual property protection last August that enhances the ability of U.S. inventors to apply for and be granted patent protection in Japan. In procurement, the United States reached agreements in telecommunications equipment and services covering purchases both by the government and by the dominant Japanese telecommunications firm (in which the government still owns the majority share), a combined market of $11 billion per year. The agreements call for more complete information about procurement plans to be made available at an earlier stage, full consideration of international standards for equipment, and the use of overall best value to judge competing bids. A similar agreement was reached in medical technology products and services, a market of $2.6 billion per year.

Two agreements were reached in financial services. In insurance, a market worth $320 billion per year, Japan agreed to ease restrictions on the introduction of new products, ease rate restrictions on policies to large customers, and deregulate the industry in such a way as not to prejudice the interests of foreign insurers, who are now active in only a small, specialized segment of the market. In January 1995 the United States and Japan reached an agreement to further liberalize the Japanese financial sector. The Japanese Government agreed to open the $200 billion public pension fund market to foreign investment advisory services, relaxed the conditions for issuing corporate debt, agreed to introduce a domestic derivatives market, and eliminated various restrictions on cross-border capital movements.

In the $4.5 billion flat glass industry, where the existence of restrictive practices had been confirmed by Japan's Fair Trade Commission, an agreement was reached in December committing Japanese distributors to carry imported glass, and requiring the Japanese Government to consider foreign glass in public procurement.

The one critical area where no agreement has been reached is automobiles and parts, the largest single sector in the Framework talks. The issues in these negotiations are access to the Japanese auto dealership network, the removal of regulations that limit foreign sales of replacement auto parts, and increased participation in the original-equipment auto parts market, including participation in the design stage. In response to the meager progress in the automobile trade talks, the Administration initiated a Section 301 investigation in October covering the replacement parts sector, where the involvement of the Japanese Government is clearly defined, and made it clear that the United States expected progress in the original-equipment parts and automobile markets as well.

From the beginning, the Administration has insisted that the Framework negotiations should lead to agreements that produce significant, measurable results. The two countries agreed that objective criteria, either qualitative, quantitative, or both, be used to evaluate the agreements over time as to whether tangible progress was being achieved. Arguments over these criteria were the most controversial part of the Framework. The Administration was widely criticized, both in Japan and elsewhere, for attempting to "manage trade" or set market share targets.

These criticisms are and were disingenuous. None of the agreements set market share targets, either for U.S. firms or for foreign firms generally. A wide range of objective indicators was suggested and ultimately agreed to, with different indicators for different sectors depending on the characteristics of each sector. Furthermore, none of the market access concessions are limited to U.S. firms; Japanese market-opening measures are available to all on an MFN basis.

The Administration intends to continue to explore market-opening measures with Japan, and to ensure that agreements lead to tangible increases in opportunities for U.S. and other foreign suppliers to sell in Japan. In addition to the negotiations on automobiles and auto parts, the Administration is now engaged in discussions on reducing barriers to foreign investment in Japan and more rigorous enforcement of Japanese antitrust laws.

The Framework negotiations on deregulation have recently taken on increased importance due to internal developments in Japan. The high cost to Japan of its extensive regulation of the economy has become increasingly apparent, and there is growing demand within the Japanese business community for deregulation. The United States has both specific and general interests in a thoroughgoing deregulation of the Japanese economy. Many of the sectoral issues concern regulatory barriers, and the United States has presented detailed requests for regulatory changes. But the United States also has a strong interest in generalized deregulation of the Japanese economy, which would reduce barriers to entry for all firms in Japan, both domestic and foreign.

Despite the length and occasional acrimony surrounding sectoral liberalization negotiations with Japan, the talks work. One study has shown that U.S. exports to Japan in those sectors covered by trade negotiations increased almost twice as fast as total U.S. merchandise exports to Japan, and estimated that the negotiations were responsible for an additional $5 billion in annual U.S. exports. It is also important to emphasize that it is not only the United States but also the Japanese consumer who gains from these agreements, in the form of lower prices and a wider choice of goods.

CHINA

The Administration is pursuing a carefully balanced economic policy toward China that takes into account the tremendous opportunities for U.S. exports associated with that country's rapid growth, as well as its geopolitical importance and Americans' concerns about China's protection of human rights. The goals of U.S. policy are threefold: promotion of U.S. commercial interests, to raise standards of living in the United States; encouragement of continued economic reform within China and its integration into the world economy, with the expectation that these will help realize U.S. foreign policy goals including democratization and protection of human rights and the environment; and promotion of global cooperation and integration in the interests of peace and prosperity.

Economic Importance

China's economy is large, dynamic, and relatively poor. Although it is estimated to be the world's third-largest economy in purchasing-power-parity terms, China's per capita income even by that measure is roughly one-tenth that of the United States. Measures based on current exchange rates rank China eighth in total output and yield a per capita income nearly 50 times smaller than that of the United States. Even if China's recent real growth rates of 9 percent per year (the highest in the world) are maintained, it will be decades before per capita income in China approaches those of developed countries today.

For much of its history since the 1949 communist revolution, China maintained a virtually closed, centrally planned economy, which was accompanied by economic stagnation. Sweeping economic reforms undertaken since the late 1970s have contributed to explosive growth and a decline in central government control. In the agricultural sector this has taken the form of decollectivization and a return to smallholder farming. In the industrial sphere the management of state-controlled firms has been decentralized, and the government has permitted the rapid growth of township and village enterprises; private enterprises now account for half of industrial output. By the early 1990s prices for 95 percent of retail sales, 90 percent of sales of agricultural commodities, and 85 percent of capital goods sales were determined by the market. Factor markets have also been liberalized: state control of labor markets has been reduced, and previously repressed capital markets have been allowed to develop in fits and starts, although they remain primitive by Western standards.

As the government has instituted market reforms and liberalized, China's economy has become increasingly integrated into the global economy. China's share of world trade grew from 0.6 percent in 1977 to 2.5 percent in 1993—making it the world's 11th-largest exporter. Similarly, flows of foreign direct investment into China exceeded $25 billion in 1993, in marked contrast to the prereform years when such investment was prohibited. And these two trends are closely related: firms with foreign equity participation accounted for two-thirds of the expansion of exports in 1992 and 1993.

China has run global trade deficits in most years since reforms were initiated—indeed, China registered a deficit last year of $12.2 billion. However, China has run a growing bilateral trade surplus with the United States, which reached $22.8 billion in 1993. China's persistent surplus with the United States in part reflects its specialization in inexpensive mass-market consumer goods. China similarly runs bilateral surpluses with Japan and Europe for this reason. Moreover, increases in the bilateral surplus with the United States since the mid-1980s in large part reflect the movement of labor-intensive production of goods such as shoes, garments, and toys from Hong Kong and Taiwan to China, to take advantage of lower wages. Table 6–2 makes clear that the increase in the U.S. deficit with China has partially been offset by declines in the deficits with Hong Kong and Taiwan.

TABLE 6–2.— *U.S. Trade Deficits with China, Hong Kong, and Taiwan*
[Millions of dollars]

Year	Total	China	Hong Kong	Taiwan
1987	25,876	2,796	5,871	17,209
1993	31,392	22,777	–319	8,934

Source: Department of Commerce, Bureau of the Census.

The Chinese trade regime has been liberalized in several ways. The role of state trading firms in intermediating international trade has been greatly reduced. Export subsidies have largely been eliminated. The former system of multiple exchange rates for differing types of transactions was unified and the currency devalued; the yuan is now convertible for most categories of transactions. As trade has been liberalized, China's trade pattern has increasingly conformed to conventional theories, with China exporting labor-intensive products and importing capital goods. Nonetheless, China's trade regime has remained selectively protectionist, with multiple overlapping barriers to trade in some goods and discriminatory rules on investment and services. The absence of effective protection for intellectual property rights has cost U.S. businesses hundreds of millions of dollars in lost sales.

Ultimately the combination of rapid economic growth and greater, albeit uneven, trade openness means that China will be a major market for U.S. goods and services. China's market presents the greatest growth opportunities in aerospace, power generation equipment, environmental technologies, and computers, among merchandise exports. Among services there are opportunities in financial (including insurance), information, distribution, accounting, audiovisual, and legal services.

Most-Favored-Nation Status

China is subject to the Jackson-Vanik Amendment to the Trade Act of 1974, since the U.S. Government defines China as a nonmarket economy. The amendment requires that each year, in order for China to qualify for MFN status, the President must issue a waiver certifying either that China does not impede emigration or that providing MFN status will lead to increased emigration. In May 1994 the President renewed MFN status for China in the context of a broader policy that includes delinking MFN renewal from human rights issues other than emigration; a ban on imports of Chinese munitions; maintenance of the U.S. economic sanctions imposed in response to the Tiananmen Square tragedy, including denial of Chinese participation in Overseas Private Investment Corporation and Trade and Development Agency programs; and a vigorous and broad-based human rights policy. The President determined that renewal of MFN status offered the best way to promote the full range of U.S. interests in China, including human rights, strategic, and economic interests. Moreover, the President determined that China had made sufficient progress on the conditions he had imposed when renewing China's MFN status in May 1993—in particular, on compliance with a 1992 agreement on the treatment of prison labor, in addition to guaranteeing freedom of emigration.

The decision to pursue a vigorous human rights policy separately from MFN renewal reflected a determination that protection of human rights is most likely to be achieved through a combination of carefully targeted initiatives and China's continued economic reform and integration with the world economy. The Administration is promoting human rights in China by a variety of means including increasing international broadcasting to China, support for nongovernmental organizations (NGOs) there, encouragement of multilateral participation in our human rights initiatives, and development, in consultation with the business and NGO communities, of a set of ethical principles for business conduct as models for all companies engaged in international business.

The decision also recognized that substantial economic disruption in both China and the United States would accompany MFN revocation, along with significant damage to the broader bilateral relationship. Revocation of MFN status would result in tariff increases on Chinese imports of 5 to 10 times their current level, depending on the product. The ultimate effect on consumer prices and consumption would depend on the particular demand and supply elasticities in each product market, but they would likely be large, with estimates of decreased Chinese imports ranging from $6 billion to $15 billion annually.

MFN renewal ultimately will promote the goal of improved human rights protection more effectively than revocation would, because increased foreign trade contributes to China's integration with the world economy, economic decentralization, and the growth of a middle class. As the economy has grown and become increasingly decentralized, a new business society has developed that is independent of the state. Further, with greater wealth and access to foreign goods and to modern telecommunications, Chinese citizens are increasingly exposed to a broader set of ideas, undermining the government's monopoly on information. The result is a diffusion of economic power and information, creating the preconditions for a civil society, and with it more pluralistic forms of governance and a greater respect for human rights.

Bilateral Issues

Despite China's economic reforms, a variety of barriers still frustrate U.S. exporters, and lack of enforcement of intellectual property laws costs U.S. firms in the computer software, publishing, and audiovisual industries hundreds of millions of dollars a year. Although China committed itself to protect copyrights, patents, and trademarks for foreign goods in the U.S.-China Bilateral Trade Agreement of 1979, compliance has been a recurrent problem. In May 1991 the U.S. Government launched an investigation under the Special 301 provision of the trade act of 1988. In January 1992 the United States and China signed a memorandum of understanding that committed the Chinese Government to strengthen patent, copyright, and trade secret laws; to provide patent protection for products as well as processes; to join two international conventions on copyrights; and to treat software as a literary work under Chinese law, resulting in protection for 50 years.

Although China subsequently carried out all the institutional and legal changes, enforcement has remained a problem. China continues to be a major producer of pirated compact discs and computer software, often in joint ventures with Taiwanese and Hong Kong partners; the pirated goods are increasingly exported to third markets. In response, negotiations were begun in 1993 to strengthen Chinese enforcement of existing laws, and the United States initiated a second Special 301 investigation in June 1994. In January 1995 the U.S. Trade Representative released a preliminary retaliation list in an attempt to persuade the Chinese to be more forthcoming in the negotiations. China itself would benefit by improving its protection of intellectual property rights. Other countries in the region have significantly strengthened their protection of intellectual property rights in recent years, recognizing that it is an essential step in order to have access to cutting-edge technology and investment from abroad, as well as to encourage innovation at home.

U.S. exporters also encounter a wide array of market access problems. Starting in the mid-1980s, the U.S. Government has held a series of bilateral negotiations to persuade Chinese authorities to reduce the number, secrecy, and severity of administrative barriers to imports, including import licensing requirements, quantitative restrictions, and product testing and certification requirements, as well as to increase the transparency of trade rules.

The United States initiated an investigation under Section 301 in October 1991. The Chinese Government signed a memorandum of understanding in October 1992, following publication of a U.S. retaliation list. Under the agreement China committed itself to dismantle 90 percent of all import restrictions, to eliminate import substitution regulations, to reduce tariffs and eliminate the import regulatory tax, to improve transparency, and to base all phytosanitary and sanitary standards and testing on sound scientific principles. In return, the United States agreed to terminate the Section 301 investigation, to work with China on its accession to the GATT (now the WTO) and to liberalize restrictions on Chinese access to technology. To date, there has been little progress in increasing the transparency of approval processes for import licenses or quotas, or in eliminating restrictions on the imports of agricultural products through sanitary and phytosanitary standards; however, negotiations with China to resolve these issues are continuing.

WTO Accession

China has applied for membership in the WTO, and formal negotiations for accession have been in progress since 1988. The United States has consistently made clear that it wants China to become a member of the WTO, and the Administration is working with China and our other trade partners toward this goal. But the United States and the other WTO members are determined that China must join on commercial, not concessional, terms. This is critical for maintaining the integrity of the global trading system and integrating China into it. Moreover, implementing transparent trade rules and promoting open trade and investment should strengthen China's economy and lock in its economic gains.

Every country that joined the GATT in the past agreed to adhere to basic obligations. These include transparency of the trade regime, uniform application of trade rules, national treatment for goods, and a foreign exchange regime that does not obstruct trade. These basic obligations are the foundation of GATT rules; without them the other disciplines are meaningless. Thus, for instance, there is no point in agreeing on disciplines for trade laws if, as is

239

currently the case in China, they are not uniformly applied throughout the country. Similarly, there is no point in negotiating market access agreements if, as in China today, the trade rules are not transparent.

Although U.S. relations with Japan and China are both very important, they are only part of a large number of bilateral trade relationships. Market-opening negotiations and, on occasion, trade disputes are a normal and continuing part of U.S. trade policy. This Administration has put strong emphasis on opening markets for U.S. exports. But its bilateral negotiations are only part of a broader strategy to promote U.S. exports.

THE NATIONAL EXPORT STRATEGY

The Administration has focused on encouraging American exports by eliminating U.S. export barriers and by improving the efficiency of U.S. export promotion efforts. The Administration's Trade Promotion Coordinating Committee unveiled the National Export Strategy in September 1993. Since then the Administration has succeeded in meeting the goals it had set out: removing obstacles to exporting, improving trade finance, supporting U.S. bidders in global competition, helping small and medium-sized U.S. firms enter export markets, and promoting U.S. exports of environmental technologies and services.

The Administration has implemented almost all of the 65 objectives laid out in the 1993 National Export Strategy report:

- Unnecessary export controls have been eliminated for computers, affecting $30 billion worth of exports. Most authorization requirements for the export of telecommunications equipment have been eliminated.
- The value of exports requiring licenses has fallen to one-third its previous level, and the licensing process has been streamlined.
- Trade finance has been buttressed by increasing the limit on project finance through the Overseas Private Investment Corporation from $50 million to $200 million. Coordination with State and local sources of trade finance has improved, and partnerships with the private sector are being encouraged.
- Export assistance centers have been opened throughout the country, providing "one-stop shopping" for small businesses seeking Federal export information and financing assistance.
- The Administration has countered the advocacy efforts of foreign governments with efforts of its own on behalf of U.S. exporters, helping U.S. firms compete and win over 90 major contracts worth a total of $20 billion. These contracts include a multi-billion-dollar Saudi Arabian telecommunications procurement, power and energy projects throughout Asia, and a

project to build an environmental surveillance and air traffic control system in Brazil.

Efforts have also been made to discourage and counter the "tied aid" practices of other nations: concessional loans or grants that are only available to recipient governments if they procure equipment produced by the donor country's firms. Worldwide, the proportion of aid that is tied has decreased dramatically since 1992—the result of new tied aid guidelines adopted through the Organization for Economic Cooperation and Development (OECD, whose membership includes the major donor countries), and of the U.S. Government's subsequent aggressive enforcement of these guidelines. These guidelines make many new aid projects ineligible for tied aid financing and therefore open to international market competition.

Further, the National Export Strategy has focused on new opportunities in the economies expected to grow especially quickly in the coming years. These "big emerging markets" include China, Taiwan, Hong Kong, Korea, Indonesia, India, Mexico, Argentina, Brazil, Poland, Turkey, and South Africa.

A year ago the Administration set the goal of raising total U.S. exports to $1 trillion by 2000. The success of this past year has led the Administration to raise this goal to $1.2 trillion, which would represent almost a doubling of the 1993 export level.

NEW ISSUES IN TRADE NEGOTIATIONS

Since the mid-1980s, when the blueprint for the Uruguay Round negotiations was determined, a series of new trade issues have arisen that will occupy negotiators for the next several years. While these issues—trade and the environment, competition policy, rules on investment, and trade and labor standards—have already made a limited appearance in multilateral discussion, they have played a greater role in recent plurilateral and bilateral negotiations. Progress achieved in those negotiations will likely have a significant influence on future negotiations at the multilateral, plurilateral, and bilateral levels.

TRADE AND THE ENVIRONMENT

Protection of the environment and an open trading system are sometimes seen as conflicting goals. Many environmentalists are concerned that free trade will come at the expense of the environment, and many free traders are concerned that efforts to incorporate environmental concerns into the international trading system will degenerate into disguised protectionism. However, there is no inherent conflict between liberalizing trade and protecting the environment, and the Administration has focused on potential complementarities between good trade policies and sound environmental policies.

In fact, free trade and environmentalism have much in common. In both cases the benefits from achieving progress are spread across a wide group of people, while the interests that are harmed are more concentrated. Trade liberalization benefits consumers (and workers producing exports) but may harm workers in import-competing sectors. Similarly, environmental protection benefits a diffuse group of people, while the cost is concentrated on a smaller group, those overusing environmental resources. Thus, while the gains from liberalized trade and a cleaner environment outweigh the losses in the aggregate, it still can be difficult to achieve progress, since the costs of the action are concentrated on a small group who vociferously oppose action, while the benefits may be so diffuse as to make it difficult to mobilize potential supporters.

Moreover, both trade liberalization and international environmental issues require the use of multilateral tools. Without such tools there is a tendency for countries to engage in damaging environmental and trade policies designed to further their own interests at the expense of their neighbors. Multilateralism can ensure that progress is made on enough fronts so that all countries gain from trade and a protected environment. The GATT and its successor the WTO are well suited for tackling world trade issues. But there is as yet no analogous forum for comprehensively addressing global environmental issues. Instead there are a variety of international agreements and organizations committed to working on environmental problems.

There are also complementarities between good trade policies and good environmental policies. Agricultural protection in industrialized countries is a case in point. The protection of developed-country agriculture leads to more intensive farming, often of lands that are of marginal use, causing unnecessary soil erosion, loss of biological diversity, and the excessive use of pesticides and chemicals. Liberalizing trade in agriculture and lowering agriculture production subsidies can lead to a pattern of world farming that causes less environmental damage.

Also, high trade barriers to labor-intensive imports, such as clothing, from developing countries lead these countries instead to export products that are intensive in natural resources, causing environmental damage. In addition, high-value-added natural resource-based products such as wood or paper products often face high tariff barriers, whereas the raw natural resource itself does not; this forces developing countries to rely on exports of unprocessed natural resources while denying them the revenue gains from the downstream products.

242

Just as trade policy improvements have the potential to help the environment, environmental policy improvements can lead to economic gains. For instance, making polluters pay for the cost of the environmental resources they use encourages efficient resource allocation and undistorted world trade. The elimination of government underpricing of public natural resources can also reduce trade distortions.

Empirical evidence on the relationship between trade and the environment reinforces the notion that the two are not in conflict. For instance, trade liberalization may act to increase income levels through more-efficient resource allocation. In fact, the evidence suggests that openness to world trade is one of the strongest predictors of rapid income growth in less developed countries. Income growth in turn has beneficial effects on the environment. One study suggests that, as a country's income per capita rises beyond a point around $5,000, its environmental record improves. As people can afford to, they devote more resources to environmental protection, and political pressures for environmental protection increase.

Most evidence suggests that international differences in environmental compliance costs have not had a significant impact on trade and investment flows, primarily because these costs are almost always a very small fraction of value added in production. In the United States, for example, pollution abatement costs in over 93 percent of all industries are less than 2 percent of value added. Such small differences are unlikely to cause firms to migrate to take advantage of differential costs of environmental regulation; other considerations are far more important.

It is important to put aside the notion that trade itself is the cause of environmental degradation. Although economic activity certainly may diminish environmental resources, international trade, like trade among the States, is simply a means of making economic activity more efficient. The above examples and the available empirical evidence suggest that trade *itself* need not pose a particular threat to the environment. By the same token, most often the best response to an environmental problem is not to restrict trade. Instead, policies aimed *directly* at an environmental problem are likely to be more effective. For instance, if the use of a particular input in a firm's production is causing pollution, it is most effective to address the use of the input itself, rather than limit trade in the resulting product.

NAFTA demonstrates how trade liberalization can serve as an impetus for improved environmental policies. NAFTA specifically ensures its members' right to safeguard the environment, and it encourages all the NAFTA parties to strengthen their environmental efforts. NAFTA maintains all existing U.S. health, safety, and environmental standards. It allows States and cities to enact even tougher standards, while providing mechanisms to encourage all parties to harmonize their standards upward. The NAFTA side agreement on the environment created a new North American Commission on Environmental Cooperation, with a council made up of the three countries' top environmental officials. There is a mechanism to ensure that countries effectively enforce their own environmental laws, and a provision that guarantees public participation in monitoring of environmental laws. Finally, two new institutions have been established to fund and implement environmental infrastructure projects along the U.S.-Mexican border. The North American Development Bank (NADBank) will make loans for environmental cleanup and community adjustment on both sides of the U.S.-Mexican border. The NADBank will work closely with the new U.S.-Mexican Border Environment Cooperation Commission, which will review and certify proposals for environmental infrastructure projects.

NAFTA shows that it is possible to use trade concessions as a carrot to encourage environmental improvements, rather than using trade penalties as a stick to punish poor environmental behavior. Without NAFTA it is unlikely that there would have been an incentive for the member countries to strengthen their commitments to environmental cooperation. NAFTA also sets an example for other trade agreements in the use of international mechanisms and national commitments to ensure that free trade is compatible with enhanced environmental protection and sustainable development.

Environmental concerns were also addressed in the most recent Uruguay Round negotiations. The preamble of the agreement establishing the WTO recognizes the importance of environmental concerns. This is the first time that a broad multilateral trade agreement has recognized sustainable development as a guiding principle. The WTO negotiators have agreed to establish a full WTO Committee on Trade and the Environment to ensure the responsiveness of the multilateral trading system to environmental objectives. Issues this committee will tackle include, first, whether countries may use their trade policies in a way that discriminates between like products on the basis of the processes and production methods used; second, the relationship of the GATT to international environmental agreements; third, the circumstances under which countries may use trade measures to protect the environment; and fourth, the scope of the exceptions for environmental measures provided by the GATT under Article XX, which covers measures necessary to protect human, animal, and plant life.

COMPETITION POLICY AND TRADE

The relationship between national competition policies and international trade has emerged as an important issue for future negotiations. Historically, concern with international cartels has motivated discussions of competition and trade policy; the current revival of interest, however, is driven primarily by questions of market access. As tariffs and other formal trade measures have fallen, domestic barriers to competition have come under increasing scrutiny. Barriers to foreign entry can arise for numerous reasons. Government procurement practices, either through explicit "buy national" policies or through carefully drawn or nontransparent product specifications, can favor domestic over foreign producers. Health and safety standards, inspection procedures, and other product regulations can also operate as protectionist barriers. These areas have already been subject to extensive negotiation, and agreements were concluded in the last two GATT negotiating rounds that require transparency and nondiscrimination in procurement and product standards.

The most intense interest, however, now falls on barriers that can arise from the practices of private firms. These are often vertical restraints—control over distribution channels, exclusive sales arrangements or refusals to deal, rebates on sales—that impede new entrants. These barriers may also derive from close affiliations among firms within corporate groups that effectively limit sales by outsiders. Vertical and other private restraints on trade have been the subject of negotiations between the United States and Japan in the SII and the Framework negotiations (discussed above). Since GATT rules do not cover restrictive practices by private parties, except as they are supported by government measures, there is particular interest in the role of national competition policy authorities in fostering market access in these cases.

The second area of concern about anticompetitive business practices is the advantages they might create for sales in other markets. If industries are characterized by economies of scale or learning effects (in which production efficiency rises as cumulative output grows), greater output or longer production runs resulting from limited imports could confer a cost advantage on domestic producers. Restrictions on competition at home may also change the character of global competition among oligopolistic firms. When restrictions are successful in creating monopoly power at home (a less price-elastic home than foreign demand), sales in foreign markets at a lower price than at home (dumping) are a predictable result. Alternatively, collusion among domestic producers in the home market to maintain prices in the face of declining demand, perhaps under the auspices of an officially sponsored recession cartel, can result in venting of surplus production in foreign markets, increasing the instability and operating risks in markets that are open.

Although there is increasing overlap between trade and competition policies, there has been little coordination of international trade policy with antitrust policy. In large part this is because the practices that trade and competition policy deal with are distinct. International trade negotiations under the GATT have dealt with government actions that restrict trade or discriminate against foreign goods. Private practices that discourage imports have been beyond the GATT's reach, except to the extent that government measures support or are necessary to sustain those restraints. Antitrust policies, in contrast, can be effective in dealing with the actions of private parties. However, antitrust laws in some countries do not cover government-owned firms, and antitrust laws seldom apply to other governmental activities.

The extension of international trade disciplines in the GATT has clearly increased competition. As trade barriers have dropped, the extent of effective competition in domestic traded-goods industries has risen. Indeed, Justice Department guidelines now take the extent of international competition explicitly into account, as do the agencies in charge of competition policy in other nations.

However, the extent to which existing competition policy can be harnessed to increase trade liberalization is less clear-cut. Many of the private barriers to entry fall in the area of nonprice vertical restraints to trade, where there is appropriately no presumption of illegality. In many instances vertical restraints, such as exclusive dealing arrangements or ownership interests in distributors, can increase efficiency and ensure product and service quality, even as they act as barriers to new entry. Competition, and not entry opportunities for individual firms, is protected under U.S. antitrust law, and in the absence of evidence of restraints on competition in the domestic market it may be difficult to win a case on the grounds that a new firm cannot gain entry.

One area in which competition policy may have beneficial results is antidumping policy, the most prominent of U.S. policies against unfair trade. In the United States, duties are assessed on imports sold at "less than fair value," in other words, at a price that is either less than the price at which the good is sold in the home market, less than the sales price in a third-country market, or less than the calculated cost of production. If dumping is found, and if the dumped goods are determined to cause injury to the domestic industry, duties are assessed to bring the price of the goods up to "fair value."

There are two rationales for antidumping laws. The first is that the sale of imported goods at less than fair value may be part of a strategy of predatory pricing, designed to force American com-

246

petitors out of business. The second rationale, and one that directly addresses why only foreign firms are subject to antidumping procedures, is that dumping arises from an asymmetry in competitive conditions between the home market of the dumping firm and the market in which goods are sold. Restricted competition in the dumper's home market creates a situation in which dumping is profitable, creates opportunities for the dumping firm that are not available to firms based in the more competitive market in which goods are dumped, and is therefore seen as unfair. Recent advances in trade theory suggest that such advantages may be possible, depending on the competitive characteristics of the industry.

The value of a competition policy approach is that it may allow a more careful distinction between pricing practices that are unfair and those that simply reflect normal cyclical and market variations. A well-developed body of antitrust law exists to deal with predatory pricing. The courts consider such factors as the size and strength of rivals, the ease of entry in the industry, whether the pricing practices are likely to force firms out of business, and whether the alleged predator could eventually recover its losses from its current low price. Foreign firms selling in the U.S. market are subject to U.S. antitrust law, and the Justice Department and the Federal Trade Commission have brought cases against foreign firms that affect U.S. competition. Competition policy addresses not only predation but also other unfair trade practices, such as vertical restraints, and seeks to avoid the conditions that enable firms to engage in unfair practices.

Ideally, the problem of competitive asymmetry could be addressed by policies that increase competition in the home market of the dumping firm. The progressive reduction of trade barriers, the negotiated elimination of other market access barriers, and the interpenetration of major markets by foreign direct investment all tend to both increase and equalize the competitive environment across markets. Indeed, within some regional groupings where integration has proceeded sufficiently, such as the European Union and the Closer Economic Relations arrangement between Australia and New Zealand, competition policy has entirely replaced dumping review as a means to control unfair trade practices, just as within a single national economy.

Efforts on competition policy and trade will take place on a variety of fronts. Differences in antitrust philosophy and accumulated case law across major countries make harmonization of competition policies unlikely in the foreseeable future, except in closely integrated regional groups. But the global character of most markets has been the impetus for increasing consultation and cooperation among competition policy agencies, and this is likely to lead to some convergence in practice and approach. There is also likely to

247

be increased cooperation in cases that span international boundaries, such as a recent case involving the leading U.S. software producer. As this cooperation increases, one possible step would be an agreement to remove the antitrust exemptions for market division and price fixing by exporters; these exemptions are contained in various national laws including the Webb-Pomerene Act and the Export Trading Company Act of 1982 in the United States and the Export Trade Act of 1952 in Japan. In addition, to facilitate future cooperation, the United States is preparing to negotiate antitrust mutual assistance agreements. These agreements would provide a framework for joint prosecution of international cartels and for effective case-by-case assistance.

Trade negotiations, from the bilateral to the multilateral level, will continue to focus on market access issues, and thus inevitably deal with entry barriers and competition policy. The approach so far has been piecemeal, barrier by barrier and sector by sector; this is particularly evident in services negotiations, but also true of recent U.S.-Japan bilateral negotiations. The key to faster progress will be whether general principles that cut across sectors can be formulated. For example, these might deal with the definition of national treatment in markets where entry is by individual license, or the access of foreign firms to private industry associations that have a regulatory role or provide services necessary for participation in the domestic market.

INVESTMENT

Increasing emphasis on market access will push investment issues to the fore of future trade negotiations, just as it has elevated competition policy issues. This is particularly true of trade in services, where delivery often depends on having a physical presence in the market where the services are sold. But such presence is also crucial for many manufactured goods, where design must be tailored to market requirements, where service and reputation are important, or where fast response is key.

Thus, whereas foreign direct investment was once seen as a substitute for international trade, it is increasingly viewed as a complement or even a necessary component of trade. The evidence on U.S. outward foreign direct investment bears this out. Roughly 60 percent of U.S. exports are sold by American firms that have operations abroad. The evidence also indicates that the countries where U.S. exports are most successful are the same countries where U.S. firms have the largest investments, and where investment restrictions are lowest. Furthermore, nearly $1 of every $5 in sales by U.S. companies abroad is earned by American sales affiliates or wholesaling companies that have established local facilities to sell U.S. exports. Access to foreign markets is the strongest motivation for investing overseas, not lower production costs. Only about 8 percent of the production of U.S. companies abroad is exported back to the United States; the vast majority is sold abroad in the local market.

The investment issue is a clear example of the progress that can be achieved when negotiations are limited to a small group of nations. The investment rules in NAFTA contain most of what is desired in an investment accord, including guarantees on right of establishment, national treatment for foreign investors once established, freedom to repatriate earnings, and transparency in the rules governing foreign investment. The Administration is encouraging similar liberalization in its regional efforts in Latin America and Asia. These principles have also been advanced in U.S. bilateral investment treaties; 12 comprehensive treaties have been signed since 1993, including treaties with the former Soviet republics of Georgia, Ukraine, and Belarus.

Progress in regional and bilateral negotiations should spur multilateral agreements on investment issues. Last September the Administration called for a June 1995 launch of negotiations in the OECD to establish a multilateral investment accord. This agreement would go beyond bilateral investment treaties and existing OECD undertakings, and would require the removal of existing barriers to investment in all OECD countries.

TRADE AND LABOR STANDARDS

The international promotion of labor standards is an important goal of this Administration. The Administration negotiated an innovative NAFTA side agreement on labor standards, and it pressed for and got agreement to include discussion of the relationship between workers' rights and international trade in the meetings of the Preparatory Committee of the WTO. In the Uruguay Round implementing legislation, the Congress directed the President to seek a working party on labor standards within the WTO.

The labor side agreement to NAFTA, the North American Agreement on Labor Cooperation, provides a mechanism for the three NAFTA partners to address interactions between national labor standards in an environment of expanded trade and investment. The agreement commits each country to promote a set of guiding principles subject to its domestic law, but does not establish common minimum standards. The principles include freedom of association and the rights to organize and bargain collectively, as well as prohibitions on forced labor and restrictions on child labor. The agreement emphasizes a cooperative program aimed at improving labor standards in all three countries through technical assistance and the exchange of information. It also contains mechanisms to encourage the enforcement of national labor laws in the three countries and provisions to make the laws more transparent. Enforcement mechanisms include public channels of communication, exchanges of information, and consultations at a variety of levels. If a conflict arises between countries over a persistent pattern of failure to enforce national occupational safety and health, child labor, minimum wage laws, or technical labor standards, in circumstances that are related to trade, the agreement provides for binding arbitration and assessment of penalties.

The promotion of labor standards has a long history in international diplomacy and U.S. policy. The International Labor Organization (ILO) was established shortly after the First World War to promote agreement on labor standards and to monitor progress in achieving them. The United States tried, unsuccessfully, to add a labor article to the GATT in 1953, and tried to incorporate these issues in the Tokyo Round and the Uruguay Round negotiations. Adherence to labor standards is also a condition for country participation in the Caribbean Basin Initiative and the U.S. Generalized System of Preferences, and for eligibility for Overseas Private Investment Corporation insurance. Furthermore, since 1988, denial of workers' rights has been defined as an unfair trade practice in Section 301 of the Trade Act of 1974 and may be subject to action if it harms U.S. economic interests.

Although there is no fixed definition of core labor standards, widely accepted standards reflected in ILO Conventions and U.S. trade law include freedom of association, the right to organize and bargain collectively, freedom from forced labor, and a minimum age for the employment of children. Core labor standards represent fundamental human and democratic rights in the workplace, rights that should prevail in all societies whatever their level of development. They are also necessary to ensure that individuals have the freedom and the information necessary to make their own choices about occupations, earnings, and working conditions. The observance of labor standards can strengthen work force productivity as a whole by raising health and worker morale, and raise the general educational level by keeping children in school. In the absence of such standards, firms may find it difficult to respect workers' rights on their own.

A related concern is that countries could, by routinely abusing workers' rights, lower labor costs so as to gain an unfair advantage in international trade. This would certainly be the case if a particular foreign industry obtained the advantages of a labor force whose rights were not guaranteed—for example, because it had access to a conscript labor force. Whether foreign industries can reap the advantages of abuse of labor rights when such abuse pervades an entire economy is less certain. It is possible to artificially depress labor costs in the short run, but over longer periods of time any advantage gained by the overall abuse of labor standards may be minimal or nonexistent.

The Administration is committed to a multilateral process designed to build consensus and encourage adoption of core labor standards. There is widespread agreement, for instance, that standards should be appropriate to a country's level of development. The ability to compensate workers is limited by overall productivity (output per worker) in the economy, and that compensation may be paid in some combination of wages and better workplace characteristics, in proportions that may vary across societies. The Administration's goals are to achieve broad support for trade at home and abroad by ensuring that the benefits of trade are widely shared by those engaged in the production of internationally traded goods and services, and ultimately to raise living standards worldwide.

DOMESTIC POLICY AND TRADE POLICY

International trade has been and will remain a powerful source of growth, opportunity, and challenge for the American economy. The Yankee trader and the clipper ship were trademarks of this country early in its development, and today the United States remains the world's largest exporter and importer. Recognition of the gains from liberalizing trade go back to our beginnings as a Nation, and recent changes in the nature of goods and services trade, together with advances in theoretical understanding, have served to strengthen this conclusion (Box 6–4).

However, few things bring only benefits, and structural adjustment and change are the essence of a dynamic economy. The most potent force in the modern economy has been technological change, which can result in painful adjustments for firms, workers, and communities, even as it raises overall living standards over time. The mechanization of agriculture, the replacement of mechanical technology with electronics (in cash registers, adding machines, typewriters, and aircraft), and the growth of large retail stores all displaced workers. Recent technological change associated in part with increasing computerization is likely to have increased the demand for skilled workers across a broad range of industries, leading to a rise in the wages of skilled relative to unskilled labor (an issue discussed in Chapter 5).

Trade adds to the opportunities and dynamism of the economy, and to the adjustments required over time. Attempts to estimate the relative importance of international trade in economic restructuring have assigned a much larger role to technological change and other factors, but international trade competition has surely played a part, as discussed in Chapter 5. When import competition

By allowing each country to specialize in the production of the goods and services in which it is most efficient, trade raises the value of production and welfare in all trading countries. However, the gains from international trade go well beyond this basic tenet of comparative advantage. In industries where there are increasing returns to scale, international trade creates a larger market and lower unit costs, further raising the total output that can be produced. An integrated world market also allows technological development and production startup costs to be spread over a larger number of units.

But the largest gains from international trade may come from the competition that international markets provide. When competition is imperfect, the opening of markets to trade dilutes monopoly rents, lowering prices and raising output and welfare. International trade introduces new technologies (Box 3–7 in Chapter 3), spurs domestic producers to raise product quality, increases the range of goods available to consumers, and lowers product prices. A recent cross-country study of productivity at the firm level suggests that achieving and maintaining high productivity requires that companies compete directly against the best firms in the global economy, and evidence shows that, along with rates of aggregate saving and investment, openness to international trade is a significant determinant of faster growth. This is the reason why more and more developing countries have unilaterally lowered their trade barriers, and the search for higher growth was the primary motive for the Single Market Program of the European Union.

increases, there are pressures for protection to slow or halt the fall in production and employment in the affected industry. Indeed, many of the trade barriers in the United States and other developed countries arose to protect output in industries where employment was declining.

Raising or maintaining import barriers imposes costs on the rest of the economy through higher prices. Estimates place the total costs to consumers of U.S. tariff and nontariff barriers as high as $70 billion per year. Since protection often is applied to "cheap goods" or to consumer staples such as clothing and food products, these costs fall most heavily on the poor. The costs extend beyond consumers, to higher costs for other industries that use the protected products as inputs. Furthermore, one cannot reduce imports while leaving exports unchanged; overall levels of exports and imports are linked through the macroeconomic balance between national saving and investment and through the exchange rate. Thus, reducing imports would ultimately slow the growth of U.S. exports, upon which the jobs of over 10 million Americans now depend.

In addition to its high cost, trade protection is far from a solution to industrial adjustment. In most protected industries adjustment pressures arise from changing technologies and demand, and import protection has been able to slow employment declines only marginally. Estimated costs per job saved through protection run very high; one study put the average consumer cost per job maintained at $170,000, which is six times the earnings of the average U.S. worker.

The President's policy to "compete, not retreat" rests on the recognition that a dynamic economy, with its associated opportunities and despite its hardships, provides the best prospects for increasing incomes for Americans over time. The Administration has chosen to continue to press for further trade liberalization in order to open up foreign markets for U.S. exports, while at the same time vigorously promoting U.S. commercial interests abroad. But the commitment to embrace change requires a commitment to assist individuals when they are hurt by it. In other words, sound domestic policy is a necessary concomitant of sound international trade policy and reinforces the case for liberalization. Thus the Administration has advocated income support for those who lose their jobs due to trade displacement, as in the NAFTA Transitional Adjustment Assistance program, and has advocated greater investment in human capital, through programs of training and retraining, both to ease adjustment and to raise the incomes of Americans.

CONCLUSION

While recognizing the difficult adjustments that international trade may bring about, one should not lose sight of the significant gains that this country has reaped from its engagement in international markets. Since 1987, U.S. exports have grown at a rate of almost 10 percent per year in real terms, well outstripping export growth in Japan and the European Union, and reversing the decline in the U.S. share of world exports that occurred earlier in the 1980s. Export growth has been responsible for about one-third of total output growth since 1990, and it made the most recent recession considerably less severe than it otherwise would have been. As detailed in Chapter 2, export growth was a significant component in the strong performance of the American economy in 1994. Growth of exports has also been an important contributor in moving Americans toward higher paying jobs. The accompanying rise in U.S. imports has also been beneficial, providing consumers with more choices and raising the purchasing power of American in-

253

comes. Competition from abroad has made U.S. firms more efficient, more quality-conscious, and, in the end, more competitive.

The United States will continue to reap large gains from international trade. In the near term, recoveries in Europe and Japan will boost U.S. exports and help narrow this country's trade deficit. The longer term trends are also quite favorable for the United States. The positive changes in economic policy in many developing and transition economies will lead to faster growth and a sharp rise in their imports of capital goods, a sector in which U.S. competitiveness is very high. Both multilateral and plurilateral trade agreements have led to much larger reductions in the trade barriers of our partner countries than in our own already low barriers, and this will continue as APEC and the Western Hemisphere move toward free trade. The new areas that have recently been suggested for international negotiations—agriculture, services, intellectual property, competition policy—are all areas where the competitive balance is strongly in the United States' favor. Finally, strengthening of the underlying rules and the international dispute settlement system will lead to a convergence toward a rules-based, transparent, and nondiscriminatory world trading system, much like the one the United States already has. The balance of concessions and prospective gains from this convergence are greatly to our advantage.

This Administration will continue to pursue a more open world trading system, through multilateral, plurilateral, and bilateral trade negotiations. These negotiations will seek to lower barriers to trade in conventional sectors and to extend market liberalization to newer sectors and issues. Although we negotiate on a variety of levels, the basic goal is always the same: the advancement of open markets on a nondiscriminatory basis. This goal has characterized our bilateral negotiations, which have sought open markets, not special entry for American firms. In plurilateral negotiations we have emphasized the principle of openness to new entrants. The United States also has a strong interest in strengthening the underlying rules of the trading system and the dispute settlement process, both because to do so fosters more efficient and fairer trade, and because it results in the kind of system in which American firms most comfortably operate and compete.

Appendix A
REPORT TO THE PRESIDENT ON THE ACTIVITIES OF THE COUNCIL OF ECONOMIC ADVISERS DURING 1994

LETTER OF TRANSMITTAL

COUNCIL OF ECONOMIC ADVISERS
Washington, D.C., December 30, 1994

MR. PRESIDENT:

The Council of Economic Advisers submits this report on its activities during the calendar year 1994 in accordance with the requirements of the Congress, as set forth in section 10(d) of the Employment Act of 1946 as amended by the Full Employment and Balanced Growth Act of 1978.

Sincerely,

Laura D'Andrea Tyson, *Chair*
Joseph E. Stiglitz, *Member*
Martin N. Baily, *Member-Nominee*

Council Members and their Dates of Service

Name	Position	Oath of office date	Separation date
Edwin G. Nourse	Chairman	August 9, 1946	November 1, 1949.
Leon H. Keyserling	Vice Chairman	August 9, 1946	
	Acting Chairman	November 2, 1949	
	Chairman	May 10, 1950	January 20, 1953.
John D. Clark	Member	August 9, 1946	
	Vice Chairman	May 10, 1950	February 11, 1953.
Roy Blough	Member	June 29, 1950	August 20, 1952.
Robert C. Turner	Member	September 8, 1952	January 20, 1953.
Arthur F. Burns	Chairman	March 19, 1953	December 1, 1956.
Neil H. Jacoby	Member	September 15, 1953	February 9, 1955.
Walter W. Stewart	Member	December 2, 1953	April 29, 1955.
Raymond J. Saulnier	Member	April 4, 1955	
	Chairman	December 3, 1956	January 20, 1961.
Joseph S. Davis	Member	May 2, 1955	October 31, 1958.
Paul W. McCracken	Member	December 3, 1956	January 31, 1959.
Karl Brandt	Member	November 1, 1958	January 20, 1961.
Henry C. Wallich	Member	May 7, 1959	January 20, 1961.
Walter W. Heller	Chairman	January 29, 1961	November 15, 1964.
James Tobin	Member	January 29, 1961	July 31, 1962.
Kermit Gordon	Member	January 29, 1961	December 27, 1962.
Gardner Ackley	Member	August 3, 1962	
	Chairman	November 16, 1964	February 15, 1968.
John P. Lewis	Member	May 17, 1963	August 31, 1964.
Otto Eckstein	Member	September 2, 1964	February 1, 1966.
Arthur M. Okun	Member	November 16, 1964	
	Chairman	February 15, 1968	January 20, 1969.
James S. Duesenberry	Member	February 2, 1966	June 30, 1968.
Merton J. Peck	Member	February 15, 1968	January 20, 1969.
Warren L. Smith	Member	July 1, 1968	January 20, 1969.
Paul W. McCracken	Chairman	February 4, 1969	December 31, 1971.
Hendrik S. Houthakker	Member	February 4, 1969	July 15, 1971.
Herbert Stein	Member	February 4, 1969	
	Chairman	January 1, 1972	August 31, 1974.
Ezra Solomon	Member	September 9, 1971	March 26, 1973.
Marina v.N. Whitman	Member	March 13, 1972	August 15, 1973.
Gary L. Seevers	Member	July 23, 1973	April 15, 1975.
William J. Fellner	Member	October 31, 1973	February 25, 1975.
Alan Greenspan	Chairman	September 4, 1974	January 20, 1977.
Paul W. MacAvoy	Member	June 13, 1975	November 15, 1976.
Burton G. Malkiel	Member	July 22, 1975	January 20, 1977.
Charles L. Schultze	Chairman	January 22, 1977	January 20, 1981.
William D. Nordhaus	Member	March 18, 1977	February 4, 1979.
Lyle E. Gramley	Member	March 18, 1977	May 27, 1980.
George C. Eads	Member	June 6, 1979	January 20, 1981.
Stephen M. Goldfeld	Member	August 20, 1980	January 20, 1981.
Murray L. Weidenbaum	Chairman	February 27, 1981	August 25, 1982.
William A. Niskanen	Member	June 12, 1981	March 30, 1985.
Jerry L. Jordan	Member	July 14, 1981	July 31, 1982.
Martin Feldstein	Chairman	October 14, 1982	July 10, 1984.
William Poole	Member	December 10, 1982	January 20, 1985.
Beryl W. Sprinkel	Chairman	April 18, 1985	January 20, 1989.
Thomas Gale Moore	Member	July 1, 1985	May 1, 1989.
Michael L. Mussa	Member	August 18, 1986	September 19, 1988.
Michael J. Boskin	Chairman	February 2, 1989	January 12, 1993.
John B. Taylor	Member	June 9, 1989	August 2, 1991
Richard L. Schmalensee	Member	October 3, 1989	June 21, 1991
David F. Bradford	Member	November 13, 1991	January 20, 1993.
Paul Wonnacott	Member	November 13, 1991	January 20, 1993
Alan S. Blinder	Member	July 27, 1993	June 26, 1994.
Laura D'Andrea Tyson	Chair	February 5, 1993	
Joseph E. Stiglitz	Member	July 27, 1993	

Report to the President on the Activities of the Council of Economic Advisers During 1994

The Council of Economic Advisers was established by the Employment Act of 1946 to provide the President with objective economic analysis and advice on the development and implementation of a wide range of domestic and international economic policy issues.

The Chair of the Council

Laura D'Andrea Tyson continued to chair the Council during 1994. Dr. Tyson, a member of the President's Cabinet, is on leave from the University of California, Berkeley, where she is Professor of Economics and Business Administration. As Chair, Dr. Tyson is responsible for communicating the Council's views on economic developments directly to the President through personal discussions and written reports.

Dr. Tyson also represents the Council at Cabinet meetings and various other high-level meetings including those of the National Security Council focusing on economic issues, deliberations of the National Economic Council, daily White House senior staff meetings, budget team briefings with the President, and many other formal and informal sessions with the President, senior White House staff, and other senior government officials. Dr. Tyson is also the Council's chief public spokesperson. She guides the work of the Council and exercises ultimate responsibility for the work of the professional staff.

The Members of the Council

Joseph E. Stiglitz is the other current Member of the Council of Economic Advisers. Dr. Stiglitz is on leave from Stanford University where he is the Joan Kenney Professor of Economics. The Council's other Member, Alan S. Blinder, left the Council upon his appointment by the President to be Vice Chairman of the Board of Governors of the Federal Reserve System. The President has nominated Martin Neil Baily to succeed Dr. Blinder as a Member of the Council. Dr. Baily is on leave from the University of Maryland where he is Professor of Economics. He currently serves as Dr. Tyson's chief macroeconomic adviser while awaiting a confirmation hearing before the Senate Banking Committee. Members of the

Council are involved in the full range of issues within the Council's purview and are responsible for the daily supervision of the work of the professional staff. Members represent the Council at a wide variety of interagency and international meetings and assume major responsibility for selecting issues for the Council's attention.

The small size of the Council permits the Chair and Members to work as a team on most policy issues. There continues to be, however, an informal division of subject matter among the Members. Dr. Stiglitz is primarily responsible for microeconomic and sectoral analysis and regulatory issues. Member-nominee Baily is primarily responsible for domestic and international macroeconomic analysis and economic projections. All three Members, under Dr. Tyson's lead, are also heavily involved in international trade issues. Finally, all three Council Members participate in the deliberations of the National Economic Council (NEC). Dr. Tyson is one of six members of the NEC Principals Committee.

MACROECONOMIC POLICIES

One of the primary functions of the Council is to advise the President on all major macroeconomic issues throughout the year. The Council prepared for the President, the Vice President, and the White House senior staff a comprehensive series of memoranda monitoring key economic indicators and analyzing current macroeconomic events. During 1994 the Council also prepared special analyses of economic policy issues and briefing papers on extraordinary economic events, such as California's Northridge earthquake disaster in January and the Mexican financial situation later in the year. Council senior economists also prepared in-depth studies of potential output, structural budget deficits, and a regular monitor of inflationary trends.

The Council played a leading role in discussions of macroeconomic policy issues with officials from the Department of the Treasury, the Office of Management and Budget (OMB), and other members of the President's economic policy team, and was a key participant in the formulation of the Administration's economic policies through various Cabinet and sub-Cabinet working groups. As part of this effort, the Council provided an economic assessment of various policy initiatives that are under discussion in the Congress, including the proposed balanced budget amendment to the Constitution (see Chapter 1), dynamic scoring of the budget (see Chapter 2), and welfare reform (see Chapter 1). The Council also carefully monitored the response of the interest-sensitive sectors of the economy to the series of monetary tightening steps taken by the Federal Reserve beginning in February.

The Council, the Department of the Treasury, and the OMB—the economic "Troika"—are responsible for producing the economic forecasts that underlie the Administration's budget proposals. The

Council, under the leadership of Dr. Baily collaborating with Dr. Tyson and Council senior economists, initiates the forecasting process twice each year. The first forecast is published in the summer as part of the Administration's mid-session budget review. In preparing the forecasts the Council solicits input from a wide variety of sources, and leading private sector forecasters visited the Council before each of the forecasting rounds to give their views on current conditions and the economic outlook.

At Dr. Tyson's direction, the Council established the President's Economic Policy Advisory Board, comprised of distinguished academic and other private sector economists. Members of the Board are recognized scholars in the fields of international trade, macroeconomics, microeconomics, labor markets, and financial markets. The Board meets approximately every 6 months to advise the Council and other high-ranking members of the Administration's economic policy team on current policy issues.

The Council continued its ongoing efforts to improve the general public's understanding of economic issues through regular briefings with the White House financial and general press corps, periodic discussions with distinguished outside economists and forecasters, presentations before civic groups, and meetings with business and labor leaders and with representatives from foreign countries. The Chair and the other Members made numerous presentations to outside organizations to explain the Administration's economic agenda. Dr. Tyson, Dr. Stiglitz, Dr. Blinder, and Dr. Baily also regularly exchanged views on the macroeconomy with the Chairman and Members of the Board of Governors of the Federal Reserve System.

Finally, the Council continued to work to improve the quality of government economic statistics. On several occasions the Council met with experts from other government agencies in seminars on topics ranging from the scope of forthcoming revisions to the national income statistics to measuring unemployment. The Council also sought increased funding for economic and demographic statistics in deliberations over Federal budget priorities.

INTERNATIONAL ECONOMIC POLICIES

International economic issues occupied much of the efforts of the Council in 1994. Dr. Tyson and the other Members helped formulate Administration policies that brought the Uruguay Round negotiations of the General Agreement on Tariffs and Trade to completion and subsequent Congressional approval. The Council also provided analyses of the implications of the Uruguay Round agreements and the North American Free Trade Agreement for the U.S. economy.

The Council was intensely involved in the preparatory work for the Administration's major regional initiatives at the November Asia-Pacific Economic Cooperation (APEC) meeting in Bogor, Indonesia and the December Summit of the Americas in Miami, which Dr. Tyson attended. Dr. Tyson was actively involved in the negotiations under the U.S.-Japan Framework for a New Economic Partnership and in the ongoing examination of U.S. relations with China and its place in the world trading system.

The Council continued its active role in the Organization for Economic Cooperation and Development (OECD). The Council leads the U.S. delegation to the OECD's semiannual Economic Policy Committee meetings, and Dr. Tyson is the Committee's Chair. Dr. Baily was a member of the OECD's Working Party 3 on macroeconomic policy coordination. Dr. Stiglitz headed the U.S. delegation to OECD Working Party 1 on microeconomic and structural issues. Senior staff participated in Asia-Pacific experts' meetings in Sydney and Jakarta. The Council was also active in the preparations for the economic summit of the Group of Seven (G-7) nations in Naples which Dr. Tyson attended.

MICROECONOMIC POLICIES

The Council continued to participate actively in a broad range of Administration microeconomic initiatives in 1994. The breadth of this activity reflects the Administration's belief in the utility and significance of microeconomic policy.

Dr. Tyson and Dr. Stiglitz both served on the Administration's Welfare Reform Task Force, which developed the Work and Responsibility Act. Dr. Tyson also served on the Community Empowerment Board, the committee responsible for implementation of the empowerment zone and enterprise community provisions of the Omnibus Budget Reconciliation Act of 1993. Dr. Tyson was also a member of the Administration's Health Care Task Force, with particular responsibility for assessing the likely economic effects of various reform options. In addition, Dr. Tyson served as a member of the President's National Science and Technology Council (NSTC).

Dr. Stiglitz chaired the NSTC Subcommittee on Social and Economic Sciences Research under the NSTC Committee on Environment and Natural Resources, where he was a strong advocate for the application of research findings in economics and other social sciences to the policy development process. He is an active participant in the Intergovernmental Panel on Climate Change and is a lead author in its forthcoming report. Dr. Stiglitz has been particularly active in the Administration's environmental policymaking efforts. He also participated in an interagency working group formed to assess the condition of the oil and gas industry. In addition, Dr. Stiglitz served on the Administration's Natural Disaster Task Force, the Task Force on Floodplain Management, and the Earthquake Task Force.

Dr. Tyson and Dr. Stiglitz also played key roles in the Administration's reinventing government efforts, particularly with respect to the Departments of Energy, Transportation, and Housing and Urban Development. Dr. Stiglitz continued as co-chair of the subgroup on benefit-cost analysis of the Administration's Regulatory Working Group and co-chairs the working group on reviewing regulation of financial services. Dr. Tyson and Dr. Stiglitz have also been very active in the Administration's efforts to formulate policy in telecommunications; in June, Dr. Stiglitz supervised the preparation of a Council White Paper, titled "Economic Benefits of the Administration's Legislative Proposals for Telecommunications."

The Council has engaged in a number of efforts aimed at improving the Nation's agricultural and resource management policies. With the support of the Vice President's office, the Council and the Office of Science and Technology Policy initiated an interagency working group on bioenergy. This work included the evaluation of the prospective economic viability of bioenergy in future decades and strategies for research, development, and demonstration. The Council, primarily through Dr. Tyson and Dr. Stiglitz, has been a key participant in Administration deliberations on reauthorization of the farm bill.

WEEKLY ECONOMIC BRIEFINGS

Dr. Tyson continued to conduct an oral weekly economic briefing for the President, the Vice President, and the President's other principal economic advisers. The Council, in cooperation with the Office of the Vice President, prepares a written *Weekly Economic Briefing of the President*, which serves as the basis for the oral briefing. The briefing includes analyses of current economic developments, more extended treatments of a wide range of economic issues and problems, and summaries of news on different regions and sectors of the economy.

The Staff of the Council of Economic Advisers

The professional staff of the Council consists of the Chief of Staff, the Senior Statistician, thirteen senior economists, six staff economists, and two research assistants. The professional staff and their areas of concentration at the end of 1994 were:

Chief of Staff and General Counsel

Thomas P. O'Donnell

Senior Economists

Jonathan B. Baker	Regulation, Industrial Organization, and Law
S. Lael Brainard	International Economics
Robert S. Dohner	International Economics
Michael R. Donihue	Macroeconomics and Forecasting
Robert D. Innes	Agriculture
Sally M. Kane	Science and International Environmental Policy
David I. Levine	Labor, Welfare, and Education
Eileen Mauskopf	Macroeconomics and Finance
Mark J. Mazur	Public Finance
Ellen E. Meade	International Economics
Jay S. Stowsky	Science and Technology
Michael A. Toman	Environment and Natural Resources
David W. Wilcox	Macroeconomics and the *Weekly Economic Briefing of the President*

Senior Statistician

Catherine H. Furlong

Staff Economists

Kimberly A. Clausing	International Economics
Maya N. Federman	Labor, Education and Agriculture
Carolyn Fischer	Public Finance, Environment, and Natural Resources
Christopher L. Foote	Macroeconomics
F. Halsey Rogers	Macroeconomics and the *Weekly Economic Briefing of the President*
Eric D. Wolff	Industrial Organization, Regulation, and Technology

Senior Research Assistant

D. W. Clark Dees	International Economics and Macroeconomics

Research Assistant

Timothy S. Simcoe

Statistical Office

Mrs. Furlong manages the Statistical Office. The Statistical Office maintains and updates the Council's statistical information, oversees the publication of the *Economic Indicators* and the statistical appendix to the *Economic Report*, and verifies statistics in Presidential and Council memoranda, testimony, and speeches.

Susan P. Clements	Statistician

Linda A. Reilly .... Statistical Assistant
Brian A. Amorosi .... Research Assistant
Margaret L. Snyder .... Secretary

The Administrative Office

Elizabeth A. Kaminski .... Administrative Officer
Catherine Fibich .... Administrative Assistant

Office of the Chair

Alice H. Williams .... Executive Assistant to the Chair
Sandra F. Daigle .... Executive Assistant to the Chair and
                                 Assistant to the Chief of Staff
Lisa D. Branch .... Executive Assistant to Dr. Stiglitz
Francine P. Obermiller .... Executive Assistant to Dr. Baily

Staff Secretaries

Mary E. Jones
Rosalind V. Rasin
Mary A. Thomas

Mrs. Thomas also served as Executive Assistant for the *Weekly Economic Briefing of the President.*

Michael Treadway provided editorial assistance in the preparation of the 1995 *Economic Report.*

Robert E. Cumby, Georgetown University, and David M. Cutler, Harvard University, served as consultants during the year. Student interns during the year were Kristen E. Bowers, William P. Cowin, William B. Ferretti, James C. Hritz, Ethan D. Kaplan, Christina M. McCall, Michael G. Rand, Rachelle M. Rowe, Jesse Shapiro, Megan L. Shiflet, Adam R. Skilken, Nathan K. Sleeper, Megan R. Sweeney, Chi-Hwa Holly Tang, Anna R. Tryon, and Raymond A. Wolff.

DEPARTURES

The Council's senior economists, in most cases, are on leave of absence from faculty positions at academic institutions or from other government agencies or research institutions. Their tenure with the Council is usually limited to 1 or 2 years. Most of the senior economists who resigned during the year returned to their previous affiliations. They are David M. Cutler (Harvard University), Warren E. Farb (Department of Commerce), Alan J. Krupnick (Resources for the Future), Erik R. Lichtenberg (University of Maryland), Marcus Noland (Institute for International Economics), and Matthew D. Shapiro (University of Michigan). Those going on to new positions were Robert E. Cumby (Georgetown University), William T. Dickens (The Brookings Institution), Constance R. Dunham (Office of the Comptroller of the Currency), Pamela F. Short (The

Rand Corporation), and Robert F. Wescott (International Monetary Fund).

Staff economists are generally graduate students who spend 1 year with the Council and then return to complete their dissertations. Those who returned to their graduate studies in 1994 are Kevin C. Murdock (Stanford University), Jeremy B. Rudd (Princeton University), Elizabeth A. Schneirov (University of Wisconsin), and Darryl S. Wills (Massachusetts Institute of Technology) and Peter R. Orszag (London School of Economics). Kimberly J. O'Neill accepted a position with the National Economic Council/Domestic Policy Council.

Public Information

The Council's *Annual Report* is the principal medium through which the Council informs the public of its work and its views. It is an important vehicle for presenting the Administration's domestic and international economic policies. Annual distribution of the *Report* in recent years has averaged about 45,000 copies. The Council also has primary responsibility for compiling the monthly *Economic Indicators*, which is issued by the Joint Economic Committee of the Congress and has a distribution of approximately 10,000.

Appendix B
STATISTICAL TABLES RELATING TO INCOME, EMPLOYMENT, AND PRODUCTION

CONTENTS

NATIONAL INCOME OR EXPENDITURE:

271

General Notes

Detail in these tables may not add to totals because of rounding.
Unless otherwise noted, all dollar figures are in current dollars.
Symbols used:

    p Preliminary.

    .... Not available (also, not applicable).

Data in these tables reflect revisions made by the source agencies from January 1994 through early February 1995.

NATIONAL INCOME OR EXPENDITURE

TABLE B-1.—Gross domestic product, 1959–94

[Billions of dollars, except as noted; quarterly data at seasonally adjusted annual rates]

Year or quarter	Gross domestic product	Personal consumption expenditures				Gross private domestic investment							Change in business inventories
							Fixed investment						
								Nonresidential					
		Total	Durable goods	Non-durable goods	Services	Total	Total	Total	Structures	Producers' durable equipment	Residential		
1959	494.2	318.1	42.8	148.5	126.8	78.8	74.6	46.5	18.1	28.3	28.1		4.2
1960	513.3	332.4	43.5	153.1	135.9	78.7	75.5	49.2	19.6	29.7	26.3		3.2
1961	531.8	343.5	41.9	157.4	144.1	77.9	75.0	48.6	19.7	28.9	26.4		2.9
1962	571.6	364.4	47.0	163.8	153.6	87.9	81.8	52.8	20.8	32.1	29.0		6.1
1963	603.1	384.2	51.8	169.4	163.1	93.4	87.7	55.6	21.2	34.4	32.1		5.7
1964	648.0	412.5	56.8	179.7	175.9	101.7	96.7	62.4	23.7	38.7	34.3		5.0
1965	702.7	444.6	63.5	191.9	189.2	118.0	108.3	74.1	28.3	45.8	34.2		9.7
1966	769.8	481.6	68.5	208.5	204.6	130.4	116.7	84.4	31.3	53.0	32.3		13.8
1967	814.3	509.3	70.6	216.9	221.7	128.0	117.6	85.2	31.5	53.7	32.4		10.5
1968	889.3	559.1	81.0	235.0	243.1	139.9	130.8	92.1	33.6	58.5	38.7		9.1
1969	959.5	603.7	86.2	252.2	265.3	155.2	145.5	102.9	37.7	65.2	42.6		9.7
1970	1,010.7	646.5	85.3	270.4	290.8	150.3	148.1	106.7	40.3	66.4	41.4		2.3
1971	1,097.2	700.3	97.2	283.3	319.8	175.5	167.5	111.7	42.7	69.1	55.8		8.0
1972	1,207.0	767.8	110.7	305.2	351.9	205.6	195.7	126.1	47.2	78.9	69.7		9.9
1973	1,349.6	848.1	124.1	339.6	384.5	243.1	225.4	150.0	55.0	95.1	75.3		17.7
1974	1,458.6	927.7	123.0	380.8	423.9	245.8	231.5	165.6	61.2	104.3	66.0		14.3
1975	1,585.9	1,024.9	134.3	416.0	474.5	226.0	231.7	169.0	61.4	107.6	62.7		−5.7
1976	1,768.4	1,143.1	160.0	451.8	531.2	286.4	269.6	187.2	65.9	121.2	82.5		16.7
1977	1,974.1	1,271.5	182.6	490.4	598.4	358.3	333.5	223.2	74.6	148.7	110.3		24.7
1978	2,232.7	1,421.2	202.3	541.5	677.4	434.0	406.1	274.5	93.9	180.6	131.6		27.9
1979	2,488.6	1,583.7	214.2	613.3	756.2	480.2	467.5	326.4	118.4	208.1	141.0		12.8
1980	2,708.0	1,748.1	212.5	682.9	852.7	467.6	477.1	353.8	137.5	216.4	123.3		−9.5
1981	3,030.6	1,926.2	228.5	744.2	953.5	558.0	532.5	410.0	169.1	240.9	122.5		25.4
1982	3,149.6	2,059.2	236.5	772.3	1,050.4	503.4	519.3	413.7	178.8	234.9	105.7		−15.9
1983	3,405.0	2,257.5	275.0	817.8	1,164.7	546.7	552.2	400.2	153.1	247.1	152.0		−5.5
1984	3,777.2	2,460.3	317.9	873.0	1,269.4	718.9	647.8	468.9	175.6	293.3	178.9		71.1
1985	4,038.7	2,667.4	352.9	919.4	1,395.1	714.5	689.9	504.0	193.4	310.6	185.9		24.6
1986	4,268.6	2,850.6	389.6	952.2	1,508.8	717.6	709.0	492.4	174.0	318.4	216.5		8.6
1987	4,539.9	3,052.2	403.7	1,011.1	1,637.4	749.3	723.0	497.8	171.3	326.5	225.2		26.3
1988	4,900.4	3,296.1	437.1	1,073.8	1,785.2	793.6	777.4	545.4	182.0	363.4	232.0		16.2
1989	5,250.8	3,523.1	459.4	1,149.5	1,914.2	832.3	798.9	568.1	193.3	374.8	230.9		33.3
1990	5,546.1	3,761.2	468.2	1,229.2	2,063.8	808.9	802.0	586.7	201.6	385.1	215.3		6.9
1991	5,724.8	3,902.4	456.6	1,257.8	2,188.1	744.8	746.6	557.0	182.9	374.1	189.6		−1.8
1992	6,020.2	4,136.9	492.7	1,295.5	2,348.7	788.3	785.2	561.4	171.1	390.3	223.8		3.0
1993	6,343.3	4,378.2	538.0	1,339.2	2,501.0	882.0	866.7	616.1	173.4	442.7	250.6		15.4
1994 ᵖ	6,736.9	4,627.0	590.9	1,393.8	2,642.2	1,037.5	979.8	697.5	182.6	514.9	282.3		57.7
1982: IV	3,195.1	2,128.7	246.9	787.3	1,094.6	464.2	510.5	397.7	168.9	228.8	112.8		−46.3
1983: IV	3,547.3	2,346.8	297.7	839.8	1,209.3	614.8	594.6	426.9	154.6	272.3	167.7		20.2
1984: IV	3,869.1	2,526.4	328.2	887.8	1,310.4	722.8	671.8	491.5	184.1	307.3	180.4		51.0
1985: IV	4,140.5	2,739.8	354.4	939.5	1,446.0	737.0	704.4	511.3	195.4	315.9	193.1		32.6
1986: IV	4,336.6	2,923.1	406.8	963.7	1,552.6	697.1	715.9	491.7	168.4	323.3	224.2		−18.8
1987: IV	4,683.0	3,124.6	408.8	1,029.4	1,686.4	800.2	740.9	514.3	180.0	334.3	226.5		59.3
1988: IV	5,044.6	3,398.2	452.9	1,105.8	1,839.5	814.8	797.5	560.2	186.8	373.4	237.3		17.3
1989: IV	5,344.8	3,599.1	458.3	1,173.5	1,967.3	825.2	795.0	568.8	198.0	370.8	226.2		30.2
1990: IV	5,597.9	3,836.6	459.5	1,260.7	2,116.4	756.4	780.3	584.4	195.7	388.7	195.8		−23.9
1991: I	5,636.8	3,841.4	449.3	1,253.0	2,139.0	732.8	750.7	568.1	193.1	374.9	182.6		−17.9
II	5,705.9	3,885.7	452.0	1,259.6	2,174.1	733.1	746.0	561.6	188.4	373.2	184.4		−12.9
III	5,759.9	3,927.0	463.8	1,261.3	2,202.0	756.5	747.1	554.5	178.1	376.4	192.7		9.3
IV	5,796.6	3,955.7	461.2	1,257.2	2,237.3	756.8	742.4	543.7	172.0	371.7	198.7		14.3
1992: I	5,896.8	4,044.4	480.1	1,276.5	2,287.8	747.7	754.0	544.2	173.3	370.9	209.8		−6.3
II	5,971.3	4,097.8	483.3	1,281.7	2,332.8	787.9	784.0	562.0	172.9	389.2	222.0		3.9
III	6,043.6	4,154.0	495.7	1,299.6	2,358.6	795.5	790.2	565.8	169.6	396.2	224.4		5.3
IV	6,169.3	4,251.3	511.6	1,324.3	2,415.4	822.0	812.7	573.6	168.6	405.1	239.1		9.3
1993: I	6,235.9	4,294.6	516.1	1,327.1	2,451.4	853.8	833.7	589.8	170.6	419.2	243.9		20.1
II	6,299.9	4,347.3	531.2	1,334.2	2,481.9	869.7	851.1	609.3	172.3	437.0	241.8		18.6
III	6,359.2	4,401.2	541.9	1,340.2	2,519.1	882.2	868.3	619.0	173.9	445.1	249.3		13.9
IV	6,478.1	4,469.6	562.8	1,355.2	2,551.6	922.5	913.5	646.3	176.7	469.6	267.2		9.0
1994: I	6,574.7	4,535.0	576.2	1,368.9	2,589.9	966.6	942.5	665.4	172.7	492.7	277.1		24.1
II	6,689.9	4,586.4	580.3	1,381.4	2,624.7	1,034.4	967.0	683.3	181.8	501.5	283.6		67.4
III	6,791.7	4,657.5	591.5	1,406.1	2,659.9	1,055.1	992.5	709.1	184.6	524.5	283.4		62.6
IV ᵖ	6,891.1	4,728.9	615.6	1,418.9	2,694.5	1,093.9	1,017.1	732.0	191.3	540.8	285.1		76.8

See next page for continuation of table.

[Billions of dollars, except as noted; quarterly data at seasonally adjusted annual rates]

Year or quarter	Net exports of goods and services			Government purchases					Final sales of domestic product	Gross domestic purchases [1]	Addendum: Gross national product [2]	Percent change from preceding period	
	Net exports	Exports	Imports	Total	Federal			State and local				Gross domestic product	Gross domestic purchases [1]
					Total	National defense	Non-defense						
1959........	−1.7	20.6	22.3	99.0	57.1	46.4	10.8	41.8	490.0	495.8	497.0	8.7	9.1
1960........	2.4	25.3	22.8	99.8	55.3	45.3	10.0	44.5	510.1	510.9	516.6	3.9	3.0
1961........	3.4	26.0	22.7	107.0	58.6	47.9	10.6	48.4	528.9	528.4	535.4	3.6	3.4
1962........	2.4	27.4	25.0	116.8	65.4	52.1	13.3	51.4	565.5	569.1	575.8	7.5	7.7
1963........	3.3	29.4	26.1	122.3	66.4	51.5	14.9	55.8	597.5	599.8	607.7	5.5	5.4
1964........	5.5	33.6	28.1	128.3	67.5	50.4	17.0	60.9	643.0	642.5	653.0	7.4	7.1
1965........	3.9	35.4	31.5	136.3	69.5	51.0	18.5	66.8	693.0	698.8	708.1	8.4	8.8
1966........	1.9	38.9	37.1	155.9	81.3	62.0	19.3	74.6	756.0	767.9	774.9	9.5	9.9
1967........	1.4	41.4	39.9	175.6	92.8	73.4	19.4	82.7	803.8	812.9	819.8	5.8	5.9
1968........	−1.3	45.3	46.6	191.5	99.2	79.1	20.0	92.3	880.2	890.6	895.5	9.2	9.6
1969........	−1.2	49.3	50.5	201.8	100.5	78.9	21.6	101.3	949.8	960.7	965.6	7.9	7.9
1970........	1.2	57.0	55.8	212.7	100.1	76.8	23.3	112.6	1,008.4	1,009.5	1,017.1	5.3	5.1
1971........	−3.0	59.3	62.3	224.3	100.0	74.1	25.9	124.3	1,089.2	1,100.2	1,104.9	8.6	9.0
1972........	−8.0	66.2	74.2	241.5	106.9	77.4	29.4	134.7	1,197.1	1,215.0	1,215.7	10.0	10.4
1973........	.6	91.8	91.2	257.7	108.5	77.5	31.1	149.2	1,331.9	1,349.0	1,362.3	11.8	11.0
1974........	−3.1	124.3	127.5	288.3	117.6	82.6	35.0	170.7	1,444.4	1,461.8	1,474.3	8.1	8.4
1975........	13.6	136.3	122.7	321.4	129.4	89.6	39.8	192.0	1,591.5	1,572.3	1,599.1	8.7	7.6
1976........	−2.3	148.9	151.1	341.3	135.8	93.4	42.4	205.5	1,751.7	1,770.7	1,785.5	11.5	12.6
1977........	−23.7	158.8	182.4	368.0	147.9	100.9	47.0	220.1	1,949.4	1,997.8	1,994.6	11.6	12.8
1978........	−26.1	186.1	212.3	403.6	162.2	108.9	53.3	241.4	2,204.8	2,258.8	2,254.5	13.1	13.1
1979........	−23.8	228.9	252.7	448.5	179.3	121.9	57.5	269.2	2,475.9	2,512.5	2,520.8	11.5	11.2
1980........	−14.7	279.2	293.9	507.1	209.1	142.7	66.4	298.0	2,717.5	2,722.8	2,742.1	8.8	8.4
1981........	−14.7	303.0	317.7	561.1	240.8	167.5	73.3	320.3	3,005.2	3,045.3	3,063.8	11.9	11.8
1982........	−20.6	282.6	303.2	607.6	266.6	193.8	72.7	341.1	3,165.5	3,170.2	3,179.8	3.9	4.1
1983........	−51.4	276.7	328.1	652.3	292.0	214.4	77.5	360.3	3,410.6	3,456.5	3,434.4	8.1	9.0
1984........	−102.7	302.4	405.1	700.8	310.9	233.1	77.8	389.9	3,706.1	3,879.9	3,801.5	10.9	12.2
1985........	−115.6	302.1	417.6	772.3	344.3	258.6	85.7	428.1	4,014.1	4,154.3	4,053.6	6.9	7.1
1986........	−132.5	319.2	451.7	833.0	367.8	276.7	91.1	465.3	4,260.0	4,401.2	4,277.7	5.7	5.9
1987........	−143.1	364.0	507.1	881.5	384.9	292.1	92.9	496.6	4,513.7	4,683.0	4,544.5	6.4	6.4
1988........	−108.0	444.2	552.2	918.7	387.0	295.6	91.4	531.7	4,884.2	5,008.4	4,908.2	7.9	6.9
1989........	−79.7	508.0	587.7	975.2	401.6	299.9	101.7	573.6	5,217.5	5,330.5	5,266.8	7.2	6.4
1990........	−71.4	557.1	628.5	1,047.4	426.5	314.0	112.5	620.9	5,539.3	5,617.5	5,567.8	5.6	5.4
1991........	−19.9	601.1	620.9	1,097.4	445.8	322.8	123.1	651.6	5,726.6	5,744.7	5,740.8	3.2	2.3
1992........	−30.3	638.1	668.4	1,125.3	449.0	314.2	134.8	676.3	6,017.2	6,050.5	6,025.8	5.2	5.3
1993........	−65.3	659.1	724.3	1,148.4	443.6	302.7	140.9	704.7	6,327.9	6,408.6	6,347.8	5.4	5.9
1994 ᴾ.....	−102.1	716.1	818.2	1,174.5	436.6	292.1	144.5	737.9	6,679.1	6,838.9		6.2	6.7
1982: IV....	−29.5	265.6	295.1	631.6	281.4	205.5	75.9	350.3	3,241.4	3,224.6	3,222.6	....	....
1983: IV....	−71.8	286.2	358.0	657.6	289.7	222.8	66.9	367.9	3,527.1	3,619.1	3,578.4	....	....
1984: IV....	−107.1	308.7	415.7	727.0	324.7	242.9	81.9	402.2	3,818.1	3,976.2	3,890.2	....	....
1985: IV....	−135.5	304.7	440.2	799.2	356.9	268.6	88.3	442.4	4,107.9	4,276.0	4,156.2	....	....
1986: IV....	−133.2	333.9	467.1	849.7	373.1	278.6	94.5	476.6	4,355.4	4,469.8	4,340.5	....	....
1987: IV....	−143.2	392.4	535.6	901.4	392.5	295.8	96.7	509.0	4,623.7	4,826.2	4,690.5	....	....
1988: IV....	−106.0	467.0	573.1	937.6	392.0	296.8	95.2	545.7	5,027.3	5,150.7	5,054.3	....	....
1989: IV....	−73.9	523.8	597.7	994.5	405.1	302.5	102.6	589.3	5,314.6	5,418.7	5,365.0	....	....
1990: IV....	−71.6	577.6	649.2	1,076.5	436.5	322.5	114.0	640.0	5,621.8	5,669.5	5,630.0	....	....
1991: I.....	−32.9	576.6	609.4	1,095.5	451.7	331.8	119.9	643.8	5,654.7	5,669.6	5,664.0	2.8	.0
II.....	−11.6	602.1	613.8	1,098.7	450.1	326.6	123.5	648.6	5,718.8	5,717.5	5,719.0	5.0	3.4
III....	−21.2	601.9	623.1	1,097.6	443.2	320.9	122.3	654.4	5,750.6	5,781.1	5,769.3	3.8	4.5
IV....	−13.7	623.7	637.5	1,097.9	438.3	311.6	126.6	659.7	5,782.3	5,810.4	5,810.7	2.6	2.0
1992: I.....	−9.9	631.8	641.7	1,114.5	445.2	312.2	133.0	669.3	5,903.1	5,906.6	5,907.7	7.1	6.8
II.....	−31.2	632.7	663.9	1,116.8	443.2	310.0	133.2	673.6	5,967.4	6,002.6	5,979.1	5.2	6.7
III....	−37.8	638.8	676.6	1,131.9	452.9	318.6	134.2	679.1	6,038.3	6,081.4	6,049.4	4.9	5.4
IV....	−42.2	649.2	691.4	1,138.1	454.8	316.0	138.7	683.3	6,160.0	6,211.4	6,167.0	8.6	8.8
1993: I.....	−49.6	646.8	696.4	1,137.1	446.9	307.0	139.9	690.2	6,215.8	6,285.5	6,243.9	4.4	4.9
II.....	−63.3	660.1	723.5	1,146.3	445.2	305.8	139.4	701.2	6,281.4	6,363.3	6,303.3	4.2	5.0
III....	−77.0	649.0	726.0	1,152.9	442.7	299.0	143.6	710.2	6,345.4	6,436.3	6,367.8	3.8	4.7
IV....	−71.2	680.3	751.4	1,157.2	439.8	299.1	140.7	717.4	6,469.2	6,549.3	6,476.2	7.7	7.2
1994: I.....	−86.7	674.2	760.9	1,159.8	437.8	291.7	146.1	722.0	6,550.6	6,661.4	6,574.0	6.1	7.0
II.....	−97.6	704.5	802.1	1,166.7	435.1	291.7	143.5	731.5	6,622.5	6,787.5	6,682.5	7.2	7.8
III....	−109.6	730.5	840.1	1,188.8	444.3	300.5	143.8	744.5	6,729.1	6,901.3	6,779.6	6.2	6.9
IV ᴾ....	−114.3	755.3	869.6	1,182.6	429.2	284.4	144.8	753.4	6,814.3	7,005.5		6.0	6.2

[1] Gross domestic product (GDP) less exports of goods and services plus imports of goods and services.
[2] GDP plus net receipts of factor income from rest of the world.

Source: Department of Commerce, Bureau of Economic Analysis.

TABLE B-2.—*Gross domestic product in 1987 dollars, 1959-94*

[Billions of 1987 dollars, except as noted; quarterly data at seasonally adjusted annual rates]

Year or quarter	Gross domestic product	Personal consumption expenditures				Gross private domestic investment						
						Total	Fixed investment					Change in business inventories
							Total	Nonresidential			Residential	
		Total	Durable goods	Nondurable goods	Services			Total	Structures	Producers' durable equipment		
1959	1,928.8	1,178.9	114.4	518.5	546.0	296.4	282.8	165.2	74.4	90.8	117.6	13.6
1960	1,970.8	1,210.8	115.4	526.9	568.5	290.8	282.7	173.3	80.8	92.5	109.4	8.1
1961	2,023.8	1,238.4	109.4	537.7	591.3	289.4	282.2	172.1	82.3	89.8	110.1	7.2
1962	2,128.1	1,293.3	120.2	553.0	620.0	321.2	305.6	185.0	86.1	98.9	120.6	15.6
1963	2,215.6	1,341.9	130.3	563.6	648.0	343.3	327.3	192.3	86.9	105.4	135.0	16.0
1964	2,340.6	1,417.2	140.7	588.2	688.3	371.8	356.2	214.0	95.9	118.1	142.1	15.7
1965	2,470.5	1,497.0	156.2	616.7	724.1	413.0	387.9	250.6	111.5	139.1	137.3	25.1
1966	2,616.2	1,573.8	166.0	647.6	760.2	438.0	401.3	276.7	119.1	157.6	124.5	36.7
1967	2,685.2	1,622.4	167.2	659.0	796.2	418.6	391.0	270.8	116.0	154.8	120.2	27.6
1968	2,796.9	1,707.5	184.5	686.0	837.0	440.1	416.5	280.1	117.4	162.7	136.4	23.6
1969	2,873.0	1,771.2	190.8	703.2	877.2	461.3	436.5	296.4	123.5	172.9	140.1	24.8
1970	2,873.9	1,813.5	183.7	717.2	912.5	429.7	423.8	292.0	123.3	168.7	131.8	5.9
1971	2,955.9	1,873.7	201.4	725.6	946.7	475.7	454.9	286.8	121.2	165.6	168.1	20.8
1972	3,107.1	1,978.4	225.2	755.8	997.4	532.2	509.6	311.6	124.8	186.8	198.0	22.5
1973	3,268.6	2,066.7	246.6	777.9	1,042.2	591.7	554.0	357.4	134.9	222.4	196.6	37.7
1974	3,248.1	2,053.8	227.2	759.8	1,066.8	543.0	512.0	356.5	132.3	224.2	155.6	30.9
1975	3,221.7	2,097.5	226.8	767.1	1,103.6	437.6	451.5	316.8	118.0	198.8	134.7	-13.9
1976	3,380.8	2,207.3	256.4	801.3	1,149.5	520.6	495.1	328.7	120.5	208.2	166.4	25.5
1977	3,533.3	2,296.6	280.0	819.8	1,196.8	600.4	566.2	364.3	126.1	238.2	201.9	34.3
1978	3,703.5	2,391.8	292.9	844.8	1,254.1	664.6	627.4	412.9	144.1	268.8	214.5	37.2
1979	3,796.8	2,448.4	289.0	862.8	1,296.5	669.7	656.1	448.8	163.3	285.5	207.4	13.6
1980	3,776.3	2,447.1	262.7	860.5	1,323.9	594.4	602.7	437.8	170.2	267.6	164.8	-8.3
1981	3,843.1	2,476.9	264.6	867.9	1,344.4	631.1	606.5	455.0	182.9	272.0	151.6	24.6
1982	3,760.3	2,503.7	262.5	872.2	1,368.9	540.5	558.0	433.9	181.3	252.6	124.1	-17.5
1983	3,906.6	2,619.4	297.7	900.3	1,421.4	599.5	595.1	420.8	160.3	260.5	174.2	4.4
1984	4,148.5	2,746.1	338.5	934.6	1,473.0	757.5	689.6	490.2	182.8	307.4	199.3	67.9
1985	4,279.8	2,865.8	370.1	958.7	1,537.0	745.9	723.8	521.8	197.4	324.4	202.0	22.1
1986	4,404.5	2,969.1	402.0	991.0	1,576.1	735.1	726.5	500.3	176.6	323.7	226.2	8.5
1987	4,539.9	3,052.2	403.7	1,011.1	1,637.4	749.3	723.0	497.8	171.3	326.5	225.2	26.3
1988	4,718.6	3,162.4	428.7	1,035.1	1,698.5	773.4	753.4	530.8	174.0	356.8	222.7	19.9
1989	4,838.0	3,223.3	440.7	1,051.6	1,731.0	784.0	754.2	540.0	177.6	362.5	214.2	29.8
1990	4,897.3	3,272.6	443.1	1,060.7	1,768.8	746.8	741.1	546.5	179.5	367.0	194.5	5.7
1991	4,867.6	3,259.4	425.3	1,047.7	1,786.3	683.8	684.9	515.4	160.6	354.9	169.5	-1.1
1992	4,979.3	3,349.5	452.6	1,057.7	1,839.1	725.3	722.9	525.9	149.8	376.2	196.9	2.5
1993	5,134.5	3,458.7	489.9	1,078.5	1,890.3	819.9	804.6	591.6	147.7	443.9	213.0	15.3
1994 ᴾ	5,342.3	3,578.5	531.5	1,109.3	1,937.8	955.5	903.1	672.4	150.4	522.0	230.6	52.4
1982: IV	3,759.6	2,539.3	272.3	880.7	1,386.2	503.5	548.4	417.2	173.2	244.0	131.2	-44.9
1983: IV	4,012.1	2,678.2	319.1	915.2	1,443.9	669.5	640.2	449.6	162.6	287.0	190.6	29.3
1984: IV	4,194.2	2,784.8	347.7	942.9	1,494.2	756.4	708.4	509.6	189.5	320.1	198.8	47.9
1985: IV	4,333.5	2,895.3	369.6	968.7	1,557.1	763.1	732.9	525.5	198.3	327.2	207.4	30.2
1986: IV	4,427.1	3,012.5	415.7	1,000.9	1,595.8	705.9	725.9	495.5	170.4	325.0	230.5	-20.1
1987: IV	4,625.5	3,074.7	404.7	1,014.6	1,655.5	793.8	733.9	510.6	177.9	332.7	223.3	59.9
1988: IV	4,779.7	3,202.9	439.2	1,046.8	1,716.9	785.0	764.1	538.8	175.7	363.1	225.3	20.9
1989: IV	4,856.7	3,242.0	436.8	1,058.9	1,746.3	769.5	744.6	536.7	179.8	356.9	208.0	24.9
1990: IV	4,867.2	3,265.9	433.2	1,057.5	1,775.2	695.7	716.6	540.2	172.8	367.4	176.3	-20.9
1991: I	4,842.0	3,242.9	420.6	1,049.5	1,772.8	670.0	686.4	522.2	169.8	352.5	164.2	-16.4
II	4,867.9	3,259.5	421.9	1,051.7	1,785.9	671.5	683.4	518.3	165.3	353.0	165.1	-11.9
III	4,879.9	3,269.8	431.3	1,049.3	1,789.2	696.0	685.6	514.4	155.8	358.6	171.2	10.4
IV	4,880.8	3,265.3	427.7	1,040.4	1,797.3	697.9	684.4	506.9	151.4	355.5	177.5	13.5
1992: I	4,918.5	3,311.4	443.4	1,051.1	1,817.0	687.2	693.5	506.8	152.5	354.3	186.7	-6.3
II	4,947.5	3,325.4	443.8	1,049.3	1,832.3	725.5	721.3	524.8	151.9	372.9	196.5	4.2
III	4,990.5	3,357.6	454.5	1,056.4	1,846.7	733.3	728.1	531.2	148.4	382.8	196.9	5.2
IV	5,060.7	3,403.4	468.8	1,074.2	1,860.4	755.2	748.6	540.9	146.3	394.6	207.7	6.6
1993: I	5,075.3	3,417.2	472.5	1,070.0	1,874.8	789.2	770.7	560.3	147.2	413.0	210.4	18.5
II	5,105.4	3,439.2	483.7	1,074.3	1,881.2	806.2	787.3	581.0	147.3	433.7	206.3	18.9
III	5,139.4	3,472.2	492.7	1,081.7	1,897.8	821.8	808.8	597.9	147.5	450.3	211.0	13.0
IV	5,218.0	3,506.2	510.8	1,088.0	1,907.4	862.5	851.7	627.2	148.7	478.5	224.5	10.8
1994: I	5,261.1	3,546.3	521.7	1,098.3	1,926.3	898.9	873.4	643.6	144.1	499.4	229.9	25.4
II	5,314.1	3,557.8	522.2	1,104.3	1,931.4	950.9	891.7	657.9	151.0	506.9	233.8	59.2
III	5,367.0	3,584.7	529.6	1,113.4	1,941.8	967.3	910.2	680.0	151.6	528.4	230.2	57.1
IV ᴾ	5,426.8	3,625.1	552.4	1,121.1	1,951.7	1,004.9	936.9	708.2	154.9	553.3	228.7	68.0

See next page for continuation of table.

[Billions of 1987 dollars, except as noted; quarterly data at seasonally adjusted annual rates]

Year or quarter	Net exports of goods and services			Government purchases					Final sales of domestic product	Gross domestic purchases [1]	Addendum: Gross national product [2]	Percent change from preceding period	
	Net exports	Exports	Imports	Total	Federal			State and local				Gross domestic product	Gross domestic purchases [1]
					Total	National defense	Nondefense						
1959	−21.8	73.8	95.6	475.3	265.7			209.6	1,915.2	1,950.6	1,939.6	5.5	5.8
1960	−7.6	88.4	96.1	476.9	259.0			217.9	1,962.7	1,978.5	1,982.8	2.2	1.4
1961	−5.5	89.9	95.3	501.5	270.1			231.4	2,016.6	2,029.3	2,037.1	2.7	2.6
1962	−10.5	95.0	105.5	524.2	287.3			236.9	2,112.5	2,138.6	2,143.3	5.2	5.4
1963	−5.8	101.8	107.7	536.3	285.7			250.6	2,199.6	2,221.4	2,231.8	4.1	3.9
1964	2.5	115.4	112.9	549.1	281.8			267.3	2,324.9	2,338.1	2,358.1	5.6	5.3
1965	−6.4	118.1	124.5	566.9	282.1			284.8	2,445.4	2,476.9	2,488.9	5.5	5.9
1966	−18.0	125.7	143.7	622.4	319.3			303.1	2,579.5	2,634.2	2,633.2	5.9	6.4
1967	−23.7	130.0	153.7	667.9	350.9			317.0	2,657.5	2,708.9	2,702.6	2.6	2.8
1968	−37.5	140.2	177.7	686.8	353.1			333.7	2,773.2	2,834.4	2,815.6	4.2	4.6
1969	−41.5	147.8	189.2	682.0	340.1			341.9	2,848.2	2,914.5	2,890.9	2.7	2.8
1970	−35.2	161.3	196.4	665.8	315.0			350.9	2,868.0	2,909.1	2,891.5	.0	−.2
1971	−45.9	161.9	207.8	652.4	290.8			361.6	2,935.2	3,001.8	2,975.9	2.9	3.2
1972	−56.5	173.7	230.2	653.0	284.4	209.6	74.8	368.6	3,084.5	3,163.6	3,128.8	5.1	5.4
1973	−34.1	210.3	244.4	642.2	265.3	191.3	74.1	378.9	3,230.9	3,302.7	3,298.6	5.2	4.4
1974	−4.1	234.4	238.4	655.4	262.6	185.8	76.8	392.9	3,217.2	3,252.2	3,282.4	−.6	−1.5
1975	23.1	232.9	209.8	663.5	262.7	184.9	77.8	400.8	3,235.6	3,198.6	3,247.6	−.8	−1.6
1976	−6.4	243.4	249.7	659.2	258.2	179.9	78.3	401.1	3,355.3	3,387.1	3,412.2	4.9	5.9
1977	−27.8	246.9	274.7	664.1	263.1	181.6	81.4	401.0	3,499.0	3,561.1	3,569.0	4.5	5.1
1978	−29.9	270.2	300.1	677.0	268.6	182.1	86.5	408.4	3,666.3	3,733.3	3,739.0	4.8	4.8
1979	−10.6	293.5	304.1	689.3	271.7	185.1	86.6	417.6	3,783.2	3,807.4	3,845.3	2.5	2.0
1980	30.7	320.5	289.9	704.2	284.8	194.2	90.6	419.4	3,784.6	3,745.7	3,823.4	−.5	−1.6
1981	22.0	326.1	304.1	713.2	295.8	206.4	89.4	417.4	3,818.6	3,821.2	3,884.4	1.8	2.0
1982	−7.4	296.7	304.1	723.6	306.0	221.4	84.7	417.6	3,777.8	3,767.7	3,796.1	−2.2	−1.4
1983	−56.1	285.9	342.1	743.8	320.8	234.2	86.6	423.0	3,902.2	3,962.8	3,939.6	3.9	5.2
1984	−122.0	305.7	427.7	766.9	331.0	245.8	85.1	436.0	4,080.6	4,270.5	4,174.5	6.2	7.8
1985	−145.3	309.2	454.6	813.4	355.2	265.6	89.5	458.2	4,257.6	4,425.1	4,295.0	3.2	3.6
1986	−155.1	329.6	484.7	855.4	373.0	280.6	92.4	482.4	4,395.9	4,559.6	4,413.5	2.9	3.0
1987	−143.1	364.0	507.1	881.5	384.9	292.1	92.9	496.6	4,513.7	4,683.0	4,544.5	3.1	2.7
1988	−104.0	421.6	525.7	886.8	377.3	287.0	90.2	509.6	4,698.6	4,822.5	4,726.3	3.9	3.0
1989	−73.7	471.8	545.4	904.4	376.1	281.4	94.8	528.3	4,808.3	4,911.7	4,852.7	2.5	1.8
1990	−54.7	510.5	565.1	932.6	384.1	283.6	100.4	548.5	4,891.6	4,951.9	4,916.5	1.2	.8
1991	−19.5	542.6	562.1	944.0	386.7	281.4	105.3	557.2	4,868.7	4,887.2	4,882.3	−.6	−1.3
1992	−32.3	578.8	611.2	936.9	373.5	261.4	112.2	563.3	4,976.9	5,011.6	4,985.7	2.3	2.5
1993	−73.9	602.5	676.3	929.8	356.6	243.7	113.0	573.1	5,119.3	5,208.4	5,140.3	3.1	3.9
1994 ᵖ	−114.2	654.8	769.0	922.5	337.3	226.5	110.7	585.2	5,289.8	5,456.5		4.0	4.8
1982: IV	−19.0	280.4	299.4	735.9	316.0	229.4	86.6	419.9	3,804.5	3,778.6	3,791.7		
1983: IV	−83.7	291.5	375.1	748.1	322.2	242.9	79.3	425.9	3,982.8	4,095.8	4,046.6		
1984: IV	−131.4	312.8	444.2	784.3	341.7	254.4	87.4	442.6	4,146.2	4,325.5	4,216.4		
1985: IV	−155.4	312.0	467.4	830.5	363.7	272.1	91.6	466.7	4,303.3	4,488.9	4,349.5		
1986: IV	−156.0	342.9	498.9	864.8	377.5	282.2	95.3	487.3	4,447.2	4,583.1	4,430.8		
1987: IV	−136.0	386.1	522.1	893.0	391.6	295.0	96.6	501.4	4,565.6	4,761.5	4,633.0		
1988: IV	−102.7	438.2	540.9	894.5	378.4	285.7	92.7	516.1	4,758.7	4,882.4	4,789.0		
1989: IV	−67.4	487.7	555.0	912.6	376.1	281.5	94.7	536.5	4,831.8	4,924.1	4,875.1		
1990: IV	−36.8	520.4	557.2	942.4	386.5	285.7	100.8	555.8	4,888.0	4,904.0	4,895.4		
1991: I	−20.4	519.0	539.4	949.5	395.2	292.1	103.1	554.3	4,858.4	4,862.4	4,866.1	−2.1	−3.4
II	−13.8	544.0	557.8	950.6	394.1	288.5	105.7	556.5	4,879.8	4,881.7	4,880.0	2.2	1.6
III	−27.1	544.8	571.8	941.3	383.6	279.3	104.3	557.7	4,869.5	4,907.0	4,889.1	1.0	2.1
IV	−16.9	562.6	579.4	934.4	374.1	265.8	108.2	560.4	4,867.3	4,897.6	4,893.9	.1	−.8
1992: I	−17.9	571.0	588.8	937.8	372.9	260.9	112.0	564.9	4,924.8	4,936.4	4,929.1	3.1	3.2
II	−34.1	573.1	607.1	930.7	368.3	257.5	110.8	562.4	4,943.2	4,981.5	4,955.5	2.4	3.7
III	−38.9	580.5	619.4	938.5	376.0	264.6	111.4	562.5	4,985.3	5,029.4	4,997.2	3.5	3.9
IV	−38.5	590.7	629.3	940.6	377.0	262.4	114.6	563.6	5,054.1	5,099.2	5,061.0	5.7	5.7
1993: I	−57.6	589.2	646.8	926.5	361.6	248.2	113.3	564.9	5,056.8	5,132.9	5,083.9	1.2	2.7
II	−69.3	600.2	669.6	929.3	358.3	246.8	111.5	571.0	5,086.5	5,174.7	5,110.1	2.4	3.3
III	−86.3	595.3	681.6	931.8	355.6	240.9	114.7	576.2	5,126.5	5,225.8	5,148.4	2.7	4.0
IV	−82.2	625.2	707.4	931.5	351.1	238.7	112.4	580.4	5,207.2	5,300.2	5,218.7	6.3	5.8
1994: I	−104.0	619.6	723.6	919.9	341.7	228.5	113.2	578.3	5,235.7	5,365.1	5,267.7	3.3	5.0
II	−111.8	643.9	755.6	917.1	334.7	226.1	108.7	582.4	5,254.9	5,425.8	5,310.5	4.1	4.6
III	−117.0	666.5	783.5	932.0	343.5	233.0	110.5	588.5	5,310.0	5,484.0	5,359.9	4.0	4.4
IV ᵖ	−124.1	689.0	813.1	920.9	329.2	218.6	110.6	591.8	5,358.8	5,550.9		4.5	5.0

[1] Gross domestic product (GDP) less exports of goods and services plus imports of goods and services.
[2] GDP plus net receipts of factor income from rest of the world.

Source: Department of Commerce, Bureau of Economic Analysis.

TABLE B–3.—*Implicit price deflators for gross domestic product, 1959–94*

[Index numbers, 1987=100, except as noted; quarterly data seasonally adjusted]

Year or quarter	Gross domestic product	Personal consumption expenditures				Gross private domestic investment: Fixed investment				
		Total	Durable goods	Non-durable goods	Services	Total	Nonresidential			Resi-dential
							Total	Struc-tures	Pro-ducers' durable equip-ment	
1959	25.6	27.0	37.4	28.6	23.2	26.4	28.1	24.4	31.2	23.9
1960	26.0	27.5	37.7	29.1	23.9	26.7	28.4	24.2	32.1	24.0
1961	26.3	27.7	38.3	29.3	24.4	26.6	28.2	24.0	32.2	24.0
1962	26.9	28.2	39.1	29.6	24.8	26.8	28.6	24.1	32.4	24.0
1963	27.2	28.6	39.7	30.1	25.2	26.8	28.9	24.4	32.6	23.8
1964	27.7	29.1	40.4	30.5	25.6	27.1	29.2	24.7	32.8	24.1
1965	28.4	29.7	40.6	31.1	26.1	27.9	29.6	25.4	32.9	24.9
1966	29.4	30.6	41.3	32.2	26.9	29.1	30.5	26.3	33.6	25.9
1967	30.3	31.4	42.3	32.9	27.8	30.1	31.5	27.2	34.7	26.9
1968	31.8	32.7	43.9	34.3	29.0	31.4	32.9	28.6	36.0	28.4
1969	33.4	34.1	45.2	35.9	30.2	33.3	34.7	30.5	37.7	30.4
1970	35.2	35.6	46.4	37.7	31.9	34.9	36.5	32.7	39.4	31.4
1971	37.1	37.4	48.3	39.0	33.8	36.8	39.0	35.2	41.7	33.2
1972	38.8	38.8	49.2	40.4	35.3	38.4	40.5	37.8	42.2	35.2
1973	41.3	41.0	50.3	43.7	36.9	40.7	42.0	40.7	42.7	38.3
1974	44.9	45.2	54.1	50.1	39.7	45.2	46.4	46.3	46.5	42.4
1975	49.2	48.9	59.2	54.2	43.0	51.3	53.3	52.0	54.1	46.6
1976	52.3	51.8	62.4	56.4	46.2	54.5	56.9	54.7	58.2	49.6
1977	55.9	55.4	65.2	59.8	50.0	58.9	61.3	59.2	62.4	54.6
1978	60.3	59.4	69.1	64.1	54.0	64.7	66.5	65.2	67.2	61.3
1979	65.5	64.7	74.1	71.1	58.3	71.2	72.7	72.5	72.9	68.0
1980	71.7	71.4	80.9	79.4	64.4	79.2	80.8	80.8	80.9	74.8
1981	78.9	77.8	86.4	85.7	70.9	87.8	90.1	92.5	88.5	80.9
1982	83.8	82.2	90.1	88.6	76.7	93.1	95.3	98.6	93.0	85.2
1983	87.2	86.2	92.4	90.8	81.9	92.8	95.1	95.5	94.8	87.3
1984	91.0	89.6	93.9	93.4	86.2	93.9	95.7	96.1	95.4	89.7
1985	94.4	93.1	95.4	95.9	90.8	95.3	96.6	98.0	95.7	92.0
1986	96.9	96.0	96.9	96.1	95.7	97.6	98.4	98.5	98.4	95.8
1987	100.0	100.0	100.0	100.0	100.0	100.0	100.0	100.0	100.0	100.0
1988	103.9	104.2	102.0	103.7	105.1	103.2	102.8	104.6	101.9	104.2
1989	108.5	109.3	104.2	109.3	110.6	105.9	105.2	108.9	103.4	107.8
1990	113.3	114.9	105.7	115.9	116.7	108.2	107.3	112.3	104.9	110.7
1991	117.6	119.7	107.3	120.0	122.5	109.0	108.1	113.9	105.4	111.9
1992	120.9	123.5	108.9	122.5	127.7	108.6	106.7	114.2	103.8	113.7
1993	123.5	126.6	109.8	124.2	132.3	107.7	104.1	117.4	99.7	117.6
1994 ᴾ	126.1	129.3	111.2	125.7	136.4	108.5	103.7	121.4	98.6	122.4
1982: IV	85.0	83.8	90.6	89.4	79.0	93.1	95.3	97.5	93.8	86.0
1983: IV	88.4	87.6	93.3	91.8	83.7	92.9	95.0	95.1	94.9	88.0
1984: IV	92.3	90.7	94.4	94.2	87.7	94.8	96.4	97.2	96.0	90.7
1985: IV	95.5	94.6	95.9	97.0	92.9	96.1	97.3	98.5	96.5	93.1
1986: IV	98.0	97.0	97.8	96.3	97.3	98.6	99.2	98.8	99.5	97.3
1987: IV	101.2	101.6	101.0	101.5	101.9	101.0	100.7	101.2	100.5	101.5
1988: IV	105.5	106.1	103.1	105.6	107.1	104.4	104.0	106.3	102.8	105.3
1989: IV	110.1	111.0	104.9	110.8	112.7	106.8	106.0	110.1	103.9	108.8
1990: IV	115.0	117.5	106.1	119.2	119.2	108.9	108.2	113.3	105.8	111.1
1991: I	116.4	118.5	106.8	119.4	120.7	109.4	108.8	113.8	106.4	111.2
II	117.2	119.7	107.1	119.8	121.7	109.2	108.4	114.0	105.7	111.7
III	118.0	120.1	107.5	120.2	123.1	109.0	107.8	114.3	105.0	112.5
IV	118.8	121.1	107.8	120.8	124.5	108.5	107.3	113.6	104.6	111.9
1992: I	119.9	122.1	108.3	121.4	125.9	108.7	107.4	113.7	104.7	112.4
II	120.7	123.2	108.9	122.1	127.3	108.7	107.1	113.8	104.4	113.0
III	121.1	123.7	109.1	123.0	127.7	108.5	106.5	114.3	103.5	114.0
IV	121.9	124.9	109.1	123.3	129.8	108.6	106.0	115.2	102.6	115.1
1993: I	122.9	125.7	109.2	124.0	130.8	108.2	105.3	115.9	101.5	115.9
II	123.4	126.4	109.8	124.2	131.9	108.1	104.9	116.9	100.8	117.2
III	123.7	126.8	110.0	123.9	132.7	107.4	103.5	117.9	98.8	118.2
IV	124.1	127.5	110.2	124.6	133.8	107.3	103.0	118.8	98.1	119.0
1994: I	125.0	127.9	110.5	124.6	134.4	107.9	103.4	119.8	98.7	120.5
II	125.9	128.9	111.1	125.1	135.9	108.4	103.9	120.4	98.9	121.3
III	126.5	129.9	111.7	126.3	137.0	109.0	104.3	121.8	99.2	123.1
IV ᴾ	127.0	130.4	111.4	126.6	138.1	108.6	103.4	123.5	97.7	124.7

See next page for continuation of table.

TABLE B-3.—*Implicit price deflators for gross domestic product, 1959–94*—Continued

[Index numbers, 1987=100, except as noted; quarterly data seasonally adjusted]

| Year or quarter | Exports and imports of goods and services | | Government purchases | | | | | Final sales of domestic product | Gross domestic purchases [1] | Percent change, GDP implicit price deflator [2] |
	Exports	Imports	Total	Federal Total	National defense	Non-defense	State and local			
1959	28.0	23.4	20.8	21.5			19.9	25.6	25.4	2.8
1960	28.6	23.8	20.9	21.3			20.4	26.0	25.8	1.6
1961	29.0	23.8	21.3	21.7			20.9	26.2	26.0	1.2
1962	28.9	23.7	22.3	22.8			21.7	26.8	26.6	2.3
1963	28.9	24.3	22.8	23.3			22.3	27.2	27.0	1.1
1964	29.1	24.9	23.4	23.9			22.8	27.7	27.5	1.8
1965	30.0	25.3	24.0	24.6			23.5	28.3	28.2	2.5
1966	31.0	25.8	25.0	25.5			24.6	29.3	29.2	3.5
1967	31.8	26.0	26.3	26.5			26.1	30.2	30.0	3.1
1968	32.3	26.2	27.9	28.1			27.7	31.7	31.4	5.0
1969	33.3	26.7	29.6	29.6			29.6	33.3	33.0	5.0
1970	35.3	28.4	31.9	31.8			32.1	35.2	34.7	5.4
1971	36.6	30.0	34.4	34.4			34.4	37.1	36.7	5.4
1972	38.1	32.2	37.0	37.6	36.9	39.3	36.5	38.8	38.4	4.6
1973	43.6	37.3	40.0	40.9	40.5	41.9	39.4	41.2	40.8	6.4
1974	53.0	53.5	44.0	44.8	44.5	45.5	43.5	44.9	44.9	8.7
1975	58.5	58.5	48.4	49.3	48.5	51.2	47.9	49.2	49.2	9.6
1976	61.2	60.5	51.8	52.6	51.9	54.1	51.2	52.2	52.3	6.3
1977	64.3	66.4	55.4	56.2	55.6	57.7	54.9	55.7	56.1	6.9
1978	68.9	70.7	59.6	60.4	59.8	61.7	59.1	60.1	60.5	7.9
1979	78.0	83.1	65.1	66.0	65.8	66.4	64.5	65.4	66.0	8.6
1980	87.1	101.4	72.0	73.4	73.5	73.3	71.1	71.8	72.7	9.5
1981	92.9	104.5	78.7	81.4	81.1	82.1	76.7	78.7	79.7	10.0
1982	95.2	99.7	84.0	87.1	87.6	85.9	81.7	83.8	84.1	6.2
1983	96.8	95.9	87.7	91.0	91.6	89.5	85.2	87.4	87.2	4.1
1984	98.9	94.7	91.4	93.9	94.8	91.3	89.4	90.8	90.9	4.4
1985	97.7	91.9	95.0	96.9	97.3	95.7	93.4	94.3	93.9	3.7
1986	96.9	93.2	97.4	98.6	98.6	98.6	96.4	96.9	96.5	2.6
1987	100.0	100.0	100.0	100.0	100.0	100.0	100.0	100.0	100.0	3.2
1988	105.3	105.1	103.6	102.6	103.0	101.4	104.3	103.9	103.9	3.9
1989	107.7	107.8	107.8	106.8	106.6	107.3	108.6	108.5	108.5	4.4
1990	109.1	111.2	112.3	111.0	110.7	112.0	113.2	113.2	113.4	4.4
1991	110.8	110.5	116.3	115.3	114.7	116.9	116.9	117.6	117.5	3.8
1992	110.2	109.4	120.1	120.2	120.2	120.2	120.1	120.9	120.7	2.8
1993	109.4	107.1	123.5	124.4	124.2	124.7	123.0	123.6	123.0	2.2
1994 P	109.4	106.4	127.3	129.4	128.9	130.5	126.1	126.3	125.3	2.1
1982: IV	94.7	98.5	85.8	89.0	89.6	87.7	83.4	85.2	85.3	
1983: IV	98.2	95.4	87.9	89.9	91.7	84.3	86.4	88.6	88.4	
1984: IV	98.7	93.6	92.7	95.0	95.5	93.7	90.9	92.1	91.9	
1985: IV	97.7	94.2	96.2	98.1	98.7	96.4	94.8	95.5	95.3	
1986: IV	97.4	93.6	98.3	98.8	98.7	99.2	97.8	97.9	97.5	
1987: IV	101.6	102.6	100.9	100.2	100.3	100.1	101.5	101.3	101.4	
1988: IV	106.6	106.0	104.8	103.6	103.9	102.6	105.7	105.6	105.5	
1989: IV	107.4	107.7	109.0	107.7	107.5	108.4	109.9	110.0	110.0	
1990: IV	111.0	116.5	114.2	112.9	112.9	113.1	115.2	115.0	115.6	
1991: I	111.1	113.0	115.4	114.3	113.6	116.4	116.1	116.4	116.6	5.0
II	110.7	110.0	115.6	114.2	113.2	116.9	116.5	117.2	117.1	2.8
III	110.5	109.0	116.6	115.5	114.9	117.3	117.3	118.1	117.8	2.8
IV	110.9	110.0	117.5	117.2	117.2	117.0	117.7	118.8	118.6	2.7
1992: I	110.7	109.0	118.9	119.4	119.7	118.8	118.5	119.9	119.7	3.8
II	110.4	109.4	120.0	120.4	120.4	120.3	119.8	120.7	120.5	2.7
III	110.0	109.2	120.6	120.4	120.4	120.5	120.7	121.1	120.9	1.3
IV	109.9	109.9	121.0	120.6	120.4	121.1	121.2	121.9	121.8	2.7
1993: I	109.8	107.7	122.7	123.6	123.7	123.5	122.2	122.9	122.5	3.3
II	110.0	108.1	123.4	124.2	123.9	125.0	122.8	123.5	123.0	1.6
III	109.0	106.5	123.7	124.5	124.1	125.2	123.3	123.8	123.2	1.0
IV	108.8	106.2	124.2	125.3	125.3	125.1	123.6	124.2	123.6	1.3
1994: I	108.8	105.2	126.1	128.1	127.7	129.1	124.9	125.1	124.2	2.9
II	109.4	106.1	127.2	130.0	129.0	132.0	125.6	126.0	125.1	2.9
III	109.6	107.2	127.6	129.3	129.0	130.1	126.5	126.7	125.8	1.9
IV P	109.6	106.9	128.4	130.4	130.1	130.9	127.3	127.2	126.2	1.6

[1] Gross domestic product (GDP) less exports of goods and services plus imports of goods and services.
[2] Percent change from preceding period; quarterly changes are at annual rates.

Note.—Separate deflators are not calculated for gross private domestic investment, change in business inventories, and net exports of goods and services.

Source: Department of Commerce, Bureau of Economic Analysis.

TABLE B–4.—*Fixed-weighted price indexes for gross domestic product, 1987 weights, 1959–94*

[Index numbers, 1987 = 100, except as noted; quarterly data seasonally adjusted]

Year or quarter	Gross domestic product	Personal consumption expenditures				Gross private domestic investment: Fixed investment				
		Total	Durable goods	Non-durable goods	Services	Total	Nonresidential			Resi-dential
							Total	Struc-tures	Pro-ducers' durable equip-ment	
1959	....	30.4	54.4	31.4	23.9	....	....	24.1	....	25.0
1960	....	30.8	54.1	31.8	24.5	....	....	24.1	....	25.1
1961	....	31.1	53.8	32.0	25.0	....	....	24.0	....	25.1
1962	....	31.3	53.4	32.1	25.3	....	....	24.2	....	25.0
1963	....	31.6	53.1	32.5	25.7	....	....	24.5	....	24.7
1964	....	31.9	53.1	32.8	26.1	....	....	24.9	....	24.9
1965	....	32.2	52.1	33.3	26.7	....	....	25.6	....	25.5
1966	....	32.8	51.3	34.3	27.4	....	....	26.6	....	26.4
1967	....	33.7	51.8	35.1	28.3	....	....	27.5	....	27.2
1968	....	35.0	53.1	36.5	29.6	....	....	28.8	....	28.6
1969	....	36.3	54.2	38.1	30.7	....	....	30.7	....	30.6
1970	....	37.9	55.1	39.9	32.4	....	....	32.8	....	31.7
1971	....	39.5	56.7	41.1	34.3	....	....	35.2	....	33.5
1972	....	40.8	57.1	42.4	35.9	....	....	37.9	....	35.5
1973	....	42.7	57.8	45.3	37.4	....	....	40.8	....	38.6
1974	....	46.7	61.0	51.3	40.3	....	....	46.3	....	42.7
1975	....	50.5	66.0	55.3	43.7	....	....	51.5	....	46.7
1976	....	53.3	69.1	57.5	46.9	....	....	53.7	....	49.7
1977	....	56.7	71.7	60.8	50.5	....	....	57.8	....	54.7
1978	....	60.7	75.2	64.7	54.6	....	....	63.7	....	61.4
1979	....	65.8	80.0	71.3	59.0	....	....	71.3	....	68.2
1980	....	72.6	84.7	79.6	65.3	....	....	78.5	....	75.3
1981	....	78.9	89.5	86.0	71.9	....	....	87.3	....	81.3
1982	84.8	83.2	92.4	88.8	77.4	95.6	100.3	92.9	104.2	85.3
1983	88.1	86.7	93.7	91.1	82.4	94.8	98.3	92.5	101.3	87.3
1984	91.1	89.9	94.9	93.7	86.4	94.7	96.8	94.1	98.3	89.8
1985	94.3	93.3	96.0	96.2	90.9	95.7	97.3	96.9	97.5	92.1
1986	97.0	96.1	97.1	96.1	95.8	97.9	98.8	98.5	99.0	95.8
1987	100.0	100.0	100.0	100.0	100.0	100.0	100.0	100.0	100.0	100.0
1988	104.0	104.3	102.0	103.8	105.1	103.3	102.8	104.6	101.9	104.3
1989	108.6	109.5	104.5	109.5	110.7	106.3	105.6	109.0	103.9	107.8
1990	113.6	115.2	106.3	116.2	116.8	109.1	108.4	112.4	106.2	110.7
1991	118.1	120.3	109.1	120.5	123.0	110.8	110.2	113.9	108.3	111.9
1992	121.9	124.6	111.6	123.0	128.7	112.0	111.2	114.1	109.7	113.6
1993	125.5	128.1	113.9	125.0	133.5	114.4	113.0	117.3	110.7	117.4
1994 *P*	128.9	131.2	117.0	126.6	137.6	117.5	115.5	121.2	112.5	122.1
1982: IV	86.3	84.7	92.6	89.7	79.6	95.4	99.6	93.5	102.8	86.2
1983: IV	89.3	88.2	94.5	92.0	84.2	94.6	97.6	92.4	100.3	88.0
1984: IV	92.3	91.0	95.2	94.4	87.9	95.1	97.0	95.3	97.9	90.8
1985: IV	95.5	94.8	96.3	97.2	92.9	96.4	97.9	97.8	97.9	93.1
1986: IV	98.0	97.1	97.9	96.3	97.3	98.8	99.5	99.0	99.8	97.3
1987: IV	101.3	101.6	101.0	101.5	101.9	101.0	100.7	101.2	100.5	101.5
1988: IV	105.6	106.2	103.3	105.7	107.2	104.5	104.0	106.2	102.9	105.4
1989: IV	110.2	111.2	105.2	111.0	112.8	107.3	106.6	110.3	104.7	108.8
1990: IV	115.3	117.9	106.9	119.7	119.5	110.0	109.4	113.3	107.4	111.1
1991: I	116.8	118.9	108.1	119.8	121.1	110.5	110.2	113.7	108.3	111.3
II	117.7	119.8	108.7	120.3	122.2	110.6	110.1	113.9	108.1	111.7
III	118.6	120.8	109.6	120.6	123.6	111.0	110.3	114.3	108.2	112.6
IV	119.4	121.8	110.0	121.3	125.1	110.9	110.4	113.5	108.7	112.1
1992: I	120.5	122.9	110.7	121.9	126.6	111.3	110.8	113.6	109.3	112.4
II	121.5	124.1	111.5	122.6	128.1	111.6	111.0	113.7	109.6	113.0
III	122.3	125.2	111.9	123.6	129.4	112.2	111.5	114.2	110.0	113.9
IV	123.2	126.1	112.3	124.0	130.8	112.7	111.6	115.1	109.8	115.1
1993: I	124.4	127.0	112.7	124.7	131.9	113.3	112.2	115.8	110.3	115.7
II	125.2	127.8	113.7	125.0	133.1	114.1	112.8	116.9	110.7	116.9
III	125.8	128.3	114.3	124.7	133.9	114.7	113.3	117.8	110.9	118.0
IV	126.6	129.1	115.0	125.4	135.0	115.3	113.7	118.8	111.1	118.8
1994: I	127.5	129.8	115.5	125.4	135.9	116.2	114.4	119.7	111.7	120.2
II	128.5	130.7	116.7	125.9	137.0	117.0	115.2	120.3	112.5	121.0
III	129.4	131.8	117.8	127.3	138.1	118.1	116.0	121.7	113.0	122.8
IV *P*	130.3	132.6	118.1	127.7	139.2	118.9	116.4	123.3	112.8	124.5

See next page for continuation of table.

[Index numbers, 1987=100, except as noted; quarterly data seasonally adjusted]

Year or quarter	Exports and imports of goods and services		Government purchases					Final sales of domestic product	Gross domestic purchases [1]	Percent change, GDP fixed-weighted price index [2]
	Exports	Imports	Total	Federal			State and local			
				Total	National defense	Non-defense				
1959			24.6	28.6			21.5			
1960			25.1	29.0			22.1			
1961			25.5	29.3			22.5			
1962			26.3	30.0			23.4			
1963			26.8	30.6			23.8			
1964			27.3	31.3			24.2			
1965			27.9	32.0			24.8			
1966			29.0	32.8			26.0			
1967			30.2	33.9			27.4			
1968			31.8	35.6			28.9			
1969			33.7	37.4			30.8			
1970			36.2	40.2			33.1			
1971			38.6	42.9			35.3			
1972			41.1	46.0	46.2	45.2	37.3			
1973			43.7	48.4	49.0	46.4	40.1			
1974			46.9	50.2	51.2	47.4	44.3			
1975			51.4	54.6	55.1	52.9	48.9			
1976			54.4	57.3	57.8	55.8	52.1			
1977			57.7	60.4	60.7	59.4	55.7			
1978			61.7	64.1	64.5	62.8	59.9			
1979			66.8	68.9	69.6	66.6	65.1			
1980			73.3	75.2	76.3	71.9	71.9			
1981			79.6	82.3	83.3	79.1	77.6			
1982	100.4	101.2	85.0	88.5	89.7	84.7	82.3	84.9	85.4	
1983	99.7	97.7	88.5	92.2	93.5	88.4	85.5	88.2	88.3	3.9
1984	99.9	96.8	92.2	95.6	96.9	91.4	89.6	91.2	91.0	3.4
1985	98.2	94.6	95.4	97.9	98.8	94.9	93.5	94.4	94.0	3.5
1986	97.3	93.8	97.6	99.0	99.5	97.5	96.5	97.0	96.6	2.8
1987	100.0	100.0	100.0	100.0	100.0	100.0	100.0	100.0	100.0	3.1
1988	105.7	105.4	103.7	102.8	103.1	102.0	104.3	104.0	104.0	4.0
1989	108.2	108.5	107.9	107.0	107.1	106.7	108.6	108.6	108.6	4.5
1990	110.0	112.4	112.6	111.8	112.1	110.8	113.2	113.6	113.7	4.6
1991	112.6	113.8	116.8	116.5	116.5	116.6	117.0	118.2	118.1	4.0
1992	113.9	115.4	120.8	121.5	122.0	119.8	120.3	122.0	121.8	3.2
1993	115.3	115.2	124.5	126.1	126.6	124.3	123.4	125.6	125.2	3.0
1994ᵖ	118.1	117.2	128.6	131.1	131.5	129.9	126.6	129.0	128.5	2.7
1982: IV	99.4	99.4	86.7	90.4	91.4	87.1	83.8	86.3	86.7	
1983: IV	100.3	97.3	89.3	92.7	93.9	88.7	86.7	89.4	89.3	
1984: IV	99.3	96.0	93.9	97.7	99.3	92.6	91.1	92.3	92.1	
1985: IV	97.9	96.0	96.9	99.4	100.5	95.9	94.9	95.6	95.4	
1986: IV	97.6	93.7	98.3	99.0	99.3	98.3	97.8	98.0	97.6	
1987: IV	101.7	102.8	101.0	100.2	100.3	100.1	101.5	101.3	101.4	
1988: IV	107.0	106.5	104.8	103.7	103.9	102.9	105.8	105.7	105.6	
1989: IV	108.1	108.6	109.1	108.2	108.3	107.8	109.9	110.2	110.2	
1990: IV	111.9	118.3	114.4	113.5	114.0	112.0	115.1	115.4	115.9	
1991: I	112.6	115.5	115.8	115.4	115.3	115.8	116.1	116.9	117.0	5.1
II	112.3	113.0	116.2	115.7	115.5	116.5	116.6	117.8	117.6	3.1
III	112.3	112.6	117.1	116.7	116.7	116.8	117.4	118.7	118.5	3.3
IV	113.0	114.1	118.0	118.3	118.7	117.1	117.8	119.5	119.3	2.7
1992: I	113.2	113.9	119.5	120.5	121.0	118.8	118.7	120.6	120.4	3.9
II	113.8	114.8	120.5	121.3	121.9	119.5	120.0	121.6	121.4	3.3
III	114.1	116.7	121.4	122.0	122.6	120.2	121.0	122.4	122.4	2.7
IV	114.3	116.4	121.8	122.2	122.7	120.9	121.5	123.3	123.1	2.8
1993: I	114.7	114.7	123.5	125.0	125.6	123.0	122.4	124.5	124.1	4.2
II	115.3	115.9	124.3	125.7	126.0	124.7	123.2	125.3	124.9	2.4
III	115.4	115.0	124.9	126.5	127.0	125.1	123.7	125.9	125.4	2.0
IV	115.6	115.3	125.4	127.0	127.9	124.4	124.1	126.7	126.2	2.4
1994: I	116.7	114.5	126.7	128.5	129.0	127.2	125.3	127.7	127.0	3.1
II	117.5	116.2	128.3	130.9	131.1	130.5	126.2	128.6	128.0	2.9
III	118.4	118.5	129.2	131.9	132.5	130.1	127.1	129.5	129.1	3.0
IVᵖ	119.8	119.4	130.1	133.0	133.3	131.8	127.9	130.4	129.9	2.6

[1] Gross domestic product (GDP) less exports of goods and services plus imports of goods and services.
[2] Percent change from preceding period; quarterly changes are at annual rates.

Note.—Separate price indexes are not calculated for gross private domestic investment, change in business inventories, and net exports of goods and services.

Source: Department of Commerce, Bureau of Economic Analysis.

TABLE B-5.—*Fixed-weighted and alternative quantity and price indexes for total GDP, 1959–94*

[Index numbers, 1987 = 100; quarterly data seasonally adjusted]

Year or quarter		Gross domestic product						
	Current dollars	Quantity indexes			Price indexes			Implicit price deflator
		Fixed 1987 weights	Chain-type annual weights	Benchmark years weights	Fixed 1987 weights	Chain-type annual weights	Benchmark years weights	
1959	10.9	42.5	39.2	38.8		27.8	28.0	25.6
1960	11.3	43.4	40.1	39.7		28.2	28.4	26.0
1961	11.7	44.6	41.0	40.7		28.5	28.8	26.3
1962	12.6	46.9	43.5	43.2		28.9	29.1	26.9
1963	13.3	48.8	45.4	45.1		29.3	29.5	27.2
1964	14.3	51.6	48.1	47.8		29.7	29.9	27.7
1965	15.5	54.4	51.2	50.8		30.2	30.4	28.4
1966	17.0	57.6	54.5	54.1		31.1	31.3	29.4
1967	17.9	59.1	55.9	55.5		32.1	32.3	30.3
1968	19.6	61.6	58.5	58.0		33.5	33.7	31.8
1969	21.1	63.3	60.3	59.8		35.1	35.2	33.4
1970	22.3	63.3	60.3	59.8		36.9	37.1	35.2
1971	24.2	65.1	62.3	61.8		38.8	39.0	37.1
1972	26.6	68.4	65.7	65.3		40.5	40.7	38.8
1973	29.7	72.0	69.6	69.1		42.7	43.0	41.3
1974	32.1	71.5	69.2	68.7		46.5	46.7	44.9
1975	34.9	71.0	68.7	68.1		50.9	51.1	49.2
1976	39.0	74.5	72.4	71.8		53.8	54.1	52.3
1977	43.5	77.8	76.0	75.5		57.3	57.6	55.9
1978	49.2	81.6	79.9	79.4		61.5	61.4	60.3
1979	54.8	83.6	82.2	81.7		66.7	66.6	65.5
1980	59.6	83.2	82.0	81.7		72.7	72.7	71.7
1981	66.8	84.7	84.0	83.9		79.4	79.3	78.9
1982	69.4	82.8	82.2	82.3	84.8	84.4	84.3	83.8
1983	75.0	86.0	85.3	85.5	88.1	87.9	87.7	87.2
1984	83.2	91.4	91.3	91.2	91.1	91.1	90.9	91.0
1985	89.0	94.3	94.3	94.2	94.3	94.4	94.2	94.4
1986	94.0	97.0	97.0	96.9	97.0	97.0	96.9	96.9
1987	100.0	100.0	100.0	100.0	100.0	100.0	100.0	100.0
1988	107.9	103.9	103.9	103.8	104.0	103.9	103.9	103.9
1989	115.7	106.6	106.6	106.4	108.6	108.5	108.5	108.5
1990	122.2	107.9	107.9	107.7	113.6	113.2	113.3	113.3
1991	126.1	107.2	107.2	106.9	118.1	117.7	117.8	117.6
1992	132.6	109.7	109.4	109.3	121.9	121.2	121.4	120.9
1993	139.7	113.1	112.2	112.0	125.5	124.6	124.8	123.5
1994 ᴾ	148.4	117.7	116.1	116.0	128.9	127.9	128.1	126.1
1989: I	113.4	106.1	106.1	105.9	106.9	106.9	106.8	106.9
II	115.2	106.6	106.6	106.4	108.2	108.1	108.0	108.1
III	116.3	106.6	106.6	106.4	109.2	109.0	109.0	109.1
IV	117.7	107.0	107.0	106.8	110.2	110.0	110.0	110.1
1990: I	120.3	107.9	108.0	107.7	111.7	111.5	111.5	111.5
II	122.0	108.3	108.4	108.1	112.9	112.7	112.7	112.7
III	123.0	108.1	108.1	107.9	114.3	113.9	114.0	113.8
IV	123.3	107.2	107.3	107.0	115.3	114.9	115.0	115.0
1991: I	124.2	106.7	106.7	106.4	116.8	116.4	116.5	116.4
II	125.7	107.2	107.2	106.9	117.7	117.3	117.4	117.2
III	126.9	107.5	107.4	107.2	118.6	118.2	118.3	118.0
IV	127.7	107.5	107.4	107.2	119.4	118.9	119.0	118.8
1992: I	129.9	108.3	108.2	108.0	120.5	120.0	120.2	119.9
II	131.5	109.0	108.8	108.6	121.5	120.9	121.1	120.7
III	133.1	109.9	109.6	109.5	122.3	121.6	121.8	121.1
IV	135.9	111.5	111.0	110.9	123.2	122.4	122.6	121.9
1993: I	137.4	111.8	111.2	111.0	124.4	123.6	123.8	122.9
II	138.8	112.5	111.7	111.5	125.2	124.3	124.5	123.4
III	140.1	113.2	112.2	112.0	125.8	124.9	125.1	123.7
IV	142.7	114.9	113.6	113.4	126.6	125.6	125.8	124.1
1994: I	144.8	115.9	114.5	114.3	127.5	126.6	126.8	125.0
II	147.4	117.1	115.6	115.5	128.5	127.5	127.7	125.9
III	149.6	118.2	116.7	116.5	129.4	128.4	128.5	126.5
IV ᴾ	151.8	119.5	117.7	117.6	130.3	129.1	129.3	127.0

Note.—For information on these series see *Survey of Current Business,* April 1992 and March 1993.

Source: Department of Commerce, Bureau of Economic Analysis.

TABLE B-6.—*Changes in fixed-weighted and alternative quantity and price indexes for total GDP.*
1959–94

[Percent change from preceding period; quarterly data at seasonally adjusted annual rates]

Year or quarter	Current dollars	Gross domestic product						Implicit price deflator
		Quantity indexes			Price indexes			
		Fixed 1987 weights[1]	Chain-type annual weights	Benchmark years weights	Fixed 1987 weights	Chain-type annual weights	Benchmark years weights	
1959	8.7	5.5						2.8
1960	3.9	2.2	2.3	2.3		1.5	1.4	1.6
1961	3.6	2.7	2.4	2.3		1.2	1.1	1.2
1962	7.5	5.2	6.1	6.2		1.3	1.3	2.3
1963	5.5	4.1	4.3	4.4		1.2	1.2	1.1
1964	7.4	5.6	5.9	5.9		1.4	1.3	1.8
1965	8.4	5.5	6.4	6.3		1.9	1.9	2.5
1966	9.5	5.9	6.5	6.5		2.8	2.9	3.5
1967	5.8	2.6	2.6	2.7		3.2	3.2	3.1
1968	9.2	4.2	4.6	4.5		4.4	4.3	5.0
1969	7.9	2.7	3.1	3.0		4.7	4.7	5.0
1970	5.3	0	−.1	0		5.3	5.3	5.4
1971	8.6	2.9	3.4	3.4		5.0	5.0	5.4
1972	10.0	5.1	5.5	5.7		4.3	4.5	4.6
1973	11.8	5.2	5.9	5.8		5.6	5.5	6.4
1974	8.1	−.6	−.6	−.6		8.8	8.6	8.7
1975	8.7	−.8	−.7	−.9		9.4	9.4	9.6
1976	11.5	4.9	5.3	5.5		5.8	5.9	6.3
1977	11.6	4.5	4.9	5.2		6.4	6.5	6.9
1978	13.1	4.8	5.2	5.2		7.5	6.6	7.9
1979	11.5	2.5	2.8	2.9		8.4	8.4	8.6
1980	8.8	−.5	−.2	0		9.0	9.2	9.5
1981	11.9	1.8	2.5	2.7		9.2	9.1	10.0
1982	3.9	−2.2	−2.2	−1.9		6.3	6.4	6.2
1983	8.1	3.9	3.8	3.9	3.9	4.1	4.1	4.1
1984	10.9	6.2	7.0	6.7	3.4	3.6	3.6	4.4
1985	6.9	3.2	3.2	3.3	3.5	3.6	3.6	3.7
1986	5.7	2.9	2.9	2.9	2.8	2.7	2.9	2.6
1987	6.4	3.1	3.1	3.2	3.1	3.1	3.2	3.2
1988	7.9	3.9	3.9	3.8	4.0	3.9	3.9	3.9
1989	7.2	2.5	2.6	2.5	4.5	4.4	4.4	4.4
1990	5.6	1.2	1.2	1.2	4.6	4.4	4.4	4.4
1991	3.2	−.6	−.7	−.7	4.0	3.9	4.0	3.8
1992	5.2	2.3	2.1	2.2	3.2	3.0	3.1	2.8
1993	5.4	3.1	2.5	2.5	3.0	2.8	2.8	2.2
1994 *P*	6.2	4.0	3.5	3.5	2.7	2.7	2.7	2.1
1989: I	8.6	3.2	3.4	3.1	5.0	5.0	4.9	5.4
II	6.3	1.8	1.7	1.7	4.8	4.6	4.6	4.6
III	3.8	0	0	.1	3.8	3.6	3.7	3.8
IV	5.1	1.5	1.5	1.5	3.7	3.5	3.6	3.7
1990: I	9.1	3.5	3.5	3.5	5.8	5.6	5.5	5.2
II	5.9	1.5	1.5	1.6	4.4	4.4	4.5	4.4
III	3.1	−.9	−.8	−.9	4.7	4.4	4.6	4.0
IV	1.0	−3.2	−3.0	−3.1	3.8	3.7	3.7	4.3
1991: I	2.8	−2.1	−2.3	−2.3	5.1	5.2	5.1	5.0
II	5.0	2.2	1.7	2.0	3.1	3.2	3.2	2.8
III	3.8	1.0	.8	.9	3.3	3.1	3.1	2.8
IV	2.6	.1	.2	.1	2.7	2.5	2.6	2.7
1992: I	7.1	3.1	3.0	3.1	3.9	3.8	3.9	3.8
II	5.2	2.4	2.2	2.2	3.3	3.1	3.2	2.7
III	4.9	3.5	3.1	3.3	2.7	2.3	2.4	1.3
IV	8.6	5.7	5.2	5.1	2.8	2.5	2.5	2.7
1993: I	4.4	1.2	.5	.5	4.2	4.0	4.0	3.3
II	4.2	2.4	1.8	1.8	2.4	2.3	2.3	1.6
III	3.8	2.7	1.8	1.8	2.0	1.9	1.9	1.0
IV	7.7	6.3	5.1	5.1	2.4	2.5	2.4	1.3
1994: I	6.1	3.3	3.2	3.2	3.1	3.2	3.2	2.9
II	7.2	4.1	4.2	4.1	2.9	2.7	2.7	2.9
III	6.2	4.0	3.6	3.6	3.0	2.8	2.7	1.9
IV *P*	6.0	4.5	3.6	3.7	2.6	2.5	2.5	1.6

[1] Percent change in GDP in 1987 dollars.

Source: Department of Commerce, Bureau of Economic Analysis.

TABLE B–7.—*Gross domestic product by major type of product, 1959–94*

[Billions of dollars; quarterly data at seasonally adjusted annual rates]

Year or quarter	Gross domestic product	Final sales of domestic product	Change in business inventories	Goods [1] Total — Total	Goods Total — Final sales	Goods Total — Change in business inventories	Durable goods — Final sales	Durable goods — Change in business inventories	Nondurable goods — Final sales	Nondurable goods — Change in business inventories	Services [1]	Structures	Auto output
1959	494.2	490.0	4.2	250.8	246.6	4.2	91.1	3.1	155.5	1.1	181.7	61.7	19.4
1960	513.3	510.1	3.2	257.1	253.9	3.2	93.8	1.6	160.1	1.6	195.1	61.1	21.3
1961	531.8	528.9	2.9	260.4	257.4	2.9	93.1	−.1	164.3	3.0	208.6	62.8	17.8
1962	571.6	565.5	6.1	281.5	275.4	6.1	103.4	3.4	172.0	2.7	223.0	67.0	22.4
1963	603.1	·597.5	5.7	293.2	287.5	5.7	110.0	2.7	177.5	3.0	238.1	71.9	25.1
1964	648.0	643.0	5.0	313.5	308.5	5.0	119.6	4.0	188.9	1.0	256.9	77.6	25.9
1965	702.7	693.0	9.7	342.9	333.2	9.7	132.4	6.7	200.8	3.0	276.0	83.8	31.1
1966	769.8	756.0	13.8	380.1	366.3	13.8	147.9	10.2	218.5	3.6	302.8	86.9	30.2
1967	814.3	803.8	10.5	395.1	384.6	10.5	154.5	5.5	230.2	5.0	330.7	88.5	27.8
1968	889.3	880.2	9.1	427.4	418.3	9.1	169.1	4.7	249.1	4.4	363.0	98.9	35.0
1969	959.5	949.8	9.7	456.6	446.8	9.7	180.1	6.4	266.8	3.3	395.8	107.1	34.7
1970	1,010.7	1,008.4	2.3	467.8	465.6	2.3	182.1	−.1	283.5	2.3	434.3	108.6	28.5
1971	1,097.2	1,089.2	8.0	493.0	485.0	8.0	189.4	2.8	295.5	5.2	477.0	127.2	38.9
1972	1,207.0	1,197.1	9.9	537.4	527.5	9.9	209.7	7.2	317.8	2.7	523.6	145.9	41.4
1973	1,349.6	1,331.9	17.7	616.6	598.9	17.7	242.0	15.0	356.9	2.8	571.0	161.9	45.9
1974	1,458.6	1,444.4	14.3	662.8	648.5	14.3	257.1	11.2	391.4	3.1	631.3	164.5	38.8
1975	1,585.9	1,591.5	−5.7	715.1	720.8	−5.7	288.8	−7.0	432.0	1.3	706.9	163.8	40.3
1976	1,768.4	1,751.7	16.7	798.8	782.0	16.7	323.6	10.3	458.4	6.4	782.2	187.5	55.1
1977	1,974.1	1,949.4	24.7	880.4	855.7	24.7	368.3	9.7	487.4	15.0	870.4	223.3	64.2
1978	2,232.7	2,204.8	27.9	989.1	961.2	27.9	416.9	20.3	544.3	7.6	975.5	268.1	67.9
1979	2,488.6	2,475.9	12.8	1,100.2	1,087.5	12.8	474.5	9.6	613.0	3.1	1,079.6	308.8	66.2
1980	2,708.0	2,717.5	−9.5	1,176.2	1,185.7	−9.5	502.1	−2.6	683.6	−6.8	1,215.4	316.4	59.2
1981	3,030.6	3,005.2	25.4	1,324.6	1,299.2	25.4	544.2	6.2	755.0	19.2	1,357.4	348.6	68.3
1982	3,149.6	3,165.5	−15.9	1,315.0	1,330.9	−15.9	541.6	−16.0	789.3	.1	1,494.2	340.4	65.3
1983	3,405.0	3,410.6	−5.5	1,407.3	1,412.8	−5.5	579.4	5.5	833.4	−11.0	1,636.3	361.5	88.3
1984	3,777.2	3,706.1	71.1	1,591.9	1,520.8	71.1	647.0	44.9	873.8	26.2	1,770.7	414.7	104.2
1985	4,038.7	4,014.1	24.6	1,652.6	1,628.0	24.6	704.8	8.6	923.2	16.0	1,939.0	447.1	115.8
1986	4,268.6	4,260.0	8.6	1,705.3	1,696.7	8.6	730.2	1.6	966.5	7.1	2,097.3	466.0	120.4
1987	4,539.9	4,513.7	26.3	1,794.5	1,768.2	26.3	753.5	21.6	1,014.7	4.7	2,267.2	478.2	118.9
1988	4,900.4	4,884.2	16.2	1,942.0	1,925.7	16.2	835.6	24.3	1,090.1	−8.1	2,460.9	497.5	129.1
1989	5,250.8	5,217.5	33.3	2,097.0	2,063.6	33.3	891.2	25.2	1,172.5	8.1	2,642.1	511.7	135.1
1990	5,546.1	5,539.3	6.9	2,185.2	2,178.4	6.9	933.5	−2.1	1,244.8	9.0	2,849.4	511.5	129.2
1991	5,724.8	5,726.6	−1.8	2,223.9	2,225.7	−1.8	934.3	−16.9	1,291.4	15.1	3,028.9	472.0	120.3
1992	6,020.2	6,017.2	3.0	2,295.0	2,292.0	3.0	968.6	−13.0	1,323.4	16.0	3,227.2	498.0	133.3
1993	6,343.3	6,327.9	15.4	2,405.8	2,390.4	15.4	1,032.4	8.6	1,358.0	6.7	3,405.5	532.0	143.3
1994 *P*	6,736.9	6,679.1	57.7	2,585.8	2,528.1	57.7	1,116.6	37.5	1,411.4	20.3	3,574.7	576.4	159.1
1982: IV	3,195.1	3,241.4	−46.3	1,302.2	1,348.5	−46.3	550.6	−41.1	798.0	−5.2	1,553.3	339.5	63.2
1983: IV	3,547.3	3,527.1	20.2	1,483.0	1,462.8	20.2	620.5	25.5	842.3	−5.3	1,686.1	378.2	101.9
1984: IV	3,869.1	3,818.1	51.0	1,617.5	1,566.5	51.0	676.3	38.5	890.2	12.5	1,824.7	426.9	110.4
1985: IV	4,140.5	4,107.9	32.6	1,673.7	1,641.1	32.6	705.7	10.9	935.4	21.7	2,008.9	457.9	115.1
1986: IV	4,336.6	4,355.4	−18.8	1,714.5	1,733.3	−18.8	751.5	−11.9	981.8	−7.0	2,154.1	468.1	122.5
1987: IV	4,683.0	4,623.7	59.3	1,865.4	1,806.1	59.3	769.3	37.1	1,036.9	22.2	2,327.6	490.1	120.9
1988: IV	5,044.6	5,027.3	17.3	2,007.0	1,989.7	17.3	861.0	35.3	1,128.7	−18.0	2,528.5	509.1	136.1
1989: IV	5,344.8	5,314.6	30.2	2,115.9	2,085.7	30.2	893.9	33.0	1,191.8	−2.8	2,715.2	513.7	131.0
1990: IV	5,597.9	5,621.8	−23.9	2,189.0	2,212.9	−23.9	931.0	−24.1	1,281.9	.3	2,920.5	488.4	118.8
1991: I	5,636.8	5,654.7	−17.9	2,203.5	2,221.4	−17.9	923.8	−38.5	1,297.6	20.5	2,962.3	471.0	113.2
II	5,705.9	5,718.8	−12.9	2,220.7	2,233.6	−12.9	942.2	−26.4	1,291.4	13.5	3,013.6	471.6	117.5
III	5,759.9	5,750.6	9.3	2,238.3	2,229.0	9.3	939.5	4.5	1,289.5	4.8	3,050.1	471.5	128.5
IV	5,796.6	5,782.3	14.3	2,233.1	2,218.7	14.3	931.4	−7.2	1,287.3	21.5	3,089.7	473.9	122.0
1992: I	5,896.8	5,903.1	−6.3	2,251.7	2,258.0	−6.3	946.8	−24.3	1,311.2	17.9	3,155.8	489.4	123.2
II	5,971.3	5,967.4	3.9	2,270.3	2,266.4	3.9	956.7	−1.8	1,309.7	5.7	3,203.1	498.0	136.3
III	6,043.6	6,038.3	5.3	2,300.5	2,295.2	5.3	971.5	−10.7	1,323.8	16.0	3,248.4	494.7	136.3
IV	6,169.3	6,160.0	9.3	2,357.7	2,348.3	9.3	999.5	−15.1	1,348.9	24.4	3,301.5	510.1	137.3
1993: I	6,235.9	6,215.8	20.1	2,369.6	2,349.6	20.1	999.1	6.9	1,350.4	13.1	3,350.4	515.9	142.6
II	6,299.9	6,281.4	18.6	2,396.2	2,377.6	18.6	1,030.6	3.7	1,347.0	14.8	3,383.1	520.6	146.8
III	6,359.2	6,345.4	13.9	2,395.8	2,381.9	13.9	1,026.8	14.9	1,355.1	−1.1	3,429.3	534.1	137.5
IV	6,478.1	6,469.2	9.0	2,461.6	2,452.6	9.0	1,072.9	9.0	1,379.7	.0	3,459.3	557.2	151.0
1994: I	6,574.7	6,550.6	24.1	2,513.2	2,489.1	24.1	1,098.2	20.6	1,390.9	3.5	3,503.8	557.7	162.7
II	6,689.9	6,622.5	67.4	2,561.2	2,493.7	67.4	1,099.4	38.2	1,394.3	29.2	3,555.4	573.4	153.4
III	6,791.7	6,729.1	62.6	2,606.2	2,543.6	62.6	1,125.8	44.1	1,417.8	18.5	3,603.6	581.9	158.2
IV *P*	6,891.1	6,814.3	76.8	·2,662.7	2,585.9	76.8	1,143.2	46.9	1,442.7	29.9	3,635.9	592.6	162.2

[1] Exports and imports of certain goods, primarily military equipment purchased and sold by the Federal Government, are included in services.

Source: Department of Commerce, Bureau of Economic Analysis.

TABLE B-8.—*Gross domestic product by major type of product in 1987 dollars, 1959–94*

[Billions of 1987 dollars; quarterly data at seasonally adjusted annual rates]

| Year or quarter | Gross domestic product | Final sales of domestic product | Change in business inventories | Goods [1] | | | | | | | Services [1] | Structures | Auto output |
| | | | | Total | | | Durable goods | | Nondurable goods | | | | |
				Total	Final sales	Change in business inventories	Final sales	Change in business inventories	Final sales	Change in business inventories			
1959	1,928.8	1,915.2	13.6	825.2	811.6	13.6	273.8	8.6	537.8	5.0	843.7	259.9	59.5
1960	1,970.8	1,962.7	8.1	835.3	827.1	8.1	277.8	4.6	549.3	3.5	877.3	258.2	63.8
1961	2,023.8	2,016.6	7.2	840.9	833.7	7.2	273.5	-.3	560.2	7.5	916.7	266.1	53.1
1962	2,128.1	2,112.5	15.6	889.6	874.0	15.6	296.5	8.6	577.5	7.0	956.8	281.7	63.3
1963	2,215.6	2,199.6	16.0	914.9	898.9	16.0	310.4	7.5	588.5	8.6	999.9	300.8	68.9
1964	2,340.6	2,324.9	15.7	967.6	952.0	15.7	334.3	11.3	617.6	4.4	1,052.6	320.4	69.5
1965	2,470.5	2,445.4	25.1	1,033.0	1,007.9	25.1	364.1	18.3	643.8	6.9	1,102.1	335.4	83.2
1966	2,616.2	2,579.5	36.7	1,113.3	1,076.6	36.7	399.4	27.1	677.2	9.6	1,168.4	334.5	80.4
1967	2,685.2	2,657.5	27.6	1,129.4	1,101.7	27.6	413.7	14.5	688.0	13.1	1,226.6	329.3	72.4
1968	2,796.9	2,773.2	23.6	1,168.9	1,145.3	23.6	430.4	12.8	714.9	10.9	1,277.8	350.1	86.6
1969	2,873.0	2,848.2	24.8	1,193.9	1,169.1	24.8	438.4	15.7	730.7	9.1	1,324.6	354.5	82.9
1970	2,873.9	2,868.0	5.9	1,173.0	1,167.1	5.9	428.0	-.9	739.1	6.9	1,362.0	338.9	65.4
1971	2,955.9	2,935.2	20.8	1,182.0	1,161.3	20.8	419.2	8.9	742.1	11.9	1,401.8	372.1	85.3
1972	3,107.1	3,084.5	22.5	1,251.0	1,228.4	22.5	458.4	16.2	770.0	6.4	1,454.1	401.9	89.9
1973	3,268.6	3,230.9	37.7	1,349.8	1,312.1	37.7	524.6	31.2	784.1	6.5	1,508.3	410.4	98.7
1974	3,248.1	3,217.2	30.9	1,328.2	1,297.3	30.9	524.6	19.6	772.7	11.3	1,553.9	366.1	79.0
1975	3,221.7	3,235.6	-13.9	1,291.8	1,305.7	-13.9	521.6	-11.5	784.1	-2.5	1,602.2	327.7	74.8
1976	3,380.8	3,355.3	25.5	1,372.7	1,347.2	25.5	540.6	17.0	806.6	8.5	1,649.1	359.0	96.8
1977	3,533.3	3,499.0	34.3	1,436.9	1,402.6	34.3	583.6	15.6	819.0	18.7	1,701.2	395.2	106.0
1978	3,703.5	3,666.3	37.2	1,507.3	1,470.1	37.2	623.7	28.7	846.4	8.5	1,770.6	425.6	104.2
1979	3,796.8	3,783.2	13.6	1,537.1	1,523.5	13.6	654.1	11.7	869.3	1.9	1,821.7	438.0	94.8
1980	3,776.3	3,784.6	-8.3	1,509.5	1,517.7	-8.3	626.4	-4.3	891.4	-4.0	1,864.3	402.5	79.1
1981	3,843.1	3,818.6	24.6	1,547.4	1,522.9	24.6	619.4	6.3	903.4	18.3	1,895.7	400.0	86.8
1982	3,760.3	3,777.8	-17.5	1,468.7	1,486.2	-17.5	578.9	-16.0	907.3	-1.5	1,922.8	368.8	79.2
1983	3,906.6	3,902.2	4.4	1,531.7	1,527.3	4.4	601.5	6.3	925.8	-1.8	1,976.8	398.1	101.7
1984	4,148.5	4,080.6	67.9	1,667.7	1,599.8	67.9	655.1	45.7	944.7	22.3	2,033.1	447.7	115.8
1985	4,279.8	4,257.6	22.1	1,695.0	1,672.9	22.1	703.4	9.3	969.5	12.9	2,115.3	469.4	125.0
1986	4,404.5	4,395.9	8.5	1,740.1	1,731.6	8.5	731.5	1.9	1,000.1	6.7	2,185.0	479.3	124.4
1987	4,539.9	4,513.7	26.3	1,794.5	1,768.2	26.3	753.5	21.6	1,014.7	4.7	2,267.2	478.2	118.9
1988	4,718.6	4,698.6	19.9	1,892.5	1,872.6	19.9	833.1	23.3	1,039.5	-3.4	2,349.7	476.4	127.3
1989	4,838.0	4,808.3	29.8	1,961.7	1,932.0	29.8	868.1	23.8	1,063.9	6.0	2,403.9	472.5	128.0
1990	4,897.3	4,891.6	5.7	1,973.2	1,967.5	5.7	893.1	-1.9	1,074.5	7.5	2,464.5	459.6	121.4
1991	4,867.6	4,868.7	-1.1	1,952.2	1,953.3	-1.1	878.5	-15.1	1,074.7	14.0	2,496.3	419.2	108.8
1992	4,979.3	4,976.9	2.5	1,991.0	1,988.5	2.5	906.7	-11.2	1,081.8	13.6	2,549.3	439.0	117.6
1993	5,134.5	5,119.3	15.3	2,081.8	2,066.5	15.3	977.7	8.3	1,088.8	7.0	2,597.6	455.1	121.6
1994 ᴾ	5,342.3	5,289.8	52.4	2,223.8	2,171.4	52.4	1,058.5	33.5	1,112.8	18.9	2,643.2	475.3	130.6
1982: IV	3,759.6	3,804.5	-44.9	1,447.7	1,492.6	-44.9	580.9	-41.9	911.6	-3.0	1,942.1	369.8	75.3
1983: IV	4,012.1	3,982.8	29.3	1,597.8	1,568.5	29.3	639.4	26.7	929.1	2.6	1,998.3	416.0	113.7
1984: IV	4,194.2	4,146.2	47.9	1,680.9	1,633.0	47.9	677.6	39.7	955.3	8.3	2,058.1	455.1	122.4
1985: IV	4,333.5	4,303.3	30.2	1,708.1	1,677.9	30.2	703.1	11.9	974.9	18.3	2,148.8	476.5	122.2
1986: IV	4,427.1	4,447.2	-20.1	1,741.8	1,761.8	-20.1	750.4	-11.9	1,011.4	-8.2	2,208.2	477.2	124.1
1987: IV	4,625.5	4,565.6	59.9	1,850.8	1,790.9	59.9	769.4	36.9	1,021.5	23.0	2,290.9	483.8	120.3
1988: IV	4,779.7	4,758.7	20.9	1,926.0	1,905.0	20.9	852.9	33.5	1,052.2	-12.5	2,372.4	481.3	134.6
1989: IV	4,856.7	4,831.8	24.9	1,956.9	1,932.0	24.9	862.3	31.0	1,069.6	-6.1	2,430.0	469.8	123.8
1990: IV	4,867.2	4,888.0	-20.9	1,953.5	1,974.3	-20.9	885.7	-22.4	1,088.6	1.5	2,477.3	436.5	110.3
1991: I	4,842.0	4,858.4	-16.4	1,944.0	1,960.4	-16.4	873.2	-34.8	1,087.2	18.4	2,478.3	419.7	103.6
II	4,867.9	4,879.8	-11.9	1,949.8	1,961.7	-11.9	886.3	-23.6	1,075.4	11.7	2,499.3	418.8	108.0
III	4,879.9	4,869.5	-10.4	1,961.9	1,951.6	-10.4	880.9	4.3	1,070.6	6.1	2,501.2	416.8	115.6
IV	4,880.8	4,867.3	13.5	1,952.9	1,939.4	13.5	873.6	-6.3	1,065.8	19.7	2,506.3	421.6	108.2
1992: I	4,918.5	4,924.8	-6.3	1,956.3	1,962.6	-6.3	884.5	-21.6	1,078.1	15.3	2,527.2	435.0	109.9
II	4,947.5	4,943.2	4.2	1,968.0	1,963.7	4.2	891.8	-1.3	1,072.0	5.5	2,538.7	440.8	120.7
III	4,990.5	4,985.3	5.2	1,995.4	1,990.1	5.2	910.6	-8.8	1,079.5	14.0	2,559.8	435.4	119.3
IV	5,060.7	5,054.1	6.6	2,044.3	2,037.7	6.6	940.0	-12.9	1,097.7	19.5	2,571.4	445.0	120.4
1993: I	5,075.3	5,056.8	18.5	2,043.7	2,025.2	18.5	939.6	6.2	1,085.7	12.3	2,584.7	446.9	121.7
II	5,105.4	5,086.5	18.9	2,069.9	2,051.0	18.9	968.8	4.6	1,082.2	14.3	2,588.5	447.0	123.4
III	5,139.4	5,126.5	13.0	2,078.2	2,065.3	13.0	977.9	13.5	1,087.4	-.6	2,606.1	455.1	114.2
IV	5,218.0	5,207.2	10.8	2,135.5	2,124.7	10.8	1,024.7	8.9	1,100.0	1.9	2,611.2	471.3	127.2
1994: I	5,261.1	5,235.7	25.4	2,168.8	2,143.3	25.4	1,041.7	19.7	1,101.7	5.7	2,625.8	466.5	135.1
II	5,314.1	5,254.9	59.2	2,201.3	2,142.1	59.2	1,038.2	33.7	1,103.9	25.5	2,635.8	476.9	125.9
III	5,367.0	5,310.0	57.1	2,235.5	2,178.4	57.1	1,063.2	39.3	1,115.2	17.8	2,653.9	477.6	128.3
IV ᴾ	5,426.8	5,358.8	68.0	2,289.6	2,221.6	68.0	1,091.0	41.3	1,130.6	26.6	2,657.0	480.2	133.1

[1] Exports and imports of certain goods, primarily military equipment purchased and sold by the Federal Government, are included in services.

Source: Department of Commerce, Bureau of Economic Analysis.

161–672 – 95 – 10

TABLE B-9.—*Gross domestic product by sector, 1959–94*

[Billions of dollars; quarterly data at seasonally adjusted annual rates]

Year or quarter	Gross domestic product	Business [1]				House-holds and institutions	General government [2]		
		Total [1]	Nonfarm [1]	Farm	Statistical discrepancy		Total	Federal	State and local
1959	494.2	436.9	419.8	18.9	−1.8	12.4	44.9	21.7	23.1
1960	513.3	451.4	434.7	19.8	−3.1	13.9	48.1	22.6	25.5
1961	531.8	465.7	447.9	20.1	−2.2	14.5	51.6	23.7	27.9
1962	571.6	500.5	481.4	20.2	−1.0	15.6	55.5	25.2	30.2
1963	603.1	527.1	508.7	20.4	−2.0	16.7	59.3	26.5	32.9
1964	648.0	565.7	547.2	19.3	−.7	17.9	64.4	28.5	35.9
1965	702.7	614.1	592.9	21.9	−.7	19.3	69.3	30.0	39.3
1966	769.8	670.1	644.4	22.9	2.8	21.3	78.4	34.3	44.1
1967	814.3	703.5	680.5	22.2	.8	23.4	87.4	37.9	49.5
1968	889.3	765.4	742.8	22.7	−.1	26.1	97.8	41.9	55.9
1969	959.5	822.5	799.9	25.2	−2.6	29.5	107.5	44.9	62.6
1970	1,010.7	858.7	832.5	26.2	.0	32.4	119.5	48.5	71.1
1971	1,097.2	931.2	900.0	28.1	3.1	35.6	130.4	51.1	79.3
1972	1,207.0	1,025.3	991.7	32.6	1.1	39.0	142.6	54.9	87.7
1973	1,349.6	1,151.5	1,102.2	49.8	−.5	43.0	155.1	57.2	97.9
1974	1,458.6	1,242.7	1,193.9	47.4	1.4	47.2	168.8	61.1	107.6
1975	1,585.9	1,346.1	1,291.4	48.8	6.0	52.0	187.7	66.6	121.1
1976	1,768.4	1,507.4	1,450.6	46.4	10.4	57.1	203.9	71.0	132.9
1977	1,974.1	1,691.1	1,633.0	47.2	10.9	62.4	220.6	75.6	145.0
1978	2,232.7	1,921.1	1,858.7	54.7	7.6	71.0	240.7	81.8	158.9
1979	2,488.6	2,147.9	2,069.7	64.5	13.8	78.9	261.9	87.1	174.8
1980	2,708.0	2,328.9	2,259.2	56.1	13.6	89.3	289.8	96.3	193.5
1981	3,030.6	2,611.7	2,530.9	69.9	10.9	100.5	318.4	107.7	210.7
1982	3,149.6	2,692.1	2,634.4	65.1	−7.4	111.6	345.8	117.3	228.5
1983	3,405.0	2,914.8	2,855.5	49.2	10.2	121.3	368.9	125.0	243.9
1984	3,777.2	3,251.1	3,191.6	68.5	−9.0	132.0	394.1	132.2	261.9
1985	4,038.7	3,473.5	3,420.3	67.1	−13.9	141.7	423.6	140.3	283.2
1986	4,268.6	3,665.7	3,601.5	62.9	1.2	153.3	449.6	143.7	305.9
1987	4,539.9	3,890.8	3,849.5	66.0	−24.8	170.5	478.7	151.4	327.3
1988	4,900.4	4,201.0	4,161.8	67.6	−28.4	187.6	511.7	159.8	351.9
1989	5,250.8	4,495.9	4,413.7	81.1	1.1	206.1	548.8	169.1	379.8
1990	5,546.1	4,725.9	4,633.0	85.1	7.8	227.5	592.8	180.1	412.7
1991	5,724.8	4,847.6	4,767.5	78.6	1.5	246.7	630.5	192.7	437.9
1992	6,020.2	5,090.4	4,996.1	85.6	8.8	268.6	661.2	199.5	461.7
1993	6,343.3	5,371.4	5,293.8	75.3	2.3	285.3	686.6	203.6	483.0
1994 ᵖ	6,736.9	5,721.7	5,662.7	84.6	−25.6	302.7	712.5	206.1	506.3
1982: IV	3,195.1	2,724.0	2,674.1	60.0	−10.1	115.5	355.6	121.1	234.5
1983: IV	3,547.3	3,046.6	2,986.9	45.8	13.8	125.1	375.6	126.2	249.4
1984: IV	3,869.1	3,330.3	3,283.2	67.5	−20.5	135.6	403.2	134.1	269.2
1985: IV	4,140.5	3,561.2	3,501.5	65.7	−5.9	145.6	433.6	142.4	291.2
1986: IV	4,336.6	3,718.3	3,656.0	64.3	−2.0	157.8	460.5	144.9	315.6
1987: IV	4,683.0	4,016.6	3,970.9	70.6	−24.9	177.6	488.8	153.2	335.6
1988: IV	5,044.6	4,327.3	4,291.9	60.8	−25.4	194.3	523.0	161.3	361.7
1989: IV	5,344.8	4,569.8	4,476.6	80.4	12.8	213.3	561.7	170.6	391.2
1990: IV	5,597.9	4,756.5	4,670.1	81.5	4.9	235.0	606.4	182.3	424.1
1991: I	5,636.8	4,774.2	4,705.9	78.6	−10.3	238.1	624.5	193.2	431.3
II	5,705.9	4,833.7	4,743.9	83.7	6.2	243.9	628.3	192.7	435.6
III	5,759.9	4,878.4	4,787.7	78.5	12.2	249.9	631.7	192.1	439.6
IV	5,796.6	4,904.0	4,832.4	73.7	−2.1	254.9	637.7	192.7	445.0
1992: I	5,896.8	4,983.4	4,892.8	88.6	2.0	261.2	652.2	200.2	452.0
II	5,971.3	5,045.4	4,951.2	82.6	11.5	266.1	659.9	200.5	459.4
III	6,043.6	5,108.0	5,015.9	88.4	3.7	270.9	664.7	199.2	465.5
IV	6,169.3	5,224.9	5,124.3	82.7	18.0	276.1	668.2	198.2	470.0
1993: I	6,235.9	5,276.7	5,171.8	79.4	25.5	279.7	679.5	204.1	475.4
II	6,299.9	5,332.3	5,249.3	77.3	5.7	283.4	684.2	203.6	480.6
III	6,359.2	5,382.1	5,322.3	65.4	−5.5	286.9	690.2	204.3	485.9
IV	6,478.1	5,494.4	5,431.7	79.2	−16.5	291.0	692.7	202.5	490.2
1994: I	6,574.7	5,575.7	5,524.7	87.1	−36.1	295.7	703.3	206.3	497.1
II	6,689.9	5,677.9	5,618.7	83.2	−24.0	300.1	711.8	208.4	503.4
III	6,791.7	5,771.8	5,710.7	82.3	−21.1	304.7	715.2	205.4	509.8
IV ᵖ	6,891.1	5,861.2	5,796.5	85.8	−21.1	310.4	719.5	204.4	515.1

[1] Includes compensation of employees in government enterprises.
[2] Compensation of government employees.

Source: Department of Commerce, Bureau of Economic Analysis.

[Billions of 1987 dollars; quarterly data at seasonally adjusted annual rates]

Year or quarter	Gross domestic product	Business [1]				House-holds and institu-tions	General government [2]		
		Total [1]	Nonfarm [1]	Farm	Statis-tical discrep-ancy		Total	Federal	State and local
1959	1,928.8	1,582.1	1,543.4	45.2	−6.5	80.1	266.5	130.5	136.0
1960	1,970.8	1,609.5	1,574.3	46.4	−11.2	86.5	274.8	132.1	142.7
1961	2,023.8	1,650.7	1,611.6	46.9	−7.8	87.5	285.6	135.3	150.3
1962	2,128.1	1,740.8	1,698.0	46.3	−3.6	91.1	296.2	141.6	154.7
1963	2,215.6	1,818.8	1,778.6	47.1	−6.8	93.6	303.2	140.9	162.3
1964	2,340.6	1,930.4	1,886.8	46.0	−2.4	96.5	313.7	141.7	172.0
1965	2,470.5	2,045.3	2,001.7	46.1	−2.5	100.4	324.8	142.3	182.5
1966	2,616.2	2,162.6	2,109.1	44.5	9.0	104.7	348.9	155.4	193.5
1967	2,685.2	2,208.0	2,158.8	46.5	2.6	108.3	368.9	168.1	200.8
1968	2,796.9	2,303.0	2,258.0	45.1	−.1	111.8	382.1	170.7	211.4
1969	2,873.0	2,366.2	2,326.7	46.8	−7.2	115.5	391.3	171.2	220.1
1970	2,873.9	2,368.4	2,318.9	49.5	.0	114.1	391.4	161.6	229.8
1971	2,955.9	2,447.4	2,388.6	50.5	8.3	116.7	391.8	152.4	239.5
1972	3,107.1	2,594.8	2,541.3	50.7	2.8	120.0	392.2	143.7	248.6
1973	3,268.6	2,749.7	2,702.0	48.6	−1.0	123.2	395.7	138.0	257.7
1974	3,248.1	2,719.6	2,666.0	50.7	3.0	124.3	404.1	137.9	266.2
1975	3,221.7	2,684.6	2,619.6	53.1	11.9	128.0	409.1	137.1	272.0
1976	3,380.8	2,840.1	2,768.1	52.5	19.5	128.6	412.0	137.0	275.0
1977	3,533.3	2,987.8	2,914.6	53.8	19.4	129.8	415.6	137.0	278.6
1978	3,703.5	3,144.2	3,083.8	48.2	12.2	135.1	424.2	138.4	285.8
1979	3,796.8	3,226.0	3,155.0	50.4	20.6	138.3	432.5	137.5	295.0
1980	3,776.3	3,193.4	3,123.4	51.0	19.0	142.6	440.3	139.2	301.1
1981	3,843.1	3,253.6	3,179.2	60.8	13.6	145.6	443.9	140.9	303.0
1982	3,760.3	3,167.3	3,115.8	60.2	−8.7	148.9	444.2	142.4	301.8
1983	3,906.6	3,308.2	3,243.1	53.7	11.5	151.0	447.4	144.8	302.6
1984	4,148.5	3,541.7	3,496.4	55.1	−9.8	154.9	451.9	146.4	305.4
1985	4,279.8	3,658.1	3,608.6	64.2	−14.7	159.9	461.8	148.6	313.2
1986	4,404.5	3,768.3	3,702.8	64.3	1.3	166.3	469.9	149.0	320.8
1987	4,539.9	3,890.8	3,849.5	66.0	−24.8	170.5	478.7	151.4	327.3
1988	4,718.6	4,050.6	4,014.8	63.2	−27.4	180.6	487.4	153.5	333.9
1989	4,838.0	4,150.5	4,083.4	66.2	.9	190.5	497.0	154.2	342.7
1990	4,897.3	4,190.8	4,112.4	71.6	6.9	196.9	509.5	156.2	353.3
1991	4,867.6	4,150.8	4,078.9	70.7	1.3	202.4	514.4	157.2	357.2
1992	4,979.3	4,258.7	4,170.6	80.8	7.3	208.5	512.0	151.9	360.1
1993	5,134.5	4,409.4	4,336.4	71.0	1.9	215.6	509.6	146.0	363.6
1994 [P]	5,342.3	4,611.4	4,550.3	81.7	−20.6	223.1	507.8	139.0	368.8
1982: IV	3,759.6	3,166.3	3,116.9	61.1	−11.7	149.6	443.8	143.2	300.6
1983: IV	4,012.1	3,411.5	3,349.0	47.0	15.5	151.7	448.9	145.2	303.7
1984: IV	4,194.2	3,583.0	3,548.9	56.1	−22.0	156.8	454.4	147.1	307.3
1985: IV	4,333.5	3,706.1	3,646.8	65.5	−6.2	162.3	465.1	148.7	316.5
1986: IV	4,427.1	3,786.7	3,724.4	64.4	−2.1	166.9	473.5	149.8	323.7
1987: IV	4,625.5	3,969.9	3,925.5	69.0	−24.6	173.2	482.3	152.8	329.5
1988: IV	4,779.7	4,104.2	4,074.5	53.8	−24.1	184.7	490.7	154.0	336.7
1989: IV	4,856.7	4,161.9	4,085.0	65.2	11.7	193.2	501.7	154.8	346.9
1990: IV	4,867.2	4,154.3	4,076.5	73.5	4.2	199.2	513.6	157.4	356.2
1991: I	4,842.0	4,125.0	4,062.4	71.4	−8.9	199.9	517.0	160.4	356.7
II	4,867.9	4,150.2	4,073.3	71.6	5.3	202.0	515.6	158.2	357.4
III	4,879.9	4,164.3	4,084.3	69.6	10.4	203.0	512.7	155.9	356.8
IV	4,880.8	4,163.9	4,095.6	70.1	−1.8	204.6	512.2	154.3	357.9
1992: I	4,918.5	4,199.6	4,117.3	80.6	1.7	206.6	512.3	153.3	359.0
II	4,947.5	4,228.5	4,140.3	78.5	9.7	207.0	512.0	152.1	359.9
III	4,990.5	4,269.6	4,182.0	84.5	3.1	209.4	511.5	151.1	360.4
IV	5,060.7	4,337.2	4,242.7	79.6	14.9	211.2	512.3	151.1	361.2
1993: I	5,075.3	4,352.0	4,255.3	75.7	21.0	212.2	511.2	149.0	362.1
II	5,105.4	4,380.4	4,303.4	72.3	4.7	215.0	510.0	146.9	363.1
III	5,139.4	4,413.3	4,353.8	64.0	−4.5	217.0	509.1	145.1	364.0
IV	5,218.0	4,491.7	4,433.2	72.0	−13.5	218.1	508.2	143.2	365.1
1994: I	5,261.1	4,532.6	4,486.1	75.9	−29.3	220.1	508.4	141.9	366.5
II	5,314.1	4,583.6	4,521.3	81.6	−19.3	222.5	508.0	139.9	368.1
III	5,367.0	4,635.4	4,567.9	84.4	−17.0	223.8	507.9	137.9	369.9
IV [P]	5,426.8	4,694.1	4,626.0	85.0	−16.9	225.9	506.8	136.0	370.8

[1] Includes compensation of employees in government enterprises.
[2] Compensation of government employees.

Source: Department of Commerce, Bureau of Economic Analysis.

TABLE B–11.—*Gross domestic product by industry, 1947–92*

[Billions of dollars]

Year	Gross domestic product	Agriculture, forestry, and fisheries	Mining	Construction	Manufacturing Total	Manufacturing Durable goods	Manufacturing Nondurable goods	Transportation and public utilities	Wholesale trade	Retail trade	Finance, insurance, and real estate	Services	Government	Statistical discrepancy [1]
Based on 1972 SIC:														
1947	234.3	20.8	6.8	9.1	66.2	33.5	32.7	21.0	16.6	27.5	24.0	20.2	20.2	1.8
1948	260.3	24.0	9.4	11.5	74.7	38.2	36.6	23.7	18.3	30.1	27.2	21.9	20.9	−1.2
1949	259.3	19.4	8.1	11.5	72.3	37.2	35.1	23.9	17.6	30.3	29.4	22.6	23.1	1.0
1950	287.0	20.7	9.3	13.2	84.1	45.9	38.2	26.6	19.8	31.7	32.3	24.2	24.2	1.0
1951	331.6	23.8	10.2	15.6	99.1	55.6	43.5	30.1	22.5	34.3	35.8	26.4	30.9	2.9
1952	349.7	23.2	10.2	16.9	103.4	59.0	44.3	32.1	22.7	36.3	39.4	28.2	35.6	1.8
1953	370.0	21.1	10.8	17.5	112.4	66.1	46.4	34.1	23.2	37.2	43.7	30.2	36.8	2.8
1954	370.9	20.7	11.0	17.7	106.8	61.0	45.8	33.7	23.5	38.1	47.5	31.6	37.9	2.4
1955	404.3	19.8	12.5	19.0	121.4	70.8	50.5	36.7	26.6	40.5	51.4	35.2	40.0	1.2
1956	426.2	19.7	13.6	21.2	127.4	74.0	53.5	39.5	29.0	42.4	55.0	38.7	42.5	−2.8
1957	448.6	19.6	13.7	22.1	132.0	78.0	54.0	41.5	30.5	44.6	59.2	41.8	45.4	−1.9
1958	454.7	21.9	12.7	21.8	124.6	70.1	54.5	41.7	31.1	45.3	63.9	44.1	48.9	−1.1
1959	494.2	20.3	12.5	23.7	142.2	81.7	60.5	44.9	34.2	49.1	68.9	48.4	51.7	−1.8
1960	513.3	21.3	12.9	24.2	144.8	82.6	62.2	47.1	35.3	50.4	73.5	51.6	55.4	−3.1
1961	531.8	21.7	13.0	25.2	145.3	81.7	63.6	48.7	36.4	51.7	78.0	55.0	59.1	−2.2
1962	571.6	22.1	13.2	27.0	159.1	92.1	67.1	51.7	38.8	55.4	82.4	59.3	63.5	−1.0
1963	603.1	22.3	13.5	28.9	168.6	98.3	70.4	54.6	40.5	57.9	87.1	63.4	68.4	−2.0
1964	648.0	21.4	13.9	31.5	180.5	105.9	74.6	58.1	43.6	63.5	92.9	69.1	74.1	−.7
1965	702.7	24.2	14.0	34.6	199.1	118.8	80.3	62.2	47.2	68.0	99.9	74.7	79.5	−.7
1966	769.8	25.4	14.7	37.7	218.2	131.1	87.1	67.1	51.5	72.7	108.0	82.6	89.1	2.8
1967	814.3	24.9	15.2	39.5	223.7	134.1	89.6	70.3	54.8	78.2	117.3	90.8	98.8	.8
1968	889.3	25.7	16.3	43.3	244.3	146.4	97.9	76.1	60.2	86.6	126.8	99.4	110.7	−.1
1969	959.5	28.5	17.1	48.4	257.8	154.4	103.4	82.5	65.1	94.2	136.4	110.7	121.4	−2.6
1970	1,010.7	29.8	18.7	51.1	253.1	146.2	106.9	88.0	68.6	100.2	146.3	120.5	134.2	.0
1971	1,097.2	32.1	18.9	56.1	266.7	154.2	112.5	97.1	74.3	109.2	163.1	130.3	146.2	3.1
1972	1,207.0	37.3	19.6	62.5	294.3	172.6	121.7	108.3	83.2	118.9	176.5	144.9	160.4	1.1
1973	1,349.6	55.0	23.8	69.8	327.6	195.8	131.8	119.1	93.5	131.0	193.1	163.2	173.9	−.5
1974	1,458.6	53.2	37.0	73.7	341.2	202.2	139.0	129.9	107.1	136.9	208.9	179.4	189.9	1.4
1975	1,585.9	54.9	42.8	75.2	358.8	207.1	151.7	142.3	117.0	153.0	226.7	199.3	209.8	6.0
1976	1,768.4	53.8	47.5	85.1	409.6	239.9	169.7	161.2	124.8	172.4	250.1	224.1	229.3	10.4
1977	1,974.1	54.4	54.1	93.9	466.8	277.7	189.1	179.2	137.9	190.4	283.6	255.7	247.1	10.9
1978	2,232.7	63.3	61.4	110.7	521.9	317.5	204.5	202.2	157.1	214.9	328.6	294.6	270.5	7.6
1979	2,488.6	74.6	71.2	124.8	575.7	343.8	231.9	219.1	178.6	233.2	370.8	333.0	293.9	13.8
1980	2,708.0	66.7	112.6	128.7	588.3	348.9	239.4	242.2	191.6	244.7	418.4	377.0	324.2	13.6
1981	3,030.6	81.1	148.1	129.4	653.0	385.3	267.7	273.3	212.7	269.3	469.6	425.1	358.1	10.9
1982	3,149.6	77.0	146.1	129.4	647.5	372.9	274.6	291.1	216.5	286.6	503.9	469.8	388.0	−7.4
1983	3,405.0	62.7	127.9	137.9	693.3	396.0	297.3	326.7	223.6	321.1	565.3	521.3	415.0	10.2
1984	3,777.2	83.7	137.1	161.2	773.9	461.2	312.7	358.8	258.4	361.3	619.0	586.9	445.9	−9.0
1985	4,038.7	84.3	130.6	179.2	798.5	471.5	327.0	378.0	276.6	390.9	681.8	650.9	481.8	−13.9
1986	4,268.6	81.7	82.7	201.9	829.3	480.0	349.3	393.8	290.9	418.7	743.5	712.8	512.1	1.2
1987	4,539.9	88.5	83.0	213.0	878.4	503.2	375.2	419.9	302.6	440.1	809.9	784.0	545.3	−24.8
Based on 1987 SIC:														
1987	4,539.9	88.5	83.0	213.0	877.8	501.9	375.9	419.8	303.1	441.8	809.7	782.5	545.3	−24.8
1988	4,900.4	90.8	87.9	227.6	961.0	541.1	419.9	442.1	331.0	471.7	866.3	865.5	584.8	−28.4
1989	5,250.8	104.8	84.2	235.9	1,004.6	562.6	442.0	463.3	351.6	502.5	926.5	948.8	627.6	1.1
1990	5,546.1	112.0	103.1	240.1	1,024.7	563.7	461.0	481.2	363.0	515.7	982.4	1,040.0	676.3	7.8
1991	5,724.8	107.2	92.0	223.1	1,032.5	554.4	478.2	507.0	373.4	531.9	1,041.1	1,093.3	721.8	1.5
1992	6,020.2	115.5	85.2	222.1	1,063.0	568.0	495.0	529.3	394.4	557.5	1,106.1	1,182.7	755.7	8.8

[1] Equals gross domestic product (GDP) measured as the sum of expenditures less gross domestic income—that is, GDP measured as the costs incurred and profits earned in domestic production.

Source: Department of Commerce, Bureau of Economic Analysis.

288

TABLE B-12.—*Gross domestic product by industry in 1987 dollars, fixed 1987 weights, 1977-92*

[Billions of 1987 dollars]

Year	Gross domestic product	Agriculture, forestry, and fisheries	Mining	Construction	Manufacturing			Transportation and public utilities	Wholesale trade	Retail trade	Finance, insurance, and real estate	Services	Government	Statistical discrepancy [1]	Residual [2]
					Total	Durable goods	Nondurable goods								
Based on 1972 SIC:															
1977	3,533.3	63.7	83.5	190.8	741.6	440.9	300.7	314.3	170.1	318.0	596.5	538.9	475.7	19.4	20.8
1978	3,703.5	59.2	85.0	198.8	773.1	460.9	312.2	325.1	185.8	338.1	631.0	573.5	488.3	12.2	33.4
1979	3,796.8	62.4	71.9	200.3	777.1	458.0	319.2	335.5	195.8	334.8	667.4	592.8	498.6	20.6	39.6
1980	3,776.3	63.2	79.9	185.4	725.4	424.3	301.1	336.3	190.5	320.1	692.8	609.0	508.9	19.0	45.7
1981	3,843.1	72.7	74.2	174.7	746.7	429.7	317.1	337.1	207.5	330.6	704.7	624.4	511.6	13.6	45.3
1982	3,760.3	73.3	73.1	164.9	711.1	392.4	318.7	331.3	218.2	336.8	708.4	629.2	507.1	−8.7	15.6
1983	3,906.6	68.4	71.3	170.0	733.8	402.5	331.3	351.7	224.2	365.1	727.9	649.5	512.5	11.5	20.8
1984	4,148.5	71.5	82.0	190.9	791.4	458.4	333.0	377.6	259.5	397.7	762.1	687.8	516.9	−9.8	21.0
1985	4,279.8	81.9	83.3	209.0	810.5	468.1	342.4	381.8	273.0	421.4	776.4	722.0	527.5	−14.7	7.7
1986	4,404.5	84.5	83.0	209.1	819.1	471.5	347.7	386.9	307.1	453.2	776.6	751.7	536.4	1.3	−4.4
1987	4,539.9	88.5	83.0	213.0	878.4	503.2	375.2	419.9	302.6	440.1	809.9	784.0	545.3	−24.8	.0
Based on 1987 SIC:															
1987	4,539.9	88.5	83.0	213.0	877.8	501.9	375.9	419.8	303.1	441.8	809.7	782.5	545.3	−24.8	.0
1988	4,718.6	85.1	94.2	211.7	923.5	536.4	387.2	437.1	311.3	469.7	846.5	812.8	555.9	−27.4	−1.8
1989	4,838.0	88.0	83.3	213.1	932.2	543.2	389.1	449.4	324.5	483.9	865.5	845.7	567.0	.9	−15.5
1990	4,897.3	95.8	91.8	210.2	928.5	537.0	391.5	462.6	319.5	478.1	868.3	869.4	581.5	6.9	−15.3
1991	4,867.6	98.4	92.3	194.8	910.8	525.5	385.4	479.1	324.5	473.2	868.8	871.4	586.7	1.3	−33.7
1992	4,979.3	110.3	89.0	201.4	924.6	533.6	391.0	494.5	340.9	486.7	893.4	889.9	584.2	7.3	−43.0

[1] Equals the current-dollar statistical discrepancy deflated by the implicit price deflator for gross domestic business product.
[2] Equals gross domestic product (GDP) in constant dollars measured as the sum of expenditures less the statistical discrepancy in constant dollars and GDP in constant dollars measured as the sum of gross product originating by industry.

Note.—Constant-dollar values are equal to fixed-weighted quantity indexes with 1987 weights divided by 100 and multiplied by the 1987 value of current-dollar GDP.

Source: Department of Commerce, Bureau of Economic Analysis.

289

TABLE B–13.—*Gross domestic product of nonfinancial corporate business, 1959–94*

[Billions of dollars; quarterly data at seasonally adjusted annual rates]

Year or quarter	Gross domestic product of nonfinancial corporate business	Consumption of fixed capital	Net domestic product												Net interest
			Total	Indirect business taxes [1]	Domestic income										
					Total	Compensation of employees	Corporate profits with inventory valuation and capital consumption adjustments						Inventory valuation adjustment	Capital consumption adjustment	
							Profits								
							Total	Profits before tax	Profits tax liability	Profits after tax					
										Total	Dividends	Undistributed profits			
1959	267.5	24.2	243.2	26.0	217.2	171.5	42.6	43.6	20.7	22.9	10.0	12.9	−0.3	−0.7	3.1
1960	278.1	25.2	252.9	28.3	224.6	181.2	40.0	40.3	19.2	21.1	10.6	10.6	−.2	−.2	3.5
1961	285.5	26.0	259.6	29.5	230.1	185.3	40.8	40.1	19.5	20.7	10.6	10.1	.3	.3	4.0
1962	311.7	26.9	284.8	32.0	252.8	200.1	48.2	45.0	20.6	24.3	11.4	13.0	.0	3.2	4.5
1963	331.8	28.1	303.7	34.0	269.7	211.1	53.8	49.8	22.8	27.0	12.6	14.4	.1	3.9	4.8
1964	358.1	29.5	328.6	36.6	292.0	226.7	60.0	56.0	24.0	32.1	13.7	18.4	−.5	4.5	5.3
1965	393.5	31.5	362.0	39.2	322.8	246.5	70.3	66.2	27.2	39.0	15.6	23.4	−1.2	5.3	6.1
1966	431.0	34.3	396.7	40.5	356.2	274.0	74.9	71.4	29.5	41.9	16.8	25.1	−2.1	5.6	7.4
1967	453.4	37.5	415.9	43.1	372.8	292.3	71.8	67.5	27.8	39.7	17.5	22.2	−1.6	5.8	8.8
1968	500.5	41.4	459.1	49.7	409.3	323.2	76.0	74.0	33.6	40.4	19.1	21.3	−3.7	5.6	10.1
1969	543.3	45.3	498.0	54.7	443.3	358.8	71.3	70.8	33.3	37.5	19.1	18.4	−5.9	6.3	13.2
1970	561.4	49.7	511.6	58.8	452.8	378.7	57.1	58.1	27.2	31.0	18.5	12.5	−6.6	5.5	17.1
1971	606.4	54.6	551.7	64.5	487.3	402.0	67.2	67.1	29.9	37.1	18.5	18.7	−4.6	4.7	18.1
1972	673.3	61.0	612.4	69.2	543.2	447.1	77.0	78.6	33.8	44.8	20.1	24.7	−6.6	5.0	19.2
1973	754.5	66.2	688.3	76.3	612.0	505.9	83.6	98.6	40.2	58.4	21.1	37.3	−20.0	5.0	22.5
1974	814.6	77.5	737.1	81.4	655.7	556.8	70.6	109.2	42.2	67.0	21.7	45.2	−39.5	.9	28.3
1975	881.2	93.3	788.0	87.4	700.6	580.3	91.5	109.9	41.5	68.4	24.8	43.6	−11.0	−7.4	28.7
1976	994.6	103.8	890.8	95.1	795.7	656.7	111.5	137.3	53.0	84.4	27.8	56.6	−14.9	−10.9	27.5
1977	1,124.7	116.2	1,008.5	104.1	904.4	741.8	132.0	158.6	59.9	98.7	32.0	66.8	−16.6	−10.0	30.6
1978	1,279.4	132.3	1,147.2	114.6	1,032.6	850.2	146.1	183.5	67.1	116.4	37.2	79.1	−25.0	−12.3	36.3
1979	1,423.7	153.0	1,270.7	123.3	1,147.4	964.2	138.1	195.5	69.6	125.9	39.3	86.7	−41.6	−15.9	45.1
1980	1,546.5	174.8	1,371.7	139.4	1,232.4	1,053.5	120.7	181.6	67.0	114.6	45.5	69.1	−43.0	−17.8	58.2
1981	1,748.6	207.0	1,541.5	167.9	1,373.6	1,164.8	136.9	181.0	63.9	117.1	53.4	63.7	−25.7	−18.4	71.9
1982	1,802.8	229.4	1,573.4	169.4	1,404.0	1,209.9	111.5	132.9	46.3	86.7	56.4	30.2	−9.9	−11.5	82.5
1983	1,936.1	242.1	1,694.0	185.8	1,508.2	1,271.6	159.9	155.9	59.4	96.4	66.5	29.9	−8.5	12.5	76.7
1984	2,166.5	248.1	1,918.3	206.9	1,711.4	1,409.2	214.3	189.0	73.7	115.4	69.5	45.9	−4.1	29.4	87.9
1985	2,293.6	258.0	2,035.5	220.3	1,815.3	1,503.2	221.4	165.5	69.9	95.6	74.5	21.1	.2	55.6	90.7
1986	2,386.3	271.4	2,114.9	231.4	1,883.6	1,581.5	203.8	149.1	75.6	73.5	76.3	−2.8	9.7	44.9	98.3
1987	2,547.3	281.4	2,265.9	241.0	2,024.9	1,675.0	244.2	212.0	93.5	118.5	77.9	40.6	−14.5	46.7	105.8
1988	2,764.8	297.5	2,467.3	257.1	2,210.2	1,814.2	274.4	256.6	101.7	154.9	82.0	72.9	−27.3	45.0	121.6
1989	2,913.5	317.4	2,596.2	274.2	2,322.0	1,920.2	255.2	232.9	99.5	133.3	101.9	31.5	−17.5	39.9	146.6
1990	3,045.5	329.3	2,716.2	290.4	2,425.8	2,020.9	256.4	232.1	93.9	138.3	118.1	20.1	−11.0	35.3	148.5
1991	3,089.7	341.6	2,748.2	311.7	2,436.5	2,053.1	249.2	212.4	83.1	129.3	124.7	4.6	5.8	31.1	134.2
1992	3,222.9	352.9	2,870.0	328.9	2,541.1	2,151.0	276.6	253.4	87.8	165.5	136.3	29.2	−6.4	29.7	113.5
1993	3,409.7	361.5	3,048.2	344.0	2,704.2	2,259.2	330.9	293.5	116.8	176.7	159.8	16.9	−6.2	43.6	114.0
1994 ᵖ		382.2		365.4		2,392.4							−18.7	53.3	
1982: IV	1,806.3	238.8	1,567.5	172.6	1,394.9	1,213.9	101.5	116.5	40.6	75.9	59.0	16.9	−8.6	−6.4	79.6
1983: IV	2,037.2	261.5	1,775.7	194.0	1,581.7	1,327.6	175.2	168.1	64.4	103.7	67.4	36.3	−7.6	14.7	78.9
1984: IV	2,228.2	258.9	1,969.4	212.4	1,756.9	1,449.7	211.4	169.0	62.6	106.4	68.7	37.7	3.5	38.9	95.8
1985: IV	2,338.8	263.4	2,075.4	223.8	1,851.6	1,540.1	221.4	168.4	71.1	97.2	74.7	22.5	−3.8	56.9	90.0
1986: IV	2,422.8	275.8	2,147.1	233.6	1,913.5	1,611.4	198.6	168.5	86.5	82.0	75.2	6.8	−10.7	40.8	103.5
1987: IV	2,627.6	286.1	2,341.4	245.4	2,096.0	1,730.1	256.8	224.8	99.6	125.1	84.0	41.2	−17.8	49.8	109.2
1988: IV	2,843.2	304.5	2,538.8	263.1	2,275.7	1,868.8	278.5	271.4	107.9	163.5	84.3	79.2	−31.7	38.8	128.4
1989: IV	2,951.5	326.5	2,625.0	279.0	2,346.0	1,954.6	240.7	215.9	91.1	124.8	102.3	22.5	−13.5	38.3	150.7
1990: IV	3,052.5	336.1	2,716.4	296.6	2,419.8	2,039.3	232.4	226.7	92.0	134.8	117.2	17.5	−19.5	25.2	148.2
1991: I	3,058.4	339.7	2,718.7	303.8	2,414.9	2,030.1	243.8	207.9	80.5	127.5	123.1	4.4	10.4	25.5	141.1
II	3,074.8	340.9	2,734.0	306.9	2,427.1	2,039.5	251.8	209.3	81.7	127.6	124.6	3.0	12.1	30.5	135.8
III	3,099.8	342.2	2,757.6	315.6	2,442.0	2,059.7	249.9	214.6	84.8	129.8	124.2	5.6	1.4	33.9	132.4
IV	3,125.9	343.5	2,782.4	320.4	2,462.0	2,083.0	251.3	217.6	85.4	132.2	126.9	5.3	−.8	34.4	127.7
1992: I	3,150.0	345.5	2,804.6	323.3	2,481.3	2,101.1	260.7	232.6	79.3	153.3	125.0	28.3	−4.0	32.1	119.5
II	3,194.4	347.7	2,846.7	325.3	2,521.3	2,134.4	271.7	258.6	90.3	168.3	131.5	36.8	−16.6	29.7	115.2
III	3,239.4	366.2	2,873.1	329.8	2,543.4	2,165.4	268.2	250.0	86.5	163.6	137.6	26.0	−7.3	25.4	109.8
IV	3,307.8	352.1	2,955.7	337.4	2,618.3	2,203.0	305.8	272.2	95.2	177.0	151.1	25.9	2.1	31.5	109.5
1993: I	3,324.4	356.9	2,967.4	336.1	2,631.3	2,225.2	293.5	269.3	106.2	163.0	160.0	2.4	−11.2	35.4	112.6
II	3,386.3	358.8	3,027.5	341.3	2,686.2	2,248.5	324.4	293.7	116.7	176.9	156.7	20.2	−10.0	40.7	113.3
III	3,428.7	366.5	3,062.2	344.3	2,717.9	2,269.1	334.3	285.7	113.5	172.2	159.4	12.8	3.0	45.7	114.4
IV	3,499.3	363.7	3,135.6	354.3	2,781.3	2,293.9	371.6	325.4	130.8	194.6	162.3	32.2	−6.5	52.7	115.8
1994: I	3,568.6	383.7	3,184.8	358.9	2,825.9	2,337.1	372.2	332.8	132.5	200.3	159.5	40.8	−12.3	51.7	116.6
II	3,626.7	376.3	3,250.3	362.9	2,887.5	2,373.1	394.7	355.9	143.4	212.5	164.3	48.1	−14.1	52.9	119.6
III	3,679.4	382.0	3,297.5	368.4	2,929.0	2,405.1	399.1	365.2	147.1	218.1	157.3	60.8	−19.6	53.6	124.8
IV ᵖ		386.8		371.5		2,454.2							−28.8	55.1	

[1] Indirect business tax and nontax liability plus business transfer payments less subsidies.

Source: Department of Commerce, Bureau of Economic Analysis.

TABLE B–14.—*Output, costs, and profits of nonfinancial corporate business, 1959–94*

[Quarterly data at seasonally adjusted annual rates]

| Year or quarter | Gross domestic product of nonfinancial corporate business (billions of dollars) | | Current-dollar cost and profit per unit of output (dollars) [1] | | | | | | | | Output per hour of all employees (1987 dollars) | Compensation per hour of all employees (dollars) |
| | | | | | | | Corporate profits with inventory valuation and capital consumption adjustments | | | | | |
	Current dollars	1987 dollars	Total cost and profit [2]	Consumption of fixed capital	Indirect business taxes [3]	Compensation of employees	Total	Profits tax liability	Profits after tax [4]	Net interest		
1959	267.5	928.7	0.288	0.026	0.028	0.185	0.046	0.022	0.024	0.003	15.443	2.851
1960	278.1	955.6	.291	.026	.030	.190	.042	.020	.022	.004	15.661	2.969
1961	285.5	978.2	.292	.027	.030	.189	.042	.020	.022	.004	16.182	3.066
1962	311.7	1,047.5	.298	.026	.031	.191	.046	.020	.026	.004	16.675	3.186
1963	331.8	1,104.8	.300	.025	.031	.191	.049	.021	.028	.004	17.204	3.287
1964	358.1	1,179.3	.304	.025	.031	.192	.051	.020	.031	.005	17.855	3.432
1965	393.5	1,262.2	.312	.025	.031	.195	.056	.022	.034	.005	18.074	3.529
1966	431.0	1,336.0	.323	.026	.030	.205	.056	.022	.034	.006	18.142	3.720
1967	453.4	1,367.4	.332	.027	.032	.214	.052	.020	.032	.006	18.362	3.924
1968	500.5	1,443.3	.347	.029	.034	.224	.053	.023	.029	.007	18.858	4.220
1969	543.3	1,492.5	.364	.030	.037	.240	.048	.022	.025	.009	18.749	4.508
1970	561.4	1,473.4	.381	.034	.040	.257	.039	.018	.020	.012	18.775	4.825
1971	606.4	1,525.9	.397	.036	.042	.263	.044	.020	.024	.012	19.484	5.133
1972	673.3	1,629.5	.413	.037	.042	.274	.047	.021	.027	.012	19.793	5.430
1973	754.5	1,706.9	.442	.039	.045	.296	.049	.024	.025	.013	19.762	5.857
1974	814.6	1,669.7	.488	.046	.049	.333	.042	.025	.017	.017	19.231	6.413
1975	881.2	1,625.6	.542	.057	.054	.357	.056	.026	.031	.018	19.764	7.056
1976	994.6	1,748.5	.569	.059	.054	.376	.064	.030	.033	.016	20.365	7.648
1977	1,124.7	1,866.7	.603	.062	.056	.397	.071	.032	.039	.016	20.767	8.252
1978	1,279.4	1,967.1	.650	.067	.058	.432	.074	.034	.040	.018	20.712	8.951
1979	1,423.7	1,995.7	.713	.077	.062	.483	.069	.035	.034	.023	20.221	9.770
1980	1,546.5	1,980.9	.781	.088	.070	.532	.061	.034	.027	.029	20.265	10.777
1981	1,748.6	2,035.1	.859	.102	.082	.572	.067	.031	.036	.035	20.537	11.754
1982	1,802.8	2,001.3	.901	.115	.085	.605	.056	.023	.033	.041	20.802	12.576
1983	1,936.1	2,112.3	.917	.115	.088	.602	.076	.028	.048	.036	21.594	13.000
1984	2,166.5	2,284.1	.949	.109	.091	.617	.094	.032	.062	.038	21.924	13.526
1985	2,293.6	2,364.3	.970	.109	.093	.636	.094	.030	.064	.038	22.148	14.082
1986	2,386.3	2,439.3	.978	.111	.095	.648	.084	.031	.053	.040	22.733	14.739
1987	2,547.3	2,547.3	1.000	.110	.095	.658	.096	.037	.059	.042	23.127	15.207
1988	2,764.8	2,684.8	1.030	.111	.096	.676	.102	.038	.064	.045	23.572	15.833
1989	2,913.5	2,718.9	1.072	.117	.101	.706	.094	.037	.057	.054	23.189	16.377
1990	3,045.5	2,747.4	1.109	.120	.106	.736	.093	.034	.059	.054	23.446	17.246
1991	3,089.7	2,716.7	1.137	.126	.115	.756	.092	.031	.061	.049	23.926	18.081
1992	3,222.9	2,802.8	1.150	.126	.117	.767	.099	.031	.067	.041	24.648	18.916
1993	3,409.7	2,942.9	1.159	.123	.117	.768	.112	.040	.073	.039	25.379	19.483
1982: IV	1,806.3	1,999.6	.903	.119	.086	.607	.051	.020	.030	.040	21.070	12.791
1983: IV	2,037.2	2,204.2	.924	.119	.088	.602	.079	.029	.050	.036	21.893	13.186
1984: IV	2,228.2	2,328.4	.957	.111	.091	.623	.091	.027	.064	.041	22.055	13.732
1985: IV	2,338.8	2,396.9	.976	.110	.093	.643	.092	.030	.063	.038	22.346	14.359
1986: IV	2,422.8	2,463.3	.984	.112	.095	.654	.081	.035	.045	.042	22.891	14.975
1987: IV	2,627.6	2,604.0	1.009	.110	.094	.664	.099	.038	.060	.042	23.356	15.517
1988: IV	2,843.2	2,719.0	1.046	.112	.097	.687	.102	.040	.063	.047	23.521	16.069
1989: IV	2,951.5	2,722.7	1.084	.120	.102	.718	.088	.033	.055	.055	23.146	16.616
1990: IV	3,052.5	2,725.0	1.120	.123	.109	.748	.085	.034	.052	.054	23.549	17.623
1991: I	3,058.4	2,702.0	1.132	.126	.112	.751	.090	.030	.060	.052	23.716	17.818
II	3,074.8	2,704.1	1.137	.126	.113	.754	.093	.030	.063	.050	23.846	17.984
III	3,099.8	2,719.9	1.140	.126	.116	.757	.092	.031	.061	.049	23.993	18.169
IV	3,125.9	2,740.9	1.140	.125	.117	.760	.092	.031	.061	.047	24.211	18.400
1992: I	3,150.0	2,746.9	1.147	.126	.118	.765	.095	.029	.066	.044	24.286	18.577
II	3,194.4	2,778.3	1.150	.125	.117	.768	.098	.033	.065	.041	24.460	18.791
III	3,239.4	2,815.7	1.150	.130	.117	.769	.095	.031	.065	.039	24.774	19.052
IV	3,307.8	2,870.2	1.152	.123	.118	.768	.107	.033	.073	.038	25.085	19.254
1993: I	3,324.4	2,868.4	1.159	.124	.117	.776	.102	.037	.065	.039	24.962	19.365
II	3,386.3	2,920.5	1.159	.123	.117	.770	.111	.040	.071	.039	25.239	19.432
III	3,428.7	2,963.3	1.157	.124	.116	.766	.113	.038	.075	.039	25.516	19.539
IV	3,499.3	3,019.5	1.159	.120	.117	.760	.123	.043	.080	.038	25.810	19.608
1994: I	3,568.6	3,062.6	1.165	.125	.117	.763	.122	.043	.078	.038	26.018	19.855
II	3,626.7	3,098.9	1.170	.121	.117	.766	.127	.046	.081	.039	25.923	19.852
III	3,679.4	3,131.2	1.175	.122	.118	.768	.127	.047	.080	.040	26.048	20.005

[1] Output is measured by gross domestic product of nonfinancial corporate business in 1987 dollars.
[2] This is equal to the deflator for gross domestic product of nonfinancial corporate business with the decimal point shifted two places to the left.
[3] Indirect business tax and nontax liability plus business transfer payments less subsidies.
[4] With inventory valuation and capital consumption adjustments.

Sources: Department of Commerce (Bureau of Economic Analysis) and Department of Labor (Bureau of Labor Statistics).

TABLE B–15.—*Personal consumption expenditures, 1959–94*

[Billions of dollars; quarterly data at seasonally adjusted annual rates]

Year or quarter	Personal consumption expenditures	Durable goods			Nondurable goods					Services					
		Total ¹	Motor vehicles and parts	Furniture and household equipment	Total ¹	Food	Clothing and shoes	Gasoline and oil	Fuel oil and coal	Total ¹	Housing ²	Household operation		Transportation	Medical care
												Total ¹	Electricity and gas		
1959	318.1	42.8	18.9	18.1	148.5	80.7	26.4	11.3	4.0	126.8	45.0	18.7	7.6	10.5	16.3
1960	332.4	43.5	19.7	18.0	153.1	82.6	27.0	12.0	3.8	135.9	48.2	20.3	8.3	11.2	17.4
1961	343.5	41.9	17.8	18.3	157.4	84.8	27.6	12.0	3.8	144.1	51.2	21.2	8.8	11.7	18.6
1962	364.4	47.0	21.5	19.3	163.8	87.1	29.0	12.6	3.8	153.6	54.7	22.4	9.4	12.2	20.7
1963	384.2	51.8	24.4	20.7	169.4	89.5	29.8	13.0	4.0	163.1	58.0	23.6	9.9	12.7	22.4
1964	412.5	56.8	26.0	23.2	179.7	94.6	32.4	13.6	4.1	175.9	61.4	25.0	10.4	13.4	25.7
1965	444.6	63.5	29.9	25.1	191.9	101.0	34.1	14.8	4.4	189.2	65.4	26.5	10.9	14.5	27.7
1966	481.6	68.5	30.3	28.2	208.5	109.0	37.4	16.0	4.7	204.6	69.5	28.2	11.5	15.9	30.5
1967	509.3	70.6	30.0	30.0	216.9	112.3	39.2	17.1	4.8	221.7	74.1	30.2	12.2	17.3	33.7
1968	559.1	81.0	36.1	32.9	235.0	121.6	43.2	18.6	4.7	243.1	79.7	32.3	13.0	18.9	39.0
1969	603.7	86.2	38.4	34.7	252.2	130.5	46.5	20.5	4.6	265.3	86.8	35.1	14.0	20.9	44.4
1970	646.5	85.3	35.5	35.7	270.4	142.1	47.8	21.9	4.4	290.8	94.0	37.8	15.2	23.7	50.1
1971	700.3	97.2	44.5	37.8	283.3	147.5	51.7	23.2	4.6	319.8	102.7	41.0	16.6	27.1	56.5
1972	767.8	110.7	51.1	42.4	305.2	158.5	56.4	24.4	5.1	351.9	112.1	45.3	18.4	29.8	63.5
1973	848.1	124.1	56.1	47.9	339.6	176.1	62.5	28.1	6.3	384.5	122.7	49.8	20.0	31.2	71.2
1974	927.7	123.0	49.5	51.5	380.8	198.1	66.0	36.1	7.8	423.9	134.1	55.5	23.5	33.3	80.1
1975	1,024.9	134.3	54.8	54.5	416.0	218.5	70.8	39.7	8.4	474.5	147.0	63.7	28.5	35.7	93.0
1976	1,143.1	160.0	71.3	60.2	451.8	236.0	76.6	43.0	10.1	531.2	161.5	72.4	32.5	41.3	106.2
1977	1,271.5	182.6	83.5	67.1	490.4	255.9	84.1	46.9	11.1	598.4	179.5	81.9	37.6	49.2	122.4
1978	1,421.2	202.3	92.2	74.0	541.5	280.6	94.3	50.1	11.5	677.4	201.7	91.2	42.1	53.6	139.7
1979	1,583.7	214.2	91.5	82.3	613.3	313.0	101.2	66.2	14.4	756.2	226.6	100.0	46.8	59.4	157.8
1980	1,748.1	212.5	84.0	86.0	682.9	341.8	107.3	86.7	15.4	852.7	255.2	113.0	56.3	65.1	181.3
1981	1,926.2	228.5	91.6	91.3	744.2	367.3	117.2	97.9	15.8	953.5	287.1	126.0	63.4	69.4	213.6
1982	2,059.2	236.5	97.7	92.5	772.3	386.0	120.5	94.1	14.5	1,050.4	311.1	141.4	72.6	71.6	240.5
1983	2,257.5	275.0	120.6	104.4	817.8	406.2	130.8	93.3	13.8	1,164.7	334.6	153.6	80.7	78.9	265.7
1984	2,460.3	317.9	144.6	115.3	873.0	430.2	142.5	94.5	14.2	1,269.4	362.3	165.5	84.6	89.1	290.6
1985	2,667.4	352.9	167.4	123.4	919.4	451.1	152.2	96.9	14.1	1,395.1	392.5	176.2	88.7	99.0	319.3
1986	2,850.6	389.6	184.9	135.5	952.2	476.8	163.2	79.7	12.0	1,508.8	421.8	181.1	87.1	105.8	346.4
1987	3,052.2	403.7	183.5	144.0	1,011.1	500.7	174.5	84.7	12.0	1,637.4	452.5	187.8	88.4	116.6	384.7
1988	3,296.1	437.1	197.8	156.7	1,073.8	533.6	186.4	86.9	12.1	1,785.2	484.2	199.5	93.4	128.5	427.7
1989	3,523.1	459.4	205.4	167.9	1,149.5	565.1	200.4	96.2	12.0	1,914.2	514.4	209.8	98.0	135.6	471.9
1990	3,761.2	468.2	202.9	174.2	1,229.2	604.8	207.3	108.4	13.2	2,063.8	547.5	215.6	97.4	142.5	526.2
1991	3,902.4	456.6	185.0	179.9	1,257.8	621.5	213.0	102.9	13.0	2,188.1	574.9	227.7	104.3	145.7	571.9
1992	4,136.9	492.7	204.1	192.5	1,295.5	626.8	227.7	105.5	13.0	2,348.7	601.3	239.4	105.7	156.7	628.3
1993	4,378.2	538.0	228.0	208.9	1,339.2	649.7	235.4	105.6	14.0	2,501.0	629.0	256.3	112.8	170.6	680.5
1994 ᴾ	4,627.0	590.9	250.9	229.4	1,393.8	679.1	246.5	107.3	13.7	2,642.2	659.9	263.7	112.7	179.6	727.1
1982: IV	2,128.7	246.9	105.1	95.6	787.3	394.9	122.7	93.0	14.0	1,094.6	320.2	145.8	74.9	73.6	250.9
1983: IV	2,346.8	297.7	134.8	109.7	839.8	413.9	136.7	94.9	14.1	1,209.3	344.6	159.3	84.8	82.9	274.8
1984: IV	2,526.4	328.2	149.3	118.7	887.8	436.8	145.7	94.9	13.8	1,310.4	373.8	168.8	85.9	92.5	299.9
1985: IV	2,739.8	354.4	162.9	128.1	939.5	460.7	156.2	97.6	14.3	1,446.0	404.6	180.7	90.1	101.5	333.0
1986: IV	2,923.1	406.8	188.2	140.6	963.7	486.7	165.8	73.0	11.3	1,552.6	432.7	182.5	86.8	109.0	358.4
1987: IV	3,124.6	408.8	186.3	145.9	1,029.4	507.4	177.6	87.8	12.2	1,686.4	466.6	189.7	88.6	121.3	398.5
1988: IV	3,398.2	452.9	203.4	162.5	1,105.8	549.5	194.4	88.5	11.7	1,839.5	496.0	203.8	95.3	132.7	444.4
1989: IV	3,599.1	458.3	198.1	170.8	1,173.5	575.3	205.4	95.9	13.2	1,967.3	526.6	217.7	103.7	137.6	489.2
1990: IV	3,836.6	459.5	192.9	174.5	1,260.7	615.6	207.6	123.0	13.9	2,116.4	558.6	219.1	99.6	145.4	546.6
1991: I	3,841.4	449.3	181.7	176.0	1,253.0	618.5	209.1	107.4	13.5	2,139.0	564.7	220.5	100.6	142.9	554.6
II	3,885.7	452.0	179.8	181.0	1,259.6	624.4	214.2	102.6	12.5	2,174.1	571.6	229.9	107.4	144.2	564.4
III	3,927.0	463.8	189.9	182.1	1,261.3	623.4	215.4	101.1	13.2	2,202.0	578.0	230.8	105.6	146.5	576.4
IV	3,955.7	461.2	188.8	180.7	1,257.2	619.7	213.2	100.5	12.3	2,237.3	585.3	229.7	103.7	149.2	592.2
1992: I	4,044.4	480.1	198.5	187.5	1,276.5	624.3	221.9	101.5	12.3	2,287.8	592.1	231.7	101.7	153.6	605.9
II	4,097.8	483.3	199.8	188.7	1,281.7	619.2	223.9	104.9	13.9	2,332.8	598.0	240.1	105.5	156.3	621.9
III	4,154.0	495.7	204.0	193.9	1,299.6	624.5	230.2	108.2	12.8	2,358.6	604.1	235.5	105.7	154.0	636.4
IV	4,251.3	511.6	214.0	199.9	1,324.3	639.3	234.8	107.5	13.2	2,415.4	611.2	250.2	109.8	163.0	648.8
1993: I	4,294.6	516.1	216.6	201.6	1,327.1	640.4	231.8	108.4	14.1	2,451.4	619.0	250.6	110.5	167.3	664.1
II	4,347.3	531.2	225.7	205.5	1,334.2	646.0	233.2	105.6	13.9	2,481.9	625.9	252.9	110.1	170.0	674.5
III	4,401.2	541.9	228.4	210.6	1,340.2	651.7	235.9	104.1	14.2	2,519.1	632.4	260.4	115.5	171.5	686.1
IV	4,469.6	562.8	241.4	217.7	1,355.2	660.8	240.7	104.4	13.9	2,551.6	638.8	261.3	115.1	173.6	697.3
1994: I	4,535.0	576.2	253.0	218.1	1,368.9	667.9	241.9	103.2	15.5	2,589.9	648.2	261.1	116.3	175.4	707.4
II	4,586.4	580.3	245.8	225.3	1,381.4	675.5	243.9	103.7	13.1	2,624.7	655.2	265.9	115.2	178.5	720.9
III	4,657.5	591.5	245.5	233.7	1,406.1	683.7	247.8	110.6	13.4	2,659.9	663.9	265.3	111.9	180.5	733.2
IV ᴾ	4,728.9	615.6	259.3	240.3	1,418.9	689.3	252.4	111.5	12.5	2,694.5	672.2	262.5	107.3	183.8	746.8

¹ Includes other items not shown separately.
² Includes imputed rental value of owner-occupied housing.

Source: Department of Commerce, Bureau of Economic Analysis.

TABLE B–16.—*Personal consumption expenditures in 1987 dollars, 1959–94*

[Billions of 1987 dollars; quarterly data at seasonally adjusted annual rates]

Year or quarter	Personal consumption expenditures	Durable goods Total[1]	Motor vehicles and parts	Furniture and household equipment	Nondurable goods Total[1]	Food	Clothing and shoes	Gasoline and oil	Fuel oil and coal	Services Total[1]	Housing[2]	Household operation Total[1]	Household operation Electricity and gas	Transportation	Medical care
1959	1,178.9	114.4	59.7	38.2	518.5	301.9	58.2	38.1	22.6	546.0	159.8	75.0	34.5	45.4	95.0
1960	1,210.8	115.4	61.3	37.7	526.9	305.8	58.7	39.4	21.7	568.5	168.1	78.5	36.3	46.7	98.4
1961	1,238.4	109.4	54.9	38.1	537.7	312.1	59.8	39.8	20.6	591.3	176.0	81.2	38.3	47.0	102.0
1962	1,293.3	120.2	62.2	40.4	553.0	316.3	62.4	41.5	20.6	620.0	185.8	85.2	40.9	48.7	110.2
1963	1,341.9	130.3	68.4	43.1	563.6	319.2	63.6	42.8	21.6	648.0	194.4	88.4	42.8	50.5	117.1
1964	1,417.2	140.7	71.2	48.3	588.2	331.0	68.5	45.1	22.5	688.3	203.5	92.6	45.1	53.0	129.8
1965	1,497.0	156.2	81.2	52.1	616.7	346.5	71.5	47.3	23.5	724.1	214.6	96.8	47.2	55.4	135.8
1966	1,573.8	166.0	81.8	57.6	647.6	359.1	76.3	50.2	24.2	760.2	224.4	101.4	49.7	58.6	142.3
1967	1,622.4	167.2	80.3	59.5	659.0	364.5	76.9	51.8	24.2	796.2	234.5	106.2	52.4	62.0	148.1
1968	1,707.5	184.5	91.8	62.9	686.0	380.7	80.2	55.5	23.0	837.0	246.0	110.1	55.0	65.4	159.5
1969	1,771.2	190.8	95.1	64.3	703.2	389.7	81.9	59.2	21.8	877.2	259.1	115.3	58.0	68.9	171.3
1970	1,813.5	183.7	85.6	64.4	717.2	397.5	81.0	62.9	20.2	912.5	269.3	118.9	60.4	71.0	180.7
1971	1,873.7	201.4	100.8	66.8	725.6	399.2	84.6	65.9	19.5	946.7	280.9	120.8	61.8	73.6	193.7
1972	1,978.4	225.2	114.3	73.6	755.8	411.9	90.4	68.6	21.5	997.4	295.9	126.8	64.9	77.8	207.0
1973	2,066.7	246.6	123.4	81.5	777.9	412.6	96.9	72.1	23.3	1,042.2	310.8	132.0	66.5	79.6	222.4
1974	2,053.8	227.2	102.2	81.9	759.8	404.7	95.4	68.6	18.4	1,066.8	326.9	132.5	66.9	79.9	231.1
1975	2,097.5	226.8	102.9	79.1	767.1	413.2	98.5	70.6	18.1	1,103.6	336.5	138.1	70.4	81.4	243.8
1976	2,207.3	256.4	124.6	84.2	801.3	431.9	103.2	73.4	20.3	1,149.5	346.7	143.9	72.9	84.4	255.5
1977	2,296.6	280.0	137.3	91.4	819.8	441.5	108.7	75.7	19.6	1,196.8	355.4	151.0	76.0	90.2	267.9
1978	2,391.8	292.9	141.5	96.6	844.8	442.8	119.0	77.4	19.5	1,254.1	372.9	158.0	78.8	92.9	279.2
1979	2,448.4	289.0	130.5	101.3	862.8	448.0	124.1	76.4	18.1	1,296.5	387.9	162.9	79.3	96.1	290.9
1980	2,447.1	262.7	111.4	98.5	860.5	448.8	126.0	72.0	14.0	1,323.9	399.4	167.1	81.6	91.3	302.1
1981	2,476.9	264.6	113.5	97.7	867.9	446.6	132.8	73.2	11.8	1,344.4	407.3	165.6	80.3	88.9	318.3
1982	2,503.7	262.5	115.6	94.2	872.2	451.4	133.7	73.9	10.9	1,368.9	409.6	166.7	81.2	87.4	323.7
1983	2,619.4	297.7	138.1	104.3	900.3	463.4	142.4	75.7	11.1	1,421.4	415.5	169.4	83.7	91.6	332.6
1984	2,746.1	338.5	160.3	115.3	934.6	472.3	153.1	77.9	11.2	1,473.0	426.8	173.7	84.3	100.0	341.9
1985	2,865.8	370.1	180.2	123.8	958.7	483.0	158.8	79.2	11.5	1,537.0	435.9	179.1	86.6	109.2	353.0
1986	2,969.1	402.0	193.3	136.3	991.0	494.1	170.3	82.9	12.1	1,576.1	442.1	180.8	85.6	112.6	366.2
1987	3,052.2	403.7	183.5	144.0	1,011.1	500.7	174.5	84.7	12.0	1,637.4	452.5	187.8	88.4	116.6	384.7
1988	3,162.4	428.7	194.8	155.4	1,035.1	513.4	178.9	86.1	12.0	1,698.5	461.8	196.9	92.7	122.5	399.4
1989	3,223.3	440.7	196.4	165.8	1,051.6	515.0	187.8	87.3	11.4	1,731.0	469.2	202.6	94.3	123.8	408.6
1990	3,272.6	443.1	192.7	171.6	1,060.7	523.9	186.2	86.4	10.5	1,768.8	474.6	204.3	92.2	124.0	424.6
1991	3,259.4	425.3	170.0	179.2	1,047.7	518.8	184.7	83.1	10.7	1,786.3	479.0	209.1	95.8	119.3	437.7
1992	3,349.5	452.6	181.8	193.3	1,057.7	514.7	193.2	85.6	11.2	1,839.1	485.2	217.8	95.2	122.9	454.3
1993	3,458.7	489.9	196.1	214.1	1,078.5	524.0	197.8	86.5	12.1	1,890.3	492.6	225.3	98.6	127.9	466.4
1994 *p*	3,578.5	531.5	207.9	238.3	1,109.3	535.2	208.8	87.4	11.9	1,937.8	501.3	227.8	97.9	132.6	479.0
1982: IV	2,539.3	272.3	123.7	96.4	880.7	458.3	135.7	73.4	10.5	1,386.2	411.0	166.2	80.2	88.2	327.8
1983: IV	2,678.2	319.1	151.6	109.3	915.2	467.1	147.7	76.9	11.4	1,443.9	419.7	173.3	86.8	94.2	334.8
1984: IV	2,784.8	347.7	164.3	118.7	942.9	475.1	154.7	79.0	11.1	1,494.2	431.3	174.8	84.5	103.5	344.9
1985: IV	2,895.3	369.6	173.9	128.6	968.7	488.2	161.7	79.5	11.4	1,557.1	438.1	182.6	88.5	111.2	359.1
1986: IV	3,012.5	415.7	193.6	141.4	1,000.9	496.9	171.9	84.6	12.4	1,595.8	444.8	182.8	86.8	113.4	372.0
1987: IV	3,074.7	404.7	183.6	145.9	1,014.6	502.4	174.5	85.4	11.9	1,655.5	457.0	189.3	88.6	117.9	390.7
1988: IV	3,202.9	439.2	197.7	160.3	1,046.8	518.0	182.8	87.5	12.0	1,716.9	465.6	198.6	93.0	124.2	403.0
1989: IV	3,242.0	436.8	188.3	167.9	1,058.9	515.6	190.9	88.6	12.0	1,746.3	471.3	208.5	98.8	124.3	411.8
1990: IV	3,265.9	433.2	182.1	172.3	1,057.5	525.8	184.5	84.6	9.5	1,775.2	475.9	206.0	93.8	122.7	429.4
1991: I	3,242.9	420.6	169.0	174.2	1,049.5	520.4	183.2	83.0	10.3	1,772.8	476.5	203.5	92.5	118.9	432.0
II	3,259.5	421.9	165.7	179.7	1,051.7	520.4	187.0	83.6	10.6	1,785.9	478.4	211.6	99.1	119.2	434.9
III	3,269.8	431.3	173.6	181.9	1,049.3	519.4	185.7	83.3	11.4	1,789.2	479.8	211.5	97.1	119.1	439.1
IV	3,265.3	427.7	171.6	181.2	1,040.4	514.9	182.8	82.4	10.7	1,797.3	481.4	209.8	94.4	120.0	444.7
1992: I	3,311.4	443.4	179.8	187.2	1,051.1	515.6	188.9	84.3	10.7	1,817.0	482.6	210.4	92.7	120.6	448.5
II	3,325.4	443.8	178.6	188.8	1,049.3	509.9	190.6	85.3	12.0	1,832.3	484.2	217.2	95.7	122.5	453.1
III	3,357.6	454.5	180.6	195.3	1,056.4	511.5	194.9	86.6	10.8	1,846.7	486.1	220.0	95.1	124.7	456.6
IV	3,403.4	468.8	188.2	202.0	1,074.2	522.0	198.7	86.0	11.3	1,860.4	487.8	223.4	97.5	123.9	459.0
1993: I	3,417.2	472.5	189.7	205.2	1,070.0	520.7	194.0	86.1	12.0	1,874.8	489.8	224.1	98.5	125.8	463.1
II	3,439.2	483.7	195.1	209.9	1,074.3	522.3	196.1	85.7	11.8	1,881.2	491.5	222.8	96.3	127.6	464.3
III	3,472.2	492.7	195.0	216.6	1,081.7	525.1	198.6	87.5	12.2	1,897.8	493.7	227.4	99.9	128.4	467.6
IV	3,506.2	510.8	204.7	224.6	1,088.0	528.1	202.4	86.6	12.2	1,907.4	495.4	226.9	99.6	129.8	470.4
1994: I	3,546.3	521.7	213.7	225.9	1,098.3	531.9	203.8	86.1	13.4	1,926.3	497.7	228.7	101.1	130.9	473.2
II	3,557.8	522.2	205.3	232.5	1,104.3	536.1	204.9	86.7	11.4	1,931.4	500.0	229.1	100.2	131.8	477.4
III	3,584.7	529.6	202.0	241.7	1,113.4	535.7	210.2	88.0	11.7	1,941.8	502.6	228.1	97.2	132.4	481.0
IV *p*	3,625.1	552.4	210.7	253.0	1,121.1	537.0	216.6	88.8	11.1	1,951.7	504.9	225.3	93.2	135.4	484.5

[1] Includes other items not shown separately.
[2] Includes imputed rental value of owner-occupied housing.

Source: Department of Commerce, Bureau of Economic Analysis.

TABLE B-17.—*Gross and net private domestic investment, 1959–94*

[Billions of dollars; quarterly data at seasonally adjusted annual rates]

Year or quarter	Gross private domestic invest-ment	Less: Consump-tion of fixed capital	Equals: Net private domestic investment						
			Total	Net fixed investment					Change in business inven-tories
				Total	Nonresidential			Resi-dential	
					Total	Struc-tures	Pro-ducers' durable equip-ment		
1959	78.8	44.6	34.2	30.1	12.3	6.6	5.7	17.8	4.2
1960	78.7	46.3	32.4	29.2	13.8	7.7	6.1	15.4	3.2
1961	77.9	47.7	30.3	27.3	12.2	7.6	4.6	15.1	2.9
1962	87.9	49.3	38.6	32.5	15.3	8.3	7.0	17.2	6.1
1963	93.4	51.3	42.0	36.4	16.4	8.3	8.1	20.0	5.7
1964	101.7	53.9	47.8	42.8	21.3	10.3	11.0	21.5	5.0
1965	118.0	57.3	60.7	51.0	30.3	14.1	16.2	20.7	9.7
1966	130.4	62.1	68.3	54.5	36.7	16.0	20.7	17.8	13.8
1967	128.0	67.4	60.6	50.1	33.2	15.1	18.1	16.9	10.5
1968	139.9	73.9	66.0	56.9	35.0	15.8	19.2	21.9	9.1
1969	155.2	81.5	73.7	64.0	40.5	17.9	22.6	23.5	9.7
1970	150.3	88.8	61.5	59.2	38.4	18.4	20.0	20.8	2.3
1971	175.5	97.6	78.0	69.9	36.8	18.4	18.4	33.1	8.0
1972	205.6	109.9	95.7	85.8	42.5	18.7	23.8	43.2	9.9
1973	243.1	120.4	122.7	105.0	59.0	23.8	35.2	46.0	17.7
1974	245.8	140.2	105.5	91.3	58.9	24.5	34.5	32.3	14.3
1975	226.0	165.2	60.9	66.5	41.5	18.8	22.7	25.1	−5.7
1976	286.4	182.8	103.6	86.8	45.6	19.9	25.6	41.2	16.7
1977	358.3	205.2	153.1	128.3	64.9	23.4	41.5	63.4	24.7
1978	434.0	234.8	199.3	171.3	94.1	35.5	58.6	77.3	27.9
1979	480.2	272.4	207.8	195.1	117.3	49.9	67.4	77.8	12.8
1980	467.6	311.9	155.7	165.2	113.8	59.1	54.7	51.4	−9.5
1981	558.0	362.4	195.6	170.2	127.1	75.5	51.6	43.1	25.4
1982	503.4	399.1	104.3	120.3	99.1	72.4	26.7	21.2	−15.9
1983	546.7	418.4	128.2	133.8	69.1	46.2	22.9	64.6	−5.5
1984	718.9	433.2	285.6	214.6	126.6	65.1	61.5	87.9	71.1
1985	714.5	454.5	260.0	235.4	146.1	75.2	70.9	89.3	24.6
1986	717.6	478.6	239.1	230.4	114.4	51.8	62.6	116.0	8.6
1987	749.3	502.2	247.1	220.9	103.0	46.7	56.3	117.9	26.3
1988	793.6	534.0	259.6	243.4	125.8	47.9	77.9	117.6	16.2
1989	832.3	580.4	251.9	218.6	117.1	48.6	68.5	101.5	33.3
1990	808.9	602.7	206.2	199.3	116.1	51.8	64.3	83.2	6.9
1991	744.8	626.5	118.3	120.1	68.0	28.7	39.2	52.1	−1.8
1992	788.3	658.5	129.8	126.7	55.9	13.0	42.9	70.8	3.0
1993	882.0	669.1	213.0	197.6	97.4	11.4	86.0	100.2	15.4
1994 ᵖ	1,037.5	715.5	322.0	264.3					57.7
1982: IV	464.2	412.5	51.7	98.0					−46.3
1983: IV	614.8	439.7	175.1	154.9					20.2
1984: IV	722.8	448.0	274.8	223.8					51.0
1985: IV	737.0	465.6	271.4	238.8					32.6
1986: IV	697.1	488.2	208.9	227.8					−18.8
1987: IV	800.2	512.1	288.1	228.8					59.3
1988: IV	814.8	547.2	267.6	250.3					17.3
1989: IV	825.2	600.8	224.4	194.2					30.2
1990: IV	756.4	614.8	141.5	165.4					−23.9
1991: I	732.8	620.2	112.6	130.5					−17.9
II	733.1	623.3	109.8	122.7					−12.9
III	756.5	627.1	129.4	120.1					9.3
IV	756.8	635.4	121.4	107.1					14.3
1992: I	747.7	632.9	114.8	121.1					−6.3
II	787.9	637.5	150.4	146.5					3.9
III	795.5	715.3	80.2	74.9					5.3
IV	822.0	648.4	173.6	164.3					9.3
1993: I	853.8	662.9	190.9	170.8					20.1
II	869.7	662.0	207.7	189.1					18.6
III	882.2	677.3	204.9	191.0					13.9
IV	922.5	674.0	248.5	239.5					9.0
1994: I	966.6	734.1	232.5	208.4					24.1
II	1,034.4	698.1	336.3	268.9					67.4
III	1,055.1	709.9	345.2	282.6					62.6
IV ᵖ	1,093.9	719.8	374.1	297.3					76.8

Source: Department of Commerce, Bureau of Economic Analysis.

294

TABLE B–18.—*Gross and net private domestic investment in 1987 dollars, 1959–94*

[Billions of 1987 dollars; quarterly data at seasonally adjusted annual rates]

Year or quarter	Gross private domestic investment	Less: Consumption of fixed capital	Equals: Net private domestic investment						
				Net fixed investment					Change in business inventories
			Total	Total	Nonresidential			Residential	
					Total	Structures	Producers' durable equipment		
1959	296.4	168.8	127.5	114.0	39.2	25.4	13.8	74.8	13.6
1960	290.8	173.7	117.1	109.0	44.1	30.5	13.7	64.8	8.1
1961	289.4	178.6	110.8	103.6	39.9	30.6	9.4	63.7	7.2
1962	321.2	183.6	137.6	122.0	49.5	32.9	16.6	72.5	15.6
1963	343.3	189.6	153.7	137.7	52.8	32.1	20.7	84.9	16.0
1964	371.8	196.4	175.4	159.7	69.7	39.5	30.2	90.0	15.7
1965	413.0	205.0	208.1	182.9	99.9	53.0	46.9	83.0	25.1
1966	438.0	214.9	223.0	186.3	118.1	58.3	59.8	68.2	36.7
1967	418.6	225.2	193.4	165.8	103.9	53.0	50.9	61.9	27.6
1968	440.1	235.3	204.7	181.1	105.1	52.2	52.9	76.0	23.6
1969	461.3	246.7	214.6	189.8	112.2	56.0	56.2	77.6	24.8
1970	429.7	258.0	171.7	165.8	98.7	53.5	45.2	67.1	5.9
1971	475.7	269.1	206.6	185.8	85.0	49.0	36.0	100.8	20.8
1972	532.2	285.0	247.2	224.6	98.9	49.2	49.7	125.7	22.5
1973	591.7	296.4	295.3	257.6	134.6	57.9	76.7	123.0	37.7
1974	543.0	310.3	232.6	201.7	122.3	53.4	68.9	79.4	30.9
1975	437.6	322.8	114.8	128.7	72.0	36.7	35.3	56.8	–13.9
1976	520.6	334.6	186.1	160.6	74.5	36.8	37.7	86.1	25.5
1977	600.4	348.4	252.1	217.8	99.0	39.8	59.2	118.8	34.3
1978	664.6	364.5	300.0	262.8	134.4	55.2	79.2	128.4	37.2
1979	669.7	384.5	285.2	271.6	154.1	70.1	84.0	117.5	13.6
1980	594.4	400.7	193.7	201.9	129.5	73.3	56.1	72.5	–8.3
1981	631.1	417.8	213.2	188.7	131.6	82.0	49.6	57.1	24.6
1982	540.5	429.5	111.0	128.5	101.0	75.3	25.7	27.5	–17.5
1983	599.5	447.4	152.1	147.7	71.6	50.3	21.4	76.0	4.4
1984	757.5	455.5	302.0	234.0	134.3	69.3	65.0	99.8	67.9
1985	745.9	471.5	274.4	252.3	154.0	79.4	74.6	98.3	22.1
1986	735.1	486.7	248.4	239.9	118.3	54.9	63.3	121.6	8.5
1987	749.3	502.2	247.1	220.9	103.0	46.7	56.3	117.9	26.3
1988	773.4	518.5	254.9	235.0	122.6	46.7	75.9	112.4	19.9
1989	784.0	545.5	238.5	208.7	114.8	45.9	68.9	94.0	29.8
1990	746.8	554.8	192.0	186.3	111.1	47.3	63.8	75.2	5.7
1991	683.8	570.1	113.8	114.9	68.3	26.2	42.1	46.6	–1.1
1992	725.3	595.8	129.5	127.0	64.9	12.6	52.3	62.1	2.5
1993	819.9	599.5	220.4	205.1	120.0	10.8	109.2	85.2	15.3
1994 *p*	955.5	628.6	326.9	274.5					52.4
1982: IV	503.5	439.2	64.3	109.2					–44.9
1983: IV	669.5	468.5	201.0	171.7					29.3
1984: IV	756.4	467.4	289.0	241.1					47.9
1985: IV	763.1	480.1	283.0	252.8					30.2
1986: IV	705.9	492.5	213.3	233.4					–20.1
1987: IV	793.8	508.1	285.7	225.8					59.9
1988: IV	785.0	524.7	260.3	239.3					20.9
1989: IV	769.5	559.6	209.9	185.0					24.9
1990: IV	695.7	559.9	135.8	156.7					–20.9
1991: I	670.0	563.7	106.3	122.7					–16.4
II	671.5	567.4	104.1	116.0					–11.9
III	696.0	570.5	125.5	115.1					10.4
IV	697.9	578.6	119.3	105.8					13.5
1992: I	687.2	575.5	111.7	118.0					–6.3
II	725.5	578.2	147.3	143.1					4.2
III	733.3	644.4	88.9	83.7					5.2
IV	755.2	585.2	170.0	163.4					6.6
1993: I	789.2	596.4	192.8	174.3					18.5
II	806.2	593.9	212.3	193.4					18.9
III	821.8	605.5	216.3	203.3					13.0
IV	862.5	602.0	260.5	249.7					10.8
1994: I	898.9	648.1	250.8	225.4					25.4
II	950.9	614.8	336.1	276.9					59.2
III	967.3	621.9	345.4	288.3					57.1
IV *p*	1,004.9	629.5	375.4	307.4					68.0

Source: Department of Commerce, Bureau of Economic Analysis.

[Billions of dollars, except as noted; seasonally adjusted]

Quarter	Inventories [1]							Final sales of domestic business [3]	Ratio of inventories to final sales of domestic business	
	Total [2]	Farm	Nonfarm						Total	Nonfarm
			Total [2]	Manu-facturing	Whole-sale trade	Retail trade	Other			
Fourth quarter:										
1959................	141.2	31.6	109.6	55.2	21.0	26.2	7.2	36.5	3.87	3.00
1960................	145.2	33.0	112.2	56.2	21.3	27.5	7.2	37.7	3.85	2.97
1961................	147.0	33.7	113.4	57.2	21.8	27.0	7.4	39.6	3.71	2.86
1962................	153.4	34.8	118.6	60.3	22.4	28.3	7.5	41.9	3.66	2.83
1963................	158.7	34.9	123.8	62.2	23.9	29.6	8.0	44.6	3.56	2.78
1964................	164.2	33.3	130.9	65.9	25.2	31.0	8.8	47.5	3.46	2.76
1965................	178.4	37.4	141.0	70.7	26.9	33.7	9.8	52.5	3.40	2.69
1966................	194.0	36.3	157.8	80.9	30.3	36.2	10.4	55.6	3.49	2.84
1967................	206.0	36.5	169.5	87.5	32.7	36.9	12.4	59.1	3.48	2.87
1968................	221.4	38.7	182.6	94.0	34.6	40.7	13.3	65.0	3.41	2.81
1969................	242.5	41.9	200.6	103.4	37.9	44.5	14.9	69.0	3.51	2.91
1970................	249.4	40.1	209.2	105.8	41.7	45.8	16.0	72.7	3.43	2.88
1971................	267.4	45.0	222.4	107.3	45.2	52.3	17.6	79.2	3.38	2.81
1972................	296.6	55.3	241.3	113.6	50.0	57.7	19.9	88.3	3.36	2.73
1973................	365.1	78.0	287.1	136.1	59.4	66.4	25.2	97.2	3.76	2.95
1974................	435.2	74.3	360.9	177.0	75.6	74.6	33.7	105.2	4.14	3.43
1975................	440.1	75.5	364.5	177.8	76.2	74.7	35.8	117.5	3.74	3.10
1976................	475.3	72.2	403.1	194.9	86.1	82.7	39.4	129.1	3.68	3.12
1977................	521.6	75.2	446.4	210.6	96.2	93.3	46.3	144.3	3.61	3.09
1978................	605.3	92.1	513.2	238.0	111.7	107.5	55.9	166.6	3.63	3.08
1979................	702.6	97.9	604.7	280.6	141.2	118.9	64.1	185.4	3.79	3.26
1980................	784.1	104.9	679.3	309.8	174.2	125.0	70.3	203.5	3.85	3.34
1981................	836.2	101.4	734.7	331.9	184.8	137.0	81.1	220.3	3.80	3.34
1982................	817.0	103.6	713.5	318.5	174.7	139.5	80.7	230.9	3.54	3.09
1983................	827.5	103.2	724.4	319.2	168.9	153.7	82.5	252.2	3.28	2.87
1984................	898.9	100.9	797.9	349.0	187.2	173.5	88.3	273.3	3.29	2.92
1985................	904.3	96.6	807.7	339.9	184.9	188.6	94.3	294.1	3.08	2.75
1986................	887.9	90.5	797.3	328.1	183.4	193.4	92.4	311.4	2.85	2.56
1987................	950.6	90.9	859.7	349.3	196.3	216.1	98.0	329.8	2.88	2.61
1988................	1,025.1	95.4	929.6	383.2	215.3	229.9	101.2	359.2	2.85	2.59
1989................	1,081.6	96.3	985.3	409.7	224.8	250.2	100.6	378.3	2.86	2.60
1990................	1,110.4	94.7	1,015.7	423.7	236.9	257.2	98.0	398.4	2.79	2.55
1991................	1,091.4	90.5	1,000.9	407.2	240.8	257.0	95.9	407.5	2.68	2.46
1992................	1,104.9	95.8	1,009.1	396.9	250.5	266.5	95.2	434.6	2.54	2.32
1993................	1,138.4	97.6	1,040.8	394.6	259.9	282.0	104.4	457.1	2.49	2.28
1994 *ᵖ*............	1,218.6	98.6	1,120.0	412.7	281.2	308.8	117.2	482.0	2.53	2.32
1991: I...........	1,094.4	97.8	996.6	417.4	237.0	247.7	94.4	399.3	2.74	2.50
II...........	1,090.5	100.2	990.3	411.4	234.2	249.4	95.3	403.9	2.70	2.45
III...........	1,091.0	95.6	995.4	409.1	236.4	254.2	96.1	405.8	2.69	2.45
IV...........	1,091.4	90.5	1,000.9	407.2	240.8	257.0	95.9	407.5	2.68	2.46
1992: I...........	1,094.8	95.7	999.2	403.9	241.1	257.0	97.2	415.8	2.63	2.40
II...........	1,100.0	95.4	1,004.7	402.1	245.1	261.4	96.1	420.1	2.62	2.39
III...........	1,104.8	95.9	1,008.9	402.6	247.3	264.2	94.8	425.2	2.60	2.37
IV...........	1,104.9	95.8	1,009.1	396.9	250.5	266.5	95.2	434.6	2.54	2.32
1993: I...........	1,122.0	99.5	1,022.6	397.9	252.9	276.1	95.6	438.1	2.56	2.33
II...........	1,123.0	95.6	1,027.4	397.3	254.6	277.2	98.3	442.8	2.54	2.32
III...........	1,131.3	96.7	1,034.6	397.0	257.5	279.7	100.4	447.4	2.53	2.31
IV...........	1,138.4	97.6	1,040.8	394.6	259.9	282.0	104.4	457.1	2.49	2.28
1994: I...........	1,145.7	99.1	1,046.6	395.9	260.0	283.0	107.7	462.6	2.48	2.26
II...........	1,163.7	93.8	1,070.0	400.2	266.2	292.2	111.3	467.5	2.49	2.29
III...........	1,185.2	94.0	1,091.2	405.1	272.9	299.2	114.0	475.8	2.49	2.29
IV *ᵖ*...........	1,218.6	98.6	1,120.0	412.7	281.2	308.8	117.2	482.0	2.53	2.32

[1] Inventories at end of quarter. Quarter-to-quarter change calculated from this table is not the current-dollar change in business inventories (CBI) component of GDP. The former is the difference between two inventory stocks, each valued at their respective end-of-quarter prices. The latter is the change in the physical volume of inventories valued at average prices of the quarter. In addition, changes calculated from this table are at quarterly rates, whereas CBI is stated at annual rates.

[2] Inventories of construction establishments are included in "other" nonfarm inventories.

[3] Quarterly totals at monthly rates. Final sales of domestic business equals final sales of domestic product less gross product of households and institutions and general government and includes a small amount of final sales by farms.

Note.—The industry classification of inventories is on an establishment basis and is based on the 1987 Standard Industrial Classification (SIC) beginning 1987 and on the 1972 SIC for earlier years shown.

Source: Department of Commerce, Bureau of Economic Analysis.

[Billions of 1987 dollars, except as noted; seasonally adjusted]

Quarter	Inventories [1]							Final sales of domestic business [3]	Ratio of inventories to final sales of domestic business	
	Total [2]	Farm	Nonfarm						Total	Nonfarm
			Total [2]	Manufacturing	Wholesale trade	Retail trade	Other			
Fourth quarter:										
1959...............	388.6	79.6	308.9	152.4	61.2	67.6	27.8	131.5	2.96	2.35
1960...............	396.7	80.5	316.2	153.9	62.4	71.4	28.5	134.3	2.95	2.35
1961...............	403.9	82.1	321.8	157.9	63.7	70.2	30.0	139.9	2.89	2.30
1962...............	419.5	83.9	335.7	166.1	65.9	73.8	29.9	145.3	2.89	2.31
1963...............	435.6	85.4	350.2	171.6	69.6	76.9	32.0	153.5	2.84	2.28
1964...............	451.2	83.4	367.8	179.6	73.4	80.3	34.5	161.1	2.80	2.28
1965...............	476.4	84.6	391.7	190.2	77.6	86.8	37.2	174.2	2.73	2.25
1966...............	513.1	83.5	429.6	212.1	86.5	92.5	38.4	177.3	2.89	2.42
1967...............	540.7	84.5	456.3	227.6	92.0	92.1	44.6	183.8	2.94	2.48
1968...............	564.3	86.9	477.5	237.4	94.7	99.3	46.1	192.6	2.93	2.48
1969...............	589.2	86.9	502.3	246.7	100.3	105.9	49.4	195.4	3.01	2.57
1970...............	595.1	86.3	508.8	246.1	106.9	105.8	50.0	197.6	3.01	2.57
1971...............	615.8	89.2	526.7	243.9	112.3	117.8	52.6	205.1	3.00	2.57
1972...............	638.4	90.6	547.7	249.6	116.3	125.3	56.5	220.4	2.90	2.49
1973...............	676.1	92.9	583.3	264.9	121.1	134.5	62.7	225.9	2.99	2.58
1974...............	707.0	92.5	614.5	283.7	130.8	133.6	66.4	220.9	3.20	2.78
1975...............	693.1	92.9	600.2	277.2	127.3	127.6	68.0	229.1	3.03	2.62
1976...............	718.6	90.8	627.8	289.6	135.3	134.8	68.1	238.3	3.02	2.63
1977...............	752.9	93.6	659.2	297.1	144.4	144.5	73.3	249.4	3.02	2.64
1978...............	790.1	93.0	697.1	309.2	155.8	153.7	78.3	264.6	2.99	2.63
1979...............	803.7	95.7	708.0	320.1	157.3	153.5	77.1	270.2	2.97	2.62
1980...............	795.4	92.3	703.1	319.9	161.9	146.7	74.6	268.5	2.96	2.62
1981...............	820.0	98.3	721.7	324.0	164.8	152.9	80.0	266.5	3.08	2.71
1982...............	802.5	101.4	701.0	311.3	159.9	151.7	78.1	267.6	3.00	2.62
1983...............	806.9	93.1	713.8	311.9	159.3	162.8	79.8	281.8	2.86	2.53
1984...............	874.8	94.8	780.0	339.4	174.7	181.4	84.5	294.6	2.97	2.65
1985...............	896.9	97.2	799.8	335.7	178.7	194.1	91.3	306.3	2.93	2.61
1986...............	905.5	95.1	810.4	333.6	185.7	196.7	94.4	317.2	2.85	2.55
1987...............	931.8	88.7	843.1	340.2	192.7	213.6	96.6	325.8	2.86	2.59
1988...............	951.7	81.7	870.0	355.3	199.1	219.7	95.9	340.3	2.80	2.56
1989...............	981.5	81.6	899.9	373.9	202.5	231.0	92.5	344.7	2.85	2.61
1990...............	987.2	84.1	903.1	376.9	208.8	229.4	88.0	347.9	2.84	2.60
1991...............	986.1	84.3	901.8	370.6	213.1	230.0	88.1	345.9	2.85	2.61
1992...............	988.5	88.7	899.8	360.4	219.6	233.6	86.2	360.9	2.74	2.49
1993...............	1,033.8	85.5	918.3	359.7	223.9	242.7	92.1	373.4	2.69	2.46
1994 *p*...........	1,056.2	92.6	963.6	365.2	237.6	260.3	100.6	385.5	2.74	2.50
1991: I...............	983.1	84.2	898.9	377.9	209.9	224.6	86.5	345.1	2.85	2.60
II...............	980.1	85.3	894.8	374.6	207.6	225.0	87.5	346.8	2.83	2.58
III...............	982.7	84.6	898.1	372.4	209.0	228.2	88.6	346.2	2.84	2.59
IV...............	986.1	84.3	901.8	370.6	213.1	230.0	88.1	345.9	2.85	2.61
1992: I...............	984.5	86.3	898.2	367.4	212.5	228.9	89.4	350.5	2.81	2.56
II...............	985.5	87.8	897.7	364.1	215.6	230.5	87.6	352.0	2.80	2.55
III...............	986.9	88.7	898.2	364.0	216.7	231.8	85.7	355.4	2.78	2.53
IV...............	988.5	88.7	899.8	360.4	219.6	233.6	86.2	360.9	2.74	2.49
1993: I...............	993.1	88.4	904.7	360.0	220.2	239.4	85.1	361.1	2.75	2.51
II...............	997.9	87.4	910.4	361.0	222.0	239.9	87.6	363.5	2.75	2.50
III...............	1,001.1	85.5	915.6	361.6	223.7	241.4	88.9	366.7	2.73	2.50
IV...............	1,003.8	85.5	918.3	359.7	223.9	242.7	92.1	373.4	2.69	2.46
1994: I...............	1,010.2	86.3	923.8	362.1	223.7	243.2	94.9	375.6	2.69	2.46
II...............	1,025.0	88.2	936.8	362.3	228.1	248.7	97.7	377.0	2.72	2.48
III...............	1,039.2	90.6	948.6	363.4	232.3	253.7	99.2	381.5	2.72	2.49
IV *p*...........	1,056.2	92.6	963.6	365.2	237.6	260.3	100.6	385.5	2.74	2.50

[1] Inventories at end of quarter. Quarter-to-quarter changes calculated from this table are at quarterly rates, whereas the constant-dollar change in business inventories component of GDP is stated at annual rates.

[2] Inventories of construction establishments are included in "other" nonfarm inventories.

[3] Quarterly totals at monthly rates. Final sales of domestic business equals final sales of domestic product less gross product of households and institutions and general government and includes a small amount of final sales by farms.

Note.—The industry classification of inventories is on an establishment basis and is based on the 1987 Standard Industrial Classification (SIC) beginning 1987 and on the 1972 SIC for earlier years shown.

Source: Department of Commerce, Bureau of Economic Analysis.

[Billions of dollars; quarterly data at seasonally adjusted annual rates]

Year or quarter	Receipts from rest of the world					Payments to rest of the world										
	Total [1]	Exports of goods and services			Receipts of factor income [3]	Total	Imports of goods and services			Payments of factor income [4]	Transfer payments (net)				Net foreign investment
		Total	Merchandise [2]	Services [2]			Total	Merchandise [2]	Services [2]		Total	From persons (net)	From government (net)	From business	
1959	25.0	20.6	16.5	4.2	4.3	25.0	22.3	15.3	7.0	1.5	2.4	0.4	1.8	0.1	−1.2
1960	30.2	25.3	20.5	4.8	5.0	30.2	22.8	15.2	7.6	1.8	2.4	.5	1.9	.1	3.2
1961	31.4	26.0	20.9	5.1	5.4	31.4	22.7	15.1	7.6	1.8	2.7	.5	2.1	.1	4.3
1962	33.5	27.4	21.7	5.7	6.1	33.5	25.0	16.9	8.1	1.8	2.8	.5	2.1	.1	3.9
1963	36.1	29.4	23.3	6.1	6.6	36.1	26.1	17.7	8.4	2.1	2.8	.6	2.1	.1	5.0
1964	41.0	33.6	26.7	6.9	7.4	41.0	28.1	19.4	8.7	2.4	3.0	.7	2.1	.2	7.5
1965	43.5	35.4	27.8	7.6	8.1	43.5	31.5	22.2	9.3	2.7	3.0	.8	2.1	.2	6.2
1966	47.2	38.9	30.7	8.2	8.3	47.2	37.1	26.3	10.7	3.1	3.2	.8	2.2	.2	3.9
1967	50.2	41.4	32.2	9.2	8.9	50.2	39.9	27.8	12.2	3.4	3.4	1.0	2.1	.2	3.5
1968	55.6	45.3	35.3	10.0	10.3	55.6	46.6	33.9	12.6	4.1	3.2	1.0	1.9	.3	1.7
1969	61.2	49.3	38.3	11.0	11.9	61.2	50.5	36.8	13.7	5.8	3.2	1.1	1.8	.3	1.8
1970	70.8	57.0	44.5	12.4	13.0	70.8	55.8	40.9	14.9	6.6	3.6	1.2	2.0	.4	4.9
1971	74.2	59.3	45.6	13.8	14.1	74.2	62.3	46.6	15.8	6.4	4.1	1.3	2.4	.4	1.3
1972	83.4	66.2	51.8	14.4	16.4	83.4	74.2	56.9	17.3	7.7	4.3	1.3	2.5	.5	−2.9
1973	115.6	91.8	73.9	17.8	23.8	115.6	91.2	71.8	19.3	11.1	4.6	1.4	2.5	.7	8.7
1974	152.6	124.3	101.0	23.3	30.3	152.6	127.5	104.5	22.9	14.6	5.4	1.2	3.2	1.0	5.1
1975	164.4	136.3	109.6	26.7	28.2	164.4	122.7	99.0	23.7	14.9	5.4	1.2	3.5	.7	21.4
1976	181.6	148.9	117.8	31.1	32.8	181.6	151.1	124.6	26.5	15.7	6.0	1.2	3.7	1.1	8.8
1977	196.5	158.8	123.7	35.1	37.7	196.5	182.4	152.6	29.8	17.2	6.0	1.2	3.4	1.4	−9.2
1978	233.3	186.1	145.4	40.7	47.1	233.3	212.3	177.4	34.8	25.3	6.4	1.3	3.8	1.4	−10.7
1979	299.7	228.9	184.2	44.7	69.7	299.7	252.7	212.8	39.9	37.5	7.5	1.4	4.1	2.0	2.0
1980	360.9	279.2	226.0	53.2	80.6	360.9	293.9	248.6	45.3	46.5	9.0	1.6	5.0	2.4	11.5
1981	398.2	303.0	239.3	63.7	94.1	398.2	317.7	267.7	49.9	60.9	10.0	1.8	5.0	3.2	9.5
1982	379.9	282.6	215.2	67.4	97.3	379.9	303.2	250.6	52.6	67.1	12.1	2.1	6.4	3.6	−2.5
1983	372.5	276.7	207.5	69.2	95.8	372.5	328.1	272.7	55.4	66.5	12.9	1.8	7.3	3.8	−35.0
1984	410.5	302.4	225.8	76.6	108.1	410.5	405.1	336.3	68.8	83.8	15.6	2.3	9.4	3.9	−94.0
1985	399.3	302.1	222.4	79.7	97.3	399.3	417.6	343.3	74.3	82.4	17.4	2.7	11.4	3.2	−118.1
1986	415.2	319.2	226.2	93.0	96.0	415.2	451.7	370.0	81.7	86.9	18.3	2.5	12.3	3.5	−141.7
1987	469.0	364.0	257.7	106.2	105.1	469.0	507.1	414.8	92.3	100.5	16.6	3.0	10.4	3.2	−155.1
1988	572.9	444.2	325.8	118.4	128.7	572.9	552.2	452.1	100.1	120.8	17.8	2.7	10.4	4.8	−118.0
1989	665.5	508.0	371.6	136.4	157.5	665.5	587.7	485.1	102.6	141.5	25.6	8.9	11.3	5.4	−89.3
1990	725.7	557.1	398.7	158.4	168.6	725.7	628.5	509.0	119.5	146.9	28.8	10.1	13.2	5.5	−78.5
1991	756.8	601.1	427.1	173.9	155.7	756.8	620.9	501.4	119.6	139.7	−12.0	10.4	−27.8	5.4	8.1
1992	771.6	638.1	449.7	188.5	133.5	771.6	668.4	544.6	123.8	127.9	31.8	9.5	16.5	5.8	−56.6
1993	795.6	659.1	461.0	198.1	136.6	795.6	724.3	592.1	132.2	132.1	31.5	9.9	15.7	5.9	−92.3
1994 [p]		716.1	509.8	206.3			818.2	678.2	139.9		33.3	10.5	15.7	7.1	
1982: IV	357.5	265.6	198.2	67.4	91.9	357.5	295.1	241.6	53.4	64.4	13.8	1.9	8.2	3.7	−15.8
1983: IV	388.3	286.2	218.2	67.9	102.1	388.3	358.0	300.0	58.0	71.0	17.8	2.0	11.0	4.8	−58.5
1984: IV	415.2	308.7	231.4	77.3	106.6	415.2	415.7	344.1	71.6	85.5	20.4	2.5	13.9	4.0	−103.3
1985: IV	402.9	304.7	222.6	82.1	98.1	402.9	440.2	363.0	77.2	82.4	19.4	2.5	13.5	3.4	−139.1
1986: IV	426.7	333.9	235.8	98.1	92.8	426.7	467.1	382.4	84.7	88.9	19.6	2.8	12.8	4.0	−149.0
1987: IV	506.8	392.4	283.3	109.2	114.4	506.8	535.6	437.6	98.0	106.9	21.4	3.1	14.6	3.8	−157.1
1988: IV	606.9	467.0	345.4	121.6	139.9	606.9	573.1	470.1	103.0	130.2	23.8	2.7	15.1	5.9	−120.1
1989: IV	683.1	523.8	380.7	143.1	159.3	683.1	597.7	492.2	105.6	139.1	30.3	9.8	15.1	5.4	−84.0
1990: IV	757.4	577.6	409.0	168.6	179.7	757.4	649.2	523.9	125.4	147.7	28.2	10.2	12.4	5.6	−67.7
1991: I	750.3	576.6	415.3	161.3	173.7	750.3	609.4	489.1	120.4	146.4	−61.4	10.3	−76.9	5.2	55.8
II	757.8	602.1	429.6	172.6	155.6	757.8	613.8	494.3	119.5	142.5	−16.1	10.3	−32.0	5.6	17.6
III	749.7	601.9	424.7	177.1	147.8	749.7	623.1	505.2	117.9	138.4	10.4	10.2	−5.0	5.2	−22.2
IV	769.5	623.7	439.0	184.7	145.7	769.5	637.5	516.9	120.6	131.6	19.1	10.6	2.8	5.7	−18.8
1992: I	771.1	631.8	442.6	189.2	139.3	771.1	641.7	516.9	124.8	128.3	27.7	9.4	12.5	5.7	−26.6
II	772.1	632.7	445.9	186.8	139.4	772.1	663.9	540.3	123.7	131.6	30.7	9.7	15.1	5.9	−54.1
III	769.4	638.8	448.5	190.2	130.7	769.4	676.6	556.8	119.8	124.8	27.9	9.2	13.0	5.7	−59.9
IV	773.8	649.2	461.6	187.6	124.6	773.8	691.4	564.3	127.1	126.8	41.1	9.9	25.3	5.9	−85.6
1993: I	777.1	646.8	451.6	195.3	130.2	777.1	696.4	569.3	127.1	122.2	26.7	9.8	11.4	5.5	−68.3
II	797.7	660.1	461.7	198.4	137.6	797.7	723.5	592.6	130.9	134.3	28.8	9.8	12.9	6.1	−88.9
III	786.1	649.0	450.3	198.7	137.1	786.1	726.0	593.2	132.8	128.6	30.3	9.9	14.3	6.1	−98.8
IV	821.6	680.3	480.3	200.0	141.3	821.6	751.4	613.3	138.1	143.3	40.1	9.8	24.3	5.9	−113.2
1994: I	819.6	674.2	476.0	198.3	145.4	819.6	760.9	622.3	138.6	146.1	29.0	10.5	11.6	6.9	−116.4
II	866.6	704.5	499.5	205.0	162.1	866.6	802.1	665.3	136.8	169.5	30.1	10.5	12.7	6.9	−135.1
III	907.2	730.5	521.3	209.1	176.7	907.2	840.1	700.0	140.1	188.8	31.9	10.3	14.4	7.2	−153.6
IV [p]		755.3	542.5	212.7			869.6	725.4	144.2		42.1	10.7	23.9	7.5	

[1] Includes capital grants received by the United States (net), not shown separately. See Table B-29 for data.
[2] Certain goods, primarily military equipment purchased and sold by the Federal Government, are included in services.
[3] Mainly receipts by U.S. residents of interest and dividends and reinvested earnings of foreign affiliates of U.S. corporations.
[4] Mainly payments to foreign residents of interest and dividends and reinvested earnings of U.S. affiliates of foreign corporations.

Source: Department of Commerce, Bureau of Economic Analysis.

TABLE B–22.—*Exports and imports of goods and services and receipts and payments of factor income in 1987 dollars, 1959–94*

[Billions of 1987 dollars; quarterly data at seasonally adjusted annual rates]

Year or quarter	Exports of goods and services					Re-ceipts of factor in-come [2]	Imports of goods and services					Pay-ments of factor in-come [3]
	Total	Merchandise [1]			Serv-ices [1]		Total	Merchandise [1]			Serv-ices [1]	
		Total	Dura-ble goods	Non-dura-ble goods				Total	Dura-ble goods	Non-dura-ble goods		
1959	73.8	58.0	31.5	26.5	15.8	17.0	95.6	60.2	26.0	34.2	35.4	6.2
1960	88.4	71.2	39.2	32.0	17.2	19.1	96.1	59.1	24.7	34.4	37.0	7.2
1961	89.9	71.5	39.4	32.1	18.4	20.6	95.3	59.2	23.7	35.5	36.1	7.2
1962	95.0	74.8	41.2	33.5	20.3	22.5	105.5	68.0	28.0	40.0	37.5	7.3
1963	101.8	80.3	43.6	36.7	21.5	24.4	107.7	70.9	29.6	41.2	36.8	8.2
1964	115.4	91.4	50.2	41.2	24.0	26.6	112.9	75.6	32.8	42.8	37.3	9.1
1965	118.1	92.1	52.2	39.9	25.9	28.3	124.5	86.5	40.5	46.0	37.9	9.9
1966	125.7	98.4	56.1	42.3	27.3	28.0	143.7	100.2	50.6	49.6	43.5	11.0
1967	130.0	100.1	63.8	36.3	29.9	29.2	153.7	105.2	53.1	52.1	48.6	11.8
1968	140.2	108.8	70.0	38.7	31.5	32.3	177.7	128.1	68.7	59.4	49.6	13.5
1969	147.8	114.4	75.2	39.2	33.3	35.7	189.2	137.0	74.1	62.8	52.3	17.8
1970	161.3	125.2	80.4	44.7	36.1	36.8	196.4	142.1	75.4	66.7	54.4	19.2
1971	161.9	124.1	79.3	44.9	37.8	37.9	207.8	156.1	84.4	71.7	51.7	17.9
1972	173.7	136.5	87.1	49.5	37.2	42.2	230.2	177.5	95.7	81.7	52.8	20.5
1973	210.3	166.9	108.0	58.9	43.4	57.5	244.4	194.7	100.9	93.9	49.7	27.6
1974	234.4	183.4	123.5	59.9	51.0	67.5	238.4	189.3	101.3	87.9	49.2	33.2
1975	232.9	178.5	121.3	57.2	54.4	57.4	209.8	163.3	82.1	81.2	46.5	31.6
1976	243.4	183.9	121.8	62.1	59.5	63.0	249.7	200.4	100.9	99.5	49.3	31.5
1977	246.9	183.9	119.5	64.4	63.0	67.9	274.7	223.2	112.9	110.3	51.5	32.2
1978	270.2	203.0	132.1	70.9	67.2	78.7	300.1	245.2	130.0	115.3	54.8	43.2
1979	293.5	225.7	148.1	77.6	67.8	107.1	304.1	248.7	132.1	116.7	55.3	58.6
1980	320.5	248.2	161.0	87.3	72.3	113.7	289.9	235.6	133.6	102.0	54.2	66.6
1981	326.1	244.0	154.2	89.7	82.2	120.7	304.1	246.1	143.4	102.7	58.0	79.4
1982	296.7	217.7	130.5	87.2	79.0	117.9	304.1	243.1	143.0	100.1	61.1	82.1
1983	285.9	208.3	124.6	83.8	77.6	111.0	342.1	276.5	167.6	108.9	65.6	78.0
1984	305.7	221.3	133.8	87.5	84.4	119.4	427.7	346.1	219.9	126.2	81.6	93.5
1985	309.2	224.8	139.3	85.6	84.4	103.4	454.6	366.5	237.2	129.3	88.1	88.2
1986	329.6	234.3	144.8	89.6	95.3	99.2	484.7	398.0	254.6	143.4	86.7	90.2
1987	364.0	257.7	163.0	94.7	106.2	105.1	507.1	414.8	264.2	150.6	92.3	100.5
1988	421.6	307.4	202.8	104.6	114.2	123.8	525.7	431.3	274.7	156.7	94.3	116.1
1989	471.8	343.8	230.9	112.9	128.0	144.7	545.4	450.4	287.1	163.3	95.0	130.1
1990	510.5	368.9	249.4	119.5	141.6	148.0	565.1	461.4	292.5	168.9	103.7	128.8
1991	542.6	397.1	269.4	127.7	145.5	131.3	562.1	464.4	297.2	167.2	97.7	116.7
1992	578.8	426.5	291.4	135.2	152.3	109.2	611.2	512.8	333.4	179.4	98.4	102.8
1993	602.5	446.0	312.5	133.4	156.5	109.1	676.3	572.7	380.9	191.8	103.6	103.4
1994 *p*	654.8	495.0	355.1	139.9	159.8		769.0	660.0	454.6	205.3	109.0	
1982: IV	280.4	202.8	119.0	83.7	77.6	109.7	299.4	236.3	134.6	101.7	63.1	77.6
1983: IV	291.5	215.5	131.0	84.5	75.9	116.5	375.1	306.6	191.1	115.5	68.6	82.0
1984: IV	312.8	229.0	138.5	90.5	83.8	116.1	444.2	357.9	229.3	128.6	86.3	93.9
1985: IV	312.0	226.4	139.6	86.8	85.5	102.9	467.4	380.0	243.5	136.5	87.4	86.8
1986: IV	342.9	243.5	150.0	93.5	99.4	94.8	498.9	409.1	259.8	149.3	89.8	91.2
1987: IV	386.1	278.0	180.1	97.8	108.1	112.9	522.1	427.4	273.8	153.7	94.6	105.4
1988: IV	438.2	322.0	214.7	107.2	116.2	132.3	540.9	444.8	284.0	160.8	96.1	123.0
1989: IV	487.7	354.8	237.8	116.9	132.9	144.3	555.0	458.5	290.4	168.1	96.5	125.9
1990: IV	520.4	374.6	250.9	123.8	145.8	155.4	557.2	453.1	294.4	158.8	104.1	127.1
1991: I	519.0	382.2	254.8	127.4	136.7	148.1	539.4	441.5	283.6	157.9	97.9	124.0
II	540.0	398.5	272.8	125.7	145.5	131.7	557.8	459.0	289.8	169.2	98.7	119.6
III	544.8	397.9	271.5	126.4	146.9	124.1	571.8	475.3	304.9	170.4	96.5	115.0
IV	562.6	409.8	278.6	131.3	152.7	121.5	579.4	481.8	310.6	171.2	97.6	108.3
1992: I	571.0	416.0	282.5	133.5	154.9	114.9	588.8	489.5	317.1	172.4	99.3	104.3
II	573.1	421.5	287.7	133.8	151.6	114.2	607.1	509.7	329.6	180.0	97.4	106.1
III	580.5	427.4	291.5	136.0	153.1	106.6	619.4	521.7	339.1	182.5	97.7	99.9
IV	590.7	441.1	303.7	137.4	149.6	101.0	629.3	530.2	347.6	182.6	99.0	100.7
1993: I	589.2	433.9	301.2	132.7	155.3	104.7	646.8	546.6	361.0	185.7	100.1	96.1
II	600.2	443.3	310.4	132.9	156.9	110.1	669.6	567.4	373.7	193.7	102.2	105.3
III	595.3	438.5	308.0	130.5	156.7	109.4	681.6	577.1	384.0	193.0	104.5	100.4
IV	625.2	468.1	330.6	137.5	157.1	112.4	707.4	599.9	405.1	194.8	107.6	111.7
1994: I	619.6	464.4	332.6	131.7	155.2	114.8	723.6	615.2	417.7	197.5	108.5	113.2
II	643.9	484.6	348.5	136.1	159.2	127.1	755.6	648.3	443.4	204.9	107.4	130.7
III	666.5	505.1	361.2	144.0	161.3	137.8	783.5	674.6	463.1	211.5	108.9	144.9
IV *p*	689.0	525.8	378.0	147.8	163.2		813.1	701.8	494.4	207.4	111.3	

[1] Certain goods, primarily military equipment purchased and sold by the Federal Government, are included in services.
[2] Mainly receipts by U.S. residents of interest and dividends and reinvested earnings of foreign affiliates of U.S. corporations.
[3] Mainly payments to foreign residents of interest and dividends and reinvested earnings of U.S. affiliates of foreign corporations.
Source: Department of Commerce, Bureau of Economic Analysis.

[Billions of dollars; quarterly data at seasonally adjusted annual rates]

Year or quarter	Gross domestic product	Plus: Receipts of factor income from rest of the world [1]	Less: Payments of factor income to rest of the world [2]	Equals: Gross national product	Less: Consumption of fixed capital	Equals: Net national product	Less: Indirect business tax and nontax liability	Less: Business transfer payments	Less: Statistical discrepancy	Plus: Subsidies less current surplus of government enterprises	Equals: National income
1959	494.2	4.3	1.5	497.0	44.6	452.5	41.9	1.4	−1.8	−0.9	410.1
1960	513.3	5.0	1.8	516.6	46.3	470.2	45.5	1.4	−3.1	−.8	425.7
1961	531.8	5.4	1.8	535.4	47.7	487.7	48.1	1.5	−2.2	.2	440.5
1962	571.6	6.1	1.8	575.8	49.3	526.5	51.7	1.6	−1.0	.3	474.5
1963	603.1	6.6	2.1	607.7	51.3	556.4	54.7	1.8	−2.0	−.3	501.5
1964	648.0	7.4	2.4	653.0	53.9	599.2	58.8	2.0	−.7	.1	539.1
1965	702.7	8.1	2.7	708.1	57.3	650.7	62.7	2.2	−.7	.3	586.9
1966	769.8	8.3	3.1	774.9	62.1	712.8	65.4	2.3	2.8	1.4	643.7
1967	814.3	8.9	3.4	819.8	67.4	752.4	70.4	2.5	.8	1.2	679.9
1968	889.3	10.3	4.1	895.5	73.9	821.5	79.0	2.8	−.1	1.2	741.0
1969	959.5	11.9	5.8	965.6	81.5	884.2	86.6	3.1	−2.6	1.5	798.6
1970	1,010.7	13.0	6.6	1,017.1	88.8	928.3	94.3	3.2	.0	2.6	833.5
1971	1,097.2	14.1	6.4	1,104.9	97.6	1,007.3	103.6	3.4	3.1	2.4	899.5
1972	1,207.0	16.4	7.7	1,215.7	109.9	1,105.7	111.4	3.9	1.1	3.4	992.9
1973	1,349.6	23.8	11.1	1,362.3	120.4	1,241.9	121.0	4.5	−.5	2.6	1,119.5
1974	1,458.6	30.3	14.6	1,474.3	140.2	1,334.1	129.3	5.0	1.4	.4	1,198.8
1975	1,585.9	28.2	14.9	1,599.1	165.2	1,433.9	140.0	5.2	6.0	2.6	1,285.3
1976	1,768.4	32.8	15.7	1,785.5	182.8	1,602.7	151.6	6.5	10.4	1.4	1,435.5
1977	1,974.1	37.7	17.2	1,994.6	205.2	1,789.4	165.5	7.3	10.9	3.3	1,609.1
1978	2,232.7	47.1	25.3	2,254.5	234.8	2,019.8	177.8	8.2	7.6	3.6	1,829.8
1979	2,488.6	69.7	37.5	2,520.8	272.4	2,248.4	188.7	9.9	13.8	2.9	2,038.9
1980	2,708.0	80.6	46.5	2,742.1	311.9	2,430.2	212.0	11.2	13.6	4.8	2,198.2
1981	3,030.6	94.1	60.9	3,063.8	362.4	2,701.4	249.3	13.4	10.9	4.7	2,432.5
1982	3,149.6	97.3	67.1	3,179.8	399.1	2,780.8	256.4	15.4	−7.4	6.2	2,522.5
1983	3,405.0	95.8	66.5	3,434.4	418.4	3,016.0	280.1	16.6	10.2	11.7	2,720.8
1984	3,777.2	108.1	83.8	3,801.5	433.2	3,368.3	309.5	19.0	−9.0	9.5	3,058.3
1985	4,038.7	97.3	82.4	4,053.6	454.5	3,599.1	329.9	21.0	−13.9	6.4	3,268.4
1986	4,268.6	96.0	86.9	4,277.7	478.6	3,799.2	345.5	24.2	1.2	9.7	3,437.9
1987	4,539.9	105.1	100.5	4,544.5	502.2	4,042.4	365.0	24.0	−24.8	14.1	3,692.3
1988	4,900.4	128.7	120.8	4,908.2	534.0	4,374.2	385.3	25.6	−28.4	10.9	4,002.6
1989	5,250.8	157.5	141.5	5,266.8	580.4	4,686.4	414.7	26.6	1.1	5.4	4,249.5
1990	5,546.1	168.6	146.9	5,567.8	602.7	4,965.1	444.0	26.8	7.8	4.5	4,491.0
1991	5,724.8	155.7	139.7	5,740.8	626.5	5,114.3	478.3	26.3	1.5	−.1	4,608.2
1992	6,020.2	133.5	127.9	6,025.8	658.5	5,367.3	504.4	28.1	8.8	3.5	4,829.5
1993	6,343.3	136.6	132.1	6,347.8	669.1	5,678.7	525.3	28.7	2.3	9.0	5,131.4
1994 *p*	6,736.9				715.5		553.7	30.6		1.0	
1982: IV	3,195.1	91.9	64.4	3,222.6	412.5	2,810.1	262.3	16.0	−10.1	9.6	2,551.5
1983: IV	3,547.3	102.1	71.0	3,578.4	439.7	3,138.7	291.7	18.1	13.8	19.2	2,834.3
1984: IV	3,869.1	106.6	85.5	3,890.2	448.0	3,442.2	317.7	20.2	−20.5	9.7	3,134.4
1985: IV	4,140.5	98.1	82.4	4,156.2	465.6	3,690.7	335.1	22.2	−5.9	2.6	3,341.9
1986: IV	4,336.6	92.8	88.9	4,340.5	488.2	3,852.3	351.6	24.9	−2.0	8.2	3,486.0
1987: IV	4,683.0	114.4	106.9	4,690.5	512.1	4,178.5	372.3	24.2	−24.9	22.0	3,828.8
1988: IV	5,044.6	139.9	130.2	5,054.3	547.2	4,507.2	394.2	27.2	−25.4	16.5	4,127.6
1989: IV	5,344.8	159.3	139.1	5,365.0	600.8	4,764.2	424.4	26.2	12.8	4.4	4,305.2
1990: IV	5,597.9	179.7	147.7	5,630.0	614.8	5,015.1	454.8	26.7	4.9	10.4	4,539.2
1991: I	5,636.8	173.7	146.4	5,664.0	620.2	5,043.8	465.8	26.0	−10.3	1.6	4,563.9
II	5,705.9	155.6	142.5	5,719.0	623.3	5,095.8	471.8	26.3	6.2	.8	4,592.3
III	5,759.9	147.8	138.4	5,769.3	627.1	5,142.2	483.7	26.0	12.2	−7.7	4,612.7
IV	5,796.6	145.7	131.6	5,810.7	635.4	5,175.4	491.8	26.8	−2.1	5.0	4,663.9
1992: I	5,896.8	139.3	128.3	5,907.7	632.9	5,274.8	496.3	27.6	2.0	3.6	4,752.4
II	5,971.3	139.4	131.6	5,979.1	637.5	5,341.7	499.6	28.1	11.5	4.4	4,806.8
III	6,043.6	130.7	124.8	6,049.4	715.3	5,334.1	505.3	28.2	3.7	−2.9	4,793.9
IV	6,169.3	124.6	126.8	6,167.0	648.4	5,518.6	516.2	28.6	18.0	9.1	4,964.9
1993: I	6,235.9	130.2	122.2	6,243.9	662.9	5,581.1	515.5	28.2	25.5	19.3	5,031.1
II	6,299.9	137.6	134.3	6,303.3	662.0	5,641.2	521.4	28.9	5.7	8.8	5,094.0
III	6,359.2	137.1	128.6	6,367.8	677.3	5,690.5	524.7	28.9	−5.5	−3.9	5,138.5
IV	6,478.1	141.3	143.3	6,476.2	674.0	5,802.2	539.7	28.6	−16.5	11.7	5,262.0
1994: I	6,574.7	145.4	146.1	6,574.0	734.1	5,840.0	544.7	30.1	−36.1	7.4	5,308.7
II	6,689.9	162.1	169.5	6,682.5	698.1	5,984.5	550.3	30.3	−24.0	3.0	5,430.7
III	6,791.7	176.7	188.8	6,779.6	709.9	6,069.8	557.2	30.8	−21.1	−8.0	5,494.9
IV *p*	6,891.1				719.8		562.8	31.4		1.6	

[1] Mainly receipts by U.S. residents of interest and dividends and reinvested earnings of foreign affiliates of U.S. corporations.
[2] Mainly payments to foreign residents of interest and dividends and reinvested earnings of U.S. affiliates of foreign corporations.

Source: Department of Commerce, Bureau of Economic Analysis.

[Billions of dollars; quarterly data at seasonally adjusted annual rates]

Year or quarter	National income	Less: Corporate profits with inventory valuation and capital consumption adjustments	Less: Net interest	Less: Contributions for social insurance	Less: Wage accruals less disbursements	Plus: Personal interest income	Plus: Personal dividend income	Plus: Government transfer payments to persons	Plus: Business transfer payments to persons	Equals: Personal income
1959	410.1	52.3	10.2	18.8	0.0	22.7	12.7	25.7	1.3	391.2
1960	425.7	50.7	11.2	21.9	.0	25.0	13.4	27.5	1.3	409.2
1961	440.5	51.6	13.1	22.9	.0	26.9	14.0	31.5	1.4	426.5
1962	474.5	59.6	14.6	25.4	.0	29.3	15.0	32.6	1.5	453.4
1963	501.5	65.1	16.1	28.5	.0	32.4	16.1	34.5	1.7	476.4
1964	539.1	72.1	18.2	30.1	.0	36.1	18.0	36.0	1.8	510.7
1965	586.9	82.9	21.1	31.6	.0	40.3	20.2	39.1	2.0	552.9
1966	643.7	88.6	24.3	40.6	.0	44.9	20.9	43.6	2.1	601.7
1967	679.9	86.0	28.1	45.5	.0	49.5	22.1	52.3	2.3	646.5
1968	741.0	92.6	30.4	50.4	.0	54.6	24.5	60.6	2.5	709.9
1969	798.6	89.6	33.6	57.9	.0	60.8	25.1	67.5	2.8	773.7
1970	833.5	77.5	40.0	62.2	.0	69.2	23.5	81.8	2.8	831.0
1971	899.5	90.3	45.4	68.9	.6	75.7	23.5	97.0	3.0	893.5
1972	992.9	103.2	49.3	79.0	.0	81.8	25.5	108.4	3.4	980.5
1973	1,119.5	116.4	56.5	97.6	−.1	94.1	27.7	124.1	3.8	1,098.7
1974	1,198.8	104.5	71.8	110.5	−.5	112.4	29.6	147.4	4.0	1,205.7
1975	1,285.3	121.9	80.0	118.5	.1	123.0	29.2	185.7	4.5	1,307.3
1976	1,435.5	147.1	85.1	134.5	.1	134.6	34.7	202.8	5.5	1,446.3
1977	1,609.1	175.7	100.7	149.8	.1	155.7	39.4	217.5	5.9	1,601.3
1978	1,829.8	199.7	120.5	171.8	.3	184.5	44.2	234.8	6.8	1,807.9
1979	2,038.9	202.5	149.9	197.8	−.2	223.2	50.4	262.8	7.9	2,033.1
1980	2,198.2	177.7	191.2	216.6	.0	274.0	57.1	312.6	8.8	2,265.4
1981	2,432.5	182.0	233.4	251.3	.1	336.1	66.9	355.7	10.2	2,534.7
1982	2,522.5	151.5	262.4	269.6	.0	376.8	67.1	396.3	11.8	2,690.9
1983	2,720.8	212.7	270.0	290.2	−.4	397.5	77.8	426.1	12.8	2,862.5
1984	3,058.3	264.2	307.9	325.0	.2	461.9	78.8	437.8	15.1	3,154.6
1985	3,268.4	280.8	326.2	353.8	−.2	498.1	87.9	468.1	17.8	3,379.8
1986	3,437.9	271.6	350.2	379.8	.0	531.7	104.7	497.1	20.7	3,590.4
1987	3,692.3	319.8	360.4	400.7	.0	548.1	100.4	521.3	20.8	3,802.0
1988	4,002.6	365.0	387.7	442.3	.0	583.2	108.4	555.9	20.8	4,075.9
1989	4,249.5	362.8	452.7	473.2	.0	668.2	126.5	603.8	21.1	4,380.3
1990	4,491.0	380.6	463.7	503.1	.1	698.2	144.4	666.3	21.3	4,673.8
1991	4,608.2	390.3	447.4	525.9	−.1	695.1	150.5	749.2	20.8	4,860.3
1992	4,829.5	405.1	420.0	556.4	−20.0	665.2	161.0	837.9	22.3	5,154.3
1993	5,131.4	485.8	399.5	585.6	20.0	637.9	181.3	892.6	22.8	5,375.1
1994 *p*	....	....	....	626.3	.0	664.3	194.3	940.2	23.5	5,701.8
1982: IV	2,551.5	150.3	256.8	272.8	.0	373.6	69.4	419.9	12.3	2,746.8
1983: IV	2,834.3	229.1	281.8	298.3	.0	418.7	80.6	428.0	13.2	2,965.8
1984: IV	3,134.4	261.3	321.1	332.2	.6	485.4	79.3	442.3	16.2	3,242.5
1985: IV	3,341.9	284.9	331.9	362.3	.0	507.5	92.7	474.8	18.8	3,456.7
1986: IV	3,486.0	264.6	349.7	388.7	.0	532.6	105.6	505.8	20.9	3,647.8
1987: IV	3,828.8	343.3	368.6	409.6	−.2	562.3	100.1	528.1	20.4	3,918.5
1988: IV	4,127.6	378.3	408.1	453.5	.0	608.9	113.8	563.5	21.3	4,195.2
1989: IV	4,305.2	354.5	459.8	480.4	.0	681.2	132.9	624.0	20.8	4,469.4
1990: IV	4,539.2	362.8	474.4	509.5	.2	710.3	144.4	690.9	21.1	4,759.1
1991: I	4,563.9	385.4	465.1	520.4	.2	710.1	148.6	725.0	20.8	4,797.2
II	4,592.3	391.5	448.0	522.7	−.4	697.3	149.9	742.2	20.7	4,840.5
III	4,612.7	389.6	444.7	528.0	.0	691.0	152.2	754.7	20.8	4,869.1
IV	4,663.9	394.7	431.8	532.7	.0	682.2	151.2	775.1	21.1	4,934.2
1992: I	4,752.4	412.1	421.6	546.3	.0	669.1	151.2	817.7	21.9	5,032.4
II	4,806.8	412.6	421.9	552.6	.0	670.2	156.7	833.0	22.2	5,101.9
III	4,793.9	363.2	418.7	558.9	.0	663.2	164.3	845.0	22.5	5,148.1
IV	4,964.9	432.5	418.0	567.8	−80.0	658.2	171.8	855.7	22.7	5,335.0
1993: I	5,031.1	442.5	414.6	568.3	80.0	653.2	178.0	875.8	22.8	5,255.5
II	5,094.0	473.1	397.6	586.1	.0	636.6	180.4	887.6	22.8	5,364.5
III	5,138.5	493.5	396.7	590.9	.0	634.1	182.8	898.8	22.8	5,395.9
IV	5,262.0	533.9	389.1	597.2	.0	627.7	184.1	908.3	22.7	5,484.6
1994: I	5,308.7	508.2	394.2	614.7	.0	631.1	185.7	924.2	23.2	5,555.8
II	5,430.7	546.4	399.7	623.5	.0	649.4	191.7	934.3	23.4	5,659.9
III	5,494.9	556.0	415.7	628.9	.0	674.2	196.9	945.4	23.6	5,734.5
IV *p*	....	....	....	637.9	.0	702.3	202.7	956.8	23.8	5,857.1

Source: Department of Commerce, Bureau of Economic Analysis.

TABLE B-25.—*National income by type of income, 1959-94*

[Billions of dollars; quarterly data at seasonally adjusted annual rates]

| Year or quarter | National income [1] | Compensation of employees | | | Proprietors' income with inventory valuation and capital consumption adjustments | | | | | | | |
| | | Total | Wages and salaries | Supplements to wages and salaries [2] | Total | Farm | | | Nonfarm | | | |
						Total	Proprietors' income [3]	Capital consumption adjustment	Total	Proprietors' income	Inventory valuation adjustment	Capital consumption adjustment
1959	410.1	281.2	259.8	21.4	51.7	10.7	11.6	−0.9	41.1	40.2	0.0	0.9
1960	425.7	296.7	272.8	23.8	51.9	11.2	12.1	−.8	40.6	39.8	.0	.8
1961	440.5	305.6	280.5	25.1	54.3	11.9	12.7	−.8	42.4	41.8	.0	.6
1962	474.5	327.4	299.3	28.1	56.4	11.9	12.7	−.8	44.5	43.9	.0	.6
1963	501.5	345.5	314.8	30.7	57.7	11.8	12.5	−.7	45.9	45.2	.0	.7
1964	539.1	371.0	337.7	33.2	60.5	10.6	11.3	−.7	49.8	49.2	−.1	.7
1965	586.9	399.8	363.7	36.1	65.0	12.9	13.7	−.7	52.1	51.9	−.2	.4
1966	643.7	443.0	400.3	42.7	69.4	14.0	14.8	−.8	55.3	55.4	−.2	.2
1967	679.9	475.5	428.9	46.6	70.9	12.7	13.5	−.8	58.2	58.3	−.2	.1
1968	741.0	524.7	471.9	52.8	75.1	12.7	13.6	−.9	62.4	63.0	−.4	−.2
1969	798.6	578.4	518.3	60.1	78.9	14.4	15.6	−1.1	64.5	65.0	−.5	.0
1970	833.5	618.3	551.5	66.8	79.9	14.6	15.9	−1.3	65.3	66.0	−.5	−.1
1971	899.5	659.4	584.5	74.9	86.2	15.2	16.6	−1.4	70.9	72.0	−.6	−.5
1972	992.9	726.2	638.7	87.6	97.4	19.1	20.9	−1.8	78.3	79.3	−.7	−.2
1973	1,119.5	812.8	708.6	104.2	116.5	32.2	34.3	−2.0	84.3	86.5	−2.0	−.2
1974	1,198.8	891.3	772.2	119.1	115.3	25.5	28.2	−2.8	89.8	94.2	−3.8	−.6
1975	1,285.3	948.7	814.7	134.0	121.2	23.7	27.5	−3.8	97.5	100.2	−1.2	−1.4
1976	1,435.5	1,058.3	899.6	158.7	132.9	18.3	22.5	−4.2	114.6	117.6	−1.3	−1.7
1977	1,609.1	1,177.3	994.0	183.3	146.4	17.1	21.8	−4.8	129.4	132.5	−1.3	−1.8
1978	1,829.8	1,333.0	1,120.9	212.1	167.7	21.5	27.0	−5.5	146.2	150.2	−2.1	−2.0
1979	2,038.9	1,496.4	1,255.3	241.1	181.8	24.7	31.2	−6.4	157.0	161.8	−2.9	−1.9
1980	2,198.2	1,644.4	1,376.6	267.8	171.8	11.5	19.4	−7.9	160.3	165.8	−3.0	−2.5
1981	2,432.5	1,815.5	1,515.6	299.8	180.8	21.2	30.2	−9.0	159.6	160.9	−1.4	.0
1982	2,522.5	1,916.0	1,593.3	322.7	170.7	13.5	23.1	−9.7	157.3	157.8	−.6	.0
1983	2,720.8	2,029.4	1,684.2	345.2	186.7	2.4	12.1	−9.7	184.3	176.1	−.6	8.7
1984	3,058.3	2,226.9	1,850.0	376.9	236.0	21.3	30.8	−9.4	214.7	197.1	−.5	18.1
1985	3,268.4	2,382.8	1,986.3	396.5	259.9	21.5	30.5	−9.0	238.4	212.4	−.2	26.1
1986	3,437.9	2,523.8	2,105.4	418.4	283.7	22.3	31.0	−8.7	261.5	230.6	−.1	30.9
1987	3,692.3	2,698.7	2,261.2	437.4	310.2	31.3	39.6	−8.3	279.0	252.4	−.8	27.4
1988	4,002.6	2,921.3	2,443.0	478.3	324.3	30.9	38.8	−8.0	293.4	266.8	−1.5	28.1
1989	4,249.5	3,100.2	2,586.4	513.8	347.3	40.2	48.3	−8.1	307.0	281.1	−1.2	27.2
1990	4,491.0	3,297.6	2,745.0	552.5	363.3	41.9	49.8	−7.8	321.4	305.6	−.4	16.2
1991	4,608.2	3,404.8	2,816.0	588.8	376.2	36.7	44.3	−7.6	339.5	328.3	−.2	11.4
1992	4,829.5	3,591.2	2,954.8	636.4	418.7	44.4	51.9	−7.5	374.4	362.0	−.5	12.9
1993	5,131.4	3,780.4	3,100.8	679.6	441.6	37.3	44.5	−7.2	404.3	390.2	−.8	14.9
1994 [p]		4,005.1	3,279.2	725.9	473.1	39.2	46.6	−7.3	433.9	419.8	−1.2	15.2
1982: IV	2,551.5	1,940.4	1,611.8	328.6	179.9	10.2	20.0	−9.8	169.6	168.0	.6	1.1
1983: IV	2,834.3	2,101.2	1,747.3	353.9	200.1	6.3	15.8	−9.5	193.8	182.5	−1.6	12.9
1984: IV	3,134.4	2,288.1	1,903.9	384.2	239.6	21.9	31.2	−9.3	217.7	196.6	.1	21.0
1985: IV	3,341.9	2,442.5	2,039.1	403.3	268.7	17.8	26.7	−8.9	250.9	223.2	−1.4	29.1
1986: IV	3,486.0	2,582.5	2,153.9	428.6	284.4	23.6	32.1	−8.6	260.9	230.0	.7	30.1
1987: IV	3,828.8	2,785.1	2,336.7	448.4	325.0	42.4	50.6	−8.2	282.6	254.2	1.7	26.7
1988: IV	4,127.6	3,004.9	2,510.6	494.3	333.4	30.9	38.8	−7.9	302.5	274.9	−1.4	29.0
1989: IV	4,305.2	3,162.8	2,637.9	524.9	349.7	38.4	46.4	−8.0	311.4	288.7	−.7	23.4
1990: IV	4,539.2	3,344.2	2,781.3	562.9	368.9	43.8	51.7	−7.9	325.1	318.4	−5.6	12.4
1991: I	4,563.9	3,359.5	2,785.3	574.2	364.2	37.0	44.8	−7.8	327.2	316.0	−.2	11.4
II	4,592.3	3,383.2	2,800.5	582.6	380.3	43.4	51.1	−7.7	336.9	325.9	−.2	11.2
III	4,612.7	3,417.6	2,823.9	593.8	373.8	29.6	37.2	−7.6	344.2	333.0	.0	11.3
IV	4,663.9	3,459.1	2,854.3	604.7	386.4	36.6	44.1	−7.5	349.8	338.2	−.2	11.8
1992: I	4,752.4	3,514.2	2,893.9	620.3	410.9	49.0	56.4	−7.4	361.9	350.3	−.7	12.3
II	4,806.8	3,564.9	2,933.4	631.5	412.8	43.7	51.0	−7.3	369.1	357.3	−.9	12.8
III	4,793.9	3,614.7	2,973.1	641.7	412.8	38.8	47.0	−8.2	374.0	361.8	−.3	12.5
IV	4,964.9	3,671.0	3,018.8	652.2	438.4	46.0	53.2	−7.2	392.4	378.6	.0	13.9
1993: I	5,031.1	3,713.1	3,053.9	659.2	444.4	49.6	56.7	−7.2	394.8	381.8	−1.3	14.4
II	5,094.0	3,761.1	3,085.1	676.0	438.8	39.4	46.5	−7.2	399.4	385.5	−.8	14.7
III	5,138.5	3,801.7	3,115.9	685.9	420.3	15.8	23.2	−7.4	404.5	389.8	−.1	14.8
IV	5,262.0	3,845.8	3,148.4	697.4	462.9	44.4	51.5	−7.0	418.5	403.7	−.9	15.7
1994: I	5,308.7	3,920.0	3,208.3	711.7	471.0	47.2	54.5	−7.3	423.8	409.3	−.6	15.2
II	5,430.7	3,979.3	3,257.2	722.0	471.3	39.3	46.6	−7.3	431.9	417.5	−1.1	15.5
III	5,494.9	4,023.7	3,293.9	729.7	467.0	29.8	37.2	−7.4	437.1	423.1	−1.1	15.2
IV [p]		4,097.4	3,357.4	740.0	483.3	40.7	47.9	−7.3	442.7	429.4	−1.8	15.1

[1] National income is the total net income earned in production. It differs from gross domestic product mainly in that it excludes depreciation charges and other allowances for business and institutional consumption of durable capital goods and indirect business taxes. See Table B-23.

See next page for continuation of table.

302

[Billions of dollars; quarterly data at seasonally adjusted annual rates]

Year or quarter	Rental income of persons with capital consumption adjustment			Corporate profits with inventory valuation and capital consumption adjustments								Capital consumption adjustment	Net interest
					Profits with inventory valuation adjustment and without capital consumption adjustment						Inventory valuation adjustment		
	Total	Rental income of persons	Capital consumption adjustment	Total	Profits								
					Total	Profits before tax	Profits tax liability	Profits after tax					
								Total	Dividends	Undistributed profits			
1959	14.7	18.0	-3.4	52.3	53.1	53.4	23.6	29.7	12.7	17.0	-0.3	-0.8	10.2
1960	15.3	18.7	-3.4	50.7	51.0	51.1	22.7	28.4	13.4	15.0	-.2	-.3	11.2
1961	15.8	19.2	-3.3	51.6	51.3	51.0	22.8	28.2	14.0	14.3	.3	.3	13.1
1962	16.5	19.8	-3.3	59.6	56.4	56.4	24.0	32.4	15.0	17.4	.0	3.2	14.6
1963	17.1	20.3	-3.2	65.1	61.2	61.2	26.2	34.9	16.1	18.8	.1	3.9	16.1
1964	17.3	20.5	-3.2	72.1	67.5	68.0	28.0	40.0	18.0	22.0	-.5	4.6	18.2
1965	18.0	21.3	-3.3	82.9	77.6	78.8	30.9	47.9	20.2	27.8	-1.2	5.3	21.1
1966	18.5	22.1	-3.6	88.6	83.0	85.1	33.7	51.4	20.9	30.5	-2.1	5.6	24.3
1967	19.4	23.4	-3.9	86.0	80.3	81.8	32.7	49.2	22.1	27.1	-1.6	5.7	28.1
1968	18.2	22.8	-4.6	92.6	86.9	90.6	39.4	51.2	24.6	26.6	-3.7	5.6	30.4
1969	18.0	23.9	-5.9	89.6	83.2	89.0	39.7	49.4	25.2	24.1	-5.9	6.4	33.6
1970	17.8	24.2	-6.4	77.5	71.8	78.4	34.4	44.0	23.7	20.3	-6.6	5.6	40.0
1971	18.2	25.6	-7.4	90.3	85.5	90.1	37.7	52.4	23.7	28.6	-4.6	4.8	45.4
1972	16.8	26.1	-9.3	103.2	97.9	104.5	41.9	62.6	25.8	36.9	-6.6	5.3	49.3
1973	17.3	28.2	-10.9	116.4	110.9	130.9	49.3	81.6	28.1	53.5	-20.0	5.5	56.5
1974	15.8	29.3	-13.5	104.5	103.4	142.8	51.8	91.0	30.4	60.6	-39.5	1.2	71.8
1975	13.5	29.5	-15.9	121.9	129.4	140.4	50.9	89.5	30.1	59.4	-11.0	-7.6	80.0
1976	12.1	29.9	-17.8	147.1	158.8	173.7	64.2	109.5	35.6	73.9	-14.9	-11.7	85.1
1977	9.0	30.0	-21.0	175.7	186.7	203.3	73.0	130.3	40.7	89.5	-16.6	-11.0	100.7
1978	8.9	34.4	-25.5	199.7	212.8	237.9	83.5	154.4	45.9	108.5	-25.0	-13.1	120.5
1979	8.4	39.1	-30.8	202.5	219.8	261.4	88.0	173.4	52.4	121.0	-41.6	-17.3	149.9
1980	13.2	49.0	-35.8	177.7	197.8	240.9	84.8	156.1	59.0	97.1	-43.0	-20.2	191.2
1981	20.8	61.1	-40.2	182.0	203.2	228.9	81.1	147.8	69.2	78.6	-25.7	-21.2	233.4
1982	21.9	64.4	-42.4	151.5	166.4	176.3	63.1	113.2	70.0	43.2	-9.9	-14.9	262.4
1983	22.1	64.8	-42.8	212.7	202.2	210.7	77.2	133.5	81.2	52.3	-8.5	10.4	270.0
1984	23.3	66.5	-43.2	264.2	236.4	240.5	94.0	146.4	82.7	63.8	-4.1	27.8	307.9
1985	18.7	63.4	-44.6	280.8	225.3	225.0	96.5	128.5	92.4	36.1	.2	55.5	326.2
1986	8.7	53.4	-44.7	271.6	227.6	217.8	106.5	111.3	109.8	1.6	9.7	44.1	350.2
1987	3.2	50.0	-46.8	319.8	273.4	287.9	127.1	160.8	106.2	54.6	-14.5	46.4	360.4
1988	4.3	53.4	-49.1	365.0	320.3	347.5	137.0	210.5	115.3	95.2	-27.3	44.7	387.7
1989	-13.5	44.2	-57.7	362.8	325.4	342.9	141.3	201.6	134.6	67.1	-17.5	37.4	452.7
1990	-14.2	42.7	-56.9	380.6	354.7	365.7	138.7	227.1	153.5	73.6	-11.0	25.9	463.7
1991	-10.5	47.4	-58.0	390.3	370.9	365.2	131.1	234.1	160.0	74.1	5.8	19.4	447.4
1992	-5.5	61.2	-66.7	405.1	389.4	395.9	139.7	256.2	171.1	85.1	-6.4	15.7	420.0
1993	24.1	86.3	-62.2	485.8	456.2	462.4	173.2	289.2	191.7	97.5	-6.2	29.5	399.5
1994 p	27.7	98.8	-71.2	....	....	....	....	205.2	....	....	-18.7	37.7	....
1982: IV	24.1	66.5	-42.3	150.3	160.0	168.6	58.7	109.9	72.5	37.5	-8.6	-9.6	256.8
1983: IV	22.2	64.5	-42.4	229.1	216.2	223.8	82.2	141.6	84.2	57.4	-7.6	12.9	281.8
1984: IV	24.3	67.6	-43.4	261.3	223.6	220.1	83.8	136.3	83.4	52.9	3.5	37.7	321.1
1985: IV	14.0	60.0	-46.0	284.9	228.0	231.8	97.6	134.2	97.4	36.9	-3.8	56.9	331.9
1986: IV	4.7	50.2	-45.5	264.6	225.0	235.7	116.6	119.2	111.0	8.2	-10.7	39.6	349.7
1987: IV	6.8	54.2	-47.4	343.3	293.4	311.2	135.2	176.0	106.3	69.7	-17.8	49.9	368.6
1988: IV	2.8	52.6	-49.7	378.3	340.5	372.2	146.2	226.0	121.0	105.0	-31.7	37.9	408.1
1989: IV	-21.6	39.8	-61.3	354.5	320.6	334.1	134.2	200.0	141.3	58.7	-13.5	33.9	459.8
1990: IV	-11.1	46.4	-57.4	362.8	349.3	368.9	137.0	231.8	153.7	78.1	-19.5	13.5	474.4
1991: I	-10.3	46.4	-56.7	385.4	371.8	361.4	127.3	234.1	158.0	76.1	10.4	13.7	465.1
II	-10.7	46.0	-56.7	391.5	372.6	360.5	130.0	230.5	159.4	71.1	12.1	18.9	448.0
III	-13.0	44.3	-57.3	389.6	367.1	365.7	134.0	231.6	161.6	70.0	1.4	22.5	444.7
IV	-8.1	53.0	-61.1	394.7	372.3	373.1	133.1	240.0	160.9	79.1	-.8	22.4	431.8
1992: I	-6.4	50.2	-56.5	412.1	393.0	397.0	139.6	257.4	161.0	96.4	-4.0	19.0	421.6
II	-5.4	51.4	-56.8	412.6	396.9	413.5	146.0	267.5	166.8	100.8	-16.6	15.8	421.9
III	-15.5	79.4	-94.9	363.2	352.3	359.5	124.6	234.9	174.4	60.5	-7.3	10.9	418.7
IV	5.1	63.8	-58.7	432.5	415.6	413.5	148.6	264.8	182.1	82.7	2.1	16.9	418.0
1993: I	16.5	80.3	-63.8	442.5	421.5	432.7	159.8	273.0	188.2	84.7	-11.2	21.0	414.6
II	23.4	83.6	-60.3	473.1	446.6	456.6	171.8	284.8	190.7	94.1	-10.0	26.5	397.6
III	26.3	88.9	-62.6	493.5	461.7	458.7	169.9	288.9	193.2	95.6	3.0	31.7	396.7
IV	30.3	92.4	-62.1	533.9	495.1	501.7	191.5	310.2	194.6	115.6	-6.5	38.8	389.1
1994: I	15.3	101.7	-86.4	508.2	471.2	483.5	184.1	299.4	196.3	103.0	-12.3	37.0	394.2
II	34.1	98.6	-64.5	546.4	509.0	523.1	201.7	321.4	202.5	118.9	-14.1	37.4	399.7
III	32.6	98.8	-66.2	556.0	518.5	538.1	208.6	329.5	207.9	121.6	-19.6	37.5	415.7
IV p	28.7	96.2	-67.5	....	....	....	....	213.9	....	....	-28.8	38.6	....

[2] Consists mainly of employer contributions for social insurance and to private pension, health, and welfare funds.
[3] With inventory valuation adjustment.

Source: Department of Commerce, Bureau of Economic Analysis.

TABLE B-26.—*Sources of personal income, 1959-94*

[Billions of dollars; quarterly data at seasonally adjusted annual rates]

Year or quarter	Personal income	Wage and salary disbursements [1]							Other labor income [1]	Proprietors' income with inventory valuation and capital consumption adjustments	
		Total	Commodity-producing industries		Distrib-utive indus-tries	Service indus-tries	Govern-ment			Farm	Nonfarm
			Total	Manu-facturing							
1959	391.2	259.8	109.9	86.9	65.1	38.8	46.0		10.6	10.7	41.1
1960	409.2	272.8	113.4	89.8	68.6	41.7	49.2		11.2	11.2	40.6
1961	426.5	280.5	114.0	89.9	69.6	44.4	52.4		11.8	11.9	42.4
1962	453.4	299.3	122.2	96.8	73.3	47.6	56.3		13.0	11.9	44.5
1963	476.4	314.8	127.4	100.7	76.8	50.7	60.0		14.0	11.8	45.9
1964	510.7	337.7	136.0	107.3	82.0	54.9	64.9		15.7	10.6	49.8
1965	552.9	363.7	146.6	115.7	87.9	59.4	69.9		17.8	12.9	52.1
1966	601.7	400.3	161.6	128.2	95.1	65.3	78.3		19.9	14.0	55.3
1967	646.5	428.9	169.0	134.3	101.6	72.0	86.4		21.7	12.7	58.2
1968	709.9	471.9	184.1	146.0	110.8	80.4	96.6		25.2	12.7	62.4
1969	773.7	518.3	200.4	157.7	121.7	90.6	105.5		28.5	14.4	64.5
1970	831.0	551.5	203.7	158.4	131.2	99.4	117.1		32.5	14.6	65.3
1971	893.5	583.9	209.1	160.5	140.4	107.9	126.5		36.7	15.2	70.9
1972	980.5	638.7	228.2	175.6	153.3	119.7	137.4		43.0	19.1	78.3
1973	1,098.7	708.7	255.9	196.6	170.3	133.9	148.7		49.2	32.2	84.3
1974	1,205.7	772.6	276.5	211.8	186.8	148.6	160.9		56.5	25.5	89.8
1975	1,307.3	814.6	277.1	211.6	198.1	163.4	176.0		65.9	23.7	97.5
1976	1,446.3	899.5	309.7	238.0	219.5	181.6	188.6		79.7	18.3	114.6
1977	1,601.3	993.9	346.1	266.7	242.7	202.8	202.3		94.7	17.1	129.4
1978	1,807.9	1,120.7	392.6	300.1	274.9	233.7	219.4		110.1	21.5	146.2
1979	2,033.1	1,255.4	442.1	334.9	308.4	267.7	237.3		124.3	24.7	157.0
1980	2,265.4	1,376.6	471.9	355.7	336.4	306.9	261.4		139.8	11.5	160.3
1981	2,534.7	1,515.6	513.7	386.9	368.1	348.1	285.7		153.0	21.2	159.6
1982	2,690.9	1,593.3	513.5	384.3	385.8	386.5	307.5		165.4	13.5	157.3
1983	2,862.5	1,684.7	525.1	397.7	406.2	427.4	325.9		174.6	2.4	184.3
1984	3,154.6	1,849.8	580.8	439.8	445.4	475.8	347.8		184.7	21.3	214.7
1985	3,379.8	1,986.5	612.2	461.3	475.9	524.5	373.9		191.8	21.5	238.4
1986	3,590.4	2,105.4	628.5	473.8	501.7	579.5	395.7		200.7	22.3	261.5
1987	3,802.0	2,261.2	651.8	490.1	536.9	650.7	421.8		210.4	31.3	279.0
1988	4,075.9	2,443.0	699.1	524.5	575.3	719.6	449.0		230.5	30.9	293.4
1989	4,380.3	2,586.4	724.2	542.2	607.0	776.8	478.5		251.9	40.2	307.0
1990	4,673.8	2,745.0	745.7	555.6	635.1	848.3	515.9		274.3	41.9	321.4
1991	4,860.3	2,816.1	738.4	557.4	648.0	884.2	545.5		299.0	36.7	339.5
1992	5,154.3	2,974.8	757.6	578.3	682.3	967.6	567.3		328.7	44.4	374.4
1993	5,375.1	3,080.8	773.8	588.4	701.9	1,021.4	583.8		355.3	37.3	404.3
1994 *p*	5,701.8	3,279.2	818.2	617.6	748.6	1,109.6	602.7		381.1	39.2	433.9
1982: IV	2,746.8	1,611.7	503.9	378.0	391.2	400.9	315.6		169.2	10.2	169.6
1983: IV	2,965.8	1,747.3	547.6	415.7	422.4	445.8	331.5		179.0	6.3	193.8
1984: IV	3,242.5	1,903.3	594.5	450.5	458.4	494.4	356.1		187.7	21.9	217.7
1985: IV	3,456.7	2,039.1	622.6	469.1	487.6	546.8	382.2		193.9	17.8	250.9
1986: IV	3,647.8	2,153.9	635.3	478.5	512.5	602.1	404.0		205.3	23.6	260.9
1987: IV	3,918.5	2,337.0	668.4	501.6	551.9	685.0	431.7		216.5	42.4	282.6
1988: IV	4,195.2	2,510.6	715.3	537.5	589.9	746.8	458.5		240.3	30.9	302.5
1989: IV	4,469.4	2,637.9	732.1	545.7	616.1	800.0	489.7		259.1	38.4	311.4
1990: IV	4,759.1	2,781.1	744.8	556.9	641.0	866.8	528.5		281.3	43.8	325.1
1991: I	4,797.2	2,785.1	737.4	552.7	639.6	866.9	541.2		288.1	37.0	327.2
II	4,840.5	2,800.9	734.3	552.7	645.7	876.3	544.6		294.8	43.4	336.9
III	4,869.1	2,823.9	739.0	558.9	650.5	888.0	546.4		302.7	29.6	344.2
IV	4,934.2	2,854.3	743.0	565.2	656.0	905.5	549.8		310.6	36.6	349.8
1992: I	5,032.4	2,893.9	738.6	561.2	664.1	930.6	560.6		318.4	49.0	361.9
II	5,101.9	2,933.4	748.9	569.9	672.9	945.0	566.6		326.0	43.7	369.1
III	5,148.1	2,973.1	753.8	575.1	682.9	966.5	569.9		332.6	38.8	374.0
IV	5,335.0	3,098.8	789.1	607.0	709.4	1,028.3	572.1		337.8	46.0	392.4
1993: I	5,255.5	2,973.9	746.3	565.8	681.2	966.1	580.3		344.1	49.6	394.8
II	5,364.5	3,085.1	776.4	591.4	704.0	1,023.7	580.9		351.4	39.4	399.4
III	5,395.9	3,115.9	781.4	594.9	709.6	1,038.8	586.1		358.8	15.8	404.5
IV	5,484.6	3,148.4	791.0	601.7	712.6	1,057.0	587.8		366.8	44.4	418.5
1994: I	5,555.8	3,208.3	801.9	609.4	728.6	1,082.0	595.7		373.2	47.2	423.8
II	5,659.9	3,257.2	811.6	612.8	742.5	1,101.2	601.9		378.4	39.3	431.9
III	5,734.5	3,293.9	821.8	618.3	753.5	1,114.3	604.4		383.7	29.8	437.1
IV *p*	5,857.1	3,357.4	837.7	630.0	769.9	1,140.9	608.9		389.1	40.7	442.7

[1] The total of wage and salary disbursements and other labor income differs from compensation of employees in Table B-25 in that it excludes employer contributions for social insurance and the excess of wage accruals over wage disbursements.

See next page for continuation of table.

304

[Billions of dollars; quarterly data at seasonally adjusted annual rates]

Year or quarter	Rental income of persons with capital consumption adjustment	Personal dividend income	Personal interest income	Transfer payments to persons							Less: Personal contributions for social insurance	Nonfarm personal income [2]
				Total	Old-age, survivors, disability, and health insurance benefits	Government unemployment insurance benefits	Veterans benefits	Government employees retirement benefits	Aid to families with dependent children (AFDC)	Other		
1959	14.7	12.7	22.7	27.0	10.2	2.8	4.6	2.8	0.9	5.7	7.9	376.7
1960	15.3	13.4	25.0	28.8	11.1	3.0	4.6	3.1	1.0	6.1	9.3	393.7
1961	15.8	14.0	26.9	32.8	12.6	4.3	5.0	3.4	1.1	6.5	9.7	410.4
1962	16.5	15.0	29.3	34.1	14.3	3.1	4.7	3.7	1.3	7.0	10.3	437.0
1963	17.1	16.1	32.4	36.2	15.2	3.0	4.8	4.2	1.4	7.6	11.8	460.0
1964	17.3	18.0	36.1	37.9	16.0	2.7	4.7	4.7	1.5	8.2	12.6	495.3
1965	18.0	20.2	40.3	41.1	18.1	2.3	4.9	5.2	1.7	9.0	13.3	534.9
1966	18.5	20.9	44.9	45.7	20.8	1.9	4.9	6.1	1.9	10.3	17.8	582.4
1967	19.4	22.1	49.5	54.6	25.5	2.2	5.6	6.9	2.3	12.2	20.6	628.3
1968	18.2	24.5	54.6	63.2	30.2	2.1	5.9	7.6	2.8	14.5	22.9	691.4
1969	18.0	25.1	60.8	70.3	32.9	2.2	6.7	8.7	3.5	16.2	26.2	753.1
1970	17.8	23.5	69.2	84.6	38.5	4.0	7.7	10.2	4.8	19.4	27.9	809.8
1971	18.2	23.5	75.7	100.1	44.5	5.8	8.8	11.8	6.2	23.0	30.7	871.5
1972	16.8	25.5	81.8	111.8	49.6	5.7	9.7	13.8	6.9	26.1	34.5	954.2
1973	17.3	27.7	94.1	127.9	60.4	4.4	10.4	16.0	7.2	29.5	42.6	1,058.1
1974	15.8	29.6	112.4	151.3	70.1	6.8	11.8	19.0	7.9	35.7	47.9	1,170.2
1975	13.5	29.2	123.0	190.2	81.4	17.6	14.5	22.7	9.2	44.7	50.4	1,272.5
1976	12.1	34.7	134.6	208.3	92.9	15.8	14.4	26.1	10.1	49.1	55.5	1,415.1
1977	9.0	39.4	155.7	223.3	104.9	12.7	13.8	29.0	10.6	52.4	61.2	1,569.9
1978	8.9	44.2	184.5	241.6	116.2	9.7	13.9	32.7	10.7	58.4	69.8	1,770.3
1979	8.4	50.4	223.2	270.7	131.8	9.8	14.4	36.9	11.0	66.8	81.0	1,989.3
1980	13.2	57.1	274.0	321.5	154.2	16.1	15.0	43.0	12.4	80.8	88.6	2,231.6
1981	20.8	66.9	336.1	365.9	182.0	15.9	16.1	49.4	13.0	89.7	104.5	2,488.5
1982	21.9	67.1	376.8	408.1	204.5	25.2	16.4	54.6	13.3	94.1	112.3	2,649.8
1983	22.1	77.8	397.5	438.9	221.7	26.3	16.6	58.0	14.2	102.1	119.7	2,832.6
1984	23.3	78.8	461.9	452.9	235.7	15.8	16.4	60.9	14.8	109.2	132.8	3,106.1
1985	18.7	87.9	498.1	485.9	253.4	15.7	16.7	66.6	15.4	118.1	149.1	3,333.2
1986	8.7	104.7	531.7	517.8	269.2	16.3	16.7	70.7	16.4	128.5	162.1	3,545.6
1987	3.2	100.4	548.1	542.2	282.9	14.5	16.6	76.0	16.7	135.5	173.6	3,749.4
1988	4.3	108.4	583.2	576.7	300.4	13.4	16.9	82.2	17.3	146.5	194.5	4,023.9
1989	−13.5	126.5	668.2	625.0	325.1	14.4	17.3	87.5	18.0	162.6	211.4	4,318.0
1990	−14.2	144.4	698.2	687.6	352.0	19.0	17.8	94.5	19.8	184.5	224.9	4,608.6
1991	−10.5	150.5	695.1	770.1	382.3	26.7	18.3	102.4	22.0	218.4	236.2	4,801.8
1992	−5.5	161.0	665.2	860.2	414.0	38.9	19.3	109.9	23.3	254.9	248.7	5,089.4
1993	24.1	181.3	637.9	915.4	444.4	33.9	20.1	118.7	23.9	274.4	261.3	5,316.6
1994 *p*	27.7	194.3	664.3	963.7	473.7	23.3	20.1	126.9	24.3	295.4	281.5	5,639.8
1982: IV	24.1	69.4	373.6	432.2	216.4	31.8	16.6	56.1	13.6	97.6	113.3	2,708.5
1983: IV	22.2	80.6	418.7	441.3	226.7	19.9	16.5	59.5	14.5	104.2	123.4	2,932.0
1984: IV	24.3	79.3	485.4	458.5	241.3	15.6	16.4	58.0	14.8	112.5	135.6	3,193.8
1985: IV	14.0	92.7	507.5	493.6	256.7	15.3	16.5	68.0	15.7	121.3	152.8	3,414.9
1986: IV	4.7	105.6	532.6	526.6	273.3	16.7	16.4	72.4	16.7	131.1	165.4	3,602.3
1987: IV	6.8	100.1	562.3	548.5	285.8	13.4	16.5	77.7	16.7	138.3	177.7	3,854.9
1988: IV	2.8	113.8	608.9	584.8	303.8	13.0	16.8	83.0	17.5	150.6	199.5	4,142.9
1989: IV	−21.6	132.9	681.2	644.8	334.4	15.6	17.3	89.3	18.4	169.9	214.7	4,408.5
1990: IV	−11.1	144.4	710.3	712.0	358.6	22.0	17.8	96.5	20.5	196.6	227.9	4,692.2
1991: I	−10.3	148.6	710.1	745.8	374.5	24.3	18.0	102.2	21.1	205.5	234.3	4,737.7
II	−10.7	149.9	697.3	762.9	380.0	27.4	18.6	101.7	21.8	213.4	234.9	4,775.0
III	−13.0	152.2	691.0	775.5	384.7	26.0	18.4	102.4	22.2	221.7	236.9	4,818.0
IV	−8.1	151.2	682.2	796.1	390.0	29.2	18.2	103.2	22.7	232.8	238.6	4,876.6
1992: I	−6.4	151.2	669.1	839.6	405.2	39.1	20.4	108.3	22.9	243.6	244.4	4,962.6
II	−5.4	156.7	670.2	855.3	412.1	40.4	18.9	109.3	23.1	251.4	247.0	5,037.8
III	−15.5	164.3	663.2	867.5	416.9	38.9	18.8	110.0	23.5	259.4	249.9	5,088.9
IV	5.1	171.8	658.2	878.4	421.6	37.2	19.1	111.9	23.5	265.0	253.4	5,268.5
1993: I	16.5	178.0	653.2	898.6	436.8	34.3	20.0	116.0	23.6	267.8	253.2	5,185.2
II	23.4	180.4	636.6	910.4	441.9	34.0	20.2	118.0	24.0	272.2	261.5	5,304.0
III	26.3	182.8	634.1	921.6	446.8	34.5	20.2	119.6	24.0	276.5	263.8	5,358.8
IV	30.3	184.1	627.7	931.0	452.1	32.7	20.0	121.1	24.1	281.0	266.6	5,418.5
1994: I	15.3	185.7	631.1	947.4	463.8	27.9	20.0	122.8	24.2	288.7	276.3	5,486.4
II	34.1	191.7	649.4	957.6	470.7	23.5	19.8	126.2	24.3	293.1	279.9	5,598.0
III	32.6	196.9	674.2	969.0	476.5	21.4	20.3	128.5	24.3	298.0	282.9	5,681.7
IV *p*	28.7	202.7	702.3	980.7	483.7	20.5	20.3	130.1	24.3	301.8	287.0	5,793.2

[2] Personal income exclusive of the farm component of wages and salaries, other labor income, proprietors' income with inventory valuation and capital consumption adjustments, and net interest.

Note.—The industry classification of wage and salary disbursements and proprietors' income is on an establishment basis and is based on the 1987 Standard Industrial Classification (SIC) beginning 1987 and on the 1972 SIC for earlier years shown.

Source: Department of Commerce, Bureau of Economic Analysis.

[Billions of dollars, except as noted; quarterly data at seasonally adjusted annual rates]

Year or quarter	Personal income	Less: Personal tax and nontax payments	Equals: Disposable personal income	Less: Personal outlays				Equals: Personal saving	Percent of disposable personal income [1]		
				Total	Personal consumption expenditures	Interest paid by persons	Personal transfer payments to rest of the world (net)		Personal outlays		Personal saving
									Total	Personal consumption expenditures	
1959	391.2	44.5	346.7	324.7	318.1	6.1	0.4	22.0	93.7	91.8	6.3
1960	409.2	48.7	360.5	339.9	332.4	7.0	.5	20.6	94.3	92.2	5.7
1961	426.5	50.3	376.2	351.3	343.5	7.3	.5	24.9	93.4	91.3	6.6
1962	453.4	54.8	398.7	372.8	364.4	7.8	.5	25.9	93.5	91.4	6.5
1963	476.4	58.0	418.4	393.7	384.2	8.9	.6	24.6	94.1	91.8	5.9
1964	510.7	56.0	454.7	423.1	412.5	10.0	.7	31.6	93.1	90.7	6.9
1965	552.9	61.9	491.0	456.4	444.6	11.1	.8	34.6	93.0	90.5	7.0
1966	601.7	71.0	530.7	494.4	481.6	12.0	.8	36.3	93.2	90.7	6.8
1967	646.5	77.9	568.6	522.8	509.3	12.5	1.0	45.8	91.9	89.6	8.1
1968	709.9	92.1	617.8	573.9	559.1	13.8	1.0	43.9	92.9	90.5	7.1
1969	773.7	109.9	663.8	620.5	603.7	15.7	1.1	43.3	93.5	90.9	6.5
1970	831.0	109.0	722.0	664.5	646.5	16.8	1.2	57.5	92.0	89.5	8.0
1971	893.5	108.7	784.9	719.4	700.3	17.8	1.3	65.4	91.7	89.2	8.3
1972	980.5	132.0	848.5	788.7	767.8	19.6	1.3	59.7	93.0	90.5	7.0
1973	1,098.7	140.6	958.1	872.0	848.1	22.4	1.4	86.1	91.0	88.5	9.0
1974	1,205.7	159.1	1,046.5	953.1	927.7	24.2	1.2	93.4	91.1	88.6	8.9
1975	1,307.3	156.4	1,150.9	1,050.6	1,024.9	24.5	1.2	100.3	91.3	89.1	8.7
1976	1,446.3	182.3	1,264.0	1,170.9	1,143.1	26.7	1.2	93.0	92.6	90.4	7.4
1977	1,601.3	210.0	1,391.3	1,303.4	1,271.5	30.7	1.2	87.9	93.7	91.4	6.3
1978	1,807.9	240.1	1,567.8	1,460.0	1,421.2	37.5	1.3	107.8	93.1	90.7	6.9
1979	2,033.1	280.2	1,753.0	1,629.6	1,583.7	44.5	1.4	123.3	93.0	90.3	7.0
1980	2,265.4	312.4	1,952.9	1,799.1	1,748.1	49.4	1.6	153.8	92.1	89.5	7.9
1981	2,534.7	360.2	2,174.5	1,982.6	1,926.2	54.6	1.8	191.8	91.2	88.6	8.8
1982	2,690.9	371.4	2,319.6	2,120.1	2,059.2	58.8	2.1	199.5	91.4	88.8	8.6
1983	2,862.5	368.8	2,493.7	2,325.1	2,257.5	65.7	1.8	168.7	93.2	90.5	6.8
1984	3,154.6	395.1	2,759.5	2,537.5	2,460.3	75.0	2.3	222.0	92.0	89.2	8.0
1985	3,379.8	436.8	2,943.0	2,753.7	2,667.4	83.6	2.7	189.3	93.6	90.6	6.4
1986	3,590.4	459.0	3,131.5	2,944.0	2,850.6	90.9	2.5	187.5	94.0	91.0	6.0
1987	3,802.0	512.5	3,289.5	3,147.5	3,052.2	92.3	3.0	142.0	95.7	92.8	4.3
1988	4,075.9	527.7	3,548.2	3,392.5	3,296.1	93.7	2.7	155.7	95.6	92.9	4.4
1989	4,380.3	593.3	3,787.0	3,634.9	3,523.1	103.0	8.9	152.1	96.0	93.0	4.0
1990	4,673.8	623.3	4,050.5	3,880.6	3,761.2	109.3	10.1	170.0	95.8	92.9	4.2
1991	4,860.3	623.7	4,236.6	4,025.0	3,902.4	112.2	10.4	211.6	95.0	92.1	5.0
1992	5,154.3	648.6	4,505.8	4,257.8	4,136.9	111.4	9.5	247.9	94.5	91.8	5.5
1993	5,375.1	686.4	4,688.7	4,496.2	4,378.2	108.2	9.9	192.6	95.9	93.4	4.1
1994 *p*	5,701.8	742.5	4,959.3	4,755.1	4,627.0	117.7	10.5	204.2	95.9	93.3	4.1
1982: IV	2,746.8	372.1	2,374.7	2,190.9	2,128.7	60.2	1.9	183.8	92.3	89.6	7.7
1983: IV	2,965.8	371.6	2,594.3	2,417.9	2,346.8	69.2	2.0	176.3	93.2	90.5	6.8
1984: IV	3,242.5	413.4	2,829.1	2,606.5	2,526.4	77.6	2.5	222.6	92.1	89.3	7.9
1985: IV	3,456.7	448.8	3,007.9	2,828.7	2,739.8	86.4	2.5	179.2	94.0	91.1	6.0
1986: IV	3,647.8	478.5	3,169.3	3,018.2	2,923.1	92.3	2.8	151.1	95.2	92.2	4.8
1987: IV	3,918.5	528.6	3,389.9	3,220.1	3,124.6	92.4	3.1	169.8	95.0	92.2	5.0
1988: IV	4,195.2	542.0	3,653.2	3,496.7	3,398.2	95.8	2.7	156.4	95.7	93.0	4.3
1989: IV	4,469.4	605.1	3,864.3	3,715.5	3,599.1	106.7	9.8	148.8	96.2	93.1	3.9
1990: IV	4,759.1	625.2	4,133.9	3,957.7	3,836.6	110.9	10.2	176.2	95.7	92.8	4.3
1991: I	4,797.2	620.5	4,176.7	3,963.9	3,841.4	112.2	10.3	212.8	94.9	92.0	5.1
II	4,840.5	620.2	4,220.4	4,008.5	3,885.7	112.5	10.3	211.9	95.0	92.1	5.0
III	4,869.1	622.8	4,246.3	4,049.4	3,927.0	112.2	10.2	196.9	95.4	92.5	4.6
IV	4,934.2	631.2	4,303.0	4,078.4	3,955.7	112.1	10.6	224.6	94.8	91.9	5.2
1992: I	5,032.4	631.3	4,401.1	4,166.4	4,044.4	112.6	9.4	234.7	94.7	91.9	5.3
II	5,101.9	638.7	4,463.2	4,219.4	4,097.8	112.0	9.7	243.8	94.5	91.8	5.5
III	5,148.1	648.1	4,500.0	4,274.2	4,154.0	111.0	9.2	225.8	95.0	92.3	5.0
IV	5,335.0	676.2	4,658.8	4,371.4	4,251.3	110.2	9.9	287.4	93.8	91.3	6.2
1993: I	5,255.5	657.3	4,598.2	4,413.7	4,294.6	109.3	9.8	184.6	96.0	93.4	4.0
II	5,364.5	685.9	4,678.6	4,464.6	4,347.3	107.5	9.8	214.0	95.4	92.9	4.6
III	5,395.9	695.4	4,700.5	4,518.2	4,401.2	107.2	9.9	182.3	96.1	93.6	3.9
IV	5,484.6	707.0	4,777.6	4,588.2	4,469.6	108.7	9.8	189.4	96.0	93.6	4.0
1994: I	5,555.8	723.0	4,832.8	4,657.3	4,535.0	111.7	10.5	175.5	96.4	93.8	3.6
II	5,659.9	746.4	4,913.5	4,712.4	4,586.4	115.5	10.5	201.1	95.9	93.3	4.1
III	5,734.5	744.1	4,990.3	4,787.0	4,657.5	119.3	10.3	203.3	95.9	93.3	4.1
IV *p*	5,857.1	756.5	5,100.7	4,863.8	4,728.9	124.2	10.7	236.9	95.4	92.7	4.6

[1] Percents based on data in millions of dollars.

Source: Department of Commerce, Bureau of Economic Analysis.

TABLE B-28.—*Total and per capita disposable personal income and personal consumption expenditures in current and 1987 dollars, 1959–94*

[Quarterly data at seasonally adjusted annual rates, except as noted]

Year or quarter	Disposable personal income				Personal consumption expenditures				Popula-tion (thou-sands)[1]
	Total (billions of dollars)		Per capita (dollars)		Total (billions of dollars)		Per capita (dollars)		
	Current dollars	1987 dollars	Current dollars	1987 dollars	Current dollars	1987 dollars	Current dollars	1987 dollars	
1959	346.7	1,284.9	1,958	7,256	318.1	1,178.9	1,796	6,658	177,073
1960	360.5	1,313.0	1,994	7,264	332.4	1,210.8	1,839	6,698	180,760
1961	376.2	1,356.4	2,048	7,382	343.5	1,238.4	1,869	6,740	183,742
1962	398.7	1,414.8	2,137	7,583	364.4	1,293.3	1,953	6,931	186,590
1963	418.4	1,461.1	2,210	7,718	384.2	1,341.9	2,030	7,089	189,300
1964	454.7	1,562.2	2,369	8,140	412.5	1,417.2	2,149	7,384	191,927
1965	491.0	1,653.5	2,527	8,508	444.6	1,497.0	2,287	7,703	194,347
1966	530.7	1,734.3	2,699	8,822	481.6	1,573.8	2,450	8,005	196,599
1967	568.6	1,811.4	2,861	9,114	509.3	1,622.4	2,562	8,163	198,752
1968	617.8	1,886.8	3,077	9,399	559.1	1,707.5	2,785	8,506	200,745
1969	663.8	1,947.4	3,274	9,606	603.7	1,771.2	2,978	8,737	202,736
1970	722.0	2,025.3	3,521	9,875	646.5	1,813.5	3,152	8,842	205,089
1971	784.9	2,099.9	3,779	10,111	700.3	1,873.7	3,372	9,022	207,692
1972	848.5	2,186.2	4,042	10,414	767.8	1,978.4	3,658	9,425	209,924
1973	958.1	2,334.1	4,521	11,013	848.1	2,066.7	4,002	9,752	211,939
1974	1,046.5	2,317.0	4,893	10,832	927.7	2,053.8	4,337	9,602	213,898
1975	1,150.9	2,355.4	5,329	10,906	1,024.9	2,097.5	4,745	9,711	215,981
1976	1,264.0	2,440.9	5,796	11,192	1,143.1	2,207.3	5,241	10,121	218,086
1977	1,391.3	2,512.6	6,316	11,406	1,271.5	2,296.6	5,772	10,425	220,289
1978	1,567.8	2,638.4	7,042	11,851	1,421.2	2,391.8	6,384	10,744	222,629
1979	1,753.0	2,710.1	7,787	12,039	1,583.7	2,448.4	7,035	10,876	225,106
1980	1,952.9	2,733.6	8,576	12,005	1,748.1	2,447.1	7,677	10,746	227,715
1981	2,174.5	2,795.8	9,455	12,156	1,926.2	2,476.9	8,375	10,770	229,989
1982	2,319.6	2,820.4	9,989	12,146	2,059.2	2,503.7	8,868	10,782	232,201
1983	2,493.7	2,893.6	10,642	12,349	2,257.5	2,619.4	9,634	11,179	234,326
1984	2,759.5	3,080.1	11,673	13,029	2,460.3	2,746.1	10,408	11,617	236,393
1985	2,943.0	3,162.1	12,339	13,258	2,667.4	2,865.8	11,184	12,015	238,510
1986	3,131.5	3,261.9	13,010	13,552	2,850.6	2,969.1	11,843	12,336	240,691
1987	3,289.5	3,289.5	13,545	13,545	3,052.2	3,052.2	12,568	12,568	242,860
1988	3,548.2	3,404.3	14,477	13,890	3,296.1	3,162.4	13,448	12,903	245,093
1989	3,787.0	3,464.9	15,307	14,005	3,523.1	3,223.3	14,241	13,029	247,397
1990	4,050.5	3,524.5	16,205	14,101	3,761.2	3,272.6	15,048	13,093	249,951
1991	4,236.6	3,538.5	16,766	14,003	3,902.4	3,259.4	15,444	12,899	252,688
1992	4,505.8	3,648.1	17,636	14,279	4,136.9	3,349.5	16,192	13,110	255,484
1993	4,688.7	3,704.1	18,153	14,341	4,378.2	3,458.7	16,951	13,391	258,290
1994 *p*	4,959.3	3,835.4	19,002	14,696	4,627.0	3,578.5	17,728	13,711	260,991
1982: IV	2,374.7	2,832.6	10,189	12,154	2,128.7	2,539.3	9,134	10,895	233,060
1983: IV	2,594.3	2,960.6	11,033	12,591	2,346.8	2,678.2	9,980	11,390	235,146
1984: IV	2,829.1	3,118.5	11,925	13,145	2,526.4	2,784.8	10,649	11,739	237,231
1985: IV	3,007.9	3,178.7	12,565	13,278	2,739.8	2,895.3	11,445	12,095	239,387
1986: IV	3,169.3	3,266.2	13,121	13,522	2,923.1	3,012.5	12,101	12,472	241,550
1987: IV	3,389.9	3,335.8	13,907	13,685	3,124.6	3,074.7	12,819	12,615	243,745
1988: IV	3,653.2	3,443.1	14,850	13,996	3,398.2	3,202.9	13,814	13,020	246,004
1989: IV	3,864.3	3,480.9	15,558	14,015	3,599.1	3,242.0	1.491	13,053	248,372
1990: IV	4,133.9	3,519.0	16,467	14,018	3,836.6	3,265.9	15,283	13,010	251,035
1991: I	4,176.7	3,526.0	16,597	14,011	3,841.4	3,242.9	15,264	12,886	251,658
II	4,220.4	3,540.2	16,728	14,032	3,885.7	3,259.5	15,401	12,919	252,300
III	4,246.3	3,535.6	16,781	13,973	3,927.0	3,269.8	15,520	12,922	253,036
IV	4,303.0	3,552.1	16,957	13,998	3,955.7	3,265.3	15,588	12,868	253,758
1992: I	4,401.1	3,603.5	17.302	14,166	4,044.4	3,311.4	15,900	13,018	254,369
II	4,463.2	3,621.9	17,498	14,199	4,097.8	3,325.4	16,065	13,037	255,076
III	4,500.0	3,637.2	17,587	14,215	4,154.0	3,357.6	16,235	13,122	255,865
IV	4,658.8	3,729.6	18,154	14,533	4,251.3	3,403.4	16,566	13,262	256,626
1993: I	4,598.2	3,658.9	17,874	14,222	4,294.6	3,417.2	16,693	13,283	257,262
II	4,678.6	3,701.3	18,141	14,351	4,347.3	3,439.2	16,856	13,335	257.908
III	4,700.5	3,708.4	18,174	14,338	4,401.2	3,472.2	17,017	13,425	258,635
IV	4,777.6	3,747.8	18,421	14,451	4,469.6	3,506.2	17,233	13,519	259,356
1994: I	4,832.8	3,779.2	18,588	14,535	4,535.0	3,546.3	17,443	13,640	259,997
II	4,913.5	3,811.5	18,853	14,625	4,586.4	3,557.8	17,598	13,651	260,627
III	4,990.3	3,840.9	19,095	14,697	4,657.5	3,584.7	17,821	13,717	261,340
IV *p*	5,100.7	3,910.1	19,468	14,924	4,728.9	3,625.1	18,049	13,836	262,000

[1] Population of the United States including Armed Forces overseas; includes Alaska and Hawaii beginning 1960. Annual data are averages of quarterly data. Quarterly data are averages for the period.

Source: Department of Commerce (Bureau of Economic Analysis and Bureau of the Census).

TABLE B-29.—Gross saving and investment, 1959-94

[Billions of dollars; quarterly data at seasonally adjusted annual rates]

Year or quarter	Gross saving								Gross investment			Statistical discrepancy
	Total	Gross private saving			Government surplus or deficit (−), national income and product accounts			Capital grants received by the United States (net) [2]	Total	Gross private domestic investment	Net foreign investment [3]	
		Total	Personal saving	Gross business saving [1]	Total	Federal	State and local					
1959	79.4	82.5	22.0	60.5	−3.1	−2.6	−0.5	....	77.6	78.8	−1.2	−1.8
1960	85.1	81.5	20.6	60.9	3.6	3.5	.0	....	82.0	78.7	3.2	−3.1
1961	84.4	87.4	24.9	62.5	−3.0	−2.6	−.4	....	82.2	77.9	4.3	−2.2
1962	92.8	95.8	25.9	69.9	−2.9	−3.4	.5	....	91.8	87.9	3.9	−1.0
1963	100.4	98.8	24.6	74.1	1.6	1.1	.4	....	98.4	93.4	5.0	−2.0
1964	110.0	111.5	31.6	80.0	−1.6	−2.6	1.0	....	109.3	101.7	7.5	−.7
1965	125.0	123.7	34.6	89.2	1.2	1.3	.0	....	124.2	118.0	6.2	−.7
1966	131.5	132.5	36.3	96.1	−1.0	−1.4	.5	....	134.3	130.4	3.9	2.8
1967	130.8	144.5	45.8	98.7	−13.7	−12.7	−1.1	....	131.6	128.0	3.5	.8
1968	141.7	146.4	43.8	102.5	−4.6	−4.7	.1	....	141.7	139.9	1.7	−.1
1969	159.5	149.5	43.3	106.2	10.0	8.5	1.5	....	157.0	155.2	1.8	−2.6
1970	155.2	165.8	57.5	108.2	−11.5	−13.3	1.8	0.9	155.2	150.3	4.9	.0
1971	173.7	192.2	65.4	126.8	−19.2	−21.7	2.5	.7	176.8	175.5	1.3	3.1
1972	201.7	204.9	59.7	145.1	−3.9	−17.3	13.4	.7	202.7	205.6	−2.9	1.1
1973	252.3	245.4	86.1	159.3	6.9	−6.6	13.4	0	251.8	243.1	8.7	−.5
1974	249.5	256.0	93.4	162.6	−4.5	−11.6	7.1	[4] −2.0	250.9	245.8	5.1	1.4
1975	241.4	306.3	100.3	206.0	−64.8	−69.4	4.6	0	247.4	226.0	21.4	6.0
1976	284.8	323.1	93.0	230.0	−38.3	−52.9	14.6	0	295.2	286.4	8.8	10.4
1977	338.2	355.0	87.9	267.1	−16.8	−42.4	25.6	0	349.1	358.3	−9.2	10.9
1978	415.7	412.8	107.8	305.0	2.9	−28.1	31.1	0	423.3	434.0	−10.7	7.6
1979	468.5	457.9	123.3	334.5	9.4	−15.7	25.1	1.1	482.2	480.2	2.0	13.8
1980	465.4	499.6	153.8	345.7	−35.3	−60.1	24.8	1.2	479.1	467.6	11.5	13.6
1981	556.6	585.9	191.8	394.1	−30.3	−58.8	28.5	1.1	567.5	558.0	9.5	10.9
1982	508.4	616.9	199.5	417.5	−108.6	−135.5	26.9	0	500.9	503.4	−2.5	−7.4
1983	501.6	641.3	168.7	472.7	−139.8	−180.1	40.3	0	511.7	546.7	−35.0	10.2
1984	633.9	742.7	222.0	520.7	−108.8	−166.9	58.1	0	624.9	718.9	−94.0	−9.0
1985	610.4	735.7	189.3	546.4	−125.3	−181.4	56.1	0	596.5	714.5	−118.1	−13.9
1986	574.6	721.4	187.5	533.9	−146.8	−201.0	54.3	0	575.9	717.6	−141.7	1.2
1987	619.0	730.7	142.0	588.7	−111.7	−151.8	40.1	0	594.2	749.3	−155.1	−24.8
1988	704.0	802.3	155.7	646.6	−98.3	−136.6	38.4	0	675.6	793.6	−118.0	−28.4
1989	741.8	819.4	152.1	667.3	−77.5	−122.3	44.8	0	742.9	832.3	−89.3	1.1
1990	722.7	861.1	170.0	691.2	−138.4	−163.5	25.1	0	730.4	808.9	−78.5	7.8
1991	751.4	937.3	211.6	725.7	−185.9	−202.9	17.0	0	752.9	744.8	8.1	1.5
1992	722.9	980.8	247.9	732.8	−257.8	−282.7	24.8	0	731.7	788.3	−56.6	8.8
1993	787.5	1,002.5	192.6	809.9	−215.0	−241.4	26.3	0	789.8	882.0	−92.3	2.3
1994 *p*	....	....	204.2					0	....	1,037.5		....
1982: IV	458.5	615.4	183.8	431.6	−156.9	−183.4	26.5	0	448.4	464.2	−15.8	−10.1
1983: IV	542.4	678.7	176.3	502.4	−136.3	−184.6	48.3	0	556.3	614.8	−58.5	13.8
1984: IV	637.0	764.7	222.6	542.1	−127.8	−186.8	59.0	0	616.5	722.8	−106.3	−20.5
1985: IV	603.8	734.7	179.2	555.5	−130.9	−187.2	56.3	0	597.8	737.0	−139.1	−5.9
1986: IV	550.1	676.3	151.1	525.3	−126.2	−177.5	51.2	0	548.1	697.1	−149.0	−2.0
1987: IV	667.9	783.7	169.8	613.9	−115.8	−152.7	37.0	0	643.0	800.2	−157.1	−24.9
1988: IV	720.1	814.8	156.4	658.3	−94.7	−134.9	40.2	0	694.7	814.8	−120.1	−25.4
1989: IV	728.4	828.6	148.8	679.8	−100.2	−141.5	41.3	0	741.3	825.2	−84.0	12.8
1990: IV	683.8	863.1	176.2	686.9	−179.3	−191.0	11.7	0	688.7	756.4	−67.7	4.9
1991: I	798.8	933.2	212.8	720.3	−134.4	−144.4	10.0	0	788.5	732.8	55.8	−10.3
II	744.5	937.3	211.9	725.4	−192.8	−207.6	14.9	0	750.7	733.1	17.6	6.2
III	722.1	917.9	196.9	721.0	−195.8	−213.6	17.8	0	734.3	756.5	−22.2	12.2
IV	740.1	960.7	224.6	736.1	−220.7	−245.8	25.1	0	738.0	756.8	−18.8	−2.1
1992: I	719.1	979.1	234.7	744.4	−260.0	−279.9	19.9	0	721.1	747.7	−26.6	2.0
II	722.3	981.2	243.8	737.4	−258.9	−284.8	25.9	0	733.8	787.9	−54.1	11.5
III	731.9	1,005.3	225.8	779.5	−273.5	−293.9	20.4	0	735.6	795.5	−59.9	3.7
IV	718.5	957.5	287.4	670.1	−239.1	−272.1	33.1	0	736.5	822.0	−85.6	18.0
1993: I	760.1	1,022.0	184.6	837.4	−261.9	−283.5	21.6	0	785.5	853.8	−68.3	25.5
II	775.0	986.6	214.0	772.7	−211.6	−237.0	25.3	0	780.8	869.7	−88.9	5.7
III	788.9	989.9	182.3	807.7	−201.0	−224.9	23.9	0	783.4	882.2	−98.8	−5.5
IV	825.8	1,011.4	189.4	821.9	−185.6	−220.1	34.5	0	809.3	922.5	−113.2	−16.5
1994: I	886.2	1,037.3	175.5	861.8	−151.1	−176.2	25.2	0	850.2	966.6	−116.4	−36.1
II	923.3	1,041.4	201.1	840.3	−118.1	−145.1	27.0	0	899.3	1,034.4	−135.1	−24.0
III	922.6	1,052.7	203.3	849.4	−130.1	−154.0	23.9	0	901.5	1,055.1	−153.6	−21.1
IV *p*	....	....	236.9					0	....	1,093.9		....

[1] Undistributed corporate profits with inventory valuation and capital consumption adjustments, corporate and noncorporate consumption of fixed capital, and private wage accruals less disbursements.
[2] Consists mainly of allocations of special drawing rights (SDRs).
[3] Net exports of goods and services plus net receipts of factor income from rest of the world less net transfers plus net capital grants received by the United States. See also Table B-21.
[4] Consists of a U.S. payment to India under the Agricultural Trade Development and Assistance Act. This payment is included in capital grants received by the United States, net.

Source: Department of Commerce, Bureau of Economic Analysis.

TABLE B-30.—*Personal saving, flow of funds accounts, 1946-94* [1]

[Billions of dollars; quarterly data at seasonally adjusted annual rates]

Year or quarter	Personal saving	Increase in financial assets									Net investment in tangible assets [7]			Less: Net increase in debt		
		Total	Checkable deposits and currency	Time and savings deposits	Money market fund shares	Government securities [2]	Corporate equities [3]	Other securities [4]	Insurance and pension reserves [5]	Other financial assets [6]	Owner-occupied homes	Consumer durables	Noncorporate business assets [8]	Mortgage debt on nonfarm homes	Consumer credit	Other debt [8][9]
1946	17.1	19.4	5.6	6.3		-1.5	1.2	-0.8	5.1	3.6	5.8	1.5	0.1	4.1	2.9	2.6
1947	18.9	12.3	.0	3.5		.5	1.2	-.8	5.4	2.5	6.8	9.4	1.5	4.9	3.5	2.7
1948	24.9	8.7	-3.0	2.3		1.0	1.0	.2	5.3	2.0	9.3	10.2	7.0	4.8	3.1	2.5
1949	20.7	8.6	-2.0	2.6		.5	.8	-.3	5.6	1.4	8.5	10.9	2.2	4.2	3.1	2.2
1950	32.4	14.7	2.7	2.4		.9	.7	-.9	6.1	2.7	11.9	14.9	7.4	7.0	4.6	5.0
1951	35.0	19.2	4.6	4.8		-.7	1.9	.7	6.3	1.6	11.9	11.4	4.6	6.4	1.4	4.3
1952	38.2	30.1	1.6	7.4		7.4	1.5	-.1	8.5	3.8	11.6	8.7	2.8	6.4	5.2	3.4
1953	35.9	24.6	.9	8.2		3.7	1.1	.3	8.0	2.4	12.6	10.3	2.3	7.4	4.1	2.3
1954	26.6	20.8	2.2	9.1		.1	.8	-1.4	8.0	2.0	13.0	7.0	1.8	9.0	1.3	5.6
1955	34.1	28.2	1.3	8.5		6.4	1.2	.4	8.7	1.7	17.1	12.7	2.2	12.2	7.0	6.8
1956	38.2	32.1	1.9	9.3		4.5	2.1	1.2	9.7	3.4	16.0	8.8	.7	10.8	3.6	5.0
1957	37.9	29.8	-.3	11.8		3.7	1.6	1.4	9.7	1.9	13.6	7.9	1.8	8.6	2.6	3.9
1958	36.5	32.6	3.9	13.8		-2.7	1.9	.9	10.7	4.3	12.3	3.7	4.2	9.5	.3	6.6
1959	34.2	34.7	1.0	10.5		8.2	.7	.2	12.2	1.9	19.2	7.7	.9	12.9	7.7	7.8
1960	37.3	34.2	1.0	12.0		2.0	.3	3.4	11.9	3.7	17.2	7.2	2.2	11.0	4.0	8.4
1961	35.8	36.1	-.8	18.1		.8	1.1	.0	12.5	4.4	16.3	4.5	2.9	12.2	2.2	9.7
1962	42.4	40.6	-1.1	25.8		1.0	-1.4	.2	13.5	2.5	18.2	8.6	4.3	13.8	5.9	9.6
1963	47.5	46.0	4.4	25.9		-1.1	-1.1	1.2	14.5	2.1	20.5	11.9	4.7	16.2	8.5	11.0
1964	61.9	57.2	6.2	25.9		3.7	.0	1.2	17.1	3.2	22.1	15.1	4.4	16.8	9.5	10.6
1965	69.3	57.4	6.8	27.5		3.8	-1.5	-.1	17.8	3.2	21.6	20.2	8.4	16.8	10.1	11.4
1966	82.9	64.3	2.7	18.8		13.6	.0	4.9	20.2	4.1	19.0	23.2	7.9	12.7	5.9	12.9
1967	84.9	72.7	10.6	34.9		-2.6	-3.0	6.4	19.6	6.8	18.5	21.3	7.3	13.1	5.1	16.7
1968	83.9	69.2	9.7	30.3		1.2	-6.0	7.2	21.1	5.7	19.8	26.9	10.2	16.7	10.8	14.7
1969	85.7	71.8	-1.2	9.7		28.8	-10.9	10.7	23.3	11.3	19.9	26.2	11.7	17.4	9.9	16.6
1970	95.1	80.5	7.8	42.5		-7.2	-2.2	5.8	25.8	7.9	17.7	19.6	10.1	13.0	4.6	15.3
1971	103.2	108.3	13.8	65.5		-12.5	-11.0	3.3	30.3	19.0	27.8	25.4	15.1	26.3	15.6	31.5
1972	124.6	135.2	13.6	72.6		-2.0	-14.3	-3.3	50.4	18.1	36.7	34.3	18.1	39.3	19.0	41.4
1973	158.0	148.0	13.4	63.0		14.3	-12.1	6.8	41.8	20.8	40.2	40.6	23.2	43.6	22.7	27.8
1974	123.2	152.6	6.4	55.3	2.4	17.2	-4.6	17.0	44.6	14.3	30.5	29.1	11.6	34.2	9.4	56.9
1975	154.5	178.3	7.0	79.9	1.3	12.1	-3.7	11.5	71.5	4.9	28.3	27.4	6.1	39.3	8.0	38.2
1976	173.8	211.8	15.9	104.1	-.3	4.2	1.3	1.4	60.3	24.8	44.9	41.5	4.0	62.0	22.9	43.4
1977	202.8	256.4	19.6	107.3	-.4	6.9	-6.2	16.0	80.3	32.9	66.1	51.5	16.3	93.0	36.7	57.7
1978	212.5	288.2	21.5	105.0	5.4	26.5	-11.6	4.3	94.3	42.8	78.7	56.8	23.1	109.9	45.1	79.3
1979	231.5	331.3	36.9	77.0	29.8	57.4	-17.8	-.2	103.5	44.7	75.4	50.4	32.0	116.2	38.3	102.9
1980	221.5	329.6	9.3	121.6	23.5	27.4	-2.2	-11.6	126.9	34.7	51.5	26.3	14.2	94.1	4.8	101.3
1981	255.5	327.5	36.3	70.1	85.9	34.0	-38.9	-10.4	126.7	23.6	50.8	27.3	27.5	69.6	16.9	91.0
1982	259.8	380.0	24.7	113.6	31.5	36.2	-20.8	-5.0	178.1	21.6	30.2	22.4	10.1	56.1	16.4	110.4
1983	319.9	498.0	21.7	198.4	-31.2	76.1	4.3	20.4	176.2	32.3	71.5	50.6	-11.8	117.1	48.9	122.5
1984	369.2	532.2	4.2	225.2	43.3	101.9	-46.7	-7.6	162.4	49.4	93.7	81.8	24.3	135.6	81.7	145.5
1985	404.0	631.9	29.0	117.2	2.3	87.4	-35.7	57.6	282.5	91.7	93.7	95.8	26.8	171.7	82.3	190.4
1986	475.5	593.9	94.9	94.2	35.7	-50.8	16.1	28.2	306.6	69.1	119.5	111.4	16.0	203.4	57.5	104.2
1987	396.1	511.8	-2.0	92.5	22.0	126.9	-45.7	21.6	227.4	69.1	123.5	102.9	12.3	240.9	32.9	80.6
1988	392.1	508.5	27.2	136.2	15.9	172.5	-78.6	9.5	157.5	68.3	126.7	112.6	7.4	234.3	50.1	78.7
1989	476.9	594.9	-1.2	79.6	76.8	122.5	-73.1	-26.2	350.0	66.5	114.6	109.0	18.4	223.8	45.8	90.4
1990	443.3	502.3	5.4	38.5	28.6	145.6	16.0	29.8	190.8	47.7	98.3	90.0	4.8	185.0	16.0	51.2
1991	391.7	442.2	63.0	-117.4	8.7	-.1	81.3	-24.5	386.0	45.2	75.7	52.2	-18.7	163.3	-15.0	11.4
1992	472.4	532.1	131.1	-112.1	-41.8	66.7	190.2	-5.7	276.9	20.6	94.0	62.6	-24.5	179.0	5.5	7.2
1993	409.8	526.4	81.6	-91.1	-10.2	-9.4	158.3	-9.3	340.0	66.5	123.1	88.9	-19.3	183.3	62.3	63.8
1992: I	496.8	579.8	183.2	-65.2	-30.5	233.6	135.9	-71.4	210.0	-15.7	87.5	55.6	-13.8	232.7	-4.6	-15.8
II	447.7	429.1	51.9	-140.3	22.2	16.8	201.6	21.4	249.0	6.5	98.1	54.8	-12.8	92.1	-15.0	44.3
III	446.1	592.1	166.7	-123.7	-99.1	47.3	271.7	-84.3	354.6	58.9	73.1	56.0	-46.1	226.9	12.0	-9.8
IV	499.1	527.3	122.4	-119.2	-60.0	-30.8	151.8	136.2	294.3	32.6	117.2	83.9	-25.1	164.4	29.6	10.2
1993: I	333.9	352.2	64.6	-188.9	-53.7	18.6	160.9	-110.5	370.3	90.9	123.6	71.1	-27.5	120.4	20.3	44.9
II	561.1	636.5	131.0	-45.7	54.5	-62.8	185.5	-27.2	369.0	32.1	121.6	86.8	-23.9	193.0	41.6	25.5
III	356.7	579.1	74.9	-107.6	-37.4	-97.0	220.4	38.5	406.5	80.9	103.7	87.3	-9.2	235.9	76.2	92.1
IV	387.3	537.9	56.0	-22.4	-4.2	103.8	66.5	62.1	214.0	62.0	143.5	110.4	-16.6	183.9	111.3	92.7
1994: I	483.4	638.3	95.5	51.1	-41.0	456.2	-4.5	-.9	1.2	74.7	128.1	71.9	-16.7	179.7	72.7	85.8
II	513.3	609.8	40.2	-22.5	13.7	402.8	85.8	-21.7	72.4	39.0	154.9	100.7	3.9	144.3	121.9	89.9
III	345.1	492.7	-9.2	-10.7	23.3	283.3	-65.6	46.4	221.6	3.6	152.4	104.6	8.9	199.0	127.1	87.4

[1] Saving by households, nonprofit institutions, farms, and other noncorporate business.
[2] Consists of U.S. savings bonds, other U.S. Treasury securities, U.S. Government agency securities and government-sponsored enterprise securities, federally-related mortgage pool securities, and State and local obligations.
[3] Includes mutual fund shares.
[4] Corporate and foreign bonds and open-market paper.
[5] Private life insurance reserves, private insured and noninsured pension reserves, and government insurance and pension reserves.
[6] Consists of security credit, mortgages, accident and health insurance reserves, nonlife insurance claims, and investment in bank personal trusts for households; of consumer credit, equity in government-sponsored enterprises, and nonlife insurance claims for noncorporate business.
[7] Purchases of physical assets less depreciation.
[8] Includes data for corporate farms.
[9] Other debt consists of security credit, U.S. Government and policy loans, and noncorporate business debt.

Source: Board of Governors of the Federal Reserve System.

309

TABLE B-31.—*Median money income (in 1993 dollars) and poverty status of families and persons, by race, selected years, 1973-93*

Year	Families [1] Number (millions)	Median money income (in 1993 dollars) [2]	Below poverty level Total Number (millions)	Below poverty level Total Percent	Below poverty level Female householder Number (millions)	Below poverty level Female householder Percent	Persons below poverty level Number (millions)	Persons below poverty level Percent	Median money income (in 1993 dollars) of persons 15 years old and over with income [2][3] Males All persons	Males Year-round full-time workers	Females All persons	Females Year-round full-time workers
ALL RACES												
1973	55.1	$36,893	4.8	8.8	2.2	32.2	23.0	11.1	$24,663	$35,109	$8,560	$19,863
1975 [4]	56.2	35,274	5.5	9.7	2.4	32.5	25.9	12.3	22,763	33,256	8,703	19,847
1977	57.2	36,603	5.3	9.3	2.6	31.7	24.7	11.6	23,145	34,456	9,011	20,152
1978	57.8	37,763	5.3	9.1	2.7	31.4	24.5	11.4	23,409	34,385	8,709	20,639
1979 [5]	59.6	38,248	5.5	9.2	2.6	30.4	26.1	11.7	23,001	34,131	8,498	20,564
1980	60.3	36,912	6.2	10.3	3.0	32.7	29.3	13.0	22,000	33,663	8,638	20,351
1981	61.0	35,905	6.9	11.2	3.3	34.6	31.8	14.0	21,608	33,185	8,753	19,978
1982	61.4	35,419	7.5	12.2	3.4	36.3	34.4	15.0	21,086	32,732	8,898	20,652
1983 [6]	62.0	35,797	7.6	12.3	3.6	36.0	35.3	15.2	21,270	32,655	9,292	21,006
1984	62.7	36,762	7.3	11.6	3.5	34.5	33.7	14.4	21,696	33,384	9,552	21,448
1985	63.6	37,246	7.2	11.4	3.5	34.0	33.1	14.0	21,905	33,572	9,692	21,825
1986	64.5	38,838	7.0	10.9	3.6	34.6	32.4	13.6	22,564	34,139	10,033	22,206
1987 [4]	65.2	39,394	7.0	10.7	3.7	34.2	32.2	13.4	22,624	33,938	10,551	22,342
1988	65.8	39,320	6.9	10.4	3.6	33.4	31.7	13.0	23,096	33,397	10,852	22,652
1989	66.1	39,869	6.8	10.3	3.5	32.2	31.5	12.8	23,182	33,117	11,215	22,885
1990	66.3	39,086	7.1	10.7	3.8	33.4	33.6	13.5	22,436	32,039	11,133	22,765
1991	67.2	38,129	7.7	11.5	4.2	35.6	35.7	14.2	21,716	32,179	11,114	22,540
1992 [7]	68.2	37,668	8.1	11.9	4.3	35.4	38.0	14.8	21,067	31,755	11,035	22,754
1993	68.5	36,959	8.4	12.3	4.4	35.6	39.3	15.1	21,102	31,077	11,046	22,469
WHITE												
1973	48.9	38,559	3.2	6.6	1.2	24.5	15.1	8.4	25,878	36,125	8,642	20,199
1975 [4]	49.9	36,686	3.8	7.7	1.4	25.9	17.8	9.7	23,912	34,024	8,793	19,893
1977	50.5	38,274	3.5	7.0	1.4	24.0	16.4	8.9	24,243	35,160	9,148	20,280
1978	50.9	39,321	3.5	6.9	1.4	23.5	16.3	8.7	24,518	35,023	8,813	20,834
1979 [5]	52.2	39,911	3.6	6.9	1.4	22.3	17.2	9.0	24,028	35,117	8,578	20,744
1980	52.7	38,458	4.2	8.0	1.6	25.7	19.7	10.2	23,401	34,624	8,686	20,548
1981	53.3	37,716	4.7	8.8	1.8	27.4	21.6	11.1	22,928	33,965	8,851	20,312
1982	53.4	37,188	5.1	9.6	1.8	27.9	23.5	12.0	22,292	33,604	9,019	20,930
1983 [6]	53.9	37,484	5.2	9.7	1.9	28.3	24.0	12.1	22,377	33,534	9,455	21,293
1984	54.4	38,505	4.9	9.1	1.9	27.1	23.0	11.5	22,902	34,527	9,664	21,661
1985	55.0	39,149	5.0	9.1	2.0	27.4	22.9	11.4	22,979	34,504	9,880	22,134
1986	55.7	40,620	4.8	8.6	2.0	28.2	22.2	11.0	23,811	35,093	10,231	22,546
1987 [4]	56.1	41,194	4.6	8.1	2.0	26.9	21.2	10.4	24,047	34,730	10,821	22,755
1988	56.5	41,426	4.5	7.9	1.9	26.5	20.7	10.1	24,379	34,521	11,119	22,992
1989	56.6	41,922	4.4	7.8	1.9	25.4	20.8	10.0	24,312	34,577	11,434	23,156
1990	56.8	40,813	4.6	8.1	2.0	26.8	22.3	10.7	23,405	33,257	11,406	23,039
1991	57.2	40,085	5.0	8.8	2.2	28.4	23.7	11.3	22,699	32,839	11,374	22,869
1992 [7]	57.7	39,828	5.3	9.1	2.2	28.5	25.3	11.9	22,047	32,510	11,291	23,018
1993	57.9	39,300	5.5	9.4	2.4	29.2	26.2	12.2	21,981	31,832	11,266	22,979
BLACK												
1973	5.4	22,254	1.5	28.1	1.0	52.7	7.4	31.4	15,653	24,348	7,801	17,129
1975 [4]	5.6	22,572	1.5	27.1	1.0	50.1	7.5	31.3	14,296	25,321	7,989	19,006
1977	5.8	21,865	1.6	28.2	1.2	51.0	7.7	31.3	14,386	24,240	7,899	18,954
1978	5.9	23,289	1.6	27.5	1.2	50.6	7.6	30.6	14,688	26,823	7,936	19,309
1979 [5]	6.2	22,601	1.7	27.8	1.2	49.4	8.1	31.0	14,874	25,309	7,807	19,008
1980	6.3	22,253	1.8	28.9	1.3	49.4	8.6	32.5	14,062	24,361	8,041	19,164
1981	6.4	21,276	2.0	30.8	1.4	52.9	9.2	34.2	13,634	24,031	7,863	18,344
1982	6.5	20,553	2.2	33.0	1.5	56.2	9.7	35.6	13,359	23,867	7,955	18,706
1983 [6]	6.7	21,125	2.2	32.3	1.5	53.7	9.9	35.7	13,086	23,808	8,080	18,860
1984	6.8	21,461	2.1	30.9	1.5	51.7	9.5	33.8	13,140	23,564	8,573	19,521
1985	6.9	22,543	2.0	28.7	1.5	50.5	8.9	31.3	14,461	24,134	8,430	19,593
1986	7.1	23,210	2.0	28.0	1.5	50.1	9.0	31.1	14,268	24,742	8,657	19,729
1987 [4]	7.2	23,413	2.1	29.4	1.6	51.1	9.5	32.4	14,266	24,832	8,839	20,324
1988	7.4	23,610	2.1	28.2	1.6	49.0	9.4	31.3	14,711	25,304	8,977	20,603
1989	7.5	23,550	2.1	27.8	1.5	46.5	9.3	30.7	14,694	24,127	9,177	20,825
1990	7.5	23,685	2.2	29.3	1.6	48.1	9.8	31.9	14,227	23,749	9,207	20,502
1991	7.7	22,861	2.3	30.4	1.8	51.2	10.2	32.7	13,752	24,007	9,353	20,300
1992 [7]	8.0	21,735	2.5	31.1	1.9	50.2	10.8	33.4	13,455	23,679	9,153	20,864
1993	8.0	21,542	2.5	31.3	1.9	49.9	10.9	33.1	14,605	23,566	9,508	20,315

[1] The term "family" refers to a group of two or more persons related by birth, marriage, or adoption and residing together; all such persons are considered members of the same family. Beginning 1979, based on householder concept and restricted to primary families.
[2] Current dollar median money income deflated by CPI-U-X1.
[3] Prior to 1979, data are for persons 14 years and over.
[4] Based on revised methodology; comparable with succeeding years.
[5] Based on 1980 census population controls; comparable with succeeding years.
[6] Reflects implementation of Hispanic population controls; comparable with succeeding years.
[7] Based on 1990 census population controls; comparable with succeeding years.

Note.—Poverty rates (percent of persons below poverty level) for all races for years not shown above are: 1959, 22.4; 1960, 22.2; 1961, 21.9; 1962, 21.0; 1963, 19.5; 1964, 19.0; 1965, 17.3; 1966, 14.7; 1967, 14.2; 1968, 12.8; 1969, 12.1; 1970, 12.6; 1971, 12.5; 1972, 11.9; 1974, 11.2; and 1976, 11.8.
Poverty thresholds are updated each year to reflect changes in the consumer price index (CPI-U).
For details see "Current Population Reports," Series P-60.

Source: Department of Commerce, Bureau of the Census.

TABLE B–32.—*Population by age group, 1929–94*

[Thousands of persons]

July 1	Total	Age (years)						
		Under 5	5–15	16–19	20–24	25–44	45–64	65 and over
1929	121,767	11,734	26,800	9,127	10,694	35,862	21,076	6,474
1933	125,579	10,612	26,897	9,302	11,152	37,319	22,933	7,363
1939	130,880	10,418	25,179	9,822	11,519	39,354	25,823	8,764
1940	132,122	10,579	24,811	9,895	11,690	39,868	26,249	9,031
1941	133,402	10,850	24,516	9,840	11,807	40,383	26,718	9,288
1942	134,860	11,301	24,231	9,730	11,955	40,861	27,196	9,584
1943	136,739	12,016	24,093	9,607	12,064	41,420	27,671	9,867
1944	138,397	12,524	23,949	9,561	12,062	42,016	28,138	10,147
1945	139,928	12,979	23,907	9,361	12,036	42,521	28,630	10,494
1946	141,389	13,244	24,103	9,119	12,004	43,027	29,064	10,828
1947	144,126	14,406	24,468	9,097	11,814	43,657	29,498	11,185
1948	146,631	14,919	25,209	8,952	11,794	44,288	29,931	11,538
1949	149,188	15,607	25,852	8,788	11,700	44,916	30,405	11,921
1950	152,271	16,410	26,721	8,542	11,680	45,672	30,849	12,397
1951	154,878	17,333	27,279	8,446	11,552	46,103	31,362	12,803
1952	157,553	17,312	28,894	8,414	11,350	46,495	31,884	13,203
1953	160,184	17,638	30,227	8,460	11,062	46,786	32,394	13,617
1954	163,026	18,057	31,480	8,637	10,832	47,001	32,942	14,076
1955	165,931	18,566	32,682	8,744	10,714	47,194	33,506	14,525
1956	168,903	19,003	33,994	8,916	10,616	47,379	34,057	14,938
1957	171,984	19,494	35,272	9,195	10,603	47,440	34,591	15,388
1958	174,882	19,887	36,445	9,543	10,756	47,337	35,109	15,806
1959	177,830	20,175	37,368	10,215	10,969	47,192	35,663	16,248
1960	180,671	20,341	38,494	10,683	11,134	47,140	36,203	16,675
1961	183,691	20,522	39,765	11,025	11,483	47,084	36,722	17,089
1962	186,538	20,469	41,205	11,180	11,959	47,013	37,255	17,457
1963	189,242	20,342	41,626	12,007	12,714	46,994	37,782	17,778
1964	191,889	20,165	42,297	12,736	13,269	46,958	38,338	18,127
1965	194,303	19,824	42,938	13,516	13,746	46,912	38,916	18,451
1966	196,560	19,208	43,702	14,311	14,050	47,001	39,534	18,755
1967	198,712	18,563	44,244	14,200	15,248	47,194	40,193	19,071
1968	200,706	17,913	44,622	14,452	15,786	47,721	40,846	19,365
1969	202,677	17,376	44,840	14,800	16,480	48,064	41,437	19,680
1970	205,052	17,166	44,816	15,289	17,202	48,473	41,999	20,107
1971	207,661	17,244	44,591	15,688	18,159	48,936	42,482	20,561
1972	209,896	17,101	44,203	16,039	18,153	50,482	42,898	21,020
1973	211,909	16,851	43,582	16,446	18,521	51,749	43,235	21,525
1974	213,854	16,487	42,989	16,769	18,975	53,051	43,522	22,061
1975	215,973	16,121	42,508	17,017	19,527	54,302	43,801	22,696
1976	218,035	15,617	42,099	17,194	19,986	55,852	44,008	23,278
1977	220,239	15,564	41,298	17,276	20,499	57,561	44,150	23,892
1978	222,585	15,735	40,428	17,288	20,946	59,400	44,286	24,502
1979	225,055	16,063	39,552	17,242	21,297	61,379	44,390	25,134
1980	227,726	16,451	38,838	17,167	21,590	63,470	44,504	25,707
1981	229,966	16,893	38,144	16,812	21,869	65,528	44,500	26,221
1982	232,188	17,228	37,784	16,332	21,902	67,692	44,462	26,787
1983	234,307	17,547	37,526	15,823	21,844	69,733	44,474	27,361
1984	236,348	17,695	37,461	15,295	21,737	71,735	44,547	27,878
1985	238,466	17,842	37,450	15,005	21,478	73,673	44,602	28,416
1986	240,651	17,963	37,404	15,024	20,942	75,651	44,660	29,008
1987	242,804	18,052	37,333	15,215	20,385	77,338	44,854	29,626
1988	245,021	18,195	37,593	15,198	19,846	78,595	45,471	30,124
1989	247,342	18,508	37,972	14,913	19,442	79,943	45,882	30,682
1990	249,911	18,849	38,588	14,449	19,305	81,196	46,288	31,235
1991	252,643	19,195	39,195	13,926	19,347	82,455	46,759	31,765
1992	255,407	19,501	39,900	13,668	19,176	82,541	48,348	32,272
1993	258,120	19,691	40,538	13,795	18,874	82,862	49,586	32,773
1994	260,651	19,727	41,213	14,030	18,429	83,199	50,894	33,158

Note.—Includes Armed Forces overseas beginning 1940. Includes Alaska and Hawaii beginning 1950.
All estimates are consistent with decennial census enumerations.

Source: Department of Commerce, Bureau of the Census.

311

[Monthly data seasonally adjusted, except as noted]

Year or month	Civilian noninstitutional population [1]	Civilian labor force					Not in labor force	Civilian labor force participation rate [2]	Civilian employment/population ratio [3]	Unemployment rate, civilian workers [4]
		Total	Employment			Unemployment				
			Total	Agricultural	Nonagricultural					
	Thousands of persons 14 years of age and over							Percent		
1929		49,180	47,630	10,450	37,180	1,550				3.2
1933		51,590	38,760	10,090	28,670	12,830				24.9
1939		55,230	45,750	9,610	36,140	9,480				17.2
1940	99,840	55,640	47,520	9,540	37,980	8,120	44,200	55.7	47.6	14.6
1941	99,900	55,910	50,350	9,100	41,250	5,560	43,990	56.0	50.4	9.9
1942	98,640	56,410	53,750	9,250	44,500	2,660	42,230	57.2	54.5	4.7
1943	94,640	55,540	54,470	9,080	45,390	1,070	39,100	58.7	57.6	1.9
1944	93,220	54,630	53,960	8,950	45,010	670	38,590	58.6	57.9	1.2
1945	94,090	53,860	52,820	8,580	44,240	1,040	40,230	57.2	56.1	1.9
1946	103,070	57,520	55,250	8,320	46,930	2,270	45,550	55.8	53.6	3.9
1947	106,018	60,168	57,812	8,256	49,557	2,356	45,850	56.8	54.5	3.9
	Thousands of persons 16 years of age and over									
1947	101,827	59,350	57,038	7,890	49,148	2,311	42,477	58.3	56.0	3.9
1948	103,068	60,621	58,343	7,629	50,714	2,276	42,447	58.8	56.6	3.8
1949	103,994	61,286	57,651	7,658	49,993	3,637	42,708	58.9	55.4	5.9
1950	104,995	62,208	58,918	7,160	51,758	3,288	42,787	59.2	56.1	5.3
1951	104,621	62,017	59,961	6,726	53,235	2,055	42,604	59.2	57.3	3.3
1952	105,231	62,138	60,250	6,500	53,749	1,883	43,093	59.0	57.3	3.0
1953 [5]	107,056	63,015	61,179	6,260	54,919	1,834	44,041	58.9	57.1	2.9
1954	108,321	63,643	60,109	6,205	53,904	3,532	44,678	58.8	55.5	5.5
1955	109,683	65,023	62,170	6,450	55,722	2,852	44,660	59.3	56.7	4.4
1956	110,954	66,552	63,799	6,283	57,514	2,750	44,402	60.0	57.5	4.1
1957	112,265	66,929	64,071	5,947	58,123	2,859	45,336	59.6	57.1	4.3
1958	113,727	67,639	63,036	5,586	57,450	4,602	46,088	59.5	55.4	6.8
1959	115,329	68,369	64,630	5,565	59,065	3,740	46,960	59.3	56.0	5.5
1960 [5]	117,245	69,628	65,778	5,458	60,318	3,852	47,617	59.4	56.1	5.5
1961	118,771	70,459	65,746	5,200	60,546	4,714	48,312	59.3	55.4	6.7
1962 [5]	120,153	70,614	66,702	4,944	61,759	3,911	49,539	58.8	55.5	5.5
1963	122,416	71,833	67,762	4,687	63,076	4,070	50,583	58.7	55.4	5.7
1964	124,485	73,091	69,305	4,523	64,782	3,786	51,394	58.7	55.7	5.2
1965	126,513	74,455	71,088	4,361	66,726	3,366	52,058	58.9	56.2	4.5
1966	128,058	75,770	72,895	3,979	68,915	2,875	52,288	59.2	56.9	3.8
1967	129,874	77,347	74,372	3,844	70,527	2,975	52,527	59.6	57.3	3.8
1968	132,028	78,737	75,920	3,817	72,103	2,817	53,291	59.6	57.5	3.6
1969	134,335	80,734	77,902	3,606	74,296	2,832	53,602	60.1	58.0	3.5
1970	137,085	82,771	78,678	3,463	75,215	4,093	54,315	60.4	57.4	4.9
1971	140,216	84,382	79,367	3,394	75,972	5,016	55,834	60.2	56.6	5.9
1972 [5]	144,126	87,034	82,153	3,484	78,669	4,882	57,091	60.4	57.0	5.6
1973 [5]	147,096	89,429	85,064	3,470	81,594	4,365	57,667	60.8	57.8	4.9
1974	150,120	91,949	86,794	3,515	83,279	5,156	58,171	61.3	57.8	5.6
1975	153,153	93,775	85,846	3,408	82,438	7,929	59,377	61.2	56.1	8.5
1976	156,150	96,158	88,752	3,331	85,421	7,406	59,991	61.6	56.8	7.7
1977	159,033	99,009	92,017	3,283	88,734	6,991	60,025	62.3	57.9	7.1
1978 [5]	161,910	102,251	96,048	3,387	92,661	6,202	59,659	63.2	59.3	6.1
1979	164,863	104,962	98,824	3,347	95,477	6,137	59,900	63.7	59.9	5.8
1980	167,745	106,940	99,303	3,364	95,938	7,637	60,806	63.8	59.2	7.1
1981	170,130	108,670	100,397	3,368	97,030	8,273	61,460	63.9	59.0	7.6
1982	172,271	110,204	99,526	3,401	96,125	10,678	62,067	64.0	57.8	9.7
1983	174,215	111,550	100,834	3,383	97,450	10,717	62,665	64.0	57.9	9.6
1984	176,383	113,544	105,005	3,321	101,685	8,539	62,839	64.4	59.5	7.5
1985	178,206	115,461	107,150	3,179	103,971	8,312	62,744	64.8	60.1	7.2
1986 [5]	180,587	117,834	109,597	3,163	106,434	8,237	62,752	65.3	60.7	7.0
1987	182,753	119,865	112,440	3,208	109,232	7,425	62,888	65.6	61.5	6.2
1988	184,613	121,669	114,968	3,169	111,800	6,701	62,944	65.9	62.3	5.5
1989	186,393	123,869	117,342	3,199	114,142	6,528	62,523	66.5	63.0	5.3
1990	188,049	124,787	117,914	3,186	114,728	6,874	63,262	66.4	62.7	5.5
1991	189,765	125,303	116,877	3,233	113,644	8,426	64,462	66.0	61.6	6.7
1992	191,576	126,982	117,598	3,207	114,391	9,384	64,593	66.3	61.4	7.4
1993	193,550	128,040	119,306	3,074	116,232	8,734	65,509	66.2	61.6	6.8
1994 [5]	196,814	131,056	123,060	3,409	119,651	7,996	65,758	66.6	62.5	6.1

[1] Not seasonally adjusted.
[2] Civilian labor force as percent of civilian noninstitutional population.
[3] Civilian employment as percent of civilian noninstitutional population.
[4] Unemployed as percent of civilian labor force.
See next page for continuation of table.

[Monthly data seasonally adjusted, except as noted]

Year or month	Civilian noninstitutional population [1]	Civilian labor force					Not in labor force	Civilian labor force participation rate [2]	Civilian employment/population ratio [3]	Unemployment rate, civilian workers [4]
		Total	Employment			Unemployment				
			Total	Agricultural	Nonagricultural					
	Thousands of persons 16 years of age and over							Percent		
1991: Jan	188,977	124,787	116,967	3,173	113,794	7,820	64,190	66.0	61.9	6.3
Feb	189,115	125,027	116,869	3,228	113,641	8,158	64,088	66.1	61.8	6.5
Mar	189,243	125,256	116,791	3,131	113,660	8,465	63,987	66.2	61.7	6.8
Apr	189,380	125,721	117,411	3,189	114,222	8,310	63,659	66.4	62.0	6.6
May	189,522	125,185	116,646	3,269	113,377	8,539	64,337	66.1	61.5	6.8
June	189,668	125,367	116,878	3,281	113,597	8,489	64,301	66.1	61.6	6.8
July	189,839	125,102	116,738	3,258	113,480	8,364	64,737	65.9	61.5	6.7
Aug	189,973	124,949	116,505	3,273	113,232	8,444	65,024	65.8	61.3	6.8
Sept	190,122	125,607	117,142	3,275	113,867	8,465	64,515	66.1	61.6	6.7
Oct	190,289	125,578	116,997	3,231	113,766	8,581	64,711	66.0	61.5	6.8
Nov	190,452	125,519	116,848	3,255	113,593	8,671	64,933	65.9	61.4	6.9
Dec	190,605	125,641	116,636	3,141	113,495	9,005	64,964	65.9	61.2	7.2
1992: Jan	190,759	126,149	117,130	3,136	113,994	9,019	64,610	66.1	61.4	7.1
Feb	190,884	126,209	116,919	3,218	113,701	9,290	64,675	66.1	61.3	7.4
Mar	191,022	126,545	117,255	3,208	114,047	9,290	64,477	66.2	61.4	7.3
Apr	191,168	126,917	117,670	3,220	114,450	9,247	64,251	66.4	61.6	7.3
May	191,307	127,036	117,534	3,192	114,342	9,502	64,271	66.4	61.4	7.5
June	191,455	127,269	117,498	3,248	114,250	9,771	64,186	66.5	61.4	7.7
July	191,622	127,358	117,763	3,217	114,546	9,595	64,264	66.5	61.5	7.5
Aug	191,790	127,339	117,749	3,237	114,512	9,590	64,451	66.4	61.4	7.5
Sept	191,947	127,306	117,772	3,211	114,561	9,534	64,641	66.3	61.4	7.5
Oct	192,131	126,933	117,723	3,188	114,535	9,210	65,198	66.1	61.3	7.3
Nov	192,316	127,287	117,974	3,170	114,804	9,313	65,029	66.2	61.3	7.3
Dec	192,509	127,469	118,155	3,222	114,933	9,314	65,040	66.2	61.4	7.3
1993: Jan	192,644	127,224	118,178	3,182	114,996	9,046	65,420	66.0	61.3	7.1
Feb	192,786	127,400	118,442	3,116	115,326	8,958	65,386	66.1	61.4	7.0
Mar	192,959	127,440	118,562	3,099	115,463	8,878	65,519	66.0	61.4	7.0
Apr	193,126	127,539	118,585	3,071	115,514	8,954	65,587	66.0	61.4	7.0
May	193,283	128,075	119,180	3,074	116,106	8,895	65,208	66.3	61.7	6.9
June	193,456	128,056	119,187	3,031	116,156	8,869	65,400	66.2	61.6	6.9
July	193,633	128,102	119,370	3,043	116,327	8,732	65,531	66.2	61.6	6.8
Aug	193,793	128,334	119,692	3,005	116,687	8,642	65,459	66.2	61.8	6.7
Sept	193,971	128,108	119,568	3,093	116,475	8,540	65,863	66.0	61.6	6.7
Oct	194,151	128,580	119,941	3,021	116,920	8,639	65,571	66.2	61.8	6.7
Nov	194,321	128,662	120,332	3,114	117,218	8,330	65,659	66.2	61.9	6.5
Dec	194,472	128,898	120,661	3,096	117,565	8,237	65,574	66.3	62.0	6.4
1994: Jan [5]	195,953	130,643	121,903	3,328	118,575	8,740	65,310	66.7	62.2	6.7
Feb	196,090	130,784	122,208	3,368	118,840	8,576	65,306	66.7	62.3	6.6
Mar	196,213	130,706	122,160	3,396	118,764	8,546	65,507	66.6	62.3	6.5
Apr	196,363	130,787	122,402	3,438	118,964	8,385	65,576	66.6	62.3	6.4
May	196,510	130,699	122,703	3,413	119,290	7,996	65,811	66.5	62.4	6.1
June	196,693	130,538	122,635	3,294	119,341	7,903	66,155	66.4	62.3	6.1
July	196,859	130,774	122,781	3,333	119,448	7,993	66,085	66.4	62.4	6.1
Aug	197,043	131,086	123,197	3,436	119,761	7,889	65,957	66.5	62.5	6.0
Sept	197,248	131,291	123,644	3,411	120,233	7,647	65,957	66.6	62.7	5.8
Oct	197,430	131,646	124,141	3,494	120,647	7,505	65,784	66.7	62.9	5.7
Nov	197,607	131,718	124,403	3,500	120,903	7,315	65,889	66.7	63.0	5.6
Dec	197,765	131,725	124,570	3,532	121,038	7,155	66,040	66.6	63.0	5.4

[5] Not strictly comparable with earlier data due to population adjustments as follows: Beginning 1953, introduction of 1950 census data added about 600,000 to population and 350,000 to labor force, total employment, and agricultural employment. Beginning 1960, inclusion of Alaska and Hawaii added about 500,000 to population, 300,000 to labor force, and 240,000 to nonagricultural employment. Beginning 1962, introduction of 1960 census data reduced population by about 50,000 and labor force and employment by 200,000. Beginning 1972, introduction of 1970 census data added about 800,000 to civilian noninstitutional population and 333,000 to labor force and employment. A subsequent adjustment based on 1970 census in March 1973 added 60,000 to labor force and to employment. Beginning 1978, changes in sampling and estimation procedures introduced into the household survey added about 250,000 to labor force and to employment. Unemployment levels and rates were not significantly affected. Beginning 1986, the introduction of revised population controls added about 400,000 to the civilian population and labor force and 350,000 to civilian employment. Unemployment levels and rates were not significantly affected.

Beginning 1994, introduction of adjusted 1990 census-based population controls together with a major redesign of the household survey added about 1.3 million to civilian population, 2.0 million to civilian labor force, 1.1 million to civilian employment, and 900,000 to unemployment. Unemployment rates were not significantly affected.

Note.—Labor force data in Tables B-33 through B-42 are based on household interviews and relate to the calendar week including the 12th of the month. For definitions of terms, area samples used, historical comparability of the data, comparability with other series, etc., see "Employment and Earnings."

Source: Department of Labor, Bureau of Labor Statistics.

TABLE B-34.—*Civilian employment and unemployment by sex and age, 1947–94*

[Thousands of persons 16 years of age and over; monthly data seasonally adjusted]

| Year or month | Civilian employment | | | | | | | Unemployment | | | | | | |
| | Total | Males | | | Females | | | Total | Males | | | Females | | |
		Total	16–19 years	20 years and over	Total	16–19 years	20 years and over		Total	16–19 years	20 years and over	Total	16–19 years	20 years and over
1947	57,038	40,995	2,218	38,776	16,045	1,691	14,354	2,311	1,692	270	1,422	619	144	475
1948	58,343	41,725	2,344	39,382	16,617	1,682	14,936	2,276	1,559	256	1,305	717	153	564
1949	57,651	40,925	2,124	38,803	16,723	1,588	15,137	3,637	2,572	353	2,219	1,065	223	841
1950	58,918	41,578	2,186	39,394	17,340	1,517	15,824	3,288	2,239	318	1,922	1,049	195	854
1951	59,961	41,780	2,156	39,626	18,181	1,611	16,570	2,055	1,221	191	1,029	834	145	689
1952	60,250	41,682	2,107	39,578	18,568	1,612	16,958	1,883	1,185	205	980	698	140	559
1953	61,179	42,430	2,136	40,296	18,749	1,584	17,164	1,834	1,202	184	1,019	632	123	510
1954	60,109	41,619	1,985	39,634	18,490	1,490	17,000	3,532	2,344	310	2,035	1,188	191	997
1955	62,170	42,621	2,095	40,526	19,551	1,547	18,002	2,852	1,854	274	1,580	998	176	823
1956	63,799	43,379	2,164	41,216	20,419	1,654	18,767	2,750	1,711	269	1,442	1,039	209	832
1957	64,071	43,357	2,115	41,239	20,714	1,663	19,052	2,859	1,841	300	1,541	1,018	197	821
1958	63,036	42,423	2,012	40,411	20,613	1,570	19,043	4,602	3,098	416	2,681	1,504	262	1,242
1959	64,630	43,466	2,198	41,267	21,164	1,640	19,524	3,740	2,420	398	2,022	1,320	256	1,063
1960	65,778	43,904	2,361	41,543	21,874	1,768	20,105	3,852	2,486	426	2,060	1,366	286	1,080
1961	65,746	43,656	2,315	41,342	22,090	1,793	20,296	4,714	2,997	479	2,518	1,717	349	1,368
1962	66,702	44,177	2,362	41,815	22,525	1,833	20,693	3,911	2,423	408	2,016	1,488	313	1,175
1963	67,762	44,657	2,406	42,251	23,105	1,849	21,257	4,070	2,472	501	1,971	1,598	383	1,216
1964	69,305	45,474	2,587	42,886	23,831	1,929	21,903	3,786	2,205	487	1,718	1,581	385	1,195
1965	71,088	46,340	2,918	43,422	24,748	2,118	22,630	3,366	1,914	479	1,435	1,452	395	1,056
1966	72,895	46,919	3,253	43,668	25,976	2,468	23,510	2,875	1,551	432	1,120	1,324	405	921
1967	74,372	47,479	3,186	44,294	26,893	2,496	24,397	2,975	1,508	448	1,060	1,468	391	1,078
1968	75,920	48,114	3,255	44,859	27,807	2,526	25,281	2,817	1,419	426	993	1,397	412	985
1969	77,902	48,818	3,430	45,388	29,084	2,687	26,397	2,832	1,403	440	963	1,429	413	1,015
1970	78,678	48,990	3,409	45,581	29,688	2,735	26,952	4,093	2,238	599	1,638	1,855	506	1,349
1971	79,367	49,390	3,478	45,912	29,976	2,730	27,246	5,016	2,789	693	2,097	2,227	568	1,658
1972	82,153	50,896	3,765	47,130	31,257	2,980	28,276	4,882	2,659	711	1,948	2,222	598	1,625
1973	85,064	52,349	4,039	48,310	32,715	3,231	29,484	4,365	2,275	653	1,624	2,089	583	1,507
1974	86,794	53,024	4,103	48,922	33,769	3,345	30,424	5,156	2,714	757	1,957	2,441	665	1,777
1975	85,846	51,857	3,839	48,018	33,989	3,263	30,726	7,929	4,442	966	3,476	3,486	802	2,684
1976	88,752	53,138	3,947	49,190	35,615	3,389	32,226	7,406	4,036	939	3,098	3,369	780	2,588
1977	92,017	54,728	4,174	50,555	37,289	3,514	33,775	6,991	3,667	874	2,794	3,324	789	2,535
1978	96,048	56,479	4,336	52,143	39,569	3,734	35,836	6,202	3,142	813	2,328	3,061	769	2,292
1979	98,824	57,607	4,300	53,308	41,217	3,783	37,434	6,137	3,120	811	2,308	3,018	743	2,276
1980	99,303	57,186	4,085	53,101	42,117	3,625	38,492	7,637	4,267	913	3,353	3,370	755	2,615
1981	100,397	57,397	3,815	53,582	43,000	3,411	39,590	8,273	4,577	962	3,615	3,696	800	2,895
1982	99,526	56,271	3,379	52,891	43,256	3,170	40,086	10,678	6,179	1,090	5,089	4,499	886	3,613
1983	100,834	56,787	3,300	53,487	44,047	3,043	41,004	10,717	6,260	1,003	5,257	4,457	825	3,632
1984	105,005	59,091	3,322	55,769	45,915	3,122	42,793	8,539	4,744	812	3,932	3,794	687	3,107
1985	107,150	59,891	3,328	56,562	47,259	3,105	44,154	8,312	4,521	806	3,715	3,791	661	3,129
1986	109,597	60,892	3,323	57,569	48,706	3,149	45,556	8,237	4,530	779	3,751	3,707	675	3,032
1987	112,440	62,107	3,381	58,726	50,334	3,260	47,074	7,425	4,101	732	3,369	3,324	616	2,709
1988	114,968	63,273	3,492	59,781	51,696	3,313	48,383	6,701	3,655	667	2,987	3,046	558	2,487
1989	117,342	64,315	3,477	60,837	53,027	3,282	49,745	6,528	3,525	658	2,867	3,003	536	2,467
1990	117,914	64,435	3,237	61,198	53,479	3,024	50,455	6,874	3,799	629	3,170	3,075	519	2,555
1991	116,877	63,593	2,879	60,714	53,284	2,749	50,535	8,426	4,817	709	4,109	3,609	581	3,028
1992	117,598	63,805	2,786	61,019	53,793	2,613	51,181	9,384	5,380	761	4,619	4,005	591	3,413
1993	119,306	64,700	2,836	61,865	54,606	2,694	51,912	8,734	4,932	728	4,204	3,801	568	3,234
1994	123,060	66,450	3,156	63,294	56,610	3,005	53,606	7,996	4,367	740	3,627	3,629	580	3,049
1993: Jan	118,178	64,237	2,819	61,418	53,941	2,633	51,308	9,046	4,977	737	4,240	4,069	594	3,475
Feb	118,442	64,329	2,852	61,477	54,113	2,634	51,479	8,958	5,067	742	4,325	3,891	596	3,295
Mar	118,562	64,355	2,857	61,498	54,207	2,591	51,616	8,878	5,147	729	4,418	3,731	588	3,143
Apr	118,585	64,416	2,802	61,614	54,169	2,636	51,533	8,954	5,098	810	4,288	3,856	575	3,281
May	119,180	64,687	2,838	61,849	54,493	2,716	51,777	8,895	5,016	731	4,285	3,879	640	3,239
June	119,187	64,642	2,837	61,805	54,545	2,670	51,875	8,869	5,041	759	4,282	3,828	571	3,257
July	119,370	64,728	2,859	61,869	54,642	2,741	51,901	8,732	5,002	731	4,271	3,730	531	3,199
Aug	119,692	64,904	2,898	62,006	54,788	2,704	52,084	8,642	4,943	728	4,215	3,699	534	3,165
Sept	119,568	64,756	2,855	61,901	54,812	2,740	52,072	8,540	4,824	687	4,137	3,716	537	3,179
Oct	119,941	64,971	2,799	62,172	54,970	2,727	52,243	8,639	4,849	715	4,134	3,790	571	3,219
Nov	120,332	65,144	2,829	62,315	55,188	2,765	52,423	8,330	4,586	703	3,883	3,744	546	3,198
Dec	120,661	65,259	2,815	62,444	55,402	2,771	52,631	8,237	4,554	677	3,877	3,683	531	3,152
1994: Jan	121,903	65,846	3,101	62,745	56,057	2,990	53,067	8,740	4,863	808	4,055	3,877	571	3,306
Feb	122,208	65,887	3,120	62,767	56,321	2,966	53,355	8,576	4,752	766	3,986	3,824	587	3,237
Mar	122,160	65,981	3,104	62,877	56,179	3,003	53,176	8,546	4,626	755	3,871	3,920	585	3,335
Apr	122,402	66,058	3,099	62,959	56,344	3,026	53,318	8,385	4,567	785	3,782	3,818	670	3,148
May	122,703	66,197	3,117	63,080	56,506	3,025	53,481	7,996	4,348	776	3,572	3,648	584	3,064
June	122,635	66,255	3,212	63,043	56,380	3,052	53,328	7,903	4,266	707	3,559	3,637	581	3,056
July	122,781	66,226	3,150	63,076	56,555	3,014	53,541	7,993	4,429	758	3,671	3,564	569	2,995
Aug	123,197	66,458	3,187	63,271	56,739	3,017	53,722	7,889	4,283	737	3,546	3,606	581	3,025
Sept	123,644	66,682	3,165	63,517	56,962	2,918	54,044	7,647	4,109	717	3,392	3,538	551	2,987
Oct	124,141	67,059	3,239	63,820	57,082	2,992	54,090	7,505	4,074	717	3,357	3,431	570	2,861
Nov	124,403	67,244	3,193	64,051	57,159	3,030	54,129	7,315	3,924	630	3,294	3,391	536	2,855
Dec	124,570	67,483	3,202	64,281	57,087	3,050	54,037	7,155	3,896	727	3,169	3,259	571	2,688

Note.—See footnote 5 and Note, Table B-33.

Source: Department of Labor, Bureau of Labor Statistics.

314

TABLE B-35.—*Civilian employment by demographic characteristic, 1954–94*

[Thousands of persons 16 years of age and over; monthly data seasonally adjusted]

Year or month	All civilian workers	White				Black and other				Black			
		Total	Males	Females	Both sexes 16–19	Total	Males	Females	Both sexes 16–19	Total	Males	Females	Both sexes 16–19
1954	60,109	53,957	37,846	16,111	3,078	6,152	3,773	2,379	396				
1955	62,170	55,833	38,719	17,114	3,225	6,341	3,904	2,437	418				
1956	63,799	57,269	39,368	17,901	3,389	6,534	4,013	2,521	430				
1957	64,071	57,465	39,349	18,116	3,374	6,604	4,006	2,598	407				
1958	63,036	56,613	38,591	18,022	3,216	6,423	3,833	2,590	365				
1959	64,630	58,006	39,494	18,512	3,475	6,623	3,971	2,652	362				
1960	65,778	58,850	39,755	19,095	3,700	6,928	4,149	2,779	430				
1961	65,746	58,913	39,588	19,325	3,693	6,833	4,068	2,765	414				
1962	66,702	59,698	40,016	19,682	3,774	7,003	4,160	2,843	420				
1963	67,762	60,622	40,428	20,194	3,851	7,140	4,229	2,911	404				
1964	69,305	61,922	41,115	20,807	4,076	7,383	4,359	3,024	440				
1965	71,088	63,446	41,844	21,602	4,562	7,643	4,496	3,147	474				
1966	72,895	65,021	42,331	22,690	5,176	7,877	4,588	3,289	545				
1967	74,372	66,361	42,833	23,528	5,114	8,011	4,646	3,365	568				
1968	75,920	67,750	43,411	24,339	5,195	8,169	4,702	3,467	584				
1969	77,902	69,518	44,048	25,470	5,508	8,384	4,770	3,614	609				
1970	78,678	70,217	44,178	26,039	5,571	8,464	4,813	3,650	574				
1971	79,367	70,878	44,595	26,283	5,670	8,488	4,796	3,692	538				
1972	82,153	73,370	45,944	27,426	6,173	8,783	4,952	3,832	573	7,802	4,368	3,433	509
1973	85,064	75,708	47,085	28,623	6,623	9,356	5,265	4,092	647	8,128	4,527	3,601	570
1974	86,794	77,184	47,674	29,511	6,796	9,610	5,352	4,258	652	8,203	4,527	3,677	554
1975	85,846	76,411	46,697	29,714	6,487	9,435	5,161	4,275	615	7,894	4,275	3,618	507
1976	88,752	78,853	47,775	31,078	6,724	9,899	5,363	4,536	611	8,227	4,404	3,823	508
1977	92,017	81,700	49,150	32,550	7,068	10,317	5,579	4,739	619	8,540	4,565	3,975	508
1978	96,048	84,936	50,544	34,392	7,367	11,112	5,936	5,177	703	9,102	4,796	4,307	571
1979	98,824	87,259	51,452	35,807	7,356	11,565	6,156	5,409	727	9,359	4,923	4,436	579
1980	99,303	87,715	51,127	36,587	7,021	11,588	6,059	5,529	689	9,313	4,798	4,515	547
1981	100,397	88,709	51,315	37,394	6,588	11,688	6,083	5,606	637	9,355	4,794	4,561	505
1982	99,526	87,903	50,287	37,615	5,984	11,624	5,983	5,641	565	9,189	4,637	4,552	428
1983	100,834	88,893	50,621	38,272	5,799	11,941	6,166	5,775	543	9,375	4,753	4,622	416
1984	105,005	92,120	52,462	39,659	5,836	12,885	6,629	6,256	607	10,119	5,124	4,995	474
1985	107,150	93,736	53,046	40,690	5,768	13,414	6,845	6,569	666	10,501	5,270	5,231	532
1986	109,597	95,660	53,785	41,876	5,792	13,937	7,107	6,830	681	10,814	5,428	5,386	536
1987	112,440	97,789	54,647	43,142	5,898	14,652	7,459	7,192	742	11,309	5,661	5,648	587
1988	114,968	99,812	55,550	44,262	6,030	15,156	7,722	7,434	774	11,658	5,824	5,834	601
1989	117,342	101,584	56,352	45,232	5,946	15,757	7,963	7,795	813	11,953	5,928	6,025	625
1990	117,914	102,087	56,432	45,654	5,518	15,827	8,003	7,825	743	11,966	5,915	6,051	573
1991	116,877	101,039	55,557	45,482	4,989	15,838	8,036	7,802	639	11,863	5,880	5,983	474
1992	117,598	101,479	55,709	45,770	4,761	16,119	8,096	8,023	637	11,933	5,846	6,087	474
1993	119,306	102,812	56,397	46,415	4,887	16,494	8,303	8,191	642	12,146	5,957	6,189	474
1994	123,060	105,190	57,452	47,738	5,398	17,870	8,998	8,872	763	12,835	6,241	6,595	552
1993: Jan	118,178	102,029	56,086	45,943	4,808	16,126	8,157	7,969	635	11,864	5,895	5,969	485
Feb	118,442	102,076	56,100	45,976	4,824	16,439	8,284	8,155	653	12,157	6,009	6,148	487
Mar	118,562	102,251	56,175	46,076	4,829	16,306	8,162	8,144	593	11,991	5,884	6,107	443
Apr	118,585	102,190	56,166	46,024	4,826	16,354	8,210	8,144	618	11,965	5,846	6,119	436
May	119,180	102,612	56,304	46,308	4,878	16,507	8,307	8,200	675	12,140	5,961	6,179	494
June	119,187	102,721	56,362	46,359	4,835	16,408	8,249	8,159	640	12,076	5,931	6,145	451
July	119,370	102,835	56,336	46,499	4,902	16,459	8,367	8,092	688	12,134	6,008	6,126	513
Aug	119,692	103,179	56,523	46,656	4,930	16,522	8,366	8,156	681	12,225	6,031	6,194	514
Sept	119,568	103,094	56,467	46,627	4,939	16,512	8,302	8,210	652	12,202	5,960	6,242	484
Oct	119,941	103,273	56,627	46,646	4,906	16,697	8,380	8,317	630	12,292	5,991	6,301	463
Nov	120,332	103,662	56,799	46,863	4,991	16,705	8,363	8,342	616	12,297	5,951	6,346	461
Dec	120,661	103,807	56,794	47,013	4,970	16,876	8,476	8,400	628	12,397	6,013	6,384	467
1994: Jan	121,903	104,268	57,043	47,225	5,305	17,603	8,818	8,785	809	12,544	6,044	6,500	597
Feb	122,208	104,612	57,053	47,559	5,336	17,637	8,881	8,756	747	12,624	6,124	6,500	537
Mar	122,160	104,412	57,042	47,370	5,355	17,689	8,921	8,768	740	12,718	6,186	6,532	547
Apr	122,402	104,591	57,113	47,478	5,398	17,778	8,948	8,830	742	12,775	6,199	6,576	546
May	122,703	104,978	57,213	47,765	5,427	17,811	9,009	8,802	718	12,810	6,271	6,539	497
June	122,635	104,687	57,273	47,414	5,477	17,850	8,944	8,906	774	12,838	6,214	6,624	552
July	122,781	105,006	57,352	47,654	5,424	17,731	8,856	8,875	759	12,767	6,150	6,617	542
Aug	123,197	105,401	57,558	47,843	5,463	17,811	8,911	8,915	757	12,795	6,168	6,627	541
Sept	123,644	105,740	57,650	48,090	5,254	17,997	9,053	8,944	801	12,927	6,286	6,641	570
Oct	124,141	106,010	57,877	48,133	5,414	18,131	9,167	8,964	778	13,022	6,369	6,653	569
Nov	124,403	106,242	58,028	48,214	5,431	18,161	9,192	8,969	778	13,054	6,393	6,661	579
Dec	124,570	106,352	58,185	48,167	5,493	18,202	9,260	8,942	744	13,119	6,458	6,661	534

Note.—See footnote 5 and Note, Table B–33.

Source: Department of Labor, Bureau of Labor Statistics.

[Thousands of persons 16 years of age and over; monthly data seasonally adjusted]

Year or month	All civilian workers	White				Black and other				Black			
		Total	Males	Fe-males	Both sexes 16–19	Total	Males	Fe-males	Both sexes 16–19	Total	Males	Fe-males	Both sexes 16–19
1954	3,532	2,859	1,913	946	423	673	431	242	79				
1955	2,852	2,252	1,478	774	373	601	376	225	77				
1956	2,750	2,159	1,366	793	382	591	345	246	95				
1957	2,859	2,289	1,477	812	401	570	364	206	96				
1958	4,602	3,680	2,489	1,191	541	923	610	313	138				
1959	3,740	2,946	1,903	1,043	525	793	517	276	128				
1960	3,852	3,065	1,988	1,077	575	788	498	290	138				
1961	4,714	3,743	2,398	1,345	669	971	599	372	159				
1962	3,911	3,052	1,915	1,137	580	861	509	352	142				
1963	4,070	3,208	1,976	1,232	708	863	496	367	176				
1964	3,786	2,999	1,779	1,220	708	787	426	361	165				
1965	3,366	2,691	1,556	1,135	705	678	360	318	171				
1966	2,875	2,255	1,241	1,014	651	622	310	312	186				
1967	2,975	2,338	1,208	1,130	635	638	300	338	203				
1968	2,817	2,226	1,142	1,084	644	590	277	313	194				
1969	2,832	2,260	1,137	1,123	660	571	267	304	193				
1970	4,093	3,339	1,857	1,482	871	754	380	374	235				
1971	5,016	4,085	2,309	1,777	1,011	930	481	450	249				
1972	4,882	3,906	2,173	1,733	1,021	977	486	491	288	906	448	458	279
1973	4,365	3,442	1,836	1,606	955	924	440	484	280	846	395	451	262
1974	5,156	4,097	2,169	1,927	1,104	1,058	544	514	318	965	494	470	297
1975	7,929	6,421	3,627	2,794	1,413	1,507	815	692	355	1,369	741	629	330
1976	7,406	5,914	3,258	2,656	1,364	1,492	779	713	355	1,334	698	637	330
1977	6,991	5,441	2,883	2,558	1,284	1,550	784	766	379	1,393	698	695	354
1978	6,202	4,698	2,411	2,287	1,189	1,505	731	774	394	1,330	641	690	360
1979	6,137	4,664	2,405	2,260	1,193	1,473	714	759	362	1,319	636	683	333
1980	7,637	5,884	3,345	2,540	1,291	1,752	922	830	377	1,553	815	738	343
1981	8,273	6,343	3,580	2,762	1,374	1,930	997	933	388	1,731	891	840	357
1982	10,678	8,241	4,846	3,395	1,534	2,437	1,334	1,104	443	2,142	1,167	975	396
1983	10,717	8,128	4,859	3,270	1,387	2,588	1,401	1,187	441	2,272	1,213	1,059	392
1984	8,539	6,372	3,600	2,772	1,116	2,167	1,144	1,022	384	1,914	1,003	911	353
1985	8,312	6,191	3,426	2,765	1,074	2,121	1,095	1,026	394	1,864	951	913	357
1986	8,237	6,140	3,433	2,708	1,070	2,097	1,097	999	383	1,840	946	894	347
1987	7,425	5,501	3,132	2,369	995	1,924	969	955	353	1,684	826	858	312
1988	6,701	4,944	2,766	2,177	910	1,757	888	869	316	1,547	771	776	288
1989	6,528	4,770	2,636	2,135	863	1,757	889	868	331	1,544	773	772	300
1990	6,874	5,091	2,866	2,225	856	1,783	933	850	292	1,527	793	734	258
1991	8,426	6,447	3,775	2,672	977	1,979	1,043	936	313	1,679	874	805	270
1992	9,384	7,047	4,121	2,926	983	2,337	1,259	1,079	369	1,958	1,046	912	313
1993	8,734	6,547	3,753	2,793	943	2,187	1,179	1,008	353	1,796	954	842	302
1994	7,996	5,892	3,275	2,617	960	2,104	1,092	1,011	360	1,666	848	818	300
1993: Jan	9,046	6,750	3,847	2,903	951	2,355	1,227	1,128	371	1,953	1,006	947	312
Feb	8,958	6,670	3,849	2,821	963	2,266	1,207	1,059	375	1,857	968	889	311
Mar	8,878	6,671	3,909	2,762	945	2,222	1,248	974	380	1,871	1,034	837	325
Apr	8,954	6,601	3,825	2,776	962	2,318	1,253	1,065	416	1,903	1,034	869	361
May	8,895	6,622	3,781	2,841	983	2,204	1,213	991	379	1,804	970	834	323
June	8,869	6,652	3,818	2,834	945	2,231	1,209	1,022	380	1,846	976	870	321
July	8,732	6,558	3,833	2,725	909	2,169	1,158	1,011	344	1,786	929	857	293
Aug	8,642	6,467	3,756	2,711	934	2,156	1,171	985	319	1,744	931	813	259
Sept	8,540	6,398	3,657	2,741	912	2,132	1,169	963	306	1,750	950	800	275
Oct	8,639	6,736	3,788	2,948	1,003	2,040	1,088	952	314	1,653	863	790	269
Nov	8,330	6,142	3,386	2,756	922	2,133	1,151	982	337	1,760	950	810	301
Dec	8,237	6,209	3,509	2,700	894	2,013	1,046	967	317	1,614	825	789	274
1994: Jan	8,740	6,401	3,607	2,794	1,023	2,274	1,207	1,067	338	1,879	976	903	292
Feb	8,576	6,284	3,540	2,744	996	2,250	1,183	1,067	342	1,838	954	884	291
Mar	8,546	6,229	3,479	2,750	986	2,258	1,116	1,142	347	1,807	856	951	289
Apr	8,385	6,218	3,489	2,729	1,116	2,159	1,086	1,073	361	1,732	868	864	300
May	7,996	5,851	3,244	2,607	992	2,113	1,075	1,038	362	1,700	868	832	307
June	7,903	5,836	3,191	2,645	917	2,063	1,074	989	372	1,643	839	804	312
July	7,993	5,905	3,295	2,610	934	2,044	1,120	924	385	1,613	872	741	323
Aug	7,889	5,785	3,168	2,617	933	2,107	1,119	988	378	1,634	851	783	306
Sept	7,647	5,641	3,077	2,564	912	2,034	1,053	981	342	1,550	780	770	269
Oct	7,505	5,545	3,059	2,486	912	2,095	1,070	1,025	404	1,627	805	822	341
Nov	7,315	5,395	2,950	2,445	849	1,967	1,007	960	339	1,524	762	762	285
Dec	7,155	5,363	2,987	2,376	946	1,846	953	893	349	1,422	710	712	283

Note.—See footnote 5 and Note, Table B-33.

Source: Department of Labor, Bureau of Labor Statistics.

TABLE B–37.—*Civilian labor force participation rate and employment/population ratio, 1948–94*

[Percent;[1] monthly data seasonally adjusted]

Year or month	Labor force participation rate							Employment/population ratio						
	All civilian workers	Males	Females	Both sexes 16–19 years	White	Black and other	Black	All civilian workers	Males	Females	Both sexes 16–19 years	White	Black and other	Black
1948	58.8	86.6	32.7	52.5				56.6	83.5	31.3	47.7			
1949	58.9	86.4	33.1	52.2				55.4	81.3	31.2	45.2			
1950	59.2	86.4	33.9	51.8				56.1	82.0	32.0	45.5			
1951	59.2	86.3	34.6	52.2				57.3	84.0	33.1	47.9			
1952	59.0	86.3	34.7	51.3				57.3	83.9	33.4	46.9			
1953	58.9	86.0	34.4	50.2				57.1	83.6	33.3	46.4			
1954	58.8	85.5	34.6	48.3	58.2	64.0		55.5	81.0	32.5	42.3	55.2	58.0	
1955	59.3	85.4	35.7	48.9	58.7	64.2		56.7	81.8	34.0	43.5	56.5	58.7	
1956	60.0	85.5	36.9	50.9	59.4	64.9		57.5	82.3	35.1	45.3	57.3	59.5	
1957	59.6	84.8	36.9	49.6	59.1	64.4		57.1	81.3	35.1	43.9	56.8	59.3	
1958	59.5	84.2	37.1	47.4	58.9	64.8		55.4	78.5	34.5	39.9	55.3	56.7	
1959	59.3	83.7	37.1	46.7	58.7	64.3		56.0	79.3	35.0	39.9	55.9	57.5	
1960	59.4	83.3	37.7	47.5	58.8	64.5		56.1	78.9	35.5	40.5	55.9	57.9	
1961	59.3	82.9	38.1	46.9	58.8	64.1		55.4	77.6	35.4	39.1	55.3	56.2	
1962	58.8	82.0	37.9	46.1	58.8	63.2		55.5	77.7	35.6	39.4	55.4	56.3	
1963	58.7	81.4	38.3	45.2	58.2	63.0		55.4	77.1	35.8	37.4	55.3	56.2	
1964	58.7	81.0	38.7	44.5	58.2	63.1		55.7	77.3	36.3	37.3	55.5	57.0	
1965	58.9	80.7	39.3	45.7	58.4	62.9		56.2	77.5	37.1	38.9	56.0	57.8	
1966	59.2	80.4	40.3	48.2	58.7	63.0		56.9	77.9	38.3	42.1	56.8	58.4	
1967	59.6	80.4	41.1	48.4	59.2	62.8		57.3	78.0	39.0	42.2	57.2	58.2	
1968	59.6	80.1	41.6	48.3	59.3	62.2		57.5	77.8	39.6	42.2	57.4	58.0	
1969	60.1	79.8	42.7	49.4	59.9	62.1		58.0	77.6	40.7	43.4	58.0	58.1	
1970	60.4	79.7	43.3	49.9	60.2	61.8		57.4	76.2	40.8	42.3	57.5	56.8	
1971	60.2	79.1	43.4	49.7	60.1	60.9		56.6	74.9	40.4	41.3	56.8	54.9	
1972	60.4	78.9	43.9	51.9	60.4	60.2	59.9	57.0	75.0	41.0	43.5	57.4	54.1	53.7
1973	60.8	78.8	44.7	53.7	60.8	60.5	60.2	57.8	75.5	42.0	45.9	58.2	55.0	54.5
1974	61.3	78.7	45.7	54.8	61.4	60.3	59.8	57.8	74.9	42.6	46.0	58.3	54.3	53.5
1975	61.2	77.9	46.3	54.0	61.5	59.6	58.8	56.1	71.7	42.0	43.3	56.7	51.4	50.1
1976	61.6	77.5	47.3	54.5	61.8	59.8	59.0	56.8	72.0	43.2	44.2	57.5	52.0	50.8
1977	62.3	77.7	48.4	56.0	62.5	60.4	59.8	57.9	72.8	44.5	46.1	58.6	52.5	51.4
1978	63.2	77.9	50.0	57.8	63.3	62.2	61.5	59.3	73.8	46.4	48.3	60.0	54.7	53.6
1979	63.7	77.8	50.9	57.9	63.9	62.2	61.4	59.9	73.8	47.5	48.5	60.6	55.2	53.8
1980	63.8	77.4	51.5	56.7	64.1	61.7	61.0	59.2	72.0	47.7	46.6	60.0	53.6	52.3
1981	63.9	77.0	52.1	55.4	64.3	61.3	60.8	59.0	71.3	48.0	44.6	60.0	52.6	51.3
1982	64.0	76.6	52.6	54.1	64.3	61.6	61.0	57.8	69.0	47.7	41.5	58.8	50.9	49.4
1983	64.0	76.4	52.9	53.5	64.3	62.1	61.5	57.9	68.8	48.0	41.5	58.9	51.0	49.5
1984	64.4	76.4	53.6	53.9	64.6	62.6	62.2	59.5	70.7	49.5	43.7	60.5	53.6	52.3
1985	64.8	76.3	54.5	54.5	65.0	63.3	62.9	60.1	70.9	50.4	44.4	61.0	54.7	53.4
1986	65.3	76.3	55.3	54.7	65.5	63.7	63.3	60.7	71.0	51.4	44.6	61.5	55.4	54.1
1987	65.6	76.2	56.0	54.7	65.8	64.3	63.8	61.5	71.5	52.5	45.5	62.3	56.8	55.6
1988	65.9	76.2	56.6	55.3	66.2	64.0	63.8	62.3	72.0	53.4	46.8	63.1	57.4	56.3
1989	66.5	76.4	57.4	55.9	66.7	64.7	64.2	63.0	72.5	54.3	47.5	63.8	58.2	56.9
1990	66.4	76.1	57.5	53.7	66.8	63.7	63.3	62.7	71.9	54.3	45.4	63.6	57.3	56.2
1991	66.0	75.5	57.3	51.7	66.6	63.1	62.6	61.6	70.2	53.7	42.1	62.6	56.1	54.9
1992	66.3	75.6	57.8	51.3	66.7	63.8	63.3	61.4	69.7	53.8	41.0	62.4	55.7	54.3
1993	66.2	75.2	57.9	51.5	66.7	63.1	62.4	61.6	69.9	54.1	41.7	62.7	55.7	54.4
1994	66.6	75.1	58.8	52.7	67.1	63.9	63.4	62.5	70.4	55.3	43.4	63.5	57.2	56.1
1993: Jan	66.0	75.1	57.7	51.4	66.6	63.1	62.4	61.3	69.7	53.7	41.3	62.5	55.0	53.5
Feb	66.1	75.3	57.7	51.9	66.5	63.7	63.2	61.4	69.8	53.8	41.7	62.5	56.0	54.8
Mar	66.0	75.3	57.6	51.5	66.6	63.0	62.4	61.4	69.7	53.9	41.4	62.5	55.4	54.0
Apr	66.0	75.2	57.6	51.8	66.5	63.3	62.3	61.4	69.7	53.8	41.4	62.4	55.5	53.8
May	66.3	75.4	57.9	52.5	66.7	63.4	62.6	61.7	69.9	54.1	42.1	62.7	55.9	54.5
June	66.2	75.3	57.9	51.5	66.7	63.0	62.4	61.6	69.8	54.1	41.5	62.7	55.4	54.1
July	66.2	75.2	57.8	51.8	66.7	62.8	62.3	61.6	69.8	54.1	42.2	62.7	55.5	54.3
Aug	66.2	75.3	57.9	51.6	66.8	62.8	62.4	61.8	70.0	54.2	42.1	62.9	55.6	54.6
Sept	66.0	74.9	57.9	51.2	66.7	62.6	62.3	61.6	69.7	54.2	42.0	62.8	55.4	54.5
Oct	66.2	75.1	58.1	51.1	67.0	62.8	62.1	61.8	69.9	54.3	41.4	62.9	56.0	54.8
Nov	66.2	75.0	58.2	51.2	66.8	63.0	62.5	61.9	70.0	54.5	41.8	63.0	55.9	54.7
Dec	66.3	75.0	58.3	50.9	66.9	63.1	62.3	62.0	70.1	54.7	41.9	63.1	56.3	55.1
1994: Jan	66.7	75.3	58.7	53.1	67.1	64.2	63.5	62.2	70.1	54.9	43.3	63.2	56.9	55.2
Feb	66.7	75.2	58.9	52.7	67.2	64.2	63.6	62.3	70.1	55.2	43.1	63.4	56.9	55.5
Mar	66.6	75.1	58.8	52.9	67.0	64.3	63.8	62.3	70.2	55.0	43.4	63.2	57.0	55.8
Apr	66.6	75.0	58.8	53.6	67.1	64.1	63.6	62.3	70.2	55.1	43.3	63.3	57.2	56.0
May	66.5	74.9	58.8	52.9	67.0	63.9	63.6	62.4	70.3	55.2	43.3	63.5	57.2	56.1
June	66.4	74.8	58.6	53.2	66.8	63.8	63.4	62.3	70.3	55.1	44.1	63.3	57.2	56.2
July	66.4	74.9	58.7	52.5	67.0	63.2	62.8	62.4	70.2	55.2	43.2	63.4	56.7	55.8
Aug	66.5	74.9	58.8	52.8	67.1	63.6	63.0	62.5	70.3	55.3	43.5	63.6	56.9	55.8
Sept	66.6	74.9	58.9	51.5	67.2	63.8	63.1	62.7	70.5	55.5	42.6	63.8	57.3	56.3
Oct	66.7	75.1	58.9	52.7	67.2	64.3	63.7	62.9	70.8	55.5	43.7	63.9	57.6	56.6
Nov	66.7	75.1	58.9	51.8	67.2	63.8	63.3	63.0	71.0	55.6	43.6	64.0	57.6	56.7
Dec	66.6	75.3	58.6	52.9	67.2	63.5	63.1	63.0	71.1	55.5	43.8	64.0	57.6	56.9

[1] Civilian labor force or civilian employment as percent of civilian noninstitutional population in group specified.

Note.—Data relate to persons 16 years of age and over.
See footnote 5 and Note, Table B–33.

Source: Department of Labor, Bureau of Labor Statistics.

[Percent;[1] monthly data seasonally adjusted]

Year or month	All civilian workers	White Total	White Males Total	White Males 16–19 years	White Males 20 years and over	White Females Total	White Females 16–19 years	White Females 20 years and over	Black and other or black Total	Black and other or black Males Total	Black and other or black Males 16–19 years	Black and other or black Males 20 years and over	Black and other or black Females Total	Black and other or black Females 16–19 years	Black and other or black Females 20 years and over
									Black and other						
1954	58.8	58.2	85.6	57.6	87.8	33.3	40.6	32.7	64.0	85.2	61.2	87.1	46.1	31.0	47.7
1955	59.3	58.7	85.4	58.6	87.5	34.5	40.7	34.0	64.2	85.1	60.8	87.8	46.1	32.7	47.5
1956	60.0	59.4	85.6	60.4	87.6	35.7	43.1	35.1	64.9	85.1	61.5	87.8	47.3	36.3	48.4
1957	59.6	59.1	84.8	59.2	86.9	35.7	42.2	35.2	64.4	84.2	58.8	87.0	47.1	33.2	48.6
1958	59.5	58.9	84.3	56.5	86.6	35.8	40.1	35.5	64.8	84.1	57.3	87.1	48.0	31.9	49.8
1959	59.3	58.7	83.8	55.9	86.3	36.0	39.6	35.6	64.3	83.4	55.5	86.7	47.7	28.2	49.8
1960	59.4	58.8	83.4	55.9	86.0	36.5	40.3	36.2	64.5	83.0	57.6	86.2	48.2	32.9	49.9
1961	59.3	58.8	83.0	54.5	85.7	36.9	40.6	36.6	64.1	82.2	55.8	85.5	48.3	32.8	50.1
1962	58.8	58.3	82.1	53.8	84.9	36.7	39.8	36.5	63.2	80.8	53.5	84.2	48.0	33.1	49.6
1963	58.7	58.2	81.5	53.1	84.4	37.2	38.7	37.0	63.0	80.2	51.5	83.9	48.1	32.6	49.9
1964	58.7	58.2	81.1	52.7	84.2	37.5	37.8	37.5	63.1	80.1	49.9	84.1	48.6	31.7	50.7
1965	58.9	58.4	80.8	54.1	83.9	38.1	39.2	38.0	62.9	79.6	51.3	83.7	48.6	29.5	51.1
1966	59.2	58.7	80.6	55.9	83.6	39.2	42.6	38.8	63.0	79.0	51.4	83.3	49.4	33.5	51.6
1967	59.6	59.2	80.6	56.3	83.5	40.1	42.5	39.8	62.8	78.5	51.1	82.9	49.5	35.2	51.6
1968	59.6	59.3	80.4	55.9	83.2	40.7	43.0	40.4	62.2	77.7	49.7	82.2	49.3	34.8	51.4
1969	60.1	59.9	80.2	56.8	83.0	41.8	44.6	41.5	62.1	76.9	49.6	81.4	49.8	34.6	52.0
1970	60.4	60.2	80.0	57.5	82.8	42.6	45.6	42.2	61.8	76.5	47.4	81.4	49.5	34.1	51.8
1971	60.2	60.1	79.6	57.9	82.3	42.6	45.4	42.3	60.9	74.9	44.7	80.0	49.2	31.2	51.8
1972	60.4	60.4	79.6	60.1	82.0	43.2	48.1	42.7	60.2	73.9	46.0	78.6	48.8	32.3	51.2
									Black						
1972	60.4	60.4	79.6	60.1	82.0	43.2	48.1	42.7	59.9	73.6	46.3	78.5	48.7	32.2	51.2
1973	60.8	60.8	79.4	62.0	81.6	44.1	50.1	43.5	60.2	73.4	45.7	78.4	49.3	34.2	51.6
1974	61.3	61.4	79.4	62.9	81.4	45.2	51.7	44.4	59.8	72.9	46.7	77.6	49.0	33.4	51.4
1975	61.2	61.5	78.7	61.9	80.7	45.9	51.5	45.3	58.8	70.9	42.6	76.0	48.8	34.2	51.1
1976	61.6	61.8	78.4	62.3	80.3	46.9	52.8	46.2	59.0	70.0	41.3	75.4	49.8	32.9	52.5
1977	62.3	62.5	78.5	64.0	80.2	48.0	54.5	47.3	59.8	70.6	43.2	75.6	50.8	32.9	53.6
1978	63.2	63.3	78.6	65.0	80.1	49.4	56.7	48.7	61.5	71.5	44.9	76.2	53.1	37.3	55.5
1979	63.7	63.9	78.6	64.8	80.1	50.5	57.4	49.8	61.4	71.3	43.6	76.3	53.1	36.8	55.4
1980	63.8	64.1	78.2	63.7	79.8	51.2	56.2	50.6	61.0	70.3	43.2	75.1	53.1	34.9	55.6
1981	63.9	64.3	77.9	62.4	79.5	51.9	55.4	51.5	60.8	70.0	41.6	74.5	53.5	34.0	56.0
1982	64.0	64.3	77.4	60.0	79.2	52.4	55.0	52.2	61.0	70.1	39.8	74.7	53.7	33.5	56.2
1983	64.0	64.3	77.1	59.4	78.9	52.7	54.5	52.5	61.5	70.6	39.9	75.2	54.2	33.0	56.8
1984	64.4	64.6	77.1	59.0	78.7	53.3	55.4	53.1	62.2	70.8	41.7	74.8	55.2	35.0	57.6
1985	64.8	65.0	77.0	59.7	78.5	54.1	55.2	54.0	62.9	70.8	44.6	74.4	56.5	37.9	58.6
1986	65.3	65.5	76.9	59.3	78.5	55.0	56.3	54.9	63.3	71.2	43.7	74.8	56.9	39.1	58.9
1987	65.6	65.8	76.8	59.0	78.4	55.7	56.5	55.6	63.8	71.1	43.6	74.7	58.0	39.6	60.0
1988	65.9	66.2	76.9	60.0	78.3	56.4	57.2	56.3	63.8	71.0	43.8	74.6	58.0	37.9	60.1
1989	66.5	66.7	77.1	61.0	78.5	57.2	57.1	57.2	64.2	71.0	44.6	74.4	58.7	40.4	60.6
1990	66.4	66.8	76.9	59.4	78.3	57.5	55.4	57.6	63.3	70.1	40.6	73.8	57.8	36.7	60.0
1991	66.0	66.6	76.4	57.2	77.8	57.4	54.3	57.7	62.6	69.5	37.4	73.4	57.0	33.5	59.3
1992	66.3	66.7	76.4	56.7	77.8	57.8	52.6	58.1	63.3	69.7	40.7	73.1	58.0	35.2	60.1
1993	66.2	66.7	76.1	56.5	77.5	58.0	53.7	58.3	62.4	68.6	39.5	72.0	57.4	34.5	59.5
1994	66.6	67.1	75.9	57.7	77.3	58.9	55.1	59.2	63.4	69.1	40.8	72.5	58.7	36.3	60.9
1993: Jan	66.0	66.6	76.1	56.4	77.5	57.7	53.0	58.1	62.4	69.1	41.1	72.3	56.8	35.5	58.9
Feb	66.1	66.5	76.1	56.7	77.5	57.7	53.2	58.0	63.2	69.7	41.7	73.0	57.8	34.9	59.9
Mar	66.0	66.6	76.2	57.0	77.6	57.7	52.5	58.0	62.4	69.0	41.3	72.2	56.9	32.4	59.2
Apr	66.0	66.5	76.0	56.6	77.4	57.6	53.1	57.9	62.3	68.6	44.6	71.3	57.2	31.8	59.6
May	66.3	66.7	76.1	56.1	77.5	58.0	55.0	58.2	62.6	68.9	42.7	72.0	57.4	35.5	59.4
June	66.2	66.7	76.1	56.8	77.5	58.0	52.6	58.4	62.4	68.6	39.8	71.9	57.3	34.0	59.5
July	66.2	66.7	76.1	56.5	77.5	58.0	53.3	58.3	62.3	68.8	41.0	72.0	57.0	36.0	58.9
Aug	66.2	66.8	76.1	57.3	77.5	58.1	53.3	58.5	62.4	68.9	39.2	72.4	57.1	34.5	59.2
Sept	66.0	66.7	75.9	56.1	77.3	58.1	54.1	58.4	62.3	68.3	38.0	71.8	57.3	33.8	59.5
Oct	66.2	67.0	76.2	56.1	77.7	58.3	55.2	58.5	62.1	67.6	34.9	71.5	57.6	34.1	59.8
Nov	66.2	66.8	75.8	56.7	77.2	58.3	54.4	58.6	62.5	68.0	34.9	71.8	58.1	36.9	60.1
Dec	66.3	66.9	75.9	56.0	77.4	58.4	54.2	58.7	62.3	67.3	35.2	70.9	58.1	35.1	60.3
1994: Jan	66.7	67.1	76.0	58.5	77.4	58.7	54.6	59.0	63.5	68.9	40.4	72.3	59.0	40.6	60.8
Feb	66.7	67.2	75.9	58.1	77.3	59.0	54.9	59.3	63.6	69.4	39.4	73.0	58.8	36.1	61.0
Mar	66.6	67.0	75.8	57.6	77.2	58.7	55.4	59.0	63.8	69.0	39.9	72.4	59.5	36.3	61.8
Apr	66.6	67.1	75.9	58.9	77.2	58.8	57.0	58.9	63.6	69.2	40.4	72.6	59.1	36.6	61.3
May	66.5	67.0	75.6	58.1	77.0	59.0	56.0	59.2	63.6	69.8	39.8	73.3	58.5	33.4	61.0
June	66.4	66.8	75.6	57.5	77.0	58.6	56.0	58.8	63.4	68.8	41.8	72.0	58.9	36.6	61.1
July	66.4	67.0	75.7	57.6	77.1	58.8	55.0	59.0	62.8	68.4	41.6	71.7	58.3	35.9	60.5
Aug	66.5	67.1	75.8	57.9	77.2	59.0	55.3	59.2	63.0	68.3	41.4	71.5	58.6	35.3	60.9
Sept	66.6	67.2	75.7	56.3	77.2	59.2	52.7	59.6	63.1	68.6	39.4	72.1	58.5	36.3	60.7
Oct	66.7	67.2	75.9	57.6	77.3	59.1	54.3	59.4	63.7	69.6	42.9	72.7	59.0	39.1	60.9
Nov	66.7	67.2	75.9	56.3	77.4	59.1	54.7	59.4	63.3	69.3	41.4	72.6	58.5	36.3	60.7
Dec	66.6	67.2	76.1	57.7	77.5	58.9	56.0	59.1	63.1	69.3	40.7	72.7	58.0	32.7	60.5

[1] Civilian labor force as percent of civilian noninstitutional population in group specified.

Note.—Data relate to persons 16 years of age and over.

See footnote 5 and Note, Table B-33.

Source: Department of Labor, Bureau of Labor Statistics.

TABLE B-39.—*Civilian employment/population ratio by demographic characteristic, 1954–94*

[Percent;[1] monthly data seasonally adjusted]

Year or month	All civilian workers	White						Black and other or black					
		Total	Males			Females			Total	Males			Females		
			Total	16–19 years	20 years and over	Total	16–19 years	20 years and over	Total	Total	16–19 years	20 years and over	Total	16–19 years	20 years and over

									Black and other						
1954	55.5	55.2	81.5	49.9	84.0	31.4	36.4	31.1	58.0	76.5	52.4	79.2	41.9	24.7	43.7
1955	56.7	56.5	82.2	52.0	84.7	33.0	37.0	32.7	58.7	77.6	52.7	80.4	42.2	26.4	43.9
1956	57.5	57.3	82.7	54.1	85.0	34.2	38.9	33.8	59.5	78.4	52.2	81.3	43.0	28.0	44.7
1957	57.1	56.8	81.8	52.4	84.1	34.2	38.2	33.9	59.3	77.2	48.0	80.5	43.7	26.5	45.5
1958	55.4	55.3	79.2	47.6	81.8	33.6	35.0	33.5	56.7	72.5	42.0	76.0	42.8	22.8	45.0
1959	56.0	55.9	79.9	48.1	82.8	34.0	34.8	34.0	57.5	73.8	41.4	77.6	43.2	20.3	45.7
1960	56.1	55.9	79.4	48.1	82.4	34.6	35.1	34.5	57.9	74.1	43.8	77.9	43.6	24.8	45.8
1961	55.4	55.3	78.2	45.9	81.4	34.5	34.6	34.5	56.2	71.7	41.0	75.5	42.6	23.2	44.8
1962	55.5	55.4	78.4	46.4	81.5	34.7	34.8	34.7	56.3	72.0	41.7	75.7	42.7	23.1	44.9
1963	55.4	55.3	77.7	44.7	81.1	35.0	32.9	35.2	56.2	71.8	37.4	76.2	42.7	21.3	45.2
1964	55.7	55.5	77.8	45.0	81.3	35.5	32.2	35.8	57.0	72.9	37.8	77.7	43.4	21.8	46.1
1965	56.2	56.0	77.9	47.1	81.5	36.2	33.7	36.5	57.8	73.7	39.4	78.7	44.1	20.2	47.3
1966	56.9	56.8	78.3	50.1	81.7	37.5	37.5	37.5	58.4	74.0	40.5	79.2	45.1	23.1	48.2
1967	57.3	57.2	78.4	50.2	81.7	38.3	37.7	38.3	58.2	73.8	38.8	79.4	45.0	24.8	47.9
1968	57.5	57.4	78.3	50.3	81.6	38.9	37.8	39.1	58.0	73.3	38.7	78.9	45.2	24.7	48.2
1969	58.0	58.0	78.2	51.1	81.4	40.1	39.5	40.1	58.1	72.8	39.0	78.4	45.9	25.1	48.9
1970	57.4	57.5	76.8	49.6	80.1	40.3	39.5	40.4	56.8	70.9	35.5	76.8	44.9	22.4	48.2
1971	56.6	56.8	75.7	49.2	79.0	39.9	38.6	40.1	54.9	68.1	31.8	74.2	43.9	20.2	47.3
1972	57.0	57.4	76.0	51.5	79.0	40.7	41.3	40.6	54.1	67.3	32.4	73.2	43.3	19.9	46.7

									Black						
1972	57.0	57.4	76.0	51.5	79.0	40.7	41.3	40.6	53.7	66.8	31.6	73.0	43.0	19.2	46.5
1973	57.8	58.2	76.5	54.3	79.2	41.8	43.6	41.6	54.5	67.5	32.8	73.7	43.8	22.0	47.2
1974	57.8	58.3	75.9	54.4	78.6	42.4	44.3	42.2	53.5	65.8	31.4	71.9	43.5	20.9	46.9
1975	56.1	56.7	73.0	50.6	75.7	42.0	42.5	41.9	50.1	60.6	26.3	66.5	41.6	20.2	44.9
1976	56.8	57.5	73.4	51.5	76.0	43.2	44.2	43.1	50.8	60.6	25.8	66.8	42.8	19.2	46.4
1977	57.9	58.6	74.1	54.4	76.5	44.5	45.9	44.4	51.4	61.4	26.4	67.5	43.3	18.5	47.0
1978	59.3	60.0	75.0	56.3	77.2	46.3	48.5	46.1	53.6	63.3	28.5	69.1	45.8	22.1	49.3
1979	59.9	60.6	75.1	55.7	77.3	47.5	49.4	47.3	53.8	63.4	28.7	69.1	46.0	22.4	49.3
1980	59.2	60.0	73.4	53.4	75.6	47.8	47.9	47.8	52.3	60.4	27.0	65.8	45.7	21.0	49.1
1981	59.0	60.0	72.8	51.3	75.1	48.3	46.2	48.5	51.3	59.1	24.6	64.5	45.1	19.7	48.5
1982	57.8	58.8	70.6	47.0	73.0	48.1	44.6	48.4	49.4	56.0	20.3	61.4	44.2	17.7	47.5
1983	57.9	58.9	70.4	47.4	72.6	48.5	44.5	48.9	49.5	56.3	20.4	61.6	44.1	17.0	47.4
1984	59.5	60.5	72.1	49.1	74.3	49.8	47.0	50.0	52.3	59.2	23.9	64.1	46.7	20.1	49.8
1985	60.1	61.0	72.3	49.9	74.3	50.7	47.1	51.0	53.4	60.0	26.3	64.6	48.1	23.1	50.9
1986	60.7	61.5	72.3	49.6	74.3	51.7	47.9	52.0	54.1	60.6	26.5	65.1	48.8	23.8	51.6
1987	61.5	62.3	72.7	49.9	74.7	52.8	49.0	53.1	55.6	62.0	28.5	66.4	50.3	25.8	53.0
1988	62.3	63.1	73.2	51.7	75.1	53.8	50.2	54.0	56.3	62.7	29.4	67.1	51.2	25.8	53.9
1989	63.0	63.8	73.7	52.6	75.4	54.6	50.5	54.9	56.9	62.8	30.4	67.0	52.0	27.1	54.6
1990	62.7	63.6	73.2	51.0	75.0	54.8	48.5	55.2	56.2	61.8	27.6	66.1	51.6	25.7	54.2
1991	61.6	62.6	71.5	47.2	73.3	54.3	46.1	54.8	54.9	60.5	23.8	64.9	50.3	21.4	53.1
1992	61.4	62.4	71.1	46.3	72.9	54.3	44.3	54.9	54.3	59.1	23.6	63.3	50.4	22.1	53.1
1993	61.6	62.7	71.3	46.6	73.1	54.7	45.8	55.3	54.4	59.1	23.6	63.2	50.5	21.6	53.2
1994	62.5	63.5	71.8	48.3	73.6	55.8	47.5	56.4	56.1	60.8	25.4	65.0	52.3	24.5	55.0
1993: Jan	61.3	62.5	71.2	46.3	73.0	54.3	45.0	54.9	53.5	59.0	24.8	63.0	49.1	21.8	51.6
Feb	61.4	62.5	71.2	46.6	73.0	54.3	45.0	54.9	54.8	60.1	25.2	64.1	50.5	21.5	53.2
Mar	61.4	62.5	71.2	47.3	73.0	54.4	44.3	55.1	54.0	58.7	23.1	62.8	50.1	19.4	53.0
Apr	61.4	62.4	71.2	46.1	73.0	54.3	45.4	54.9	53.8	58.3	23.7	62.2	50.1	18.0	53.1
May	61.7	62.7	71.3	46.4	73.1	54.6	46.0	55.2	54.5	59.3	25.6	63.2	50.5	21.7	53.2
June	61.6	62.7	71.3	46.3	73.1	54.7	45.2	55.3	54.1	58.9	24.4	62.9	50.2	18.8	53.1
July	61.6	62.7	71.2	46.5	73.0	54.8	46.2	55.4	54.3	59.6	25.5	63.5	50.0	23.5	52.5
Aug	61.8	62.9	71.4	47.2	73.2	54.9	45.9	55.5	54.6	59.7	25.5	63.7	50.5	23.5	53.0
Sept	61.6	62.8	71.3	46.7	73.1	54.9	46.3	55.4	54.5	58.9	22.9	63.1	50.8	22.9	53.4
Oct	61.8	62.9	71.4	46.0	73.3	54.9	46.3	55.4	54.7	58.6	20.8	63.6	51.2	22.9	53.9
Nov	61.9	63.0	71.6	46.7	73.4	55.1	47.2	55.6	54.7	58.6	21.2	63.0	51.5	22.2	54.2
Dec	62.0	63.1	71.5	46.5	73.3	55.2	46.9	55.8	55.1	59.1	21.5	63.5	51.7	22.8	54.5
1994: Jan	62.2	63.2	71.5	48.0	73.3	55.4	46.9	56.0	55.2	59.4	24.5	63.5	51.8	29.8	54.0
Feb	62.3	63.4	71.5	48.3	73.3	55.8	46.9	56.4	55.5	60.1	23.7	64.4	51.8	25.2	54.4
Mar	62.3	63.2	71.4	47.9	73.3	55.5	47.6	56.1	55.8	60.6	24.5	64.9	52.0	25.3	54.6
Apr	62.3	63.3	71.5	48.1	73.3	55.6	48.0	56.1	56.0	60.7	24.4	65.0	52.3	25.3	54.9
May	62.4	63.5	71.6	48.2	73.4	55.9	48.3	56.5	56.1	61.3	23.5	65.8	51.9	21.7	54.9
June	62.3	63.3	71.6	48.9	73.3	55.5	48.4	56.0	56.2	60.6	25.4	64.8	52.5	24.7	55.3
July	62.4	63.4	71.6	48.3	73.4	55.7	47.8	56.3	55.8	59.9	24.4	64.2	52.4	24.2	55.2
Aug	62.5	63.6	71.8	49.0	73.6	55.9	47.7	56.5	55.8	60.0	24.9	64.2	52.4	24.0	55.2
Sept	62.7	63.8	71.9	47.8	73.8	56.2	45.7	56.9	56.3	61.1	27.3	65.1	52.5	24.2	55.2
Oct	62.9	63.9	72.1	48.8	73.9	56.2	46.9	56.8	56.6	61.8	27.5	65.8	52.5	23.8	55.3
Nov	63.0	64.0	72.2	48.3	74.1	56.2	47.8	56.8	56.7	61.9	28.2	65.9	52.5	23.9	55.3
Dec	63.0	64.0	72.4	48.5	74.2	56.2	48.6	56.7	56.9	62.4	26.7	66.7	52.4	21.2	55.5

[1] Civilian employment as percent of civilian noninstitutional population in group specified.

Note.—Data relate to persons 16 years of age and over.
See footnote 5 and Note, Table B–33.

Source: Department of Labor, Bureau of Labor Statistics.

TABLE B–40.—*Civilian unemployment rate, 1948–94*

[Percent;[1] monthly data seasonally adjusted]

Year or month	All civilian workers	Males			Females			Both sexes 16–19 years	White	Black and other	Black	Experienced wage and salary workers	Married men, spouse present[2]	Women who maintain families
		Total	16–19 years	20 years and over	Total	16–19 years	20 years and over							
1948	3.8	3.6	9.8	3.2	4.1	8.3	3.6	9.2	3.5	5.9		4.3		
1949	5.9	5.9	14.3	5.4	6.0	12.3	5.3	13.4	5.6	8.9		6.8	3.5	
1950	5.3	5.1	12.7	4.7	5.7	11.4	5.1	12.2	4.9	9.0		6.0	4.6	
1951	3.3	2.8	8.1	2.5	4.4	8.3	4.0	8.2	3.1	5.3		3.7	1.5	
1952	3.0	2.8	8.9	2.4	3.6	8.0	3.2	8.5	2.8	5.4		3.4	1.4	
1953	2.9	2.8	7.9	2.5	3.3	7.2	2.9	7.6	2.7	4.5		3.2	1.7	
1954	5.5	5.3	13.5	4.9	6.0	11.4	5.5	12.6	5.0	9.9		6.2	4.0	
1955	4.4	4.2	11.6	3.8	4.9	10.2	4.4	11.0	3.9	8.7		4.8	2.6	
1956	4.1	3.8	11.1	3.4	4.8	11.2	4.2	11.1	3.6	8.3		4.4	2.3	
1957	4.3	4.1	12.4	3.6	4.7	10.6	4.1	11.6	3.8	7.9		4.6	2.8	
1958	6.8	6.8	17.1	6.2	6.8	14.3	6.1	15.9	6.1	12.6		7.3	5.1	
1959	5.5	5.2	15.3	4.7	5.9	13.5	5.2	14.6	4.8	10.7		5.7	3.6	
1960	5.5	5.4	15.3	4.7	5.9	13.9	5.1	14.7	5.0	10.2		5.7	3.7	
1961	6.7	6.4	17.1	5.7	7.2	16.3	6.3	16.8	6.0	12.4		6.8	4.6	
1962	5.5	5.2	14.7	4.6	6.2	14.6	5.4	14.7	4.9	10.9		5.6	3.6	
1963	5.7	5.2	17.2	4.5	6.5	17.2	5.4	17.2	5.0	10.8		5.6	3.4	
1964	5.2	4.6	15.8	3.9	6.2	16.6	5.2	16.2	4.6	9.6		5.0	2.8	
1965	4.5	4.0	14.1	3.2	5.5	15.7	4.5	14.8	4.1	8.1		4.3	2.4	
1966	3.8	3.2	11.7	2.5	4.8	14.1	3.8	12.8	3.4	7.3		3.5	1.9	
1967	3.8	3.1	12.3	2.3	5.2	13.5	4.2	12.9	3.4	7.4		3.6	1.8	4.9
1968	3.6	2.9	11.6	2.2	4.8	14.0	3.8	12.7	3.2	6.7		3.4	1.6	4.4
1969	3.5	2.8	11.4	2.1	4.7	13.3	3.7	12.2	3.1	6.4		3.3	1.5	4.4
1970	4.9	4.4	15.0	3.5	5.9	15.6	4.8	15.3	4.5	8.2		4.8	2.6	5.4
1971	5.9	5.3	16.6	4.4	6.9	17.2	5.7	16.9	5.4	9.9		5.7	3.2	7.3
1972	5.6	5.0	15.9	4.0	6.6	16.7	5.4	16.2	5.1	10.0	10.4	5.3	2.8	7.2
1973	4.9	4.2	13.9	3.3	6.0	15.3	4.9	14.5	4.3	9.0	9.4	4.5	2.3	7.1
1974	5.6	4.9	15.6	3.8	6.7	16.6	5.5	16.0	5.0	9.9	10.5	5.3	2.7	7.0
1975	8.5	7.9	20.1	6.8	9.3	19.7	8.0	19.9	7.8	13.8	14.8	8.2	5.1	10.0
1976	7.7	7.1	19.2	5.9	8.6	18.7	7.4	19.0	7.0	13.1	14.0	7.3	4.2	10.1
1977	7.1	6.3	17.3	5.2	8.2	18.3	7.0	17.8	6.2	13.1	14.0	6.6	3.6	9.4
1978	6.1	5.3	15.8	4.3	7.2	17.1	6.0	16.4	5.2	11.9	12.8	5.6	2.8	8.5
1979	5.8	5.1	15.9	4.2	6.8	16.4	5.7	16.1	5.1	11.3	12.3	5.5	2.8	8.3
1980	7.1	6.9	18.3	5.9	7.4	17.2	6.4	17.8	6.3	13.1	14.3	6.9	4.2	9.2
1981	7.6	7.4	20.1	6.3	7.9	19.0	6.8	19.6	6.7	14.2	15.6	7.3	4.3	10.4
1982	9.7	9.9	24.4	8.8	9.4	21.9	8.3	23.2	8.6	17.3	18.9	9.3	6.5	11.7
1983	9.6	9.9	23.3	8.9	9.2	21.3	8.1	22.4	8.4	17.8	19.5	9.2	6.5	12.2
1984	7.5	7.4	19.6	6.6	7.6	18.0	6.8	18.9	6.5	14.4	15.9	7.1	4.6	10.3
1985	7.2	7.0	19.5	6.2	7.4	17.6	6.6	18.6	6.2	13.7	15.1	6.8	4.3	10.4
1986	7.0	6.9	19.0	6.1	7.1	17.6	6.2	18.3	6.0	13.1	14.5	6.6	4.4	9.8
1987	6.2	6.2	17.8	5.4	6.2	15.9	5.4	16.9	5.3	11.6	13.0	5.8	3.9	9.2
1988	5.5	5.5	16.0	4.8	5.6	14.4	4.9	15.3	4.7	10.4	11.7	5.2	3.3	8.1
1989	5.3	5.2	15.9	4.5	5.4	14.0	4.7	15.0	4.5	10.0	11.4	5.0	3.0	8.1
1990	5.5	5.6	16.3	4.9	5.4	14.7	4.8	15.5	4.7	10.1	11.3	5.3	3.4	8.2
1991	6.7	7.0	19.8	6.3	6.3	17.4	5.7	18.6	6.0	11.1	12.4	6.5	4.4	9.1
1992	7.4	7.8	21.5	7.0	6.9	18.5	6.3	20.0	6.5	12.7	14.1	7.1	5.0	9.9
1993	6.8	7.1	20.4	6.4	6.5	17.4	5.9	19.0	6.0	11.7	12.9	6.5	4.4	9.5
1994	6.1	6.2	19.0	5.4	6.0	16.2	5.4	17.6	5.3	10.5	11.5	5.9	3.7	8.9
1993: Jan	7.1	7.2	20.7	6.5	7.0	18.4	6.3	19.6	6.2	12.7	14.1	6.8	4.5	10.4
Feb	7.0	7.3	20.6	6.6	6.7	18.5	6.0	19.6	6.1	12.1	13.3	6.7	4.6	10.1
Mar	7.0	7.4	20.3	6.7	6.4	18.5	5.7	19.5	6.1	12.0	13.5	6.7	4.7	9.0
Apr	7.0	7.3	22.4	6.5	6.6	17.9	6.0	20.3	6.1	12.4	13.7	6.7	4.5	9.6
May	6.9	7.2	20.5	6.5	6.6	19.1	5.9	19.8	6.1	11.8	12.9	6.6	4.5	9.8
June	6.9	7.2	21.1	6.5	6.6	17.6	5.9	19.5	6.1	12.0	13.3	6.6	4.4	9.7
July	6.8	7.2	20.4	6.5	6.4	16.2	5.8	18.4	6.0	11.6	12.8	6.5	4.5	9.6
Aug	6.7	7.1	20.1	6.4	6.3	16.5	5.7	18.4	5.9	11.5	12.5	6.4	4.4	9.0
Sept	6.7	6.9	19.4	6.3	6.3	16.4	5.8	17.9	5.8	11.4	12.5	6.3	4.2	9.0
Oct	6.7	6.9	20.3	6.2	6.4	17.3	5.8	18.9	6.1	10.9	11.9	6.4	4.4	9.3
Nov	6.5	6.6	19.9	5.9	6.4	16.5	5.7	18.3	5.6	11.3	12.5	6.2	4.0	9.0
Dec	6.4	6.5	19.4	5.8	6.2	16.1	5.7	17.8	5.6	10.7	11.5	6.2	3.9	10.2
1994: Jan	6.7	6.9	20.7	6.1	6.5	16.0	5.9	18.5	5.8	11.4	13.0	6.6	4.2	9.3
Feb	6.6	6.9	19.7	6.0	6.4	16.5	5.7	18.2	5.7	11.3	12.7	6.4	4.3	9.5
Mar	6.5	6.6	19.6	5.8	6.5	16.3	5.9	18.0	5.6	11.3	12.4	6.4	4.1	9.4
Apr	6.4	6.5	20.2	5.7	6.3	18.1	5.6	19.2	5.6	10.8	11.9	6.2	3.9	9.1
May	6.1	6.2	19.9	5.4	6.1	16.2	5.4	18.1	5.3	10.6	11.7	5.9	3.7	8.9
June	6.1	6.0	18.0	5.3	6.1	16.0	5.4	17.1	5.3	10.4	11.3	5.9	3.6	8.8
July	6.1	6.3	19.4	5.5	5.9	15.9	5.3	17.7	5.3	10.3	11.2	6.0	3.6	7.9
Aug	6.0	6.1	18.8	5.3	6.0	16.1	5.3	17.5	5.2	10.6	11.3	5.8	3.5	8.8
Sept	5.8	5.8	18.5	5.1	5.8	15.9	5.2	17.2	5.1	10.2	10.7	5.7	3.4	8.9
Oct	5.7	5.7	18.1	5.0	5.7	16.0	5.0	17.1	5.0	10.4	11.1	5.5	3.3	8.9
Nov	5.6	5.5	16.5	4.9	5.6	15.0	5.0	15.8	4.8	9.8	10.5	5.4	3.2	8.7
Dec	5.4	5.5	18.5	4.7	5.4	15.8	4.7	17.2	4.8	9.2	9.8	5.3	3.2	8.8

[1] Unemployed as percent of civilian labor force in group specified.
[2] Data for 1949 and 1951–54 are for April; 1950, for March.

Note.—Data relate to persons 16 years of age and over.
See footnote 5 and Note, Table B–33.

Source: Department of Labor, Bureau of Labor Statistics.

[Percent; [1] monthly data seasonally adjusted]

Year or month	All civilian workers	White							Black and other or black						
		Total	Males			Females			Total	Males			Females		
			Total	16–19 years	20 years and over	Total	16–19 years	20 years and over		Total	16–19 years	20 years and over	Total	16–19 years	20 years and over
									Black and other						
1954	5.5	5.0	4.8	13.4	4.4	5.5	10.4	5.1	9.9	10.3	14.4	9.9	9.2	20.6	8.4
1955	4.4	3.9	3.7	11.3	3.3	4.3	9.1	3.9	8.7	8.8	13.4	8.4	8.5	19.2	7.7
1956	4.1	3.6	3.4	10.5	3.0	4.2	9.7	3.7	8.3	7.9	15.0	7.4	8.9	22.8	7.8
1957	4.3	3.8	3.6	11.5	3.2	4.3	9.5	3.8	7.9	8.3	18.4	7.6	7.3	20.2	6.4
1958	6.8	6.1	6.1	15.7	5.5	6.2	12.7	5.6	12.6	13.7	26.8	12.7	10.8	28.4	9.5
1959	5.5	4.8	4.6	14.0	4.1	5.3	12.0	4.7	10.7	11.5	25.2	10.5	9.4	27.7	8.3
1960	5.5	5.0	4.8	14.0	4.2	5.3	12.7	4.6	10.2	10.7	24.0	9.6	9.4	24.8	8.3
1961	6.7	6.0	5.7	15.7	5.1	6.5	14.8	5.7	12.4	12.8	26.8	11.7	11.9	29.2	10.6
1962	5.5	4.9	4.6	13.7	4.0	5.5	12.8	4.7	10.9	10.9	22.0	10.0	11.0	30.2	9.6
1963	5.7	5.0	4.7	15.9	3.9	5.8	15.1	4.8	10.8	10.5	27.3	9.2	11.2	34.7	9.4
1964	5.2	4.6	4.1	14.7	3.4	5.5	14.9	4.6	9.6	8.9	24.3	7.7	10.7	31.6	9.0
1965	4.5	4.1	3.6	12.9	2.9	5.0	14.0	4.0	8.1	7.4	23.3	6.0	9.2	31.7	7.5
1966	3.8	3.4	2.8	10.5	2.2	4.3	12.1	3.3	7.3	6.3	21.3	4.9	8.7	31.3	6.6
1967	3.8	3.4	2.7	10.7	2.1	4.6	11.5	3.8	7.4	6.0	23.9	4.3	9.1	29.6	7.1
1968	3.6	3.2	2.6	10.1	2.0	4.3	12.1	3.4	6.7	5.6	22.1	3.9	8.3	28.7	6.3
1969	3.5	3.1	2.5	10.0	1.9	4.2	11.5	3.4	6.4	5.3	21.4	3.7	7.8	27.6	5.8
1970	4.9	4.5	4.0	13.7	3.2	5.4	13.4	4.4	8.2	7.3	25.0	5.6	9.3	34.5	6.9
1971	5.9	5.4	4.9	15.1	4.0	6.3	15.1	5.3	9.9	9.1	28.8	7.3	10.9	35.4	8.7
1972	5.6	5.1	4.5	14.2	3.6	5.9	14.2	4.9	10.0	8.9	29.7	6.9	11.4	38.4	8.8
									Black						
1972	5.6	5.1	4.5	14.2	3.6	5.9	14.2	4.9	10.4	9.3	31.7	7.0	11.8	40.5	9.0
1973	4.9	4.3	3.8	12.3	3.0	5.3	13.0	4.3	9.4	8.0	27.8	6.0	11.1	36.1	8.6
1974	5.6	5.0	4.4	13.5	3.5	6.1	14.5	5.1	10.5	9.8	33.1	7.4	11.3	37.4	8.8
1975	8.5	7.8	7.2	18.3	6.2	8.6	17.4	7.5	14.8	14.8	38.1	12.5	14.8	41.0	12.2
1976	7.7	7.0	6.4	17.3	5.4	7.9	16.4	6.8	14.0	13.7	37.5	11.4	14.3	41.6	11.7
1977	7.1	6.2	5.5	15.0	4.7	7.3	15.9	6.2	14.0	13.3	39.2	10.7	14.9	43.4	12.3
1978	6.1	5.2	4.6	13.5	3.7	6.2	14.4	5.2	12.8	11.8	36.7	9.3	13.8	40.8	11.2
1979	5.8	5.1	4.5	13.9	3.6	5.9	14.0	5.0	12.3	11.4	34.2	9.3	13.3	39.1	10.9
1980	7.1	6.3	6.1	16.2	5.3	6.5	14.8	5.6	14.3	14.5	37.5	12.4	14.0	39.8	11.9
1981	7.6	6.7	6.5	17.9	5.6	6.9	16.6	5.9	15.6	15.7	40.7	13.5	15.6	42.2	13.4
1982	9.7	8.6	8.8	21.7	7.8	8.3	19.0	7.3	18.9	20.1	48.9	17.8	17.6	47.1	15.4
1983	9.6	8.4	8.8	20.2	7.9	7.9	18.3	6.9	19.5	20.3	48.8	18.1	18.6	48.2	16.5
1984	7.5	6.5	6.4	16.8	5.7	6.5	15.2	5.8	15.9	16.4	42.7	14.3	15.4	42.6	13.5
1985	7.2	6.2	6.1	16.5	5.4	6.4	14.8	5.7	15.1	15.3	41.0	13.2	14.9	39.2	13.1
1986	7.0	6.0	6.0	16.3	5.3	6.1	14.9	5.4	14.5	14.8	39.3	12.9	14.2	39.2	12.4
1987	6.2	5.3	5.4	15.5	4.8	5.2	13.4	4.6	13.0	12.7	34.4	11.1	13.2	34.9	11.6
1988	5.5	4.7	4.7	13.9	4.1	4.7	12.3	4.1	11.7	11.7	32.7	10.1	11.7	32.0	10.4
1989	5.3	4.5	4.5	13.7	3.9	4.5	11.5	4.0	11.4	11.5	31.9	10.0	11.4	33.0	9.8
1990	5.5	4.7	4.8	14.2	4.3	4.6	12.6	4.1	11.3	11.8	32.1	10.4	10.8	30.0	9.6
1991	6.7	6.0	6.4	17.5	5.7	5.5	15.2	4.9	12.4	12.9	36.5	11.5	11.9	36.1	10.5
1992	7.4	6.5	6.9	18.4	6.3	6.0	15.7	5.4	14.1	15.2	42.0	13.4	13.0	37.2	11.7
1993	6.8	6.0	6.2	17.6	5.6	5.7	14.6	5.1	12.9	13.8	40.1	12.1	12.0	37.5	10.6
1994	6.1	5.3	5.4	16.3	4.8	5.2	13.8	4.6	11.5	12.0	37.6	10.3	11.0	32.6	9.8
1993: Jan	7.1	6.2	6.4	17.9	5.8	5.9	15.0	5.4	14.1	14.6	39.7	12.9	13.7	38.5	12.3
Feb	7.0	6.1	6.4	17.8	5.8	5.8	15.3	5.2	13.3	13.9	39.5	12.2	12.6	38.4	11.2
Mar	7.0	6.1	6.5	17.1	5.9	5.7	15.5	5.1	13.5	14.4	44.1	13.0	12.1	40.1	10.6
Apr	7.0	6.1	6.4	18.5	5.7	5.7	14.5	5.2	13.7	15.0	46.8	12.7	12.4	43.2	10.9
May	6.9	6.1	6.3	17.2	5.7	5.8	16.3	5.1	12.9	14.0	40.2	12.2	11.9	38.7	10.4
June	6.9	6.1	6.3	18.4	5.7	5.8	14.0	5.3	13.3	14.1	38.8	12.6	12.4	44.8	10.7
July	6.8	6.0	6.4	17.7	5.8	5.5	13.4	5.1	12.8	13.4	37.9	11.8	12.3	34.7	11.0
Aug	6.7	5.9	6.2	17.7	5.6	5.5	14.0	5.0	12.5	13.4	34.9	12.0	11.6	32.0	10.5
Sept	6.7	5.8	6.1	16.8	5.5	5.6	14.3	5.0	12.5	13.7	39.7	12.1	11.4	32.3	10.2
Oct	6.7	6.1	6.3	17.9	5.7	5.9	16.0	5.3	11.9	12.6	40.6	11.0	11.1	32.8	10.0
Nov	6.5	5.6	5.6	17.7	5.0	5.6	13.3	5.1	12.5	13.8	39.2	12.3	11.3	39.7	9.7
Dec	6.4	5.6	5.8	16.9	5.2	5.4	13.4	4.9	11.5	12.1	38.8	10.5	11.0	35.2	9.7
1994: Jan	6.7	5.8	5.9	18.0	5.2	5.6	14.1	5.0	13.0	13.9	39.3	12.2	12.2	26.7	11.3
Feb	6.6	5.7	5.8	16.9	5.2	5.5	14.4	4.9	12.7	13.5	39.9	11.8	12.0	30.2	10.9
Mar	6.5	5.6	5.7	16.8	5.1	5.5	14.2	4.9	12.4	12.2	38.6	10.4	12.7	30.3	11.7
Apr	6.4	5.6	5.8	18.3	5.0	5.4	15.9	4.7	11.9	12.3	39.7	10.5	11.6	31.0	10.5
May	6.1	5.3	5.4	17.0	4.7	5.2	13.7	4.6	11.7	12.2	40.9	10.3	11.3	35.0	10.0
June	6.1	5.3	5.3	15.1	4.7	5.3	13.6	4.7	11.3	11.9	39.3	10.0	10.8	32.6	9.5
July	6.1	5.3	5.4	16.1	4.8	5.2	13.1	4.7	11.2	12.4	41.4	10.4	10.1	32.7	8.8
Aug	6.0	5.2	5.2	15.4	4.6	5.2	13.7	4.6	11.3	12.1	39.9	10.2	10.6	31.9	9.4
Sept	5.8	5.1	5.1	16.2	4.4	5.1	13.3	4.6	10.7	11.0	30.8	9.8	10.4	33.4	9.0
Oct	5.7	5.0	5.0	15.2	4.4	4.9	13.5	4.4	11.1	11.2	35.9	9.5	11.0	39.1	9.2
Nov	5.6	4.8	4.8	14.3	4.3	4.8	12.6	4.3	10.5	10.6	32.0	9.2	10.3	34.1	8.9
Dec	5.4	4.8	4.9	16.0	4.2	4.7	13.2	4.1	9.8	9.9	34.3	8.3	9.7	35.0	8.3

[1] Unemployed as percent of civilian labor force in group specified.

Note.—See Note, Table B–40.

Source: Department of Labor, Bureau of Labor Statistics.

TABLE B–42.—*Unemployment by duration and reason, 1950–94*

[Thousands of persons, except as noted; monthly data seasonally adjusted [1]]

Year or month	Unem-ploy-ment	Duration of unemployment						Reason for unemployment					
		Less than 5 weeks	5–14 weeks	15–26 weeks	27 weeks and over	Average (mean) dura-tion (weeks)	Median dura-tion (weeks)	Job losers [3]			Job leav-ers	Reen-trants	New en-trants
								Total	On layoff	Other			
1950	3,288	1,450	1,055	425	357	12.1							
1951	2,055	1,177	574	166	137	9.7							
1952	1,883	1,135	516	148	84	8.4							
1953	1,834	1,142	482	132	78	8.0							
1954	3,532	1,605	1,116	495	317	11.8							
1955	2,852	1,335	815	366	336	13.0							
1956	2,750	1,412	805	301	232	11.3							
1957	2,859	1,408	891	321	239	10.5							
1958	4,602	1,753	1,396	785	667	13.9							
1959	3,740	1,585	1,114	469	571	14.4							
1960	3,852	1,719	1,176	503	454	12.8							
1961	4,714	1,806	1,376	728	804	15.6							
1962	3,911	1,663	1,134	534	585	14.7							
1963	4,070	1,751	1,231	535	553	14.0							
1964	3,786	1,697	1,117	491	482	13.3							
1965	3,366	1,628	983	404	351	11.8							
1966	2,875	1,573	779	287	239	10.4							
1967 [2]	2,975	1,634	893	271	177	8.7	2.3	1,229	394	836	438	945	396
1968	2,817	1,594	810	256	156	8.4	4.5	1,070	334	736	431	909	407
1969	2,832	1,629	827	242	133	7.8	4.4	1,017	339	678	436	965	413
1970	4,093	2,139	1,290	428	235	8.6	4.9	1,811	675	1,137	550	1,228	504
1971	5,016	2,245	1,585	668	519	11.3	6.3	2,323	735	1,588	590	1,472	630
1972	4,882	2,242	1,472	601	566	12.0	6.2	2,108	582	1,526	641	1,456	677
1973	4,365	2,224	1,314	483	343	10.0	5.2	1,694	472	1,221	683	1,340	649
1974	5,156	2,604	1,597	574	381	9.8	5.2	2,242	746	1,495	768	1,463	681
1975	7,929	2,940	2,484	1,303	1,203	14.2	8.4	4,386	1,671	2,714	827	1,892	823
1976	7,406	2,844	2,196	1,018	1,348	15.8	8.2	3,679	1,050	2,628	903	1,928	895
1977	6,991	2,919	2,132	913	1,028	14.3	7.0	3,166	865	2,300	909	1,963	953
1978	6,202	2,865	1,923	766	648	11.9	5.9	2,585	712	1,873	874	1,857	885
1979	6,137	2,950	1,946	706	535	10.8	5.4	2,635	851	1,784	880	1,806	817
1980	7,637	3,295	2,470	1,052	820	11.9	6.5	3,947	1,488	2,459	891	1,927	872
1981	8,273	3,449	2,539	1,122	1,162	13.7	6.9	4,267	1,430	2,837	923	2,102	981
1982	10,678	3,883	3,311	1,708	1,776	15.6	8.7	6,268	2,127	4,141	840	2,384	1,185
1983	10,717	3,570	2,937	1,652	2,559	20.0	10.1	6,258	1,780	4,478	830	2,412	1,216
1984	8,539	3,350	2,451	1,104	1,634	18.2	7.9	4,421	1,171	3,250	823	2,184	1,110
1985	8,312	3,498	2,509	1,025	1,280	15.6	6.8	4,139	1,157	2,982	877	2,256	1,039
1986	8,237	3,448	2,557	1,045	1,187	15.0	6.9	4,033	1,090	2,943	1,015	2,160	1,029
1987	7,425	3,246	2,196	943	1,040	14.5	6.5	3,566	943	2,623	965	1,974	920
1988	6,701	3,084	2,007	801	809	13.5	5.9	3,092	851	2,241	983	1,809	816
1989	6,528	3,174	1,978	730	646	11.9	4.8	2,983	850	2,133	1,024	1,843	677
1990	6,874	3,169	2,201	809	695	12.1	5.4	3,322	1,018	2,305	1,014	1,883	654
1991	8,426	3,380	2,724	1,225	1,098	13.8	6.9	4,608	1,279	3,329	979	2,087	753
1992	9,384	3,270	2,760	1,424	1,930	17.9	8.8	5,291	1,246	4,045	975	2,228	890
1993	8,734	3,160	2,522	1,274	1,778	18.1	8.4	4,769	1,104	3,664	946	2,145	874
1994	7,996	2,728	2,408	1,237	1,623	18.8	9.2	3,815	977	2,838	791	2,786	604
1993: Jan	9,046	3,262	2,543	1,372	1,921	18.5	8.6	4,934	1,072	3,862	834	2,295	950
Feb	8,958	3,232	2,549	1,284	1,890	18.2	8.4	4,799	1,081	3,718	1,020	2,281	899
Mar	8,878	3,148	2,583	1,275	1,835	17.7	8.4	4,856	1,096	3,760	1,061	2,059	922
Apr	8,954	3,309	2,537	1,311	1,675	17.7	8.5	4,862	1,068	3,794	990	2,187	920
May	8,895	3,242	2,526	1,270	1,776	17.8	8.3	4,752	1,144	3,608	960	2,237	890
June	8,869	3,232	2,758	1,257	1,768	17.8	8.3	4,845	1,131	3,714	940	2,201	894
July	8,732	3,223	2,543	1,258	1,749	17.9	8.3	4,872	1,183	3,689	915	2,117	870
Aug	8,642	3,046	2,608	1,259	1,741	18.3	8.4	4,864	1,190	3,674	882	2,081	834
Sept	8,540	3,052	2,457	1,297	1,750	18.4	8.9	4,699	1,112	3,587	926	2,075	843
Oct	8,639	3,156	2,491	1,284	1,746	18.4	8.3	4,779	1,216	3,563	957	2,084	839
Nov	8,330	2,946	2,401	1,216	1,755	18.9	8.5	4,444	963	3,481	960	2,084	833
Dec	8,237	3,063	2,247	1,150	1,714	18.2	8.2	4,442	1,060	3,382	932	2,018	797
1994: Jan	8,740	3,319	2,351	1,308	1,738	18.4	8.5	4,395	1,149	3,246	817	2,824	644
Feb	8,576	2,677	2,670	1,318	1,748	18.8	8.9	4,163	1,091	3,072	852	2,936	636
Mar	8,546	2,749	2,574	1,264	1,792	19.2	9.1	4,068	1,011	3,057	823	2,989	630
Apr	8,385	2,772	2,482	1,237	1,735	19.1	9.2	3,880	979	2,901	810	3,164	679
May	7,996	2,651	2,461	1,160	1,693	19.4	9.2	3,640	811	2,829	796	2,863	611
June	7,903	2,754	2,452	1,193	1,547	18.4	9.1	3,734	931	2,803	788	2,785	498
July	7,993	2,768	2,365	1,234	1,589	19.0	9.2	3,863	1,031	2,832	770	2,766	594
Aug	7,889	2,655	2,572	1,198	1,575	18.9	9.2	3,706	1,012	2,694	786	2,758	621
Sept	7,647	2,675	2,294	1,213	1,555	18.8	9.5	3,574	824	2,750	874	2,620	600
Oct	7,505	2,434	2,256	1,344	1,590	19.3	10.1	3,513	848	2,665	755	2,626	614
Nov	7,315	2,599	2,163	1,187	1,474	18.2	9.1	3,495	881	2,614	710	2,575	578
Dec	7,155	2,587	2,149	1,088	1,368	17.8	8.7	3,442	930	2,512	704	2,525	555

[1] Because of independent seasonal adjustment of the various series, detail will not add to totals.
[2] Data for 1967 by reason for unemployment are not not equal to total unemployment.
[3] Beginning January 1994, job losers and persons who completed temporary jobs.
Note.—Data relate to persons 16 years of age and over.
See footnote 5 and Note, Table B–33.
Source: Department of Labor, Bureau of Labor Statistics.

Year or month	All programs			State programs				
	Covered employ-ment [1]	Insured unemploy-ment (weekly aver-age) [2][3]	Total benefits paid (millions of dollars) [2][4]	Insured unem-ployment	Initial claims	Exhaus-tions [5]	Insured unemploy-ment as percent of covered employ-ment	Benefits paid	
								Total (millions of dollars) [4]	Average weekly check (dollars) [6]
	Thousands			Weekly average; thousands					
1962	47,776	1,946	3,145	1,783	302	32	4.4	2,675	34.56
1963	48,434	[7]1,973	3,026	[7]1,806	[7]298	30	4.3	2,775	35.27
1964	49,637	1,753	2,749	1,605	268	26	3.8	2,522	35.92
1965	51,580	1,450	2,360	1,328	232	21	3.0	2,166	37.19
1966	54,739	1,129	1,891	1,061	203	15	2.3	1,771	39.75
1967	56,342	1,270	2,222	1,205	226	17	2.5	2,092	41.25
1968	57,977	1,187	2,191	1,111	201	16	2.2	2,032	43.43
1969	59,999	1,177	2,299	1,101	200	16	2.1	2,128	46.17
1970	59,526	2,070	4,209	1,805	296	25	3.4	3,849	50.34
1971	59,375	2,608	6,154	2,150	295	39	4.1	4,957	54.02
1972	66,458	2,192	5,491	1,848	261	35	3.5	4,471	56.76
1973	69,897	1,793	4,517	1,632	247	29	2.7	4,008	59.00
1974	72,451	2,558	6,934	2,262	363	37	3.5	5,975	64.25
1975	71,037	4,937	16,802	3,986	478	81	6.0	11,755	70.23
1976	73,459	3,846	12,345	2,991	386	63	4.6	8,975	75.16
1977	76,419	3,308	10,999	2,655	375	55	3.9	8,357	78.79
1978	88,804	2,645	9,007	2,359	346	39	3.3	7,717	83.67
1979	92,062	2,592	9,401	2,434	388	39	2.9	8,613	89.67
1980	92,659	3,837	16,175	3,350	488	59	3.9	13,761	98.95
1981	93,300	3,410	15,287	3,047	460	57	3.5	13,262	106.70
1982	91,628	4,592	23,775	4,059	583	80	4.6	20,650	119.34
1983	91,898	3,774	20,206	3,395	438	80	3.9	17,763	123.59
1984	96,474	2,560	13,109	2,475	377	50	2.8	12,595	123.47
1985	99,186	2,699	15,056	2,617	397	49	2.9	14,131	128.14
1986	101,099	2,739	16,293	2,643	378	52	2.8	15,329	135.65
1987	103,936	2,369	14,929	2,300	328	46	2.4	13,607	140.55
1988	107,157	2,135	13,694	2,081	310	38	2.0	12,565	144.97
1989	109,918	2,205	14,948	2,158	330	37	2.1	13,760	151.73
1990	111,490	2,575	18,721	2,522	388	45	2.4	17,356	161.56
1991	109,641	3,406	26,717	3,342	447	67	3.2	24,526	169.88
1992	110,170	3,348	[9]26,460	3,245	408	74	3.1	23,869	173.64
1993 [p]	[8]112,106	2,845	[9]22,950	2,751	341	62	2.6	20,535	179.62
1994 [p]		2,746	22,216	2,671	340	57	2.5	19,778	182.19
				**	**		**		
1993: Jan		3,400	2,162.7	2,697	350	70	2.6	2,075.5	177.36
Feb		3,355	2,109.8	2,631	341	66	2.5	2,024.3	179.47
Mar		3,405	2,456.4	2,679	358	66	2.6	2,361.5	180.70
Apr		2,939	2,034.9	2,759	350	66	2.6	1,958.0	180.50
May		2,604	1,696.8	2,789	348	59	2.7	1,631.5	180.52
June		2,812	1,882.9	2,840	348	61	2.7	1,811.0	179.88
July		2,660	1,750.1	2,851	352	61	2.7	1,684.3	178.30
Aug		2,725	1,814.4	2,819	329	61	2.7	1,746.4	179.71
Sept		2,426	1,616.9	2,823	328	57	2.7	1,552.2	179.61
Oct		2,330	1,472.9	2,815	341	56	2.7	1,402.5	180.46
Nov		2,570	1,710.3	2,776	335	56	2.6	1,609.7	180.07
Dec		2,802	2,015.6	2,694	325	57	2.6	1,905.9	179.10
1994: Jan		3,521	2,281.1	2,720	369	64	2.6	2,170.7	181.46
Feb		3,517	2,292.7	2,791	351	60	2.6	2,195.4	183.95
Mar		3,406	2,548.0	2,744	340	61	2.6	2,459.4	183.72
Apr		2,880	1,961.8	2,722	350	64	2.6	1,891.6	183.68
May		2,631	1,814.0	2,755	367	60	2.6	1,746.4	182.60
June		2,638	1,856.1	2,760	351	59	2.6	1,770.7	181.44
July		2,581	1,691.0	2,738	349	60	2.6	1,610.8	179.80
Aug		2,579	1,849.0	2,679	327	57	2.5	1,757.1	178.61
Sept		2,185	1,522.6	2,622	320	49	2.4	1,459.8	181.76
Oct		2,206	1,429.4	2,567	325	51	2.4	1,368.1	182.45
Nov		2,347	1,588.4	2,517	325	51	2.3	1,520.7	181.78
Dec [p]		2,530	1,780.2	2,507	327	51	2.3	1,713.1	184.00

**Monthly data are seasonally adjusted.
[1] Includes persons under the State, UCFE (Federal employee, effective January 1955), RRB (Railroad Retirement Board) programs, and UCX (unemployment compensation for ex-servicemembers, effective October 1958) programs.
[2] Includes State, UCFE, RR, UCX, UCV (unemployment compensation for veterans, October 1952-January 1960), and SRA (Servicemen's Readjustment Act, September 1944-September 1951) programs. Also includes Federal and State extended benefit programs. Does not include FSB (Federal supplemental benefits), SUA (special unemployment assistance), Federal Supplemental Compensation, and Emergency Unemployment Compensation programs, except as noted in footnote 9.
[3] Covered workers who have completed at least 1 week of unemployment.
[4] Annual data are net amounts and monthly data are gross amounts.
[5] Individuals receiving final payments in benefit year.
[6] For total unemployment only.
[7] Programs include Puerto Rican sugarcane workers for initial claims and insured unemployment beginning July 1963.
[8] Latest data available for all programs combined. Workers covered by State programs account for about 97 percent of wage and salary earners.
[9] Including Emergency Unemployment Compensation and Federal Supplemental Compensation, total benefits paid for 1992 and 1993 would be (in millions of dollars): for 1992, 39,889.6 and for 1993, 34,876.2.

Source: Department of Labor, Employment and Training Administration.

[Thousands of persons; monthly data seasonally adjusted]

Year or month	Total	Goods-producing industries					
		Total	Mining	Construc-tion	Manufacturing		
					Total	Durable goods	Nondura-ble goods
1946	41,652	17,248	862	1,683	14,703	7,785	6,918
1947	43,857	18,509	955	2,009	15,545	8,358	7,187
1948	44,866	18,774	994	2,198	15,582	8,298	7,285
1949	43,754	17,565	930	2,194	14,441	7,462	6,979
1950	45,197	18,506	901	2,364	15,241	8,066	7,175
1951	47,819	19,959	929	2,637	16,393	9,059	7,334
1952	48,793	20,198	898	2,668	16,632	9,320	7,313
1953	50,202	21,074	866	2,659	17,549	10,080	7,468
1954	48,990	19,751	791	2,646	16,314	9,101	7,213
1955	50,641	20,513	792	2,839	16,882	9,511	7,370
1956	52,369	21,104	822	3,039	17,243	9,802	7,442
1957	52,855	20,967	828	2,962	17,176	9,825	7,351
1958	51,322	19,513	751	2,817	15,945	8,801	7,144
1959	53,270	20,411	732	3,004	16,675	9,342	7,333
1960	54,189	20,434	712	2,926	16,796	9,429	7,367
1961	53,999	19,857	672	2,859	16,326	9,041	7,285
1962	55,549	20,451	650	2,948	16,853	9,450	7,403
1963	56,653	20,640	635	3,010	16,995	9,586	7,410
1964	58,283	21,005	634	3,097	17,274	9,785	7,489
1965	60,763	21,926	632	3,232	18,062	10,374	7,688
1966	63,901	23,158	627	3,317	19,214	11,250	7,963
1967	65,803	23,308	613	3,248	19,447	11,408	8,039
1968	67,897	23,737	606	3,350	19,781	11,594	8,187
1969	70,384	24,361	619	3,575	20,167	11,862	8,304
1970	70,880	23,578	623	3,588	19,367	11,176	8,190
1971	71,211	22,935	609	3,704	18,623	10,604	8,019
1972	73,675	23,668	628	3,889	19,151	11,022	8,129
1973	76,790	24,893	642	4,097	20,154	11,863	8,291
1974	78,265	24,794	697	4,020	20,077	11,897	8,181
1975	76,945	22,600	752	3,525	18,323	10,662	7,661
1976	79,382	23,352	779	3,576	18,997	11,051	7,946
1977	82,471	24,346	813	3,851	19,682	11,570	8,112
1978	86,697	25,585	851	4,229	20,505	12,245	8,259
1979	89,823	26,461	958	4,463	21,040	12,730	8,310
1980	90,406	25,658	1,027	4,346	20,285	12,159	8,127
1981	91,152	25,497	1,139	4,188	20,170	12,082	8,089
1982	89,544	23,812	1,128	3,904	18,780	11,014	7,766
1983	90,152	23,330	952	3,946	18,432	10,707	7,725
1984	94,408	24,718	966	4,380	19,372	11,476	7,896
1985	97,387	24,842	927	4,668	19,248	11,458	7,790
1986	99,344	24,533	777	4,810	18,947	11,195	7,752
1987	101,958	24,674	717	4,958	18,999	11,154	7,845
1988	105,210	25,125	713	5,098	19,314	11,363	7,951
1989	107,895	25,254	692	5,171	19,391	11,394	7,997
1990	109,419	24,905	709	5,120	19,076	11,109	7,968
1991	108,256	23,745	689	4,650	18,406	10,569	7,837
1992	108,604	23,231	635	4,492	18,104	10,277	7,827
1993 ᵖ	110,525	23,256	611	4,642	18,003	10,172	7,831
1994 ᵖ	113,427	23,583	605	4,916	18,063	10,267	7,796
1993: Jan	109,490	23,235	622	4,519	18,094	10,244	7,850
Feb	109,856	23,324	613	4,595	18,116	10,256	7,860
Mar	109,804	23,263	615	4,549	18,099	10,238	7,861
Apr	110,096	23,261	614	4,587	18,060	10,207	7,853
May	110,285	23,281	616	4,636	18,029	10,176	7,853
June	110,372	23,225	608	4,632	17,985	10,145	7,840
July	110,628	23,232	606	4,653	17,973	10,135	7,838
Aug	110,714	23,207	602	4,659	17,946	10,121	7,825
Sept	110,923	23,206	605	4,667	17,934	10,123	7,811
Oct	111,112	23,245	605	4,700	17,940	10,135	7,805
Nov	111,366	23,281	604	4,733	17,944	10,142	7,802
Dec	111,610	23,298	618	4,738	17,942	10,153	7,789
1994: Jan	111,711	23,328	616	4,744	17,968	10,182	7,786
Feb	111,919	23,327	612	4,745	17,970	10,182	7,788
Mar	112,298	23,395	609	4,806	17,980	10,190	7,790
Apr	112,699	23,506	606	4,893	18,007	10,216	7,791
May	112,951	23,519	603	4,907	18,009	10,217	7,792
June	113,334	23,576	605	4,927	18,044	10,253	7,791
July	113,624	23,590	601	4,944	18,045	10,249	7,796
Aug	113,914	23,640	603	4,942	18,095	10,290	7,805
Sept	114,186	23,673	605	4,972	18,096	10,306	7,790
Oct	114,348	23,715	599	4,974	18,142	10,335	7,807
Nov ᵖ	114,882	23,827	600	5,044	18,183	10,371	7,812
Dec ᵖ	115,092	23,858	596	5,044	18,218	10,400	7,818

Note.—Data in Tables B-44 and B-45 are based on reports from employing establishments and relate to full- and part-time wage and salary workers in nonagricultural establishments who received pay for any part of the pay period which includes the 12th of the month. Not comparable with labor force data (Tables B-33 through B-42), which include proprietors, self-employed persons, domestic servants,

See next page for continuation of table.

TABLE B-44.—*Employees on nonagricultural payrolls, by major industry, 1946-94—Continued*

[Thousands of persons; monthly data seasonally adjusted]

Year or month		Service-producing industries							
	Total	Transportation and public utilities	Wholesale trade	Retail trade	Finance, insurance, and real estate	Services	Government		
							Total	Federal	State and local
1946	24,404	4,061	2,298	6,077	1,675	4,697	5,595	2,254	3,341
1947	25,348	4,166	2,478	6,477	1,728	5,025	5,474	1,892	3,582
1948	26,092	4,189	2,612	6,659	1,800	5,181	5,650	1,863	3,787
1949	26,189	4,001	2,610	6,654	1,828	5,239	5,856	1,908	3,948
1950	26,691	4,034	2,643	6,743	1,888	5,356	6,026	1,928	4,098
1951	27,860	4,226	2,735	7,007	1,956	5,547	6,389	2,302	4,087
1952	28,595	4,248	2,821	7,184	2,035	5,699	6,609	2,420	4,188
1953	29,128	4,290	2,862	7,385	2,111	5,835	6,645	2,305	4,340
1954	29,239	4,084	2,875	7,360	2,200	5,969	6,751	2,188	4,563
1955	30,128	4,141	2,934	7,601	2,298	6,240	6,914	2,187	4,727
1956	31,264	4,244	3,027	7,831	2,389	6,497	7,278	2,209	5,069
1957	31,889	4,241	3,037	7,848	2,438	6,708	7,616	2,217	5,399
1958	31,811	3,976	2,989	7,761	2,481	6,765	7,839	2,191	5,648
1959	32,857	4,011	3,092	8,035	2,549	7,087	8,083	2,233	5,850
1960	33,755	4,004	3,153	8,238	2,628	7,378	8,353	2,270	6,083
1961	34,142	3,903	3,142	8,195	2,688	7,619	8,594	2,279	6,315
1962	35,098	3,906	3,207	8,359	2,754	7,982	8,890	2,340	6,550
1963	36,013	3,903	3,258	8,520	2,830	8,277	9,225	2,358	6,868
1964	37,278	3,951	3,347	8,812	2,911	8,660	9,596	2,348	7,248
1965	38,839	4,036	3,477	9,239	2,977	9,036	10,074	2,378	7,696
1966	40,743	4,158	3,608	9,637	3,058	9,498	10,784	2,564	8,220
1967	42,495	4,268	3,700	9,906	3,185	10,045	11,391	2,719	8,672
1968	44,158	4,318	3,791	10,308	3,337	10,567	11,839	2,737	9,102
1969	46,023	4,442	3,919	10,785	3,512	11,169	12,195	2,758	9,437
1970	47,302	4,515	4,006	11,034	3,645	11,548	12,554	2,731	9,823
1971	48,276	4,476	4,014	11,338	3,772	11,797	12,881	2,696	10,185
1972	50,007	4,541	4,127	11,822	3,908	12,276	13,334	2,684	10,649
1973	51,897	4,656	4,291	12,315	4,046	12,857	13,732	2,663	11,068
1974	53,471	4,725	4,447	12,539	4,148	13,441	14,170	2,724	11,446
1975	54,345	4,542	4,430	12,630	4,165	13,892	14,686	2,748	11,937
1976	56,030	4,582	4,562	13,193	4,271	14,551	14,871	2,733	12,138
1977	58,125	4,713	4,723	13,792	4,467	15,302	15,127	2,727	12,399
1978	61,113	4,923	4,985	14,556	4,724	16,252	15,672	2,753	12,919
1979	63,363	5,136	5,221	14,972	4,975	17,112	15,947	2,773	13,174
1980	64,748	5,146	5,292	15,018	5,160	17,890	16,241	2,866	13,375
1981	65,655	5,165	5,375	15,171	5,298	18,615	16,031	2,772	13,259
1982	65,732	5,081	5,295	15,158	5,340	19,021	15,837	2,739	13,098
1983	66,821	4,952	5,283	15,587	5,466	19,664	15,869	2,774	13,096
1984	69,690	5,156	5,568	16,512	5,684	20,746	16,024	2,807	13,216
1985	72,544	5,233	5,727	17,315	5,948	21,927	16,394	2,875	13,519
1986	74,811	5,247	5,761	17,880	6,273	22,957	16,693	2,899	13,794
1987	77,284	5,362	5,848	18,422	6,533	24,110	17,010	2,943	14,067
1988	80,086	5,514	6,030	19,023	6,630	25,504	17,386	2,971	14,415
1989	82,642	5,625	6,187	19,475	6,668	26,907	17,779	2,988	14,791
1990	84,514	5,793	6,173	19,601	6,709	27,934	18,304	3,085	15,219
1991	84,511	5,762	6,081	19,284	6,646	28,336	18,402	2,966	15,436
1992	85,373	5,721	5,997	19,356	6,602	29,052	18,645	2,969	15,676
1993	87,269	5,787	5,958	19,717	6,712	30,278	18,817	2,915	15,902
1994 ᵖ	89,844	5,843	6,059	20,309	6,789	31,803	19,041	2,870	16,171
1993: Jan	86,255	5,768	5,957	19,500	6,661	29,642	18,727	2,940	15,787
Feb	86,532	5,782	5,952	19,607	6,669	29,767	18,755	2,939	15,816
Mar	86,541	5,777	5,945	19,564	6,676	29,818	18,761	2,933	15,828
Apr	86,835	5,784	5,950	19,642	6,688	29,992	18,779	2,923	15,856
May	87,004	5,788	5,959	19,672	6,694	30,103	18,788	2,914	15,874
June	87,147	5,789	5,949	19,695	6,704	30,206	18,804	2,908	15,896
July	87,396	5,800	5,962	19,735	6,718	30,355	18,826	2,903	15,923
Aug	87,507	5,786	5,954	19,770	6,724	30,451	18,822	2,906	15,916
Sept	87,717	5,783	5,962	19,805	6,735	30,545	18,887	2,902	15,985
Oct	87,867	5,798	5,965	19,822	6,748	30,661	18,873	2,901	15,972
Nov	88,085	5,800	5,971	19,848	6,763	30,816	18,887	2,900	15,987
Dec	88,312	5,792	5,976	19,931	6,769	30,926	18,918	2,915	16,003
1994: Jan	88,383	5,793	5,990	19,924	6,771	31,004	18,901	2,893	16,008
Feb	88,592	5,803	6,003	19,965	6,776	31,129	18,916	2,892	16,024
Mar	88,903	5,816	6,013	20,026	6,781	31,326	18,941	2,884	16,057
Apr	89,193	5,759	6,028	20,137	6,791	31,497	18,981	2,882	16,099
May	89,432	5,843	6,037	20,153	6,787	31,598	19,014	2,870	16,144
June	89,758	5,849	6,049	20,279	6,798	31,765	19,018	2,859	16,159
July	90,034	5,857	6,053	20,386	6,797	31,918	19,023	2,859	16,164
Aug	90,274	5,866	6,079	20,405	6,801	32,036	19,087	2,858	16,229
Sept	90,513	5,865	6,095	20,470	6,794	32,138	19,151	2,863	16,288
Oct	90,633	5,867	6,106	20,523	6,786	32,231	19,120	2,858	16,262
Nov ᵖ	91,055	5,888	6,117	20,655	6,791	32,414	19,190	2,854	16,336
Dec ᵖ	91,234	5,915	6,132	20,736	6,791	32,497	19,163	2,869	16,294

Note (cont'd).—which count persons as employed when they are not at work because of industrial disputes, bad weather, etc., even if they are not paid for the time off; and which are based on a sample of the working-age population. For description and details of the various establishment data, see "Employment and Earnings."

Source: Department of Labor, Bureau of Labor Statistics.

325

TABLE B–45.—*Hours and earnings in private nonagricultural industries, 1959–94*[1]

[Monthly data seasonally adjusted, except as noted]

Year or month	Average weekly hours			Average hourly earnings			Average weekly earnings, total private			
	Total private	Manufacturing		Total private		Manufacturing (current dollars)	Level		Percent change from year earlier [3]	
		Total	Over-time	Current dollars	1982 dollars [2]		Current dollars	1982 dollars [2]	Current dollars	1982 dollars [2]
1959	39.0	40.3	2.7	$2.02	$6.69	$2.19	$78.78	$260.86	4.9	4.2
1960	38.6	39.7	2.5	2.09	6.79	2.26	80.67	261.92	2.4	.4
1961	38.6	39.8	2.4	2.14	6.88	2.32	82.60	265.59	2.4	1.4
1962	38.7	40.4	2.8	2.22	7.07	2.39	85.91	273.60	4.0	3.0
1963	38.8	40.5	2.8	2.28	7.17	2.45	88.46	278.18	3.0	1.7
1964	38.7	40.7	3.1	2.36	7.33	2.53	91.33	283.63	3.2	2.0
1965	38.8	41.2	3.6	2.46	7.52	2.61	95.45	291.90	4.5	2.9
1966	38.6	41.4	3.9	2.56	7.62	2.71	98.82	294.11	3.5	.8
1967	38.0	40.6	3.4	2.68	7.72	2.82	101.84	293.49	3.1	−.2
1968	37.8	40.7	3.6	2.85	7.89	3.01	107.73	298.42	5.8	1.7
1969	37.7	40.6	3.6	3.04	7.98	3.19	114.61	300.81	6.4	.8
1970	37.1	39.8	3.0	3.23	8.03	3.35	119.83	298.08	4.6	−.9
1971	36.9	39.9	2.9	3.45	8.21	3.57	127.31	303.12	6.2	1.7
1972	37.0	40.5	3.5	3.70	8.53	3.82	136.90	315.44	7.5	4.1
1973	36.9	40.7	3.8	3.94	8.55	4.09	145.39	315.38	6.2	−.0
1974	36.5	40.0	3.3	4.24	8.28	4.42	154.76	302.27	6.4	−4.2
1975	36.1	39.5	2.6	4.53	8.12	4.83	163.53	293.06	5.7	−3.0
1976	36.1	40.1	3.1	4.86	8.24	5.22	175.45	297.37	7.3	1.5
1977	36.0	40.3	3.5	5.25	8.36	5.68	189.00	300.96	7.7	1.2
1978	35.8	40.4	3.6	5.69	8.40	6.17	203.70	300.89	7.8	−.0
1979	35.7	40.2	3.3	6.16	8.17	6.70	219.91	291.66	8.0	−3.1
1980	35.3	39.7	2.8	6.66	7.78	7.27	235.10	274.65	6.9	−5.8
1981	35.2	39.8	2.8	7.25	7.69	7.99	255.20	270.63	8.5	−1.5
1982	34.8	38.9	2.3	7.68	7.68	8.49	267.26	267.26	4.7	−1.2
1983	35.0	40.1	3.0	8.02	7.79	8.83	280.70	272.52	5.0	2.0
1984	35.2	40.7	3.4	8.32	7.80	9.19	292.86	274.73	4.3	.8
1985	34.9	40.5	3.3	8.57	7.77	9.54	299.09	271.16	2.1	−1.3
1986	34.8	40.7	3.4	8.76	7.81	9.73	304.85	271.94	1.9	.3
1987	34.8	41.0	3.7	8.98	7.73	9.91	312.50	269.16	2.5	−1.0
1988	34.7	41.1	3.9	9.28	7.69	10.19	322.02	266.79	3.0	−.9
1989	34.6	41.0	3.8	9.66	7.64	10.48	334.24	264.22	3.8	−1.0
1990	34.5	40.8	3.6	10.01	7.52	10.83	345.35	259.47	3.3	−1.8
1991	34.3	40.7	3.6	10.32	7.45	11.18	353.98	255.40	2.5	−1.6
1992	34.4	41.0	3.8	10.57	7.41	11.46	363.61	254.99	2.7	−.2
1993	34.5	41.4	4.1	10.83	7.39	11.74	373.64	254.87	2.8	−.0
1994 ᴾ	34.6	42.0	4.7	11.12	7.40	12.06	384.75	255.99	3.0	.4
1993: Jan	34.4	41.3	4.0	10.72	7.40	11.60	368.77	254.50	3.3	.1
Feb	34.4	41.5	4.2	10.73	7.38	11.62	369.11	254.03	2.1	−1.0
Mar	34.2	41.1	4.0	10.77	7.40	11.64	368.33	252.97	2.0	−1.0
Apr	34.4	41.4	4.1	10.77	7.38	11.69	370.49	253.76	2.8	−.3
May	34.7	41.4	4.1	10.81	7.38	11.69	375.11	256.22	3.6	.5
June	34.4	41.3	4.1	10.81	7.38	11.71	371.86	253.83	2.7	−.1
July	34.5	41.4	4.1	10.82	7.38	11.73	373.29	254.46	2.9	.2
Aug	34.6	41.5	4.1	10.86	7.39	11.77	375.76	255.62	2.8	.1
Sept	34.4	41.5	4.2	10.88	7.40	11.82	374.27	254.43	3.0	.5
Oct	34.5	41.6	4.3	10.92	7.39	11.84	376.74	255.07	3.1	.5
Nov	34.6	41.7	4.4	10.94	7.39	11.87	378.52	255.76	2.3	−.2
Dec	34.5	41.7	4.4	10.96	7.40	11.93	378.12	255.14	3.2	.7
1994: Jan	34.8	41.7	4.5	11.02	7.43	11.95	383.50	258.60	3.7	1.3
Feb	34.3	41.3	4.5	11.03	7.42	12.01	378.33	254.60	2.5	.1
Mar	34.6	42.1	4.7	11.02	7.39	12.00	381.29	255.73	3.5	1.2
Apr	34.7	42.2	4.8	11.05	7.40	12.00	383.44	256.83	3.5	1.3
May	34.8	42.1	4.7	11.09	7.42	12.00	385.93	258.15	2.8	.7
June	34.6	42.0	4.7	11.08	7.39	12.03	383.37	255.58	3.1	.6
July	34.6	42.0	4.6	11.11	7.38	12.05	384.41	255.25	3.0	.3
Aug	34.4	42.0	4.6	11.13	7.36	12.08	382.87	253.22	1.8	−1.0
Sept	34.6	42.0	4.7	11.17	7.38	12.12	386.48	255.27	3.3	.3
Oct	34.9	42.1	4.7	11.25	7.43	12.14	392.63	259.16	3.8	1.2
Nov ᴾ	34.6	42.1	4.8	11.23	7.39	12.17	388.56	255.80	2.7	.0
Dec ᴾ	34.6	42.2	4.8	11.25	7.39	12.19	389.25	255.75	3.0	.3

[1] For production or nonsupervisory workers; total includes private industry groups shown in Table B–44.
[2] Current dollars divided by the consumer price index for urban wage earners and clerical workers on a 1982=100 base.
[3] Percent changes are based on data that are not seasonally adjusted.

Note.—See Note, Table B–44.

Source: Department of Labor, Bureau of Labor Statistics.

TABLE B-46.—*Employment cost index, private industry, 1980-94*

Year and month	Total private			Goods-producing			Service-producing			Manufacturing			Nonmanufacturing		
	Total compensation	Wages and salaries	Benefits [1]	Total compensation	Wages and salaries	Benefits [1]	Total compensation	Wages and salaries	Benefits [1]	Total compensation	Wages and salaries	Benefits [1]	Total compensation	Wages and salaries	Benefits [1]
Index, June 1989 = 100; not seasonally adjusted															
December:															
1980	64.8	67.1	59.4	66.7	69.7	60.5	63.3	65.3	58.4	66.0	68.9	59.9	64.2	66.2	59.1
1981	71.2	73.0	66.6	73.3	75.7	68.2	69.5	71.1	65.1	72.5	74.9	67.5	70.4	72.1	66.1
1982	75.8	77.6	71.4	77.8	80.0	73.2	74.1	75.9	69.6	76.9	79.1	72.4	75.1	76.8	70.6
1983	80.1	81.4	76.7	81.6	83.2	78.3	78.9	80.2	75.2	80.8	82.5	77.5	79.6	81.0	76.2
1984	84.0	84.8	81.7	85.4	86.4	83.2	82.9	83.7	80.4	85.0	86.1	82.7	83.4	84.2	81.1
1985	87.3	88.3	84.6	88.2	89.4	85.7	86.6	87.7	83.6	87.8	89.2	85.0	87.0	88.0	84.4
1986	90.1	91.1	87.5	91.0	92.3	88.3	89.3	90.3	86.8	90.7	92.1	87.5	89.7	90.6	87.5
1987	93.1	94.1	90.5	93.8	95.2	90.9	92.6	93.4	90.2	93.4	95.2	89.8	92.9	93.7	91.0
1988	97.6	98.0	96.7	97.9	98.2	97.3	97.3	97.8	96.1	97.6	98.1	96.6	97.5	97.8	96.8
1989	102.3	102.0	102.6	102.1	102.0	102.6	102.3	102.2	102.6	102.0	101.9	102.3	102.3	102.2	102.8
1990	107.0	106.1	109.4	107.0	105.8	109.9	107.0	106.3	109.0	107.2	106.2	109.5	106.9	106.1	109.3
1991	111.7	110.0	116.2	111.9	109.7	116.7	111.6	110.2	115.7	112.2	110.3	116.1	111.5	109.8	116.2
1992	115.6	112.9	122.2	116.1	112.8	123.4	115.2	113.0	121.2	116.5	113.7	122.6	115.1	112.6	122.0
1993	119.8	116.4	128.3	120.6	116.1	130.3	119.3	116.6	126.7	121.3	117.3	130.0	119.0	116.0	127.4
1994	123.5	119.7	133.0	124.3	119.6	134.8	122.8	119.7	131.5	125.1	120.8	134.3	122.6	119.1	132.3
1993: Mar	117.1	113.9	125.2	118.0	113.8	127.3	116.4	113.9	123.4	118.6	114.7	126.8	116.3	113.4	124.2
June	118.0	114.6	126.7	119.1	114.5	129.0	117.3	114.7	124.6	119.7	115.5	128.6	117.2	114.2	125.5
Sept	119.1	115.7	127.7	119.9	115.3	130.0	118.5	115.9	125.7	120.6	116.3	129.7	118.4	115.4	126.5
Dec	119.8	116.4	128.3	120.6	116.1	130.3	119.3	116.6	126.7	121.3	117.3	130.0	119.0	116.0	127.4
1994: Mar	121.0	117.2	130.7	121.8	116.9	132.7	120.4	117.3	128.9	122.5	118.0	132.0	120.3	116.8	129.9
June	122.0	118.1	131.7	123.0	118.0	133.9	121.2	118.2	129.7	123.5	119.0	133.0	121.2	117.7	130.8
Sept	123.0	119.1	132.8	123.9	118.9	134.8	122.3	119.2	131.2	124.4	120.0	133.9	122.3	118.7	132.2
Dec	123.5	119.7	133.0	124.3	119.6	134.8	122.8	119.7	131.5	125.1	120.8	134.3	122.6	119.1	132.3
Index, June 1989 = 100; seasonally adjusted															
1993: Mar	116.9	113.9	124.8	117.7	113.8	126.8	116.3	113.9	123.1	118.4	114.7	126.1	116.2	113.4	123.8
June	117.9	114.6	126.5	118.8	114.5	128.7	117.2	114.7	124.5	119.6	115.5	128.3	117.2	114.2	125.3
Sept	118.9	115.6	127.7	119.7	115.3	129.9	118.3	115.8	125.7	120.6	116.3	129.7	118.3	115.3	126.5
Dec	119.9	116.4	129.1	120.7	116.1	131.2	119.4	116.7	127.2	121.6	117.3	131.0	119.2	116.1	127.9
1994: Mar	120.8	117.3	130.2	121.5	116.9	132.2	120.2	117.4	128.5	122.3	118.0	131.3	120.2	116.8	129.5
June	121.8	118.3	131.5	122.7	118.0	133.5	121.1	118.2	129.6	123.4	119.0	132.7	121.2	117.7	130.7
Sept	122.8	119.1	132.8	123.7	118.9	134.7	122.1	119.1	131.2	124.5	120.0	133.9	122.2	118.6	132.2
Dec	123.6	119.7	133.8	124.5	119.6	135.8	122.9	119.7	132.0	125.4	120.8	135.3	122.8	119.2	132.9
Percent change from 12 months earlier, not seasonally adjusted															
December:															
1980	9.6	9.1	11.7	9.9	9.4	10.8	9.7	8.8	12.5	9.8	9.4	10.5	9.7	8.9	12.6
1981	9.9	8.8	12.1	9.9	8.6	12.7	9.8	8.9	11.5	9.8	8.7	12.7	9.7	8.9	11.8
1982	6.5	6.3	7.2	6.1	5.7	7.3	6.6	6.8	6.9	6.1	5.6	7.3	6.7	6.5	6.8
1983	5.7	4.9	7.4	4.9	4.0	7.0	6.5	5.7	8.0	5.1	4.3	7.0	6.0	5.5	7.9
1984	4.9	4.2	6.5	4.7	3.8	6.3	5.1	4.4	6.9	5.2	4.4	6.7	4.8	4.0	6.4
1985	3.9	4.1	3.5	3.3	3.5	3.0	4.5	4.8	4.0	3.3	3.6	2.8	4.3	4.5	4.1
1986	3.2	3.2	3.4	3.2	3.2	3.0	3.1	3.0	3.8	3.3	3.3	2.9	3.1	3.0	3.7
1987	3.3	3.3	3.4	3.1	3.1	2.9	3.7	3.4	3.9	3.0	3.4	2.6	3.6	3.4	4.0
1988	4.8	4.1	6.9	4.4	3.2	7.0	5.1	4.7	6.5	4.5	3.0	7.6	5.0	4.4	6.4
1989	4.8	4.1	6.1	4.3	3.9	5.4	5.1	4.5	6.8	4.5	3.9	5.9	4.9	4.5	6.2
1990	4.6	4.0	6.6	4.8	3.7	7.1	4.6	4.0	6.2	5.1	4.2	7.0	4.5	3.8	6.3
1991	4.4	3.7	6.2	4.6	3.7	6.2	4.3	3.7	6.1	4.7	3.9	6.0	4.3	3.5	6.3
1992	3.5	2.6	5.2	3.8	2.8	5.7	3.2	2.5	4.8	3.8	3.1	5.6	3.2	2.6	5.0
1993	3.6	3.1	5.0	3.9	2.9	5.6	3.6	3.2	4.5	4.1	3.2	6.0	3.4	3.0	4.4
1994	3.1	2.8	3.7	3.1	3.0	3.5	2.9	2.7	3.8	3.1	3.0	3.3	3.0	2.7	3.8
1993: Mar	3.5	2.7	5.6	4.0	2.8	6.3	3.2	2.5	4.8	4.0	2.9	6.3	3.2	2.4	5.1
June	3.6	2.7	5.8	4.2	2.8	7.0	3.3	2.7	4.9	4.4	2.9	7.1	3.3	2.6	5.1
Sept	3.7	3.1	5.4	4.0	2.9	6.3	3.6	3.2	4.4	4.2	3.0	6.7	3.5	3.1	4.5
Dec	3.6	3.1	5.0	3.9	2.9	5.6	3.6	3.2	4.5	4.1	3.2	6.0	3.4	3.0	4.4
1994: Mar	3.3	2.9	4.4	3.2	2.7	4.2	3.4	3.0	4.5	3.3	2.9	4.1	3.4	3.0	4.6
June	3.4	3.1	3.9	3.3	3.1	3.8	3.3	3.1	4.1	3.2	3.0	3.4	3.4	3.1	4.2
Sept	3.3	2.9	4.0	3.3	3.1	3.7	3.2	2.8	4.4	3.2	3.2	3.2	3.3	2.9	4.5
Dec	3.1	2.8	3.7	3.1	3.0	3.5	2.9	2.7	3.8	3.1	3.0	3.3	3.0	2.7	3.8
Percent change from 3 months earlier, seasonally adjusted															
1993: Mar	1.0	0.8	1.5	1.2	0.9	2.1	0.9	0.7	1.2	1.4	0.9	2.1	0.8	0.6	1.1
June	.9	.6	1.4	.9	.6	1.5	.8	.7	1.1	1.0	.7	1.7	.9	.7	1.2
Sept	.8	.9	.9	.8	.7	.9	.9	1.0	1.0	.8	.7	1.1	.9	1.0	1.0
Dec	.8	.7	1.1	.8	.7	1.0	.9	.8	1.2	.8	.9	1.0	.8	.7	1.1
1994: Mar	.8	.8	.9	.7	.7	.8	.7	.6	1.0	.6	.6	.2	.8	.6	1.3
June	.8	.9	1.0	1.0	.9	1.0	.7	.7	.9	.9	.8	1.1	.8	.8	.9
Sept	.8	.7	1.0	.8	.8	.9	.8	.8	1.2	.9	.8	.9	.8	.8	1.1
Dec	.7	.6	.8	.6	.6	.8	.7	.5	.6	.7	.7	1.0	.5	.5	.5

[1] Employer costs for employee benefits.

Note.—The employment cost index is a measure of the change in the cost of labor, free from the influence of employment shifts among occupations and industries.

Data exclude farm and household workers.

Through December 1981, percent changes are based on unrounded data; thereafter changes are based on indexes as published.

Source: Department of Labor, Bureau of Labor Statistics.

TABLE B–47.—*Productivity and related data, business sector, 1950–94*

[1982 = 100; quarterly data seasonally adjusted]

Year or quarter	Output per hour of all persons		Output [1]		Hours of all persons [2]		Compensation per hour [3]		Real compensation per hour [4]		Unit labor costs		Implicit price deflator [5]	
	Business sector	Nonfarm business sector	Business sector	Nonfarm business sector	Business sector	Nonfarm business sector	Business sector	Nonfarm business sector	Business sector	Nonfarm business sector	Business sector	Nonfarm business sector	Business sector	Nonfarm business sector
1950	49.9	56.9	38.6	37.9	77.4	66.6	12.3	13.5	49.4	54.0	24.7	23.7	25.8	24.8
1951	51.7	58.2	41.1	40.5	79.6	69.7	13.5	14.6	50.3	54.4	26.2	25.2	27.5	26.4
1952	53.6	59.8	42.6	42.1	79.6	70.4	14.4	15.5	52.4	56.3	26.9	25.9	27.8	26.8
1953	55.3	60.7	44.4	43.8	80.3	72.1	15.4	16.4	55.6	59.1	27.8	26.9	28.1	27.5
1954	56.7	62.2	44.0	43.3	77.6	69.6	15.9	16.9	57.0	60.6	28.0	27.1	28.2	27.6
1955	58.6	64.3	47.1	46.5	80.4	72.4	16.3	17.5	58.7	63.1	27.8	27.3	28.9	28.5
1956	59.4	64.5	48.4	47.9	81.6	74.2	17.4	18.6	61.7	65.9	29.3	28.8	29.9	29.5
1957	61.0	65.8	49.0	48.6	80.3	73.8	18.5	19.6	63.6	67.5	30.4	29.8	30.9	30.5
1958	63.0	67.6	48.2	47.8	76.6	70.7	19.4	20.4	64.7	68.2	30.8	30.2	31.3	30.8
1959	64.6	69.2	51.4	51.0	79.6	73.7	20.2	21.3	67.1	70.5	31.3	30.8	32.1	31.8
1960	65.6	69.9	52.2	51.8	79.7	74.2	21.1	22.2	68.8	72.4	32.2	31.8	32.6	32.3
1961	68.1	72.2	53.3	52.9	78.3	73.3	21.9	23.0	70.8	74.1	32.2	31.8	32.8	32.5
1962	70.5	74.5	56.1	55.7	79.6	74.8	23.0	23.9	73.4	76.3	32.6	32.1	33.5	33.1
1963	73.3	77.1	58.7	58.3	80.0	75.7	23.8	24.7	75.1	78.0	32.5	32.1	33.7	33.4
1964	76.5	80.0	62.2	61.9	81.3	77.4	25.1	25.9	78.0	80.5	32.8	32.3	34.1	33.9
1965	78.6	81.8	65.9	65.7	83.8	80.3	26.0	26.7	79.7	81.9	33.1	32.7	35.0	34.6
1966	80.7	83.4	69.3	69.3	85.8	83.1	27.8	28.3	82.9	84.3	34.5	33.9	36.1	35.8
1967	82.8	85.2	70.8	70.8	85.5	83.0	29.4	30.0	85.0	86.6	35.5	35.2	37.2	36.9
1968	85.3	87.7	74.0	74.0	86.7	84.4	31.8	32.3	88.3	89.6	37.3	36.8	38.8	38.6
1969	85.8	87.7	76.2	76.2	88.8	86.9	34.1	34.5	89.8	90.8	39.8	39.4	40.6	40.4
1970	87.0	88.5	75.8	75.7	87.2	85.6	36.7	37.0	91.3	92.0	42.2	41.8	42.4	42.2
1971	89.8	91.3	78.0	77.9	86.8	85.3	39.1	39.4	93.1	93.8	43.5	43.1	44.5	44.3
1972	92.7	94.2	83.0	83.0	89.5	88.1	41.6	42.0	95.9	96.9	44.8	44.5	46.2	45.8
1973	95.1	96.4	88.2	88.4	92.7	91.6	45.1	45.4	98.1	98.7	47.5	47.1	49.0	47.9
1974	93.3	94.5	86.6	86.7	92.9	91.8	49.6	49.9	97.0	97.6	53.1	52.8	53.7	52.8
1975	95.5	96.7	85.0	84.9	89.0	87.9	54.5	54.9	97.8	98.4	57.1	56.8	59.0	58.3
1976	98.3	99.2	89.9	90.0	91.5	90.7	59.5	59.6	100.9	101.1	60.5	60.1	62.4	61.9
1977	99.9	100.7	94.9	95.0	95.0	94.4	64.3	64.4	102.4	102.5	64.3	63.9	66.5	66.1
1978	100.5	101.4	100.1	100.5	99.6	99.1	70.0	70.1	103.6	103.7	69.6	69.1	71.8	71.2
1979	99.4	99.9	102.1	102.5	102.7	102.6	76.8	76.7	102.1	102.0	77.3	76.8	78.3	77.5
1980	98.6	99.0	100.5	100.8	101.9	101.8	85.0	84.9	99.5	99.4	86.2	85.7	85.9	85.6
1981	99.9	99.9	102.4	102.4	102.5	102.5	93.0	93.0	98.7	98.8	93.1	93.1	94.5	94.2
1982	100.0	100.0	100.0	100.0	100.0	100.0	100.0	100.0	100.0	100.0	100.0	100.0	100.0	100.0
1983	102.3	102.5	104.1	104.4	101.8	101.9	103.8	104.0	100.6	100.8	101.5	101.5	103.4	104.0
1984	104.8	104.7	112.6	113.0	107.4	107.9	108.3	108.3	100.6	100.6	103.4	103.4	107.7	107.6
1985	106.3	105.6	116.7	116.8	109.8	110.7	113.2	112.8	101.5	101.1	106.5	106.8	111.2	111.6
1986	108.5	107.7	119.9	120.1	110.5	111.5	118.8	118.4	104.6	104.3	109.5	110.0	113.6	114.2
1987	109.6	108.6	124.8	125.0	113.8	115.1	123.1	122.5	104.6	104.1	112.3	112.8	116.6	117.2
1988	110.7	109.6	130.1	130.6	117.5	119.1	128.5	127.7	104.8	104.2	116.0	116.5	120.8	121.4
1989	110.9	108.6	132.3	132.7	120.4	122.2	133.0	132.0	103.5	102.7	121.0	121.5	126.1	126.5
1990	110.7	109.1	133.3	133.5	120.5	122.4	140.6	139.2	103.8	102.8	127.1	127.6	131.2	131.8
1991	112.1	110.7	132.0	132.2	117.7	119.5	147.4	146.2	104.4	103.6	131.5	132.1	135.9	136.7
1992	115.5	113.7	135.5	135.5	117.4	119.2	154.9	153.7	106.6	105.7	134.2	135.2	138.8	139.9
1993	117.2	115.4	140.0	141.0	120.0	122.2	160.5	158.7	107.2	106.0	136.9	137.5	141.5	142.6
1982: IV	101.1	101.1	100.0	100.0	98.9	98.9	102.1	102.1	100.6	100.6	101.0	101.0	101.1	101.4
1983: IV	103.1	103.3	107.5	108.1	104.3	104.7	105.3	105.2	100.5	100.4	102.1	101.9	104.8	105.2
1984: IV	105.4	105.3	114.4	114.8	108.5	109.0	109.9	109.9	100.7	100.7	104.3	104.4	109.0	109.0
1985: IV	107.0	106.0	118.0	118.2	110.2	111.4	115.6	115.0	102.4	101.8	108.0	108.5	112.4	112.9
1986: IV	108.3	107.4	120.6	120.8	111.3	112.5	120.9	120.5	105.6	105.2	111.6	112.2	114.6	115.2
1987: IV	110.6	109.5	127.4	127.6	115.1	116.5	125.8	125.1	105.1	104.6	113.7	114.3	117.9	118.5
1988: IV	110.8	110.0	131.7	132.5	118.8	120.5	130.6	129.8	104.7	104.1	117.9	118.0	122.8	123.4
1989: IV	109.7	108.5	132.3	132.7	120.6	122.3	134.9	133.9	103.4	102.6	123.0	123.4	127.8	128.2
1990: IV	110.5	108.9	132.1	132.2	119.6	121.4	143.5	142.2	103.4	102.5	129.8	130.5	133.2	134.0
1991: IV	113.0	111.5	132.6	132.8	117.4	119.2	150.1	148.8	105.1	104.2	132.9	133.5	136.9	137.9
1992: I	114.5	112.6	133.7	133.6	116.8	118.6	152.2	150.9	105.9	105.0	133.0	134.0	138.0	139.0
II	114.8	113.1	134.4	134.4	117.1	118.9	153.7	152.6	106.1	105.3	133.9	134.9	138.8	139.9
III	115.9	113.9	136.1	135.9	117.4	119.3	156.0	154.7	106.8	106.0	134.7	135.9	138.3	139.5
IV	116.8	115.0	137.9	137.9	118.1	120.0	157.7	156.4	107.1	106.3	135.1	136.1	140.1	141.2
1993: I	116.2	114.4	138.1	138.3	118.9	120.9	158.8	157.2	107.0	106.0	136.6	137.5	140.8	142.0
II	116.4	114.5	139.6	139.9	119.9	122.1	160.0	158.2	107.0	105.8	137.5	138.1	141.4	142.5
III	117.3	115.6	140.9	141.5	120.1	122.4	161.2	159.3	107.3	106.1	137.4	137.7	141.6	142.8
IV	119.0	117.0	143.9	144.3	121.0	123.3	162.1	160.2	107.2	105.9	136.3	136.9	142.1	143.1
1994: I	119.8	117.9	145.8	146.1	121.7	124.0	164.6	162.6	108.3	106.9	137.4	137.9	142.6	143.5
II	119.2	117.2	147.2	147.3	123.5	125.6	164.7	162.9	107.6	106.4	138.2	138.9	143.8	145.1
III	120.2	118.1	148.7	148.8	123.7	126.0	166.1	164.1	107.5	106.2	138.2	138.9	144.5	145.9

[1] Output refers to gross domestic product originating in the sector in 1987 dollars.
[2] Hours at work of all persons engaged in the sector, including hours of proprietors and unpaid family workers. Estimates based primarily on establishment data.
[3] Wages and salaries of employees plus employers' contributions for social insurance and private benefit plans. Also includes an estimate of wages, salaries, and supplemental payments for the self-employed.
[4] Hourly compensation divided by the consumer price index for all urban consumers.
[5] Current dollar gross domestic product divided by constant dollar gross domestic product.

Source: Department of Labor, Bureau of Labor Statistics.

[Percent change from preceding period; quarterly data at seasonally adjusted annual rates]

Year or quarter	Output per hour of all persons		Output [1]		Hours of all persons [2]		Compensation per hour [3]		Real compensation per hour [4]		Unit labor costs		Implicit price deflator [5]	
	Business sector	Nonfarm business sector	Business sector	Nonfarm business sector	Business sector	Nonfarm business sector	Business sector	Nonfarm business sector	Business sector	Nonfarm business sector	Business sector	Nonfarm business sector	Business sector	Nonfarm business sector
1950	8.5	6.5	9.5	9.6	0.9	3.0	7.4	6.2	6.1	4.8	-0.9	-0.3	1.6	1.8
1951	3.6	2.3	6.6	7.0	2.8	4.6	9.8	8.7	1.8	.7	6.0	6.2	6.7	6.1
1952	3.7	2.8	3.7	3.8	.0	1.0	6.3	5.6	4.3	3.6	2.6	2.8	1.0	1.6
1953	3.2	1.6	4.1	4.0	.9	2.4	6.8	5.7	6.0	4.9	3.5	4.1	1.3	2.5
1954	2.5	2.5	-.9	-1.0	-3.3	-3.4	3.3	3.3	2.5	2.5	.7	.8	.4	.7
1955	3.4	3.2	7.1	7.3	3.6	3.9	2.6	3.7	3.0	4.1	-.7	.5	2.5	3.2
1956	1.3	.4	2.8	3.0	1.5	2.5	6.7	6.1	5.1	4.5	5.3	5.6	3.3	3.5
1957	2.8	2.0	1.3	1.5	-1.5	-.5	6.6	5.7	3.1	2.3	3.6	3.7	3.2	3.3
1958	3.2	2.7	-1.6	-1.7	-4.6	-4.2	4.6	4.0	1.7	1.2	1.4	1.3	1.4	.9
1959	2.5	2.3	6.5	6.7	3.8	4.3	4.3	4.1	3.6	3.4	1.7	1.7	2.7	3.4
1960	1.6	1.1	1.7	1.7	.1	.6	4.3	4.4	2.6	2.6	2.7	3.3	1.5	1.5
1961	3.8	3.3	2.1	2.1	-1.6	-1.2	4.0	3.4	2.9	2.3	.1	0	.5	.6
1962	3.5	3.1	5.1	5.3	1.6	2.1	4.7	4.1	3.6	3.0	1.2	1.0	2.0	2.1
1963	4.1	3.6	4.6	4.7	.5	1.1	3.8	3.5	2.4	2.2	-.3	-.1	.8	.9
1964	4.3	3.8	6.0	6.2	1.6	2.3	5.2	4.6	3.9	3.3	.9	.8	1.1	1.4
1965	2.7	2.2	6.0	6.1	3.2	3.8	3.8	3.3	2.2	1.7	1.1	1.0	2.5	2.2
1966	2.8	1.9	5.2	5.4	2.3	3.4	7.0	5.9	4.0	2.9	4.1	3.9	3.3	3.3
1967	2.6	2.2	2.2	2.2	-.3	-.1	5.7	5.9	2.6	2.7	3.1	3.5	2.9	3.3
1968	3.0	2.9	4.5	4.6	1.4	1.7	8.1	7.9	3.8	3.5	5.0	4.8	4.4	4.5
1969	.5	-.0	2.9	2.9	2.4	2.9	7.3	6.8	1.7	1.3	6.7	6.9	4.7	4.6
1970	1.4	1.0	-.5	-.6	-1.8	-1.5	7.5	7.2	1.7	1.4	6.1	6.2	4.3	4.5
1971	3.3	3.1	2.9	2.9	-.4	-.3	6.4	6.4	1.9	2.0	3.0	3.2	4.9	5.0
1972	3.2	3.2	6.4	6.5	3.1	3.3	6.4	6.5	3.1	3.2	3.1	3.3	3.8	3.5
1973	2.5	2.4	6.2	6.4	3.6	4.0	8.6	8.2	2.3	1.9	5.9	5.7	6.1	4.5
1974	-1.9	-2.0	-1.8	-1.9	.1	.2	9.8	9.8	-1.1	-1.1	11.9	12.1	9.5	10.2
1975	2.4	2.3	-1.9	-2.0	-4.2	-4.2	10.0	10.0	.8	.8	7.5	7.5	10.0	10.4
1976	2.9	2.6	5.8	5.9	2.8	3.2	9.1	8.7	3.2	2.7	6.0	5.9	5.8	6.3
1977	1.7	1.5	5.6	5.6	3.8	4.1	8.0	8.0	1.5	1.4	6.3	6.4	6.5	6.8
1978	.6	.7	5.5	5.8	4.9	5.0	8.9	8.9	1.2	1.2	8.2	8.1	8.0	7.6
1979	-1.1	-1.4	2.0	2.0	3.2	3.5	9.7	9.5	-1.5	-1.7	11.0	11.0	9.1	8.9
1980	-.8	-.9	-1.6	-1.7	-.9	-.8	10.7	10.7	-2.5	-2.5	11.5	11.7	9.7	10.4
1981	1.3	.9	1.9	1.6	.6	.7	9.4	9.6	-.8	-.7	8.0	8.6	10.1	10.1
1982	.1	.1	-2.3	-2.4	-2.5	-2.4	7.6	7.5	1.3	1.2	7.4	7.4	5.8	6.1
1983	2.3	2.5	4.1	4.4	1.8	1.9	3.8	4.0	.6	.8	1.5	1.5	3.4	4.0
1984	2.4	2.2	8.2	8.2	5.6	5.9	4.3	4.1	.0	-.2	1.9	1.9	4.1	3.5
1985	1.4	.8	3.6	3.4	2.1	2.5	4.5	4.1	.9	.6	3.0	3.3	3.3	3.7
1986	2.1	2.0	2.8	2.8	.6	.8	5.0	5.0	3.1	3.1	2.8	2.9	2.2	2.4
1987	1.0	.8	4.1	4.1	3.0	3.2	3.6	3.5	-.1	-.2	2.5	2.6	2.6	2.6
1988	1.0	1.0	4.3	4.4	3.3	3.4	4.4	4.2	.2	.1	3.4	3.3	3.6	3.6
1989	-.7	-.9	1.7	1.7	2.5	2.6	3.5	3.3	-1.3	-1.4	4.3	4.3	4.4	4.2
1990	.7	.4	.7	.6	.1	.2	5.7	5.5	.3	.1	5.0	5.1	4.1	4.2
1991	1.3	1.5	-1.0	-1.0	-2.3	-2.4	4.8	5.0	.6	.8	3.5	3.5	3.5	3.7
1992	3.0	2.7	2.7	2.4	-.3	-.3	5.1	5.1	2.0	2.0	2.1	2.4	2.2	2.3
1993	1.5	1.5	3.8	4.1	2.2	2.5	3.6	3.3	.6	.2	2.0	1.7	1.9	1.9
1992: I	5.5	4.2	3.4	2.4	-1.9	-1.8	5.8	5.7	3.1	3.0	.3	1.4	3.3	3.2
II	1.1	1.9	2.2	2.5	1.1	.6	4.0	4.6	.7	1.2	2.8	2.6	2.2	2.5
III	3.7	2.8	4.9	4.4	1.2	1.6	6.1	5.8	3.0	2.6	2.4	2.9	-1.3	-1.2
IV	3.2	3.8	5.6	6.2	2.3	2.3	4.4	4.5	1.2	1.2	1.2	.6	5.1	5.1
1993: I	-1.9	-2.0	.6	1.0	2.5	3.0	2.6	2.1	-.4	-.9	4.6	4.1	2.3	2.2
II	.6	.4	4.2	4.7	3.6	4.3	3.1	2.4	-.0	-.7	2.5	2.0	1.7	1.6
III	3.3	4.0	4.0	4.9	.7	.9	3.0	2.8	1.1	.9	-.3	-1.2	.6	.7
IV	5.7	4.9	8.6	7.9	2.8	2.9	2.4	2.4	-.6	-.6	-3.1	-2.4	1.2	.8
1994: I	2.9	2.9	5.5	5.2	2.5	2.3	6.3	6.1	4.1	3.9	3.3	3.1	1.5	1.2
II	-2.0	-2.1	3.7	3.2	5.9	5.5	.2	.7	-2.5	-2.0	2.3	2.9	3.5	4.5
III	3.5	2.9	4.4	4.2	.9	1.2	3.4	3.0	-.1	-.6	0	0	1.8	2.2

[1] Output refers to gross domestic product originating in the sector in 1987 dollars.
[2] Hours at work of all persons engaged in the sector, including hours of proprietors and unpaid family workers. Estimates based primarily on establishment data.
[3] Wages and salaries of employees plus employers' contributions for social insurance and private benefit plans. Also includes an estimate of wages, salaries, and supplemental payments for the self-employed.
[4] Hourly compensation divided by the consumer price index for all urban consumers.
[5] Current dollar gross domestic product divided by constant dollar gross domestic product.

Note.—Percent changes are based on original data and may differ slightly from percent changes based on indexes in Table B–47.

Source: Department of Labor, Bureau of Labor Statistics.

329

TABLE B-49.—*Industrial production indexes, major industry divisions, 1947-94*

[1987 = 100; monthly data seasonally adjusted]

Year or month	Total industrial production	Manufacturing			Mining	Utilities
		Total	Durable	Nondurable		
1947	22.7	21.2	19.9	22.6	55.5	11.7
1948	23.6	22.0	20.8	23.4	58.3	13.0
1949	22.3	20.8	18.9	23.0	51.7	13.9
1950	25.8	24.2	23.0	25.6	57.7	15.8
1951	28.0	26.1	25.9	26.4	63.4	18.1
1952	29.1	27.2	27.5	26.9	62.8	19.6
1953	31.6	29.6	31.1	28.0	64.5	21.3
1954	29.9	27.7	27.4	28.2	63.2	22.9
1955	33.7	31.3	31.3	31.3	70.5	25.6
1956	35.1	32.5	32.4	32.9	74.2	28.1
1957	35.6	32.9	32.6	33.5	74.3	30.0
1958	33.3	30.6	28.5	33.7	68.1	31.4
1959	37.3	34.5	32.8	37.1	71.3	34.5
1960	38.1	35.2	33.3	38.0	72.7	36.9
1961	38.4	35.3	32.7	39.1	73.1	39.0
1962	41.6	38.4	36.3	41.5	75.2	41.9
1963	44.0	40.7	38.7	43.8	78.2	44.8
1964	47.0	43.5	41.4	46.6	81.4	48.7
1965	51.7	48.2	47.1	49.8	84.4	51.7
1966	56.3	52.6	52.3	52.9	88.9	55.6
1967	57.5	53.6	52.9	54.6	90.6	58.4
1968	60.7	56.6	55.5	58.1	94.1	63.1
1969	63.5	59.1	57.7	61.1	97.8	68.7
1970	61.4	56.4	53.3	61.1	100.4	72.9
1971	62.2	57.3	53.1	63.6	97.8	76.4
1972	68.3	63.3	59.3	69.3	99.9	81.3
1973	73.8	68.9	66.2	72.7	100.8	84.5
1974	72.7	67.9	64.8	72.3	100.3	83.5
1975	66.3	61.1	56.7	67.7	98.0	84.3
1976	72.4	67.4	62.6	74.6	98.9	87.6
1977	78.2	73.3	68.7	80.1	101.5	89.9
1978	82.6	77.8	73.9	83.5	104.6	92.7
1979	85.7	80.9	78.3	84.6	106.6	95.3
1980	84.1	78.8	75.7	83.1	110.0	95.9
1981	85.7	80.3	77.4	84.5	114.3	94.3
1982	81.9	76.6	72.7	82.5	109.3	91.8
1983	84.9	80.9	76.8	87.0	104.8	93.6
1984	92.8	89.3	88.4	90.8	111.9	97.0
1985	94.4	91.6	91.8	91.5	109.0	99.5
1986	95.3	94.3	93.9	94.9	101.0	96.3
1987	100.0	100.0	100.0	100.0	100.0	100.0
1988	104.4	104.7	106.6	102.3	101.3	105.0
1989	106.0	106.4	108.6	103.7	100.0	108.7
1990	106.0	106.1	107.4	104.4	102.0	109.9
1991	104.3	103.9	104.2	103.6	100.2	112.3
1992	107.6	108.0	109.3	106.5	98.9	111.9
1993	112.0	112.9	116.1	109.3	98.2	116.2
1994 ᵖ	118.1	119.7	125.6	113.2	99.8	118.1
1993: Jan	110.6	111.5	114.0	108.6	99.1	112.9
Feb	111.3	112.0	114.6	109.1	98.0	117.2
Mar	111.4	112.2	115.0	108.9	97.5	117.4
Apr	111.4	112.3	115.2	109.0	97.7	115.1
May	111.1	112.1	114.9	108.8	97.6	113.1
June	111.5	112.3	115.0	109.3	98.5	115.5
July	112.0	112.9	115.6	109.7	97.5	117.2
Aug	112.2	112.9	115.9	109.5	97.6	118.3
Sept	112.5	113.4	116.9	109.4	99.1	116.4
Oct	112.7	113.6	117.5	109.1	98.6	115.8
Nov	113.7	114.8	119.1	110.0	98.2	116.7
Dec	114.7	116.1	121.2	110.4	98.4	115.6
1994: Jan	114.7	115.8	121.0	110.0	97.8	120.3
Feb	115.6	116.7	122.1	110.7	99.5	119.6
Mar	116.6	118.0	122.9	112.5	100.5	117.9
Apr	116.7	118.4	123.7	112.4	100.7	114.7
May	117.4	119.0	124.0	113.4	100.7	115.8
June	118.0	119.3	124.6	113.4	100.6	121.1
July	118.2	119.8	125.2	113.6	100.1	119.0
Aug	119.1	120.9	127.0	114.0	100.0	118.8
Sept	119.0	120.9	127.2	113.7	100.1	116.5
Oct ᵖ	119.4	121.4	128.2	113.8	99.2	117.2
Nov ᵖ	120.3	122.6	129.5	115.0	98.7	115.8
Dec ᵖ	121.4	123.9	131.2	115.8	99.9	114.9

Source: Board of Governors of the Federal Reserve System.

TABLE B-50.—*Industrial production indexes, market groupings, 1947-94*

[1987=100; monthly data seasonally adjusted]

Year or month	Total industrial production	Final products									Intermediate products	Materials			
		Total	Consumer goods				Equipment					Total	Durable	Nondurable	Energy
			Total	Automotive products	Other durable goods	Nondurable goods	Total¹	Business	Defense and space						
1947	22.7	20.8	25.4	21.7	22.8	27.0	15.0	14.7	7.5	22.4	25.1	21.5	....	....
1948	23.6	21.5	26.2	22.6	23.8	27.7	15.8	15.3	8.8	23.6	26.2	22.1	....	....
1949	22.3	20.9	26.1	22.5	22.0	27.9	14.1	13.4	9.2	22.4	23.9	19.8	....	....
1950	25.8	23.5	29.7	28.3	30.4	30.3	15.3	14.3	10.8	26.1	28.6	24.9	....	....
1951	28.0	25.4	29.4	25.0	26.2	31.3	21.2	17.5	26.5	27.4	31.6	28.3	....	....
1952	29.1	27.3	30.1	22.5	26.2	32.6	25.5	19.8	37.2	27.2	32.1	28.9	....	....
1953	31.6	29.1	31.9	28.4	29.6	33.5	27.6	20.6	44.6	29.1	35.6	33.8	....	....
1954	29.9	27.6	31.7	26.5	27.3	33.9	24.2	18.1	39.3	29.0	32.9	29.2	25.2	52.7
1955	33.7	29.8	35.4	35.2	32.2	36.5	24.7	19.6	35.9	32.9	38.9	35.7	28.9	59.3
1956	35.1	31.6	36.7	28.9	33.9	38.8	27.1	22.7	35.1	34.4	39.9	35.8	30.2	62.7
1957	35.6	32.5	37.6	30.3	33.2	40.1	28.2	23.6	36.7	34.4	39.9	35.8	30.1	63.4
1958	33.3	31.0	37.2	24.1	31.3	41.3	25.2	19.9	36.8	33.6	35.9	30.1	29.9	58.8
1959	37.3	34.0	40.9	30.2	36.0	44.1	27.7	22.4	38.8	37.1	41.4	35.9	34.2	62.3
1960	38.1	35.1	42.4	34.6	36.2	45.5	28.5	23.0	39.9	37.4	42.0	36.3	34.8	63.1
1961	38.4	35.4	43.3	31.6	37.3	47.0	28.1	22.3	40.6	38.1	42.0	35.5	36.2	63.6
1962	41.6	38.4	46.2	38.3	40.5	49.2	31.3	24.3	46.9	40.4	45.8	39.4	39.2	65.8
1963	44.0	40.6	48.8	41.9	43.7	51.4	33.1	25.5	50.6	42.7	48.7	42.1	41.6	69.7
1964	47.0	42.9	51.5	43.9	47.7	54.0	35.0	28.5	49.0	45.5	52.6	45.9	45.2	72.5
1965	51.7	47.1	55.5	54.1	54.1	56.3	39.6	32.6	54.3	48.4	58.7	52.6	49.6	75.8
1966	56.3	51.6	58.4	53.9	59.6	59.0	46.1	37.8	63.7	51.4	63.9	57.9	53.6	80.6
1967	57.5	53.7	59.8	47.4	60.4	62.0	49.0	38.6	72.7	53.5	63.3	55.9	54.5	83.4
1968	60.7	56.3	63.4	56.4	64.7	64.5	50.4	40.3	72.9	56.6	67.5	59.2	59.9	87.2
1969	63.5	58.1	65.8	56.7	69.0	66.7	51.8	42.9	69.4	59.6	71.5	62.3	64.9	91.7
1970	61.4	56.0	65.0	47.7	66.9	67.8	48.1	41.3	58.7	58.7	69.0	56.5	65.2	96.2
1971	62.2	56.5	68.8	60.8	70.8	69.7	45.0	39.3	52.8	60.5	70.0	56.8	68.0	97.1
1972	68.3	61.3	74.3	65.6	81.0	74.2	49.3	44.8	51.3	67.6	77.2	64.2	74.9	100.8
1973	73.8	65.9	77.6	72.4	85.7	76.5	55.0	52.4	50.1	71.9	84.5	73.3	80.4	101.5
1974	72.7	65.7	75.2	62.6	79.3	76.5	56.8	54.7	49.4	69.4	82.8	71.2	80.8	98.8
1975	66.3	61.8	72.3	59.0	69.8	74.9	52.0	48.8	48.5	62.6	72.6	59.3	71.9	96.7
1976	72.4	66.2	79.4	73.2	78.2	80.4	53.8	50.6	49.2	69.0	81.2	68.4	81.4	99.0
1977	78.2	71.6	85.1	84.0	87.4	84.4	58.8	56.7	49.2	74.9	87.3	75.3	86.7	101.1
1978	82.6	76.1	88.4	86.3	91.2	87.8	64.2	63.1	49.5	79.1	91.8	81.4	89.7	102.2
1979	85.7	79.0	87.3	78.5	89.8	87.7	71.0	71.5	51.5	81.2	95.4	85.3	92.9	105.0
1980	84.1	80.0	85.3	59.5	85.1	89.1	74.6	73.5	57.4	77.0	91.3	79.3	88.7	106.2
1981	85.7	82.1	85.8	59.2	86.3	89.6	78.2	76.1	58.5	77.0	92.8	82.1	90.5	104.3
1982	81.9	80.8	84.5	57.5	78.1	89.7	77.0	72.9	65.7	75.1	85.1	73.4	82.1	100.7
1983	84.9	83.0	88.8	71.9	86.2	91.9	76.8	71.9	71.8	80.3	88.3	79.2	89.2	98.9
1984	92.8	91.0	92.8	86.6	94.6	93.4	89.2	85.4	78.9	86.2	96.6	92.1	93.0	103.8
1985	94.4	94.2	93.7	92.7	90.6	94.4	94.8	91.1	89.4	88.3	96.6	92.9	91.7	103.4
1986	95.3	95.7	96.8	95.3	93.9	97.6	94.5	93.1	96.0	91.9	95.9	93.7	94.4	99.5
1987	100.0	100.0	100.0	100.0	100.0	100.0	100.0	100.0	100.0	100.0	100.0	100.0	100.0	100.0
1988	104.4	104.8	102.9	106.4	103.0	102.4	107.6	110.7	99.7	101.8	105.0	106.4	104.4	102.2
1989	106.0	106.8	104.0	108.2	105.2	103.2	110.9	115.5	100.1	102.0	106.7	108.4	107.1	103.1
1990	106.0	107.0	103.4	100.7	103.6	103.8	112.1	116.9	98.8	101.2	106.8	107.6	108.0	104.2
1991	104.3	105.6	103.0	89.9	100.5	105.2	109.4	116.5	91.3	96.9	105.4	105.4	106.8	104.3
1992	107.6	109.0	105.9	99.9	105.0	106.9	113.4	124.1	86.5	98.8	109.2	111.8	110.2	103.7
1993	112.0	113.4	109.4	111.3	110.1	109.2	119.3	134.6	78.5	102.4	114.1	119.8	113.4	103.6
1994ᵖ	118.1	118.4	113.1	125.5	114.2	111.6	126.7	146.9	71.1	108.1	121.4	131.2	118.3	105.2
1993: Jan	110.6	112.4	108.7	112.5	108.4	108.4	118.0	131.0	82.6	100.9	112.2	117.1	111.7	103.3
Feb	111.3	112.8	109.6	112.1	109.5	109.5	117.4	131.0	81.9	102.1	113.0	118.1	112.0	104.0
Mar	111.4	112.9	109.4	112.2	109.3	109.2	118.1	132.8	80.7	101.9	113.2	118.3	112.1	104.4
Apr	111.4	112.5	108.6	110.3	108.9	108.5	118.5	133.3	80.5	102.4	113.4	118.5	113.0	103.8
May	111.1	112.5	108.4	109.4	108.2	108.4	118.6	133.6	79.3	101.7	113.1	118.4	112.8	103.2
June	111.5	112.8	108.8	106.8	109.2	109.1	118.7	133.9	78.5	101.4	113.7	118.8	113.5	104.3
July	112.0	113.6	109.8	105.5	112.2	110.1	119.3	134.8	77.6	102.1	113.7	119.2	113.4	103.5
Aug	112.2	113.6	109.6	105.7	110.9	110.0	119.5	134.8	77.6	102.6	114.2	119.7	114.2	103.6
Sept	112.5	113.9	109.4	108.1	110.1	109.6	120.6	136.0	77.4	103.0	114.6	120.8	113.5	103.5
Oct	112.7	114.0	109.8	114.1	112.2	109.1	120.3	136.4	76.4	103.0	114.7	121.1	113.9	103.0
Nov	113.7	115.0	110.6	119.4	112.3	109.5	121.5	138.3	76.3	103.9	115.9	122.8	115.0	103.5
Dec	114.7	115.5	110.9	123.1	112.0	109.5	122.6	140.0	75.2	104.7	117.5	125.4	116.3	103.2
1994: Jan	114.7	115.9	111.5	126.6	111.8	109.8	122.7	140.4	74.5	104.6	117.1	125.2	114.6	103.8
Feb	115.6	117.0	112.4	131.5	112.2	110.4	123.8	142.0	73.6	104.9	118.1	126.2	115.6	104.7
Mar	116.6	117.4	112.9	126.4	112.7	111.5	124.3	142.6	73.7	106.3	119.5	128.3	116.7	105.0
Apr	116.7	117.3	112.3	124.1	112.5	111.0	124.9	143.5	73.6	106.9	119.7	129.2	115.9	104.8
May	117.4	117.8	112.8	120.1	113.2	112.0	125.4	144.5	72.4	107.7	120.5	129.8	118.2	104.6
June	118.0	118.4	113.5	121.0	115.4	112.5	125.8	145.5	71.3	108.5	121.2	130.0	118.1	106.7
July	118.2	118.5	113.3	119.5	116.7	112.2	126.4	146.9	69.9	109.1	121.4	130.9	118.6	105.2
Aug	119.1	119.2	113.8	124.9	117.1	112.2	127.5	148.9	69.2	109.2	122.8	132.6	120.3	106.1
Sept	119.0	118.9	113.0	123.8	115.2	111.7	128.0	149.5	68.8	108.6	122.9	133.3	119.8	105.6
Oct ᵖ	119.4	119.1	112.6	124.5	115.3	111.0	129.2	151.4	68.8	109.9	123.4	134.2	120.0	105.2
Nov ᵖ	120.3	119.8	113.6	127.1	115.5	111.9	129.6	152.0	69.0	110.8	124.3	136.0	121.0	104.6
Dec ᵖ	121.4	121.0	114.6	130.5	116.7	112.7	130.9	153.7	69.3	110.8	125.9	138.4	121.7	105.3

¹ Two components—oil and gas well drilling and manufactured homes—are included in total equipment, but not in detail shown.
Source: Board of Governors of the Federal Reserve System.

Year or month	Durable manufactures								Nondurable manufactures				
	Primary metals		Fabri- cated metal prod- ucts	Indus- trial ma- chin- ery and equip- ment	Electri- cal machin- ery	Transportation equipment		Lumber and prod- ucts	Apparel prod- ucts	Textile mill prod- ucts	Printing and publish- ing	Chem- icals and prod- ucts	Foods
	Total	Iron and steel				Total	Motor vehicles and parts						
1947	70.2	102.1	37.5	12.0	8.5	19.6	27.3	38.8	43.1	35.2	22.1	8.7	33.1
1948	73.0	106.8	38.2	12.1	8.8	21.4	29.6	40.4	45.0	37.7	23.2	9.4	32.8
1949	61.4	91.2	34.4	10.3	8.3	21.5	30.4	35.7	44.5	34.8	23.8	9.3	33.1
1950	77.3	112.4	42.2	11.6	11.3	25.7	39.0	43.4	47.9	39.6	24.9	11.6	34.3
1951	84.1	125.7	45.1	14.7	11.4	28.7	35.8	43.2	47.0	39.2	25.4	13.1	35.0
1952	76.8	110.6	44.0	16.0	13.0	33.3	30.7	42.7	49.5	38.9	25.3	13.7	35.7
1953	87.0	127.5	49.6	16.7	14.9	41.8	38.7	45.1	50.1	39.9	26.5	14.8	36.4
1954	70.4	99.1	44.7	14.2	13.3	36.4	33.3	44.8	49.5	37.3	27.6	15.0	37.2
1955	91.5	131.8	51.0	15.6	15.3	41.9	44.6	50.1	54.7	42.5	30.3	17.6	39.3
1956	90.9	129.3	51.8	17.9	16.5	40.6	36.2	49.5	56.0	43.7	32.3	18.9	41.5
1957	87.1	124.6	53.1	17.9	16.4	43.5	38.0	45.4	55.8	41.6	33.4	19.9	42.2
1958	69.0	93.9	47.6	15.0	15.0	34.3	28.0	46.1	54.3	41.1	32.6	20.6	43.2
1959	80.7	108.1	53.4	17.5	18.2	38.9	36.4	52.3	59.7	46.4	34.8	24.0	45.4
1960	80.4	109.9	53.4	17.6	19.8	40.3	41.1	49.3	60.9	45.6	36.2	24.9	46.6
1961	78.9	104.9	52.1	17.1	21.0	37.8	36.0	51.6	61.3	46.9	36.4	26.1	47.9
1962	84.6	109.3	56.7	19.2	24.1	43.7	43.9	54.4	63.8	50.1	37.7	29.0	49.5
1963	91.2	119.1	58.5	20.5	24.8	48.0	48.6	56.9	66.4	51.9	39.7	31.7	51.2
1964	102.9	135.5	62.1	23.3	26.2	49.2	49.9	61.1	68.7	56.0	42.1	34.8	53.6
1965	113.2	148.7	68.3	26.2	31.3	58.5	63.7	63.5	72.6	61.0	44.8	38.7	54.8
1966	120.2	153.1	73.1	30.5	37.5	62.7	62.6	65.9	74.5	64.7	48.3	42.2	56.9
1967	111.1	141.5	76.5	31.1	37.7	61.3	55.1	65.3	74.1	64.8	50.9	44.2	59.4
1968	115.1	146.1	80.6	31.3	39.8	66.6	66.0	67.2	76.0	72.3	51.7	49.6	61.0
1969	123.8	159.2	81.9	33.9	42.3	66.1	66.3	67.1	78.4	76.0	54.2	53.7	63.0
1970	115.2	148.2	75.9	32.8	40.5	55.5	53.3	66.7	75.3	74.4	52.7	55.9	64.0
1971	109.2	135.5	75.6	30.5	40.7	60.1	66.9	68.5	76.2	78.5	53.2	59.5	66.0
1972	122.4	150.6	82.9	35.4	46.5	64.1	73.0	78.4	80.9	86.0	56.7	66.9	69.5
1973	138.9	171.5	92.1	41.4	53.0	73.0	85.0	78.7	81.5	89.6	58.3	73.1	70.9
1974	134.5	166.1	88.4	44.1	52.4	66.4	73.4	71.4	77.9	81.5	57.4	75.8	71.9
1975	107.2	133.5	76.7	38.1	45.1	59.7	62.2	66.5	71.1	77.7	53.7	69.1	71.4
1976	119.9	147.1	84.9	40.0	50.7	68.0	81.9	75.6	83.9	86.3	58.7	77.3	75.5
1977	121.5	145.1	92.7	45.1	58.4	73.7	94.7	82.3	91.6	91.6	64.3	83.3	79.0
1978	130.7	155.3	96.2	50.2	64.0	79.5	99.2	83.6	93.9	92.0	68.1	88.0	81.8
1979	133.0	156.5	99.5	56.9	71.3	81.0	91.0	82.4	89.0	95.0	69.9	91.3	82.6
1980	110.8	126.0	92.5	60.6	73.3	72.3	67.0	76.9	89.2	92.1	70.3	87.8	84.6
1981	117.5	135.1	91.1	65.9	75.4	68.7	64.4	74.7	91.0	89.4	72.1	89.2	86.5
1982	83.2	86.2	83.2	63.9	75.9	64.8	58.8	67.3	90.1	83.0	75.2	81.8	87.7
1983	91.0	96.1	85.5	64.3	80.3	72.7	74.5	79.9	93.8	93.2	79.0	87.5	90.1
1984	102.4	105.9	93.3	80.8	94.1	83.1	90.6	86.0	95.7	93.7	84.5	91.4	92.1
1985	101.8	104.5	94.5	86.8	93.1	91.8	99.0	88.0	92.6	89.7	87.6	91.4	94.9
1986	93.7	90.8	93.8	90.3	94.3	96.9	98.5	95.1	96.3	93.9	90.6	94.6	97.4
1987	100.0	100.0	100.0	100.0	100.0	100.0	100.0	100.0	100.0	100.0	100.0	100.0	100.0
1988	108.7	112.7	104.2	113.0	108.5	105.2	105.7	100.1	98.1	98.6	100.9	106.0	101.5
1989	107.2	111.2	102.8	117.3	111.0	109.6	106.9	99.4	95.0	100.3	101.1	109.2	102.5
1990	106.5	111.5	99.5	117.6	111.4	107.0	101.0	97.1	92.2	97.1	100.8	111.8	103.7
1991	98.7	100.5	95.3	115.0	113.4	101.3	94.3	90.5	92.9	96.6	97.0	111.1	105.3
1992	101.9	105.1	98.8	124.6	121.9	105.1	107.4	95.8	95.0	103.9	97.2	114.7	107.0
1993	106.9	111.4	103.7	141.1	139.3	105.5	121.1	100.2	94.9	105.7	99.3	119.1	109.4
1994 ᵖ	114.2	117.8	110.7	160.0	160.2	109.9	138.0	106.1	96.2	109.0	101.3	123.9	112.8
1993: Jan	105.8	110.4	102.2	132.2	131.4	109.6	122.5	98.5	95.8	105.7	99.6	116.9	108.0
Feb	106.8	110.4	102.9	133.5	133.8	108.6	121.2	101.0	96.9	104.8	99.7	116.9	109.5
Mar	105.7	110.0	103.3	135.9	135.3	107.6	120.8	98.8	95.4	105.4	99.8	118.6	108.4
Apr	105.0	108.8	103.6	138.2	136.2	106.4	119.0	97.5	95.1	104.1	101.0	118.4	107.6
May	105.2	109.0	102.8	139.3	136.6	105.1	117.6	98.3	95.1	106.0	99.5	118.7	108.0
June	107.3	112.6	102.4	139.9	138.3	103.0	116.0	97.7	95.2	106.5	99.3	119.2	109.7
July	104.6	108.9	103.6	143.0	140.3	101.3	113.6	99.2	95.1	107.0	98.9	119.2	109.8
Aug	107.5	112.6	103.7	142.8	141.7	101.1	114.3	100.1	95.0	105.9	98.3	119.4	110.5
Sept	108.0	112.2	104.2	144.8	143.4	102.2	117.8	101.2	94.2	105.2	98.9	119.5	111.0
Oct	106.7	111.4	104.1	145.4	143.9	105.1	124.9	102.9	93.9	106.0	99.0	119.6	110.9
Nov	109.1	114.0	105.6	147.3	145.0	108.5	132.4	103.5	94.5	105.7	99.3	120.7	110.1
Dec	113.4	118.6	107.1	151.3	147.3	109.8	135.9	104.6	94.7	105.7	98.8	120.9	110.3
1994: Jan	108.0	110.8	107.2	150.3	148.1	110.8	138.7	105.3	93.5	106.0	98.2	121.3	110.9
Feb	111.6	116.0	106.6	151.9	150.1	112.3	142.6	103.8	94.9	106.4	98.8	121.8	110.9
Mar	112.1	116.7	108.5	154.0	152.6	110.7	138.8	104.0	95.7	107.9	101.3	123.1	112.9
Apr	114.8	121.5	109.6	156.1	154.3	109.5	136.2	103.9	96.2	108.6	101.7	122.4	111.9
May	114.8	120.9	110.0	157.7	156.5	107.6	131.6	106.0	97.1	108.9	101.6	124.0	112.8
June	113.7	118.2	112.2	158.9	159.5	107.5	132.2	106.2	97.0	108.7	102.4	124.4	112.8
July	112.7	116.1	111.7	160.6	161.5	105.7	129.6	106.8	97.0	109.4	102.1	124.7	113.4
Aug	113.5	113.0	112.4	162.6	164.1	109.5	138.1	105.5	96.8	109.0	101.5	124.7	113.7
Sept	116.0	118.2	111.6	164.6	165.0	108.8	137.4	107.6	96.8	108.3	100.9	123.7	114.6
Oct ᵖ	115.8	118.6	112.4	166.6	167.1	109.3	138.4	106.7	97.1	110.4	101.6	123.7	113.0
Nov ᵖ	117.9	120.1	113.4	167.9	169.6	111.1	141.5	108.3	96.4	111.4	102.5	125.3	114.5
Dec ᵖ	121.0	124.8	114.1	169.7	173.4	113.2	145.0	108.8	96.9	113.3	102.7	126.3	115.1

Source: Board of Governors of the Federal Reserve System.

TABLE B-52.—*Capacity utilization rates, 1948–94*

[Percent;[1] monthly data seasonally adjusted]

| Year or month | Total industry | Manufacturing | | | | | Mining | Utilities |
		Total	Durable goods	Non-durable goods	Primary processing	Advanced processing		
1948		82.5			87.3	80.0		
1949		74.2			76.2	73.2		
1950		82.8			88.5	79.8		
1951		85.8			90.2	83.4		
1952		85.4			84.9	85.9		
1953		89.3			89.4	89.3		
1954		80.1			80.6	80.0		
1955		87.0			92.0	84.2		
1956		86.1			89.4	84.4		
1957		83.6			84.7	83.1		
1958		75.0			75.4	74.9		
1959		81.6			83.0	81.1		
1960		80.1			79.8	80.5		
1961		77.3			77.9	77.2		
1962		81.4			81.5	81.6		
1963		83.5			83.8	83.4		
1964		85.6			87.8	84.6		
1965		89.5			91.0	88.8		
1966		91.1			91.4	91.1		
1967	86.4	87.2	87.1	86.3	85.4	88.0	81.2	93.4
1968	86.8	87.2	86.8	86.6	86.3	87.4	83.5	94.1
1969	86.9	86.8	86.3	86.6	86.9	86.5	86.6	95.8
1970	80.8	79.7	76.7	82.9	80.4	79.1	88.9	95.4
1971	79.2	78.2	74.3	82.8	79.3	77.4	87.4	93.9
1972	84.3	83.7	80.9	86.6	86.4	82.5	90.4	94.6
1973	88.4	88.1	87.5	87.5	91.5	86.5	92.5	92.9
1974	84.2	83.8	82.7	84.0	86.0	82.8	92.5	86.8
1975	74.6	73.2	70.2	76.4	72.9	73.5	89.9	84.0
1976	79.3	78.5	75.4	81.8	80.1	77.8	90.0	84.8
1977	83.3	82.8	80.3	85.2	84.0	81.9	90.9	84.6
1978	85.5	85.1	83.5	86.2	86.3	84.3	91.3	84.8
1979	86.2	85.4	84.9	85.1	86.4	84.8	91.9	85.9
1980	82.1	80.2	78.6	81.4	78.0	81.3	94.0	85.5
1981	80.9	78.8	76.6	81.0	78.0	79.1	94.6	82.8
1982	75.0	72.8	69.0	78.0	69.0	74.6	86.5	79.5
1983	75.8	74.9	70.5	81.1	74.8	74.9	79.9	80.3
1984	81.1	80.4	78.3	83.1	80.4	80.3	84.4	82.5
1985	80.3	79.5	77.8	81.9	79.8	79.4	82.9	83.5
1986	79.2	79.1	76.2	83.0	80.9	78.3	78.2	80.2
1987	81.5	81.6	78.6	85.6	84.9	80.1	79.9	82.0
1988	83.7	83.6	81.9	85.9	86.9	82.2	84.1	84.2
1989	83.7	83.2	81.6	85.3	86.2	82.0	85.4	86.0
1990	82.1	81.3	79.1	84.0	84.1	80.1	88.4	85.7
1991	79.2	78.0	75.0	81.7	79.9	77.2	87.4	85.8
1992	80.2	79.2	76.7	82.5	82.3	78.0	86.9	84.7
1993	81.7	80.9	79.5	82.7	84.6	79.4	87.4	86.7
1994 ᴾ	84.0	83.4	83.2	83.8	87.8	81.6	89.5	87.0
1993: Jan	81.5	80.7	78.9	83.0	83.7	79.5	87.7	84.9
Feb	81.8	80.9	79.1	83.2	84.2	79.6	86.8	88.0
Mar	81.7	80.8	79.2	82.9	84.0	79.6	86.5	88.1
Apr	81.6	80.8	79.2	82.9	84.1	79.4	86.7	86.3
May	81.2	80.5	78.8	82.6	83.9	79.1	86.8	84.7
June	81.4	80.5	78.7	82.8	84.3	78.9	87.7	86.5
July	81.6	80.7	78.9	82.9	84.3	79.2	86.9	87.6
Aug	81.6	80.6	79.0	82.6	84.6	79.0	87.1	88.4
Sept	81.7	80.8	79.5	82.4	84.7	79.2	88.5	86.9
Oct	81.7	80.7	79.7	82.1	84.8	79.1	88.2	86.4
Nov	82.3	81.4	80.7	82.5	85.8	79.7	87.9	87.0
Dec	82.9	82.2	81.9	82.7	86.9	80.3	88.2	86.1
1994: Jan	82.7	81.8	81.5	82.2	85.9	80.1	87.7	89.5
Feb	83.2	82.2	82.0	82.6	86.1	80.7	89.3	88.9
Mar	83.7	82.9	82.3	83.8	86.8	81.3	90.2	87.5
Apr	83.6	83.0	82.6	83.6	87.2	81.3	90.3	85.1
May	83.8	83.2	82.5	84.1	88.0	81.3	90.3	85.8
June	84.1	83.2	82.7	84.0	87.5	81.5	90.3	89.6
July	84.1	83.3	82.8	84.0	87.7	81.5	89.8	88.0
Aug	84.5	83.8	83.7	84.1	88.3	82.1	89.7	87.8
Sept	84.2	83.6	83.6	83.8	88.2	81.8	89.8	86.0
Oct ᴾ	84.3	83.8	84.0	83.6	88.3	82.0	89.0	86.4
Nov ᴾ	84.7	84.4	84.6	84.4	89.3	82.5	88.5	85.3
Dec ᴾ	85.4	85.1	85.5	84.8	90.0	83.1	89.6	84.5

[1] Output as percent of capacity.
Source: Board of Governors of the Federal Reserve System.

TABLE B–53.—New construction activity, 1929–94

[Value put in place, billions of dollars; monthly data at seasonally adjusted annual rates]

Year or month	Total new construction	Private construction Total	Residential buildings [1] Total [2]	New housing units	Nonresidential buildings and other construction [1] Total	Commercial [3]	Industrial	Other [4]	Public construction Total	Federal	State and local [5]
1929	10.8	8.3	3.6	3.0	4.7	1.1	0.9	2.6	2.5	0.2	2.3
1933	2.9	1.2	.5	.3	.8	.1	.2	.5	1.6	.5	1.1
1939	8.2	4.4	2.7	2.3	1.7	.3	.3	1.2	3.8	.8	3.1
1940	8.7	5.1	3.0	2.6	2.1	.3	.4	1.3	3.6	1.2	2.4
1941	12.0	6.2	3.5	3.0	2.7	.4	.8	1.5	5.8	3.8	2.0
1942	14.1	3.4	1.7	1.4	1.7	.2	.3	1.2	10.7	9.3	1.3
1943	8.3	2.0	.9	.7	1.1	.0	.2	.9	6.3	5.6	.7
1944	5.3	2.2	.8	.6	1.4	.1	.2	1.1	3.1	2.5	.6
1945	5.8	3.4	1.3	.7	2.1	.2	.6	1.3	2.4	1.7	.7
1946	14.3	12.1	6.2	4.8	5.8	1.2	1.7	3.0	2.2	.9	1.4
New series											
1947	20.0	16.7	9.9	7.8	6.9	1.0	1.7	4.2	3.3	.8	2.5
1948	26.1	21.4	13.1	10.5	8.2	1.4	1.4	5.5	4.7	1.2	3.5
1949	26.7	20.5	12.4	10.0	8.0	1.2	1.0	5.9	6.3	1.5	4.8
1950	33.6	26.7	18.1	15.6	8.6	1.4	1.1	6.1	6.9	1.6	5.2
1951	35.4	26.2	15.9	13.2	10.3	1.5	2.1	6.7	9.3	3.0	6.3
1952	36.8	26.0	15.8	12.9	10.2	1.1	2.3	6.8	10.8	4.2	6.6
1953	39.1	27.9	16.6	13.4	11.3	1.8	2.2	7.3	11.2	4.1	7.1
1954	41.4	29.7	18.2	14.9	11.5	2.2	2.0	7.2	11.7	3.4	8.3
1955	46.5	34.8	21.9	18.2	12.9	3.2	2.4	7.3	11.7	2.8	8.9
1956	47.6	34.9	20.2	16.1	14.7	3.6	3.1	8.0	12.7	2.7	10.0
1957	49.1	35.1	19.0	14.7	16.1	3.6	3.6	9.0	14.1	3.0	11.1
1958	50.0	34.6	19.8	15.4	14.8	3.6	2.4	8.8	15.5	3.4	12.1
1959	55.4	39.3	24.3	19.2	15.1	3.9	2.1	9.0	16.1	3.7	12.3
1960	54.7	38.9	23.0	17.3	15.9	4.2	2.9	8.9	15.9	3.6	12.2
1961	56.4	39.3	23.1	17.1	16.2	4.7	2.8	8.7	17.1	3.9	13.3
1962	60.2	42.3	25.2	19.4	17.2	5.1	2.8	9.2	17.9	3.9	14.0
1963	64.8	45.5	27.9	21.7	17.6	5.0	2.9	9.7	19.4	4.0	15.4
New series											
1964	72.1	51.9	30.5	24.1	21.4	6.8	3.6	11.0	20.2	3.7	16.5
1965	78.0	56.1	30.2	23.8	25.8	8.1	5.1	12.6	21.9	3.9	18.0
1966	81.2	57.4	28.6	21.8	28.8	8.1	6.6	14.1	23.8	3.8	20.0
1967	83.0	57.6	28.7	21.5	28.8	8.0	6.0	14.9	25.4	3.3	22.1
1968	92.4	65.0	34.2	26.7	30.8	9.0	6.0	15.8	27.4	3.2	24.2
1969	99.8	72.0	37.2	29.2	34.8	10.8	6.8	17.2	27.8	3.2	24.6
1970	100.7	72.8	35.9	27.1	37.0	11.2	6.6	19.2	27.9	3.1	24.8
1971	117.3	87.6	48.5	38.7	39.1	13.1	5.5	20.5	29.7	3.8	25.9
1972	133.3	103.3	60.7	50.1	42.6	15.7	4.8	22.1	30.0	4.2	25.8
1973	146.8	114.5	65.1	54.6	49.4	18.1	6.4	24.9	32.3	4.7	27.6
1974	147.5	109.3	56.0	43.4	53.4	18.1	8.1	27.2	38.1	5.1	33.0
1975	145.6	102.3	51.6	36.3	50.7	14.3	8.3	28.2	43.3	6.1	37.2
1976	165.4	121.5	68.3	50.8	53.2	14.1	7.4	31.6	44.0	6.8	37.2
1977	193.1	150.0	92.0	72.2	58.0	16.4	8.0	33.7	43.1	7.1	36.0
1978	230.2	180.0	109.8	85.6	70.2	20.6	11.5	38.2	50.1	8.1	42.0
1979	259.8	203.2	116.4	89.3	86.8	28.3	15.6	42.8	56.6	8.6	48.1
1980	259.7	196.1	100.4	69.6	95.7	34.6	14.6	46.6	63.6	9.6	54.0
1981	272.0	207.3	99.2	69.4	108.0	40.2	18.0	49.8	64.7	10.4	54.3
1982	260.6	197.5	84.7	57.0	112.9	44.1	18.5	50.2	63.1	10.0	53.1
1983	294.9	231.5	125.5	94.6	106.0	43.9	13.8	48.2	63.5	10.6	52.9
1984	348.8	278.6	153.8	113.8	124.8	59.1	14.8	50.8	70.2	11.2	59.0
1985	377.4	299.5	158.5	114.7	141.1	72.6	17.1	51.3	77.8	12.0	65.8
1986	407.7	323.1	187.1	133.2	136.0	69.5	14.9	51.6	84.6	12.4	72.2
1987	419.4	328.7	194.7	139.9	134.1	68.9	15.0	50.1	90.6	14.1	76.6
1988	432.3	337.5	198.1	138.9	139.4	71.5	16.5	51.5	94.7	12.3	82.5
1989	443.7	345.5	196.6	139.2	148.9	73.9	20.4	54.6	98.2	12.2	86.0
1990	442.2	334.7	182.9	128.0	151.8	72.5	23.8	55.4	107.5	12.1	95.4
1991	403.6	293.5	157.8	110.6	135.7	54.8	22.3	58.7	110.1	12.8	97.3
1992	435.4	316.1	187.9	129.6	128.2	45.0	20.7	62.5	119.2	14.3	104.9
1993	466.4	341.1	210.5	144.1	130.6	46.9	19.5	64.2	125.3	14.3	110.9
1994 [p]	506.8	377.6	238.0	167.5	139.7	52.3	21.7	65.7	129.2	14.2	115.0

See next page for continuation of table.

[Value put in place, billions of dollars; monthly data at seasonally adjusted annual rates]

Year or month	Total new construc-tion	Private construction							Public construction		
		Total	Residential buildings [1]		Nonresidential buildings and other construction [1]				Total	Federal	State and local [5]
			Total [2]	New housing units	Total	Com-mer-cial [3]	Indus-trial	Other [4]			
1993: Jan	450.5	333.9	206.1	138.4	127.8	45.1	20.0	62.7	116.6	14.1	102.5
Feb	452.2	332.5	207.2	142.0	125.3	45.4	20.0	60.0	119.7	14.5	105.2
Mar	452.5	334.6	206.1	140.0	128.4	45.0	21.5	61.9	117.9	16.4	101.5
Apr	449.3	326.5	201.6	136.7	125.0	44.4	18.4	62.2	122.7	15.4	107.3
May	452.3	332.5	203.8	138.4	128.7	46.8	19.1	62.8	119.8	12.8	107.0
June	461.0	335.4	206.2	139.6	129.2	46.8	18.7	63.8	125.6	13.2	112.4
July	463.1	335.8	206.5	141.0	129.2	45.4	19.2	64.6	127.4	14.3	113.1
Aug	464.7	339.3	208.5	143.1	130.7	46.4	19.4	64.9	125.4	13.6	111.8
Sept	470.8	342.5	211.5	145.3	131.0	46.5	19.6	65.0	128.3	14.8	113.5
Oct	477.8	350.2	216.6	149.5	133.6	48.1	19.2	66.3	127.6	13.9	113.7
Nov	490.2	360.4	222.4	154.1	138.0	51.5	19.3	67.3	129.8	14.1	115.6
Dec	499.9	367.3	228.5	159.5	138.7	51.4	20.4	67.0	132.7	14.4	118.3
1994: Jan	488.5	363.9	229.8	160.8	134.1	47.7	19.7	66.7	124.6	14.3	110.3
Feb	485.9	361.9	233.3	164.2	128.6	46.3	20.0	62.3	124.0	16.5	107.5
Mar	496.0	371.7	236.8	167.0	134.9	50.4	19.9	64.6	124.4	13.5	110.8
Apr	497.0	374.1	238.0	168.4	136.0	52.0	21.2	62.8	122.9	13.1	109.9
May	504.4	378.2	241.2	170.1	137.1	52.3	21.3	63.4	126.1	13.5	112.7
June	506.1	379.3	240.7	168.9	138.7	52.6	21.0	65.1	126.8	13.1	113.7
July	505.4	376.5	237.8	168.8	138.7	52.3	21.1	65.3	129.0	13.3	115.7
Aug	505.5	376.2	236.9	167.9	139.3	52.0	22.0	65.4	129.3	13.7	115.6
Sept	514.2	382.3	238.5	168.9	143.8	53.7	22.6	67.4	131.9	14.3	117.6
Oct	521.4	384.9	239.3	167.8	145.6	54.4	22.3	68.8	136.5	15.5	121.0
Nov [P]	524.4	392.3	242.4	169.3	149.9	56.1	24.8	69.0	132.1	15.2	116.9
Dec [P]	530.0	394.4	244.4	170.8	150.0	56.8	23.8	69.4	135.7	15.7	120.0

[1] Beginning 1960, farm residential buildings included in residential buildings; prior to 1960, included in nonresidential buildings and other construction.

[2] Includes residential improvements, not shown separately. Prior to 1964, also includes nonhousekeeping units (hotels, motels, etc.).

[3] Office buildings, warehouses, stores, restaurants, garages, etc., and, beginning 1964, hotels and motels; prior to 1964 hotels and motels are included in total residential.

[4] Religious, educational, hospital and institutional, miscellaneous nonresidential, farm (see also footnote 1), public utilities (telecommunications, gas, electric, railroad, and petroleum pipelines), and all other private.

[5] Includes Federal grants-in-aid for State and local projects.

Source: Department of Commerce, Bureau of the Census.

TABLE B-54.—*New housing units started and authorized, 1959–94*

[Thousands of units]

Year or month	New housing units started							New private housing units authorized [2]			
	Private and public [1]		Private (farm and nonfarm) [1]					Total	Type of structure		
	Total (farm and nonfarm)	Nonfarm	Total	Type of structure					1 unit	2 to 4 units	5 units or more
				1 unit	2 to 4 units	5 units or more					
1959	1,553.7	1,531.3	1,517.0	1,234.0	282.9			1,208.3	938.3	77.1	192.9
1960	1,296.1	1,274.0	1,252.2	994.7	257.5			998.0	746.1	64.6	187.4
1961	1,365.0	1,336.8	1,313.0	974.3	338.7			1,064.2	722.8	67.6	273.8
1962	1,492.5	1,468.7	1,462.9	991.4	471.5			1,186.6	716.2	87.1	383.3
1963	1,634.9	1,614.8	1,603.2	1,012.4	590.7			1,334.7	750.2	118.9	465.6
1964	1,561.0	1,534.0	1,528.8	970.5	108.4	450.0		1,285.8	720.1	100.8	464.9
1965	1,509.7	1,487.5	1,472.8	963.7	86.6	422.5		1,239.8	709.9	84.8	445.1
1966	1,195.8	1,172.8	1,164.9	778.6	61.1	325.1		971.9	563.2	61.0	347.7
1967	1,321.9	1,298.8	1,291.6	843.9	71.6	376.1		1,141.0	650.6	73.0	417.5
1968	1,545.4	1,521.4	1,507.6	899.4	80.9	527.3		1,353.4	694.7	84.3	574.4
1969	1,499.5	1,482.3	1,466.8	810.6	85.0	571.2		1,323.7	625.9	85.2	612.7
1970	1,469.0	([3])	1,433.6	812.9	84.8	535.9		1,351.5	646.8	88.1	616.7
1971	2,084.5	([3])	2,052.2	1,151.0	120.3	780.9		1,924.6	906.1	132.9	885.7
1972	2,378.5	([3])	2,356.6	1,309.2	141.3	906.2		2,218.9	1,033.1	148.6	1,037.2
1973	2,057.5	([3])	2,045.3	1,132.0	118.3	795.0		1,819.5	882.1	117.0	820.5
1974	1,352.5	([3])	1,337.7	888.1	68.1	381.6		1,074.4	643.8	64.3	366.2
1975	1,171.4	([3])	1,160.4	892.2	64.0	204.3		939.2	675.5	63.9	199.8
1976	1,547.6	([3])	1,537.5	1,162.4	85.9	289.2		1,296.2	893.6	93.1	309.5
1977	2,001.7	([3])	1,987.1	1,450.9	121.7	414.4		1,690.0	1,126.1	121.3	442.7
1978	2,036.1	([3])	2,020.3	1,433.3	125.0	462.0		1,800.5	1,182.6	130.6	487.3
1979	1,760.0	([3])	1,745.1	1,194.1	122.0	429.0		1,551.8	981.5	125.4	444.8
1980	1,312.6	([3])	1,292.2	852.2	109.5	330.5		1,190.6	710.4	114.5	365.7
1981	1,100.3	([3])	1,084.2	705.4	91.1	287.7		985.5	564.3	101.8	319.4
1982	1,072.1	([3])	1,062.2	662.6	80.0	319.6		1,000.5	546.4	88.3	365.8
1983	1,712.5	([3])	1,703.0	1,067.6	113.5	522.0		1,605.2	901.5	133.6	570.1
1984	1,755.8	([3])	1,749.5	1,084.2	121.4	544.0		1,681.8	922.4	142.6	616.8
1985	1,745.0	([3])	1,741.8	1,072.4	93.4	576.1		1,733.3	956.6	120.1	656.6
1986	1,807.1	([3])	1,805.4	1,179.4	84.0	542.0		1,769.4	1,077.6	108.4	583.5
1987	1,622.7	([3])	1,620.5	1,146.4	65.3	408.7		1,534.8	1,024.4	89.3	421.1
1988	([4])	([3])	1,488.1	1,081.3	58.8	348.0		1,455.6	993.8	75.7	386.1
1989	([4])	([3])	1,376.1	1,003.3	55.2	317.6		1,338.4	931.7	67.0	339.8
1990	([4])	([3])	1,192.7	894.8	37.5	260.4		1,110.8	793.9	54.3	262.6
1991	([4])	([3])	1,013.9	840.4	35.6	137.9		948.8	753.5	43.1	152.1
1992	([4])	([3])	1,199.7	1,029.9	30.7	139.0		1,094.9	910.7	45.8	138.4
1993	([4])	([3])	1,287.6	1,125.7	29.4	132.6		1,199.1	986.5	52.3	160.2
1994 [p]	([4])	([3])	1,453.1	1,195.6	35.5	221.9		1,363.3	1,061.2	61.6	240.5
	Seasonally adjusted annual rates										
1993: Jan	([4])	([3])	1,170	1,049	25	96		1,150	965	48	137
Feb	([4])	([3])	1,194	1,048	24	122		1,152	951	51	150
Mar	([4])	([3])	1,092	957	30	105		1,046	875	45	126
Apr	([4])	([3])	1,232	1,082	27	123		1,107	921	51	135
May	([4])	([3])	1,241	1,100	26	115		1,113	915	49	149
June	([4])	([3])	1,238	1,067	30	141		1,122	926	50	146
July	([4])	([3])	1,245	1,076	53	116		1,169	973	54	142
Aug	([4])	([3])	1,319	1,178	17	124		1,234	1,004	51	179
Sept	([4])	([3])	1,359	1,160	32	167		1,265	1,036	58	171
Oct	([4])	([3])	1,409	1,231	31	147		1,298	1,078	58	162
Nov	([4])	([3])	1,406	1,248	30	128		1,363	1,132	59	172
Dec	([4])	([3])	1,612	1,383	21	208		1,474	1,181	53	240
1994: Jan	([4])	([3])	1,271	1,125	23	123		1,312	1,071	57	184
Feb	([4])	([3])	1,328	1,121	33	174		1,252	1,054	47	151
Mar	([4])	([3])	1,519	1,271	33	215		1,313	1,068	55	190
Apr	([4])	([3])	1,471	1,211	32	228		1,380	1,069	58	253
May	([4])	([3])	1,491	1,200	36	255		1,357	1,083	62	212
June	([4])	([3])	1,358	1,163	19	176		1,316	1,046	58	212
July	([4])	([3])	1,439	1,219	32	188		1,337	1,034	63	240
Aug	([4])	([3])	1,463	1,176	39	248		1,354	1,046	57	251
Sept	([4])	([3])	1,509	1,234	42	233		1,425	1,052	70	303
Oct	([4])	([3])	1,436	1,153	37	246		1,398	1,047	60	291
Nov [p]	([4])	([3])	1,545	1,193	65	287		1,388	1,035	69	284
Dec [p]	([4])	([3])	1,529	1,226	40	263		1,405	1,089	70	246

[1] Units in structures built by private developers for sale upon completion to local public housing authorities under the Department of Housing and Urban Development "Turnkey" program are classified as private housing. Military housing starts, including those financed with mortgages insured by FHA under Section 803 of the National Housing Act, are included in publicly owned starts and excluded from total private starts.
[2] Authorized by issuance of local building permit: in 17,000 permit-issuing places beginning 1984; in 16,000 places for 1978–83; in 14,000 places for 1972–77; in 13,000 places for 1967–71; in 12,000 places for 1963–66; and in 10,000 places prior to 1963.
[3] Not available separately beginning January 1970.
[4] Series discontinued December 1988.

Source: Department of Commerce, Bureau of the Census.

TABLE B-55.—Business expenditures for new plant and equipment, 1947-94

[Billions of dollars; quarterly data at seasonally adjusted annual rates]

Year or quarter	All indus-tries	Manufacturing Total	Dura-ble goods	Non-durable goods	Nonmanufacturing Total [2]	Min-ing	Trans-porta-tion	Public utili-ties	Com-mercial and other	Total non-farm busi-ness [3]	Manu-fac-tur-ing	Nonmanufacturing Total	Sur-veyed quar-terly	Sur-veyed annu-ally [4]
1947	20.11	8.73	3.39	5.34	11.38	0.69	2.69	1.64	6.38	22.27	8.73	13.54	11.38	2.16
1948	22.78	9.25	3.54	5.71	13.53	.93	3.17	2.67	6.77	25.97	9.25	16.73	13.53	3.19
1949	20.28	7.32	2.67	4.64	12.96	.88	2.80	3.28	6.01	24.03	7.32	16.72	12.96	3.76
1950	21.56	7.73	3.22	4.51	13.83	.84	2.87	3.42	6.70	25.81	7.73	18.08	13.83	4.25
1951	26.81	11.07	5.12	5.95	15.74	1.11	3.60	3.75	7.29	31.38	11.07	20.31	15.74	4.57
1952	28.16	12.12	5.75	6.37	16.04	1.21	3.56	3.96	7.31	32.16	12.12	20.04	16.04	4.00
1953	29.96	12.43	5.71	6.72	17.53	1.25	3.58	4.61	8.09	34.20	12.43	21.77	17.53	4.23
1954	28.86	12.00	5.49	6.51	16.85	1.29	2.91	4.23	8.42	33.62	12.00	21.62	16.85	4.76
1955	30.94	12.50	5.87	6.62	18.44	1.31	3.10	4.26	9.77	37.08	12.50	24.58	18.44	6.14
1956	37.90	16.33	8.19	8.15	21.57	1.64	3.56	4.78	11.59	45.25	16.33	28.91	21.57	7.35
1957	40.54	17.50	8.59	8.91	23.04	1.69	3.84	5.95	11.56	48.62	17.50	31.11	23.04	8.08
1958	33.84	12.98	6.21	6.77	20.86	1.43	2.72	5.74	10.97	42.55	12.98	29.57	20.86	8.72
1959	35.88	13.76	6.72	7.04	22.12	1.35	3.42	5.46	11.84	45.17	13.76	31.41	22.12	9.29
1960	39.44	16.36	8.28	8.08	23.08	1.29	3.54	5.40	12.86	48.99	16.36	32.63	23.08	9.55
1961	38.34	15.53	7.43	8.10	22.80	1.26	3.14	5.20	13.21	48.14	15.53	32.60	22.80	9.80
1962	40.86	16.03	7.81	8.22	24.83	1.41	3.59	5.12	14.71	51.61	16.03	35.58	24.83	10.75
1963	43.67	17.27	8.64	8.63	26.40	1.26	3.64	5.33	16.17	53.59	17.27	36.33	26.40	9.93
1964	51.26	21.23	10.98	10.25	30.04	1.33	4.71	5.80	18.20	62.02	21.23	40.80	30.04	10.76
1965	59.52	25.41	13.49	11.92	34.12	1.36	5.66	6.49	20.60	70.79	25.41	45.39	34.12	11.27
1966	70.40	31.37	17.23	14.15	39.03	1.42	6.68	7.82	23.11	82.62	31.37	51.25	39.03	12.22
1967	72.75	32.25	17.83	14.42	40.50	1.38	6.57	9.33	23.22	83.82	32.25	51.57	40.50	11.07
1968	76.42	32.34	17.93	14.40	44.08	1.44	6.91	10.52	25.22	88.92	32.34	56.58	44.08	12.50
1969	85.74	36.27	19.97	16.31	49.47	1.77	7.23	11.70	28.77	100.02	36.27	63.74	49.47	14.27
1970	91.91	36.99	19.80	17.19	54.92	2.02	7.17	13.03	32.71	106.15	36.99	69.16	54.92	14.24
1971	92.91	33.60	16.78	16.82	59.31	2.67	6.42	14.70	35.52	109.18	33.60	75.58	59.31	16.26
1972	103.40	35.42	18.22	17.20	67.98	2.88	7.14	16.26	41.69	120.91	35.42	85.49	67.98	17.51
1973	120.03	42.35	22.63	19.72	77.67	3.30	8.00	17.99	48.39	139.26	42.35	96.91	77.67	19.24
1974	139.67	52.48	26.77	25.71	87.19	4.58	9.16	19.96	53.49	159.83	52.48	107.35	87.19	20.16
1975	142.42	53.66	25.37	28.28	88.76	6.12	9.95	20.23	52.47	162.60	53.66	108.95	88.76	20.19
1976	158.44	58.53	27.50	31.03	99.91	7.63	11.10	22.90	58.29	179.91	58.53	121.38	99.91	21.47
1977	184.82	67.48	32.77	34.71	117.34	9.81	12.20	27.83	67.51	208.15	67.48	140.67	117.34	23.33
1978	216.81	78.13	39.02	39.10	138.69	10.55	12.07	32.10	83.96	244.40	78.13	166.27	138.69	27.58
1979	255.26	95.13	47.72	47.41	160.13	11.05	13.91	37.53	97.64	285.24	95.13	190.11	160.13	29.98
1980	286.40	112.60	54.82	57.77	173.80	12.71	13.56	41.32	106.21	318.08	112.60	205.48	173.80	31.68
1981	324.73	128.68	58.93	69.75	196.06	15.81	12.67	47.17	120.41	358.77	128.68	230.09	196.06	34.04
1982	326.19	123.97	54.58	69.39	202.22	14.11	11.75	53.58	122.79	363.08	123.97	239.11	202.22	36.89
1983	321.16	117.35	51.61	65.74	203.82	10.64	10.81	52.95	129.41	359.73	117.35	242.38	203.82	38.56
1984	373.83	139.61	64.57	75.04	234.22	11.86	13.44	57.53	151.39	418.38	139.61	278.77	234.22	44.55
1985	410.12	152.88	70.87	82.01	257.24	12.00	14.57	59.58	171.09	454.93	152.88	302.05	257.24	44.81
1986	399.36	137.95	65.68	72.28	261.40	8.15	15.05	56.61	181.59	447.11	137.95	309.16	261.40	47.75
1987	410.52	141.06	68.03	73.03	269.46	8.28	15.07	56.26	189.84	461.51	141.06	320.45	269.46	50.99
1988	455.49	163.45	77.04	86.41	292.04	9.29	16.63	60.37	205.76	508.22	163.45	344.77	292.04	52.73
1989	507.40	183.80	82.56	101.24	323.60	9.21	18.84	66.28	229.28	563.93	183.80	380.13	323.60	56.53
1990	532.61	192.61	82.58	110.04	339.99	9.88	21.47	67.21	241.43	591.96	192.61	399.34	339.99	59.35
1991	528.39	182.81	77.64	105.17	345.58	10.02	22.66	66.57	246.32	587.93	182.81	405.12	345.58	59.54
1992	546.60	174.02	73.32	100.69	372.58	8.88	22.64	72.21	268.84	607.71	174.02	433.69	372.58	61.11
1993	586.73	179.47	81.45	98.02	407.26	10.08	21.77	75.98	299.44	650.41	179.47	470.95	407.26	63.68
1994 [5]	638.37	192.56	92.78	99.77	445.81	11.24	21.19	76.44	336.93		192.56		445.81	
1992: I	534.23	173.14	73.26	99.87	361.09	8.99	21.82	69.09	261.19		173.14		361.09	
II	541.29	172.52	73.74	98.78	368.77	9.20	23.32	72.56	263.69		172.52		368.77	
III	547.82	173.05	72.63	100.42	374.77	8.96	23.66	72.48	269.67		173.05		374.77	
IV	559.39	176.74	73.64	103.09	382.65	8.43	21.66	73.79	278.77		176.74		382.65	
1993: I	563.48	173.99	78.19	95.80	389.49	8.98	22.38	73.78	284.35		173.99		389.49	
II	578.95	177.55	80.33	97.22	401.40	9.10	21.50	74.45	296.35		177.55		401.40	
III	594.56	182.48	82.74	99.74	412.09	11.09	21.32	75.94	303.74		182.48		412.09	
IV	604.51	182.15	83.64	98.51	422.36	10.92	21.84	78.87	310.73		182.15		422.36	
1994: I	619.34	185.04	86.03	99.02	434.29	11.43	22.47	73.20	327.20		185.04		434.29	
II	637.08	193.99	91.71	102.28	443.09	10.70	19.59	76.51	336.28		193.99		443.09	
III [5]	651.92	197.36	98.97	98.39	454.56	11.57	20.73	78.50	343.76		197.36		454.56	
IV [5]	645.13	193.83	94.44	99.39	451.30	11.27	21.98	77.57	340.48		193.83		451.30	

[1] These industries accounted for 90 percent of total nonfarm spending in 1993.

[2] Excludes forestry, fisheries, and agricultural services; professional services; social services and membership organizations; and real estate, which, effective with the April–May 1984 survey, are no longer surveyed quarterly. See last column ("nonmanufacturing surveyed annually") for data for these industries.

[3] "All industries" plus the part of nonmanufacturing that is surveyed annually.

[4] Consists of forestry, fisheries, and agricultural services; professional services; social services and membership organizations; and real estate.

[5] Planned capital expenditures as reported by business in July and August 1994, corrected for biases.

Source: Department of Commerce, Bureau of the Census.

TABLE B-56.—*Manufacturing and trade sales and inventories, 1952-94*

[Amounts in millions of dollars; monthly data seasonally adjusted]

Year or month	Total manufacturing and trade			Manufacturing			Merchant wholesalers			Retail trade		
	Sales [1]	Inventories [2]	Ratio [3]	Sales [1]	Inventories [2]	Ratio [3]	Sales [1]	Inventories [2]	Ratio [3]	Sales [1]	Inventories [2]	Ratio [3]
1952	44,840	72,377	1.58	22,529	41,136	1.78	8,782	10,210	1.12	13,529	21,031	1.52
1953	47,987	76,122	1.58	24,843	43,948	1.76	9,052	10,686	1.17	14,091	21,488	1.53
1954	46,443	73,175	1.60	23,355	41,612	1.81	8,993	10,637	1.18	14,095	20,926	1.51
1955	51,694	79,516	1.47	26,480	45,069	1.62	9,893	11,678	1.13	15,321	22,769	1.43
1956	54,063	87,304	1.55	27,740	50,642	1.73	10,513	13,260	1.19	15,811	23,402	1.47
1957	55,879	89,052	1.59	28,736	51,871	1.80	10,475	12,730	1.23	16,667	24,451	1.44
1958	54,201	87,055	1.61	27,248	50,203	1.84	10,257	12,739	1.24	16,696	24,113	1.44
1959	59,729	92,097	1.54	30,286	52,913	1.75	11,491	13,879	1.21	17,951	25,305	1.41
1960	60,827	94,719	1.56	30,878	53,786	1.74	11,656	14,120	1.21	18,294	26,813	1.47
1961	61,159	95,580	1.56	30,922	54,871	1.77	11,988	14,488	1.21	18,249	26,221	1.44
1962	65,662	101,049	1.54	33,358	58,172	1.74	12,674	14,936	1.18	19,630	27,941	1.42
1963	68,995	105,463	1.53	35,058	60,029	1.71	13,382	16,048	1.20	20,556	29,386	1.43
1964	73,682	111,504	1.51	37,331	63,410	1.70	14,529	17,000	1.17	21,823	31,094	1.42
1965	80,283	120,929	1.51	40,995	68,207	1.66	15,611	18,317	1.17	23,677	34,405	1.45
1966	87,181	136,824	1.57	44,870	77,986	1.74	16,987	20,765	1.22	25,330	38,073	1.50
1967	90,918	145,681	1.60	46,486	84,646	1.82	19,675	25,786	1.31	24,757	35,249	1.42
1968	98,794	156,611	1.59	50,229	90,560	1.80	21,121	27,166	1.29	27,445	38,885	1.42
1969	105,812	170,400	1.61	53,501	98,145	1.83	22,940	29,800	1.30	29,371	42,455	1.45
1970	108,352	178,594	1.65	52,805	101,599	1.92	24,298	33,354	1.37	31,249	43,641	1.40
1971	117,023	188,991	1.61	55,906	102,567	1.83	26,619	36,568	1.37	34,497	49,856	1.45
1972	131,227	203,227	1.55	63,027	108,121	1.72	30,011	40,297	1.34	38,189	54,809	1.44
1973	153,881	234,406	1.52	72,931	124,499	1.71	38,319	46,918	1.22	42,631	62,989	1.48
1974	178,201	287,144	1.61	84,790	157,625	1.86	48,271	58,667	1.22	45,141	70,852	1.57
1975	182,412	288,992	1.58	86,589	159,708	1.84	46,848	57,774	1.23	48,975	71,510	1.46
1976	204,386	318,345	1.56	98,797	174,636	1.77	50,934	64,622	1.27	54,655	79,087	1.45
1977	229,786	350,706	1.53	113,201	188,378	1.66	56,409	73,179	1.30	60,176	89,149	1.48
1978	260,755	400,931	1.54	126,905	211,691	1.67	66,849	86,934	1.30	67,002	102,306	1.53
1979	298,328	452,640	1.52	143,936	242,157	1.68	79,678	99,679	1.25	74,713	110,804	1.48
1980	328,112	510,126	1.55	154,391	265,215	1.72	93,977	123,833	1.32	79,743	121,078	1.52
1981	356,909	547,181	1.53	168,129	283,413	1.69	102,267	131,049	1.28	86,514	132,719	1.53
1982	348,771	575,504	1.67	163,351	311,852	1.95	96,357	129,024	1.36	89,062	134,628	1.49
1983	370,501	591,875	1.56	172,547	312,379	1.78	100,440	131,663	1.28	97,514	147,833	1.44
1984	411,427	651,551	1.53	190,682	339,516	1.73	113,502	144,223	1.23	107,243	167,812	1.49
1985	423,940	665,835	1.55	194,538	334,799	1.73	114,816	149,155	1.28	114,586	181,881	1.52
1986	431,786	664,624	1.55	194,657	322,669	1.68	116,326	155,445	1.32	120,803	186,510	1.56
1987	459,107	711,725	1.50	206,326	338,075	1.59	124,340	165,814	1.29	128,442	207,836	1.56
1988	496,819	767,538	1.49	223,541	367,422	1.58	135,170	180,535	1.30	138,108	219,581	1.54
1989	523,260	813,637	1.53	232,724	386,911	1.64	143,754	188,566	1.29	146,782	238,160	1.58
1990	542,349	837,120	1.53	239,459	399,068	1.65	148,859	196,935	1.30	154,031	241,117	1.56
1991	537,598	832,852	1.54	235,518	386,348	1.67	146,834	201,462	1.35	155,246	245,042	1.55
1992	559,799	841,831	1.50	244,511	379,238	1.57	152,031	208,757	1.35	163,258	253,836	1.52
1993	592,201	865,584	1.45	258,520	377,425	1.47	160,213	216,586	1.33	173,468	271,573	1.52
1993: Jan	581,571	844,777	1.45	252,845	378,624	1.50	159,197	209,865	1.32	169,529	256,288	1.51
Feb	584,401	846,955	1.45	256,800	379,232	1.48	158,771	209,213	1.32	168,830	258,510	1.53
Mar	583,028	851,101	1.46	258,979	379,539	1.47	156,755	210,261	1.34	167,294	261,301	1.56
Apr	585,385	853,751	1.46	255,114	380,307	1.49	159,741	211,761	1.33	170,530	261,683	1.53
May	587,850	855,316	1.45	254,007	381,591	1.50	161,819	211,568	1.31	172,024	262,157	1.52
June	589,578	856,313	1.45	258,299	381,326	1.48	158,980	212,090	1.33	172,299	262,897	1.53
July	585,564	857,693	1.46	251,680	381,561	1.52	160,502	213,106	1.33	173,382	263,026	1.52
Aug	591,660	859,113	1.45	256,556	381,392	1.49	160,739	214,553	1.33	174,365	263,168	1.51
Sept	595,305	861,176	1.45	260,088	380,689	1.46	160,743	214,992	1.34	174,474	265,495	1.52
Oct	600,099	862,672	1.44	260,471	380,301	1.46	161,920	214,368	1.32	177,708	268,003	1.51
Nov	606,641	866,240	1.43	265,574	380,181	1.43	162,305	215,500	1.33	178,762	270,559	1.51
Dec	612,390	865,584	1.41	269,722	377,425	1.40	161,797	216,586	1.34	180,871	271,573	1.50
1994: Jan	610,456	867,692	1.42	268,330	378,908	1.41	163,483	217,278	1.33	178,643	271,506	1.52
Feb	619,103	871,842	1.41	271,815	380,068	1.40	165,330	218,820	1.32	181,958	272,954	1.50
Mar	627,781	870,189	1.39	274,497	379,772	1.38	167,981	217,359	1.29	185,303	273,058	1.47
Apr	625,080	874,989	1.40	274,243	380,645	1.39	167,408	219,605	1.31	183,429	274,739	1.50
May	627,524	885,185	1.41	276,232	382,382	1.38	167,897	223,213	1.33	183,395	279,590	1.52
June	632,863	889,100	1.40	278,566	383,106	1.38	169,208	223,098	1.32	185,089	282,896	1.53
July	630,573	894,689	1.42	275,485	386,645	1.40	169,801	226,639	1.33	185,287	281,405	1.52
Aug	651,210	902,514	1.39	288,080	387,012	1.34	175,157	227,600	1.30	187,973	287,902	1.53
Sept	649,932	906,731	1.40	286,134	386,531	1.35	174,333	228,755	1.31	189,465	291,445	1.54
Oct	651,917	913,385	1.40	283,975	388,063	1.37	176,153	232,224	1.32	191,789	293,098	1.53
Nov [p]	659,251	919,786	1.40	291,191	389,988	1.34	175,978	235,121	1.34	192,082	294,677	1.53

[1] Annual data are averages of monthly not seasonally adjusted figures.

[2] Seasonally adjusted, end of period. Inventories beginning January 1982 for manufacturing and December 1980 for wholesale and retail trade are not comparable with earlier periods.

[3] Inventory/sales ratio. Annual data are: beginning 1982, averages of monthly ratios; for 1958-81, ratio of December inventories to monthly average sales for the year; and for earlier years, weighted averages. Monthly data are ratio of inventories at end of month to sales for month.

Note.—Earlier data are not strictly comparable with data beginning 1958 for manufacturing and beginning 1967 for wholesale and retail trade.

Source: Department of Commerce, Bureau of the Census.

[Millions of dollars; monthly data seasonally adjusted]

Year or month	Shipments [1]			Inventories [2]								
					Durable goods industries				Nondurable goods industries			
	Total	Durable goods industries	Nondurable goods industries	Total	Total	Materials and supplies	Work in process	Finished goods	Total	Materials and supplies	Work in process	Finished goods
1952	22,529	11,313	11,216	41,136	23,731				17,405			
1953	24,843	13,349	11,494	43,948	25,878	8,966	10,720	6,206	18,070	8,317	2,472	7,409
1954	23,355	11,828	11,527	41,612	23,710	7,894	9,721	6,040	17,902	8,167	2,440	7,415
1955	26,480	14,071	12,409	45,069	26,405	9,194	10,756	6,348	18,664	8,556	2,571	7,666
1956	27,740	14,715	13,025	50,642	30,447	10,417	12,317	7,565	20,195	8,971	2,721	8,622
1957	28,736	15,237	13,499	51,871	31,728	10,608	12,837	8,125	20,143	8,775	2,864	8,624
1958	27,248	13,553	13,695	50,203	30,194	9,970	12,408	7,816	20,009	8,676	2,827	8,506
1959	30,286	15,597	14,689	52,913	32,012	10,709	13,086	8,217	20,901	9,094	2,942	8,865
1960	30,878	15,870	15,008	53,786	32,337	10,306	12,809	9,222	21,449	9,097	2,947	9,405
1961	30,922	15,601	15,321	54,871	32,496	10,246	13,211	9,039	22,375	9,505	3,108	9,762
1962	33,358	17,247	16,111	58,172	34,565	10,794	14,124	9,647	23,607	9,836	3,304	10,467
1963	35,058	18,255	16,803	60,029	35,776	11,053	14,835	9,888	24,253	10,009	3,420	10,824
1964	37,331	19,611	17,720	63,410	38,421	11,946	16,158	10,317	24,989	10,167	3,531	11,291
1965	40,995	22,193	18,802	68,207	42,189	13,298	18,055	10,836	26,018	10,487	3,825	11,706
1966	44,870	24,617	20,253	77,986	49,852	15,464	21,908	12,480	28,134	11,197	4,226	12,711
1967	46,486	25,233	21,253	84,646	54,896	16,423	24,933	13,540	29,750	11,760	4,431	13,559
1968	50,229	27,624	22,605	90,560	58,732	17,344	27,213	14,175	31,828	12,328	4,852	14,648
1969	53,501	29,403	24,098	98,145	64,598	18,636	30,282	15,680	33,547	12,753	5,120	15,674
1970	52,805	28,156	24,649	101,599	66,651	19,149	29,745	17,757	34,948	13,168	5,271	16,509
1971	55,906	29,924	25,982	102,567	66,136	19,679	28,550	17,907	36,431	13,686	5,678	17,067
1972	63,027	33,987	29,040	108,121	70,067	20,807	30,713	18,547	38,054	14,677	5,998	17,379
1973	72,931	39,635	33,296	124,499	81,192	25,944	35,490	19,758	43,307	18,147	6,729	18,431
1974	84,790	44,173	40,617	157,625	101,493	35,070	42,530	23,893	56,132	23,744	8,189	24,199
1975	86,589	43,598	42,991	159,708	102,590	33,903	43,227	25,460	57,118	23,565	8,834	24,719
1976	98,797	50,623	48,174	174,636	111,988	37,457	46,074	28,457	62,648	25,847	9,929	26,872
1977	113,201	59,168	54,033	188,378	120,877	40,186	50,226	30,465	67,501	27,387	10,961	29,153
1978	126,905	67,731	59,174	211,691	138,181	45,198	58,848	34,135	73,510	29,619	12,085	31,806
1979	143,936	75,927	68,009	242,157	160,734	52,670	69,325	38,739	81,423	32,814	13,910	34,699
1980	154,391	77,419	76,972	265,215	174,788	55,173	76,945	42,670	90,427	36,606	15,884	37,937
1981	168,129	83,727	84,402	283,413	186,443	57,998	80,998	47,447	96,970	38,165	16,194	42,611
1982	163,351	79,212	84,139	311,852	200,444	59,336	86,707	54,601	111,408	44,039	18,612	48,757
1983	172,547	85,481	87,066	312,379	199,854	60,325	86,899	52,630	112,525	44,816	18,691	49,018
1984	190,682	97,940	92,742	339,516	221,330	66,031	98,251	57,048	118,186	45,692	19,328	53,166
1985	194,538	101,279	93,259	334,799	218,212	64,005	98,085	56,122	116,587	44,087	19,445	53,055
1986	194,657	103,238	91,419	322,669	212,006	61,409	96,926	53,671	110,663	42,309	18,124	50,230
1987	206,326	108,128	98,198	338,075	220,776	63,614	102,328	54,834	117,299	45,287	19,279	52,733
1988	223,541	117,993	105,549	367,422	241,402	69,388	112,380	59,634	126,020	49,030	20,446	56,544
1989	232,724	121,703	111,022	386,911	256,065	71,942	121,919	62,204	130,846	49,632	21,261	59,953
1990	239,459	122,387	117,072	399,068	259,988	72,788	122,520	64,680	139,080	51,606	22,447	65,027
1991	235,518	119,151	116,367	386,348	249,117	69,987	115,107	64,023	137,231	51,556	21,886	63,789
1992	244,511	125,553	118,958	379,238	237,717	68,165	107,140	62,412	141,521	52,194	22,887	66,440
1993 *p*	258,520	135,981	122,539	377,425	236,303	68,434	105,358	62,511	141,122	51,866	23,347	65,909
1994 *p*	280,787	151,032	129,756	391,277	247,263	74,772	104,782	67,709	144,014	52,756	23,951	67,307
1993: Jan	252,845	130,805	122,040	378,624	236,332	67,707	106,426	62,199	142,292	52,286	22,962	67,044
Feb	256,800	134,133	122,667	379,232	237,034	67,839	106,552	62,643	142,198	52,121	23,161	66,916
Mar	258,979	135,537	123,442	379,539	236,849	67,864	106,071	62,914	142,690	52,329	23,128	67,233
Apr	255,114	132,763	122,351	380,307	237,043	68,089	105,671	63,283	143,264	52,672	23,099	67,493
May	254,007	132,307	121,700	381,591	237,734	68,401	106,042	63,291	143,857	52,965	22,990	67,902
June	258,299	135,042	123,257	381,326	237,514	68,163	106,306	63,045	143,812	53,055	23,097	67,660
July	251,680	129,257	122,423	381,561	237,937	68,357	106,545	63,035	143,624	52,647	23,202	67,775
Aug	256,556	134,521	122,035	381,392	237,688	68,678	106,463	62,547	143,704	52,594	23,280	67,830
Sept	260,088	137,521	122,567	380,689	237,571	68,441	106,704	62,426	143,118	52,489	23,329	67,300
Oct	260,471	138,153	122,318	380,301	237,632	68,522	106,943	62,167	142,669	52,259	23,437	66,973
Nov	265,574	142,665	122,909	380,181	237,886	68,670	106,119	63,097	142,295	52,363	23,477	66,455
Dec	269,722	146,182	123,540	377,425	236,303	68,434	105,358	62,511	141,122	51,866	23,347	65,909
1994: Jan	268,330	144,709	123,621	378,908	238,172	68,157	105,770	64,245	140,736	51,434	23,349	65,953
Feb	271,815	146,260	125,555	380,068	238,832	68,803	105,305	64,724	141,236	51,485	23,278	66,473
Mar	274,497	147,388	127,109	379,772	238,195	68,780	105,075	64,340	141,577	51,785	23,417	66,375
Apr	274,243	146,932	127,311	380,645	239,164	69,576	104,959	64,629	141,481	51,705	23,205	66,571
May	276,232	148,510	127,722	382,382	240,539	70,231	105,506	64,802	141,843	51,953	23,403	66,487
June	278,566	150,010	128,556	383,106	241,039	70,763	106,108	64,168	142,067	52,001	23,652	66,414
July	275,485	146,472	129,013	386,645	243,392	71,732	106,531	65,129	143,253	52,044	23,888	67,321
Aug	288,080	155,619	132,461	387,012	244,116	72,238	106,207	65,671	142,896	52,093	23,752	67,051
Sept	286,134	154,350	131,784	386,531	243,814	72,713	105,458	65,643	142,717	52,571	23,905	66,241
Oct	283,975	152,586	131,389	388,063	244,925	73,367	105,215	66,343	143,138	52,536	24,026	66,576
Nov	291,191	157,292	133,899	389,988	246,374	74,404	104,954	67,016	143,614	52,600	24,198	66,816
Dec *p*	295,319	158,827	136,492	391,277	247,263	74,772	104,782	67,709	144,014	52,756	23,951	67,307

[1] Annual data are averages of monthly not seasonally adjusted figures.
[2] Seasonally adjusted, end of period. Data beginning 1982 are not comparable with data for prior periods.

Note.—Data beginning 1958 are not strictly comparable with earlier data.

Source: Department of Commerce, Bureau of the Census.

TABLE B-58.—Manufacturers' new and unfilled orders, 1952-94

[Amounts in millions of dollars; monthly data seasonally adjusted]

Year or month	New orders [1]				Unfilled orders [2]			Unfilled orders—shipments ratio [3]		
	Total	Durable goods industries		Non-durable goods industries	Total	Durable goods industries	Non-durable goods industries	Total	Durable goods industries	Non-durable goods industries
		Total	Capital goods industries, non-defense							
1952	23,204	12,061		11,143	75,857	72,680	3,177			
1953	23,586	12,147		11,439	61,178	58,637	2,541			
1954	22,335	10,768		11,566	48,266	45,250	3,016	3.42	4.12	0.96
1955	27,465	14,996		12,469	60,004	56,241	3,763	3.63	4.27	1.12
1956	28,368	15,365		13,003	67,375	63,880	3,495	3.87	4.55	1.04
1957	27,559	14,111		13,448	53,183	50,352	2,831	3.35	4.00	.85
1958	27,193	13,387		13,805	46,609	43,807	2,802	3.02	3.62	.85
1959	30,711	15,979		14,732	51,717	48,369	3,348	2.94	3.47	.92
1960	30,232	15,288		14,944	44,213	41,650	2,563	2.71	3.29	.71
1961	31,112	15,753		15,359	46,624	43,582	3,042	2.58	3.08	.78
1962	33,440	17,363		16,078	47,798	45,170	2,628	2.64	3.18	.68
1963	35,511	18,671		16,840	53,417	50,346	3,071	2.74	3.31	.72
1964	38,240	20,507		17,732	64,518	61,315	3,203	2.99	3.59	.71
1965	42,137	23,286		18,851	78,249	74,459	3,790	3.25	3.86	.79
1966	46,420	26,163		20,258	96,846	93,002	3,844	3.74	4.48	.75
1967	47,067	25,803		21,265	103,711	99,735	3,976	3.66	4.37	.73
1968	50,657	28,051	6,314	22,606	108,377	104,393	3,984	3.79	4.58	.69
1969	53,990	29,876	7,046	24,114	114,341	110,161	4,180	3.71	4.45	.69
1970	52,022	27,340	6,072	24,682	105,008	100,412	4,596	3.61	4.36	.76
1971	55,921	29,905	6,682	26,016	105,247	100,225	5,022	3.32	4.00	.76
1972	64,182	35,038	7,745	29,144	119,349	113,034	6,315	3.26	3.85	.86
1973	76,003	42,627	9,926	33,376	156,561	149,204	7,357	3.80	4.51	.91
1974	87,327	46,862	11,594	40,465	187,043	181,519	5,524	4.09	4.93	.62
1975	85,139	41,957	9,886	43,181	169,546	161,664	7,882	3.69	4.45	.82
1976	99,513	51,307	11,490	48,206	178,128	169,857	8,271	3.24	3.88	.74
1977	115,109	61,035	13,681	54,073	202,024	193,323	8,701	3.24	3.85	.71
1978	131,629	72,278	17,588	59,351	259,169	248,281	10,888	3.57	4.20	.81
1979	147,604	79,483	21,154	68,121	303,593	291,321	12,272	3.89	4.62	.82
1980	156,359	79,392	21,135	76,967	327,416	315,202	12,214	3.85	4.58	.75
1981	168,025	83,654	21,806	84,371	326,547	314,707	11,840	3.87	4.68	.69
1982	162,140	78,064	19,213	84,077	311,887	300,798	11,089	3.84	4.74	.62
1983	175,451	88,140	19,624	87,311	347,273	333,114	14,159	3.53	4.29	.69
1984	192,879	100,164	23,669	92,715	373,529	359,651	13,878	3.60	4.37	.64
1985	195,706	102,356	24,545	93,351	387,095	372,027	15,068	3.67	4.46	.68
1986	195,204	103,647	23,983	91,557	393,412	376,622	16,790	3.59	4.40	.70
1987	209,389	110,809	26,095	98,579	430,288	408,602	21,686	3.63	4.42	.83
1988	227,026	121,445	30,729	105,581	471,951	450,002	21,949	3.64	4.45	.76
1989	235,932	124,933	32,725	110,999	510,459	488,780	21,679	4.00	4.91	.78
1990	240,646	123,556	32,254	117,090	524,846	502,914	21,932	4.14	5.13	.76
1991	234,354	117,878	29,468	116,476	511,122	487,892	23,230	4.08	5.06	.81
1992	241,545	122,614	29,653	118,932	475,304	452,383	22,921	3.46	4.21	.77
1993	255,701	133,273	31,889	122,428	441,947	420,288	21,659	3.04	3.65	.72
1994 [p]	281,889	151,851	37,541	130,038	456,635	431,195	25,440	2.87	3.44	.76
1993: Jan	253,626	131,266	28,645	122,360	476,085	452,844	23,241	3.56	4.35	.79
Feb	257,250	134,533	32,748	122,717	476,535	453,244	23,291	3.51	4.27	.79
Mar	253,007	129,903	29,122	123,104	470,563	447,610	22,953	3.42	4.14	.78
Apr	252,369	129,838	30,453	122,531	467,818	444,685	23,133	3.46	4.20	.79
May	248,335	126,783	29,931	121,552	462,146	439,161	22,985	3.42	4.15	.78
June	255,462	132,252	33,850	123,210	459,309	436,371	22,938	3.33	4.02	.78
July	250,566	128,520	30,093	122,046	458,195	435,634	22,561	3.41	4.17	.76
Aug	253,461	131,752	31,992	121,709	455,100	432,865	22,235	3.30	3.99	.76
Sept	255,309	133,176	30,992	122,133	450,321	428,520	21,801	3.22	3.89	.73
Oct	258,270	136,613	32,825	121,657	448,120	426,980	21,140	3.21	3.89	.71
Nov	262,773	139,675	34,878	123,098	445,319	423,990	21,329	3.12	3.75	.72
Dec	266,351	142,481	35,059	123,870	441,947	420,288	21,659	3.04	3.65	.72
1994: Jan	272,616	148,549	36,630	124,067	446,233	424,128	22,105	3.11	3.73	.74
Feb	271,786	145,882	36,382	125,904	446,204	423,750	22,454	3.07	3.69	.74
Mar	274,691	146,906	36,127	127,785	446,398	423,268	23,130	3.03	3.63	.76
Apr	275,182	147,345	35,815	127,837	447,337	423,681	23,656	3.04	3.64	.77
May	277,441	149,412	35,498	128,029	448,546	424,583	23,963	3.01	3.60	.76
June	279,788	151,212	38,055	128,576	449,767	425,784	23,983	2.98	3.58	.76
July	274,305	145,251	36,310	129,054	448,587	424,563	24,024	2.99	3.60	.75
Aug	287,222	154,675	37,595	132,547	447,729	423,619	24,110	2.89	3.47	.73
Sept	287,248	155,433	39,056	131,815	448,843	424,702	24,141	2.90	3.48	.74
Oct	285,985	154,150	38,276	131,835	450,853	426,266	24,587	2.94	3.52	.76
Nov	293,716	159,321	40,781	134,395	453,378	428,295	25,083	2.88	3.45	.76
Dec [p]	298,576	161,727	37,988	136,849	456,635	431,195	25,440	2.87	3.44	.76

[1] Annual data are averages of monthly not seasonally adjusted figures.
[2] Seasonally adjusted, end of period.
[3] Ratio of unfilled orders at end of period to shipments for period; excludes industries with no unfilled orders. Annual figures relate to seasonally adjusted data for December.

Note.—Data beginning 1958 are not strictly comparable with earlier data.

Source: Department of Commerce, Bureau of the Census.

PRICES

TABLE B–59.—*Consumer price indexes for major expenditure classes, 1950–94*

[For all urban consumers; 1982–84 = 100]

Year or month	All items (CPI–U)	Food and beverages Total¹	Food	Housing Total	Shelter	Fuel and other utilities	House-hold furnish-ings and oper-ation	Apparel and upkeep	Trans-por-ta-tion	Medical care	Enter-tainment	Other goods and services	Ener-gy²
1950	24.1		25.4					40.3	22.7	15.1			
1951	26.0		28.2					43.9	24.1	15.9			
1952	26.5		28.7					43.5	25.7	16.7			
1953	26.7		28.3		22.0	22.5		43.1	26.5	17.3			
1954	26.9		28.2		22.5	22.6		43.1	26.1	17.8			
1955	26.8		27.8		22.7	23.0		42.9	25.8	18.2			
1956	27.2		28.0		23.1	23.6		43.7	26.2	18.9			
1957	28.1		28.9		24.0	24.3		44.5	27.7	19.7			21.5
1958	28.9		30.2		24.5	24.8		44.6	28.6	20.6			21.5
1959	29.1		29.7		24.7	25.4		45.0	29.8	21.5			21.9
1960	29.6		30.0		25.2	26.0		45.7	29.8	22.3			22.4
1961	29.9		30.4		25.4	26.3		46.1	30.1	22.9			22.5
1962	30.2		30.6		25.8	26.3		46.3	30.8	23.5			22.6
1963	30.6		31.1		26.1	26.6		46.9	30.9	24.1			22.6
1964	31.0		31.5		26.5	26.6		47.3	31.4	24.6			22.5
1965	31.5		32.2		27.0	26.6		47.8	31.9	25.2			22.9
1966	32.4		33.8		27.8	26.7		49.0	32.3	26.3			23.3
1967	33.4	35.0	34.1	30.8	28.8	27.1	42.0	51.0	33.3	28.2	40.7	35.1	23.8
1968	34.8	36.2	35.3	32.0	30.1	27.4	43.6	53.7	34.3	29.9	43.0	36.9	24.2
1969	36.7	38.1	37.1	34.0	32.6	28.0	45.2	56.8	35.7	31.9	45.2	38.7	24.8
1970	38.8	40.1	39.2	36.4	35.5	29.1	46.8	59.2	37.5	34.0	47.5	40.9	25.5
1971	40.5	41.4	40.4	38.0	37.0	31.1	48.6	61.1	39.5	36.1	50.0	42.9	26.5
1972	41.8	43.1	42.1	39.4	38.7	32.5	49.7	62.3	39.9	37.3	51.5	44.7	27.2
1973	44.4	48.8	48.2	41.2	40.5	34.3	51.1	64.6	41.2	38.8	52.9	46.4	29.4
1974	49.3	55.5	55.1	45.8	44.4	40.7	56.8	69.4	45.8	42.4	56.9	49.8	38.1
1975	53.8	60.2	59.8	50.7	48.8	45.4	63.4	72.5	50.1	47.5	62.0	53.9	42.1
1976	56.9	62.1	61.6	53.8	51.5	49.4	67.3	75.2	55.1	52.0	65.1	57.0	45.1
1977	60.6	65.8	65.5	57.4	54.9	54.7	70.4	78.6	59.0	57.0	68.3	60.4	49.4
1978	65.2	72.2	72.0	62.4	60.5	58.5	74.7	81.4	61.7	61.8	71.9	64.3	52.5
1979	72.6	79.9	79.9	70.1	68.9	64.8	79.9	84.9	70.5	67.5	76.7	68.9	65.7
1980	82.4	86.7	86.8	81.1	81.0	75.4	86.3	90.9	83.1	74.9	83.6	75.2	86.0
1981	90.9	93.5	93.6	90.4	90.5	86.4	93.0	95.3	93.2	82.9	90.1	82.6	97.7
1982	96.5	97.3	97.4	96.9	96.9	94.9	98.0	97.8	97.0	92.5	96.0	91.1	99.2
1983	99.6	99.5	99.4	99.5	99.1	100.2	100.2	100.2	99.3	100.6	100.1	101.1	99.9
1984	103.9	103.2	103.2	103.6	104.0	104.8	101.9	102.1	103.7	106.8	103.8	107.9	100.9
1985	107.6	105.6	105.6	107.7	109.8	106.5	103.8	105.0	106.4	113.5	107.9	114.5	101.6
1986	109.6	109.1	109.0	110.9	115.8	104.1	105.2	105.9	102.3	122.0	111.6	121.4	88.2
1987	113.6	113.5	113.5	114.2	121.3	103.0	107.1	110.6	105.4	130.1	115.3	128.5	88.6
1988	118.3	118.2	118.2	118.5	127.1	104.4	109.4	115.4	108.7	138.6	120.3	137.0	89.3
1989	124.0	124.9	125.1	123.0	132.8	107.8	111.2	118.6	114.1	149.3	126.5	147.7	94.3
1990	130.7	132.1	132.4	128.5	140.0	111.6	113.3	124.1	120.5	162.8	132.4	159.0	102.1
1991	136.2	136.8	136.3	133.6	146.3	115.3	116.0	128.7	123.8	177.0	138.4	171.6	102.5
1992	140.3	138.7	137.9	137.5	151.2	117.8	118.0	131.9	126.5	190.1	142.3	183.3	103.0
1993	144.5	141.6	140.9	141.2	155.7	121.3	119.3	133.7	130.4	201.4	145.8	192.9	104.2
1994	148.2	144.9	144.3	144.8	160.5	122.8	121.0	133.4	134.3	211.0	150.1	198.5	104.6
1993: Jan	142.6	140.5	139.8	139.3	153.7	119.2	118.2	129.7	129.1	196.4	144.3	191.0	103.4
Feb	143.1	140.7	139.9	139.7	154.4	118.4	118.6	133.4	129.2	198.0	144.5	191.5	102.2
Mar	143.6	140.9	140.1	140.2	154.8	119.5	118.7	136.2	129.0	198.6	144.8	192.0	102.5
Apr	144.0	141.4	140.6	140.4	155.0	119.6	119.2	136.9	129.4	199.4	145.3	192.4	103.1
May	144.2	141.8	141.1	140.5	154.9	120.5	119.1	135.0	130.2	200.5	145.0	193.2	104.4
June	144.4	141.1	140.4	141.5	155.7	122.7	119.1	131.9	130.3	201.1	145.5	193.1	106.5
July	144.4	141.1	140.3	141.9	156.3	123.2	118.8	129.4	130.3	202.2	145.3	193.7	105.8
Aug	144.8	141.5	140.8	142.3	156.8	123.3	119.2	131.9	130.2	202.9	145.8	193.4	105.2
Sept	145.1	141.8	141.1	142.3	156.6	123.9	119.6	134.6	130.1	203.3	146.6	193.1	105.2
Oct	145.7	142.3	141.6	142.2	156.8	122.4	120.0	136.1	131.8	204.4	147.3	193.4	105.4
Nov	145.8	142.6	141.9	142.0	156.7	121.2	120.3	136.2	132.6	204.9	147.7	193.8	103.7
Dec	-145.8	143.3	142.7	142.3	157.1	121.7	120.3	132.6	132.1	205.2	147.8	194.2	102.4
1994: Jan	146.2	144.3	143.7	142.9	158.1	121.6	120.5	130.4	131.6	206.4	148.5	195.1	101.3
Feb	146.7	143.6	142.9	143.7	159.1	122.4	120.4	132.4	131.9	207.7	149.1	195.2	102.0
Mar	147.2	143.9	143.2	144.1	159.8	122.4	120.6	136.1	132.2	208.3	149.6	195.5	101.9
Apr	147.4	144.0	143.4	143.9	159.6	121.6	120.6	136.4	132.6	209.2	149.7	196.4	102.0
May	147.5	144.1	143.5	144.1	159.6	122.2	121.1	135.6	132.8	209.7	149.9	197.1	102.9
June	148.0	144.2	143.5	144.9	160.1	124.2	121.4	133.8	133.8	210.4	149.8	197.6	105.7
July	148.4	144.8	144.2	145.4	160.8	124.3	121.5	130.9	134.6	211.5	150.2	198.0	106.8
Aug	149.0	145.3	144.8	145.9	161.7	124.3	121.4	131.1	135.9	212.2	150.2	199.4	108.5
Sept	149.4	145.6	145.0	145.8	161.6	124.2	121.4	134.2	135.9	212.8	150.7	201.4	108.2
Oct	149.5	145.6	145.0	145.7	162.0	122.4	121.4	135.2	136.1	214.0	-151.0	201.9	105.8
Nov	149.7	145.9	145.3	145.5	162.1	121.8	121.1	134.2	137.1	214.7	151.6	202.3	105.7
Dec	149.7	147.2	146.8	145.4	161.8	122.0	120.8	130.5	137.1	215.3	151.2	202.4	104.7

¹ Includes alcoholic beverages, not shown separately.
² Household fuels—gas (piped), electricity, fuel oil, etc.—and motor fuel. Motor oil, coolant, etc. also included through 1982.
Note.—Data beginning 1983 incorporate a rental equivalence measure for homeowners' costs.
Source: Department of Labor, Bureau of Labor Statistics.

TABLE B-60.—*Consumer price indexes for selected expenditure classes, 1950–94*

[For all urban consumers; 1982–84 = 100, except as noted]

Year or month	Food and beverages Total [1]	Food Total	Food At home	Food Away from home	Shelter Total	Renters' costs Total [2]	Renters' costs Rent, residential	Home-owners' costs [2]	Maintenance and repairs	Fuel and other utilities Total	Fuels Total	Fuels Fuel oil and other household fuel commodities	Fuels Gas (piped) and electricity (energy services)	Other utilities and public services
1950		25.4	27.3				29.7					11.3	19.2	
1951		28.2	30.3				30.9					11.8	19.3	
1952		28.7	30.8				32.2					12.1	19.5	
1953		28.3	30.3	21.5	22.0		33.9		20.5	22.5		12.6	19.9	
1954		28.2	30.1	21.9	22.5		35.1		20.9	22.6		12.6	20.2	
1955		27.8	29.5	22.1	22.7		35.6		21.4	23.0		12.7	20.7	
1956		28.0	29.6	22.6	23.1		36.3		22.3	23.6		13.3	20.9	
1957		28.9	30.6	23.4	24.0		37.0		23.2	24.3		14.0	21.1	
1958		30.2	32.0	24.1	24.5		37.6		23.6	24.8		13.7	21.9	
1959		29.7	31.2	24.8	24.7		38.2		24.0	25.4		13.9	22.4	
1960		30.0	31.5	25.4	25.2		38.7		24.4	26.0		13.8	23.3	
1961		30.4	31.8	26.0	25.4		39.2		24.8	26.3		14.1	23.5	
1962		30.6	32.0	26.7	25.8		39.7		25.0	26.3		14.2	23.5	
1963		31.1	32.4	27.3	26.1		40.1		25.3	26.6		14.4	23.5	
1964		31.5	32.7	27.8	26.5		40.5		25.8	26.6		14.4	23.5	
1965		32.2	33.5	28.4	27.0		40.9		26.3	26.6		14.6	23.5	
1966		33.8	35.2	29.7	27.8		41.5		27.5	26.7		15.0	23.6	
1967	35.0	34.1	35.1	31.3	28.8		42.2		28.9	27.1	21.4	15.5	23.7	46.6
1968	36.2	35.3	36.3	32.9	30.1		43.3		30.6	27.4	21.7	16.0	23.9	47.1
1969	38.1	37.1	38.0	34.9	32.6		44.7		33.2	28.0	22.1	16.3	24.3	48.4
1970	40.1	39.2	39.9	37.5	35.5		46.5		35.8	29.1	23.1	17.0	25.4	50.0
1971	41.4	40.4	40.9	39.4	37.0		48.7		38.6	31.1	24.7	18.2	27.1	53.4
1972	43.1	42.1	42.7	41.0	38.7		50.4		40.6	32.5	25.7	18.3	28.5	56.2
1973	48.8	48.2	49.7	44.2	40.5		52.5		43.6	34.3	27.5	21.1	29.9	57.8
1974	55.5	55.1	57.1	49.8	44.4		55.2		49.5	40.7	34.4	33.2	34.5	60.7
1975	60.2	59.8	61.8	54.5	48.8		58.0		54.1	45.4	39.4	36.4	40.1	63.9
1976	62.1	61.6	63.1	58.2	51.5		61.1		57.6	49.4	43.3	38.8	44.7	67.7
1977	65.8	65.5	66.8	62.6	54.9		64.8		62.0	54.7	49.0	43.9	50.5	70.8
1978	72.2	72.0	73.8	68.3	60.5		69.3		67.2	58.5	53.0	46.2	55.0	73.7
1979	79.9	79.9	81.8	75.9	68.9		74.3		74.0	64.8	61.3	62.4	61.0	74.3
1980	86.7	86.8	88.4	83.4	81.0		80.9		82.4	75.4	74.8	86.1	71.4	77.0
1981	93.5	93.6	94.8	90.9	90.5		87.9		90.7	86.4	87.2	104.6	81.9	84.3
1982	97.3	97.4	98.1	95.8	96.9		94.6		96.4	94.9	95.6	103.4	93.2	93.3
1983	99.5	99.4	99.1	100.0	99.1	103.0	100.1	102.5	99.9	100.2	100.5	97.2	101.5	99.5
1984	103.2	103.2	102.8	104.2	104.0	108.6	105.3	107.3	103.7	104.8	104.0	99.4	105.4	107.2
1985	105.6	105.6	104.3	108.3	109.8	115.4	111.8	113.1	106.5	106.5	104.5	95.9	107.1	112.1
1986	109.1	109.0	107.3	112.5	115.8	121.9	118.3	119.4	107.9	104.1	99.2	77.6	105.7	117.9
1987	113.5	113.5	111.9	117.0	121.3	128.1	123.1	124.8	111.8	103.0	97.3	77.9	103.8	120.1
1988	118.2	118.2	116.6	121.8	127.1	133.6	127.8	131.1	114.7	104.4	98.0	78.1	104.6	122.9
1989	124.9	125.1	124.2	127.4	132.8	138.9	132.8	137.3	118.0	107.8	100.9	81.7	107.5	127.1
1990	132.1	132.4	132.3	133.4	140.0	146.7	138.4	144.6	122.2	111.6	104.5	99.3	109.3	131.7
1991	136.8	136.3	135.8	137.9	146.3	155.6	143.3	150.2	126.3	115.3	106.7	94.6	112.6	137.9
1992	138.7	137.9	136.8	140.7	151.2	160.9	146.9	155.3	128.6	117.8	108.1	90.7	114.8	142.5
1993	141.6	140.9	140.1	143.2	155.7	165.0	150.3	160.2	130.6	121.3	111.2	90.3	118.5	147.0
1994	144.9	144.3	144.1	145.7	160.5	169.4	154.0	165.5	130.8	122.8	111.7	88.8	119.2	150.2
1993: Jan	140.5	139.8	139.1	142.0	153.7	162.5	148.9	158.2	129.7	119.2	109.2	92.3	115.9	144.3
Feb	140.7	139.9	139.1	142.2	154.4	164.4	149.1	158.5	130.5	118.4	107.5	92.5	113.8	145.3
Mar	140.9	140.1	139.4	142.4	154.8	165.2	149.1	158.7	131.5	119.5	108.6	92.8	115.1	146.3
Apr	141.4	140.6	140.0	142.7	155.0	164.9	149.7	159.2	131.8	119.6	108.8	92.6	115.3	146.2
May	141.8	141.1	140.7	142.9	154.9	164.2	149.9	159.4	131.6	120.5	110.3	91.3	117.3	146.3
June	141.1	140.4	139.3	143.2	155.7	165.2	150.3	160.1	131.2	122.9	114.1	90.4	122.0	146.5
July	141.1	140.3	139.1	143.4	156.3	166.8	150.4	160.3	131.3	123.2	114.2	89.1	122.2	147.1
Aug	141.5	140.8	139.7	143.6	156.8	167.3	150.8	160.8	131.6	123.3	114.1	87.8	122.2	147.8
Sept	141.8	141.1	140.0	143.8	156.6	165.3	151.0	161.4	131.3	123.9	114.8	87.9	123.1	148.1
Oct	142.3	141.6	140.8	144.0	156.8	165.4	151.4	161.6	130.8	122.4	112.1	89.1	119.7	148.4
Nov	142.6	141.9	141.2	144.2	156.7	164.4	151.6	162.0	127.9	121.2	110.1	89.4	117.3	148.6
Dec	143.3	142.7	142.3	144.3	157.1	164.4	151.9	162.5	127.6	121.7	110.7	88.3	118.1	148.8
1994: Jan	144.9	144.3	144.1	145.7	160.5	169.4	154.0	165.5	130.8	122.8	111.7	88.8	119.2	150.2
Feb	143.6	142.9	142.6	144.6	159.1	168.9	152.8	163.7	129.4	122.4	111.1	93.6	117.9	150.0
Mar	143.9	143.2	142.8	144.8	159.8	170.1	153.2	164.1	129.3	122.4	111.1	92.5	118.1	150.1
Apr	144.0	143.4	143.0	145.1	159.6	169.1	153.3	164.2	130.2	121.6	109.8	90.2	116.9	150.0
May	144.1	143.5	143.0	145.3	159.6	168.5	153.3	164.5	131.0	122.2	110.6	88.7	118.0	150.4
June	144.2	143.5	142.9	145.5	160.1	169.6	153.4	164.8	131.5	124.2	113.9	87.7	122.1	150.4
July	144.8	144.2	144.0	145.6	160.8	171.0	153.9	165.3	131.3	124.3	114.1	87.1	122.3	150.4
Aug	145.3	144.8	144.7	145.9	161.7	172.1	154.5	166.1	131.2	124.3	114.0	86.8	122.2	150.6
Sept	145.6	145.0	145.0	146.2	161.6	169.4	155.0	167.1	131.6	124.2	113.8	86.8	122.1	150.6
Oct	145.6	145.0	144.8	146.4	162.0	169.8	155.2	167.5	130.8	122.4	110.8	87.0	118.5	150.4
Nov	145.9	145.3	145.1	146.8	162.1	168.9	155.6	167.9	131.2	121.8	109.9	87.7	117.3	150.5
Dec	147.2	146.8	147.3	147.1	161.8	168.2	155.7	167.8	132.7	122.0	110.1	88.4	117.4	150.6

[1] Includes alcoholic beverages, not shown separately.
[2] December 1982 = 100.

See next page for continuation of table.

TABLE B-60.—*Consumer price indexes for selected expenditure classes, 1950–94*—Continued

[For all urban consumers; 1982–84 = 100, except as noted]

Year or month	Transportation								Medical care		
		Private transportation									
	Total	Total³	New cars	Used cars	Motor fuel⁴	Automobile maintenance and repair	Other	Public transportation	Total	Medical care commodities	Medical care services
1950	22.7	24.5	41.1		19.0	18.9		13.4	15.1	39.7	12.8
1951	24.1	25.6	43.1		19.5	20.4		14.8	15.9	40.8	13.4
1952	25.7	27.3	46.8		20.0	20.8		15.8	16.7	41.2	14.3
1953	26.5	27.8	47.2	26.7	21.2	22.0		16.8	17.3	41.5	14.8
1954	26.1	27.1	46.5	22.7	21.8	22.7		18.0	17.8	42.0	15.3
1955	25.8	26.7	44.8	21.5	22.1	23.2		18.5	18.2	42.5	15.7
1956	26.2	27.1	46.1	20.7	22.8	24.2		19.2	18.9	43.4	16.3
1957	27.7	28.6	48.5	23.2	23.8	25.0		19.9	19.7	44.6	17.0
1958	28.6	29.5	50.0	24.0	23.4	25.4		20.9	20.6	46.1	17.9
1959	29.8	30.8	52.2	26.8	23.7	26.0		21.5	21.5	46.8	18.7
1960	29.8	30.6	51.5	25.0	24.4	26.5		22.2	22.3	46.9	19.5
1961	30.1	30.8	51.5	26.0	24.1	27.1		23.2	22.9	46.3	20.2
1962	30.8	31.4	51.3	28.4	24.3	27.5		24.0	23.5	45.6	20.9
1963	30.9	31.6	51.0	28.7	24.2	27.8		24.3	24.1	45.2	21.5
1964	31.4	32.0	50.9	30.0	24.1	28.2		24.7	24.6	45.1	22.0
1965	31.9	32.5	49.7	29.8	25.1	28.7		25.2	25.2	45.0	22.7
1966	32.3	32.9	48.8	29.0	25.6	29.2		26.1	26.3	45.1	23.9
1967	33.3	33.8	49.3	29.9	26.4	30.4	37.9	27.4	28.2	44.9	26.0
1968	34.3	34.8	50.7		26.8	32.1	39.2	28.7	29.9	45.0	27.9
1969	35.7	36.0	51.5	30.9	27.6	34.1	41.6	30.9	31.9	45.4	30.2
1970	37.5	37.5	53.0	31.2	27.9	36.6	45.2	35.2	34.0	46.5	32.3
1971	39.5	39.4	55.2	33.0	28.1	39.3	48.6	37.8	36.1	47.3	34.7
1972	39.9	39.7	54.7	33.1	28.4	41.1	48.9	39.3	37.3	47.4	35.9
1973	41.2	41.0	54.8	35.2	31.2	43.2	48.4	39.7	38.8	47.5	37.5
1974	45.8	46.2	57.9	36.7	42.2	47.6	50.2	40.6	42.4	49.2	41.4
1975	50.1	50.6	62.9	43.8	45.1	53.7	53.5	43.5	47.5	53.3	46.6
1976	55.1	55.6	66.9	50.3	47.0	57.6	61.8	47.8	52.0	56.5	51.3
1977	59.0	59.7	70.4	54.7	49.7	61.9	67.2	50.0	57.0	60.2	56.4
1978	61.7	62.5	75.8	55.8	51.8	67.0	69.9	51.5	61.8	64.4	61.2
1979	70.5	71.7	81.8	60.2	70.1	73.7	75.2	54.9	67.5	69.0	67.2
1980	83.1	84.2	88.4	62.3	97.4	81.5	84.3	69.0	74.9	75.4	74.8
1981	93.2	93.8	93.7	76.9	108.5	89.2	91.4	85.6	82.9	83.7	82.8
1982	97.0	97.1	97.4	88.8	102.8	96.0	97.7	94.9	92.5	92.3	92.6
1983	99.3	99.3	99.9	98.7	99.4	100.3	98.8	99.5	100.6	100.2	100.7
1984	103.7	103.6	102.8	112.5	97.9	103.8	103.5	105.7	106.8	107.5	106.7
1985	106.4	106.2	106.1	113.7	98.7	106.8	109.0	110.5	113.5	115.2	113.2
1986	102.3	101.2	110.6	108.8	77.1	110.3	115.1	117.0	122.0	122.8	121.9
1987	105.4	104.2	114.6	113.1	80.2	114.8	120.8	121.1	130.1	131.0	130.0
1988	108.7	107.6	116.9	118.0	80.9	119.7	127.9	123.3	138.6	139.9	138.3
1989	114.1	112.9	119.2	120.4	88.5	124.9	135.8	129.5	149.3	150.8	148.9
1990	120.5	118.8	121.0	117.6	101.2	130.1	142.5	142.6	162.8	163.4	162.7
1991	123.8	121.9	125.3	118.1	99.4	136.0	149.1	148.9	177.0	176.8	177.1
1992	126.5	124.6	128.4	123.2	99.0	141.3	153.2	151.4	190.1	188.1	190.5
1993	130.4	127.5	131.5	133.9	98.0	145.9	156.8	167.0	201.4	195.0	202.9
1994	134.3	131.4	136.0	141.7	98.5	150.2	162.1	172.0	211.0	200.7	213.4
1993: Jan	129.1	126.6	130.9	127.4	98.6	143.4	156.5	161.6	196.4	191.8	197.5
Feb	129.2	126.5	130.9	126.0	98.0	144.3	156.8	164.1	198.0	193.2	199.1
Mar	129.0	126.3	130.9	126.6	97.3	144.7	156.3	163.5	198.6	193.9	199.7
Apr	129.4	126.8	131.1	128.7	98.4	145.2	156.1	162.8	199.4	193.7	200.7
May	130.2	127.5	131.3	131.5	99.7	145.4	156.1	165.5	200.5	194.2	202.0
June	130.3	127.6	131.0	134.3	99.8	145.8	155.8	164.5	201.1	194.7	202.6
July	130.3	127.4	130.9	136.1	98.1	146.2	156.0	167.7	202.2	195.7	203.8
Aug	130.2	127.3	130.8	137.5	97.0	146.2	156.4	168.1	202.9	196.1	204.5
Sept	130.1	127.1	130.6	138.7	96.1	146.8	156.1	168.4	203.2	196.2	205.0
Oct	131.8	129.0	131.9	139.8	99.7	147.1	157.8	168.2	204.4	196.6	206.2
Nov	132.6	129.5	133.4	140.7	98.4	147.4	159.1	173.0	204.9	196.6	206.8
Dec	132.1	128.6	134.2	139.3	94.8	147.7	159.0	176.5	205.2	197.0	207.1
1994: Jan	131.6	128.2	134.7	136.8	92.6	148.1	159.5	175.3	206.4	197.8	208.4
Feb	131.9	128.5	135.0	134.1	93.6	148.6	159.7	175.9	207.7	198.7	209.8
Mar	132.2	128.6	135.3	133.6	93.3	149.0	160.2	178.5	208.3	199.1	210.4
Apr	132.6	129.2	135.4	135.3	94.8	149.4	160.4	176.5	209.2	199.7	211.4
May	132.8	130.0	135.7	137.9	96.0	149.7	160.8	169.9	209.7	200.1	212.0
June	133.8	131.0	135.8	140.9	98.2	149.8	161.3	169.9	210.4	200.5	212.6
July	134.6	131.8	135.8	142.6	100.5	150.0	161.5	171.4	211.5	201.3	213.8
Aug	135.9	133.0	135.6	144.0	104.1	150.7	162.0	173.2	212.2	201.7	214.7
Sept	135.9	133.1	135.7	145.4	103.7	151.2	162.1	171.7	212.8	201.7	215.4
Oct	136.1	133.6	136.6	147.7	101.8	151.7	164.1	168.4	214.0	202.2	216.8
Nov	137.1	134.8	137.7	150.1	102.7	151.8	166.2	167.2	214.7	202.7	217.5
Dec	137.1	134.9	138.5	151.5	100.4	151.9	167.6	165.6	215.3	202.9	218.2

³ Includes other new vehicles, not shown separately. Includes direct pricing of new trucks and motorcycles beginning 1982.
⁴ Includes direct pricing of diesel fuel and gasohol beginning 1981.

Note.—See Note, Table B-59.

Source: Department of Labor, Bureau of Labor Statistics.

TABLE B–61.—*Consumer price indexes for commodities, services, and special groups, 1950–94*

[For all urban consumers; 1982–84=100, except as noted]

Year or month	All items (CPI–U)	Commodities			Services			Special indexes				
		All commodities	Food	Commodities less food	All services	Medical care services	Services less medical care services	All items less food	All items less energy	All items less food and energy	All items less medical care	CPI–U–X1 (all items) (Dec. 1982 =97.6) [1]
1950	24.1	29.0	25.4	31.4	16.9	12.8		23.8				26.2
1951	26.0	31.6	28.2	33.8	17.8	13.4		25.3				28.3
1952	26.5	32.0	28.7	34.1	18.6	14.3		25.9				28.8
1953	26.7	31.9	28.3	34.2	19.4	14.8		26.4				29.0
1954	26.9	31.6	28.2	33.8	20.0	15.3		26.6				29.2
1955	26.8	31.3	27.8	33.6	20.4	15.7		26.6				29.1
1956	27.2	31.6	28.0	33.9	20.9	16.3		27.1				29.6
1957	28.1	32.6	28.9	34.9	21.8	17.0	22.8	28.0	28.9	28.9	28.7	30.5
1958	28.9	33.3	30.2	35.3	22.6	17.9	23.6	28.6	29.7	29.6	29.5	31.4
1959	29.1	33.3	29.7	35.8	23.3	18.7	24.2	29.2	29.9	30.2	29.8	31.6
1960	29.6	33.6	30.0	36.0	24.1	19.5	25.0	29.7	30.4	30.6	30.2	32.2
1961	29.9	33.8	30.4	36.1	24.5	20.2	25.4	30.0	30.7	31.0	30.5	32.5
1962	30.2	34.1	30.6	36.3	25.0	20.9	25.9	30.3	31.1	31.4	30.8	32.8
1963	30.6	34.4	31.1	36.6	25.5	21.5	26.3	30.7	31.5	31.8	31.1	33.3
1964	31.0	34.8	31.5	36.9	26.0	22.0	26.8	31.1	32.0	32.3	31.5	33.7
1965	31.5	35.2	32.2	37.2	26.6	22.7	27.4	31.6	32.5	32.7	32.0	34.2
1966	32.4	36.1	33.8	37.7	27.6	23.9	28.3	32.3	33.5	33.5	33.0	35.2
1967	33.4	36.8	34.1	38.6	28.8	26.0	29.3	33.4	34.4	34.7	33.7	36.3
1968	34.8	38.1	35.3	40.0	30.3	27.9	30.8	34.9	35.9	36.3	35.1	37.7
1969	36.7	39.9	37.1	41.7	32.4	30.2	32.9	36.8	38.0	38.4	37.0	39.4
1970	38.8	41.7	39.2	43.4	35.0	32.3	35.6	39.0	40.3	40.8	39.2	41.3
1971	40.5	43.2	40.4	45.1	37.0	34.7	37.5	40.8	42.0	42.7	40.8	43.1
1972	41.8	44.5	42.1	46.1	38.4	35.9	38.9	42.0	43.4	44.0	42.1	44.4
1973	44.4	47.8	48.2	47.7	40.1	37.5	40.6	43.7	46.1	45.6	44.8	47.2
1974	49.3	53.5	55.1	52.8	43.8	41.4	44.3	48.0	50.6	49.4	49.8	51.9
1975	53.8	58.2	59.8	57.6	48.0	46.6	48.3	52.5	55.1	53.9	54.3	56.2
1976	56.9	60.7	61.6	60.5	52.0	51.3	52.2	56.0	58.2	57.4	57.2	59.4
1977	60.6	64.2	65.5	63.8	56.0	56.4	55.9	59.6	61.9	61.0	60.8	63.2
1978	65.2	68.8	72.0	67.5	60.8	61.2	60.7	63.9	66.7	65.5	65.4	67.5
1979	72.6	76.6	79.9	75.3	67.5	67.2	67.5	71.2	73.4	71.9	72.9	74.0
1980	82.4	86.0	86.8	85.7	77.9	74.8	78.2	81.5	81.9	80.8	82.8	82.3
1981	90.9	93.2	93.6	93.1	88.1	82.8	88.7	90.4	90.1	89.2	91.4	90.1
1982	96.5	97.0	97.4	96.9	96.0	92.6	96.4	96.3	96.1	95.8	96.8	95.6
1983	99.6	99.8	99.4	100.0	99.4	100.7	99.2	99.7	99.6	99.6	99.6	99.6
1984	103.9	103.2	103.2	103.1	104.6	106.7	104.4	104.0	104.3	104.6	103.7	103.9
1985	107.6	105.4	105.6	105.2	109.9	113.2	109.6	108.0	108.4	109.1	107.2	107.6
1986	109.6	104.4	109.0	101.7	115.4	121.9	114.6	109.8	112.6	113.5	108.8	109.6
1987	113.6	107.7	113.5	104.3	120.2	130.0	119.1	113.6	117.2	118.2	112.6	113.6
1988	118.3	111.5	118.2	107.7	125.7	138.3	124.3	118.3	122.3	123.4	117.0	118.3
1989	124.0	116.7	125.1	112.0	131.9	148.9	130.1	123.7	128.1	129.0	122.4	124.0
1990	130.7	122.8	132.4	117.4	139.2	162.7	136.8	130.3	134.7	135.5	128.8	130.7
1991	136.2	126.6	136.3	121.3	146.3	177.1	143.3	136.1	140.9	142.1	133.8	136.2
1992	140.3	129.1	137.9	124.2	152.0	190.5	148.4	140.8	145.4	147.3	137.5	140.3
1993	144.5	131.5	140.9	126.3	157.9	202.9	153.6	145.1	150.0	152.2	141.2	144.5
1994	148.2	133.8	144.3	127.9	163.1	213.4	158.4	149.0	154.1	156.5	144.7	148.2
1993: Jan	142.6	130.4	139.8	125.1	155.2	197.5	151.2	143.1	147.9	149.9	139.5	142.6
Feb	143.1	130.9	139.9	125.8	155.8	199.1	151.7	143.7	148.7	150.8	140.0	143.1
Mar	143.6	131.4	140.1	126.4	156.2	199.7	152.1	144.2	149.1	151.4	140.4	143.6
Apr	144.0	131.9	140.6	127.0	156.5	200.7	152.3	144.6	149.5	151.7	140.8	144.0
May	144.2	132.0	141.1	126.9	156.9	202.0	152.6	144.8	149.6	151.7	141.0	144.2
June	144.4	131.4	140.4	126.3	157.8	202.6	153.6	145.1	149.6	151.8	141.1	144.4
July	144.4	130.9	140.3	125.5	158.4	203.8	154.1	145.2	149.7	152.0	141.1	144.4
Aug	144.8	131.1	140.8	125.7	159.0	204.5	154.7	145.6	150.3	152.6	141.6	144.8
Sept	145.1	131.3	141.1	125.9	159.3	205.0	155.0	145.9	150.6	152.9	141.8	145.1
Oct	145.7	132.3	141.6	127.1	159.5	206.2	155.1	146.4	151.2	153.5	142.3	145.7
Nov	145.8	132.5	141.9	127.3	159.6	206.8	155.2	146.6	151.5	153.9	142.5	145.8
Dec	145.8	132.0	142.7	126.1	160.0	207.1	155.6	146.4	151.7	153.9	142.5	145.8
1994: Jan	146.2	132.0	143.7	125.6	160.7	208.4	156.2	146.6	152.2	154.3	142.8	146.2
Feb	146.7	132.2	142.9	126.2	161.5	209.8	157.0	147.3	152.6	155.0	143.2	146.7
Mar	147.2	132.8	143.2	127.0	162.1	210.4	157.5	148.0	153.3	155.8	143.8	147.2
Apr	147.4	133.1	143.4	127.4	162.0	211.4	157.4	148.1	153.4	155.9	143.9	147.4
May	147.5	133.4	143.5	127.8	162.0	212.0	157.4	148.3	153.5	156.0	144.0	147.5
June	148.0	133.5	143.5	127.9	162.8	212.6	158.2	148.8	153.7	156.2	144.5	148.0
July	148.4	133.7	144.2	127.8	163.4	213.8	158.7	149.1	154.0	156.4	144.8	148.4
Aug	149.0	134.3	144.8	128.4	164.2	214.7	159.4	149.8	154.6	157.0	145.5	149.0
Sept	149.4	134.8	145.0	129.0	164.4	215.4	159.6	150.2	155.0	157.5	145.8	149.4
Oct	149.5	134.9	145.0	129.3	164.6	216.8	159.7	150.4	155.5	158.0	145.9	149.5
Nov	149.7	135.2	145.3	129.5	164.7	217.5	159.8	150.6	155.7	158.2	146.1	149.7
Dec	149.7	135.1	146.8	128.5	164.7	218.2	159.7	150.2	155.7	157.9	146.0	149.7

[1] CPI–U–X1 is a rental equivalence approach to homeowners' costs for the consumer price index for years prior to 1983, the first year for which the official index (CPI–U) incorporates such a measure. CPI–U–X1 is rebased to the December 1982 value of the CPI–U (1982–84=100); thus it is identical with CPI–U data for December 1982 and all subsequent periods. Data prior to 1967 estimated by moving the series at the same rate as the CPI–U for each year.

Note.—See Note, Table B–59.

Source: Department of Labor, Bureau of Labor Statistics.

TABLE B-62.—Changes in special consumer price indexes, 1958-94

[For all urban consumers; percent change]

Year or month	All items (CPI-U)		All items less food		All items less energy		All items less food and energy		All items less medical care	
	Dec. to Dec.[1]	Year to year	Dec. to Dec.[1]	Year to year	Dec. to Dec.[1]	Year to year	Dec. to Dec.[1]	Year to year	Dec. to Dec.[1]	Year to year
1958	1.8	2.8	1.8	2.1	2.1	2.8	1.7	2.4	1.7	2.8
1959	1.7	.7	2.1	2.1	1.3	.7	2.0	2.0	1.4	1.0
1960	1.4	1.7	1.0	1.7	1.3	1.7	1.0	1.3	1.3	1.3
1961	.7	1.0	1.3	1.0	.7	1.0	1.3	1.3	.3	1.0
1962	1.3	1.0	1.0	1.0	1.3	1.3	1.3	1.3	1.3	1.0
1963	1.6	1.3	1.6	1.3	1.9	1.3	1.6	1.3	1.6	1.0
1964	1.0	1.3	1.0	1.3	1.3	1.6	1.2	1.6	1.0	1.3
1965	1.9	1.6	1.6	1.6	1.9	1.6	1.5	1.2	1.9	1.6
1966	3.5	2.9	3.5	2.2	3.4	3.1	3.3	2.4	3.4	3.1
1967	3.0	3.1	3.3	3.4	3.2	2.7	3.8	3.6	2.7	2.1
1968	4.7	4.2	5.0	4.5	4.9	4.4	5.1	4.6	4.7	4.2
1969	6.2	5.5	5.6	5.4	6.5	5.8	6.2	5.8	6.1	5.4
1970	5.6	5.7	6.6	6.0	5.4	6.1	6.6	6.3	5.2	5.9
1971	3.3	4.4	3.0	4.6	3.4	4.2	3.1	4.7	3.2	4.1
1972	3.4	3.2	2.9	2.9	3.5	3.3	3.0	3.0	3.4	3.2
1973	8.7	6.2	5.6	4.0	8.2	6.2	4.7	3.6	9.1	6.4
1974	12.3	11.0	12.2	9.8	11.7	9.8	11.1	8.3	12.2	11.2
1975	6.9	9.1	7.3	9.4	6.6	8.9	6.7	9.1	6.7	9.0
1976	4.9	5.8	6.1	6.7	4.8	5.6	6.1	6.5	4.5	5.3
1977	6.7	6.5	6.4	6.4	6.7	6.4	6.5	6.3	6.7	6.3
1978	9.0	7.6	8.3	7.2	9.1	7.8	8.5	7.4	9.1	7.6
1979	13.3	11.3	14.0	11.4	11.1	10.0	11.3	9.8	13.4	11.5
1980	12.5	13.5	13.0	14.5	11.7	11.6	12.2	12.4	12.5	13.6
1981	8.9	10.3	9.8	10.9	8.5	10.0	9.5	10.4	8.8	10.4
1982	3.8	6.2	4.1	6.5	4.2	6.7	4.5	7.4	3.6	5.9
1983	3.8	3.2	4.1	3.5	4.5	3.6	4.8	4.0	3.6	2.9
1984	3.9	4.3	3.9	4.3	4.4	4.7	4.7	5.0	3.9	4.1
1985	3.8	3.6	4.1	3.8	4.0	3.9	4.3	4.3	3.5	3.4
1986	1.1	1.9	.5	1.7	3.8	3.9	3.8	4.0	.7	1.5
1987	4.4	3.6	4.6	3.5	4.1	4.1	4.2	4.1	4.3	3.5
1988	4.4	4.1	4.2	4.1	4.7	4.4	4.7	4.4	4.2	3.9
1989	4.6	4.8	4.5	4.6	4.6	4.7	4.4	4.5	4.5	4.6
1990	6.1	5.4	6.3	5.3	5.2	5.2	5.2	5.0	5.9	5.2
1991	3.1	4.2	3.3	4.5	3.9	4.6	4.4	4.9	2.7	3.9
1992	2.9	3.0	3.2	3.5	3.0	3.2	3.3	3.7	2.7	2.8
1993	2.7	3.0	2.7	3.1	3.1	3.2	3.2	3.3	2.6	2.7
1994	2.7	2.6	2.6	2.7	2.6	2.7	2.6	2.8	2.5	2.5

	Percent change from preceding period									
	Unadjusted	Seasonally adjusted	Unadjusted	Seasonally adjusted	Unadjusted	Seasonally adjusted	Unadjusted	Seasonally adjusted	Unadjusted	Seasonally adjusted
1993: Jan	0.5	0.2	0.4	0.4	0.5	0.3	0.5	0.3	0.4	0.3
Feb	.4	.4	.4	.3	.5	.3	.6	.4	.4	.3
Mar	.3	.2	.3	.3	.3	.3	.4	.2	.3	.2
Apr	.3	.3	.3	.3	.3	.3	.2	.3	.3	.3
May	.1	.2	.1	.2	.1	.3	0	.3	.1	.2
June	.1	.1	.2	.1	0	.1	.1	.2	.1	.1
July	0	.1	.1	.1	.1	.1	.1	.2	0	.1
Aug	.3	.3	.3	.2	.4	.3	.4	.3	.4	.2
Sept	.2	.1	.2	.1	.2	.1	.2	.1	.1	0
Oct	.4	.3	.3	.3	.4	.3	.4	.3	.4	.4
Nov	.1	.3	.1	.3	.2	.3	.3	.4	.1	.2
Dec	0	.2	-.1	.1	.1	.3	0	.2	0	.2
1994: Jan	.3	0	.1	.1	.3	.1	.3	.1	.2	0
Feb	.3	.3	.5	.3	.3	.1	.5	.3	.3	.3
Mar	.3	.3	.5	.4	.5	.3	.5	.3	.4	.3
Apr	.1	.1	.1	.1	.1	.2	.1	.2	.1	.1
May	.1	.2	.1	.2	.1	.3	.1	.3	.1	.1
June	.3	.3	.3	.3	.1	.3	.1	.3	.3	.3
July	.3	.3	.2	.3	.2	.3	.1	.2	.2	.3
Aug	.4	.3	.5	.3	.4	.3	.4	.3	.5	.3
Sept	.3	.2	.3	.1	.3	.2	.3	.2	.2	.2
Oct	.1	.1	.1	.1	.3	.2	.3	.2	.1	0
Nov	.1	.3	.1	.3	.1	.2	.1	.2	.1	.3
Dec	0	.2	-.3	0	0	.3	-.2	.1	-.1	.1

[1] Changes from December to December are based on unadjusted indexes.

Note.—See Note, Table B-59.

Source: Department of Labor, Bureau of Labor Statistics.

TABLE B-63.—*Changes in consumer price indexes for commodities and services, 1929–94*

[For all urban consumers; percent change]

Year	All items (CPI–U)		Commodities				Services				Medical care [2]		Energy [3]	
			Total		Food		Total		Medical care					
	Dec. to Dec.[1]	Year to year	Dec. to Dec.[1]	Year to year	Dec. to Dec.[1]	Year to year	Dec. to Dec.[1]	Year to year	Dec. to Dec.[1]	Year to year	Dec. to Dec.[1]	Year to year	Dec. to Dec.[1]	Year to year
1929	0.6	0			2.5	1.2								
1933	.8	−5.1			6.9	−2.8								
1939	0	−1.4	−0.7	−2.0	−2.5	−2.5	0	0	1.2	1.2	1.0	0		
1940	.7	.7	1.4	.7	2.5	1.7	.8	.8	0	0	0	1.0		
1941	9.9	5.0	13.3	6.7	15.7	9.2	2.4	.8	1.2	0	1.0	0		
1942	9.0	10.9	12.9	14.5	17.9	17.6	2.3	3.1	3.5	3.5	3.8	2.9		
1943	3.0	6.1	4.2	9.3	3.0	11.0	2.3	2.3	5.6	4.5	4.6	4.7		
1944	2.3	1.7	2.0	1.0	0	−1.2	2.2	2.2	3.2	4.3	2.6	3.6		
1945	2.2	2.3	2.9	3.0	3.5	2.4	.7	1.5	3.1	3.1	2.6	2.6		
1946	18.1	8.3	24.8	10.6	31.3	14.5	3.6	1.4	9.0	5.1	8.3	5.0		
1947	8.8	14.4	10.3	20.5	11.3	21.7	5.6	4.3	6.4	8.7	6.9	8.0		
1948	3.0	8.1	1.7	7.2	−.8	8.3	5.9	6.1	6.9	7.1	5.8	6.7		
1949	−2.1	−1.2	−4.1	−2.7	−3.9	−4.2	3.7	5.1	1.6	3.3	1.4	2.8		
1950	5.9	1.3	7.8	.7	9.8	1.6	3.6	3.0	4.0	2.4	3.4	2.0		
1951	6.0	7.9	5.9	9.0	7.1	11.0	5.2	5.3	5.3	4.7	5.8	5.3		
1952	.8	1.9	−.9	1.3	−1.0	1.8	4.4	4.5	5.8	6.7	4.3	5.0		
1953	.7	.8	−.3	−.3	−1.1	−1.4	4.2	4.3	3.4	3.5	3.5	3.6		
1954	−.7	.7	−1.6	−.9	−1.8	−.4	2.0	3.1	2.6	3.4	2.3	2.9		
1955	.4	−.4	−.3	−.9	−.7	−1.4	2.0	2.0	3.2	2.6	3.3	2.2		
1956	3.0	1.5	2.6	1.0	2.9	.7	3.4	2.5	3.8	3.8	3.2	3.8		
1957	2.9	3.3	2.8	3.2	2.8	3.2	4.2	4.3	4.8	4.3	4.7	4.2		
1958	1.8	2.8	1.2	2.1	2.4	4.5	2.7	3.7	4.6	5.3	4.5	4.6	−0.9	0
1959	1.7	.7	.6	0	−1.0	−1.7	3.9	3.1	4.9	4.5	3.8	4.4	4.7	1.9
1960	1.4	1.7	1.2	.9	3.1	1.0	2.5	3.4	3.7	4.3	3.2	3.7	1.3	2.3
1961	.7	1.0	0	.6	−.7	1.3	2.1	1.7	3.5	3.6	3.1	2.7	−1.3	.4
1962	1.3	1.0	.9	.9	1.3	.7	1.6	2.0	2.9	3.5	2.2	2.6	2.2	.4
1963	1.6	1.3	1.5	.9	2.0	1.6	2.4	2.0	2.8	2.9	2.5	2.6	−.9	0
1964	1.0	1.3	.9	1.2	1.3	1.3	1.6	2.0	2.3	2.3	2.1	2.1	0	−.4
1965	1.9	1.6	1.4	1.1	3.5	2.2	2.7	2.3	3.6	3.2	2.8	2.4	1.8	1.8
1966	3.5	2.9	2.5	2.6	4.0	5.0	4.8	3.8	8.3	5.3	6.7	4.4	1.7	1.7
1967	3.0	3.1	2.5	1.9	1.2	.9	4.3	4.3	8.0	8.8	6.3	7.2	1.7	2.1
1968	4.7	4.2	4.0	3.5	4.4	3.5	5.8	5.2	7.1	7.3	6.2	6.0	1.7	1.7
1969	6.2	5.5	5.4	4.7	7.0	5.1	7.7	6.9	7.3	8.2	6.2	6.7	2.9	2.5
1970	5.6	5.7	3.9	4.5	2.3	5.7	8.1	8.0	8.1	7.0	7.4	6.6	4.8	2.8
1971	3.3	4.4	2.8	3.6	4.3	3.1	4.1	5.7	5.4	7.4	4.6	6.2	3.1	3.9
1972	3.4	3.2	3.4	3.0	4.6	4.2	3.4	3.8	3.7	3.5	3.3	3.3	2.6	2.6
1973	8.7	6.2	10.4	7.4	20.3	14.5	6.2	4.4	6.0	4.5	5.3	4.0	17.0	8.1
1974	12.3	11.0	12.8	11.9	12.0	14.3	11.4	9.2	13.2	10.4	12.6	9.3	21.6	29.6
1975	6.9	9.1	6.2	8.8	6.6	8.5	8.2	9.6	10.3	12.6	9.8	12.0	11.4	10.5
1976	4.9	5.8	3.3	4.3	.5	3.0	7.2	8.3	10.8	10.1	10.0	9.5	7.1	7.1
1977	6.7	6.5	6.1	5.8	8.1	6.3	8.0	7.7	9.0	9.9	8.9	9.6	7.2	9.5
1978	9.0	7.6	8.8	7.2	11.8	9.9	9.3	8.6	9.3	8.5	8.8	8.4	7.9	6.3
1979	13.3	11.3	13.0	11.3	10.2	11.0	13.6	11.0	10.5	9.8	10.1	9.2	37.5	25.1
1980	12.5	13.5	11.0	12.3	10.2	8.6	14.2	15.4	10.1	11.3	9.9	11.0	18.0	30.9
1981	8.9	10.3	6.0	8.4	4.3	7.8	13.0	13.1	12.6	10.7	12.5	10.7	11.9	13.6
1982	3.8	6.2	3.6	4.1	3.1	4.1	4.3	9.0	11.2	11.8	11.0	11.6	1.3	1.5
1983	3.8	3.2	2.9	2.9	2.7	2.1	4.8	3.5	6.2	8.7	6.4	8.8	−.5	.7
1984	3.9	4.3	2.7	3.4	3.8	3.8	5.4	5.2	5.8	6.0	6.1	6.2	.2	1.0
1985	3.8	3.6	2.5	2.1	2.6	2.3	5.1	5.1	6.8	6.1	6.8	6.3	1.8	.7
1986	1.1	1.9	−2.0	−.9	3.8	3.2	4.5	5.0	7.9	7.7	7.7	7.5	−19.7	−13.2
1987	4.4	3.6	4.6	3.2	3.5	4.1	4.3	4.2	5.6	6.6	5.8	6.6	8.2	.5
1988	4.4	4.1	3.8	3.5	5.2	4.1	4.8	4.6	6.9	6.4	6.9	6.5	.5	.8
1989	4.6	4.8	4.1	4.7	5.6	5.8	5.1	4.9	8.6	7.7	8.5	7.7	5.1	5.6
1990	6.1	5.4	6.6	5.2	5.3	5.8	5.7	5.5	9.9	9.3	9.6	9.0	18.1	8.3
1991	3.1	4.2	1.2	3.1	1.9	2.9	4.6	5.1	8.0	8.9	7.9	8.7	−7.4	.4
1992	2.9	3.0	2.0	2.0	1.5	1.2	3.6	3.9	7.0	7.6	6.6	7.4	2.0	.5
1993	2.7	3.0	1.5	1.9	2.9	2.2	3.8	3.9	5.9	6.5	5.4	5.9	−1.4	1.2
1994	2.7	2.6	2.3	1.7	2.9	2.4	2.9	3.3	5.4	5.2	4.9	4.8	2.2	.4

[1] Changes from December to December are based on unadjusted indexes.

[2] Commodities and services.

[3] Household fuels—gas (piped), electricity, fuel oil, etc.—and motor fuel. Motor oil, coolant, etc. also included through 1982.

Note.—See Note, Table B–59.

Source: Department of Labor, Bureau of Labor Statistics.

TABLE B–64.—*Producer price indexes by stage of processing, 1950–94*

[1982 = 100]

Year or month	Total finished goods	Finished goods								Total finished consumer goods
		Consumer foods			Finished goods excluding consumer foods					
		Total	Crude	Processed	Total	Consumer goods			Capital equipment	
						Total	Durable	Non-durable		
1950	28.2	32.7	36.5	32.4		29.0	36.5	25.1	23.2	29.9
1951	30.8	36.7	41.9	36.2		31.1	38.9	27.0	25.5	32.7
1952	30.6	36.4	44.6	35.4		30.7	39.2	26.3	25.9	32.3
1953	30.3	34.5	41.6	33.6		31.0	39.5	26.6	26.3	31.7
1954	30.4	34.2	37.5	34.0		31.1	39.8	26.7	26.7	31.7
1955	30.5	33.4	39.1	32.7		31.3	40.2	26.8	27.4	31.5
1956	31.3	33.3	39.1	32.7		32.1	41.6	27.3	29.5	32.0
1957	32.5	34.4	38.5	34.1		32.9	42.8	27.9	31.3	32.9
1958	33.2	36.5	41.0	36.1		32.9	43.4	27.8	32.1	33.6
1959	33.1	34.8	37.3	34.7		33.3	43.9	28.2	32.7	33.3
1960	33.4	35.5	39.8	35.2		33.5	43.8	28.4	32.8	33.6
1961	33.4	35.4	38.0	35.3		33.4	43.6	28.4	32.9	33.6
1962	33.5	35.7	38.4	35.6		33.4	43.4	28.4	33.0	33.7
1963	33.4	35.3	37.8	35.2		33.4	43.1	28.5	33.1	33.5
1964	33.5	35.4	38.9	35.2		33.3	43.3	28.4	33.4	33.6
1965	34.1	36.8	39.0	36.8		33.6	43.2	28.8	33.8	34.2
1966	35.2	39.2	41.5	39.2		34.1	43.4	29.3	34.6	35.4
1967	35.6	38.5	39.6	38.8	35.0	34.7	44.1	30.0	35.8	35.6
1968	36.6	40.0	42.5	40.0	35.9	35.5	45.1	30.6	37.0	36.5
1969	38.0	42.4	45.9	42.3	36.9	36.3	45.9	31.5	38.3	37.9
1970	39.3	43.8	46.0	43.9	38.2	37.4	47.2	32.5	40.1	39.1
1971	40.5	44.5	45.8	44.7	39.6	38.7	48.9	33.5	41.7	40.2
1972	41.8	46.9	48.0	47.2	40.4	39.4	50.0	34.1	42.8	41.5
1973	45.6	56.5	63.6	55.8	42.0	41.2	50.9	36.1	44.2	46.0
1974	52.6	64.4	71.6	63.9	48.8	48.2	55.5	44.0	50.5	53.1
1975	58.2	69.8	71.7	70.3	54.7	53.2	61.0	48.9	58.2	58.2
1976	60.8	69.6	76.7	69.0	58.1	56.5	63.7	52.4	62.1	60.4
1977	64.7	73.3	79.5	72.7	62.2	60.6	67.4	56.8	66.1	64.3
1978	69.8	79.9	85.8	79.4	66.7	64.9	73.6	60.0	71.3	69.4
1979	77.6	87.3	92.3	86.8	74.6	73.5	80.8	69.3	77.5	77.5
1980	88.0	92.4	93.9	92.3	86.7	87.1	91.0	85.1	85.8	88.6
1981	96.1	97.8	104.4	97.2	95.6	96.1	96.4	95.8	94.6	96.6
1982	100.0	100.0	100.0	100.0	100.0	100.0	100.0	100.0	100.0	100.0
1983	101.6	101.0	102.4	100.9	101.8	101.2	102.8	100.5	102.8	101.3
1984	103.7	105.4	111.4	104.9	103.2	102.2	104.5	101.1	105.2	103.3
1985	104.7	104.6	102.9	104.8	104.6	103.3	106.5	101.7	107.5	103.8
1986	103.2	107.3	105.6	107.4	101.9	98.5	108.9	93.3	109.7	101.4
1987	105.4	109.5	107.1	109.6	104.0	100.7	111.5	94.9	111.7	103.6
1988	108.0	112.6	109.8	112.7	106.5	103.1	113.8	97.3	114.3	106.2
1989	113.6	118.7	119.6	118.6	111.8	108.9	117.6	103.8	118.8	112.1
1990	119.2	124.4	123.0	124.4	117.4	115.3	120.4	111.5	122.9	118.2
1991	121.7	124.1	119.3	124.4	120.9	118.7	123.9	115.0	126.7	120.5
1992	123.2	123.3	107.6	124.4	123.1	120.8	125.7	117.3	129.1	121.7
1993	124.7	125.7	114.4	126.5	124.4	121.7	128.0	117.6	131.4	123.0
1994	125.5	126.8	111.2	127.9	125.1	121.6	130.9	116.2	134.1	123.3
1993: Jan	124.2	124.3	114.8	125.0	124.0	121.4	127.2	117.6	130.8	122.5
Feb	124.5	124.5	114.5	125.2	124.4	121.8	127.6	117.9	131.1	122.8
Mar	124.7	124.8	113.8	125.6	124.6	122.1	127.6	118.4	131.2	123.1
Apr	125.5	126.5	126.5	126.5	125.1	122.7	127.9	119.1	131.2	124.0
May	125.8	126.9	125.2	127.0	125.4	123.3	127.8	119.9	131.2	124.5
June	125.5	125.4	102.3	127.1	125.5	123.4	127.7	120.1	131.0	124.1
July	125.3	125.0	100.7	126.8	125.3	123.0	127.9	119.5	131.3	123.8
Aug	124.2	125.4	107.4	126.7	123.8	120.9	127.9	116.6	131.2	122.4
Sept	123.8	125.7	108.6	126.9	123.2	120.5	126.0	116.8	130.3	122.2
Oct	124.6	125.4	105.8	126.8	124.3	121.2	129.1	116.5	132.3	122.6
Nov	124.5	126.6	123.4	126.9	123.7	120.3	129.7	115.0	132.5	122.3
Dec	124.1	127.2	130.1	127.0	123.1	119.4	129.7	113.7	132.5	121.9
1994: Jan	124.5	127.0	124.2	127.2	123.7	119.9	130.5	114.0	133.3	122.2
Feb	124.8	126.7	109.4	128.0	124.1	120.5	130.5	114.9	133.5	122.5
Mar	124.9	127.5	112.2	128.7	124.1	120.4	130.5	114.7	133.6	122.6
Apr	125.0	127.1	105.3	128.7	124.3	120.7	130.4	115.1	133.8	122.7
May	125.3	126.6	103.1	128.3	124.8	121.2	130.9	115.6	134.1	122.9
June	125.6	125.9	103.5	127.6	125.4	122.0	130.8	116.9	134.2	123.3
July	126.0	126.2	106.3	127.7	125.8	122.5	130.9	117.5	134.2	123.8
Aug[1]	126.5	126.6	104.7	128.2	126.4	123.4	131.0	118.7	134.3	124.5
Sept	125.5	126.4	106.5	127.8	125.2	122.0	128.9	117.6	133.5	123.4
Oct	125.8	126.1	103.8	127.8	125.6	122.0	132.0	116.4	134.8	123.4
Nov	126.1	126.8	113.9	127.7	125.8	122.3	132.0	116.8	134.8	123.8
Dec	126.2	128.5	142.0	127.5	125.5	121.7	132.2	115.8	135.1	123.9

[1] Data have been revised through August 1994 to reflect the availability of late reports and corrections by respondents. All data are subject to revision 4 months after original publication.

See next page for continuation of table.

[1982 = 100]

Year or month	Intermediate materials, supplies, and components								Crude materials for further processing				
				Materials and components		Processed fuels and lubricants	Containers	Supplies			Other		
	Total	Foods and feeds²	Other	For manufacturing	For construction				Total	Foodstuffs and feedstuffs	Total	Fuel	Other
1950	25.3		24.6	26.9	26.2	15.2	25.2	29.0	32.7	43.4		8.8	27.8
1951	28.4		27.6	30.5	28.7	15.9	29.6	32.6	37.6	50.2		9.0	32.0
1952	27.5		26.7	29.3	28.5	15.7	28.0	32.6	34.5	47.3		9.0	27.8
1953	27.7		27.0	29.7	29.0	15.8	28.0	31.0	31.9	42.3		9.3	26.6
1954	27.9		27.2	29.8	29.1	15.8	28.5	31.7	31.6	42.3		8.9	26.1
1955	28.4		28.0	30.5	30.3	15.8	28.9	31.2	30.4	38.4		8.9	27.5
1956	29.6		29.3	32.0	31.8	16.3	31.0	32.0	30.6	37.6		9.5	28.6
1957	30.3		30.1	32.7	32.0	17.2	32.4	32.3	31.2	39.2		10.1	28.2
1958	30.4		30.1	32.8	32.0	16.2	33.2	33.1	31.9	41.6		10.2	27.1
1959	30.8		30.5	33.3	32.9	16.2	33.0	33.5	31.1	38.8		10.4	28.1
1960	30.8		30.7	33.3	32.7	16.6	33.4	33.3	30.4	38.4		10.5	26.9
1961	30.6		30.3	32.9	32.2	16.8	33.2	33.7	30.2	37.9		10.5	27.2
1962	30.6		30.2	32.7	32.1	16.7	33.6	34.5	30.5	38.6		10.4	27.1
1963	30.7		30.1	32.7	32.2	16.6	33.2	35.0	29.9	37.5		10.5	26.7
1964	30.8		30.3	33.1	32.5	16.2	32.9	34.7	29.6	36.6		10.5	27.2
1965	31.2		30.7	33.6	32.8	16.5	33.5	35.0	31.1	39.2		10.6	27.7
1966	32.0		31.3	34.3	33.6	16.8	34.5	36.5	33.1	42.7		10.9	28.3
1967	32.2	41.8	31.7	34.5	34.0	16.9	35.0	36.8	31.3	40.3	21.1	11.3	26.5
1968	33.0	41.5	32.5	35.3	35.7	16.5	35.9	37.1	31.8	40.9	21.6	11.5	27.1
1969	34.1	42.9	33.6	36.5	37.7	16.6	37.2	37.8	33.9	44.1	22.5	12.0	28.4
1970	35.4	45.6	34.8	38.0	38.3	17.7	39.0	39.7	35.2	45.2	23.8	13.8	29.1
1971	36.8	46.7	36.2	38.9	40.8	19.5	40.8	40.8	36.0	46.1	24.7	15.7	29.4
1972	38.2	49.5	37.7	40.4	43.0	20.1	42.7	42.5	39.9	51.5	27.0	16.8	32.3
1973	42.4	70.3	40.6	44.1	46.5	22.2	45.2	51.7	54.5	72.6	34.3	18.6	42.9
1974	52.5	83.6	50.5	56.0	55.0	33.6	53.3	56.8	61.4	76.4	44.1	24.8	54.5
1975	58.0	81.6	56.6	61.7	60.1	39.4	60.0	61.8	61.6	77.4	43.7	30.6	50.0
1976	60.9	77.4	60.0	64.0	64.1	42.3	63.1	65.8	63.4	76.8	48.2	34.5	54.9
1977	64.9	79.6	64.1	67.4	69.3	47.7	65.9	69.3	65.5	77.5	51.7	42.0	56.3
1978	69.5	84.8	68.6	72.0	76.5	49.9	71.0	72.9	73.4	87.3	57.5	48.2	61.9
1979	78.4	94.5	77.4	80.9	84.2	61.6	79.4	80.2	85.9	100.0	69.6	57.3	75.5
1980	90.3	105.5	89.4	91.7	91.3	85.0	89.1	89.9	95.3	104.6	84.6	69.4	91.8
1981	98.6	104.6	98.2	98.7	97.9	100.6	96.7	96.9	103.0	103.9	101.8	84.8	109.8
1982	100.0	100.0	100.0	100.0	100.0	100.0	100.0	100.0	100.0	100.0	100.0	100.0	100.0
1983	100.6	103.6	100.5	101.2	102.8	95.4	100.4	101.8	101.3	101.8	100.7	105.1	98.8
1984	103.1	105.7	103.0	104.1	105.6	95.7	105.9	104.1	103.5	104.7	102.2	105.1	101.0
1985	102.7	97.3	103.0	103.3	107.3	92.8	109.0	104.4	95.8	94.8	96.9	102.7	94.3
1986	99.1	96.2	99.3	102.2	108.1	72.7	110.3	105.6	87.7	93.2	81.6	92.2	76.0
1987	101.5	99.2	101.7	105.3	109.8	73.3	114.5	107.7	93.7	96.2	87.9	84.1	88.5
1988	107.1	109.5	106.9	113.2	116.1	71.2	120.1	113.7	96.0	106.1	85.5	82.1	85.9
1989	112.0	113.8	111.9	118.1	121.3	76.4	125.4	118.1	103.1	111.2	93.4	85.3	95.8
1990	114.5	113.3	114.5	118.7	122.9	85.9	127.7	119.4	108.9	113.1	101.5	84.8	107.3
1991	114.4	111.1	114.6	118.1	124.5	85.3	128.1	121.4	101.2	105.5	94.6	82.9	97.5
1992	114.7	110.7	114.9	117.9	126.5	84.5	127.7	122.7	100.4	105.1	93.5	84.0	94.2
1993	116.2	112.7	116.4	118.9	132.0	84.7	126.4	125.0	102.4	108.4	94.7	87.1	94.1
1994	118.5	114.8	118.7	122.1	136.6	83.1	129.7	127.0	101.7	106.5	94.8	82.5	96.9
1993: Jan	115.2	110.9	115.4	118.4	129.1	83.2	126.7	124.2	101.4	105.6	94.8	90.6	92.4
Feb	115.6	109.8	115.9	118.7	130.9	83.3	126.8	124.3	101.4	106.0	94.6	83.4	96.1
Mar	116.0	109.9	116.3	118.8	132.5	83.8	126.7	124.3	102.6	108.3	95.0	81.4	97.9
Apr	116.3	111.2	116.6	119.1	132.8	84.3	126.5	124.8	103.9	110.4	95.8	82.4	98.5
May	116.2	111.8	116.5	118.9	132.0	85.2	126.5	124.7	106.5	112.2	98.8	89.4	99.1
June	116.7	111.1	117.0	118.8	131.3	88.1	126.5	124.7	104.2	107.2	98.3	94.9	95.3
July	116.6	114.0	116.7	118.9	131.1	87.1	126.4	125.2	101.5	107.5	93.9	85.5	93.8
Aug	116.6	114.3	116.7	119.0	131.6	86.3	126.1	125.5	100.6	108.0	92.1	84.4	91.7
Sept	116.8	113.7	117.0	119.0	132.3	87.1	126.1	125.4	101.0	107.7	92.8	87.6	91.0
Oct	116.5	113.6	116.7	118.9	132.5	85.4	126.2	125.5	102.8	105.7	97.0	90.8	95.5
Nov	116.4	114.7	116.5	119.1	133.3	83.3	126.3	125.7	102.2	110.2	93.2	87.5	91.6
Dec	116.0	116.8	116.0	119.2	134.2	80.0	126.3	126.1	101.0	112.1	90.1	87.9	86.8
1994: Jan	116.2	116.8	116.2	119.5	135.0	79.5	126.2	126.4	103.2	112.2	93.5	93.8	88.6
Feb	116.6	117.2	116.6	119.7	135.1	81.3	126.1	126.6	101.8	113.1	90.7	86.1	88.7
Mar	116.8	117.4	116.8	120.0	135.5	81.0	126.0	126.6	104.1	114.2	93.7	91.0	90.5
Apr	116.9	117.1	116.9	120.4	135.1	80.7	126.3	126.5	104.1	113.1	94.4	88.7	92.8
May	117.2	116.5	117.3	120.7	135.3	81.3	127.5	126.6	103.0	109.7	94.7	83.0	96.5
June	118.2	115.5	118.3	121.2	136.2	84.4	127.9	126.9	103.2	107.8	96.4	82.1	99.5
July	118.7	113.4	119.0	121.7	136.3	85.9	128.2	126.9	102.2	103.6	97.3	78.3	103.0
Aug [1]	119.5	113.6	119.8	122.5	136.8	87.5	129.4	126.9	101.9	101.8	98.0	80.7	102.7
Sept	120.0	114.0	120.3	123.5	137.4	86.4	131.8	127.0	99.5	101.2	94.6	78.6	98.8
Oct	120.0	112.1	120.4	124.4	137.8	83.2	134.0	127.5	98.6	98.8	94.7	77.2	99.7
Nov	120.9	112.2	121.3	125.5	139.0	83.7	136.0	127.9	99.4	100.2	95.1	74.7	101.7
Dec	121.1	111.5	121.6	126.2	139.4	82.4	137.3	128.2	99.9	101.7	94.9	76.0	100.7

² Intermediate materials for food manufacturing and feeds.

Source: Department of Labor, Bureau of Labor Statistics.

TABLE B-65.—*Producer price indexes by stage of processing, special groups, 1974-94*

[1982 = 100]

Year or month	Finished goods						Intermediate materials, supplies, and components				Crude materials for further processing			
	Total	Foods	Energy	Excluding foods and energy			Total	Foods and feeds[1]	Energy	Other	Total	Food-stuffs and feed-stuffs	Energy	Other
				Total	Capital equip-ment	Con-sumer goods exclud-ing foods and energy								
1974................	52.6	64.4	26.2	53.6	50.5	55.5	52.5	83.6	33.1	54.0	61.4	76.4	27.8	83.3
1975................	58.2	69.8	30.7	59.7	58.2	60.6	58.0	81.6	38.7	60.2	61.6	77.4	33.3	69.3
1976................	60.8	69.6	34.3	63.1	62.1	63.7	60.9	77.4	41.5	63.8	63.4	76.8	35.3	80.2
1977................	64.7	73.3	39.7	66.9	66.1	67.3	64.9	79.6	46.8	67.6	65.5	77.5	40.4	79.8
1978................	69.8	79.9	42.3	71.9	71.3	72.2	69.5	84.8	49.1	72.5	73.4	87.3	45.2	87.8
1979................	77.6	87.3	57.1	78.3	77.5	78.8	78.4	94.5	61.1	80.7	85.9	100.0	54.9	106.2
1980................	88.0	92.4	85.2	87.1	85.8	87.8	90.3	105.5	84.9	90.3	95.3	104.6	73.1	113.1
1981................	96.1	97.8	101.5	94.6	94.6	94.6	98.6	104.6	100.5	97.7	103.0	103.9	97.7	111.7
1982................	100.0	100.0	100.0	100.0	100.0	100.0	100.0	100.0	100.0	100.0	100.0	100.0	100.0	100.0
1983................	101.6	101.0	95.2	103.0	102.8	103.1	100.6	103.6	95.3	101.6	101.3	101.8	98.7	105.3
1984................	103.7	105.4	91.2	105.5	105.2	105.7	103.1	105.7	95.5	104.7	103.5	104.7	98.0	111.7
1985................	104.7	104.6	87.6	108.1	107.5	108.4	102.7	97.3	92.6	105.2	95.8	94.8	93.3	104.9
1986................	103.2	107.3	63.0	110.6	109.7	111.1	99.1	96.2	72.6	104.9	87.7	93.2	71.8	103.1
1987................	105.4	109.5	61.8	113.3	111.7	114.2	101.5	99.2	73.0	107.8	93.7	96.2	75.0	115.7
1988................	108.0	112.6	59.8	117.0	114.3	118.5	107.1	109.5	70.9	115.2	96.0	106.1	67.7	133.0
1989................	113.6	118.7	65.7	122.1	118.8	124.0	112.0	113.8	76.1	120.2	103.1	111.2	75.9	137.9
1990................	119.2	124.4	75.0	126.6	122.9	128.8	114.5	113.3	85.5	120.9	108.9	113.1	85.9	136.3
1991................	121.7	124.1	78.1	131.1	126.7	133.7	114.4	111.1	85.1	121.4	101.2	105.5	80.4	128.2
1992................	123.2	123.3	77.8	134.2	129.1	137.3	114.7	110.7	84.3	122.0	100.4	105.1	78.8	128.4
1993................	124.7	125.7	78.0	135.8	131.4	138.5	116.2	112.7	84.6	123.8	102.4	108.4	76.7	140.2
1994................	125.5	126.8	77.0	137.1	134.1	138.9	118.5	114.8	83.0	127.1	101.7	106.5	72.2	156.1
1993: Jan	124.2	124.3	76.6	135.9	130.8	139.0	115.2	110.9	83.1	122.9	101.4	105.6	78.6	134.3
Feb	124.5	124.5	76.9	136.2	131.1	139.4	115.6	109.8	83.2	123.5	101.4	106.0	77.5	137.4
Mar	124.7	124.8	77.5	136.3	131.2	139.5	116.0	109.9	83.7	123.9	102.6	108.3	77.7	138.2
Apr	125.5	126.5	78.3	136.7	131.2	140.0	116.3	111.2	84.2	124.1	103.9	110.4	78.0	140.7
May	125.8	126.9	79.6	136.6	131.2	140.0	116.2	111.8	85.1	123.8	106.5	112.2	81.3	142.2
June	125.5	125.4	80.5	136.3	131.0	139.5	116.7	111.1	87.9	123.7	104.2	107.2	80.9	141.7
July..........	125.3	125.0	79.6	136.4	131.3	139.5	116.6	114.0	87.0	123.6	101.5	107.5	75.0	142.6
Aug	124.2	125.4	79.1	134.6	131.2	136.7	116.6	114.3	86.1	123.8	100.6	108.0	73.6	139.8
Sept	123.8	125.7	79.5	133.7	130.3	135.7	116.8	113.7	86.9	123.9	101.0	107.7	74.5	139.8
Oct	124.6	125.4	78.8	135.4	132.3	137.3	116.5	113.6	85.3	124.0	102.8	105.7	79.4	140.8
Nov..........	124.5	126.6	76.2	135.6	132.5	137.6	116.4	114.7	83.3	124.2	102.2	110.2	74.4	141.8
Dec..........	124.1	127.2	73.3	135.9	132.5	138.0	116.0	116.8	79.9	124.4	101.0	112.1	70.0	143.6
1994: Jan	124.5	127.0	73.6	136.6	133.3	138.6	116.2	116.8	79.5	124.8	103.2	112.2	72.9	147.9
Feb	124.8	126.7	74.9	136.7	133.5	138.7	116.6	117.2	81.1	124.9	101.8	113.1	68.3	152.0
Mar	124.9	127.5	74.7	136.7	133.6	138.6	116.8	117.4	80.9	125.2	104.1	114.2	71.7	153.1
Apr	125.0	127.1	75.5	136.7	133.8	138.5	116.9	117.1	80.6	125.4	104.1	113.1	72.5	153.3
May	125.3	126.6	76.2	137.0	134.1	138.8	117.2	116.5	81.2	125.7	103.0	109.7	73.4	151.4
June	125.6	125.9	78.3	137.1	134.2	138.9	118.2	115.5	84.2	126.3	103.2	107.8	75.2	152.4
July..........	126.0	126.2	79.6	137.1	134.2	138.9	118.7	113.4	85.8	126.7	102.2	103.6	75.3	155.6
Aug [2]	126.5	126.6	81.4	137.2	134.3	139.0	119.5	113.6	87.3	127.3	101.9	101.8	75.6	157.9
Sept	125.5	126.4	79.5	136.3	133.5	138.1	120.0	114.0	86.3	128.2	99.5	101.2	71.0	159.0
Oct	125.8	126.1	77.1	137.8	134.8	139.6	120.0	112.1	83.1	129.1	98.6	98.8	71.0	159.2
Nov..........	126.1	126.8	77.8	137.8	134.8	139.7	120.9	112.2	83.6	130.2	99.4	100.2	70.3	163.6
Dec..........	126.2	128.5	75.8	138.1	135.1	139.9	121.1	111.5	82.3	130.8	99.9	101.7	68.7	168.0

[1] Intermediate materials for food manufacturing and feeds.
[2] Data have been revised through August 1994 to reflect the availability of late reports and corrections by respondents. All data are subject to revision 4 months after original publication.

Source: Department of Labor, Bureau of Labor Statistics.

161-672 - 95 - 12

TABLE B-66.—*Producer price indexes for major commodity groups, 1950–94*

[1982 = 100]

Year or month	Farm products and processed foods and feeds			Industrial commodities				
	Total	Farm products	Processed foods and feeds	Total	Textile products and apparel	Hides, skins, leather, and related products	Fuels and related products and power [1]	Chemicals and allied products [1]
1950	37.7	44.0	33.2	25.0	50.2	32.9	12.6	30.4
1951	43.0	51.2	36.9	27.6	56.0	37.7	13.0	34.8
1952	41.3	48.4	36.4	26.9	50.5	30.5	13.0	33.0
1953	38.6	43.8	34.8	27.2	49.3	31.0	13.4	33.4
1954	38.5	43.2	35.4	27.2	48.2	29.5	13.2	33.8
1955	36.6	40.5	33.8	27.8	48.2	29.4	13.2	33.7
1956	36.4	40.0	33.8	29.1	48.2	31.2	13.6	33.9
1957	37.7	41.1	34.8	29.9	48.3	31.2	14.3	34.6
1958	39.4	42.9	36.5	30.0	47.4	31.6	13.7	34.9
1959	37.6	40.2	35.6	30.5	48.1	35.9	13.7	34.8
1960	37.7	40.1	35.6	30.5	48.6	34.6	13.9	34.8
1961	37.7	39.7	36.2	30.4	47.8	34.9	14.0	34.5
1962	38.1	40.4	36.5	30.4	48.2	35.3	14.0	33.9
1963	37.7	39.6	36.8	30.3	48.2	34.3	13.9	33.5
1964	37.5	39.0	36.7	30.5	48.5	34.4	13.5	33.6
1965	39.0	40.7	38.0	30.9	48.8	35.9	13.8	33.9
1966	41.6	43.7	40.2	31.5	48.9	39.4	14.1	34.0
1967	40.2	41.3	39.8	32.0	48.9	38.1	14.4	34.2
1968	41.1	42.3	40.6	32.8	50.7	39.3	14.3	34.1
1969	43.4	45.0	42.7	33.9	51.8	41.5	14.6	34.2
1970	44.9	45.8	44.6	35.2	52.4	42.0	15.3	35.0
1971	45.8	46.6	45.5	36.5	53.3	43.4	16.6	35.6
1972	49.2	51.6	48.0	37.8	55.5	50.0	17.1	35.6
1973	63.9	72.7	58.9	40.3	60.5	54.5	19.4	37.6
1974	71.3	77.4	68.0	49.2	68.0	55.2	30.1	50.2
1975	74.0	77.0	72.6	54.9	67.4	56.5	35.4	62.0
1976	73.6	78.8	70.8	58.4	72.4	63.9	38.3	64.0
1977	75.9	79.4	74.0	62.5	75.3	68.3	43.6	65.9
1978	83.0	87.7	80.6	67.0	78.1	76.1	46.5	68.0
1979	92.3	99.6	88.5	75.7	82.5	96.1	58.9	76.0
1980	98.3	102.9	95.9	88.0	89.7	94.7	82.8	89.0
1981	101.1	105.2	98.9	97.4	97.6	99.3	100.2	98.4
1982	100.0	100.0	100.0	100.0	100.0	100.0	100.0	100.0
1983	102.0	102.4	101.8	101.1	100.3	103.2	95.9	100.3
1984	105.5	105.5	105.4	103.3	102.7	109.0	94.8	102.9
1985	100.7	95.1	103.5	103.7	102.9	108.9	91.4	103.7
1986	101.2	92.9	105.4	100.0	103.2	113.0	69.8	102.6
1987	103.7	95.5	107.9	102.6	105.1	120.4	70.2	106.4
1988	110.0	104.9	112.7	106.3	109.2	131.4	66.7	116.3
1989	115.4	110.9	117.8	111.6	112.3	136.3	72.9	123.0
1990	118.6	112.2	121.9	115.8	115.0	141.7	82.3	123.6
1991	116.4	105.7	121.9	116.5	116.3	138.9	81.2	125.6
1992	115.9	103.6	122.1	117.4	117.8	140.4	80.4	125.9
1993	118.4	107.1	124.0	119.0	118.0	143.7	80.0	128.2
1994	119.1	106.3	125.5	120.7	118.3	148.6	77.8	132.1
1993: Jan	116.6	104.3	122.7	118.3	118.0	143.6	79.4	127.6
Feb	116.6	104.4	122.7	118.7	117.9	142.5	79.2	128.1
Mar	117.5	106.4	122.9	119.0	117.9	142.9	79.7	127.8
Apr	119.1	109.7	123.7	119.4	118.1	143.6	80.3	128.6
May	119.8	111.0	124.2	119.7	118.0	143.8	81.9	128.2
June	117.5	104.3	124.0	119.9	118.0	143.7	83.2	128.5
July	118.0	105.4	124.3	119.4	118.2	143.5	81.0	128.2
Aug	118.4	106.6	124.3	118.8	118.3	143.9	80.2	128.3
Sept	118.3	106.3	124.3	118.8	118.1	144.1	80.9	128.1
Oct	117.7	104.2	124.5	119.4	118.1	143.7	81.2	128.2
Nov	119.9	110.1	124.8	118.8	118.0	144.1	78.3	128.5
Dec	121.3	113.0	125.4	118.1	117.9	144.4	74.7	127.9
1994: Jan	121.4	112.0	126.0	118.7	117.9	145.1	75.4	128.3
Feb	121.6	112.3	126.2	118.8	117.9	143.8	75.4	128.2
Mar	122.2	112.8	126.8	119.2	117.9	144.6	76.0	128.3
Apr	121.6	111.5	126.6	119.4	117.9	146.1	76.4	129.3
May	120.3	108.7	126.1	119.8	118.0	146.7	77.2	130.2
June	119.3	107.2	125.4	120.7	118.1	147.2	79.5	130.7
July	117.5	102.8	124.9	121.2	118.4	148.7	80.6	131.2
Aug [2]	117.1	101.0	125.2	121.9	118.5	149.0	82.0	132.6
Sept	117.2	101.2	125.2	121.5	118.5	150.8	79.7	134.6
Oct	115.9	98.7	124.5	121.8	118.6	153.4	77.7	136.4
Nov	116.8	101.2	124.6	122.4	118.6	153.7	77.9	137.2
Dec	118.1	105.6	124.3	122.4	118.8	153.6	76.3	138.6

[1] Prices for some items in this grouping are lagged and refer to 1 month earlier than the index month.
[2] Data have been revised through August 1994 to reflect the availability of late reports and corrections by respondents. All data are subject to revision 4 months after original publication.

See next page for continuation of table.

[1982 = 100]

Year or month	Rubber and plastic products	Lumber and wood products	Pulp, paper, and allied products	Metals and metal products	Machinery and equipment	Furniture and household durables	Non-metallic mineral products	Transportation equipment		Miscellaneous products
								Total	Motor vehicles and equipment	
1950	35.6	31.4	25.7	22.0	22.6	40.9	23.5	....	30.0	28.6
1951	43.7	34.1	30.5	24.5	25.3	44.4	25.0	....	31.6	30.3
1952	39.6	33.2	29.7	24.5	25.3	43.5	25.0	....	33.4	30.2
1953	36.9	33.1	29.6	25.3	25.9	44.4	26.0	....	33.3	31.0
1954	37.5	32.5	29.6	25.5	26.3	44.9	26.6	....	33.4	31.3
1955	42.4	34.1	30.4	27.2	27.2	45.1	27.3	....	34.3	31.3
1956	43.0	34.6	32.4	29.6	29.3	46.3	28.5	....	36.3	31.7
1957	42.8	32.8	33.0	30.2	31.4	47.5	29.6	....	37.9	32.6
1958	42.8	32.5	33.4	30.0	32.1	47.9	29.9	....	39.0	33.3
1959	42.6	34.7	33.7	30.6	32.8	48.0	30.3	....	39.9	33.4
1960	42.7	33.5	34.0	30.6	33.0	47.8	30.4	....	39.3	33.6
1961	41.1	32.0	33.0	30.5	33.0	47.5	30.5	....	39.2	33.7
1962	39.9	32.2	33.4	30.2	33.0	47.2	30.5	....	39.2	33.9
1963	40.1	32.8	33.1	30.3	33.1	46.9	30.3	....	38.9	34.2
1964	39.6	33.5	33.0	31.1	33.3	47.1	30.4	....	39.1	34.4
1965	39.7	33.7	33.3	32.0	33.7	46.8	30.4	....	39.2	34.7
1966	40.5	35.2	34.2	32.8	34.7	47.4	30.7	....	39.2	35.3
1967	41.4	35.1	34.6	33.2	35.9	48.3	31.2	....	39.8	36.2
1968	42.8	39.8	35.0	34.0	37.0	49.7	32.4	....	40.9	37.0
1969	43.6	44.0	36.0	36.0	38.2	50.7	33.6	40.4	41.7	38.1
1970	44.9	39.9	37.5	38.7	40.0	51.9	35.3	41.9	43.3	39.8
1971	45.2	44.7	38.1	39.4	41.4	53.1	38.2	44.2	45.7	40.8
1972	45.3	50.7	39.3	40.9	42.3	53.8	39.4	45.5	47.0	41.5
1973	46.6	62.2	42.3	44.0	43.7	55.7	40.7	46.1	47.4	43.3
1974	56.4	64.5	52.5	57.0	50.0	61.8	47.8	50.3	51.4	48.1
1975	62.2	62.1	59.0	61.5	57.9	67.5	54.4	56.7	57.6	53.4
1976	66.0	72.2	62.1	65.0	61.3	70.3	58.2	60.5	61.2	55.6
1977	69.4	83.0	64.6	69.3	65.2	73.2	62.6	64.6	65.2	59.4
1978	72.4	96.9	67.7	75.3	70.3	77.5	69.6	69.5	70.0	66.7
1979	80.5	105.5	75.9	86.0	76.7	82.8	77.6	75.3	75.8	75.5
1980	90.1	101.5	86.3	95.0	86.0	90.7	88.4	82.9	83.1	93.6
1981	96.4	102.8	94.8	99.6	94.4	95.9	96.7	94.3	94.6	96.1
1982	100.0	100.0	100.0	100.0	100.0	100.0	100.0	100.0	100.0	100.0
1983	100.8	107.9	103.3	101.8	102.7	103.4	101.6	102.8	102.2	104.8
1984	102.3	108.0	110.3	104.8	105.1	105.7	105.4	105.2	104.1	107.0
1985	101.9	106.6	113.3	104.4	107.2	107.1	108.6	107.9	106.4	109.4
1986	101.9	107.2	116.1	103.2	108.8	108.2	110.0	110.5	109.1	111.6
1987	103.0	112.8	121.8	107.1	110.4	109.9	110.0	112.5	111.7	114.9
1988	109.3	118.9	130.4	118.7	113.2	113.1	111.2	114.3	113.1	120.2
1989	112.6	126.7	137.8	124.1	117.4	116.9	112.6	117.7	116.2	126.5
1990	113.6	129.7	141.2	122.9	120.7	119.2	114.7	121.5	118.2	134.2
1991	115.1	132.1	142.9	120.2	123.0	121.2	117.2	126.4	122.1	140.8
1992	115.1	146.6	145.2	119.2	123.4	122.2	117.3	130.4	124.9	145.3
1993	116.0	174.0	147.3	119.2	124.0	123.7	120.0	133.7	128.0	145.4
1994	117.6	180.1	152.4	124.8	125.1	126.1	124.1	137.1	131.3	141.8
1993: Jan	115.7	160.2	147.0	118.9	123.9	122.6	118.4	132.7	127.1	148.6
Feb	115.7	169.3	147.1	119.2	123.9	122.9	118.6	133.1	127.8	149.4
Mar	115.6	176.9	147.3	119.0	123.9	123.0	118.9	133.3	127.8	149.4
Apr	116.0	181.2	147.7	118.7	124.0	123.2	119.6	133.4	127.7	150.4
May	115.8	179.8	147.7	118.4	123.9	123.4	119.7	133.3	127.6	150.7
June	115.9	174.1	147.1	118.9	124.0	123.6	120.0	133.3	127.7	149.6
July	115.9	171.7	147.1	119.5	124.0	123.8	120.2	133.6	127.8	149.6
Aug	116.0	171.1	147.1	119.5	124.0	124.0	120.5	133.5	127.7	138.9
Sept	116.4	173.2	147.1	119.5	124.1	124.0	120.8	131.7	124.9	138.9
Oct	116.5	174.0	147.6	119.4	124.2	124.5	121.0	135.2	129.7	138.8
Nov	116.4	177.3	147.6	119.6	124.2	124.8	121.2	135.5	129.9	139.1
Dec	116.5	179.6	147.8	120.2	124.2	124.8	121.4	135.6	130.0	140.9
1994: Jan	116.2	184.6	148.6	120.7	124.6	125.2	121.8	136.5	130.7	141.9
Feb	116.2	183.3	148.8	121.7	124.7	125.4	122.2	136.6	130.9	141.8
Mar	116.2	184.2	149.2	122.3	124.9	125.5	122.9	136.6	130.8	141.6
Apr	116.2	180.3	149.4	122.5	125.1	125.8	123.4	136.7	130.8	141.7
May	116.5	178.2	150.1	122.7	125.2	126.1	123.7	137.1	131.4	141.5
June	116.7	179.4	151.0	123.5	125.2	126.2	124.3	137.0	131.3	141.6
July	117.1	177.4	152.0	124.7	125.3	126.4	124.5	137.2	131.5	141.8
Aug [2]	117.4	177.7	153.1	125.5	125.2	126.3	124.8	137.2	131.6	141.8
Sept	118.1	178.7	154.4	126.4	125.1	126.1	125.0	135.3	128.7	141.9
Oct	119.2	177.8	155.9	127.2	125.2	126.3	125.3	138.4	132.8	141.7
Nov	120.5	179.7	157.5	129.2	125.4	126.6	125.7	138.2	132.4	142.1
Dec	120.6	179.4	159.1	130.7	125.4	126.7	125.8	138.6	133.0	142.5

Source: Department of Labor, Bureau of Labor Statistics.

TABLE B-67.—*Changes in producer price indexes for finished goods, 1958-94*

[Percent change]

Year or month	Total finished goods Dec. to Dec.[1]	Total finished goods Year to year	Finished consumer foods Dec. to Dec.[1]	Finished consumer foods Year to year	Finished goods excluding consumer foods — Total Dec. to Dec.[1]	Total Year to year	Consumer goods Dec. to Dec.[1]	Consumer goods Year to year	Capital equipment Dec. to Dec.[1]	Capital equipment Year to year	Finished energy goods Dec. to Dec.[1]	Finished energy goods Year to year	Finished goods excluding foods and energy Dec. to Dec.[1]	Finished goods excluding foods and energy Year to year
1958	0.3	2.2	0.6	6.1			0.3	0	1.2	2.6				
1959	-.3	-.3	-3.7	-4.7			.9	1.2	.9	1.9				
1960	1.8	.9	5.3	2.0			.3	.6	.3	.3				
1961	-.6	0	-1.9	-.3			-.3	-.3	0	.3				
1962	.3	.3	.6	.8			0	0	.3	.3				
1963	-.3	-.3	-1.4	-1.1			0	0	.6	.3				
1964	.6	.3	.6	.3			.3	-.3	.9	.9				
1965	3.3	1.8	9.1	4.0			.9	.9	1.5	1.2				
1966	2.0	3.2	1.3	6.5			1.8	1.5	3.8	2.4				
1967	1.7	1.1	-.3	-1.8			2.0	1.8	3.1	3.5				
1968	3.1	2.8	4.6	3.9	2.5	2.6	2.0	2.3	3.0	3.4				
1969	4.9	3.8	8.1	6.0	3.3	2.8	2.8	2.3	4.8	3.5				
1970	2.1	3.4	-2.3	3.3	4.3	3.5	3.8	3.0	4.8	4.7				
1971	3.3	3.1	5.8	1.6	2.0	3.7	2.1	3.5	2.4	4.0				
1972	3.9	3.2	7.9	5.4	2.3	2.0	2.1	1.8	2.1	2.6				
1973	11.7	9.1	22.7	20.5	6.6	4.0	7.5	4.6	5.1	3.3				
1974	18.3	15.4	12.8	14.0	21.1	16.2	20.3	17.0	22.7	14.3			17.7	11.4
1975	6.6	10.6	5.6	8.4	7.2	12.1	6.8	10.4	8.1	15.2	16.3	17.2	6.0	11.4
1976	3.8	4.5	-2.5	-.3	6.2	6.2	6.0	6.2	6.5	6.7	11.6	11.7	5.7	5.7
1977	6.7	6.4	6.9	5.3	6.8	7.1	6.7	7.3	7.2	6.4	12.0	15.7	6.2	6.0
1978	9.3	7.9	11.7	9.0	8.3	7.2	8.5	7.1	8.0	7.9	8.5	6.5	8.4	7.5
1979	12.8	11.2	7.4	9.3	14.8	11.8	17.6	13.3	8.8	8.7	58.1	35.0	9.4	8.9
1980	11.8	13.4	7.5	5.8	13.4	16.2	14.1	18.5	11.4	10.7	27.9	49.2	10.8	11.2
1981	7.1	9.2	1.5	5.8	8.7	10.3	8.6	10.3	9.2	10.3	14.1	19.1	7.7	8.6
1982	3.6	4.1	2.0	2.2	4.2	4.6	4.2	4.1	3.9	5.7	-.1	-1.5	4.9	5.7
1983	.6	1.6	2.3	1.0	0	1.8	-.9	1.2	2.0	2.8	-9.2	-4.8	1.9	3.0
1984	1.7	2.1	3.5	4.4	1.1	1.4	.8	1.0	1.8	2.3	-4.2	-4.2	2.0	2.4
1985	1.8	1.0	.6	-.8	2.2	1.4	2.1	1.1	2.7	2.2	-.2	-3.9	2.7	2.5
1986	-2.3	-1.4	2.8	2.6	-4.0	-2.6	-6.6	-4.6	2.1	2.0	-38.1	-28.1	2.7	2.3
1987	2.2	2.1	-.2	2.1	3.2	2.1	4.1	2.2	1.3	1.8	11.2	-1.9	2.1	2.4
1988	4.0	2.5	5.7	2.8	3.2	2.4	3.1	2.4	3.6	2.3	-3.6	-3.2	4.3	3.3
1989	4.9	5.2	5.2	5.4	4.8	5.0	5.3	5.6	3.8	3.9	9.5	9.9	4.2	4.4
1990	5.7	4.9	2.6	4.8	6.9	5.0	8.7	5.9	3.4	3.5	30.7	14.2	3.5	3.7
1991	-.1	2.1	-1.5	-.2	.3	3.0	-.7	2.9	2.5	3.1	-9.6	4.1	3.1	3.6
1992	1.6	1.2	1.6	-.6	1.6	1.8	1.6	1.8	1.7	1.9	-.3	-.4	2.0	2.4
1993	.2	1.2	2.4	1.9	-.4	1.1	-1.4	.7	1.8	1.8	-4.1	.3	.4	1.2
1994	1.7	.6	1.0	.9	1.9	.6	1.9	-.1	2.0	2.1	3.4	-1.3	1.6	1.0

Percent change from preceding month

	Total finished goods Unadjusted	Seasonally adjusted	Finished consumer foods Unadjusted	Seasonally adjusted	Finished goods excluding consumer foods — Total Unadjusted	Seasonally adjusted	Consumer goods Unadjusted	Seasonally adjusted	Capital equipment Unadjusted	Seasonally adjusted	Finished energy goods Unadjusted	Seasonally adjusted	Finished goods excluding foods and energy Unadjusted	Seasonally adjusted
1993: Jan	0.3	0.3	0.1	-0.2	0.3	0.5	0.2	0.5	0.5	0.5	0.3	1.0	0.4	0.4
Feb	.2	.4	.2	0	.3	.5	.3	.6	.2	.3	.4	1.4	.2	.3
Mar	.2	.2	.2	.2	.2	.3	.2	.3	.1	.2	.8	.9	.1	.1
Apr	.6	.5	1.4	1.3	.4	.2	.5	.3	0	.2	1.0	0	.3	.3
May	.2	0	.3	-.4	.2	0	.5	0	0	0	1.7	-.5	-.1	.2
June	-.2	-.5	-1.2	-.6	.1	-.4	.1	-.6	-.2	-.1	1.1	-.9	-.2	-.3
July	-.2	0	-.3	-.1	-.2	0	-.3	-.1	.2	.3	-1.1	-.8	.1	.1
Aug	-.9	-.8	.3	.3	-1.2	-1.0	-1.7	-1.6	-.1	-.2	-.6	-1.0	-1.3	-1.1
Sept	-.3	.2	.2	.6	-.5	0	-.3	-.1	-.7	.1	.5	-.1	-.7	.1
Oct	.6	-.1	-.2	-.2	.9	-.1	.6	.1	1.5	-.4	-.9	.8	1.3	-.3
Nov	-.1	.1	1.0	.8	-.5	-.1	-.7	-.2	.2	.3	-3.3	-2.1	.1	.4
Dec	-.3	-.1	.5	.6	-.5	-.4	-.7	-.6	0	.2	-3.8	-2.9	.2	.1
1994: Jan	.3	.3	-.2	-.4	.5	.7	.4	.6	.6	.7	.4	1.1	.5	.5
Feb	.2	.4	-.2	-.3	.3	.6	.5	.7	.2	.2	1.8	2.8	.1	.1
Mar	.1	.2	.6	-.6	0	0	-.1	-.1	.1	.2	-.3	-.3	0	.1
Apr	.1	0	-.3	-.5	.2	.2	.2	0	.1	.4	1.1	.3	0	.1
May	.2	-.2	-.4	-.9	.4	.1	.4	.1	.2	.3	.9	-1.2	.2	.4
June	.2	.1	-.6	0	.5	.2	.7	.2	.1	.1	2.8	.7	.1	.1
July	.3	.5	.2	.4	.3	.4	.4	.5	0	.1	1.7	2.0	0	.1
Aug[2]	.4	.5	.3	.3	.5	.6	.7	.8	.1	.2	2.3	1.8	.1	.4
Sept	-.8	-.3	-.2	.2	-.9	-.5	-1.1	-.7	-.6	-.2	-2.3	-2.9	-.7	.1
Oct	.2	-.5	-.2	-.2	.3	-.6	0	-.6	1.0	-1.0	-3.0	-1.2	1.1	-.5
Nov	.2	.5	.6	.2	.2	.6	.2	.7	0	.1	.9	2.1	0	.1
Dec	.1	.2	1.3	1.6	-.2	-.2	-.5	-.3	.2	.4	-2.6	-1.5	.2	.2

[1] Changes from December to December are based on unadjusted indexes.

[2] Data have been revised through August 1994 to reflect the availability of late reports and corrections by respondents. All data are subject to revision 4 months after original publication.

Source: Department of Labor, Bureau of Labor Statistics.

TABLE B-68.—*Money stock, liquid assets, and debt measures, 1959-94*

[Averages of daily figures; billions of dollars, seasonally adjusted]

Year and month	M1 — Sum of currency, demand deposits, travelers checks, and other checkable deposits (OCDs)	M2 — M1 plus overnight RPs and Eurodollars, MMMF balances (general purpose and broker/dealer), MMDAs, and savings and small time deposits	M3 — M2 plus large time deposits, term RPs, term Eurodollars, and institution-only MMMF balances	L — M3 plus other liquid assets	Debt¹ — Debt of domestic nonfinancial sectors (monthly average)	Percent change from year or 6 months earlier² M1	M2	M3	Debt
December:									
1959	140.0	297.8	299.8	388.6	687.7	....	4.9	5.2	7.6
1960	140.7	312.3	315.3	403.6	723.1	0.5	4.9	5.2	5.1
1961	145.2	335.5	341.0	430.8	765.8	3.2	7.4	8.2	5.9
1962	147.8	362.7	371.4	466.1	818.6	1.8	8.1	8.9	6.9
1963	153.3	393.2	406.0	503.8	873.5	3.7	8.4	9.3	6.7
1964	160.3	424.8	442.5	540.4	937.0	4.6	8.0	9.0	7.3
1965	167.9	459.3	482.2	584.4	1,003.8	4.7	8.1	9.0	7.1
1966	172.0	480.0	505.1	614.7	1,071.2	2.4	4.5	4.7	6.7
1967	183.3	524.3	557.1	666.5	1,145.4	6.6	9.2	10.3	6.9
1968	197.4	566.3	606.2	728.9	1,236.8	7.7	8.0	8.8	8.0
1969	203.9	589.5	615.0	763.5	1,326.9	3.3	4.1	1.5	7.3
1970	214.4	628.1	677.4	816.2	1,416.0	5.1	6.5	10.1	6.7
1971	228.3	712.7	776.1	902.9	1,549.5	6.5	13.5	14.6	9.4
1972	249.2	805.2	886.0	1,022.9	1,704.4	9.2	13.0	14.2	10.0
1973	262.8	861.0	984.9	1,142.4	1,890.7	5.5	6.9	11.2	10.9
1974	274.3	908.5	1,070.3	1,250.2	2,064.0	4.4	5.5	8.7	9.2
1975	287.5	1,023.2	1,172.2	1,366.9	2,251.5	4.8	12.6	9.5	9.1
1976	306.3	1,163.6	1,311.7	1,516.5	2,496.3	6.5	13.7	11.9	10.9
1977	331.1	1,286.5	1,472.5	1,705.3	2,813.7	8.1	10.6	12.3	12.7
1978	358.2	1,388.6	1,646.4	1,910.7	3,192.2	8.2	7.9	11.8	13.5
1979	382.5	1,497.0	1,803.9	2,117.1	3,568.1	6.8	7.8	9.6	11.8
1980	408.5	1,629.3	1,988.8	2,325.8	3,896.9	6.8	8.8	10.3	9.2
1981	436.3	1,793.3	2,235.9	2,598.7	4,279.3	6.8	10.1	12.4	9.8
1982	474.3	1,953.2	2,443.2	2,853.1	4,692.2	8.7	8.9	9.3	9.6
1983	521.0	2,187.6	2,696.2	3,157.6	5,244.3	9.8	12.0	10.4	11.8
1984	552.1	2,377.9	2,994.6	3,536.0	6,011.4	6.0	8.7	11.1	14.6
1985	619.9	2,575.0	3,211.6	3,838.9	6,902.1	12.3	8.3	7.2	14.8
1986	724.5	2,818.2	3,497.3	4,137.5	7,785.2	16.9	9.4	8.9	12.8
1987	750.1	2,920.1	3,681.3	4,340.2	8,544.6	3.5	3.6	5.3	9.8
1988	787.4	3,081.4	3,920.4	4,674.6	9,315.0	5.0	5.5	6.5	9.0
1989	794.7	3,239.8	4,067.3	4,897.3	10,045.1	.9	5.1	3.7	7.8
1990	826.4	3,353.0	4,125.7	4,974.8	10,690.2	4.0	3.5	1.4	6.4
1991	897.7	3,455.2	4,180.4	4,992.9	11,171.1	8.6	3.0	1.3	4.5
1992	1,024.8	3,509.0	4,183.0	5,057.1	11,706.1	14.2	1.6	.1	4.8
1993	1,128.4	3,567.9	4,232.0	5,135.0	12,335.4	10.1	1.7	1.2	5.4
1994	1,147.6	3,600.0	4,282.4	....	....	1.7	.9	1.2	....
1993: Jan	1,033.0	3,502.7	4,162.6	5,040.2	11,743.8	14.3	1.3	-1.1	4.3
Feb	1,035.4	3,494.1	4,156.7	5,036.2	11,779.3	12.2	.3	-1.9	4.0
Mar	1,040.2	3,494.7	4,155.6	5,037.5	11,830.4	10.3	-.1	-2.1	4.0
Apr	1,047.1	3,497.9	4,163.2	5,055.6	11,892.8	8.5	-.5	-1.6	4.6
May	1,067.7	3,521.8	4,188.8	5,089.4	11,953.9	10.1	.6	-.2	5.1
June	1,076.6	3,528.6	4,189.0	5,090.7	12,009.0	10.1	1.1	.3	5.2
July	1,086.4	3,533.2	4,187.9	5,087.2	12,063.9	10.3	1.7	1.2	5.5
Aug	1,095.3	3,536.0	4,188.4	5,096.4	12,121.7	11.6	2.4	1.5	5.8
Sept	1,105.1	3,544.3	4,197.6	5,089.6	12,174.9	12.5	2.8	2.0	5.8
Oct	1,113.4	3,548.0	4,205.3	5,100.3	12,211.4	12.7	2.9	2.0	5.4
Nov	1,122.4	3,560.3	4,219.0	5,113.8	12,268.4	10.2	2.2	1.4	5.3
Dec	1,128.4	3,567.9	4,232.0	5,135.0	12,335.4	9.6	2.2	2.1	5.4
1994: Jan	1,133.5	3,574.9	4,238.3	5,157.2	12,379.6	8.7	2.4	2.4	5.2
Feb	1,138.5	3,572.1	4,213.2	5,146.4	12,430.4	7.9	2.0	1.2	5.1
Mar	1,142.3	3,584.3	4,220.4	5,144.6	12,496.0	6.7	2.3	1.0	5.3
Apr	1,141.1	3,591.5	4,229.6	5,165.4	12,555.2	5.0	2.5	1.2	5.6
May	1,142.8	3,595.2	4,228.9	5,171.6	12,613.6	3.6	2.0	.5	5.6
June	1,146.3	3,588.9	4,230.4	5,162.0	12,655.5	3.2	1.2	-.1	5.2
July	1,153.1	3,604.6	4,252.8	5,189.1	12,683.4	3.5	1.7	.7	4.9
Aug	1,151.0	3,598.9	4,245.9	5,182.1	12,749.1	2.2	1.5	1.6	5.1
Sept	1,151.9	3,597.6	4,250.9	5,176.9	12,809.5	1.7	.7	1.4	5.0
Oct	1,148.5	3,592.6	4,259.6	5,205.5	12,856.8	1.3	.1	1.4	4.8
Nov	1,147.6	3,594.2	4,267.0	5,217.8	12,924.3	.8	-.1	1.8	4.9
Dec	1,147.6	3,600.0	4,282.4	....	....	.2	.6	2.5	....

¹ Consists of outstanding credit market debt of the U.S. Government, State and local governments, and private nonfinancial sectors; data derived from flow of funds accounts.

² Annual changes are from December to December; monthly changes are from 6 months earlier at a simple annual rate.

Note.—See Table B-69 for components.

Note.—See Table B-69 for components.

Data do not reflect revisions released on February 2, 1995.

Source: Board of Governors of the Federal Reserve System.

TABLE B–69.—*Components of money stock measures and liquid assets, 1959–94*

[Averages of daily figures; billions of dollars, seasonally adjusted, except as noted]

Year and month	Currency	Travelers checks	Demand deposits	Other checkable deposits (OCDs)	Overnight repurchase agreements (RPs) net, plus overnight Eurodollars [1] NSA	Money market mutual fund (MMMF) balances		Savings deposits, including money market deposit accounts (MMDAs) [3]
						General purpose and broker/ dealer [2]	Institution only [2]	
December:								
1959	28.8	0.3	110.8	0.0	0.0	0.0	0.0	146.5
1960	28.7	.3	111.6	.0	.0	.0	.0	159.1
1961	29.3	.4	115.5	.0	.0	.0	.0	175.5
1962	30.3	.4	117.1	.0	.0	.0	.0	194.7
1963	32.2	.4	120.6	.1	.0	.0	.0	214.4
1964	33.9	.5	125.8	.1	.0	.0	.0	235.3
1965	36.0	.5	131.3	.1	.0	.0	.0	256.9
1966	38.0	.6	133.4	.1	.0	.0	.0	253.2
1967	40.0	.6	142.5	.1	.0	.0	.0	263.7
1968	43.0	.7	153.6	.1	.0	.0	.0	268.9
1969	45.7	.8	157.3	.2	2.2	.0	.0	263.6
1970	48.6	.9	164.8	.1	1.3	.0	.0	260.9
1971	52.0	1.0	175.1	.2	2.3	.0	.0	292.2
1972	56.2	1.2	191.6	.2	2.8	.0	.0	321.4
1973	60.8	1.4	200.3	.3	5.3	.0	.0	326.7
1974	67.0	1.7	205.1	.4	5.7	1.7	.2	338.6
1975	72.8	2.1	211.6	.9	6.0	2.7	.4	388.9
1976	79.5	2.6	221.5	2.7	10.8	2.4	.6	453.3
1977	87.4	2.9	236.7	4.2	15.0	2.4	.9	492.4
1978	96.0	3.3	250.4	8.4	20.8	6.4	3.1	482.2
1979	104.8	3.5	257.4	16.8	22.4	33.4	9.5	424.1
1980	115.4	3.9	261.2	28.0	29.3	61.6	15.2	400.6
1981	122.6	4.1	231.2	78.4	37.6	150.6	38.0	344.2
1982	132.5	4.1	233.8	103.9	40.8	185.6	50.0	400.4
1983	146.2	4.7	238.2	132.0	57.3	139.0	41.4	685.1
1984	156.1	5.0	243.7	147.4	63.0	167.9	62.5	704.8
1985	167.9	5.6	266.6	179.8	75.6	177.4	64.7	815.4
1986	180.7	6.1	302.1	235.6	83.3	209.8	85.3	941.0
1987	196.9	6.6	287.1	259.5	85.7	223.5	92.0	937.7
1988	212.2	7.0	287.2	280.9	84.1	244.4	91.5	926.7
1989	222.6	6.9	279.8	285.4	80.2	320.4	108.5	891.0
1990	246.7	7.8	277.9	294.0	77.3	355.5	135.0	920.4
1991	267.1	7.7	290.0	332.8	80.6	370.4	181.0	1,041.1
1992	292.2	8.1	339.6	384.9	80.6	352.0	201.5	1,183.6
1993	321.4	7.9	384.8	414.3	92.3	348.8	197.0	1,215.5
1994	353.6	8.4	383.3	402.3	117.2	374.5	176.6	1,145.5
1993: Jan	294.5	8.0	341.9	388.6	77.8	350.3	196.6	1,183.8
Feb	297.0	8.0	342.7	387.7	77.7	345.3	198.0	1,183.7
Mar	299.3	8.0	344.3	388.5	78.8	345.9	197.7	1,182.4
Apr	301.8	8.1	349.0	388.2	77.2	345.9	196.3	1,185.5
May	304.4	8.1	358.8	396.4	75.2	348.5	198.0	1,195.1
June	307.2	8.0	362.2	399.2	78.5	347.5	194.7	1,200.4
July	309.7	7.9	366.0	402.8	81.2	346.6	192.6	1,202.1
Aug	312.4	7.8	370.9	404.2	82.2	345.5	190.1	1,205.9
Sept	315.4	7.8	375.4	406.6	85.5	345.0	190.8	1,208.4
Oct	317.6	7.8	378.4	409.5	89.5	344.4	194.3	1,208.8
Nov	319.5	7.9	383.2	411.8	90.6	347.0	194.8	1,211.9
Dec	321.4	7.9	384.8	414.3	92.3	348.8	197.0	1,215.5
1994: Jan	325.2	7.9	388.3	412.0	95.1	349.3	192.7	1,220.3
Feb	329.2	7.9	390.3	411.2	93.5	345.8	176.9	1,220.9
Mar	332.4	8.0	390.0	411.9	98.5	348.2	177.4	1,221.9
Apr	334.8	8.1	388.9	409.3	97.1	359.4	177.0	1,220.7
May	337.6	8.1	385.7	411.2	100.3	361.9	169.3	1,215.9
June	340.3	8.1	386.5	411.4	104.7	356.3	169.5	1,207.2
July	343.2	8.2	389.1	412.5	109.9	361.7	170.9	1,202.5
Aug	345.4	8.3	387.5	409.7	111.6	361.1	169.3	1,194.8
Sept	347.4	8.4	388.0	408.2	113.1	360.5	167.9	1,186.6
Oct	350.0	8.4	385.8	404.3	114.9	363.3	175.3	1,173.4
Nov	352.9	8.4	383.4	402.8	113.6	368.1	175.6	1,159.8
Dec	353.6	8.4	383.3	402.3	117.2	374.5	176.6	1,145.5

[1] Includes continuing contract RPs.
[2] Data prior to 1983 are not seasonally adjusted.
[3] Data prior to 1982 are savings deposits only; MMDA data begin December 1982.

See next page for continuation of table.

[Averages of daily figures; billions of dollars, seasonally adjusted, except as noted]

Year and month	Small denomination time deposits [4]	Large denomination time deposits [4]	Term repurchase agreements (RPs) NSA	Term Euro-dollars NSA	Savings bonds	Short-term Treasury securities	Bankers acceptances	Commercial paper
December:								
1959	11.4	1.2	0.0	0.7	46.1	38.6	0.6	3.6
1960	12.5	2.0	.0	.8	45.7	36.7	.9	5.1
1961	14.8	3.9	.0	1.5	46.5	37.0	1.1	5.2
1962	20.1	7.0	.0	1.6	46.9	39.8	1.1	6.8
1963	25.6	10.8	.0	1.9	48.1	40.7	1.2	7.7
1964	29.2	15.2	.0	2.4	49.0	38.5	1.3	9.1
1965	34.5	21.2	.0	1.8	49.6	40.7	1.6	10.2
1966	55.0	23.1	.0	2.2	50.2	43.2	1.8	14.4
1967	77.8	30.9	.0	2.2	51.2	38.7	1.8	17.8
1968	100.6	37.4	.0	2.9	51.8	46.1	2.3	22.5
1969	120.4	20.4	2.7	2.7	51.7	59.5	3.3	34.0
1970	151.2	45.1	1.6	2.2	52.0	48.8	3.5	34.5
1971	189.8	57.6	2.7	2.7	54.3	36.0	3.8	32.7
1972	231.7	73.3	3.5	3.6	57.6	40.7	3.5	35.2
1973	265.8	111.0	6.7	5.5	60.4	49.3	5.0	42.8
1974	287.9	144.7	7.8	8.1	63.3	52.8	12.6	51.2
1975	337.8	129.7	8.1	9.8	67.2	68.4	10.7	48.5
1976	390.7	118.1	13.9	14.8	71.8	69.8	10.8	52.5
1977	445.4	145.2	18.9	20.2	76.4	78.3	14.1	64.0
1978	520.9	195.6	26.2	31.8	80.3	81.3	22.0	80.7
1979	634.2	223.2	29.1	44.7	79.5	108.2	27.1	98.3
1980	728.5	260.3	33.5	50.3	72.3	133.9	32.0	98.8
1981	823.1	303.0	35.3	67.5	67.8	149.8	39.9	105.3
1982	850.8	327.2	33.4	81.7	68.0	183.8	44.5	113.6
1983	784.1	327.7	49.9	91.5	71.1	212.1	45.0	133.2
1984	888.8	416.6	57.6	82.9	74.2	261.0	45.4	160.7
1985	885.7	434.3	62.4	76.5	79.5	298.3	42.1	207.5
1986	859.0	431.5	80.6	83.8	91.8	280.0	37.1	231.3
1987	922.7	475.5	106.0	91.0	100.6	253.1	44.5	260.6
1988	1,038.6	525.5	121.8	105.7	109.4	269.3	40.2	335.4
1989	1,153.7	549.1	99.0	79.5	117.5	325.5	40.6	346.5
1990	1,174.5	489.5	89.6	68.7	126.0	332.0	35.9	355.2
1991	1,067.4	425.8	72.5	57.6	137.9	316.2	23.6	334.8
1992	870.5	360.3	81.1	45.7	156.6	332.5	20.6	364.3
1993	785.7	339.0	96.8	47.0	171.7	329.9	14.6	386.8
1994	818.1	363.6	103.6	53.7	....			
1993: Jan	860.8	353.2	80.3	43.6	158.7	337.3	20.6	361.0
Feb	853.7	350.1	82.9	46.8	160.8	339.4	20.0	359.4
Mar	846.7	344.8	87.0	49.9	162.4	338.5	19.4	361.5
Apr	839.3	348.8	90.1	48.8	163.6	342.4	19.3	367.1
May	832.3	348.2	91.0	48.8	164.7	344.8	19.2	371.8
June	823.8	345.3	94.1	45.5	165.9	346.5	18.5	370.9
July	814.4	341.8	97.8	41.9	167.1	344.3	17.4	370.4
Aug	806.5	341.6	97.6	44.1	168.2	343.8	16.5	379.5
Sept	799.9	340.4	97.3	45.2	169.2	328.0	16.4	378.4
Oct	794.9	341.6	95.9	45.0	170.1	323.7	16.4	384.7
Nov	790.6	339.4	95.6	48.9	170.8	324.6	15.3	384.1
Dec	785.7	339.0	96.8	47.0	171.7	329.9	14.6	386.8
1994: Jan	779.7	341.8	92.9	46.0	172.7	339.8	14.9	391.6
Feb	775.1	336.5	91.5	48.1	173.4	341.5	15.3	403.0
Mar	772.2	332.2	94.0	47.2	174.1	344.8	15.7	389.6
Apr	770.0	332.3	97.9	47.5	174.8	361.9	14.2	384.9
May	770.9	335.5	97.1	48.7	175.7	364.5	11.5	391.0
June	772.8	336.2	101.1	51.3	176.6	351.8	10.6	392.6
July	774.8	338.5	102.2	52.1	177.5	355.3	10.8	392.7
Aug	779.8	341.0	100.6	52.5	178.4	359.5	11.3	387.0
Sept	785.3	346.7	101.6	53.2	179.0	344.1	12.0	391.0
Oct	795.7	353.0	101.4	54.1	179.4	346.8	11.9	407.8
Nov	807.9	359.0	102.1	55.9	179.9	354.3	10.7	405.9
Dec	818.1	363.6	103.6	53.7				

[4] Small denomination and large denomination deposits are those issued in amounts of less than $100,000 and more than $100,000, respectively.

Note.—NSA indicates data are not seasonally adjusted.

See also Table B-68.

Data do not reflect revisions released on February 2, 1995.

Source: Board of Governors of the Federal Reserve System.

[Averages of daily figures [1]; millions of dollars; seasonally adjusted, except as noted]

| Year and month | Adjusted for changes in reserve requirements [2] | | | | | Borrowings of depository institutions from the Federal Reserve, NSA | | |
| | Reserves of depository institutions | | | | Mone-tary base | | | |
	Total	Nonbor-rowed	Nonbor-rowed plus extended credit	Required		Total	Seasonal	Extended credit
December:								
1959	11,109	10,168	10,168	10,603	40,880	941		
1960	11,247	11,172	11,172	10,503	40,977	74		
1961	11,499	11,366	11,366	10,915	41,853	133		
1962	11,604	11,344	11,344	11,033	42,957	260		
1963	11,730	11,397	11,397	11,239	45,003	332		
1964	12,011	11,747	11,747	11,605	47,161	264		
1965	12,316	11,872	11,872	11,892	49,620	444		
1966	12,223	11,690	11,690	11,884	51,565	532		
1967	13,180	12,952	12,952	12,805	54,579	228		
1968	13,767	13,021	13,021	13,341	58,357	746		
1969	14,168	13,049	13,049	13,882	61,569	1,119		
1970	14,558	14,225	14,225	14,309	65,013	332		
1971	15,230	15,104	15,104	15,049	69,108	126		
1972	16,645	15,595	15,595	16,361	75,167	1,050		
1973	17,021	15,723	15,723	16,717	81,073	1,298	41	
1974	17,550	16,823	16,970	17,292	87,535	727	32	147
1975	17,822	17,692	17,704	17,556	93,887	130	14	12
1976	18,388	18,335	18,335	18,115	101,515	53	13	
1977	18,990	18,420	18,420	18,800	110,323	569	55	
1978	19,753	18,885	18,885	19,521	120,445	868	135	
1979	20,720	19,248	19,248	20,279	131,143	1,473	82	
1980	22,015	20,325	20,328	21,501	142,004	1,690	116	3
1981	22,443	21,807	21,956	22,124	149,021	636	54	148
1982	23,600	22,966	23,152	23,100	160,127	634	33	186
1983	25,367	24,593	24,595	24,806	175,467	774	96	2
1984	26,847	23,661	26,265	25,992	187,224	3,186	113	2,604
1985	31,451	30,132	30,632	30,414	203,543	1,318	56	499
1986	38,935	38,108	38,411	37,565	223,576	827	38	303
1987	38,849	38,072	38,555	37,803	239,775	777	93	483
1988	40,396	38,681	39,925	39,349	256,870	1,716	130	1,244
1989	40,496	40,231	40,251	39,574	267,696	265	84	20
1990	41,769	41,444	41,466	40,105	293,157	326	76	23
1991	45,532	45,340	45,340	44,553	317,122	192	38	1
1992	54,341	54,218	54,218	53,186	350,609	124	18	1
1993	60,476	60,394	60,394	59,413	385,855	82	31	0
1994	59,003	58,794	58,794	57,856	417,076	209	100	0
1993: Jan	54,684	54,519	54,520	53,425	353,152	165	11	1
Feb	54,906	54,861	54,861	53,802	355,913	45	18	0
Mar	55,228	55,137	55,137	54,015	358,590	91	26	0
Apr	55,306	55,233	55,233	54,210	361,166	73	41	0
May	56,740	56,618	56,618	55,743	365,294	121	84	0
June	57,048	56,867	56,867	56,138	368,194	181	142	0
July	57,546	57,302	57,302	56,457	371,286	244	210	0
Aug	58,011	57,659	57,659	57,059	374,340	352	234	0
Sept	58,813	58,386	58,386	57,723	378,076	428	236	0
Oct	59,749	59,464	59,464	58,660	381,400	285	192	0
Nov	60,320	60,231	60,231	59,219	384,029	89	75	0
Dec	60,476	60,394	60,394	59,413	385,855	82	31	0
1994: Jan	60,603	60,529	60,529	59,155	389,613	73	15	0
Feb	60,763	60,693	60,693	59,623	393,960	70	15	0
Mar	60,588	60,533	60,533	59,621	397,014	55	24	0
Apr	60,333	60,208	60,208	59,181	399,198	124	57	0
May	59,910	59,709	59,709	58,995	401,725	200	134	0
June	59,708	59,374	59,374	58,603	404,319	333	226	0
July	59,819	59,361	59,361	58,712	407,043	458	364	0
Aug	59,518	59,050	59,050	58,514	409,200	469	445	0
Sept	59,483	58,996	58,996	58,423	411,084	487	444	0
Oct	59,170	58,790	58,790	58,366	413,399	380	339	0
Nov	59,012	58,763	58,763	58,004	416,463	249	164	0
Dec	59,025	58,816	58,816	57,856	417,076	209	100	0

[1] Data are prorated averages of biweekly (maintenance period) averages of daily figures.
[2] Aggregate reserves incorporate adjustments for discontinuities associated with regulatory changes to reserve requirements. For details on aggregate reserves series see *Federal Reserve Bulletin.*

Note.—NSA indicates data are not seasonally adjusted.

Monetary base data do not reflect revisions released on February 2, 1995.

Source: Board of Governors of the Federal Reserve System.

TABLE B-71.—*Bank credit at all commercial banks, 1972–94*

[Monthly average; billions of dollars, seasonally adjusted [1]]

Year and month	Total bank credit	Securities in bank credit			Loans and leases in bank credit							
		Total securities	U.S. Government securities	Other securities	Total loans and leases [2]	Commercial and industrial	Real estate			Consumer	Security	Other
							Total	Revolving home equity	Other			
December:												
1972	572.5	182.4	89.0	93.4	390.1	137.1	98.1			86.3	15.6	53.0
1973	647.8	187.6	88.2	99.4	460.2	165.0	117.3			98.6	12.9	66.4
1974	713.7	193.8	86.3	107.5	519.9	196.6	130.1			102.4	12.7	78.1
1975	745.1	227.9	116.7	111.2	517.2	189.3	134.4			104.9	13.5	75.1
1976	804.6	249.8	136.3	113.5	554.8	190.9	148.8			116.3	17.7	81.1
1977	891.5	259.3	136.6	122.7	632.3	211.0	175.2			138.3	21.0	86.8
1978	1,013.9	266.8	137.6	129.2	747.1	246.2	210.5			164.7	19.7	106.0
1979	1,135.6	286.2	144.3	141.9	849.4	291.4	241.9			184.5	18.7	112.9
1980	1,238.6	325.0	170.6	154.4	913.5	325.7	262.6			179.2	18.0	128.0
1981	1,307.0	339.8	179.3	160.5	967.3	355.4	284.1			182.5	21.4	123.9
1982	1,400.4	366.5	201.7	164.8	1,033.9	392.5	299.9			188.2	25.3	128.0
1983	1,552.2	428.3	259.2	169.1	1,123.9	414.2	331.0			212.9	28.0	137.8
1984	1,722.9	400.7	259.8	140.9	1,322.2	473.2	376.3			254.2	35.0	183.5
1985	1,910.4	449.8	270.8	179.0	1,460.6	500.2	425.9			295.0	43.3	196.2
1986	2,093.7	504.0	310.1	193.9	1,589.7	536.7	494.1			315.4	40.3	203.2
1987	2,241.2	531.6	335.8	195.8	1,709.6	566.4	587.2			328.2	34.5	193.3
New series												
1988	2,435.7	562.4	367.1	195.3	1,873.3	607.9	674.5	40.1	634.5	357.7	41.0	192.1
1989	2,608.6	584.5	400.0	184.5	2,024.1	639.0	769.6	50.3	719.3	378.2	41.9	195.4
1990	2,749.7	633.8	455.6	178.2	2,115.9	640.0	854.5	62.3	792.2	383.5	45.2	192.8
1991	2,852.5	743.4	563.9	179.5	2,109.1	618.6	878.9	69.6	809.3	366.4	54.7	190.5
1992	2,949.7	839.7	663.3	176.3	2,110.0	594.2	900.3	73.6	826.7	358.8	64.6	192.1
1993	3,105.3	911.6	727.3	184.4	2,193.6	583.4	940.8	73.2	867.6	391.2	87.7	190.5
1994	3,323.4	950.5	717.6	232.8	2,372.9	644.3	999.9	75.9	924.0	450.4	76.6	201.7
1993: Jan	2,954.2	843.9	668.5	175.4	2,110.3	594.3	899.2	73.6	825.7	361.3	63.8	191.6
Feb	2,968.8	856.8	679.6	177.2	2,112.0	594.8	900.5	73.9	826.6	363.4	62.6	190.7
Mar	2,984.5	870.5	690.7	179.8	2,114.0	592.5	902.3	74.7	827.6	364.9	64.8	189.5
Apr	2,991.9	878.9	697.3	181.6	2,113.0	587.7	902.7	75.1	827.6	367.1	63.7	191.9
May	3,015.6	883.9	701.4	182.5	2,131.7	591.2	907.5	75.2	832.3	369.3	69.4	194.3
June	3,037.9	892.2	710.4	181.8	2,145.7	592.4	913.2	75.1	838.1	371.1	73.1	195.9
July	3,060.7	896.5	714.2	182.2	2,164.2	590.5	916.9	75.0	841.9	375.3	83.1	198.4
Aug	3,065.2	902.7	718.3	184.4	2,162.6	588.8	919.8	74.7	845.1	378.1	80.4	195.5
Sept	3,072.8	904.5	720.4	184.1	2,168.3	586.6	923.1	74.4	848.7	380.3	82.4	196.0
Oct	3,074.7	899.6	717.5	182.1	2,175.1	586.0	927.2	73.8	853.3	384.8	81.8	195.4
Nov	3,090.9	902.8	720.8	181.9	2,188.1	584.3	934.0	73.5	860.5	388.4	88.2	193.2
Dec	3,105.3	911.6	727.3	184.4	2,193.6	583.4	940.8	73.2	867.6	391.2	87.7	190.5
1994: Jan	3,142.0	941.9	732.5	209.5	2,200.1	588.3	942.8	73.0	869.8	394.3	81.1	193.5
Feb	3,153.0	943.2	731.9	211.3	2,209.8	590.7	942.2	73.2	869.1	398.0	82.3	196.6
Mar	3,178.5	960.2	746.7	213.4	2,218.4	595.3	943.0	73.3	869.8	402.5	83.4	194.0
Apr	3,206.1	976.2	757.0	219.2	2,229.9	602.1	946.3	73.4	872.9	408.9	77.0	195.6
May	3,211.8	972.0	750.1	221.9	2,239.8	607.2	949.0	73.7	875.2	412.5	77.5	193.6
June	3,224.0	974.6	750.9	223.6	2,249.4	610.4	956.0	74.1	881.9	416.3	76.2	190.5
July	3,260.3	979.5	751.5	228.0	2,280.8	618.9	962.9	74.2	888.7	424.3	77.7	197.1
Aug	3,270.9	971.9	746.8	225.1	2,299.0	623.6	971.6	74.4	897.2	430.3	75.0	198.4
Sept	3,280.5	968.1	741.1	227.0	2,312.4	628.0	979.2	74.7	904.4	435.2	69.1	200.9
Oct	3,287.7	957.6	727.9	229.7	2,330.2	634.1	983.9	75.0	908.9	442.1	72.1	197.9
Nov	3,297.2	950.6	719.9	230.7	2,346.6	639.4	990.3	75.6	914.8	444.9	73.3	198.6
Dec	3,323.4	950.5	717.6	232.8	2,372.9	644.3	999.9	75.9	924.0	450.4	76.6	201.7

[1] Data are Wednesday values or prorated averages of Wednesday values for domestically chartered commercial banks, branches and agencies of foreign banks, New York State investment companies, and foreign-related institutions. Beginning 1988, data are adjusted for breaks caused by reclassifications of assets and liabilities.

[2] Excludes Federal funds sold to, reverse repurchase agreements (RPs) with, and loans to commercial banks in the United States.

Note.—Data are not strictly comparable because of breaks in the series.

Source: Board of Governors of the Federal Reserve System.

[Percent per annum]

Year and month	U.S. Treasury securities					Corporate bonds (Moody's)		High-grade munici-pal bonds (Stand-ard & Poor's) [3]	New-home mort-gage yields [3]	Com-mer-cial paper, 6 months [4]	Prime rate charged by banks [5]	Discount rate, Federal Reserve Bank of New York [5]	Federal funds rate [6]
	Bills (new issues) [1]		Constant maturities [2]										
	3-month	6-month	3-year	10-year	30-year	Aaa	Baa						
1929						4.73	5.90	4.27		5.85	5.50–6.00	5.16	
1933	0.515					4.49	7.76	4.71		1.73	1.50–4.00	2.56	
1939	.023					3.01	4.96	2.76		.59	1.50	1.00	
1940	.014					2.84	4.75	2.50		.56	1.50	1.00	
1941	.103					2.77	4.33	2.10		.53	1.50	1.00	
1942	.326					2.83	4.28	2.36		.66	1.50	[7]1.00	
1943	.373					2.73	3.91	2.06		.69	1.50	[7]1.00	
1944	.375					2.72	3.61	1.86		.73	1.50	[7]1.00	
1945	.375					2.62	3.29	1.67		.75	1.50	[7]1.00	
1946	.375					2.53	3.05	1.64		.81	1.50	[7]1.00	
1947	.594					2.61	3.24	2.01		1.03	1.50–1.75	1.00	
1948	1.040					2.82	3.47	2.40		1.44	1.75–2.00	1.34	
1949	1.102					2.66	3.42	2.21		1.49	2.00	1.50	
1950	1.218					2.62	3.24	1.98		1.45	2.07	1.59	
1951	1.552					2.86	3.41	2.00		2.16	2.56	1.75	
1952	1.766					2.96	3.52	2.19		2.33	3.00	1.75	
1953	1.931		2.47	2.85		3.20	3.74	2.72		2.52	3.17	1.99	
1954	.953		1.63	2.40		2.90	3.51	2.37		1.58	3.05	1.60	
1955	1.753		2.47	2.82		3.06	3.53	2.53		2.18	3.16	1.89	1.78
1956	2.658		3.19	3.18		3.36	3.88	2.93		3.31	3.77	2.77	2.73
1957	3.267		3.98	3.65		3.89	4.71	3.60		3.81	4.20	3.12	3.11
1958	1.839		2.84	3.32		3.79	4.73	3.56		2.46	3.83	2.15	1.57
1959	3.405	3.832	4.46	4.33		4.38	5.05	3.95		3.97	4.48	3.36	3.30
1960	2.928	3.247	3.98	4.12		4.41	5.19	3.73		3.85	4.82	3.53	3.22
1961	2.378	2.605	3.54	3.88		4.35	5.08	3.46		2.97	4.50	3.00	1.96
1962	2.778	2.908	3.47	3.95		4.33	5.02	3.18		3.26	4.50	3.00	2.68
1963	3.157	3.253	3.67	4.00		4.26	4.86	3.23	5.89	3.55	4.50	3.23	3.18
1964	3.549	3.686	4.03	4.19		4.40	4.83	3.22	5.83	3.97	4.50	3.55	3.50
1965	3.954	4.055	4.22	4.28		4.49	4.87	3.27	5.81	4.38	4.54	4.04	4.07
1966	4.881	5.082	5.23	4.92		5.13	5.67	3.82	6.25	5.55	5.63	4.50	5.11
1967	4.321	4.630	5.03	5.07		5.51	6.23	3.98	6.46	5.10	5.61	4.19	4.22
1968	5.339	5.470	5.68	5.65		6.18	6.94	4.51	6.97	5.90	6.30	5.16	5.66
1969	6.677	6.853	7.02	6.67		7.03	7.81	5.81	7.81	7.83	7.96	5.87	8.20
1970	6.458	6.562	7.29	7.35		8.04	9.11	6.51	8.45	7.71	7.91	5.95	7.18
1971	4.348	4.511	5.65	6.16		7.39	8.56	5.70	7.74	5.11	5.72	4.88	4.66
1972	4.071	4.466	5.72	6.21		7.21	8.16	5.27	7.60	4.73	5.25	4.50	4.43
1973	7.041	7.178	6.95	6.84		7.44	8.24	5.18	7.96	8.15	8.03	6.44	8.73
1974	7.886	7.926	7.82	7.56		8.57	9.50	6.09	8.92	9.84	10.81	7.83	10.50
1975	5.838	6.122	7.49	7.99		8.83	10.61	6.89	9.00	6.32	7.86	6.25	5.82
1976	4.989	5.266	6.77	7.61		8.43	9.75	6.49	9.00	5.34	6.84	5.50	5.04
1977	5.265	5.510	6.69	7.42	7.75	8.02	8.97	5.56	9.02	5.61	6.83	5.46	5.54
1978	7.221	7.572	8.29	8.41	8.49	8.73	9.49	5.90	9.56	7.99	9.06	7.46	7.93
1979	10.041	10.017	9.71	9.44	9.28	9.63	10.69	6.39	10.78	10.91	12.67	10.28	11.19
1980	11.506	11.374	11.55	11.46	11.27	11.94	13.67	8.51	12.66	12.29	15.27	11.77	13.36
1981	14.029	13.776	14.44	13.91	13.45	14.17	16.04	11.23	14.70	14.76	18.87	13.42	16.38
1982	10.686	11.084	12.92	13.00	12.76	13.79	16.11	11.57	15.14	11.89	14.86	11.02	12.26
1983	8.63	8.75	10.45	11.10	11.18	12.04	13.55	9.47	12.57	8.89	10.79	8.50	9.09
1984	9.58	9.80	11.89	12.44	12.41	12.71	14.19	10.15	12.38	10.16	12.04	8.80	10.23
1985	7.48	7.66	9.64	10.62	10.79	11.37	12.72	9.18	11.55	8.01	9.93	7.69	8.10
1986	5.98	6.03	7.06	7.68	7.78	9.02	10.39	7.38	10.17	6.39	8.33	6.33	6.81
1987	5.82	6.05	7.68	8.39	8.59	9.38	10.58	7.73	9.31	6.85	8.21	5.66	6.66
1988	6.69	6.92	8.26	8.85	8.96	9.71	10.83	7.76	9.19	7.68	9.32	6.20	7.57
1989	8.12	8.04	8.55	8.49	8.45	9.26	10.18	7.24	10.13	8.80	10.87	6.93	9.21
1990	7.51	7.47	8.26	8.55	8.61	9.32	10.36	7.25	10.05	7.95	10.01	6.98	8.10
1991	5.42	5.49	6.82	7.86	8.14	8.77	9.80	6.89	9.32	5.85	8.46	5.45	5.69
1992	3.45	3.57	5.30	7.01	7.67	8.14	8.98	6.41	8.24	3.80	6.25	3.25	3.52
1993	3.02	3.14	4.44	5.87	6.59	7.22	7.93	5.63	7.20	3.30	6.00	3.00	3.02
1994	4.29	4.66	6.27	7.09	7.37	7.97	8.63	6.19	7.49	4.93	7.15	3.60	4.21

[1] Rate on new issues within period; bank-discount basis.

[2] Yields on the more actively traded issues adjusted to constant maturities by the Treasury Department.

[3] Effective rate (in the primary market) on conventional mortgages, reflecting fees and charges as well as contract rate and assuming, on the average, repayment at end of 10 years. Rates beginning January 1973 not strictly comparable with prior rates.

[4] Bank-discount basis; prior to November 1979, data are for 4–6 months paper.

[5] For monthly data, high and low for the period. Prime rate for 1929–33 and 1947–48 are ranges of the rate in effect during the period.

[6] Since July 19, 1975, the daily effective rate is an average of the rates on a given day weighted by the volume of transactions at these rates. Prior to that date, the daily effective rate was the rate considered most representative of the day's transactions, usually the one at which most transactions occurred.

[7] From October 30, 1942, to April 24, 1946, a preferential rate of 0.50 percent was in effect for advances secured by Government securities maturing in 1 year or less.

See next page for continuation of table.

[Percent per annum]

Year and month	U.S. Treasury securities					Corporate bonds (Moody's)		High-grade municipal bonds (Standard & Poor's)	New home mortgage yields[3]	Commercial paper, 6 months[4]	Prime rate charged by banks[5]	Discount rate, Federal Reserve Bank of New York[5]	Federal funds rate[6]
	Bills (new issues)[1]		Constant maturities[2]										
	3-month	6-month	3-year	10-year	30-year	Aaa	Baa				High-low	High-low	
1990:													
Jan	7.64	7.52	8.13	8.21	8.26	8.99	9.94	7.13	9.91	7.96	10.50–10.00	7.00–7.00	8.23
Feb	7.76	7.72	8.39	8.47	8.50	9.22	10.14	7.21	9.88	8.04	10.00–10.00	7.00–7.00	8.24
Mar	7.87	7.83	8.63	8.59	8.56	9.37	10.21	7.29	10.03	8.23	10.00–10.00	7.00–7.00	8.28
Apr	7.78	7.82	8.78	8.79	8.76	9.46	10.30	7.36	10.17	8.29	10.00–10.00	7.00–7.00	8.26
May	7.78	7.82	8.69	8.76	8.73	9.47	10.41	7.34	10.28	8.23	10.00–10.00	7.00–7.00	8.18
June	7.74	7.64	8.40	8.48	8.46	9.26	10.22	7.22	10.13	8.06	10.00–10.00	7.00–7.00	8.29
July	7.66	7.57	8.26	8.47	8.50	9.24	10.20	7.15	10.08	7.90	10.00–10.00	7.00–7.00	8.15
Aug	7.44	7.36	8.22	8.75	8.86	9.41	10.41	7.31	10.11	7.77	10.00–10.00	7.00–7.00	8.13
Sept	7.38	7.33	8.27	8.89	9.03	9.56	10.64	7.40	9.90	7.83	10.00–10.00	7.00–7.00	8.20
Oct	7.19	7.20	3.07	8.72	8.86	9.53	10.74	7.40	9.98	7.81	10.00–10.00	7.00–7.00	8.11
Nov	7.07	7.04	7.74	8.39	8.54	9.30	10.62	7.10	9.90	7.74	10.00–10.00	7.00–7.00	7.81
Dec	6.81	6.76	7.47	8.08	8.24	9.05	10.43	7.04	9.76	7.49	10.00–10.00	7.00–6.50	7.31
1991:													
Jan	6.30	6.34	7.38	8.09	8.27	9.04	10.45	7.05	9.65	7.02	10.00– 9.50	6.50–6.50	6.91
Feb	5.95	5.93	7.08	7.85	8.03	8.83	10.07	6.90	9.57	6.41	9.50– 9.00	6.50–6.00	6.25
Mar	5.91	5.91	7.35	8.11	8.29	8.93	10.09	7.07	9.43	6.36	9.00– 9.00	6.00–6.00	6.12
Apr	5.67	5.73	7.23	8.04	8.21	8.86	9.94	7.05	9.60	6.07	9.00– 9.00	6.00–5.50	5.91
May	5.51	5.65	7.12	8.07	8.27	8.86	9.86	6.95	9.52	5.94	9.00– 8.50	5.50–5.50	5.78
June	5.60	5.76	7.39	8.28	8.47	9.01	9.96	7.09	9.46	6.16	8.50– 8.50	5.50–5.50	5.90
July	5.58	5.71	7.38	8.27	8.45	9.00	9.89	7.03	9.43	6.14	8.50– 8.50	5.50–5.50	5.82
Aug	5.39	5.47	6.80	7.90	8.14	8.75	9.65	6.89	9.48	5.76	8.50– 8.50	5.50–5.50	5.66
Sept	5.25	5.29	6.50	7.65	7.95	8.61	9.51	6.80	9.30	5.59	8.50– 8.00	5.50–5.00	5.45
Oct	5.03	5.08	6.23	7.53	7.93	8.55	9.49	6.59	9.04	5.33	8.00– 8.00	5.00–5.00	5.21
Nov	4.60	4.66	5.90	7.42	7.92	8.48	9.45	6.64	8.64	4.93	8.00– 7.50	5.00–4.50	4.81
Dec	4.12	4.16	5.39	7.09	7.70	8.31	9.26	6.63	8.53	4.49	7.50– 6.50	4.50–3.50	4.43
1992:													
Jan	3.84	3.88	5.40	7.03	7.58	8.20	9.13	6.41	8.49	4.06	6.50–6.50	3.50–3.50	4.03
Feb	3.84	3.94	5.72	7.34	7.85	8.29	9.23	6.67	8.65	4.13	6.50–6.50	3.50–3.50	4.06
Mar	4.05	4.19	6.18	7.54	7.97	8.35	9.25	6.69	8.51	4.38	6.50–6.50	3.50–3.50	3.98
Apr	3.81	3.93	5.93	7.48	7.96	8.33	9.21	6.64	8.58	4.13	6.50–6.50	3.50–3.50	3.73
May	3.66	3.78	5.81	7.39	7.89	8.28	9.13	6.57	8.59	3.97	6.50–6.50	3.50–3.50	3.82
June	3.70	3.81	5.60	7.26	7.84	8.22	9.05	6.50	8.43	3.99	6.50–6.50	3.50–3.50	3.76
July	3.28	3.36	4.91	6.84	7.60	8.07	8.84	6.12	8.00	3.53	6.50–6.00	3.50–3.00	3.25
Aug	3.14	3.23	4.72	6.59	7.39	7.95	8.65	6.08	8.00	3.44	6.00–6.00	3.00–3.00	3.30
Sept	2.97	3.01	4.42	6.42	7.34	7.92	8.62	6.24	7.93	3.26	6.00–6.00	3.00–3.00	3.22
Oct	2.84	2.98	4.64	6.59	7.53	7.99	8.84	6.43	7.90	3.33	6.00–6.00	3.00–3.00	3.10
Nov	3.14	3.35	5.14	6.87	7.61	8.10	8.96	6.35	8.07	3.67	6.00–6.00	3.00–3.00	3.09
Dec	3.25	3.39	5.21	6.77	7.44	7.98	8.81	6.24	7.88	3.70	6.00–6.00	3.00–3.00	2.92
1993:													
Jan	3.06	3.17	4.93	6.60	7.34	7.91	8.67	6.18	7.82	3.35	6.00–6.00	3.00–3.00	3.02
Feb	2.95	3.08	4.58	6.26	7.09	7.71	8.39	5.87	7.77	3.27	6.00–6.00	3.00–3.00	3.03
Mar	2.97	3.08	4.40	5.98	6.82	7.58	8.15	5.65	7.46	3.24	6.00–6.00	3.00–3.00	3.07
Apr	2.89	3.00	4.30	5.97	6.85	7.46	8.14	5.78	7.46	3.19	6.00–6.00	3.00–3.00	2.96
May	2.96	3.07	4.40	6.04	6.92	7.43	8.21	5.81	7.37	3.20	6.00–6.00	3.00–3.00	3.00
June	3.10	3.23	4.53	5.96	6.81	7.33	8.07	5.73	7.23	3.38	6.00–6.00	3.00–3.00	3.04
July	3.05	3.15	4.43	5.81	6.63	7.17	7.93	5.60	7.20	3.35	6.00–6.00	3.00–3.00	3.06
Aug	3.05	3.17	4.36	5.68	6.32	6.85	7.60	5.50	7.05	3.33	6.00–6.00	3.00–3.00	3.03
Sept	2.96	3.06	4.17	5.36	6.00	6.66	7.34	5.31	6.95	3.25	6.00–6.00	3.00–3.00	3.09
Oct	3.04	3.13	4.18	5.33	5.94	6.67	7.31	5.29	6.80	3.27	6.00–6.00	3.00–3.00	2.99
Nov	3.12	3.27	4.50	5.72	6.21	6.93	7.66	5.47	6.80	3.43	6.00–6.00	3.00–3.00	3.02
Dec	3.08	3.25	4.54	5.77	6.25	6.93	7.69	5.35	6.92	3.40	6.00–6.00	3.00–3.00	2.96
1994:													
Jan	3.02	3.19	4.48	5.75	6.29	6.92	7.65	5.30	6.95	3.30	6.00–6.00	3.00–3.00	3.05
Feb	3.21	3.38	4.83	5.97	6.49	7.08	7.76	5.44	6.85	3.62	6.00–6.00	3.00–3.00	3.25
Mar	3.52	3.79	5.40	6.48	6.91	7.48	8.13	5.93	6.99	4.08	6.00–6.25	3.00–3.00	3.34
Apr	3.74	4.13	5.99	6.97	7.27	7.88	8.52	6.28	7.31	4.40	6.25–6.75	3.00–3.00	3.56
May	4.19	4.64	6.34	7.18	7.41	7.99	8.62	6.26	7.43	4.92	6.75–7.25	3.00–3.50	4.01
June	4.18	4.58	6.27	7.10	7.40	7.97	8.65	6.14	7.62	4.86	7.25–7.25	3.50–3.50	4.25
July	4.39	4.81	6.48	7.30	7.58	8.11	8.80	6.19	7.71	5.13	7.25–7.25	3.50–3.50	4.26
Aug	4.50	4.91	6.50	7.24	7.49	8.07	8.74	6.19	7.67	5.19	7.25–7.75	3.50–4.00	4.47
Sept	4.64	5.02	6.69	7.46	7.71	8.34	8.98	6.33	7.70	5.32	7.75–7.75	4.00–4.00	4.73
Oct	4.96	5.39	7.04	7.74	7.94	8.57	9.20	6.50	7.76	5.70	7.75–7.75	4.00–4.00	4.76
Nov	5.25	5.69	7.44	7.96	8.08	8.68	9.32	6.96	7.81	6.01	7.75–8.50	4.00–4.75	5.29
Dec	5.64	6.21	7.71	7.81	7.87	8.46	9.10	6.76	7.83	6.62	8.50–8.50	4.75–4.75	5.45

Sources: Department of the Treasury, Board of Governors of the Federal Reserve System, Federal Housing Finance Board, Moody's Investors Service, and Standard & Poor's Corporation.

TABLE B–73.—*Total funds raised in credit markets, 1985–94*

[Billions of dollars; quarterly data at seasonally adjusted annual rates]

Item	1985	1986	1987	1988	1989	1990	1991	1992	1993
NONFINANCIAL:									
Total net borrowing by domestic nonfinancial sectors	937.6	854.3	733.0	762.8	729.0	635.ö	475.8	536.1	628.1
U.S. Government	225.7	216.0	143.9	155.1	146.4	246.9	278.2	304.0	256.1
Treasury securities	225.8	215.6	142.4	137.7	144.7	238.7	292.0	303.8	248.3
Agency issues and mortgages	−.1	.4	1.5	17.4	1.6	8.2	−13.8	.2	7.8
Private domestic nonfinancial sectors	712.0	638.3	589.1	607.7	582.7	388.7	197.5	232.1	372.0
Tax-exempt securities	179.5	41.4	75.5	46.3	69.8	48.7	68.7	31.1	78.1
Corporate bonds	83.2	127.1	78.8	103.1	73.8	47.1	78.8	67.5	75.2
Mortgages	261.7	305.6	335.7	299.9	281.2	199.5	161.4	123.9	155.6
Home mortgages	172.3	204.2	241.6	234.9	224.5	185.6	163.8	179.5	183.9
Multifamily residential	30.3	36.4	24.9	17.5	11.5	4.8	−3.1	−11.2	−6.1
Commercial	65.6	75.1	76.2	52.2	47.8	9.3	.4	−45.5	−22.5
Farm	−6.6	−10.1	−6.9	−4.8	−2.5	−.3	.4	1.1	.5
Consumer credit	82.3	57.5	32.9	50.1	45.8	16.0	−15.0	5.5	62.3
Bank loans n.e.c.	43.8	58.9	14.7	38.2	27.3	.4	−40.9	−13.8	5.0
Commercial paper	14.6	−9.3	1.6	11.9	21.4	9.7	−18.4	8.6	10.0
Other	47.0	57.1	49.9	58.2	63.3	67.4	−37.1	9.2	−14.3
By borrowing sector:	712.0	638.3	589.1	607.7	582.7	388.7	197.5	232.1	372.0
Households	299.1	268.1	285.4	291.4	281.6	218.9	170.9	217.7	284.5
Nonfinancial domestic business	278.0	315.3	228.7	274.8	233.1	123.7	−35.9	−2.0	21.9
Farm	−14.5	−16.9	−11.1	−10.2	.6	−2.1	2.1	1.0	2.0
Nonfarm noncorporate	123.3	99.1	75.0	60.4	40.3	10.1	−28.5	−43.9	−26.0
Corporate	169.2	233.0	164.8	224.5	192.1	111.3	−9.6	40.9	45.8
State and local governments	134.9	54.9	75.1	41.5	68.0	46.0	62.6	16.4	65.7
Foreign net borrowing in United States	1.2	9.7	6.2	6.4	10.2	23.9	13.9	21.3	46.9
Bonds	3.8	3.1	7.4	6.9	4.9	21.4	14.1	14.4	59.4
Bank loans n.e.c.	−2.8	−1.0	−3.6	−1.8	−.1	−2.9	3.1	2.3	.7
Commercial paper	6.2	11.5	3.8	8.7	13.1	12.3	6.4	5.2	−9.0
U.S. Government and other loans	−6.0	−3.9	−1.4	−7.5	−7.6	−7.0	−9.8	−.6	−4.2
Total domestic plus foreign	938.8	864.0	739.2	769.2	739.2	659.4	489.6	557.4	675.0
FINANCIAL:									
Total net borrowing by domestic financial sectors	204.1	327.0	293.7	249.5	225.1	202.9	152.6	237.1	286.1
U.S. Government related	101.5	178.1	171.8	119.8	149.5	167.4	145.7	155.8	161.2
Private domestic financial sectors	102.5	148.9	121.9	129.7	75.7	35.5	6.8	81.3	125.0
By borrowing sector:	204.1	327.0	293.7	249.5	225.1	202.9	152.6	237.1	286.1
Government-sponsored enterprises	21.7	14.9	29.5	44.9	25.2	17.0	9.1	40.2	80.6
Federally related mortgage pools	79.9	163.3	142.3	74.9	124.3	150.3	136.6	115.6	80.6
Private domestic financial sectors	102.5	148.9	121.9	129.7	75.7	35.5	6.8	81.3	125.0
Commercial banks	−4.9	−3.6	6.2	−3.0	−1.4	−.7	−11.7	8.8	5.6
Bank holding companies	16.6	10.7	14.3	5.2	6.2	−27.7	−2.5	2.3	8.8
Savings institutions	20.7	24.1	28.3	21.7	−15.1	−30.2	−44.5	−6.7	11.1
Funding corporations	10.7	12.0	9.7	38.0	12.5	15.4	−6.5	13.2	2.9
Finance companies	40.7	51.5	23.2	23.9	27.4	24.0	18.6	−3.6	.2
Asset-backed securities issuers	16.0	42.0	49.9	37.6	28.3	52.3	51.0	56.3	81.5
Other	2.7	12.3	−9.6	6.3	17.8	2.3	2.5	11.0	14.9
ALL SECTORS, BY TRANSACTION:	1,142.9	1,191.0	1,032.9	1,018.7	964.4	862.3	642.2	794.5	961.2
U.S. Government securities	326.2	394.5	316.4	274.9	295.8	414.4	424.0	459.8	417.3
Tax-exempt securities	179.5	41.4	75.5	46.3	69.8	48.7	68.7	31.1	78.1
Corporate and foreign bonds	143.4	222.5	164.7	162.2	120.2	114.7	160.5	160.4	252.9
Mortgages	261.7	305.8	336.0	300.2	281.6	200.1	161.9	124.5	159.2
Consumer credit	82.3	57.5	32.9	50.1	45.8	16.0	−15.0	5.5	62.3
Bank loans n.e.c.	40.7	70.2	2.8	39.1	40.7	2.2	−29.1	−9.4	−8.3
Open-market paper	52.8	26.4	32.3	75.4	65.9	30.7	−44.0	13.1	−5.1
Other loans	56.3	72.7	72.2	70.5	44.7	35.6	−84.9	9.5	4.7

See next page for continuation of table.

[Billions of dollars; quarterly data at seasonally adjusted annual rates]

Item	1992				1993				1994		
	I	II	III	IV	I	II	III	IV	I	II	III
NONFINANCIAL:											
Total net borrowing by domestic nonfinancial sectors	618.4	505.1	564.8	456.0	481.4	740.5	613.3	677.2	651.2	543.4	612.3
U.S. Government	331.3	347.4	294.6	242.7	240.5	336.4	173.4	274.2	210.6	122.9	134.1
Treasury securities	342.4	347.0	285.5	240.0	237.4	332.3	157.2	266.5	211.8	118.2	129.8
Agency issues and mortgages	−11.2	.4	9.0	2.7	3.2	4.1	16.3	7.7	−1.3	4.7	4.4
Private domestic nonfinancial sectors	287.1	157.7	270.3	213.3	240.9	404.1	439.9	403.0	440.6	420.5	478.1
Tax-exempt securities	42.5	52.1	45.6	−15.8	88.7	130.3	66.2	27.4	22.6	−9.8	−41.2
Corporate bonds	76.5	77.8	61.7	54.0	85.7	75.7	72.0	67.4	35.1	38.9	24.6
Mortgages	195.9	52.5	160.7	86.6	99.8	152.2	222.1	148.5	151.5	162.2	219.4
Home mortgages	233.2	92.6	227.4	164.9	120.9	193.5	236.5	184.5	180.2	144.9	199.6
Multifamily residential	10.2	−16.9	−11.5	−26.5	−5.5	−11.4	−4.9	−2.6	−6.1	4.3	7.1
Commercial	−46.9	−25.9	−58.0	−51.4	−15.7	−30.9	−9.9	−33.6	−23.4	7.1	8.9
Farm	−.6	2.7	2.8	−.5	.2	1.0	.4	.2	.8	6.0	3.7
Consumer credit	−4.6	−15.0	12.0	29.6	20.3	41.6	76.2	111.3	72.7	121.9	127.1
Bank loans n.e.c.	−30.8	−20.5	−23.0	19.1	−16.2	−.2	7.8	28.5	74.2	73.0	93.5
Commercial paper	10.3	−2.0	4.0	22.3	−14.1	33.2	17.2	3.8	8.0	16.4	33.8
Other	−2.7	12.8	9.3	17.5	−23.3	−28.6	−21.7	16.2	76.5	17.8	20.9
By borrowing sector:	287.1	157.7	270.3	213.3	240.9	404.1	439.9	403.0	440.6	420.5	478.1
Households	238.6	121.0	261.6	249.6	167.5	264.1	368.5	337.7	299.4	303.6	370.5
Nonfinancial domestic business	13.3	2.2	−25.4	1.9	−11.6	26.7	24.1	48.2	131.4	144.7	156.4
Farm	−.2	5.1	1.6	−2.4	−2.3	2.7	4.1	3.6	3.1	11.8	3.6
Nonfarm noncorporate	−22.1	−45.3	−54.3	−53.9	−28.6	−33.4	−26.2	−15.6	8.4	16.5	26.9
Corporate	35.6	42.4	27.4	58.2	19.3	57.4	46.3	60.2	119.9	116.4	125.9
State and local governments	35.2	34.5	34.1	−38.2	85.0	113.2	47.3	17.1	9.9	−27.8	−48.8
Foreign net borrowing in United States	−3.8	55.0	30.6	3.6	38.9	42.8	83.1	22.9	−66.3	−1.9	−3.4
Bonds	1.0	18.7	12.1	26.0	66.5	45.3	84.5	41.4	29.0	11.1	6.6
Bank loans n.e.c.	1.5	14.1	3.9	−10.3	1.5	6.6	1.0	−6.3	6.0	−.8	.9
Commercial paper	−8.0	27.8	13.1	−12.1	−21.7	−.6	−1.6	−12.0	−101.8	−5.2	−8.1
U.S. Government and other loans	1.8	−5.6	1.4	.0	−7.5	−8.4	−.8	−.1	.5	−7.0	−2.7
Total domestic plus foreign	614.6	560.1	595.4	459.6	520.3	783.3	696.4	700.2	584.9	541.5	608.9
FINANCIAL:											
Total net borrowing by domestic financial sectors	191.9	251.7	306.1	198.8	180.4	175.5	438.9	349.8	477.0	294.9	345.6
U.S. Government related	130.4	188.2	171.9	132.6	169.4	56.6	287.3	131.3	320.8	245.2	224.9
Private domestic financial sectors	61.5	63.5	134.1	66.1	11.0	118.9	151.6	218.5	156.2	49.7	120.7
By borrowing sector:	191.9	251.7	306.1	198.8	180.4	175.5	438.9	349.8	477.0	294.9	345.6
Government-sponsored enterprises	11.5	48.3	67.7	33.5	32.2	68.8	167.8	53.4	140.8	146.6	152.1
Federally related mortgage pools	118.9	139.9	104.3	99.2	137.2	−12.2	119.5	77.9	180.0	98.6	72.8
Private domestic financial sectors	61.5	63.5	134.1	66.1	11.0	118.9	151.6	218.5	156.2	49.7	120.7
Commercial banks	1.7	6.5	12.6	14.5	3.5	11.3	6.5	1.2	2.0	12.4	22.8
Bank holding companies	10.9	−9.2	6.6	.8	21.1	1.3	.5	12.2	3.5	8.2	11.7
Savings institutions	−19.1	−8.8	6.3	−5.4	9.7	12.6	13.5	8.4	−5.6	5.8	14.8
Funding corporations	18.8	16.3	14.0	3.6	−31.4	−1.6	7.9	36.7	47.4	−17.1	47.0
Finance companies	−27.3	−3.5	15.2	1.0	−19.6	−13.6	17.5	16.3	63.3	67.0	16.9
Asset-backed securities issuers	42.9	50.7	64.0	67.7	62.0	60.5	85.8	117.6	81.8	4.0	22.3
Other	33.6	11.5	15.3	−16.1	−34.2	48.3	20.0	25.6	−36.2	−30.5	−14.8
ALL SECTORS, BY TRANSACTION:	806.5	811.8	901.5	658.4	700.7	958.8	1,135.3	1,050.0	1,061.9	836.4	954.5
U.S. Government securities	461.7	535.6	466.5	375.5	409.9	393.0	460.7	405.5	550.5	368.1	359.0
Tax-exempt securities	42.5	52.1	45.6	−15.8	88.7	130.3	66.2	27.4	22.6	−9.8	−41.2
Corporate and foreign bonds	129.2	185.7	158.3	177.0	251.2	213.4	299.9	247.1	212.6	109.8	96.5
Mortgages	196.7	52.6	161.2	87.4	101.2	153.5	228.3	154.0	151.8	162.7	219.6
Consumer credit	−4.6	−15.0	12.0	29.6	20.3	41.6	76.2	111.3	72.7	121.9	127.1
Bank loans, n.e.c.	−8.9	−12.0	−1.1	−15.3	−49.2	19.2	−7.3	4.2	61.9	27.1	76.8
Open-market paper	1.8	11.9	35.1	3.7	−110.9	16.4	6.3	67.7	−57.2	13.3	67.8
Other loans	−12.0	9.6	23.9	16.3	−10.4	−8.7	4.9	32.9	47.0	43.1	49.0

Source: Board of Governors of the Federal Reserve System.

TABLE B-74.—*Mortgage debt outstanding by type of property and of financing, 1940-94*

[Billions of dollars]

End of year or quarter	All proper-ties	Farm proper-ties	Nonfarm properties				Nonfarm properties by type of mortgage					
							Government underwritten				Conventional [2]	
			Total	1- to 4- family houses	Multi-family proper-ties	Com-mercial proper-ties	Total [1]	1- to 4-family houses			Total	1- to 4- family houses
								Total	FHA insured	VA guar-anteed		
1940	36.5	6.5	30.0	17.4	5.7	6.9	2.3	2.3	2.3		27.7	15.1
1941	37.6	6.4	31.2	18.4	5.9	7.0	3.0	3.0	3.0		28.2	15.4
1942	36.7	6.0	30.8	18.2	5.8	6.7	3.7	3.7	3.7		27.1	14.5
1943	35.3	5.4	29.9	17.8	5.8	6.3	4.1	4.1	4.1		25.8	13.7
1944	34.7	4.9	29.7	17.9	5.6	6.2	4.2	4.2	4.2		25.5	13.7
1945	35.5	4.8	30.8	18.6	5.7	6.4	4.3	4.3	4.1	0.2	26.5	14.3
1946	41.8	4.9	36.9	23.0	6.1	7.7	6.3	6.1	3.7	2.4	30.6	16.9
1947	48.9	5.1	43.9	28.2	6.6	9.1	9.8	9.3	3.8	5.5	34.1	18.9
1948	56.2	5.3	50.9	33.3	7.5	10.2	13.6	12.5	5.3	7.2	37.3	20.8
1949	62.7	5.6	57.1	37.6	8.6	10.8	17.1	15.0	6.9	8.1	40.0	22.6
1950	72.8	6.1	66.7	45.2	10.1	11.5	22.1	18.8	8.5	10.3	44.7	26.3
1951	82.3	6.7	75.6	51.7	11.5	12.5	26.6	22.9	9.7	13.2	49.1	28.9
1952	91.4	7.2	84.2	58.5	12.3	13.4	29.3	25.4	10.8	14.6	54.9	33.2
1953	101.3	7.7	93.6	66.1	12.9	14.5	32.1	28.1	12.0	16.1	61.5	38.0
1954	113.7	8.2	105.4	75.7	13.5	16.3	36.2	32.1	12.8	19.3	69.3	43.6
1955	129.9	9.0	120.9	88.2	14.3	18.3	42.9	38.9	14.3	24.6	78.0	49.3
1956	144.5	9.8	134.6	99.0	14.9	20.7	47.8	43.9	15.5	28.4	86.8	55.1
1957	156.5	10.4	146.1	107.6	15.3	23.2	51.6	47.2	16.5	30.7	94.6	60.4
1958	171.8	11.1	160.7	117.7	16.8	26.1	55.2	50.1	19.7	30.4	105.5	67.6
1959	190.8	12.1	178.7	130.9	18.7	29.2	59.3	53.8	23.8	30.0	119.4	77.0
1960	207.5	12.8	194.7	141.9	20.3	32.4	62.3	56.4	26.7	29.7	132.3	85.5
1961	228.0	13.9	214.1	154.6	23.0	36.5	65.6	59.1	29.5	29.6	148.5	95.5
1962	251.4	15.2	236.2	169.3	25.8	41.1	69.4	62.2	32.3	29.9	166.9	107.1
1963	278.5	16.8	261.7	186.4	29.0	46.2	73.4	65.9	35.0	30.9	188.2	120.5
1964	305.9	18.9	287.0	203.4	33.6	50.0	77.2	69.2	38.3	30.9	209.8	134.1
1965	333.3	21.2	312.1	220.5	37.2	54.5	81.2	73.1	42.0	31.1	231.0	147.4
1966	356.5	23.1	333.4	232.9	40.3	60.1	84.1	76.1	44.8	31.3	249.3	156.9
1967	381.2	25.1	356.1	247.3	43.9	64.8	88.2	79.9	47.4	32.5	267.9	167.4
1968	411.1	27.5	383.5	264.8	47.3	71.4	93.4	84.4	50.6	33.8	290.1	180.4
1969	441.6	29.4	412.2	283.2	52.2	76.9	100.2	90.2	54.5	35.7	312.0	193.0
1970	473.7	30.5	443.2	297.4	60.1	85.6	109.2	97.3	59.9	37.3	333.9	200.2
1971	524.2	32.4	491.8	325.9	70.1	95.9	120.7	105.2	65.7	39.5	371.1	220.7
1972	597.4	35.4	562.0	366.5	82.8	112.7	131.1	113.0	68.2	44.7	430.9	253.5
1973	672.6	39.8	632.8	407.9	93.1	131.7	135.0	116.2	66.2	50.0	497.7	291.7
1974	732.5	44.9	687.5	440.7	100.0	146.9	140.2	121.3	65.1	56.2	547.3	319.4
1975	791.9	49.9	742.0	482.1	100.6	159.3	147.0	127.7	66.1	61.6	595.0	354.3
1976	878.6	55.4	823.2	546.3	105.7	171.2	154.1	133.5	66.5	67.0	669.0	412.8
1977	1,010.3	63.9	946.4	642.7	114.0	189.7	161.7	141.6	68.0	73.6	784.6	501.0
1978	1,163.0	72.8	1,090.2	753.5	124.9	211.8	176.4	153.4	71.4	82.0	913.9	600.2
1979	1,328.4	86.8	1,241.7	870.5	134.9	236.3	199.0	172.9	81.0	92.0	1,042.7	697.6
1980	1,460.4	97.5	1,362.9	965.1	142.3	255.5	225.1	195.2	93.6	101.6	1,137.8	769.9
1981	1,566.7	107.2	1,459.5	1,039.8	142.1	277.5	238.9	207.6	101.3	106.2	1,220.6	832.2
1982	1,641.1	111.3	1,529.8	1,081.7	145.8	302.2	248.9	217.9	108.0	109.9	1,280.9	863.9
1983	1,828.8	113.7	1,715.1	1,199.4	160.9	354.8	279.8	248.8	127.4	121.4	1,435.3	950.6
1984	2,054.6	112.4	1,942.2	1,335.1	185.7	421.4	294.8	265.9	136.7	129.1	1,647.3	1,069.2
1985	2,312.8	105.9	2,206.9	1,504.7	215.6	486.6	328.3	288.8	153.0	135.8	1,878.6	1,215.9
1986	2,615.4	95.2	2,520.2	1,707.1	251.8	561.3	370.5	328.6	185.5	143.1	2,149.7	1,378.5
1987	2,963.2	87.7	2,875.5	1,936.1	276.0	663.4	431.4	387.9	235.5	152.4	2,444.1	1,548.2
1988	3,205.3	83.0	3,167.3	2,171.0	293.7	702.7	459.7	414.2	258.8	155.4	2,707.6	1,756.8
1989	3,549.0	80.5	3,468.5	2,407.8	306.5	754.2	486.8	440.1	282.8	157.3	2,981.6	1,967.7
1990	3,763.6	78.9	3,684.7	2,617.0	309.4	758.3	517.9	470.9	310.9	160.0	3,166.8	2,146.1
1991	3,926.2	79.3	3,846.8	2,781.4	306.4	759.0	537.2	493.3	330.6	162.7	3,309.6	2,288.1
1992	4,056.2	80.7	3,975.5	2,963.4	295.4	716.7	533.3	489.8	326.0	163.8	3,442.2	2,473.6
1993	4,215.5	81.2	4,134.3	3,147.3	290.5	696.5	513.4	469.5	303.2	166.2	3,620.9	2,677.8
1992: I	3,961.5	79.2	3,882.3	2,825.8	309.0	747.4	538.1	494.3	330.6	163.7	3,344.3	2,331.5
II	3,986.7	79.8	3,906.8	2,859.9	304.8	742.1	536.1	492.4	328.8	163.6	3,370.8	2,367.5
III	4,029.3	80.5	3,948.8	2,918.6	302.0	728.2	537.5	493.9	329.5	164.4	3,411.3	2,424.7
IV	4,056.2	80.7	3,975.5	2,963.4	295.4	716.7	533.3	489.8	326.0	163.8	3,442.2	2,473.6
1993: I	4,067.2	80.8	3,986.4	2,979.3	294.1	713.0	530.5	487.0	323.4	163.6	3,455.9	2,492.3
II	4,116.0	81.0	4,034.9	3,038.1	291.4	705.5	522.6	479.0	315.2	163.8	3,512.3	2,559.1
III	4,174.2	81.1	4,093.1	3,098.3	290.7	704.0	520.1	476.2	312.5	163.7	3,573.0	2,622.1
IV	4,215.5	81.2	4,134.3	3,147.3	290.5	696.5	513.4	469.5	303.2	166.2	3,620.9	2,677.8
1994: I	4,239.5	81.4	4,158.1	3,178.4	289.0	690.7	521.2	476.7	309.7	167.0	3,636.9	2,701.7
II	4,290.6	82.9	4,207.8	3,225.1	290.1	692.6	533.5	488.8	318.8	170.0	3,674.2	2,736.2
III *p*	4,346.6	83.8	4,262.8	3,276.0	291.9	694.8	540.4	495.4	321.1	174.3	3,722.4	2,780.6

[1] Includes FHA insured multifamily properties, not shown separately.
[2] Derived figures. Total includes multifamily and commercial properties, not shown separately.

Source: Board of Governors of the Federal Reserve System, based on data from various Government and private organizations.

TABLE B-75.—*Mortgage debt outstanding by holder, 1940–94*

[Billions of dollars]

End of year or quarter	Total	Major financial institutions				Other holders	
		Total	Savings institutions[1]	Commercial banks[2]	Life insurance companies	Federal and related agencies[3]	Individuals and others[4]
1940	36.5	19.5	9.0	4.6	6.0	4.9	12.0
1941	37.6	20.7	9.4	4.9	6.4	4.7	12.2
1942	36.7	20.7	9.2	4.7	6.7	4.3	11.7
1943	35.3	20.2	9.0	4.5	6.7	3.6	11.5
1944	34.7	20.2	9.1	4.4	6.7	3.0	11.5
1945	35.5	21.0	9.6	4.8	6.6	2.4	12.1
1946	41.8	26.0	11.5	7.2	7.2	2.0	13.8
1947	48.9	31.8	13.8	9.4	8.7	1.8	15.3
1948	56.2	37.8	16.1	10.9	10.8	1.8	16.6
1949	62.7	42.9	18.3	11.6	12.9	2.3	17.5
1950	72.8	51.7	21.9	13.7	16.1	2.8	18.4
1951	82.3	59.5	25.5	14.7	19.3	3.5	19.3
1952	91.4	66.9	29.8	15.9	21.3	4.1	20.4
1953	101.3	75.1	34.9	16.9	23.3	4.6	21.7
1954	113.7	85.7	41.1	18.6	26.0	4.8	23.2
1955	129.9	99.3	48.9	21.0	29.4	5.3	25.3
1956	144.5	111.2	55.5	22.7	33.0	6.2	27.1
1957	156.5	119.7	61.2	23.3	35.2	7.7	29.1
1958	171.8	131.5	68.9	25.5	37.1	8.0	32.3
1959	190.8	145.5	78.1	28.1	39.2	10.2	35.1
1960	207.5	157.6	87.0	28.8	41.8	11.5	38.4
1961	228.0	172.6	98.0	30.4	44.2	12.2	43.1
1962	251.4	192.5	111.1	34.5	46.9	12.6	46.3
1963	278.5	217.1	127.2	39.4	50.5	11.8	49.5
1964	305.9	241.0	141.9	44.0	55.2	12.2	52.7
1965	333.3	264.6	154.9	49.7	60.0	13.5	55.2
1966	356.5	280.8	161.8	54.4	64.6	17.5	58.2
1967	381.2	298.8	172.3	59.0	67.5	20.9	61.4
1968	411.1	319.9	184.3	65.7	70.0	25.1	66.1
1969	441.6	339.1	196.4	70.7	72.0	31.1	71.4
1970	473.7	355.9	208.3	73.3	74.4	38.3	79.4
1971	524.2	394.2	236.2	82.5	75.5	46.4	83.6
1972	597.4	450.0	273.7	99.3	76.9	54.6	92.8
1973	672.6	505.4	305.0	119.1	81.4	64.8	102.4
1974	732.5	542.6	324.2	132.1	86.2	82.2	107.7
1975	791.9	581.2	355.8	136.2	89.2	101.1	109.6
1976	878.6	647.5	404.6	151.3	91.6	116.7	114.4
1977	1,010.3	745.2	469.4	179.0	96.8	140.5	124.6
1978	1,163.0	848.2	528.0	214.0	106.2	170.6	144.3
1979	1,328.4	938.2	574.6	245.2	118.4	216.0	174.3
1980	1,460.4	996.8	603.1	262.7	131.1	256.8	206.8
1981	1,566.7	1,040.5	618.5	284.2	137.7	289.4	236.8
1982	1,641.1	1,021.3	578.1	301.3	142.0	355.4	264.4
1983	1,828.8	1,108.2	626.7	330.5	151.0	433.4	287.2
1984	2,054.6	1,245.9	709.7	379.5	156.7	490.6	318.1
1985	2,312.8	1,361.5	760.5	429.2	171.8	581.9	369.4
1986	2,615.4	1,474.3	778.0	502.5	193.8	733.7	407.3
1987	2,963.2	1,665.3	860.5	592.4	212.4	858.9	439.0
1988	3,250.3	1,831.5	924.6	674.0	232.9	937.8	481.0
1989	3,549.0	1,931.5	910.3	767.1	254.2	1,067.3	550.1
1990	3,763.6	1,914.3	801.6	844.8	267.9	1,258.9	590.4
1991	3,926.2	1,846.7	705.4	876.1	265.3	1,422.6	656.8
1992	4,056.2	1,769.2	628.0	894.5	246.7	1,558.3	728.7
1993	4,215.5	1,767.8	598.3	940.4	229.1	1,670.1	777.5
1992: I	3,961.5	1,826.7	682.3	881.0	263.3	1,458.1	676.7
II	3,986.7	1,803.8	659.6	885.0	259.3	1,497.1	685.8
III	4,029.3	1,793.5	648.2	891.4	253.9	1,521.5	714.3
IV	4,056.2	1,769.2	628.0	894.5	246.7	1,558.3	728.7
1993: I	4,067.2	1,753.3	617.2	891.8	244.4	1,586.9	727.0
II	4,116.0	1,765.7	612.4	911.0	242.2	1,600.3	750.0
III	4,174.2	1,770.0	609.7	922.7	237.6	1,636.7	767.6
IV	4,215.5	1,767.8	598.3	940.4	229.1	1,670.1	777.5
1994: I	4,239.5	1,746.5	584.5	937.9	224.0	1,714.3	778.8
II	4,290.6	1,763.2	585.7	956.8	220.8	1,748.5	778.9
III p	4,346.6	1,784.2	587.4	981.4	215.5	1,771.9	790.6

[1] Includes savings banks and savings and loan associations. Data reported by Federal Savings and Loan Insurance Corporation-insured institutions include loans in process for 1987 and exclude loans in process beginning 1988.

[2] Includes loans held by nondeposit trust companies, but not by bank trust departments.

[3] Includes Government National Mortgage Association (GNMA), Federal Housing Administration, Veterans Administration, Farmers Home Administration (FmHA), and in earlier years Reconstruction Finance Corporation, Homeowners Loan Corporation, Federal Farm Mortgage Corporation, and Public Housing Administration. Also includes U.S.-sponsored agencies such as Federal National Mortgage Association (FNMA), Federal Land Banks, Federal Home Loan Mortgage Corporation (FHLMC), and mortgage pass-through securities issued or guaranteed by GNMA, FHLMC, FNMA or FmHA. Other U.S. agencies (amounts small or current separate data not readily available) included with "individuals and others."

[4] Includes private mortgage pools.

Source: Board of Governors of the Federal Reserve System, based on data from various Government and private organizations.

TABLE B-76.—*Consumer credit outstanding, 1952-94*

[Amount outstanding (end of month); millions of dollars, seasonally adjusted]

Year and month	Total consumer credit	Installment credit [1]				Noninstallment credit [4]
		Total	Automobile	Revolving [2]	Other [3]	
December:						
1952	29,766	20,121	7,651		12,470	9,645
1953	33,769	23,870	9,702		14,168	9,899
1954	35,027	24,470	9,755		14,715	10,557
1955	41,885	29,809	13,485		16,324	12,076
1956	45,503	32,660	14,499		18,161	12,843
1957	48,132	34,914	15,493		19,421	13,218
1958	48,356	34,736	14,267		20,469	13,620
1959	55,878	40,421	16,641		23,780	15,457
1960	60,035	44,335	18,108		26,227	15,700
1961	62,340	45,438	17,656		27,782	16,902
1962	68,231	50,375	20,001		30,374	17,856
1963	76,606	57,056	22,891		34,165	19,550
1964	85,989	64,674	25,865		38,809	21,315
1965	95,948	72,814	29,378		43,436	23,134
1966	101,839	78,162	31,024		47,138	23,677
1967	106,716	81,783	31,136		50,647	24,933
1968	117,231	90,112	34,352	2,022	53,738	27,119
1969	126,928	99,381	36,946	3,563	58,872	27,547
1970	131,600	103,905	36,348	4,900	62,657	27,695
1971	147,058	116,434	40,522	8,252	67,660	30,624
1972	166,009	131,258	47,835	9,391	74,032	34,751
1973	190,601	152,910	53,740	11,318	87,852	37,691
1974	199,365	162,203	54,241	13,232	94,730	37,162
1975	204,963	167,043	56,989	14,507	95,547	37,920
1976	228,162	187,782	66,821	16,595	104,366	40,380
1977	263,808	221,475	80,948	36,689	103,838	42,333
1978	308,272	261,976	98,739	45,202	118,035	46,296
1979	347,507	296,483	112,475	53,357	130,651	51,024
1980	350,269	298,154	111,991	55,111	131,053	52,115
1981	366,869	311,259	119,008	61,070	131,182	55,610
1982	383,132	325,805	125,945	66,454	133,406	57,327
1983	431,170	368,966	143,560	79,088	146,318	62,204
1984	511,314	442,602	173,564	100,280	168,758	68,713
1985	591,291	517,660	210,238	121,758	185,664	73,631
1986	647,982	572,006	247,772	135,825	188,408	75,976
1987	680,036	608,675	266,295	153,064	189,316	71,362
1988 [5]	729,121	662,553	285,364	174,269	202,921	66,568
1989	782,077	717,200	291,531	199,162	226,508	64,876
1990	797,339	734,898	283,072	223,517	228,309	62,441
1991	780,982	728,389	259,594	245,281	223,514	52,593
1992	787,041	731,098	257,678	257,304	216,117	55,943
1993	847,486	794,300	282,036	287,875	224,389	53,186
1993: Jan	788,426	733,686	256,395	259,871	217,419	54,740
Feb	791,379	738,275	258,959	262,070	217,245	53,104
Mar	791,425	738,918	259,289	263,531	216,098	52,507
Apr	798,090	745,176	260,647	265,723	218,806	52,914
May	799,566	745,308	262,904	267,728	214,676	54,258
June	804,813	751,104	265,689	269,385	216,030	53,709
July	811,582	758,607	268,408	273,442	216,757	52,974
Aug	816,559	763,958	270,610	275,772	217,576	52,601
Sept	824,722	772,171	273,179	279,013	219,979	52,550
Oct	832,295	779,316	278,168	280,985	220,163	52,979
Nov	838,361	786,101	280,861	285,110	220,130	52,260
Dec	847,486	794,300	282,036	287,875	224,389	53,186
1994: Jan	851,576	798,844	283,134	290,165	225,545	52,732
Feb	856,713	802,720	284,447	292,604	225,668	53,993
Mar	868,006	813,750	288,663	296,710	228,376	54,256
Apr	877,282	823,342	293,018	301,260	229,064	53,940
May	889,996	836,936	298,278	305,528	233,130	53,059
June	900,428	847,715	303,526	309,472	234,717	52,713
July	906,635	854,469	305,193	313,591	235,685	52,166
Aug	920,512	869,628	309,721	321,365	238,542	50,884
Sept	931,529	879,961	315,162	322,823	241,976	51,568
Oct	943,274	891,603	318,036	327,707	245,860	51,671
Nov [p]	953,908	904,487	322,808	334,428	247,251	49,421

[1] Installment credit covers most short- and intermediate-term credit extended to individuals through regular business channels, usually to finance the purchase of consumer goods and services or to refinance debts incurred for such purposes, and scheduled to be repaid (or with the option of repayment) in two or more installments. Credit secured by real estate is excluded.
[2] Consists of credit cards at retailers, gasoline companies, and commercial banks, and check credit at commercial banks. Excludes 30-day charge credit held by travel and entertainment companies. Prior to 1968, included in "other," except gasoline companies included in noninstallment credit prior to 1971. Beginning 1977, includes open-end credit at retailers, previously included in "other." Also beginning 1977, some retail credit was reclassified from commercial into consumer credit.
[3] Includes mobile home loans and all other installment loans not included in autombile or revolving credit, such as loans for education, boats, trailers, or vacations. These loans may be secured or unsecured.
[4] Noninstallment credit is credit scheduled to be repaid in a lump sum, including single-payment loans, charge accounts, and service credit. Because of inconsistencies in the data and infrequent benchmarking, series is no longer published by the Federal Reserve Board on a regular basis. Data are shown here as a general indication of trends.
[5] Data newly available in January 1989 result in breaks in many series between December 1988 and subsequent months.
Source: Board of Governors of the Federal Reserve System.

Table B-77.—*Federal receipts, outlays, surplus or deficit, and debt, selected fiscal years, 1929-96*

[Billions of dollars; fiscal years]

Fiscal year or period	Total			On-budget			Off-budget			Gross Federal debt (end of period)		Addendum: Gross domestic product
	Receipts	Outlays	Surplus or deficit (−)	Receipts	Outlays	Surplus or deficit (−)	Receipts	Outlays	Surplus or deficit (−)	Total	Held by the public	
1929	3.9	3.1	0.7	3.9	3.1	0.7	....	....	....	[1] 16.9	....	....
1933	2.0	4.6	−2.6	2.0	4.6	−2.6	....	....	....	[1] 22.5	....	56.8
1939	6.3	9.1	−2.8	5.8	9.2	−3.4	0.5	−0.0	0.5	48.2	41.4	87.8
1940	6.5	9.5	−2.9	6.0	9.5	−3.5	.6	−.0	.6	50.7	42.8	95.4
1941	8.7	13.7	−4.9	8.0	13.6	−5.6	.7	.0	.7	57.5	48.2	112.5
1942	14.6	35.1	−20.5	13.7	35.1	−21.3	.9	.1	.8	79.2	67.8	141.8
1943	24.0	78.6	−54.6	22.9	78.5	−55.6	1.1	.1	1.0	142.6	127.8	175.4
1944	43.7	91.3	−47.6	42.5	91.2	−48.7	1.3	.1	1.2	204.1	184.8	201.7
1945	45.2	92.7	−47.6	43.8	92.6	−48.7	1.3	.1	1.2	260.1	235.2	212.0
1946	39.3	55.2	−15.9	38.1	55.0	−17.0	1.2	.2	1.0	271.0	241.9	212.5
1947	38.5	34.5	4.0	37.1	34.2	2.9	1.5	.3	1.2	257.1	224.3	222.9
1948	41.6	29.8	11.8	39.9	29.4	10.5	1.6	.4	1.2	252.0	216.3	246.7
1949	39.4	38.8	.6	37.7	38.4	−.7	1.7	.4	1.3	252.6	214.3	262.7
1950	39.4	42.6	−3.1	37.3	42.0	−4.7	2.1	.5	1.6	256.9	219.0	265.8
1951	51.6	45.5	6.1	48.5	44.2	4.3	3.1	1.3	1.8	255.3	214.3	313.5
1952	66.2	67.7	−1.5	62.6	66.0	−3.4	3.6	1.7	1.9	259.1	214.8	340.5
1953	69.6	76.1	−6.5	65.5	73.8	−8.3	4.1	2.3	1.8	266.0	218.4	363.8
1954	69.7	70.9	−1.2	65.1	67.9	−2.8	4.6	2.9	1.7	270.8	224.5	368.0
1955	65.5	68.4	−3.0	60.4	64.5	−4.1	5.1	4.0	1.1	274.4	226.6	384.7
1956	74.6	70.6	3.9	68.2	65.7	2.5	6.4	5.0	1.5	272.7	222.2	416.3
1957	80.0	76.6	3.4	73.2	70.6	2.6	6.8	6.0	.8	272.3	219.3	438.3
1958	79.6	82.4	−2.8	71.6	74.9	−3.3	8.0	7.5	.5	279.7	226.3	448.1
1959	79.2	92.1	−12.8	71.0	83.1	−12.1	8.3	9.0	−.7	287.5	234.7	480.2
1960	92.5	92.2	.3	81.9	81.3	.5	10.6	10.9	−.2	290.5	236.8	504.6
1961	94.4	97.7	−3.3	82.3	86.0	−3.8	12.1	11.7	.4	292.6	238.4	517.0
1962	99.7	106.8	−7.1	87.4	93.3	−5.9	12.3	13.5	−1.3	302.9	248.0	555.2
1963	106.6	111.3	−4.8	92.4	96.4	−4.0	14.2	15.0	−.8	310.3	254.0	584.5
1964	112.6	118.5	−5.9	96.2	102.8	−6.5	16.4	15.7	.6	316.1	256.8	625.3
1965	116.8	118.2	−1.4	100.1	101.7	−1.6	16.7	16.5	.2	322.3	260.8	671.0
1966	130.8	134.5	−3.7	111.7	114.8	−3.1	19.1	19.7	−.6	328.5	263.7	735.4
1967	148.8	157.5	−8.6	124.4	137.0	−12.6	24.4	20.4	4.0	340.4	266.6	793.3
1968	153.0	178.1	−25.2	128.1	155.8	−27.7	24.9	22.3	2.6	368.7	289.5	847.2
1969	186.9	183.6	3.2	157.9	158.4	−.5	29.0	25.2	3.7	365.8	278.1	925.7
1970	192.8	195.6	−2.8	159.3	168.0	−8.7	33.5	27.6	5.9	380.9	283.2	985.4
1971	187.1	210.2	−23.0	151.3	177.3	−26.1	35.8	32.8	3.0	408.2	303.0	1,050.9
1972	207.3	230.7	−23.4	167.4	193.8	−26.4	39.9	36.9	3.1	435.9	322.4	1,147.8
1973	230.8	245.7	−14.9	184.7	200.1	−15.4	46.1	45.6	.5	466.3	340.9	1,274.0
1974	263.2	269.4	−6.1	209.3	217.3	−8.0	53.9	52.1	1.8	483.9	343.7	1,403.6
1975	279.1	332.3	−53.2	216.6	271.9	−55.3	62.5	60.4	2.0	541.9	394.7	1,509.8
1976	298.1	371.8	−73.7	231.7	302.2	−70.5	66.4	69.6	−3.2	629.0	477.4	1,684.2
Transition quarter	81.2	96.0	−14.7	63.2	76.6	−13.3	18.0	19.4	−1.4	643.6	495.5	445.0
1977	355.6	409.2	−53.7	278.7	328.5	−49.8	76.8	80.7	−3.9	706.4	549.1	1,917.2
1978	399.6	458.7	−59.2	314.2	369.1	−54.9	85.4	89.7	−4.3	776.6	607.1	2,155.0
1979	463.3	504.0	−40.7	365.3	404.1	−38.7	98.0	100.0	−2.0	829.5	640.3	2,429.5
1980	517.1	590.9	−73.8	403.9	476.6	−72.7	113.2	114.3	−1.1	909.1	709.8	2,644.1
1981	599.3	678.2	−79.0	469.1	543.1	−74.0	130.2	135.2	−5.0	994.8	785.3	2,964.4
1982	617.8	745.8	−128.0	474.3	594.4	−120.1	143.5	151.4	−7.9	1,137.3	919.8	3,122.2
1983	600.6	808.4	−207.8	453.2	661.3	−208.0	147.3	147.1	.2	1,371.7	1,131.6	3,316.5
1984	666.5	851.8	−185.4	500.4	686.0	−185.7	166.1	165.8	.3	1,564.7	1,300.5	3,695.0
1985	734.1	946.4	−212.3	547.9	769.6	−221.7	186.2	176.8	9.4	1,817.5	1,499.9	3,967.7
1986	769.1	990.3	−221.2	568.9	806.8	−238.0	200.2	183.5	16.7	2,120.6	1,736.7	4,219.0
1987	854.1	1,003.9	−149.8	640.7	810.1	−169.3	213.4	193.8	19.6	2,346.1	1,888.7	4,452.4
1988	909.0	1,064.1	−155.2	667.5	861.4	−194.0	241.5	202.7	38.8	2,601.3	2,050.8	4,808.4
1989	990.7	1,143.2	−152.5	727.0	932.3	−205.2	263.7	210.9	52.8	2,868.0	2,189.9	5,173.3
1990	1,031.3	1,252.7	−221.4	749.7	1,027.6	−278.0	281.7	225.1	56.6	3,206.6	2,410.7	5,481.5
1991	1,054.3	1,323.4	−269.2	760.4	1,081.8	−321.4	293.9	241.7	52.2	3,598.5	2,688.1	5,676.4
1992	1,090.5	1,380.9	−290.4	788.0	1,128.5	−340.5	302.4	252.3	50.1	4,002.1	2,998.8	5,921.5
1993	1,153.5	1,408.7	−255.1	841.6	1,142.1	−300.5	311.9	266.6	45.3	4,351.4	3,247.5	6,258.6
1994	1,257.7	1,460.9	−203.2	922.7	1,181.5	−258.8	335.0	279.4	55.7	4,643.7	3,432.2	6,633.6
1995 [2]	1,346.4	1,538.9	−192.5	995.2	1,246.9	−251.8	351.3	292.0	59.3	4,961.5	3,640.1	7,024.1
1996 [2]	1,415.5	1,612.1	−196.7	1,045.1	1,307.1	−262.0	370.4	305.0	65.3	5,299.6	3,857.3	7,407.0

[1] Not strictly comparable with later data.
[2] Estimates.

Note.—Through fiscal year 1976, the fiscal year was on a July 1–June 30 basis; beginning October 1976 (fiscal year 1977), the fiscal year is on an October 1–September 30 basis. The 3-month period from July 1, 1976 through September 30, 1976 is a separate fiscal period known as the transition quarter.

Refunds of receipts are excluded from receipts and outlays.

See *Budget of the United States Government, Fiscal Year 1996*, February 1995, for additional information.

Sources: Department of Commerce (Bureau of Economic Analysis), Department of the Treasury, and Office of Management and Budget.

TABLE B-78.—*Federal budget receipts, outlays, surplus or deficit, and debt, as percent of gross domestic product, 1934–96*

[Percent; fiscal years]

Fiscal year or period	Receipts	Outlays		Surplus or deficit (−)	Gross Federal debt (end of period)	
		Total	National defense		Total	Held by public
1934	4.9	10.8		−5.9		
1935	5.3	9.3		−4.1		
1936	5.1	10.6		−5.6		
1937	6.2	8.7		−2.5		
1938	7.7	7.8		−.1		
1939	7.2	10.4		−3.2	54.9	47.2
1940	6.9	9.9	1.7	−3.1	53.1	44.8
1941	7.7	12.1	5.7	−4.4	51.1	42.9
1942	10.3	24.8	18.1	−14.5	55.9	47.8
1943	13.7	44.8	38.0	−31.1	81.3	72.8
1944	21.7	45.3	39.2	−23.6	101.2	91.6
1945	21.3	43.7	39.1	−22.4	122.7	110.9
1946	18.5	26.0	20.1	−7.5	127.5	113.8
1947	17.3	15.5	5.7	1.8	115.4	100.6
1948	16.8	12.1	3.7	4.8	102.2	87.7
1949	15.0	14.8	5.0	.2	96.2	81.6
1950	14.8	16.0	5.2	−1.2	96.6	82.4
1951	16.5	14.5	7.5	1.9	81.4	68.4
1952	19.4	19.9	13.5	−.4	76.1	63.1
1953	19.1	20.9	14.5	−1.8	73.1	60.0
1954	18.9	19.3	13.4	−.3	73.6	61.0
1955	17.0	17.8	11.1	−.8	71.3	58.9
1956	17.9	17.0	10.2	.9	65.5	53.4
1957	18.3	17.5	10.4	.8	62.1	50.0
1958	17.8	18.4	10.4	−.6	62.4	50.5
1959	16.5	19.2	10.2	−2.7	59.9	48.9
1960	18.3	18.3	9.5	.1	57.6	46.9
1961	18.3	18.9	9.6	−.6	56.6	46.1
1962	18.0	19.2	9.4	−1.3	54.6	44.7
1963	18.2	19.0	9.1	−.8	53.1	43.5
1964	18.0	19.0	8.8	−.9	50.5	41.1
1965	17.4	17.6	7.5	−.2	48.0	38.9
1966	17.8	18.3	7.9	−.5	44.7	35.9
1967	18.8	19.8	9.0	−1.1	42.9	33.6
1968	18.1	21.0	9.7	−3.0	43.5	34.2
1969	20.2	19.8	8.9	.4	39.5	30.0
1970	19.6	19.9	8.3	−.3	38.7	28.7
1971	17.8	20.0	7.5	−2.2	38.8	28.8
1972	18.1	20.1	6.9	−2.0	38.0	28.1
1973	18.1	19.3	6.0	−1.2	36.6	26.8
1974	18.8	19.2	5.7	−.4	34.5	24.5
1975	18.5	22.0	5.7	−3.5	35.9	26.1
1976	17.7	22.1	5.3	−4.4	37.3	28.3
Transition quarter	18.3	21.6	5.0	−3.3	36.2	27.8
1977	18.5	21.3	5.1	−2.8	36.8	28.6
1978	18.5	21.3	4.8	−2.7	36.0	28.2
1979	19.1	20.7	4.8	−1.7	34.1	26.4
1980	19.6	22.3	5.1	−2.8	34.4	26.8
1981	20.2	22.9	5.3	−2.7	33.6	26.5
1982	19.8	23.9	5.9	−4.1	36.4	29.5
1983	18.1	24.4	6.3	−6.3	41.4	34.1
1984	18.0	23.1	6.2	−5.0	42.3	35.2
1985	18.5	23.9	6.4	−5.4	45.8	37.8
1986	18.2	23.5	6.5	−5.2	50.3	41.2
1987	19.2	22.5	6.3	−3.4	52.7	42.4
1988	18.9	22.1	6.0	−3.2	54.1	42.7
1989	19.2	22.1	5.9	−2.9	55.4	42.3
1990	18.8	22.9	5.5	−4.0	58.5	44.0
1991	18.6	23.3	4.8	−4.7	63.4	47.4
1992	18.4	23.3	5.0	−4.9	67.6	50.6
1993	18.4	22.5	4.7	−4.1	69.5	51.9
1994	19.0	22.0	4.2	−3.1	70.0	51.7
1995 [1]	19.2	21.9	3.9	−2.7	70.6	51.8
1996 [1]	19.1	21.8	3.5	−2.7	71.5	52.1

[1] Estimates.

Note.—Through fiscal year 1976, the fiscal year was on a July 1–June 30 basis; beginning October 1976 (fiscal year 1977), the fiscal year is on an October 1–September 30 basis. The 3-month period from July 1, 1976 through September 30, 1976 is a separate fiscal period known as the transition quarter.

See *Budget of the United States Government, Fiscal Year 1996,* February 1995, for additional information.

Sources: Department of the Treasury and Office of Management and Budget.

[Billions of dollars; fiscal years]

Fiscal year or period	Receipts (on-budget and off-budget)					Outlays (on-budget and off-budget)										Surplus or deficit (−) (on-budget and off-budget)
	Total	Individual income taxes	Corporation income taxes	Social insurance taxes and contributions	Other	Total	National defense		International affairs	Health	Medicare	Income security	Social security	Net interest	Other	
							Total	Department of Defense, military								
1940	6.5	0.9	1.2	1.8	2.7	9.5	1.7		0.1	0.1		1.5	0.0	0.9	5.3	−2.9
1941	8.7	1.3	2.1	1.9	3.3	13.7	6.4		.1	.1		1.9	.1	.9	4.1	−4.9
1942	14.6	3.3	4.7	2.5	4.2	35.1	25.7		1.0	.1		1.8	.1	1.1	5.4	−20.5
1943	24.0	6.5	9.6	3.0	4.9	78.6	66.7		1.3	.1		1.7	.2	1.5	7.0	−54.6
1944	43.7	19.7	14.8	3.5	5.7	91.3	79.1		1.4	.2		1.5	.2	2.2	6.6	−47.6
1945	45.2	18.4	16.0	3.5	7.3	92.7	83.0		1.9	.2		1.1	.3	3.1	3.1	−47.6
1946	39.3	16.1	11.9	3.1	8.2	55.2	42.7		1.9	.2		2.4	.4	4.1	3.6	−15.9
1947	38.5	17.9	8.6	3.4	8.5	34.5	12.8		5.8	.2		2.8	.5	4.2	8.2	4.0
1948	41.6	19.3	9.7	3.8	8.8	29.8	9.1		4.6	.2		2.5	.6	4.3	8.5	11.8
1949	39.4	15.6	11.2	3.8	8.9	38.8	13.2		6.1	.2		3.2	.7	4.5	11.1	.6
1950	39.4	15.8	10.4	4.3	8.9	42.6	13.7		4.7	.3		4.1	.8	4.8	14.2	−3.1
1951	51.6	21.6	14.1	5.7	10.2	45.5	23.6		3.6	.3		3.4	1.6	4.7	8.4	6.1
1952	66.2	27.9	21.2	6.4	10.6	67.7	46.1		2.7	.3		3.7	2.1	4.7	8.1	−1.5
1953	69.6	29.8	21.2	6.8	11.7	76.1	52.8		2.1	.3		3.8	2.7	5.2	9.1	−6.5
1954	69.7	29.5	21.1	7.2	11.9	70.9	49.3		1.6	.3		4.4	3.4	4.8	7.1	−1.2
1955	65.5	28.7	17.9	7.9	11.0	68.4	42.7		2.2	.3		5.1	4.4	4.9	8.9	−3.0
1956	74.6	32.2	20.9	9.3	12.2	70.6	42.5		2.4	.4		4.7	5.5	5.1	10.1	3.9
1957	80.0	35.6	21.2	10.0	13.2	76.6	45.4		3.1	.5		5.4	6.7	5.4	10.1	3.4
1958	79.6	34.7	20.1	11.2	13.6	82.4	46.8		3.4	.5		7.5	8.2	5.6	10.3	−2.8
1959	79.2	36.7	17.3	11.7	13.5	92.1	49.0		3.1	.7		8.2	9.7	5.8	15.5	−12.8
1960	92.5	40.7	21.5	14.7	15.6	92.2	48.1		3.0	.8		7.4	11.6	6.9	14.4	.3
1961	94.4	41.3	21.0	16.4	15.7	97.7	49.6		3.2	.9		9.7	12.5	6.7	15.2	−3.3
1962	99.7	45.6	20.5	17.0	16.5	106.8	52.3	50.1	5.6	1.2		9.2	14.4	6.9	17.2	−7.1
1963	106.6	47.6	21.6	19.8	17.6	111.3	53.4	51.1	5.3	1.5		9.3	15.8	7.7	18.3	−4.8
1964	112.6	48.7	23.5	22.0	18.5	118.5	54.8	52.6	4.9	1.8		9.7	16.6	8.2	22.6	−5.9
1965	116.8	48.8	25.5	22.2	20.3	118.2	50.6	48.8	5.3	1.8		9.5	17.5	8.6	25.0	−1.4
1966	130.8	55.4	30.1	25.5	19.8	134.5	58.1	56.6	5.6	2.5	.1	9.7	20.7	9.4	28.5	−3.7
1967	148.8	61.5	34.0	32.6	20.7	157.5	71.4	70.1	5.6	3.4	2.7	10.3	21.7	10.3	32.1	−8.6
1968	153.0	68.7	28.7	33.9	21.7	178.1	81.9	80.4	5.3	4.4	4.6	11.8	23.9	11.1	35.1	−25.2
1969	186.9	87.2	36.7	39.0	23.9	183.6	82.5	80.8	4.6	5.2	5.7	13.1	27.3	12.7	32.6	3.2
1970	192.8	90.4	32.8	44.4	25.2	195.6	81.7	80.1	4.3	5.9	6.2	15.6	30.3	14.4	37.2	−2.8
1971	187.1	86.2	26.8	47.3	26.8	210.2	78.9	77.5	4.2	6.8	6.6	22.9	35.9	14.8	40.0	−23.0
1972	207.3	94.7	32.2	52.6	27.8	230.7	79.2	77.6	4.8	8.7	7.5	27.6	40.2	15.5	47.3	−23.4
1973	230.8	103.2	36.2	63.1	28.3	245.7	76.7	75.0	4.1	9.4	8.1	28.3	49.1	17.3	52.8	−14.9
1974	263.2	119.0	38.6	75.1	30.6	269.4	79.3	77.9	5.7	10.7	9.6	33.7	55.9	21.4	52.9	−6.1
1975	279.1	122.4	40.6	84.5	31.5	332.3	86.5	84.9	7.1	12.9	12.9	50.2	64.7	23.2	74.9	−53.2
1976	298.1	131.6	41.4	90.8	34.3	371.8	89.6	87.9	6.4	15.7	15.8	60.8	73.9	26.7	82.8	−73.7
Transition quarter	81.2	38.8	8.5	25.2	8.8	96.0	22.3	21.8	2.5	3.9	4.3	15.0	19.8	6.9	21.4	−14.7
1977	355.6	157.6	54.9	106.5	36.6	409.2	97.2	95.1	6.4	17.3	19.3	61.0	85.1	29.9	93.0	−53.7
1978	399.6	181.0	60.0	121.0	37.7	458.7	104.5	102.3	7.5	18.5	22.8	61.5	93.9	35.5	114.7	−59.2
1979	463.3	217.8	65.7	138.9	40.8	504.0	116.3	113.6	7.5	20.5	26.5	66.4	104.1	42.6	120.2	−40.7
1980	517.1	244.1	64.6	157.8	50.6	590.9	134.0	130.9	12.7	23.2	32.1	86.5	118.5	52.5	131.4	−73.8
1981	599.3	285.9	61.1	182.7	69.5	678.2	157.5	153.9	13.1	26.9	39.1	99.7	139.6	68.8	133.5	−79.0
1982	617.8	297.7	49.2	201.5	69.3	745.8	185.3	180.7	12.3	27.4	46.6	107.7	156.0	85.0	125.4	−128.0
1983	600.6	288.9	37.0	209.0	65.6	808.4	209.9	204.4	11.8	28.6	52.6	122.6	170.7	89.8	122.3	−207.8
1984	666.5	298.4	56.9	239.4	71.8	851.8	227.4	220.9	15.9	30.4	57.5	112.7	178.2	111.1	118.6	−185.4
1985	734.1	334.5	61.3	265.2	73.0	946.4	252.7	245.2	16.2	33.5	65.8	128.2	188.6	129.5	131.8	−212.3
1986	769.1	349.0	63.1	283.9	73.1	990.3	273.4	265.5	14.2	35.9	70.2	119.8	198.8	136.0	142.1	−221.2
1987	854.1	392.6	83.9	303.3	74.3	1,003.9	282.0	274.0	11.6	40.0	75.1	123.3	207.4	138.7	125.9	−149.8
1988	909.0	401.2	94.5	334.3	78.9	1,064.1	290.4	281.9	10.5	44.5	78.9	129.3	219.3	151.8	139.4	−155.2
1989	990.7	445.7	103.3	359.4	82.3	1,143.2	303.6	294.9	9.6	48.4	85.0	136.0	232.5	169.3	158.8	−152.5
1990	1,031.3	466.9	93.5	380.0	90.9	1,252.7	299.3	289.8	13.8	57.7	98.1	147.0	248.6	184.2	203.9	−221.4
1991	1,054.3	467.8	98.1	396.0	92.3	1,323.4	273.3	262.4	15.9	71.2	104.5	170.3	269.0	194.5	224.8	−269.2
1992	1,090.5	476.0	100.3	413.7	100.5	1,380.9	298.4	286.9	16.1	89.5	119.0	196.9	287.6	199.4	173.9	−290.4
1993	1,153.5	509.7	117.5	428.3	98.0	1,408.7	291.1	278.6	17.2	99.4	130.6	207.3	304.6	198.8	159.7	−255.1
1994	1,257.7	543.1	140.4	461.5	112.8	1,460.9	281.6	268.6	17.1	107.1	144.7	214.0	319.6	203.0	173.8	−203.2
1995 [1]	1,346.4	588.5	150.9	484.4	122.7	1,538.9	271.6	260.2	18.7	115.1	157.3	223.0	336.1	234.2	182.8	−192.5
1996 [1]	1,415.5	623.4	157.4	509.3	125.3	1,612.1	261.4	250.0	16.7	124.0	177.8	233.2	354.5	257.0	187.4	−196.7

[1] Estimates.

Note.—Through fiscal year 1976, the fiscal year was on a July 1-June 30 basis; beginning October 1976 (fiscal year 1977), the fiscal year is on an October 1-September 30 basis. The 3-month period from July 1, 1976 through September 30, 1976 is a separate fiscal period known as the transition quarter.

Refunds of receipts are excluded from receipts and outlays.

See *Budget of the United States Government, Fiscal Year 1996,* February 1995, for additional information.

Sources: Department of the Treasury and Office of Management and Budget.

TABLE B-80.—*Federal receipts, outlays, and debt, fiscal years 1983–96*

[Millions of dollars; fiscal years]

Description	Actual						
	1983	1984	1985	1986	1987	1988	1989
RECEIPTS AND OUTLAYS:							
Total receipts	600,562	666,457	734,057	769,091	854,143	908,954	990,691
Total outlays	808,380	851,846	946,391	990,336	1,003,911	1,064,140	1,143,172
Total surplus or deficit (−)	−207,818	−185,388	−212,334	−221,245	−149,769	−155,187	−152,481
On-budget receipts	453,242	500,382	547,886	568,862	640,741	667,463	727,026
On-budget outlays	661,272	686,032	769,584	806,838	810,079	861,449	932,261
On-budget surplus or deficit (−)	−208,030	−185,650	−221,698	−237,976	−169,339	−193,986	−205,235
Off-budget receipts	147,320	166,075	186,171	200,228	213,402	241,491	263,666
Off-budget outlays	147,108	165,813	176,807	183,498	193,832	202,691	210,911
Off-budget surplus or deficit (−)	212	262	9,363	16,731	19,570	38,800	52,754
OUTSTANDING DEBT, END OF PERIOD:							
Gross Federal debt	1,371,710	1,564,657	1,817,521	2,120,629	2,346,125	2,601,307	2,868,039
Held by Government accounts	240,114	264,159	317,612	383,919	457,444	550,507	678,157
Held by the public	1,131,596	1,300,498	1,499,908	1,736,709	1,888,680	2,050,799	2,189,882
Federal Reserve System	155,527	155,122	169,806	190,855	212,040	229,218	220,088
Other	976,069	1,145,376	1,330,102	1,545,854	1,676,640	1,821,581	1,969,795
RECEIPTS: ON-BUDGET AND OFF-BUDGET	600,562	666,457	734,057	769,091	854,143	908,954	990,691
Individual income taxes	288,938	298,415	334,531	348,959	392,557	401,181	445,690
Corporation income taxes	37,022	56,893	61,331	63,143	83,926	94,508	103,291
Social insurance taxes and contributions	208,994	239,376	265,163	283,901	303,318	334,335	359,416
On-budget	61,674	73,301	78,992	83,673	89,916	92,845	95,751
Off-budget	147,320	166,075	186,171	200,228	213,402	241,491	263,666
Excise taxes	35,300	37,361	35,992	32,919	32,457	35,227	34,386
Estate and gift taxes	6,053	6,010	6,422	6,958	7,493	7,594	8,745
Customs duties and fees	8,655	11,370	12,079	13,327	15,085	16,198	16,334
Miscellaneous receipts:							
Deposits of earnings by Federal Reserve System	14,492	15,684	17,059	18,374	16,817	17,163	19,604
All other	1,108	1,347	1,480	1,510	2,490	2,747	3,225
OUTLAYS: ON-BUDGET AND OFF-BUDGET	808,380	851,846	946,391	990,336	1,003,911	1,064,140	1,143,172
National defense	209,903	227,413	252,748	273,375	281,999	290,361	303,559
International affairs	11,848	15,876	16,176	14,152	11,649	10,471	9,573
General science, space, and technology	7,935	8,317	8,627	8,976	9,216	10,841	12,838
Energy	9,353	7,086	5,685	4,735	4,115	2,297	2,706
Natural resources and environment	12,672	12,593	13,357	13,639	13,363	14,606	16,182
Agriculture	22,901	13,613	25,565	31,449	26,606	17,210	16,919
Commerce and housing credit	6,681	6,917	4,229	4,890	6,182	18,815	29,211
On-budget	6,681	6,917	4,229	4,890	6,182	18,815	29,520
Off-budget	....	....	....	....	....	....	−310
Transportation	21,334	23,669	25,838	28,117	26,222	27,272	27,608
Community and regional development	7,560	7,673	7,680	7,233	5,051	5,294	5,362
Education, training, employment, and social services	26,606	27,579	29,342	30,585	29,724	31,938	36,674
Health	28,641	30,417	33,542	35,936	39,967	44,487	48,390
Medicare	52,588	57,540	65,822	70,164	75,120	78,878	84,964
Income security	122,598	112,668	128,200	119,796	123,250	129,332	136,031
Social security	170,724	178,223	188,623	198,757	207,353	219,341	232,542
On-budget	19,993	7,056	5,189	8,072	4,930	4,852	5,069
Off-budget	150,731	171,167	183,434	190,684	202,422	214,489	227,473
Veterans benefits and services	24,846	25,614	26,292	26,356	26,782	29,428	30,066
Administration of justice	5,105	5,663	6,270	6,572	7,553	9,236	9,474
General government	11,235	11,817	11,588	12,564	7,565	9,464	9,017
Net interest	89,828	111,123	129,504	136,047	138,652	151,838	169,266
On-budget	91,673	114,432	133,622	140,377	143,942	159,253	180,661
Off-budget	−1,845	−3,310	−4,118	−4,329	−5,290	−7,416	−11,395
Allowances							
Undistributed offsetting receipts	−33,976	−31,957	−32,698	−33,007	−36,455	−36,967	−37,212
On-budget	−32,198	−29,913	−30,189	−30,150	−33,155	−32,585	−32,354
Off-budget	−1,778	−2,044	−2,509	−2,857	−3,300	−4,382	−4,858

Note.—Through fiscal year 1976, the fiscal year was on a July 1–June 30 basis; beginning October 1976 (fiscal year 1977), the fiscal year is on an October 1–September 30 basis. The 3-month period from July 1, 1976 through September 30, 1976 is a separate fiscal period known as the transition quarter.

Refunds of receipts are excluded from receipts and outlays.

See next page for continuation of table.

[Millions of dollars; fiscal years]

Description	Actual					Estimates	
	1990	1991	1992	1993	1994	1995	1996
RECEIPTS AND OUTLAYS:							
Total receipts	1,031,321	1,054,272	1,090,453	1,153,535	1,257,745	1,346,414	1,415,456
Total outlays	1,252,705	1,323,441	1,380,856	1,408,675	1,460,914	1,538,920	1,612,128
Total surplus or deficit (−)	− 221,384	− 269,169	− 290,403	− 255,140	− 203,169	− 192,506	− 196,671
On-budget receipts	749,666	760,388	788,027	841,601	922,719	995,158	1,045,095
On-budget outlays	1,027,640	1,081,754	1,128,518	1,142,088	1,181,542	1,246,936	1,307,105
On-budget surplus or deficit (−)	− 277,974	− 321,367	− 340,490	− 300,487	− 258,823	− 251,778	− 262,010
Off-budget receipts	281,656	293,885	302,426	311,934	335,026	351,256	370,361
Off-budget outlays	225,065	241,687	252,339	266,587	279,372	291,984	305,023
Off-budget surplus or deficit (−)	56,590	52,198	50,087	45,347	55,654	59,272	65,338
OUTSTANDING DEBT, END OF PERIOD:							
Gross Federal debt	3,206,564	3,598,498	4,002,136	4,351,416	4,643,711	4,961,529	5,299,581
Held by Government accounts	795,841	910,362	1,003,302	1,103,945	1,211,498	1,321,380	1,442,281
Held by the public	2,410,722	2,688,137	2,998,834	3,247,471	3,432,213	3,640,149	3,857,300
Federal Reserve System	234,410	258,591	296,397	325,653	355,150	....	....
Other	2,176,312	2,429,546	2,702,437	2,921,818	3,077,063	....	....
RECEIPTS: ON-BUDGET AND OFF-BUDGET	1,031,321	1,054,272	1,090,453	1,153,535	1,257,745	1,346,414	1,415,456
Individual income taxes	466,884	467,827	475,964	509,680	543,055	588,460	623,372
Corporation income taxes	93,507	98,086	100,270	117,520	140,385	150,864	157,449
Social insurance taxes and contributions	380,047	396,016	413,689	428,300	461,475	484,409	509,315
On-budget	98,392	102,131	111,263	116,366	126,450	133,153	138,954
Off-budget	281,656	293,885	302,426	311,934	335,026	351,256	370,361
Excise taxes	35,345	42,402	45,569	48,057	55,225	57,600	57,194
Estate and gift taxes	11,500	11,138	11,143	12,577	15,225	15,587	16,760
Customs duties and fees	16,707	15,949	17,359	18,802	20,099	20,913	22,332
Miscellaneous receipts:							
Deposits of earnings by Federal Reserve System	24,319	19,158	22,920	14,908	18,023	24,559	24,774
All other	3,011	3,696	3,538	3,691	4,259	4,022	4,260
OUTLAYS: ON-BUDGET AND OFF-BUDGET	1,252,705	1,323,441	1,380,856	1,408,675	1,460,914	1,538,920	1,612,128
National defense	299,331	273,292	298,350	291,086	281,563	271,600	261,424
International affairs	13,764	15,851	16,107	17,248	17,083	18,713	16,735
General science, space, and technology	14,444	16,111	16,409	17,030	16,227	16,977	16,851
Energy	3,341	2,436	4,500	4,319	5,219	4,589	4,369
Natural resources and environment	17,080	18,559	20,025	20,239	21,064	21,891	21,839
Agriculture	11,958	15,183	15,205	20,490	15,121	14,401	13,552
Commerce and housing credit	67,142	75,312	10,093	− 22,719	− 5,122	− 11,958	− 7,553
On-budget	65,516	73,994	9,434	− 24,160	− 6,225	− 12,670	− 8,178
Off-budget	1,626	1,317	659	1,441	1,103	712	625
Transportation	29,485	31,099	33,333	35,004	38,134	39,154	38,639
Community and regional development	8,498	6,811	6,838	9,052	10,454	12,598	12,815
Education, training, employment, and social services	38,755	43,354	45,248	50,012	46,307	56,065	57,173
Health	57,716	71,183	89,497	99,415	107,122	115,098	124,000
Medicare	98,102	104,489	119,024	130,552	144,747	157,288	177,824
Income security	147,022	170,276	196,948	207,250	214,036	223,006	233,153
Social security	248,623	269,015	287,585	304,585	319,565	336,149	354,548
On-budget	3,625	2,619	6,166	6,236	5,683	4,860	5,184
Off-budget	244,998	266,395	281,418	298,349	313,881	331,289	349,364
Veterans benefits and services	29,112	31,349	34,138	35,720	37,642	38,392	38,092
Administration of justice	9,993	12,276	14,426	14,955	15,256	17,631	19,732
General government	10,734	11,661	12,990	13,009	11,312	14,493	14,580
Net interest	184,221	194,541	199,421	198,811	202,957	234,224	257,001
On-budget	200,212	214,763	223,059	225,599	232,160	267,800	295,103
Off-budget	− 15,991	− 20,222	− 23,637	− 26,788	− 29,203	− 33,576	− 38,102
Allowances							− 224
Undistributed offsetting receipts	− 36,615	− 39,356	− 39,280	− 37,386	− 37,772	− 41,392	− 42,424
On-budget	− 31,048	− 33,553	− 33,179	− 30,970	− 31,362	− 34,951	− 35,560
Off-budget	− 5,567	− 5,804	− 6,101	− 6,416	− 6,409	− 6,441	− 6,864

See *Budget of the United States Government, Fiscal Year 1996,* February 1995, for additional information.

Sources: Department of the Treasury and Office of Management and Budget.

TABLE B–81.—*Relation of Federal Government receipts and expenditures in the national income and product accounts to the budget, fiscal years, 1992–96*

[Billions of dollars; fiscal years]

Receipts and expenditures	1992	1993	1994	Estimates	
				1995	1996
RECEIPTS					
Total on-budget and off-budget receipts	1,090.5	1,153.5	1,257.7	1,346.4	1,415.5
Government contributions for employee retirement (grossing)	51.5	53.5	56.9	58.0	60.2
Other netting and grossing	25.2	28.1	28.0	27.9	25.9
Timing adjustments	−5.3	7.1	8.8	5.4	4.5
Geographic exclusions	−1.9	−2.0	−2.0	−2.1	−2.2
Other	1.3	.7	.0	.0	.0
Federal sector, national income and product accounts, receipts	1,161.2	1,241.0	1,349.4	1,435.7	1,504.0
EXPENDITURES					
Total on-budget and off-budget outlays	1,380.9	1,408.7	1,460.9	1,538.9	1,612.1
Government contributions for employee retirement (grossing)	51.5	53.5	56.9	58.0	60.2
Other netting and grossing	25.2	28.1	28.0	27.9	25.9
Lending transactions	−5.7	−11.0	−12.6	−16.5	−5.7
Deposit insurance and other financial transactions	−.3	26.3	3.7	10.4	6.7
Defense timing adjustment	.6	2.4	−.3	.6	4.7
Other timing adjustments	−7.0	−2.2	−5.3	−2.8	−3.2
Payments to U.S. territories	−7.2	−6.8	−8.8	−9.3	−9.2
Bonuses on outer continental shelf land leases	.0	.0	.2	.2	.2
Other	−2.1	−3.6	−.7	1.9	3.7
Federal sector, national income and product accounts, expenditures	1,435.9	1,495.5	1,521.9	1,609.4	1,695.4

Note.—See Note, Table B–77.
For further details, see *Survey of Current Business*, February 1995.

Sources: Department of Commerce (Bureau of Economic Analysis), Department of the Treasury, and Office of Management and Budget.

TABLE B-82.—*Federal Government receipts and expenditures, national income and product accounts (NIPA), 1978–96*

[Billions of dollars; quarterly data at seasonally adjusted annual rates]

Year or quarter	Receipts Total	Personal tax and nontax receipts	Corporate profits tax accruals	Indirect business tax and nontax accruals	Contributions for social insurance	Expenditures Total [1]	Purchases Total	Purchases National defense	Transfer payments To persons	Transfer payments To rest of the world (net)	Grants-in-aid to State and local governments	Net interest paid	Subsidies less current surplus of government enterprises	Surplus or deficit (−) (NIPA)
Fiscal: [2]														
1978	423.8	185.5	67.4	27.9	143.0	458.0	158.1	106.3	179.3	3.5	74.7	33.1	9.4	−34.1
1979	490.5	221.6	75.3	29.9	163.7	505.4	174.5	117.7	198.5	4.0	79.1	40.2	9.1	−14.9
1980	538.1	249.1	70.4	36.2	182.3	587.1	201.0	136.9	235.4	4.3	86.7	50.1	9.6	−49.0
1981	623.0	287.9	69.3	54.3	211.5	679.9	232.9	160.9	274.6	5.2	90.1	66.1	11.0	−56.9
1982	642.7	308.4	51.6	51.5	231.2	747.6	259.5	187.3	305.6	5.8	83.4	81.8	11.5	−105.0
1983	646.4	290.7	56.4	52.0	247.3	829.2	289.8	210.2	339.8	6.5	86.2	89.6	16.8	−182.8
1984	711.7	300.4	75.1	57.0	279.3	875.3	302.2	228.2	342.4	8.7	91.5	107.5	23.0	−163.6
1985	777.0	337.0	75.0	59.1	305.9	952.9	335.2	251.7	360.7	11.5	98.6	125.2	21.6	−175.9
1986	813.8	353.1	80.4	53.8	326.5	1,017.6	363.7	274.3	380.6	12.5	108.3	130.5	22.1	−203.9
1987	899.1	396.3	99.4	57.8	345.5	1,051.0	379.9	287.6	399.4	9.9	103.4	133.6	24.9	−151.9
1988	955.1	403.8	107.6	59.6	384.1	1,098.5	386.3	295.1	420.7	10.2	108.4	143.8	28.9	−143.3
1989	1,050.1	456.9	119.2	62.2	411.8	1,164.5	399.4	299.5	449.6	11.6	115.8	160.5	27.6	−114.3
1990	1,092.0	475.2	115.4	63.1	438.3	1,250.0	418.1	309.0	491.3	14.4	128.3	175.1	22.8	−157.9
1991	1,121.8	476.4	109.3	77.0	459.1	1,311.3	446.0	325.9	535.9	−26.2	147.0	183.5	25.1	−189.4
1992	1,161.2	484.6	112.4	81.1	483.1	1,435.9	445.2	312.1	596.0	11.5	168.2	188.9	26.1	−274.7
1993	1,241.0	511.8	134.6	82.9	511.7	1,495.5	446.3	306.3	634.2	17.4	180.7	183.5	33.4	−254.4
1994	1,349.4	552.1	161.2	93.3	542.8	1,521.9	435.1	295.6	660.6	13.8	197.9	187.0	27.6	−172.5
1995 [3]	1,435.7	598.6	170.5	93.9	572.7	1,609.4	438.2	288.5	698.6	12.6	213.6	217.4	29.0	−173.7
1996 [3]	1,504.0	637.4	176.8	93.6	596.1	1,695.4	439.8	284.8	747.0	11.2	226.5	238.9	31.9	−191.4
Calendar:														
1978	441.2	193.8	71.4	28.9	147.1	469.3	162.2	108.9	182.4	3.8	77.3	34.6	9.2	−28.1
1979	504.7	229.7	74.4	30.1	170.4	520.3	179.3	121.9	205.7	4.1	80.5	42.1	8.7	−15.7
1980	553.0	256.2	70.3	39.6	186.8	613.1	209.1	142.7	247.0	5.0	88.7	52.7	10.6	−60.1
1981	639.0	297.2	65.7	57.3	218.8	697.8	240.8	167.5	282.1	5.0	87.9	71.7	10.3	−58.8
1982	635.4	302.9	49.0	49.7	233.8	770.9	266.6	193.8	316.4	6.4	83.9	84.4	13.3	−135.5
1983	660.0	292.6	61.3	53.5	252.6	840.0	292.0	214.4	340.2	7.3	87.0	92.7	20.4	−180.1
1984	725.8	308.0	75.2	57.8	284.8	892.7	310.9	233.1	344.3	9.4	94.4	113.1	20.8	−166.9
1985	788.6	342.8	76.3	58.6	310.9	969.9	344.3	258.6	366.8	11.4	100.3	127.0	19.9	−181.4
1986	827.2	357.4	83.8	53.5	332.5	1,028.2	367.8	276.7	386.2	12.3	107.6	131.0	23.4	−201.0
1987	913.8	400.6	103.2	58.4	351.5	1,065.6	384.9	292.1	401.8	10.4	102.8	136.6	29.1	−151.8
1988	972.3	410.1	111.0	60.9	390.4	1,109.0	387.0	295.6	425.9	10.4	111.3	146.0	28.4	−136.6
1989	1,059.3	461.9	117.1	61.9	418.5	1,181.6	401.6	299.9	460.2	11.3	118.2	164.8	25.5	−122.3
1990	1,111.4	484.3	116.4	65.8	444.8	1,274.9	426.5	314.0	500.9	13.2	132.3	176.5	25.6	−163.5
1991	1,128.7	475.8	108.1	79.9	465.0	1,331.6	445.8	322.8	550.0	−27.8	153.3	187.8	22.4	−202.9
1992	1,178.3	489.5	115.6	81.3	491.9	1,460.9	449.0	314.2	608.8	16.5	172.2	186.8	27.6	−282.7
1993	1,265.7	520.3	143.0	84.6	517.8	1,507.0	443.6	302.7	642.2	15.7	186.1	183.6	35.7	−241.4
1994 ᴾ		566.0		90.9	555.3	1,538.2	436.6	292.1	666.8	15.7	197.9	191.6	29.6	
1982: IV	632.3	301.6	45.5	49.2	235.9	815.7	281.4	205.5	337.8	8.2	84.3	86.8	17.3	−183.4
1983: IV	671.1	290.5	65.4	55.4	259.8	855.7	289.7	222.8	340.0	11.0	86.9	99.2	28.8	−184.6
1984: IV	739.8	323.5	67.0	58.2	291.1	926.6	324.7	242.9	346.2	13.9	97.7	122.3	22.2	−186.8
1985: IV	803.6	351.8	77.0	56.8	318.0	990.8	356.9	268.6	370.3	13.5	104.5	129.2	16.4	−187.2
1986: IV	856.8	371.7	91.4	54.8	338.8	1,034.3	373.1	278.6	391.4	12.8	103.8	131.1	22.1	−177.5
1987: IV	943.5	414.8	109.7	59.5	359.4	1,096.3	392.5	295.8	405.1	14.6	102.9	143.1	37.8	−152.7
1988: IV	1,000.6	420.0	118.5	61.4	400.7	1,135.5	392.0	296.8	429.4	15.1	113.0	151.2	34.9	−134.9
1989: IV	1,068.3	470.1	111.3	62.2	424.7	1,209.8	405.1	302.5	473.7	15.1	121.9	168.9	25.0	−141.5
1990: IV	1,115.8	483.9	115.1	67.1	449.7	1,306.9	436.5	322.5	514.1	12.4	137.6	174.4	32.0	−191.0
1991: I	1,120.1	477.0	105.2	77.7	460.2	1,264.5	451.7	331.8	538.4	−76.9	144.3	183.6	23.7	−144.4
II	1,121.8	474.1	107.2	78.4	462.1	1,329.4	450.1	326.6	547.2	−32.0	151.7	188.8	23.2	−207.6
III	1,132.5	474.7	110.4	80.6	466.8	1,346.0	443.2	320.9	551.2	−5.0	154.7	187.1	14.9	−213.6
IV	1,140.5	477.3	109.6	82.9	470.7	1,386.3	438.3	311.6	563.4	2.8	162.6	191.6	27.7	−245.8
1992: I	1,155.7	476.0	115.7	80.7	483.3	1,435.6	445.2	312.2	598.7	12.5	164.6	188.2	26.4	−279.9
II	1,171.0	481.3	120.8	80.5	488.5	1,455.8	443.2	310.0	607.1	15.1	172.8	189.5	28.0	−284.8
III	1,166.5	489.2	103.2	80.2	493.9	1,460.4	452.9	318.6	611.8	13.0	174.6	186.6	21.5	−293.9
IV	1,219.9	511.6	122.6	83.8	501.9	1,492.0	454.8	316.0	617.8	25.3	176.6	183.1	34.5	−272.1
1993: I	1,212.7	497.2	132.1	81.9	501.6	1,496.2	446.9	307.0	633.4	11.4	176.7	182.5	45.2	−283.5
II	1,263.7	519.8	141.8	83.5	518.6	1,500.6	445.2	305.8	639.9	12.9	182.9	184.8	35.1	−237.0
III	1,272.7	527.5	140.2	82.3	522.7	1,497.6	442.7	299.0	645.9	14.3	187.8	183.6	23.3	−224.9
IV	1,313.6	536.8	157.8	90.7	528.3	1,533.7	439.8	299.1	649.8	24.3	197.0	183.5	39.3	−220.1
1994: I	1,337.4	550.2	151.8	90.4	545.1	1,513.7	437.8	291.7	659.9	11.6	190.0	179.3	35.1	−176.2
II	1,380.7	571.1	166.3	90.4	553.0	1,525.9	435.1	291.7	663.5	12.7	194.4	188.8	31.3	−145.1
III	1,388.8	566.9	172.4	91.9	557.6	1,542.8	444.3	300.5	668.5	14.4	200.3	194.4	20.9	−154.0
IV ᴾ		575.6		91.0	565.7	1,570.3	429.2	284.4	675.4	23.9	206.9	203.9	31.1	

[1] Includes an item for the difference between wage accruals and disbursements, not shown separately.
[2] Beginning October 1976, the fiscal year is on an October 1–September 30 basis. Data are not seasonally adjusted.
[3] Estimates.

Sources: Department of Commerce (Bureau of Economic Analysis) and Office of Management and Budget.

371

[Billions of dollars; quarterly data at seasonally adjusted annual rates]

Year or quarter	Total government			Federal Government			State and local government		
	Receipts	Expenditures	Surplus or deficit (−) (NIPA)	Receipts	Expenditures	Surplus or deficit (−) (NIPA)	Receipts	Expenditures	Surplus or deficit (−) (NIPA)
1959	128.8	131.9	−3.1	90.6	93.2	−2.6	45.0	45.5	−0.5
1960	138.8	135.2	3.6	97.0	93.4	3.5	48.3	48.3	.0
1961	144.1	147.1	−3.0	99.0	101.7	−2.6	52.4	52.7	−.4
1962	155.8	158.7	−2.9	107.2	110.6	−3.4	56.6	56.1	.5
1963	167.5	165.9	1.6	115.5	114.4	1.1	61.1	60.6	.4
1964	172.9	174.5	−1.6	116.2	118.8	−2.6	67.1	66.1	1.0
1965	187.0	185.8	1.2	125.8	124.6	1.3	72.3	72.3	.0
1966	210.7	211.6	−1.0	143.5	144.9	−1.4	81.5	81.1	.5
1967	226.4	240.2	−13.7	152.6	165.2	−12.7	89.8	90.9	−1.1
1968	260.9	265.5	−4.6	176.8	181.5	−4.7	102.7	102.6	.1
1969	294.0	284.0	10.0	199.6	191.0	8.5	114.8	113.3	1.5
1970	299.8	311.2	−11.5	195.2	208.5	−13.3	129.0	127.2	1.8
1971	318.9	338.1	−19.2	202.6	224.3	−21.7	145.3	142.8	2.5
1972	364.2	368.1	−3.9	232.0	249.3	−17.3	169.7	156.3	13.4
1973	408.5	401.6	6.9	263.7	270.3	−6.6	185.3	171.9	13.4
1974	450.7	455.2	−4.5	294.0	305.6	−11.6	200.6	193.5	7.1
1975	465.8	530.6	−64.8	294.8	364.2	−69.4	225.6	221.0	4.6
1976	532.6	570.9	−38.3	339.9	392.7	−52.9	253.9	239.3	14.6
1977	598.4	615.2	−16.8	384.0	426.4	−42.4	281.9	256.3	25.6
1978	673.2	670.3	2.9	441.2	469.3	−28.1	309.3	278.2	31.1
1979	754.7	745.3	9.4	504.7	520.3	−15.7	330.6	305.4	25.1
1980	825.7	861.0	−35.3	553.0	613.1	−60.1	361.4	336.6	24.8
1981	941.9	972.3	−30.3	639.0	697.8	−58.8	390.8	362.3	28.5
1982	960.5	1,069.1	−108.6	635.4	770.9	−135.5	409.0	382.1	26.9
1983	1,016.4	1,156.2	−139.8	660.0	840.0	−180.1	443.4	403.2	40.3
1984	1,123.6	1,232.4	−108.8	725.8	892.7	−166.9	492.2	434.1	58.1
1985	1,217.0	1,342.2	−125.3	788.6	969.9	−181.4	528.7	472.6	56.1
1986	1,290.8	1,437.5	−146.8	827.2	1,028.2	−201.0	571.2	517.0	54.3
1987	1,405.2	1,516.9	−111.7	913.8	1,065.6	−151.8	594.3	554.2	40.1
1988	1,492.4	1,590.7	−98.3	972.3	1,109.0	−136.6	631.3	593.0	38.4
1989	1,622.6	1,700.1	−77.5	1,059.3	1,181.6	−122.3	681.5	636.7	44.8
1990	1,709.1	1,847.5	−138.4	1,111.4	1,274.9	−163.5	730.0	704.9	25.1
1991	1,759.0	1,944.9	−185.9	1,128.7	1,331.6	−202.9	783.6	766.6	17.0
1992	1,849.1	2,106.9	−257.8	1,178.3	1,460.9	−282.7	842.9	818.1	24.8
1993 ᴾ	1,970.6	2,185.6	−215.0	1,265.7	1,507.0	−241.4	891.0	864.7	26.3
1994 ᴾ		2,257.1			1,538.2		916.9		
1982: IV	965.9	1,122.8	−156.9	632.3	815.7	−183.4	417.9	391.4	26.5
1983: IV	1,043.7	1,180.0	−136.3	671.1	855.7	−184.6	459.5	411.1	48.3
1984: IV	1,147.1	1,274.9	−127.8	739.8	926.6	−186.8	505.1	446.1	59.0
1985: IV	1,243.8	1,374.7	−130.9	803.6	990.8	−187.2	544.8	488.4	56.3
1986: IV	1,335.4	1,461.6	−126.2	856.8	1,034.3	−177.5	582.4	531.1	51.2
1987: IV	1,445.7	1,561.5	−115.8	943.5	1,096.3	−152.7	605.1	568.1	37.0
1988: IV	1,535.8	1,630.5	−94.7	1,000.6	1,135.5	−134.9	648.2	607.9	40.2
1989: IV	1,644.1	1,744.3	−100.2	1,068.3	1,209.8	−141.5	697.7	656.4	41.3
1990: IV	1,726.5	1,905.8	−179.3	1,115.8	1,306.9	−191.0	748.3	736.5	11.7
1991: I	1,734.0	1,868.4	−134.4	1,120.1	1,264.5	−144.4	758.2	748.2	10.0
II	1,744.6	1,937.4	−192.8	1,121.8	1,329.4	−207.6	774.6	759.7	14.9
III	1,768.5	1,964.2	−195.8	1,132.5	1,346.0	−213.6	790.7	772.9	17.8
IV	1,788.8	2,009.4	−220.7	1,140.5	1,386.3	−245.8	810.8	785.7	25.1
1992: I	1,813.5	2,073.5	−260.0	1,155.7	1,435.6	−279.9	822.4	802.5	19.9
II	1,836.8	2,095.7	−258.9	1,171.0	1,455.8	−284.8	838.7	812.8	25.9
III	1,837.0	2,110.5	−273.5	1,166.5	1,460.4	−293.9	845.1	824.7	20.4
IV	1,908.8	2,147.9	−239.1	1,219.9	1,492.0	−272.1	865.5	832.5	33.1
1993: I	1,900.9	2,162.8	−261.9	1,212.7	1,496.2	−283.5	865.0	843.4	21.6
II	1,965.1	2,176.7	−211.6	1,263.7	1,500.6	−237.0	884.3	859.0	25.3
III	1,980.9	2,181.9	−201.0	1,272.7	1,497.6	−224.9	896.0	872.1	23.9
IV	2,035.4	2,221.0	−185.6	1,313.6	1,533.7	−220.1	918.8	884.3	34.5
1994: I	2,066.5	2,217.6	−151.1	1,337.4	1,513.7	−176.2	919.1	893.9	25.2
II	2,121.9	2,240.0	−118.1	1,380.7	1,525.9	−145.1	935.6	908.6	27.0
III	2,138.9	2,269.0	−130.1	1,388.8	1,542.8	−154.0	950.3	926.4	23.9
IV ᴾ		2,302.0			1,570.3		938.6		

Note.—Federal grants-in-aid to State and local governments are reflected in Federal expenditures and State and local receipts. Total government receipts and expenditures have been adjusted to eliminate this duplication.

Source: Department of Commerce, Bureau of Economic Analysis.

TABLE B–84.—*Federal and State and local government receipts and expenditures, national income and product accounts (NIPA), by major type, 1959–94*

[Billions of dollars; quarterly data at seasonally adjusted annual rates]

Year or quarter	Receipts					Expenditures								Surplus or deficit (−) (NIPA)	Addendum: Grants-in-aid to State and local governments
	Total	Personal tax and nontax receipts	Corporate profits tax accruals	Indirect business tax and nontax accruals	Contributions for social insurance	Total¹	Purchases	Transfer payments	Net interest paid			Less: Dividends received by government²	Subsidies less current surplus of government enterprises		
									Total	Interest paid	Less: Interest received by government²				
1959	128.8	44.5	23.6	41.9	18.8	131.9	99.0	27.5	6.3				−0.9	−3.1	6.8
1960	138.8	48.7	22.7	45.5	21.9	135.2	99.8	29.3	6.9	10.1	3.3		−.8	3.6	6.5
1961	144.1	50.3	22.8	48.1	22.9	147.1	107.0	33.6	6.4	9.9	3.5		.2	−3.0	7.2
1962	155.8	54.8	24.0	51.7	25.4	158.7	116.8	34.7	6.9	10.8	3.9		.3	−2.9	8.0
1963	167.5	58.0	26.2	54.7	28.5	165.9	122.3	36.6	7.4	11.6	4.2		−.3	1.6	9.1
1964	172.9	56.0	28.0	58.8	30.1	174.5	128.3	38.1	7.9	12.5	4.6		.1	−1.6	10.4
1965	187.0	61.9	30.9	62.7	31.6	185.8	136.3	41.1	8.1	13.2	5.1		.3	1.2	11.1
1966	210.7	71.0	33.7	65.4	40.6	211.6	155.9	45.8	8.5	14.5	6.0		1.4	−1.0	14.4
1967	226.4	77.9	32.7	70.4	45.5	240.2	175.6	54.5	8.9	15.7	6.8		1.2	−13.7	15.9
1968	260.9	92.1	39.4	79.0	50.4	265.5	191.5	62.6	10.3	18.1	7.7	0.1	1.2	−4.6	18.6
1969	294.0	109.9	39.7	86.6	57.9	284.0	201.8	69.3	11.5	19.8	8.3	.2	1.5	10.0	20.3
1970	299.8	109.0	34.4	94.3	62.2	311.2	212.7	83.8	12.4	22.3	9.9	.2	2.6	−11.5	24.4
1971	318.9	108.7	37.7	103.6	68.9	338.1	224.3	99.4	12.5	23.1	10.6	.3	2.4	−19.2	29.0
1972	364.2	132.0	41.9	111.4	79.0	368.1	241.5	110.9	12.9	24.8	11.9	.3	3.4	−3.9	37.5
1973	408.5	140.6	49.3	121.0	97.6	401.6	257.7	126.6	15.2	29.6	14.4	.5	2.6	6.9	40.6
1974	450.7	159.1	51.8	129.3	110.5	455.2	288.3	150.5	16.3	33.6	17.3	.9	.4	−4.5	43.9
1975	465.8	156.4	50.9	140.0	118.5	530.6	321.4	189.2	18.5	37.7	19.2	.9	2.6	−64.8	54.6
1976	532.6	182.3	64.2	151.6	134.5	570.9	341.3	206.5	22.8	43.6	20.9	.9	1.4	−38.3	61.1
1977	598.4	210.0	73.0	165.5	149.8	615.2	368.0	220.9	24.4	47.9	23.5	1.3	3.3	−16.8	67.5
1978	673.2	240.1	83.5	177.8	171.8	670.3	403.6	238.6	26.5	56.8	30.3	1.7	3.6	2.9	77.3
1979	754.7	280.2	88.0	188.7	197.8	745.3	448.5	266.9	28.7	68.6	39.9	2.0	2.9	9.4	80.5
1980	825.7	312.4	84.8	212.0	216.6	861.0	507.1	317.6	33.4	83.9	50.5	1.9	4.8	−35.3	88.7
1981	941.9	360.2	81.1	249.3	251.3	972.3	561.1	360.7	48.1	110.2	62.1	2.3	4.7	−30.3	87.9
1982	960.5	371.4	63.1	256.4	269.6	1,069.1	607.6	402.7	55.5	130.6	75.0	2.9	6.2	−108.6	83.9
1983	1,016.4	368.8	77.2	280.1	290.2	1,156.2	652.3	433.4	61.8	146.6	84.8	3.4	11.7	−139.8	87.0
1984	1,123.6	395.1	94.0	309.5	325.0	1,232.4	700.8	447.2	79.1	174.6	95.6	3.9	9.5	−108.8	94.4
1985	1,217.0	436.8	96.5	329.9	353.8	1,342.2	772.3	479.5	88.3	195.9	107.6	4.5	6.4	−125.3	100.3
1986	1,290.8	459.0	106.5	345.5	379.8	1,437.5	833.0	509.4	90.6	207.9	117.3	5.1	9.7	−146.8	107.6
1987	1,405.2	512.5	127.1	365.0	400.7	1,516.9	881.5	531.8	95.4	215.9	120.5	5.9	14.1	−111.7	102.8
1988	1,492.4	527.7	137.0	385.3	442.3	1,590.7	918.7	566.2	101.8	229.9	128.1	6.9	10.9	−98.3	111.3
1989	1,622.6	593.3	141.3	414.7	473.2	1,700.1	975.2	615.1	112.4	251.0	138.6	8.1	5.4	−77.5	118.2
1990	1,709.1	623.3	138.7	444.0	503.1	1,847.5	1,047.4	679.5	125.2	269.6	144.5	9.0	4.5	−138.4	132.3
1991	1,759.0	623.7	131.1	478.3	525.9	1,944.9	1,097.4	721.4	135.5	283.9	148.3	9.5	−.1	−185.9	153.3
1992	1,849.1	648.6	139.7	504.4	556.4	2,106.9	1,125.3	854.4	133.7	282.3	148.6	10.1	3.5	−257.8	172.2
1993	1,970.6	686.4	173.2	525.3	585.6	2,185.6	1,148.4	908.4	130.2	279.3	149.1	10.4	9.0	−215.0	186.1
1994 ᵖ		742.5		553.7	626.3	2,257.1	1,174.5	955.8	136.8	286.0	149.3	10.9	1.0		197.9
1982: IV	965.9	372.1	58.7	262.3	272.8	1,122.8	631.6	428.1	56.6	135.6	79.0	3.1	9.6	−156.9	84.3
1983: IV	1,043.7	371.6	82.2	291.7	298.3	1,180.0	657.6	439.1	67.7	156.1	88.4	3.5	19.2	−136.3	86.9
1984: IV	1,147.1	413.4	83.8	317.7	332.2	1,274.9	727.0	456.2	86.7	186.5	99.8	4.1	9.7	−127.8	97.7
1985: IV	1,243.8	448.8	97.6	335.1	362.3	1,374.7	799.2	488.3	89.2	201.6	112.3	4.7	2.6	−130.9	104.5
1986: IV	1,335.4	478.5	116.6	351.6	388.7	1,461.6	849.7	518.6	90.5	208.7	118.2	5.4	8.2	−126.2	103.8
1987: IV	1,445.7	528.6	135.2	372.3	409.6	1,561.5	901.4	542.6	101.3	222.9	121.6	6.1	22.0	−115.8	102.9
1988: IV	1,535.8	542.0	146.2	394.2	453.5	1,630.5	937.6	578.6	105.0	236.0	131.0	7.2	16.5	−94.7	113.0
1989: IV	1,644.1	605.1	134.2	424.4	480.4	1,744.3	994.5	639.0	114.8	256.0	141.2	8.5	4.4	−100.2	121.9
1990: IV	1,726.5	625.2	137.0	454.8	509.5	1,905.8	1,076.5	703.3	125.1	278.3	153.2	9.3	10.4	−179.3	137.6
1991: I	1,734.0	620.5	127.3	465.8	520.4	1,868.4	1,095.5	648.1	132.8	281.2	148.4	9.4	1.6	−134.4	144.3
II	1,744.6	620.2	130.0	471.8	522.7	1,937.4	1,098.7	710.2	136.8	284.4	147.6	9.5	.8	−192.8	151.7
III	1,768.5	622.8	134.0	483.7	528.0	1,964.2	1,097.6	749.6	134.2	283.5	149.3	9.5	−7.7	−195.8	154.7
IV	1,788.8	631.2	133.1	491.8	532.7	2,009.4	1,097.9	777.9	138.3	286.4	148.1	9.6	5.0	−220.7	162.6
1992: I	1,813.5	631.3	139.6	496.3	546.3	2,073.5	1,114.5	830.2	134.9	282.3	147.4	9.8	3.6	−260.0	164.6
II	1,836.8	638.7	146.0	499.6	552.6	2,095.7	1,116.8	848.2	136.4	284.2	147.9	10.1	4.4	−258.9	172.8
III	1,837.0	648.1	124.6	505.3	558.9	2,110.5	1,131.9	858.1	133.5	282.3	148.8	10.1	−2.9	−273.5	174.6
IV	1,908.8	676.2	148.6	516.2	567.8	2,147.9	1,138.1	881.0	130.0	280.3	150.3	10.3	9.1	−239.1	176.6
1993: I	1,900.9	657.3	159.8	515.5	568.3	2,162.8	1,137.1	887.2	129.4	277.7	148.3	10.2	19.3	−261.9	176.7
II	1,965.1	685.9	171.8	521.4	586.1	2,176.7	1,146.3	900.4	131.5	280.5	149.0	10.3	8.8	−211.6	182.9
III	1,980.9	695.4	169.9	524.7	590.9	2,181.9	1,152.9	913.1	130.2	279.9	149.7	10.4	−3.9	−201.0	187.8
IV	2,035.4	707.0	191.5	539.7	597.2	2,221.0	1,157.2	932.7	129.9	279.1	149.2	10.5	11.7	−185.6	197.0
1994: I	2,066.5	723.0	184.1	544.7	614.7	2,217.6	1,159.8	935.8	125.2	273.7	148.4	10.7	7.4	−151.1	190.0
II	2,121.9	746.4	201.7	550.7	623.5	2,240.0	1,166.7	946.9	134.2	283.2	149.0	10.8	3.0	−118.1	194.4
III	2,138.9	744.1	208.6	557.2	628.9	2,269.0	1,188.8	959.8	139.3	288.8	149.5	10.9	−8.0	−130.1	200.3
IV ᵖ		756.5		562.8	637.9	2,302.0	1,182.6	980.7	148.3	298.5	150.2	11.3	1.6		206.9

¹ Includes an item for the difference between wage accruals and disbursements, not shown separately.
² Prior to 1968, dividends received is included in interest received.

Source: Department of Commerce, Bureau of Economic Analysis.

TABLE B-85.—*State and local government receipts and expenditures, national income and product accounts (NIPA), 1959-94*

[Billions of dollars; quarterly data at seasonally adjusted annual rates]

Year or quarter	Receipts						Expenditures					Surplus or deficit (−) (NIPA)
	Total	Personal tax and nontax receipts	Corporate profits tax accruals	Indirect business tax and nontax accruals	Contributions for social insurance	Federal grants-in-aid	Total [1]	Purchases	Transfer payments to persons	Net interest paid less dividends received	Subsidies less current surplus of government enterprises	
1959	45.0	4.6	1.2	29.3	3.1	6.8	45.5	41.8	5.6	0.1	−2.0	−0.5
1960	48.3	5.2	1.2	32.0	3.4	6.5	48.3	44.5	5.9	.1	−2.2	.0
1961	52.4	5.7	1.3	34.4	3.7	7.2	52.7	48.4	6.5	.1	−2.3	−.4
1962	56.6	6.3	1.5	37.0	3.9	8.0	56.1	51.4	7.0	.2	−2.5	.5
1963	61.1	6.7	1.7	39.4	4.2	9.1	60.6	55.8	7.5	.1	−2.8	.4
1964	67.1	7.5	1.8	42.6	4.7	10.4	66.1	60.9	8.2	−.1	−2.8	1.0
1965	72.3	8.1	2.0	46.1	5.0	11.1	72.3	66.8	8.8	−.3	−3.0	.0
1966	81.5	9.5	2.2	49.7	5.7	14.4	81.1	74.6	10.1	−.6	−3.0	.5
1967	89.8	10.6	2.6	53.9	6.7	15.9	90.9	82.7	12.1	−.9	−3.1	−1.1
1968	102.7	12.7	3.3	60.8	7.2	18.6	102.6	92.3	14.5	−1.1	−3.2	.1
1969	114.8	15.2	3.6	67.4	8.3	20.3	113.3	101.3	16.7	−1.3	−3.3	1.5
1970	129.0	16.7	3.7	74.8	9.2	24.4	127.2	112.6	20.1	−2.0	−3.6	1.8
1971	145.3	18.7	4.3	83.1	10.2	29.0	142.8	124.3	24.0	−1.6	−3.7	2.5
1972	169.7	24.2	5.3	91.2	11.5	37.5	156.3	134.7	27.5	−1.8	−4.2	13.4
1973	185.3	26.3	6.0	99.5	13.0	40.6	171.9	149.2	30.4	−3.3	−4.3	13.4
1974	200.6	28.2	6.7	107.2	14.6	43.9	193.5	170.7	32.3	−5.2	−4.4	7.1
1975	225.6	31.0	7.3	115.8	16.8	54.6	221.0	192.0	38.9	−5.4	−4.5	4.6
1976	253.9	35.8	9.6	127.8	19.5	61.1	239.3	205.5	43.6	−5.0	−4.8	14.6
1977	281.9	41.0	11.4	139.9	22.1	67.5	256.3	220.1	47.4	−6.0	−5.1	25.6
1978	309.3	46.3	12.1	148.9	24.7	77.3	278.2	241.4	52.4	−9.8	−5.6	31.1
1979	330.6	50.5	13.6	158.6	27.4	80.5	305.4	269.2	57.2	−15.3	−5.7	25.1
1980	361.4	56.2	14.5	172.3	29.7	88.7	336.6	298.0	65.7	−21.2	−5.8	24.8
1981	390.8	63.0	15.4	192.0	32.5	87.9	362.3	320.3	73.6	−25.9	−5.6	28.5
1982	409.0	68.5	14.0	206.8	35.8	83.9	382.1	341.1	79.9	−31.8	−7.1	26.9
1983	443.4	76.2	15.9	226.6	37.7	87.0	403.2	360.3	85.9	−34.3	−8.7	40.3
1984	492.2	87.1	18.8	251.7	40.2	94.4	434.1	389.9	93.5	−37.9	−11.4	58.1
1985	528.7	94.0	20.2	271.4	42.8	100.3	472.6	428.1	101.2	−43.2	−13.5	56.1
1986	571.2	101.6	22.7	292.0	47.3	107.6	517.0	465.3	110.9	−45.6	−13.7	54.3
1987	594.3	111.8	23.9	306.5	49.2	102.8	554.2	496.6	119.6	−47.0	−14.9	40.1
1988	631.3	117.6	26.0	324.5	51.9	111.3	593.0	531.7	130.0	−51.1	−17.5	38.4
1989	681.5	131.4	24.2	352.8	54.8	118.2	636.7	573.6	143.6	−60.4	−20.1	44.8
1990	730.0	138.9	22.3	378.2	58.3	132.3	704.9	620.9	165.4	−60.3	−21.1	25.1
1991	783.6	147.9	23.0	398.4	61.0	153.3	766.6	651.6	199.2	−61.8	−22.5	17.0
1992	842.9	159.1	24.2	423.1	64.5	172.2	818.1	676.3	229.0	−63.2	−24.0	24.8
1993	891.0	166.1	30.3	440.7	67.8	186.1	864.7	704.7	250.4	−63.7	−26.7	26.3
1994 *p*		176.6		462.8	70.9	197.9	916.9	737.9	273.3	−65.8	−28.6	
1982: IV	417.9	70.5	13.1	213.1	36.8	84.3	391.4	350.3	82.1	−33.2	−7.7	26.5
1983: IV	459.5	81.1	16.8	236.3	38.4	86.9	411.1	367.9	88.0	−35.1	−9.6	48.3
1984: IV	505.1	89.9	16.8	259.6	41.1	97.7	446.1	402.2	96.1	−39.7	−12.5	59.0
1985: IV	544.8	97.0	20.6	278.3	44.3	104.5	488.4	442.4	104.5	−44.7	−13.8	56.3
1986: IV	582.4	106.8	25.2	296.8	49.8	103.8	531.1	476.6	114.4	−45.9	−13.9	51.2
1987: IV	605.1	113.8	25.5	312.8	50.2	102.9	568.1	509.0	122.9	−48.0	−15.8	37.0
1988: IV	648.2	122.0	27.7	332.7	52.8	113.0	607.9	545.7	134.2	−53.4	−18.5	40.2
1989: IV	697.7	135.0	22.8	362.2	55.8	121.9	656.4	589.3	150.2	−62.6	−20.6	41.3
1990: IV	748.3	141.3	21.9	387.7	59.7	137.6	736.5	640.0	176.8	−58.7	−21.6	11.7
1991: I	758.2	143.5	22.1	388.1	60.2	144.3	748.2	643.8	186.6	−60.2	−22.1	10.0
II	774.6	146.1	22.8	393.4	60.6	151.7	759.7	648.6	195.0	−61.6	−22.4	14.9
III	790.7	148.1	23.6	403.1	61.2	154.7	772.9	654.4	203.5	−62.4	−22.6	17.8
IV	810.8	153.9	23.5	408.9	62.0	162.6	785.7	659.7	211.7	−62.9	−22.7	25.1
1992: I	822.4	155.3	23.9	415.6	63.0	164.6	802.5	669.3	219.0	−63.0	−22.8	19.9
II	838.7	157.4	25.2	419.1	64.1	172.8	812.8	673.6	225.9	−63.2	−23.5	25.9
III	845.1	158.9	21.4	425.2	65.0	174.6	824.7	679.1	233.2	−63.2	−24.4	20.4
IV	865.5	164.6	26.0	432.4	65.9	176.6	832.5	683.3	237.9	−63.4	−25.4	33.1
1993: I	865.0	160.2	27.7	433.7	66.7	176.7	843.4	690.2	242.4	−63.3	−25.9	21.6
II	884.3	166.1	30.0	437.9	67.5	182.9	859.0	701.2	247.7	−63.6	−26.3	25.3
III	896.0	167.9	29.7	442.4	68.2	187.8	872.1	710.2	252.9	−63.8	−27.2	23.9
IV	918.8	170.2	33.7	449.0	68.9	197.0	884.3	717.4	258.6	−64.1	−27.6	34.5
1994: I	919.1	172.9	32.3	454.2	69.7	190.0	893.9	722.0	264.3	−64.7	−27.7	25.2
II	935.6	175.3	35.4	460.0	70.5	194.4	908.6	731.5	270.7	−65.4	−28.3	27.0
III	950.3	177.3	36.2	465.3	71.3	200.3	926.4	744.5	276.8	−66.0	−28.9	23.9
IV *p*		180.8		471.8	72.2	206.9	938.6	753.4	281.4	−66.8	−29.4	

[1] Includes an item for the difference between wage accruals and disbursements, not shown separately.

Source: Department of Commerce, Bureau of Economic Analysis.

TABLE B–86.—*State and local government revenues and expenditures, selected fiscal years, 1927–92*

[Millions of dollars]

Fiscal year [1]	General revenues by source [2]							General expenditures by function [2]				
	Total	Property taxes	Sales and gross receipts taxes	Individual income taxes	Corporation net income taxes	Revenue from Federal Government	All other [3]	Total	Education	Highways	Public welfare	All other [4]
1927	7,271	4,730	470	70	92	116	1,793	7,210	2,235	1,809	151	3,015
1932	7,267	4,487	752	74	79	232	1,643	7,765	2,311	1,741	444	3,269
1934	7,678	4,076	1,008	80	49	1,016	1,449	7,181	2,177	1,509	889	2,952
1936	8,395	4,093	1,484	153	113	948	1,604	7,644	2,177	1,425	827	3,215
1938	9,228	4,440	1,794	218	165	800	1,811	8,757	2,491	1,650	1,069	3,547
1940	9,609	4,430	1,982	224	156	945	1,872	9,229	2,638	1,573	1,156	3,862
1942	10,418	4,537	2,351	276	272	858	2,123	9,190	2,586	1,490	1,225	3,889
1944	10,908	4,604	2,289	342	451	954	2,269	8,863	2,793	1,200	1,133	3,737
1946	12,356	4,986	2,986	422	447	855	2,661	11,028	3,356	1,672	1,409	4,591
1948	17,250	6,126	4,442	543	592	1,861	3,685	17,684	5,379	3,036	2,099	7,170
1950	20,911	7,349	5,154	788	593	2,486	4,541	22,787	7,177	3,803	2,940	8,867
1952	25,181	8,652	6,357	998	846	2,566	5,763	26,098	8,318	4,650	2,788	10,342
1953	27,307	9,375	6,927	1,065	817	2,870	6,252	27,910	9,390	4,987	2,914	10,619
1954	29,012	9,967	7,276	1,127	778	2,966	6,897	30,701	10,557	5,527	3,060	11,557
1955	31,073	10,735	7,643	1,237	744	3,131	7,584	33,724	11,907	6,452	3,168	12,197
1956	34,667	11,749	8,691	1,538	890	3,335	8,465	36,711	13,220	6,953	3,139	13,399
1957	38,164	12,864	9,467	1,754	984	3,843	9,252	40,375	14,134	7,816	3,485	14,940
1958	41,219	14,047	9,829	1,759	1,018	4,865	9,699	44,851	15,919	8,567	3,818	16,547
1959	45,306	14,983	10,437	1,994	1,001	6,377	10,516	48,887	17,283	9,592	4,136	17,876
1960	50,505	16,405	11,849	2,463	1,180	6,974	11,634	51,876	18,719	9,428	4,404	19,325
1961	54,037	18,002	12,463	2,613	1,266	7,131	12,563	56,201	20,574	9,844	4,720	21,063
1962	58,252	19,054	13,494	3,037	1,308	7,871	13,489	60,206	22,216	10,357	5,084	22,549
1963	62,890	20,089	14,456	3,269	1,505	8,722	14,850	64,816	23,776	11,136	5,481	24,423
1962–63	62,269	19,833	14,446	3,267	1,505	8,663	14,556	63,977	23,729	11,150	5,420	23,678
1963–64	68,443	21,241	15,762	3,791	1,695	10,002	15,951	69,302	26,286	11,664	5,766	25,586
1964–65	74,000	22,583	17,118	4,090	1,929	11,029	17,250	74,678	28,563	12,221	6,315	27,579
1965–66	83,036	24,670	19,085	4,760	2,038	13,214	19,269	82,843	33,287	12,770	6,757	30,029
1966–67	91,197	26,047	20,530	5,825	2,227	15,370	21,197	93,350	37,919	13,932	8,218	33,281
1967–68	101,264	27,747	22,911	7,308	2,518	17,181	23,598	102,411	41,158	14,481	9,857	36,915
1968–69	114,550	30,673	26,519	8,908	3,180	19,153	26,118	116,728	47,238	15,417	12,110	41,963
1969–70	130,756	34,054	30,322	10,812	3,738	21,857	29,971	131,332	52,718	16,427	14,679	47,508
1970–71	144,927	37,852	33,233	11,900	3,424	26,146	32,374	150,674	59,413	18,095	18,226	54,940
1971–72	167,541	42,877	37,518	15,227	4,416	31,342	36,162	168,549	65,814	19,021	21,117	62,597
1972–73	190,222	45,283	42,047	17,994	5,425	39,264	40,210	181,357	69,714	18,615	23,582	69,446
1973–74	207,670	47,705	46,098	19,491	6,015	41,820	46,541	198,959	75,833	19,946	25,085	78,096
1974–75	228,171	51,491	49,815	21,454	6,642	47,034	51,735	230,722	87,858	22,528	28,156	92,180
1975–76	256,176	57,001	54,547	24,575	7,273	55,589	57,191	256,731	97,216	23,907	32,604	103,004
1976–77	285,157	62,527	60,641	29,246	9,174	62,444	61,124	274,215	102,780	23,058	35,906	112,472
1977–78	315,960	66,422	67,596	33,176	10,738	69,592	68,436	296,984	110,758	24,609	39,140	122,477
1978–79	343,236	64,944	74,247	36,932	12,128	75,164	79,821	327,517	119,448	28,440	41,898	137,731
1979–80	382,322	68,499	79,927	42,080	13,321	83,029	95,466	369,086	133,211	33,311	47,288	155,277
1980–81	423,404	74,969	85,971	46,426	14,143	90,294	111,599	407,449	145,784	34,603	54,105	172,957
1981–82	457,654	82,067	93,613	50,738	15,028	87,282	128,926	436,733	154,282	34,520	57,996	189,935
1982–83	486,753	89,105	100,247	55,129	14,258	90,007	138,008	466,516	163,876	36,655	60,906	205,079
1983–84	542,730	96,457	114,097	64,529	17,141	96,935	153,570	505,008	176,108	39,419	66,414	223,068
1984–85	598,121	103,757	126,376	70,361	19,152	106,158	172,317	553,899	192,686	44,989	71,479	244,745
1985–86	641,486	111,709	135,005	74,365	19,994	114,857	187,314	605,623	210,819	49,368	75,868	269,568
1986–87	686,860	121,203	144,091	83,935	22,425	114,857	200,350	657,134	226,619	52,355	82,650	295,510
1987–88	726,762	132,212	156,452	88,350	23,663	117,602	208,482	704,921	242,683	55,621	89,090	317,528
1988–89	786,129	142,400	166,336	97,806	25,926	125,824	227,838	762,360	263,898	58,105	97,879	342,479
1989–90	849,502	155,613	177,885	105,640	23,566	136,802	249,996	834,818	288,148	61,057	110,518	375,095
1990–91	902,207	167,999	185,570	109,341	22,242	154,099	262,956	908,108	309,302	64,937	130,402	403,467
1991–92	972,452	178,406	196,150	115,170	23,833	179,184	279,710	972,185	326,770	66,689	154,234	424,492

[1] Fiscal years not the same for all governments. See Note.
[2] Excludes revenues or expenditures of publicly owned utilities and liquor stores, and of insurance-trust activities. Intergovernmental receipts and payments between State and local governments are also excluded.
[3] Includes other taxes and charges and miscellaneous revenues.
[4] Includes expenditures for libraries, hospitals, health, employment security administration, veterans' services, air transportation, water transport and terminals, parking facilities, and transit subsidies, police protection, fire protection, correction, protective inspection and regulation, sewerage, natural resources, parks and recreation, housing and community development, solid waste management, financial administration, judicial and legal, general public buildings, other government administration, interest on general debt, and general expenditures, n.e.c.

Note.—Data for fiscal years listed from 1962–63 to 1991–92 are the aggregations of data for government fiscal years that ended in the 12-month period from July 1 to June 30 of those years. Data for 1963 and earlier years include data for government fiscal years ending during that particular calendar year.

Data are not available for intervening years.

Source: Department of Commerce, Bureau of the Census.

TABLE B-87.—*Interest-bearing public debt securities by kind of obligation, 1967–94*

[Millions of dollars]

End of year or month	Total interest-bearing public debt securities	Marketable				Nonmarketable				
		Total¹	Treasury bills	Treasury notes	Treasury bonds	Total	U.S. savings bonds	Foreign government and public series²	Government account series	Other³
Fiscal year:										
1967	322,286	⁴210,672	58,535	49,108	97,418	111,614	51,213	1,514	56,155	2,731
1968	344,401	226,592	64,440	71,073	91,079	117,808	51,712	3,741	59,526	2,828
1969	351,729	226,107	68,356	78,946	78,805	125,623	51,711	4,070	66,790	3,051
1970	369,026	232,599	76,154	93,489	62,956	136,426	51,281	4,755	76,323	4,068
1971	396,289	245,473	86,677	104,807	53,989	150,816	53,003	9,270	82,784	5,759
1972	425,360	257,202	94,648	113,419	49,135	168,158	55,921	18,985	89,598	3,654
1973	456,353	262,971	100,061	117,840	45,071	193,382	59,418	28,524	101,738	3,701
1974	473,238	266,575	105,019	128,419	33,137	206,663	61,921	25,011	115,442	4,289
1975	532,122	315,606	128,569	150,257	36,779	216,516	65,482	23,216	124,173	3,644
1976	619,254	392,581	161,198	191,758	39,626	226,673	69,733	21,500	130,557	4,883
1977	697,629	443,508	156,091	241,692	45,724	254,121	75,411	21,799	140,113	16,797
1978	766,971	485,155	160,936	267,865	56,355	281,816	79,798	21,680	153,271	27,067
1979	819,007	506,693	161,378	274,242	71,073	312,314	80,440	28,115	176,360	27,400
1980	906,402	594,506	199,832	310,903	83,772	311,896	72,727	25,158	189,848	24,164
1981	996,495	683,209	223,388	363,643	96,178	313,286	68,017	20,499	201,052	23,718
1982	1,140,883	824,422	277,900	442,890	103,631	316,461	67,274	14,641	210,462	24,085
1983	1,375,751	1,024,000	340,733	557,525	125,742	351,751	70,024	11,450	234,684	35,593
1984	1,559,570	1,176,556	356,798	661,687	158,070	383,015	72,832	8,806	259,534	41,843
1985	1,821,010	1,360,179	384,220	776,449	199,510	460,831	77,011	6,638	313,928	63,255
1986	2,122,684	¹1,564,329	410,730	896,884	241,716	558,355	85,551	4,128	365,872	102,804
1987	2,347,750	¹1,675,980	378,263	1,005,127	277,590	671,769	97,004	4,350	440,658	129,758
1988	2,599,877	¹1,802,905	398,451	1,089,578	299,875	796,972	106,176	6,320	536,455	148,023
1989	2,836,309	¹1,892,763	406,597	1,133,193	337,974	943,546	114,025	6,818	663,677	159,025
1990	3,210,943	¹2,092,759	482,454	1,218,081	377,224	1,118,184	122,152	36,041	779,412	180,581
1991	3,662,759	¹2,390,660	564,589	1,387,717	423,354	1,272,099	133,512	41,639	908,406	188,541
1992	4,061,801	¹2,677,476	634,287	1,566,349	461,840	1,384,325	148,266	37,039	1,011,020	188,000
1993	4,408,567	¹2,904,910	658,381	1,734,161	497,367	1,503,657	167,024	42,459	1,114,289	179,886
1994	4,689,524	¹3,091,602	697,295	1,867,507	511,800	1,597,922	176,413	41,996	1,211,689	167,826
1993: Jan	4,150,059	¹2,732,962	647,041	1,598,398	472,523	1,417,098	157,647	37,167	1,043,062	179,222
Feb	4,180,254	¹2,760,533	648,459	1,616,923	480,151	1,419,722	159,888	37,006	1,042,760	180,066
Mar	4,227,628	¹2,807,092	659,877	1,652,068	480,148	1,420,536	161,441	37,038	1,039,995	182,062
Apr	4,251,164	¹2,808,859	642,189	1,671,522	480,147	1,442,306	162,644	43,791	1,053,080	182,791
May	4,279,221	¹2,821,933	657,491	1,661,834	487,608	1,457,288	163,550	43,221	1,066,394	184,123
June	4,349,011	¹2,860,622	659,280	1,698,736	487,606	1,488,389	164,424	42,964	1,097,751	183,251
July	4,333,507	¹2,852,073	671,190	1,678,277	487,606	1,481,434	165,319	43,007	1,094,815	178,293
Aug	4,400,313	¹2,917,196	677,030	1,727,799	497,368	1,483,116	166,181	42,496	1,095,548	178,892
Sept	4,408,567	¹2,904,910	658,381	1,734,161	497,367	1,503,657	167,024	42,459	1,114,289	179,886
Oct	4,403,759	¹2,892,521	668,723	1,711,432	497,366	1,511,239	168,155	43,777	1,120,822	178,485
Nov	4,490,639	¹2,977,823	709,212	1,757,755	495,856	1,512,817	168,993	43,596	1,120,345	179,883
Dec	4,532,325	¹2,989,475	714,631	1,763,989	495,855	1,542,850	169,425	43,480	1,150,041	179,904
1994: Jan	4,523,027	¹2,986,024	702,292	1,772,877	495,855	1,537,002	170,736	43,222	1,147,831	175,214
Feb	4,556,241	¹3,017,122	700,686	1,797,213	504,223	1,539,120	171,750	42,724	1,148,964	175,681
Mar	4,572,619	¹3,042,902	721,146	1,802,537	504,219	1,529,717	172,632	42,724	1,138,405	175,957
Apr	4,548,547	¹3,003,364	705,340	1,778,805	504,219	1,545,183	173,533	42,708	1,152,758	176,185
May	4,605,977	¹3,046,277	700,228	1,829,211	501,838	1,559,700	174,237	42,517	1,167,948	174,998
June	4,642,523	¹3,050,989	698,446	1,835,705	501,837	1,591,534	174,859	42,229	1,200,606	173,840
July	4,616,171	¹3,034,469	706,064	1,811,569	501,837	1,581,702	175,460	41,924	1,194,806	169,512
Aug	4,688,745	¹3,103,702	716,177	1,860,724	511,800	1,585,043	175,915	41,788	1,198,058	169,283
Sept	4,689,524	¹3,091,602	697,295	1,867,507	511,800	1,597,922	176,413	41,996	1,211,689	167,826
Oct	4,730,969	¹3,123,224	721,149	1,875,275	511,799	1,607,746	177,187	42,880	1,221,401	166,278
Nov	4,775,318	¹3,164,390	745,294	1,893,798	510,297	1,610,928	177,755	42,683	1,225,944	164,544
Dec	4,769,171	¹3,126,035	733,753	1,866,986	510,296	1,643,137	177,786	42,471	1,259,827	163,053

¹ Includes Federal Financing Bank securities, not shown separately, in the amount of 15,000 million dollars.
² Nonmarketable certificates of indebtedness, notes, bonds, and bills in the Treasury foreign series of dollar-denominated and foreign-currency denominated issues.
³ Includes depository bonds, retirement plan bonds, Rural Electrification Administration bonds, State and local bonds, and special issues held only by U.S. Government agencies and trust funds and the Federal home loan banks.
⁴ Includes $5,610 million in certificates not shown separately.

Note.—Through fiscal year 1976, the fiscal year was on a July 1–June 30 basis; beginning October 1976 (fiscal year 1977), the fiscal year is on an October 1–September 30 basis.

Source: Department of the Treasury.

TABLE B–88.—*Maturity distribution and average length of marketable interest-bearing public debt securities held by private investors, 1967–94*

End of year or month	Amount outstanding, privately held	Maturity class					Average length	
		Within 1 year	1 to 5 years	5 to 10 years	10 to 20 years	20 years and over	Years	Months
		Millions of dollars					Years	Months
Fiscal year:								
1967	150,321	56,561	53,584	21,057	6,153	12,968	5	1
1968	159,671	66,746	52,295	21,850	6,110	12,670	4	5
1969	156,008	69,311	50,182	18,078	6,097	12,337	4	2
1970	157,910	76,443	57,035	8,286	7,876	8,272	3	8
1971	161,863	74,803	58,557	14,503	6,357	7,645	3	6
1972	165,978	79,509	57,157	16,033	6,358	6,922	3	3
1973	167,869	84,041	54,139	16,385	8,741	4,564	3	1
1974	164,862	87,150	50,103	14,197	9,930	3,481	2	11
1975	210,382	115,677	65,852	15,385	8,857	4,611	2	8
1976	279,782	150,296	90,578	24,169	8,087	6,652	2	7
1977	326,674	161,329	113,319	33,067	8,428	10,531	2	11
1978	356,501	163,819	132,993	33,500	11,383	14,805	3	3
1979	380,530	181,883	127,574	32,279	18,489	20,304	3	7
1980	463,717	220,084	156,244	38,809	25,901	22,679	3	9
1981	549,863	256,187	182,237	48,743	32,569	30,127	4	0
1982	682,043	314,436	221,783	75,749	33,017	37,058	3	11
1983	862,631	379,579	294,955	99,174	40,826	48,097	4	1
1984	1,017,488	437,941	332,808	130,417	49,664	66,658	4	6
1985	1,185,675	472,661	402,766	159,383	62,853	88,012	4	11
1986	1,354,275	506,903	467,348	189,995	70,664	119,365	5	3
1987	1,445,366	483,582	526,746	209,160	72,862	153,016	5	9
1988	1,555,208	524,201	552,993	232,453	74,186	171,375	5	9
1989	1,654,660	546,751	578,333	247,428	80,616	201,532	6	0
1990	1,841,903	626,297	630,144	267,573	82,713	235,176	6	1
1991	2,113,799	713,778	761,243	280,574	84,900	273,304	6	0
1992	2,363,802	808,705	866,329	295,921	84,706	308,141	5	11
1993	2,562,336	858,135	978,714	306,663	94,345	324,479	5	10
1994	2,719,861	877,932	1,128,322	289,998	88,208	335,401	5	8
1993: Jan	2,419,560	832,988	881,131	303,278	92,356	309,807	5	10
Feb	2,443,020	833,583	894,130	308,058	89,376	317,874	5	11
Mar	2,484,628	849,766	922,468	306,175	88,626	317,593	5	10
Apr	2,486,231	833,935	937,347	308,094	88,834	318,022	5	10
May	2,496,615	854,658	919,114	313,037	85,273	324,532	5	10
June	2,515,501	849,639	949,127	309,295	84,237	323,204	5	10
July	2,521,249	864,355	940,460	304,447	85,708	326,279	5	10
Aug	2,578,501	874,599	976,547	308,413	94,487	324,456	5	10
Sept	2,562,336	858,135	978,714	306,663	94,345	324,479	5	10
Oct	2,552,880	866,988	968,794	298,460	94,436	324,203	5	10
Nov	2,626,085	898,241	1,008,468	308,219	87,131	324,025	5	9
Dec	2,628,352	905,311	1,011,213	304,863	86,143	320,822	5	8
1994: Jan	2,628,451	894,898	1,029,878	296,604	86,408	320,663	5	7
Feb	2,661,872	899,813	1,041,195	300.082	86,573	334,208	5	9
Mar	2,683,420	908,889	1,054,336	299,433	86,355	334,407	5	8
Apr	2,639,251	887,454	1,041,071	289,963	86,355	334,407	5	8
May	2,680,916	893,359	1,076,198	295,356	87,866	328,138	5	8
June	2,676,695	878,396	1,087,030	295,184	87,702	328,383	5	7
July	2,667,897	888,349	1,076,723	286,051	87,621	329,153	5	7
Aug	2,731,481	899,256	1,116,418	292,971	88,235	334,601	5	8
Sept	2,719,861	877,932	1,128,322	289,998	88,208	335,401	5	8
Oct	2,750,705	904,001	1,144,298	279,896	88,058	334,451	5	7
Nov	2,782,099	926,834	1,149,907	290,468	84,856	330,035	5	6
Dec	2,737,789	906,618	1,130,084	288,781	84,157	328,150	5	6

Note.—All issues classified to final maturity.
Through fiscal year 1976, the fiscal year was on a July 1–June 30 basis; beginning October 1976 (fiscal year 1977), the fiscal year is on an October 1–September 30 basis.

Source: Department of the Treasury.

[Par values; [1] billions of dollars]

End of month	Total	Commercial banks [2]	Held by private investors — Nonbank investors				Insurance companies	Money market funds	Corporations [5]	State and local governments [6]	Foreign and international [7]	Other investors [8]
			Total	Individuals [3]								
				Total	Savings bonds [4]	Other securities						
1976: June	376.4	92.5	283.9	96.1	69.6	26.5	10.7	0.8	23.3	32.7	69.8	50.5
Dec	409.5	103.8	305.7	101.6	72.0	29.6	12.7	1.1	23.5	39.3	78.1	49.4
1977: June	421.0	102.9	318.1	104.9	74.4	30.5	13.0	.8	22.1	49.6	87.9	39.8
Dec	461.3	102.0	359.3	107.8	76.7	31.1	15.1	.9	18.2	59.1	109.6	48.6
1978: June	477.8	99.6	378.2	109.0	79.1	29.9	14.2	1.3	17.3	69.6	119.5	47.3
Dec	508.6	95.3	413.3	114.0	80.7	33.3	15.3	1.5	17.3	81.1	133.1	51.0
1979: June	516.6	94.6	422.0	115.5	80.6	34.9	16.0	3.8	18.6	86.2	114.9	67.0
Dec	540.5	95.6	444.9	118.0	79.9	38.1	15.6	5.6	17.0	86.2	119.0	83.5
1980: June	558.2	98.5	459.7	116.5	73.4	43.1	15.3	5.3	14.0	85.1	118.2	105.3
Dec	616.4	111.5	504.9	117.1	72.5	44.6	18.1	3.5	19.3	90.3	129.7	126.9
1981: June	651.2	115.0	536.2	107.4	69.2	38.2	19.9	9.0	19.9	95.9	136.6	147.5
Dec	694.5	113.8	580.7	110.8	68.1	42.7	21.6	21.5	17.9	99.9	136.6	172.4
1982: June	740.9	114.7	626.2	114.1	67.4	46.7	24.4	22.4	17.6	106.0	137.2	204.5
Dec	848.4	134.0	714.4	116.5	68.3	48.2	30.6	42.6	24.5	118.6	149.5	232.1
1983: June	948.6	167.4	781.2	121.3	69.7	51.6	37.8	28.3	32.8	138.1	160.1	262.8
Dec	1,022.6	179.5	843.1	133.4	71.5	61.9	46.0	22.8	39.7	153.0	166.3	281.9
1984: June	1,102.2	180.6	921.6	142.2	72.9	69.3	51.2	14.9	45.3	171.0	171.6	325.3
Dec	1,212.5	181.5	1,031.0	143.8	74.5	69.3	64.5	25.9	50.1	188.4	205.9	352.4
1985: June	1,292.0	195.6	1,096.4	148.7	76.7	72.0	69.1	24.8	54.9	213.4	213.8	371.7
Dec	1,417.2	189.4	1,227.8	154.8	79.8	75.0	80.5	25.1	59.0	299.0	224.8	384.6
1986: June	1,502.7	194.4	1,308.3	159.5	83.8	75.7	87.9	22.8	61.2	317.4	250.9	408.6
Dec	1,602.0	197.7	1,404.3	162.7	92.3	70.4	101.6	28.6	68.8	342.1	263.4	437.1
1987: June	1,658.1	192.5	1,465.6	165.6	96.8	68.8	104.7	20.6	79.7	375.4	281.1	438.4
Dec	1,731.4	194.4	1,537.0	172.4	101.1	71.3	108.1	14.6	84.6	403.9	299.7	453.7
1988: June	1,786.7	190.8	1,595.9	182.0	106.2	75.8	113.5	13.4	87.6	423.5	345.4	430.5
Dec	1,858.5	185.3	1,673.2	190.4	109.6	80.8	118.6	11.8	86.0	435.4	362.2	468.8
1989: June	1,909.1	178.4	1,730.7	211.7	114.0	97.7	120.6	11.3	91.0	439.2	369.1	487.8
Dec	2,015.8	165.3	1,850.5	216.4	117.7	98.7	123.9	14.9	93.4	442.5	429.6	529.8
1990: Mar	2,115.1	178.8	1,936.3	222.8	119.9	102.9	132.3	31.3	94.9	455.6	421.8	577.6
June	2,141.8	177.3	1,964.5	229.6	121.9	107.7	133.7	28.0	96.9	464.4	427.3	584.6
Sept	2,207.3	180.0	2,027.3	232.5	123.9	108.6	136.4	34.0	102.0	460.9	440.3	621.2
Dec	2,288.3	172.1	2,116.2	233.8	126.2	107.6	138.2	45.5	108.9	462.5	458.4	668.9
1991: Mar	2,360.6	187.5	2,173.1	238.3	129.7	108.6	147.2	65.4	114.9	466.7	464.3	676.2
June	2,397.9	196.2	2,201.7	243.5	133.2	110.3	156.8	55.4	130.8	471.3	473.6	670.2
Sept	2,489.4	217.5	2,271.9	257.5	135.4	122.1	171.4	64.5	142.0	472.9	477.3	686.3
Dec	2,563.2	232.5	2,330.7	263.9	138.1	125.8	181.8	80.0	150.8	485.1	491.7	677.4
1992: Mar	2,664.0	255.9	2,408.1	268.1	142.0	126.1	188.4	84.8	166.0	484.0	507.9	708.9
June	2,712.4	267.0	2,445.4	275.1	145.4	129.7	192.8	79.4	175.0	488.1	529.6	705.5
Sept	2,765.5	287.5	2,478.0	281.2	150.3	130.9	194.8	79.4	180.8	479.5	535.2	727.1
Dec	2,839.9	294.4	2,545.5	289.2	157.3	131.9	197.5	79.7	192.5	476.7	549.7	760.2
1993: Mar	2,895.0	310.2	2,584.8	297.7	163.6	134.1	208.0	77.7	199.3	488.8	564.2	749.2
June	2,938.4	307.2	2,631.2	303.0	166.5	136.4	217.8	76.2	206.1	505.4	567.7	755.0
Sept	2,983.0	313.9	2,669.1	305.8	169.1	136.7	229.4	74.8	215.6	513.8	591.3	738.3
Dec	3,047.7	322.2	2,725.5	309.9	171.9	137.9	234.5	80.5	213.0	514.2	622.6	750.9
1994: Mar	3,094.6	345.0	2,749.6	315.1	175.0	140.1	236.9	70.5	216.3	517.4	632.7	760.7
June	3,088.2	330.7	2,757.5	321.1	177.1	144.0	244.1	59.5	226.3	520.1	632.5	754.0
Sept	3,127.8	325.0	2,802.8	327.2	178.6	148.6	250.0	59.9	229.3	521.0	653.8	761.6

[1] U.S. savings bonds, series A–F and J, are included at current redemption value.

[2] Includes domestically chartered banks, U.S. branches and agencies of foreign banks, New York investment companies majority owned by foreign banks, and Edge Act corporations owned by domestically chartered and foreign banks.

[3] Includes partnerships and personal trust accounts.

[4] Includes U.S. savings notes. Sales began May 1, 1967, and were discontinued June 30, 1970.

[5] Exclusive of banks and insurance companies.

[6] Includes State and local government series (SLGs) as well as State and local pension funds.

[7] Consists of the investments of foreign and international accounts (both official and private) in U.S. public debt issues. Reflects 1978 benchmark through December 1984; December 1984 benchmark through 1989; and December 1989 benchmark thereafter.

[8] Includes savings and loan associations, credit unions, nonprofit institutions, mutual savings banks, corporate pension trust funds, dealers and brokers, certain government deposit accounts, and Government-sponsored enterprises.

Source: Department of the Treasury.

CORPORATE PROFITS AND FINANCE

TABLE B-90.—*Corporate profits with inventory valuation and capital consumption adjustments, 1959–94*

[Billions of dollars; quarterly data at seasonally adjusted annual rates]

Year or quarter	Corporate profits with inventory valuation and capital consumption adjustments	Corporate profits tax liability	Corporate profits after tax with inventory valuation and capital consumption adjustments		
			Total	Dividends	Undistributed profits with inventory valuation and capital consumption adjustments
1959	52.3	23.6	28.6	12.7	15.9
1960	50.7	22.7	28.0	13.4	14.6
1961	51.6	22.8	28.8	14.0	14.8
1962	59.6	24.0	35.6	15.0	20.6
1963	65.1	26.2	38.9	16.1	22.8
1964	72.1	28.0	44.1	18.0	26.1
1965	82.9	30.9	52.0	20.2	31.8
1966	88.6	33.7	54.9	20.9	34.0
1967	86.0	32.7	53.3	22.1	31.2
1968	92.6	39.4	53.2	24.6	28.6
1969	89.6	39.7	49.9	25.2	24.7
1970	77.5	34.4	43.1	23.7	19.4
1971	90.3	37.7	52.6	23.7	28.8
1972	103.2	41.9	61.3	25.8	35.5
1973	116.4	49.3	67.1	28.1	39.0
1974	104.5	51.8	52.7	30.4	22.3
1975	121.9	50.9	71.0	30.1	40.9
1976	147.1	64.2	82.8	35.6	47.2
1977	175.7	73.0	102.6	40.7	61.9
1978	199.7	83.5	116.2	45.9	70.3
1979	202.5	88.0	114.5	52.4	62.1
1980	177.7	84.8	92.9	59.0	33.9
1981	182.0	81.1	100.9	69.2	31.7
1982	151.5	63.1	88.4	70.0	18.4
1983	212.7	77.2	135.4	81.2	54.2
1984	264.2	94.0	170.2	82.7	87.5
1985	280.8	96.5	184.2	92.4	91.9
1986	271.6	106.5	165.1	109.8	55.4
1987	319.8	127.1	192.8	106.2	86.5
1988	365.0	137.0	228.0	115.3	112.6
1989	362.8	141.3	221.5	134.6	86.9
1990	380.6	138.7	241.9	153.5	88.5
1991	390.3	131.1	259.2	160.0	99.2
1992	405.1	139.7	265.4	171.1	94.3
1993	485.8	173.2	312.5	191.7	120.9
1994 ᵖ				205.2	
1982: IV	150.3	58.7	91.7	72.5	19.2
1983: IV	229.1	82.2	146.9	84.2	62.7
1984: IV	261.3	83.8	177.5	83.4	94.1
1985: IV	284.9	97.6	187.2	97.4	89.9
1986: IV	264.6	116.6	148.1	111.0	37.1
1987: IV	343.3	135.2	208.1	106.3	101.8
1988: IV	378.3	146.2	232.2	121.0	111.2
1989: IV	354.5	134.2	220.3	141.3	79.0
1990: IV	362.8	137.0	225.8	153.7	72.1
1991: I	385.4	127.3	258.1	158.0	100.1
II	391.5	130.0	261.5	159.4	102.1
III	389.6	134.0	255.6	161.6	93.9
IV	394.7	133.1	261.6	160.9	100.8
1992: I	412.1	139.6	272.4	161.0	111.4
II	412.6	146.0	266.6	166.8	99.9
III	363.2	124.6	238.6	174.4	64.2
IV	432.5	148.6	283.8	182.1	101.7
1993: I	442.5	159.8	282.8	188.2	94.5
II	473.1	171.8	301.3	190.7	110.7
III	493.5	169.9	323.6	193.2	130.3
IV	533.9	191.5	342.4	194.6	147.9
1994: I	508.2	184.1	324.1	196.3	127.7
II	546.4	201.7	344.8	202.5	142.3
III	556.0	208.6	347.4	207.9	139.5
IV ᵖ				213.9	

Source: Department of Commerce, Bureau of Economic Analysis.

TABLE B–91.—*Corporate profits by industry, 1959–94*

[Billions of dollars; quarterly data at seasonally adjusted annual rates]

Year or quarter	Total	Corporate profits with inventory valuation adjustment and without capital consumption adjustment									Rest of the world
		Domestic industries									
		Total	Financial [1]			Nonfinancial					
			Total	Federal Reserve banks	Other	Total	Manu-facturing [2]	Trans-portation and public utilities	Wholesale and retail trade	Other	
1959	53.1	50.4	7.0	0.7	6.3	43.4	26.5	7.1	6.2	3.6	2.7
1960	51.0	47.8	7.7	.9	6.7	40.2	23.8	7.5	5.2	3.6	3.1
1961	51.3	48.0	7.5	.8	6.8	40.4	23.4	7.9	5.5	3.6	3.3
1962	56.4	52.6	7.6	.9	6.8	45.0	26.3	8.5	6.3	3.9	3.8
1963	61.2	57.1	7.3	1.0	6.4	49.8	29.6	9.5	6.4	4.4	4.1
1964	67.5	63.0	7.5	1.1	6.4	55.5	32.4	10.2	7.9	5.1	4.5
1965	77.6	72.9	7.9	1.3	6.5	65.0	39.7	11.0	8.6	5.6	4.7
1966	83.0	78.5	9.2	1.7	7.5	69.3	42.4	11.9	8.8	6.2	4.5
1967	80.3	75.5	9.5	2.0	7.6	66.0	39.0	10.9	9.7	6.4	4.8
1968	86.9	81.3	10.9	2.5	8.4	70.4	41.7	11.0	10.9	6.8	5.6
1969	83.2	76.6	11.6	3.1	8.5	65.0	37.0	10.6	11.2	6.2	6.6
1970	71.8	64.7	13.1	3.5	9.6	51.6	27.1	8.2	10.3	5.9	7.1
1971	85.5	77.7	15.2	3.3	11.9	62.5	34.8	8.9	12.3	6.6	7.9
1972	97.9	88.4	16.4	3.3	13.1	72.0	41.4	9.4	14.1	7.1	9.5
1973	110.9	96.0	17.5	4.5	13.0	78.5	46.7	9.0	14.6	8.2	14.9
1974	103.4	85.9	16.2	5.7	10.5	69.7	40.7	7.6	13.7	7.7	17.5
1975	129.4	114.8	15.9	5.6	10.3	98.9	54.5	10.9	21.9	11.6	14.6
1976	158.8	142.3	19.9	5.9	14.0	122.4	70.7	15.3	23.1	13.3	16.5
1977	186.7	167.7	25.7	6.1	19.6	142.0	78.5	18.5	27.8	17.1	18.9
1978	212.8	190.2	31.8	7.6	24.1	158.4	89.6	21.7	27.7	19.4	22.6
1979	219.8	185.6	31.6	9.4	22.2	153.9	88.3	16.9	28.3	20.5	34.3
1980	197.8	162.9	24.3	11.8	12.6	138.5	75.8	18.3	22.8	21.6	35.0
1981	203.2	174.0	18.7	14.4	4.3	155.3	87.4	20.1	31.6	16.2	29.2
1982	166.4	138.6	15.6	15.2	.4	123.0	63.1	20.8	31.9	7.2	27.8
1983	202.2	171.9	24.5	14.6	9.9	147.4	71.4	28.9	38.7	8.4	30.4
1984	236.4	205.2	20.3	16.4	3.9	185.0	86.7	39.9	49.7	8.7	31.2
1985	225.3	194.5	28.7	16.3	12.4	165.8	80.1	34.1	43.1	8.5	30.8
1986	227.6	194.6	35.8	15.5	20.3	158.9	59.0	36.5	46.3	17.1	32.9
1987	273.4	233.9	36.4	15.7	20.7	197.5	87.0	43.4	39.9	27.2	39.5
1988	320.3	271.2	41.8	17.6	24.2	229.4	117.5	47.5	37.1	27.3	49.1
1989	325.4	266.0	50.6	20.1	30.5	215.3	108.0	42.1	39.7	25.5	59.4
1990	354.7	286.7	65.7	21.4	44.3	221.1	109.1	44.0	37.2	30.8	67.9
1991	370.9	302.4	84.3	20.3	64.0	218.1	90.1	53.6	46.7	27.7	68.5
1992	389.4	328.8	81.9	17.8	64.2	246.9	94.5	55.6	54.8	42.0	60.6
1993	456.2	391.0	103.7	16.0	87.7	287.3	114.2	65.0	61.2	46.9	65.3
1982: IV	160.0	130.8	23.0	14.6	8.3	107.8	50.1	18.2	33.8	5.7	29.2
1983: IV	216.2	182.6	22.1	15.2	6.9	160.5	90.5	19.1	40.7	10.2	33.6
1984: IV	223.6	192.9	20.3	17.2	3.2	172.6	79.2	33.5	50.8	9.0	30.7
1985: IV	228.0	193.5	29.0	16.0	13.0	164.5	83.3	31.3	39.0	11.0	34.5
1986: IV	225.0	192.5	34.7	15.2	19.5	157.8	63.9	34.2	43.1	16.6	32.6
1987: IV	293.4	246.3	39.4	16.1	23.3	207.0	98.7	43.1	39.3	25.8	47.0
1988: IV	340.5	285.9	46.1	18.9	27.2	239.7	129.3	47.6	39.3	23.5	54.6
1989: IV	320.6	254.8	52.5	20.4	32.1	202.3	94.5	38.8	39.2	29.8	65.8
1990: IV	349.3	273.8	66.6	21.4	45.2	207.2	98.5	38.7	36.2	33.8	75.5
1991: I	371.8	296.9	78.6	21.0	57.6	218.3	93.8	49.6	48.0	26.9	74.8
II	372.6	305.9	84.6	20.2	64.4	221.4	92.9	57.4	45.3	25.9	66.6
III	367.1	305.5	89.5	20.1	69.4	216.0	88.5	54.3	46.2	27.0	61.5
IV	372.3	301.4	84.6	19.7	64.8	216.8	85.3	53.3	47.4	30.8	70.9
1992: I	393.0	329.5	100.9	18.8	82.1	228.6	88.1	58.1	46.7	35.8	63.5
II	396.9	333.2	91.2	18.4	72.8	242.0	93.0	55.2	55.6	38.1	63.6
III	352.3	291.6	48.8	17.2	31.7	242.8	95.6	52.9	52.5	41.9	60.6
IV	415.6	361.0	86.7	16.6	70.1	274.3	101.3	56.3	64.6	52.1	54.6
1993: I	421.5	354.0	95.9	16.4	79.6	258.0	96.2	61.3	56.0	44.7	67.5
II	446.6	383.8	100.1	15.9	84.2	283.7	114.2	61.9	63.3	44.3	62.7
III	461.7	392.6	103.9	15.7	88.2	288.7	112.4	67.0	62.0	47.3	69.1
IV	495.1	433.4	114.6	15.8	98.8	318.8	134.2	69.7	63.7	51.3	61.7
1994: I	471.2	410.1	89.6	16.0	73.6	320.5	145.1	63.4	59.0	53.0	61.1
II	509.0	448.2	106.4	16.9	89.6	341.8	143.0	73.2	72.0	53.6	60.7
III	518.5	458.1	112.6	18.0	94.6	345.5	143.3	74.4	70.1	57.7	60.3

[1] Consists of the following industries: Depository institutions; nondepository credit institutions; security and commodity brokers; insurance carriers; regulated investment companies; small business investment companies; and real estate investment trusts.
[2] See Table B–92 for industry detail.

Note.—The industry classification is on a company basis and is based on the 1987 Standard Industrial Classification (SIC) beginning 1987, and on the 1972 SIC for earlier years shown.

Source: Department of Commerce, Bureau of Economic Analysis.

[Billions of dollars; quarterly data at seasonally adjusted annual rates]

		Corporate profits with inventory valuation adjustment and without capital consumption adjustment											
		Durable goods							Nondurable goods				
Year or quarter	Total manufac-turing	Total	Pri-mary metal indus-tries	Fabri-cated metal prod-ucts	Indus-trial machin-ery and equip-ment	Elec-tronic and other electric equip-ment	Motor vehicles and equip-ment	Other	Total	Food and kindred prod-ucts	Chemi-cals and allied prod-ucts	Petro-leum and coal prod-ucts	Other
1959	26.5	13.7	2.3	1.1	2.2	1.7	3.0	3.5	12.8	2.5	3.5	2.6	4.3
1960	23.8	11.7	2.0	.8	1.8	1.3	3.0	2.8	12.1	2.2	3.1	2.6	4.2
1961	23.4	11.4	1.6	1.0	1.9	1.3	2.5	3.1	12.0	2.4	3.3	2.2	4.2
1962	26.3	14.1	1.6	1.2	2.4	1.5	4.0	3.5	12.2	2.4	3.2	2.2	4.4
1963	29.6	16.4	2.0	1.3	2.5	1.6	4.9	4.0	13.2	2.7	3.7	2.2	4.7
1964	32.4	18.0	2.5	1.4	3.3	1.7	4.6	4.5	14.4	2.7	4.1	2.3	5.3
1965	39.7	23.2	3.1	2.1	4.0	2.7	6.2	5.2	16.4	2.8	4.6	2.9	6.1
1966	42.4	23.9	3.6	2.4	4.5	3.0	5.1	5.3	18.4	3.3	4.9	3.4	6.8
1967	39.0	21.2	2.7	2.5	4.1	3.0	4.0	5.0	17.8	3.2	4.3	3.9	6.4
1968	41.7	22.4	1.9	2.3	4.1	2.9	5.5	5.7	19.2	3.2	5.2	3.7	7.0
1969	37.0	19.0	1.4	2.0	3.7	2.3	4.8	4.9	18.0	3.0	4.6	3.3	7.0
1970	27.1	10.4	.8	1.1	3.0	1.3	1.3	3.0	16.8	3.2	3.9	3.6	6.1
1971	34.8	16.6	.8	1.5	3.0	1.9	5.1	4.2	18.2	3.5	4.5	3.7	6.5
1972	41.4	22.6	1.6	2.2	4.3	2.8	5.9	5.7	18.8	2.9	5.2	3.2	7.5
1973	46.7	25.0	2.3	2.6	4.7	3.2	5.9	6.3	21.7	2.5	6.1	5.2	7.9
1974	40.7	15.1	5.0	1.8	3.1	.5	.7	4.1	25.7	2.6	5.2	10.7	7.2
1975	54.5	20.3	2.7	3.2	4.8	2.6	2.2	4.8	34.1	8.6	6.3	9.8	9.4
1976	70.7	31.2	2.1	3.9	6.7	3.8	7.4	7.4	39.5	7.1	8.2	13.3	11.0
1977	78.5	37.6	1.0	4.5	8.3	5.8	9.3	8.6	41.0	6.8	7.7	12.9	13.6
1978	89.6	45.0	3.6	5.0	10.4	6.6	8.9	10.5	44.6	6.1	8.2	15.5	14.8
1979	88.3	36.5	3.5	5.2	9.1	5.4	4.6	8.6	51.8	5.8	7.1	24.5	14.6
1980	75.8	17.9	2.6	4.3	7.5	5.0	−4.3	2.8	57.8	6.0	5.5	33.6	12.9
1981	87.4	18.1	3.0	4.4	8.2	4.9	.2	−2.7	69.3	9.0	7.6	38.6	14.2
1982	63.1	4.8	−4.7	2.6	3.4	1.3	−.4	2.6	58.3	7.2	4.7	31.6	14.8
1983	71.4	18.4	−4.9	3.1	4.4	3.4	5.2	7.2	53.0	5.8	6.8	22.1	18.3
1984	86.7	37.2	−.4	4.5	6.3	4.8	8.9	13.1	49.5	7.3	7.3	15.9	19.1
1985	80.1	29.0	−.9	4.7	5.3	2.4	7.3	10.1	51.1	8.4	6.0	17.1	19.7
1986	59.0	30.0	.9	5.3	3.2	2.6	4.4	13.7	29.0	7.5	8.0	−8.5	21.9
1987	87.0	42.2	2.6	5.2	7.3	6.2	3.7	17.3	44.8	11.4	15.1	−3.6	21.9
1988	117.5	52.2	5.9	6.4	10.5	7.6	5.7	16.1	65.3	11.8	19.3	10.4	23.8
1989	108.0	49.3	6.1	6.6	10.3	9.3	2.3	14.6	58.8	10.7	18.5	5.7	23.9
1990	109.1	39.2	3.3	6.1	9.6	7.9	−2.2	14.6	69.9	14.0	16.2	17.3	22.5
1991	90.1	30.3	1.1	5.3	4.3	9.2	−5.6	16.0	59.8	17.7	15.5	5.0	21.6
1992	94.5	35.5	−.4	7.5	6.1	9.0	−1.5	14.8	58.9	17.5	15.8	−1.4	27.1
1993	114.2	49.4	.2	6.8	7.4	11.9	4.1	19.0	64.9	16.9	17.5	4.7	25.8
1982: IV	50.1	−5.3	−5.2	1.1	1.0	−1.0	−2.9	1.7	55.5	6.7	3.1	29.0	16.6
1983: IV	90.5	33.4	−3.7	4.9	6.5	6.6	9.4	9.7	57.1	6.1	7.7	24.1	19.2
1984: IV	79.2	34.2	−1.0	5.2	5.0	4.1	8.5	12.4	45.0	7.3	6.0	13.0	18.6
1985: IV	83.3	28.8	−1.3	4.0	7.0	2.0	7.3	9.7	54.5	7.8	3.5	24.1	19.2
1986: IV	63.9	34.2	1.7	4.7	2.6	3.3	4.5	17.4	29.7	8.2	9.5	−13.3	25.3
1987: IV	98.7	35.2	3.3	6.0	6.3	2.9	.6	16.2	63.4	13.4	18.5	7.4	24.1
1988: IV	129.3	56.4	6.5	6.4	8.0	9.7	9.6	16.2	72.9	12.3	24.0	14.2	22.4
1989: IV	94.5	43.0	4.1	5.3	12.6	10.9	−3.1	13.2	51.6	9.8	15.0	4.6	22.2
1990: IV	98.5	29.5	3.0	5.0	7.6	5.4	−5.3	13.8	69.1	16.2	12.0	22.0	18.9
1991: I	93.8	25.8	1.8	3.7	6.5	8.4	−9.6	14.9	68.0	17.2	13.3	18.0	19.5
II	92.9	34.1	1.0	6.0	4.7	9.9	−6.4	18.8	58.8	17.4	14.2	5.8	21.4
III	88.5	29.6	.2	5.5	.9	8.4	−2.8	17.4	58.9	20.0	16.2	−1.4	24.1
IV	85.3	31.9	1.5	6.1	5.1	9.9	−3.6	12.8	53.4	16.2	18.2	−2.4	21.4
1992: I	88.1	32.5	.4	7.4	4.8	8.6	−2.2	13.5	55.6	15.3	16.1	.0	24.2
II	93.0	34.0	−.2	7.7	5.7	7.2	−.7	14.2	59.0	19.7	13.9	−1.1	26.6
III	95.6	35.3	−.6	8.2	6.2	8.4	−2.5	15.6	60.2	18.5	15.4	−1.8	28.3
IV	101.3	40.3	−1.2	6.7	7.5	11.9	−.5	16.0	61.0	16.5	17.9	−2.6	29.2
1993: I	96.2	34.1	−1.3	5.7	5.6	10.4	−.9	14.6	62.1	19.1	18.6	−1.7	26.1
II	114.2	47.2	.6	7.0	7.1	9.1	4.0	19.4	67.0	16.4	16.9	6.0	27.7
III	112.4	52.2	−.2	6.7	9.1	13.0	3.1	20.4	60.2	16.3	15.7	5.4	22.9
IV	134.2	64.0	1.8	7.8	7.6	14.9	10.3	21.5	70.2	15.9	18.8	9.1	26.4
1994: I	145.1	71.4	.2	9.0	9.3	16.6	14.4	21.8	73.8	20.9	18.4	5.5	29.0
II	143.0	69.4	.9	9.0	9.0	17.9	9.7	22.9	73.5	20.3	19.1	4.6	29.5
III	143.3	70.3	.6	9.0	7.9	21.4	8.8	22.6	73.0	20.3	18.4	6.6	27.8

Note.—The industry classification is on a company basis and is based on the 1987 Standard Industrial Classification (SIC) beginning 1987 and on the 1972 SIC for earlier years shown. In the 1972 SIC, the categories shown here as "industrial machinery and equipment" and "electronic and other electric equipment" were identified as "machinery, except electrical" and "electric and electronic equipment," respectively.

Source: Department of Commerce, Bureau of Economic Analysis.

[Billions of dollars]

Year or quarter	All manufacturing corporations				Durable goods industries				Nondurable goods industries			
	Sales (net)	Profits		Stock-holders' equity [2]	Sales (net)	Profits		Stock-holders' equity [2]	Sales (net)	Profits		Stock-holders' equity [2]
		Before income taxes [1]	After income taxes			Before income taxes [1]	After income taxes			Before income taxes [1]	After income taxes	
1952	250.2	22.9	10.7	103.7	122.0	12.9	5.5	49.8	128.0	10.0	5.2	53.9
1953	265.9	24.4	11.3	108.2	137.9	14.0	5.8	52.4	128.0	10.4	5.5	55.7
1954	248.5	20.9	11.2	113.1	122.8	11.4	5.6	54.9	125.7	9.6	5.6	58.2
1955	278.4	28.6	15.1	120.1	142.1	16.5	8.1	58.8	136.3	12.1	7.0	61.3
1956	307.3	29.8	16.2	131.6	159.5	16.5	8.3	65.2	147.8	13.2	7.8	66.4
1957	320.0	28.2	15.4	141.1	166.0	15.8	7.9	70.5	154.1	12.4	7.5	70.6
1958	305.3	22.7	12.7	147.4	148.6	11.4	5.8	72.8	156.7	11.3	6.9	74.6
1959	338.0	29.7	16.3	157.1	169.4	15.8	8.1	77.9	168.5	13.9	8.3	79.2
1960	345.7	27.5	15.2	165.4	173.9	14.0	7.0	82.3	171.8	13.5	8.2	83.1
1961	356.4	27.5	15.3	172.6	175.2	13.6	6.9	84.9	181.2	13.9	8.5	87.7
1962	389.4	31.9	17.7	181.4	195.3	16.8	8.6	89.1	194.1	15.1	9.2	92.3
1963	412.7	34.9	19.5	189.7	209.0	18.5	9.5	93.3	203.6	16.4	10.0	96.3
1964	443.1	39.6	23.2	199.8	226.3	21.2	11.6	98.5	216.8	18.3	11.6	101.3
1965	492.2	46.5	27.5	211.7	257.0	26.2	14.5	105.4	235.2	20.3	13.0	106.3
1966	554.2	51.8	30.9	230.3	291.7	29.2	16.4	115.2	262.4	22.6	14.6	115.1
1967	575.4	47.8	29.0	247.6	300.6	25.7	14.6	125.0	274.8	22.0	14.4	122.6
1968	631.9	55.4	32.1	265.9	335.5	30.6	16.5	135.6	296.4	24.8	15.5	130.3
1969	694.6	58.1	33.2	289.9	366.5	31.5	16.9	147.6	328.1	26.6	16.4	142.3
1970	708.8	48.1	28.6	306.8	363.1	23.0	12.9	155.1	345.7	25.2	15.7	151.7
1971	751.1	52.9	31.0	320.8	381.8	26.5	14.5	160.4	369.3	26.5	16.5	160.5
1972	849.5	63.2	36.5	343.4	435.8	33.6	18.4	171.4	413.7	29.6	18.0	172.0
1973	1,017.2	81.4	48.1	374.1	527.3	43.6	24.8	188.7	489.9	37.8	23.3	185.4
1973: IV........	275.1	21.4	13.0	386.4	140.1	10.8	6.3	194.7	135.0	10.6	6.7	191.7
New series:												
1973: IV........	236.6	20.6	13.2	368.0	122.7	10.1	6.2	185.8	113.9	10.5	7.0	182.1
1974	1,060.6	92.1	58.7	395.0	529.0	41.1	24.7	196.0	531.6	51.0	34.1	199.0
1975	1,065.2	79.9	49.1	423.4	521.1	35.3	21.4	208.1	544.1	44.6	27.7	215.3
1976	1,203.2	104.9	64.5	462.7	589.6	50.7	30.8	224.3	613.7	54.3	33.7	238.4
1977	1,328.1	115.1	70.4	496.7	657.3	57.9	34.8	239.9	670.8	57.2	35.5	256.8
1978	1,496.4	132.5	81.1	540.5	760.7	69.6	41.8	262.6	735.7	62.9	39.3	277.9
1979	1,741.8	154.2	98.7	600.5	865.7	72.4	45.2	292.5	876.1	81.8	53.5	308.0
1980	1,912.8	145.8	92.6	668.1	889.1	57.4	35.6	317.7	1,023.7	88.4	56.9	350.4
1981	2,144.7	158.6	101.3	743.4	979.5	67.2	41.6	350.4	1,165.2	91.3	59.6	393.0
1982	2,039.4	108.2	70.9	770.2	913.1	34.7	21.7	355.5	1,126.4	73.6	49.3	414.7
1983	2,114.3	133.1	85.8	812.8	973.5	48.7	30.0	372.4	1,140.8	84.4	55.8	440.4
1984	2,335.0	165.6	107.6	864.2	1,107.6	75.5	48.9	395.6	1,227.5	90.0	58.8	468.5
1985	2,331.4	137.0	87.6	866.2	1,142.6	61.5	38.6	420.9	1,188.8	75.6	49.1	445.3
1986	2,220.9	129.3	83.1	874.7	1,125.5	52.1	32.6	436.3	1,095.4	77.2	50.5	438.4
1987	2,378.2	173.0	115.6	900.9	1,178.0	78.0	53.0	444.3	1,200.3	95.1	62.6	456.6
1988	2,596.2	216.1	154.6	957.6	1,284.7	91.7	67.1	468.7	1,311.5	124.4	87.5	488.9
1989	2,745.1	188.8	136.3	999.0	1,356.6	75.2	55.7	501.3	1,388.5	113.5	80.6	497.7
1990	2,810.7	159.6	111.6	1,043.8	1,357.2	57.6	40.9	515.0	1,453.5	102.0	70.6	528.9
1991	2,761.1	99.8	67.5	1,064.1	1,304.0	14.1	7.4	506.8	1,457.1	85.7	60.1	557.4
1992	2,890.2	32.5	23.2	1,034.7	1,389.8	−33.5	−23.7	473.9	1,500.4	66.0	47.0	560.8
1993	3,015.1	118.8	83.9	1,039.9	1,490.3	39.2	27.6	482.9	1,524.8	79.6	56.4	557.0
1992: I [3]	679.6	−65.1	−44.2	1,015.0	325.4	−59.0	−40.2	462.0	354.2	−6.1	−4.0	553.0
II	733.6	42.2	30.0	1,035.4	355.9	15.3	11.2	475.5	377.7	26.9	18.9	560.0
III	729.9	37.3	27.7	1,056.8	346.2	10.9	8.9	487.4	383.7	26.5	18.8	569.4
IV	747.1	18.1	9.6	1,031.3	362:3	−.8	−3.6	470.6	384.8	18.8	13.3	560.7
1993: I	717.7	11.3	11.1	1,019.5	349.5	−5.7	−1.7	464.8	368.2	17.0	12.8	554.7
II	767.4	37.6	25.2	1,035.1	381.0	15.7	9.4	479.8	386.4	21.9	15.9	555.3
III	752.5	37.7	25.0	1,047.1	368.3	16.2	11.5	492.0	384.2	21.5	13.5	555.0
IV	777.6	32.2	22.6	1,058.0	391.6	13.0	8.4	494.9	386.0	19.2	14.2	563.1
1994: I	757.6	50.3	35.3	1,075.4	383.7	23.4	16.3	505.8	374.0	26.9	19.0	569.6
II	819.6	64.5	46.5	1,101.4	420.3	35.6	25.8	523.8	399.2	28.8	20.7	577.6
III	824.3	65.0	46.5	1,129.9	412.7	30.6	22.2	542.6	411.5	34.4	24.2	587.2

Addendum: Impact of Accounting Change [3]—First quarter 1992

| 1992: I.......... | .... | −99.2 | −68.9 | −69.2 | .... | −69.9 | −48.0 | −48.1 | .... | −29.3 | −21.0 | −21.1 |

[1] In the old series, "income taxes" refers to Federal income taxes only, as State and local income taxes had already been deducted. In the new series, no income taxes have been deducted.

[2] Annual data are average equity for the year (using four end-of-quarter figures).

[3] Data for the first quarter of 1992 were revised significantly as a result of the early adoption of Financial Accounting Standards Board Statement 106 (Employer's Accounting for Post-Retirement Benefits Other Than Pensions) by a large number of companies during the fourth quarter of 1992. Corporations must show the cumulative effect of a change in accounting principle in the first quarter of the year in which the change is adopted.

Note.—Data are not necessarily comparable from one period to another due to changes in accounting principles, industry classifications, sampling procedures, etc. For explanatory notes concerning compilation of the series, see "Quarterly Financial Report for Manufacturing, Mining, and Trade Corporations," Department of Commerce, Bureau of the Census.

Source: Department of Commerce, Bureau of the Census.

TABLE B–94.—*Relation of profits after taxes to stockholders' equity and to sales, all manufacturing corporations, 1947–94*

Year or quarter	Ratio of profits after income taxes (annual rate) to stockholders' equity—percent [1]			Profits after income taxes per dollar of sales—cents		
	All manufacturing corporations	Durable goods industries	Nondurable goods industries	All manufacturing corporations	Durable goods industries	Nondurable goods industries
1947	15.6	14.4	16.6	6.7	6.7	6.7
1948	16.0	15.7	16.2	7.0	7.1	6.8
1949	11.6	12.1	11.2	5.8	6.4	5.4
1950	15.4	16.9	14.1	7.1	7.7	6.5
1951	12.1	13.0	11.2	4.9	5.3	4.5
1952	10.3	11.1	9.7	4.3	4.5	4.1
1953	10.5	11.1	9.9	4.3	4.2	4.3
1954	9.9	10.3	9.6	4.5	4.6	4.4
1955	12.6	13.8	11.4	5.4	5.7	5.1
1956	12.3	12.8	11.8	5.3	5.2	5.3
1957	10.9	11.3	10.6	4.8	4.8	4.9
1958	8.6	8.0	9.2	4.2	3.9	4.4
1959	10.4	10.4	10.4	4.8	4.8	4.9
1960	9.2	8.5	9.8	4.4	4.0	4.8
1961	8.9	8.1	9.6	4.3	3.9	4.7
1962	9.8	9.6	9.9	4.5	4.4	4.7
1963	10.3	10.1	10.4	4.7	4.5	4.9
1964	11.6	11.7	11.5	5.2	5.1	5.4
1965	13.0	13.8	12.2	5.6	5.7	5.5
1966	13.4	14.2	12.7	5.6	5.6	5.6
1967	11.7	11.7	11.8	5.0	4.8	5.3
1968	12.1	12.2	11.9	5.1	4.9	5.2
1969	11.5	11.4	11.5	4.8	4.6	5.0
1970	9.3	8.3	10.3	4.0	3.5	4.5
1971	9.7	9.0	10.3	4.1	3.8	4.5
1972	10.6	10.8	10.5	4.3	4.2	4.4
1973	12.8	13.1	12.6	4.7	4.7	4.8
1973: IV	13.4	12.9	14.0	4.7	4.5	5.0
New series:						
1973: IV	14.3	13.3	15.3	5.6	5.0	6.1
1974	14.9	12.6	17.1	5.5	4.7	6.4
1975	11.6	10.3	12.9	4.6	4.1	5.1
1976	13.9	13.7	14.2	5.4	5.2	5.5
1977	14.2	14.5	13.8	5.3	5.3	5.3
1978	15.0	16.0	14.2	5.4	5.5	5.3
1979	16.4	15.4	17.4	5.7	5.2	6.1
1980	13.9	11.2	16.3	4.8	4.0	5.6
1981	13.6	11.9	15.2	4.7	4.2	5.1
1982	9.2	6.1	11.9	3.5	2.4	4.4
1983	10.6	8.1	12.7	4.1	3.1	4.9
1984	12.5	12.4	12.5	4.6	4.4	4.8
1985	10.1	9.2	11.0	3.8	3.4	4.1
1986	9.5	7.5	11.5	3.7	2.9	4.6
1987	12.8	11.9	13.7	4.9	4.5	5.2
1988	16.1	14.3	17.9	6.0	5.2	6.7
1989	13.6	11.1	16.2	5.0	4.1	5.8
1990	10.7	8.0	13.4	4.0	3.0	4.9
1991	6.3	1.5	10.8	2.4	.6	4.1
1992	2.2	−5.0	8.4	.8	−1.7	3.1
1993	8.1	5.7	10.1	2.8	1.9	3.7
1992: I [2]	−17.4	−34.8	−2.9	−6.5	−12.4	−1.1
II	11.6	9.4	13.5	4.1	3.1	5.0
III	10.5	7.3	13.2	3.8	2.6	4.9
IV	3.7	−3.1	9.5	1.3	−1.0	3.4
1993: I	4.4	−1.5	9.3	1.6	−.5	3.5
II	9.7	7.8	11.4	3.3	2.5	4.1
III	9.5	9.3	9.7	3.3	3.1	3.5
IV	8.5	6.8	10.1	2.9	2.2	3.7
1994: I	13.1	12.9	13.4	4.7	4.2	5.1
II	16.9	19.7	14.3	5.7	6.1	5.2
III	16.4	16.4	16.5	5.6	5.4	5.9

[1] Annual ratios based on average equity for the year (using four end-of-quarter figures). Quarterly ratios based on equity at end of quarter only.

[2] See footnote 3, Table B–93.

Note.—Based on data in millions of dollars.
See Note, Table B–93.

Source: Department of Commerce, Bureau of the Census.

Table B-95.—*Sources and uses of funds, nonfarm nonfinancial corporate business, 1947–94*

[Billions of dollars; quarterly data at seasonally adjusted annual rates]

Year or quarter	Sources Total	Internal Total	U.S. undistributed profits	Inventory valuation and capital consumption adjustments	Capital consumption allowances	Foreign earnings retained abroad [1]	External Total	Credit market funds Total	Securities and mortgages	Loans and short-term paper	Other [2]	Uses Total	Capital expenditures [3]	Increase in financial assets	Discrepancy (sources less uses)
1947....	27.3	13.3	12.7	−8.7	9.0	0.3	14.0	8.5	5.6	2.9	5.4	26.4	18.1	8.3	0.9
1948....	29.7	19.7	14.0	−5.2	10.4	.4	10.1	7.7	6.9	.8	2.4	25.6	20.7	4.9	4.1
1949....	20.8	20.0	9.6	−1.0	11.2	.3	.8	3.3	5.2	−1.9	−2.5	18.4	14.9	3.5	2.4
1950....	42.7	18.5	14.1	−7.9	12.0	.3	24.2	8.5	4.6	3.9	15.7	40.3	24.0	16.3	2.4
1951....	36.6	20.8	10.8	−4.4	13.8	.6	15.9	10.8	6.3	4.5	5.1	37.9	30.6	7.3	−1.3
1952....	30.7	22.7	9.1	−2.0	14.8	.8	8.0	8.9	7.7	1.2	−.9	29.8	25.3	4.5	.9
1953....	28.9	22.6	9.4	−3.3	15.8	.7	6.3	5.8	6.2	−.3	.5	28.3	26.1	2.2	.5
1954....	29.6	24.7	9.3	−1.9	16.7	.5	5.0	5.8	6.2	−.5	−.8	27.8	23.0	4.8	1.8
1955....	53.9	30.3	13.7	−2.0	17.8	.8	23.6	10.8	7.0	3.8	12.8	49.0	32.6	16.4	4.8
1956....	45.1	30.5	13.1	−3.7	20.0	1.0	14.6	11.8	6.5	5.3	2.8	40.9	37.0	3.9	4.2
1957....	44.2	32.4	11.9	−2.7	22.0	1.2	11.8	12.2	10.0	2.2	−.4	39.8	35.7	4.1	4.4
1958....	42.3	31.2	8.8	−1.4	23.0	.8	11.1	9.8	9.9	−.1	1.3	38.7	28.0	10.7	3.6
1959....	55.3	37.0	13.0	−1.0	24.1	.9	18.3	10.5	6.1	4.4	7.8	51.8	37.8	14.1	3.5
1960....	48.1	36.4	10.5	−.4	25.1	1.2	11.7	9.9	5.4	4.5	1.7	41.5	37.7	3.8	6.6
1961....	53.5	37.5	10.2	.6	25.8	1.0	16.0	9.7	8.2	1.5	6.3	50.6	36.5	14.1	2.9
1962....	59.8	44.0	13.0	3.2	26.8	1.1	15.8	11.0	7.0	4.0	4.8	54.6	42.2	12.3	5.3
1963....	68.3	47.8	14.5	4.0	27.9	1.4	20.5	10.7	6.6	4.2	9.8	59.9	44.4	15.5	8.4
1964....	76.6	53.0	18.4	4.0	29.3	1.3	23.6	15.3	8.8	6.5	8.3	64.5	49.8	14.7	12.1
1965....	95.4	60.1	23.4	4.0	31.3	1.4	35.4	20.3	7.8	12.5	15.1	82.4	60.8	21.6	13.0
1966....	100.7	64.3	25.0	3.5	34.1	1.7	36.4	26.0	15.3	10.8	10.3	91.0	74.5	16.5	9.7
1967....	97.0	65.3	22.2	4.2	37.3	1.6	31.7	27.2	19.2	8.1	4.4	87.3	71.2	16.2	9.7
1968....	116.6	66.7	21.3	1.9	41.1	2.3	49.9	30.3	17.1	13.2	19.6	106.0	75.6	30.5	10.5
1969....	124.8	66.5	18.4	.4	45.0	2.8	58.3	37.6	18.3	19.3	20.7	116.5	85.2	31.3	8.3
1970....	109.9	64.0	12.6	−1.1	49.4	3.2	46.0	39.3	31.2	8.1	6.7	99.9	81.7	18.3	10.0
1971....	131.4	76.1	18.7	.0	54.2	3.2	55.3	39.0	33.9	5.1	16.3	123.5	87.4	36.1	7.8
1972....	162.4	88.1	24.6	−1.6	60.5	4.7	74.3	47.4	30.3	17.2	26.8	148.4	99.1	49.4	13.9
1973....	221.9	95.5	36.9	−15.2	65.6	8.1	126.4	80.4	47.0	33.4	46.0	192.4	122.6	69.8	29.5
1974....	191.8	91.0	45.3	−38.8	76.8	7.7	100.8	59.8	24.8	35.0	41.0	189.7	138.4	51.3	2.1
1975....	159.6	125.0	43.4	−18.6	92.2	8.1	34.6	26.6	41.7	−15.2	8.0	155.9	116.2	39.7	3.7
1976....	211.7	140.5	56.5	−26.1	102.5	7.6	71.2	51.1	40.1	11.0	20.2	207.4	155.7	51.7	4.3
1977....	263.7	162.7	66.9	−27.0	114.8	8.1	100.9	72.4	43.6	28.9	28.5	244.6	184.3	60.3	19.1
1978....	323.0	183.6	78.7	−37.8	131.1	11.7	139.4	76.7	39.9	36.8	62.6	327.6	221.9	105.7	−4.6
1979....	343.7	198.5	86.4	−58.0	151.6	18.6	145.2	75.0	20.1	54.8	70.2	369.8	242.2	127.6	−26.1
1980....	336.1	199.7	69.2	−61.4	173.2	18.7	136.4	78.4	35.9	42.4	58.0	334.5	252.4	82.1	1.6
1981....	394.4	238.9	64.2	−44.8	205.3	14.2	155.6	105.8	32.7	73.1	49.8	418.3	309.9	108.4	23.9
1982....	331.7	247.5	30.6	−22.4	227.5	11.8	84.1	70.0	11.6	58.4	14.1	343.3	278.8	64.6	−11.7
1983....	444.6	292.3	30.5	2.9	240.1	18.8	152.3	101.0	56.2	44.8	51.3	410.4	294.0	116.4	34.2
1984....	511.4	336.3	46.4	24.1	246.1	19.7	175.0	118.9	−5.6	124.5	56.1	495.4	391.6	103.8	16.0
1985....	493.8	351.9	21.7	54.4	256.0	19.8	142.0	84.7	13.2	71.5	57.3	467.2	370.2	97.0	26.7
1986....	538.8	336.7	−2.1	53.4	269.2	16.2	202.1	148.1	65.1	83.0	54.0	501.7	344.2	157.5	37.1
1987....	564.7	375.9	41.3	30.6	279.2	24.8	188.8	89.3	39.9	49.4	99.4	492.3	361.5	130.9	72.4
1988....	634.2	404.3	73.6	15.7	295.1	19.9	229.9	95.0	−4.7	99.8	134.9	575.8	391.0	184.8	58.4
1989....	567.9	399.6	32.2	19.8	314.8	32.8	168.2	68.0	−37.6	105.6	100.2	509.4	401.1	108.3	58.4
1990....	535.5	411.6	20.5	21.8	326.6	42.8	123.9	48.3	−20.1	68.3	75.6	488.7	402.8	85.9	46.7
1991....	471.7	426.0	4.7	35.2	338.6	47.6	45.7	8.7	96.1	−87.4	37.0	435.3	379.8	55.6	36.4
1992....	560.5	438.4	29.8	22.0	349.3	37.3	122.2	67.9	67.0	.9	54.3	527.8	386.0	141.8	32.8
1993....	557.4	462.3	17.5	36.5	357.6	50.8	95.1	67.1	81.2	−14.1	28.0	523.4	440.4	83.0	34.0
1992:															
I......	541.3	434.3	28.7	26.7	341.8	37.1	107.0	81.6	94.3	−12.7	25.5	512.8	362.1	150.7	28.4
II......	570.7	432.9	37.3	11.8	344.0	39.8	137.8	78.4	95.4	−16.9	59.4	528.7	389.2	139.5	42.0
III......	531.2	440.7	26.7	16.9	362.5	34.7	90.5	39.4	31.1	8.3	51.1	522.6	394.1	128.5	8.6
IV......	598.9	445.6	26.4	32.4	349.1	37.6	153.3	72.2	47.2	25.0	81.1	547.0	398.7	148.3	51.9
1993:															
I......	443.4	436.4	3.1	23.1	352.6	57.6	7.0	27.5	83.9	−56.4	−20.6	426.1	424.7	1.4	17.3
II......	548.8	450.7	20.7	29.6	355.1	45.3	98.1	80.6	68.0	12.7	17.5	530.4	441.5	88.9	18.4
III......	600.6	476.4	13.4	47.7	362.4	52.9	124.1	78.6	101.9	−23.3	45.6	550.0	444.1	105.9	50.5
IV......	636.8	485.7	32.7	45.3	360.4	47.3	151.1	81.7	71.1	10.6	69.4	587.2	451.2	136.0	49.5
1994:															
I......	653.8	502.9	41.3	38.5	381.3	41.7	150.8	110.3	12.4	97.9	40.5	648.9	474.7	174.2	4.8
II......	656.8	500.4	48.6	38.0	372.0	41.8	156.4	114.4	36.7	77.7	42.0	652.0	520.7	131.3	4.8
III......	664.5	503.1	59.6	33.2	377.9	32.5	161.5	75.9	−23.7	99.6	85.6	646.2	535.2	111.0	18.3

[1] Foreign branch profits, dividends, and subsidiaries' earnings retained abroad.
[2] Consists of tax liabilities, trade debt, direct foreign investment in the United States, and pension fund contributions payable.
[3] Plant and equipment, residential structures, inventory investment, and access rights from U.S. Government.

Source: Board of Governors of the Federal Reserve System.

TABLE B-96.—*Common stock prices and yields, 1955–94*

| Year or month | Common stock prices [1] | | | | | | | Common stock yields (S&P) (percent) [4] | |
| | New York Stock Exchange indexes (Dec. 31, 1965=50) [2] | | | | | Dow Jones industrial average [2] | Standard & Poor's composite index (1941–43=10) [2] | Dividend-price ratio [5] | Earnings-price ratio [6] |
	Composite	Industrial	Transportation	Utility [3]	Finance				
1955	21.54					442.72	40.49	4.08	7.95
1956	24.40					493.01	46.62	4.09	7.55
1957	23.67					475.71	44.38	4.35	7.89
1958	24.56					491.66	46.24	3.97	6.23
1959	30.73					632.12	57.38	3.23	5.78
1960	30.01					618.04	55.85	3.47	5.90
1961	35.37					691.55	66.27	2.98	4.62
1962	33.49					639.76	62.38	3.37	5.82
1963	37.51					714.81	69.87	3.17	5.50
1964	43.76					834.05	81.37	3.01	5.32
1965	47.39					910.88	88.17	3.00	5.59
1966	46.15	46.18	50.26	90.81	44.45	873.60	85.26	3.40	6.63
1967	50.77	51.97	53.51	90.86	49.82	879.12	91.93	3.20	5.73
1968	55.37	58.00	50.58	88.38	65.85	906.00	98.70	3.07	5.67
1969	54.67	57.44	46.96	85.60	70.49	876.72	97.84	3.24	6.08
1970	45.72	48.03	32.14	74.47	60.00	753.19	83.22	3.83	6.45
1971	54.22	57.92	44.35	79.05	70.38	884.76	98.29	3.14	5.41
1972	60.29	65.73	50.17	76.95	78.35	950.71	109.20	2.84	5.50
1973	57.42	63.08	37.74	75.38	70.12	923.88	107.43	3.06	7.12
1974	43.84	48.08	31.89	59.58	49.67	759.37	82.85	4.47	11.59
1975	45.73	50.52	31.10	63.00	47.14	802.49	86.16	4.31	9.15
1976	54.46	60.44	39.57	73.94	52.94	974.92	102.01	3.77	8.90
1977	53.69	57.86	41.09	81.84	55.25	894.63	98.20	4.62	10.79
1978	53.70	58.23	43.50	78.44	56.65	820.23	96.02	5.28	12.03
1979	58.32	64.76	47.34	76.41	61.42	844.40	103.01	5.47	13.46
1980	68.10	78.70	60.61	74.69	64.25	891.41	118.78	5.26	12.66
1981	74.02	85.44	72.61	77.81	73.52	932.92	128.05	5.20	11.96
1982	68.93	78.18	60.41	79.49	71.99	884.36	119.71	5.81	11.60
1983	92.63	107.45	89.36	93.99	95.34	1,190.34	160.41	4.40	8.03
1984	92.46	108.01	85.63	92.89	89.28	1,178.48	160.46	4.64	10.02
1985	108.09	123.79	104.11	113.49	114.21	1,328.23	186.84	4.25	8.12
1986	136.00	155.85	119.87	142.72	147.20	1,792.76	236.34	3.49	6.09
1987	161.70	195.31	140.39	148.57	146.48	2,275.99	286.83	3.08	5.48
1988	149.91	180.95	134.12	143.53	127.26	2,060.82	265.79	3.64	8.01
1989	180.02	216.23	175.28	174.87	151.88	2,508.91	322.84	3.45	7.41
1990	183.46	225.78	158.62	181.20	133.26	2,678.94	334.59	3.61	6.47
1991	206.33	258.14	173.99	185.32	150.82	2,929.33	376.18	3.24	4.79
1992	229.01	284.62	201.09	198.91	179.26	3,284.29	415.74	2.99	4.22
1993	249.58	299.99	242.49	228.90	216.42	3,522.06	451.41	2.78	4.46
1994	254.12	315.25	247.29	209.06	209.73	3,793.77	460.33	2.82	....
1993: Jan	239.67	292.11	221.00	211.04	203.38	3,277.72	435.23	2.88	
Feb	243.41	294.40	226.96	218.89	209.93	3,367.26	441.70	2.81	
Mar	248.12	298.75	229.42	225.07	217.01	3,440.74	450.16	2.76	4.39
Apr	244.72	292.19	237.97	227.56	216.02	3,423.63	443.08	2.82	
May	246.02	297.83	237.80	222.41	209.40	3,478.17	445.25	2.80	
June	247.16	298.78	234.30	226.53	209.75	3,513.81	448.06	2.81	4.29
July	247.85	295.34	238.30	232.55	218.94	3,529.43	447.29	2.81	
Aug	251.93	298.83	250.82	237.44	224.96	3,597.01	454.13	2.76	
Sept	254.86	300.92	248.15	244.21	229.35	3,592.29	459.24	2.73	4.45
Oct	257.53	306.61	254.04	240.97	228.18	3,625.81	463.90	2.72	
Nov	255.93	310.84	262.96	230.12	214.08	3,674.70	462.89	2.72	
Dec	257.73	313.22	268.11	229.95	216.00	3,744.10	465.95	2.72	4.69
1994: Jan	262.11	320.92	278.29	225.15	218.71	3,868.36	472.99	2.69	
Feb	261.97	322.41	276.67	220.85	217.12	3,905.62	471.58	2.70	
Mar	257.32	318.08	265.68	215.45	211.02	3,816.98	463.81	2.78	5.09
Apr	247.97	304.48	250.43	210.08	208.12	3,661.48	447.23	2.90	
May	249.56	307.58	244.75	205.77	211.30	3,707.99	450.90	2.89	
June	251.21	308.66	246.64	206.54	215.89	3,737.58	454.83	2.84	5.67
July	249.29	307.34	244.21	205.46	210.91	3,718.30	451.40	2.87	
Aug	256.08	316.55	244.67	211.26	214.77	3,797.48	464.24	2.78	
Sept	257.61	322.19	239.10	204.60	211.90	3,880.60	466.96	2.80	5.91
Oct	255.22	321.53	230.71	203.35	203.33	3,868.10	463.81	2.82	
Nov	252.48	319.33	227.45	200.13	198.38	3,792.43	461.01	2.86	
Dec	248.65	313.92	218.93	200.02	195.25	3,770.31	455.19	2.91	

[1] Averages of daily closing prices, except NYSE data through May 1964 are averages of weekly closing prices.

[2] Includes stocks as follows: for NYSE, all stocks listed (more than 2,000); for Dow-Jones industrial average, 30 stocks; and for S&P composite index, 500 stocks.

[3] Effective April 1993, the NYSE doubled the value of the utility index to facilitate trading of options and futures on the index. All indexes shown here reflect the doubling.

[4] Based on 500 stocks in the S&P composite index.

[5] Aggregate cash dividends (based on latest known annual rate) divided by aggregate market value based on Wednesday closing prices. Monthly data are averages of weekly figures; annual data are averages of monthly figures.

[6] Quarterly data are ratio of earnings (after taxes) for 4 quarters ending with particular quarter to price index for last day of that quarter. Annual data are averages of quarterly ratios.

Note.—All data relate to stocks listed on the New York Stock Exchange.

Sources: New York Stock Exchange (NYSE), Dow Jones & Co., Inc., and Standard & Poor's Corporation (S&P).

TABLE B–97.—*Business formation and business failures, 1950–94*

Year or month	Index of net business formation (1967=100)	New business incorporations (number)	Business failure rate [2]	Number of failures			Amount of current liabilities (millions of dollars)		
				Total	Liability size class		Total	Liability size class	
					Under $100,000	$100,000 and over		Under $100,000	$100,000 and over
1950	87.7	93,092	34.3	9,162	8,746	416	248.3	151.2	97.1
1951	86.7	83,778	30.7	8,058	7,626	432	259.5	131.6	128.0
1952	90.8	92,946	28.7	7,611	7,081	530	283.3	131.9	151.4
1953	89.7	102,706	33.2	8,862	8,075	787	394.2	167.5	226.6
1954	88.8	117,411	42.0	11,086	10,226	860	462.6	211.4	251.2
1955	96.6	139,915	41.6	10,969	10,113	856	449.4	206.4	243.0
1956	94.6	141,163	48.0	12,686	11,615	1,071	562.7	239.8	322.9
1957	90.3	137,112	51.7	13,739	12,547	1,192	615.3	267.1	348.2
1958	90.2	150,781	55.9	14,964	13,499	1,465	728.3	297.6	430.7
1959	97.9	193,067	51.8	14,053	12,707	1,346	692.8	278.9	413.9
1960	94.5	182,713	57.0	15,445	13,650	1,795	938.6	327.2	611.4
1961	90.8	181,535	64.4	17,075	15,006	2,069	1,090.1	370.1	720.0
1962	92.6	182,057	60.8	15,782	13,772	2,010	1,213.6	346.5	867.1
1963	94.4	186,404	56.3	14,374	12,192	2,182	1,352.6	321.0	1,031.6
1964	98.2	197,724	53.2	13,501	11,346	2,155	1,329.2	313.6	1,015.6
1965	99.8	203,897	53.3	13,514	11,340	2,174	1,321.7	321.7	1,000.0
1966	99.3	200,010	51.6	13,061	10,833	2,228	1,385.7	321.5	1,064.1
1967	100.0	206,569	49.0	12,364	10,144	2,220	1,265.2	297.9	967.3
1968	108.3	233,635	38.6	9,636	7,829	1,807	941.0	241.1	699.9
1969	115.8	274,267	37.3	9,154	7,192	1,962	1,142.1	231.3	910.8
1970	108.8	264,209	43.8	10,748	8,019	2,729	1,887.8	269.3	1,618.4
1971	111.1	287,577	41.7	10,326	7,611	2,715	1,916.9	271.3	1,645.6
1972	119.3	316,601	38.3	9,566	7,040	2,526	2,000.2	258.8	1,741.5
1973	119.1	329,358	36.4	9,345	6,627	2,718	2,298.6	235.6	2,063.0
1974	113.2	319,149	38.4	9,915	6,733	3,182	3,053.1	256.9	2,796.3
1975	109.9	326,345	42.6	11,432	7,504	3,928	4,380.2	298.6	4,081.6
1976	120.4	375,766	34.8	9,628	6,176	3,452	3,011.3	257.8	2,753.4
1977	130.8	436,170	28.4	7,919	4,861	3,058	3,095.3	208.3	2,887.0
1978	138.1	478,019	23.9	6,619	3,712	2,907	2,656.0	164.7	2,491.3
1979	138.3	524,565	27.8	7,564	3,930	3,634	2,667.4	179.9	2,487.5
1980	129.9	533,520	42.1	11,742	5,682	6,060	4,635.1	272.5	4,362.6
1981	124.8	581,242	61.3	16,794	8,233	8,561	6,955.2	405.8	6,549.3
1982	116.4	566,942	88.4	24,908	11,509	13,399	15,610.8	541.7	15,069.1
1983	117.5	600,420	109.7	31,334	15,572	15,762	16,072.9	635.1	15,437.8
1984	121.3	634,991	107.0	52,078	33,527	18,551	29,268.6	409.8	28,858.8
1985	120.9	664,235	115.0	57,253	36,551	20,702	36,937.4	423.9	36,513.5
1986	120.4	702,738	120.0	61,616	38,908	22,708	44,724.0	838.3	43,885.7
1987	121.2	685,572	102.0	61,111	38,949	22,162	34,723.8	746.0	33,977.8
1988	124.1	685,095	98.0	57,097	38,300	18,797	39,573.0	686.9	38,886.1
1989	124.8	676,565	65.0	50,361	33,312	17,049	42,328.8	670.5	41,658.2
1990	120.7	647,366	74.0	60,747	40,833	19,914	56,130.1	735.6	55,394.5
1991	115.2	628,604	107.0	88,140	60,617	27,523	96,825.3	1,044.9	95,780.4
1992	116.3	666,800	110.0	97,069	68,264	28,805	94,317.5	1,096.7	93,220.8
1993	121.1	706,537	96.0	86,133	61,188	24,945	47,755.5	947.6	46,807.9
1994				71,356	50,719	20,637	30,089.9	838.9	29,251.0
Seasonally adjusted									
1993: Jan	119.3	55,689		7,702	5,406	2,296	5,541.7	81.0	5,460.7
Feb	120.9	59,691		7,122	5,113	2,009	2,630.0	76.9	2,553.1
Mar	122.0	61,002		8,463	5,944	2,519	4,118.4	91.6	4,026.9
Apr	121.0	59,648		7,873	5,512	2,361	3,219.7	94.7	3,124.9
May	117.6	51,765		7,575	5,311	2,264	5,544.2	84.3	5,459.9
June	120.8	60,422		7,171	5,092	2,079	2,738.0	80.6	2,657.4
July	120.7	58,387		6,821	4,838	1,983	5,552.7	76.4	5,476.3
Aug	121.1	58,209		7,168	5,190	1,978	7,144.9	79.6	7,065.3
Sept	122.3	63,758		7,603	5,600	2,003	3,246.9	76.9	3,169.9
Oct	119.2	55,291		6,604	4,722	1,882	2,531.2	72.8	2,458.4
Nov	123.5	61,739		6,227	4,425	1,802	2,953.4	67.8	2,885.6
Dec	125.3	61,873		5,804	4,035	1,769	2,534.6	65.1	2,469.5
1994: Jan	125.2	61,978		5,768	4,041	1,727	1,736.4	65.6	1,670.8
Feb	125.1	60,680		5,888	4,181	1,707	2,141.3	68.8	2,072.5
Mar	127.5	64,058		7,117	5,079	2,038	2,166.0	82.9	2,083.1
Apr	125.4	58,992		5,233	3,721	1,512	1,688.7	62.0	1,626.7
May	124.8	58,528		6,572	4,645	1,927	2,565.0	78.0	2,487.0
June	125.9	63,097		6,150	4,364	1,786	2,328.6	72.6	2,256.0
July	122.9	56,380		5,404	3,808	1,596	2,111.7	63.1	2,048.6
Aug	125.5	64,844		6,460	4,541	1,919	2,459.5	75.6	2,383.9
Sept	124.2	64,564		5,989	4,265	1,724	3,533.5	74.0	3,459.4
Oct	126.2			5,895	4,304	1,591	3,674.4	71.7	3,602.7
Nov	130.2			5,503	3,907	1,596	2,576.9	63.1	2,513.8
Dec				5,377	3,863	1,514	3,108.0	61.5	3,046.5

[1] Commercial and industrial failures only through 1983, excluding failures of banks, railroads, real estate, insurance, holding, and financial companies, steamship lines, travel agencies, etc.

Data beginning 1984 are based on expanded coverage and new methodology and are therefore not generally comparable with earlier data. Data for 1993 and 1994 are subject to revision due to amended court filings.

[2] Failure rate per 10,000 listed enterprises.

Sources: Department of Commerce (Bureau of Economic Analysis) and The Dun & Bradstreet Corporation.

TABLE B–98.—*Farm income, 1945–94*

[Billions of dollars; quarterly data at seasonally adjusted annual rates]

Year or quarter	Income of farm operators from farming							
	Gross farm income						Net farm income	
	Total [1]	Cash marketing receipts			Value of inventory changes [2]	Production expenses	Current dollars	1987 dollars [3]
		Total	Livestock and products	Crops				
1945	25.4	21.7	12.0	9.7	−0.4	13.1	12.3	92.6
1946	29.6	24.8	13.8	11.0	.0	14.5	15.1	90.2
1947	32.4	29.6	16.5	13.1	−1.8	17.0	15.4	82.1
1948	36.5	30.2	17.1	13.1	1.7	18.8	17.7	88.3
1949	30.8	27.8	15.4	12.4	−.9	18.0	12.8	64.2
1950	33.1	28.5	16.1	12.4	.8	19.5	13.6	67.6
1951	38.3	32.9	19.6	13.2	1.2	22.3	15.9	74.8
1952	37.8	32.5	18.2	14.3	.9	22.8	15.0	69.6
1953	34.4	31.0	16.9	14.1	−.6	21.5	13.0	59.0
1954	34.2	29.8	16.3	13.6	.5	21.8	12.4	55.7
1955	33.5	29.5	16.0	13.5	.2	22.2	11.3	49.4
1956	34.0	30.4	16.4	14.0	−.5	22.7	11.3	47.7
1957	34.8	29.7	17.4	12.3	.6	23.7	11.1	45.4
1958	39.0	33.5	19.2	14.2	.8	25.8	13.2	52.9
1959	37.9	33.6	18.9	14.7	.0	27.2	10.7	41.9
1960	38.6	34.0	19.0	15.0	.4	27.4	11.2	43.1
1961	40.5	35.2	19.5	15.7	.3	28.6	12.0	45.5
1962	42.3	36.5	20.2	16.3	.6	30.3	12.1	44.8
1963	43.4	37.5	20.0	17.4	.6	31.6	11.8	43.3
1964	42.3	37.3	19.9	17.4	−.8	31.8	10.5	37.9
1965	46.5	39.4	21.9	17.5	1.0	33.6	12.9	45.4
1966	50.5	43.4	25.0	18.4	−.1	36.5	14.0	47.5
1967	50.5	42.8	24.4	18.4	.7	38.2	12.3	40.7
1968	51.8	44.2	25.5	18.7	.1	39.5	12.3	38.8
1969	56.4	48.2	28.6	19.6	.1	42.1	14.3	42.8
1970	58.8	50.5	29.5	21.0	.0	44.5	14.4	40.8
1971	62.1	52.7	30.5	22.3	1.4	47.1	15.0	40.5
1972	71.1	61.1	35.6	25.5	.9	51.7	19.5	50.1
1973	98.9	86.9	45.8	41.1	3.4	64.6	34.4	83.2
1974	98.2	92.4	41.3	51.1	−1.6	71.0	27.3	60.7
1975	100.6	88.9	43.1	45.8	3.4	75.0	25.5	51.9
1976	102.9	95.4	46.3	49.0	−1.5	82.7	20.2	38.6
1977	108.8	96.2	47.6	48.6	1.1	88.9	19.9	35.6
1978	128.4	112.4	59.2	53.2	1.9	103.3	25.2	41.8
1979	150.7	131.5	69.2	62.3	5.0	123.3	27.4	41.9
1980	149.3	139.7	68.0	71.7	−6.3	133.1	16.1	22.5
1981	166.3	141.6	69.2	72.5	6.5	139.4	26.9	34.1
1982	164.1	142.6	70.3	72.3	−1.4	140.3	23.8	28.4
1983	153.9	136.8	69.6	67.2	−10.9	139.6	14.2	16.3
1984	168.0	142.8	72.9	69.9	6.0	141.9	26.1	28.7
1985	161.2	144.1	69.8	74.3	−2.3	132.4	28.8	30.5
1986	156.1	135.4	71.6	63.8	−2.2	125.1	31.1	32.0
1987	168.5	141.8	76.0	65.9	−2.3	128.8	39.7	39.7
1988	175.8	151.2	79.4	71.7	−3.4	137.8	38.0	36.6
1989	192.8	161.1	84.1	77.0	4.8	144.9	47.9	44.1
1990	198.2	170.0	89.8	80.1	3.4	151.3	46.9	41.4
1991	192.3	168.8	86.7	82.1	−.3	151.2	41.1	35.0
1992	200.2	171.2	86.4	84.9	4.3	150.1	50.1	41.4
1993	201.4	175.1	90.6	84.5	−3.6	158.0	43.4	35.1
1992: I	200.3	165.2	82.4	82.8	5.4	147.4	52.9	44.1
II	198.8	167.7	87.2	80.4	5.0	149.7	49.2	40.7
III	202.0	181.2	89.6	91.7	4.0	151.5	50.5	41.7
IV	199.8	170.7	86.2	84.5	2.9	152.0	47.8	39.2
1993: I	203.4	172.6	84.2	88.4	−6.5	155.1	48.3	39.3
II	202.6	175.4	88.4	87.1	−5.1	157.5	45.0	36.5
III	198.3	186.0	101.9	84.1	−6.0	159.5	38.9	31.4
IV	202.8	167.6	87.8	79.8	3.0	160.0	42.8	34.5
1994: I	211.7	178.0	90.0	88.0	6.6	159.3	52.4	41.9
II	201.1	170.9	81.8	89.1	6.1	161.8	39.3	31.2
III [p]	217.0	196.2	97.3	98.8	4.9	163.8	53.2	42.1

[1] Cash marketing receipts and inventory changes plus Government payments, other farm cash income, and nonmoney income furnished by farms.
[2] Physical changes in end-of-period inventory of crop and livestock commodities valued at average prices during the period.
[3] Income in current dollars divided by the GDP implicit price deflator (Department of Commerce).

Note.—Data include net Commodity Credit Corporation loans and operator households.

Source: Department of Agriculture, except as noted.

TABLE B-99.—*Farm output and productivity indexes, 1948-91*

[1982 = 100]

Year	Farm output						Productivity indicators [5]	
	Total [1]	Livestock and products [2] [3]	Crops [2]				Farm output per unit of total factor input	Farm output per unit of farm labor
			Total [4]	Feed crops	Food grains	Oil crops		
1948	47	54	43	34	40	15	51	19
1949	46	58	38	17	34	14	50	19
1950	46	60	36	22	32	17	49	19
1951	49	63	39	20	32	15	51	21
1952	51	64	41	22	42	15	53	23
1953	51	66	41	22	36	14	53	23
1954	52	68	41	28	34	16	55	24
1955	54	70	43	31	34	19	55	26
1956	55	71	43	29	35	22	56	28
1957	54	70	42	37	30	21	55	29
1958	56	72	46	36	46	27	60	32
1959	59	76	47	35	38	24	60	34
1960	60	75	50	44	46	25	62	37
1961	62	78	50	37	42	29	64	38
1962	62	79	51	38	40	30	66	39
1963	65	82	53	42	40	31	68	42
1964	64	84	51	34	47	32	69	44
1965	67	82	56	52	46	36	71	47
1966	66	84	53	44	48	40	72	51
1967	70	86	59	60	54	43	75	56
1968	70	86	60	54	57	48	77	56
1969	72	86	62	57	54	50	77	59
1970	72	90	59	49	50	53	78	60
1971	77	91	68	77	58	52	83	65
1972	77	92	67	67	57	56	84	66
1973	81	93	73	71	63	67	88	69
1974	76	92	66	53	66	54	79	66
1975	82	87	79	78	79	67	85	72
1976	83	91	77	75	77	58	85	75
1977	89	93	86	89	74	78	93	83
1978	89	93	86	91	67	86	87	83
1979	93	93	94	95	79	104	90	87
1980	90	99	83	64	86	80	85	83
1981	100	101	100	102	102	89	97	95
1982	100	100	100	100	100	100	100	100
1983	84	102	71	31	84	75	88	88
1984	101	100	100	108	93	87	103	104
1985	105	103	106	125	87	96	111	118
1986	102	103	99	119	77	88	111	117
1987	104	106	101	101	77	88	117	123
1988	97	108	88	63	70	71	112	114
1989	108	110	105	116	77	87	124	131
1990	112	112	112	113	99	87	127	129
1991	112	114	109	113	76	92	126	127

[1] Farm output measures the annual volume of net farm production available for eventual human use through sales from farms or consumption in farm households.
[2] Gross production.
[3] Horses and mules excluded.
[4] Includes items not included in groups shown.
[5] See Table B-100 for farm inputs.

Source: Department of Agriculture.

Year	Farm population, April [1]		Farm employment (thousands) [3]			Crops harvested (millions of acres) [5]	Selected indexes of input use (1982=100)							
	Number (thousands)	As percent of total population [2]	Total	Self-employed and unpaid workers [4]	Hired workers		Total	Farm labor	Farm real estate	Durable equipment	Energy	Agricultural chemicals [6]	Feed, seed, and livestock purchases [7]	Other purchased inputs
1948	24,383	16.6	10,363	8,026	2,337	356	93	251	84	38	65	34	45	74
1949	24,194	16.2	9,964	7,712	2,252	360	91	241	86	45	72	36	40	77
1950	23,048	15.2	9,926	7,597	2,329	345	94	237	89	52	73	43	44	78
1951	21,890	14.2	9,546	7,310	2,236	344	96	228	91	58	76	42	49	80
1952	21,748	13.9	9,149	7,005	2,144	349	96	222	93	63	79	43	47	83
1953	19,874	12.5	8,864	6,775	2,089	348	97	220	95	66	81	42	50	82
1954	19,019	11.7	8,651	6,570	2,081	346	95	216	96	69	81	43	46	81
1955	19,078	11.5	8,381	6,345	2,036	340	99	211	98	70	83	45	59	83
1956	18,712	11.1	7,852	5,900	1,952	324	98	197	99	71	83	50	62	81
1957	17,656	10.3	7,600	5,660	1,940	324	97	183	99	69	82	49	68	85
1958	17,128	9.8	7,503	5,521	1,982	324	95	176	99	68	80	49	67	81
1959	16,592	9.3	7,342	5,390	1,952	324	98	173	99	68	81	56	69	99
1960	15,635	8.7	7,057	5,172	1,885	324	97	163	99	69	82	58	74	99
1961	14,803	8.1	6,919	5,029	1,890	302	96	161	97	68	84	61	68	98
1962	14,313	7.7	6,700	4,873	1,827	295	94	159	95	67	85	55	66	100
1963	13,367	7.1	6,518	4,738	1,780	298	94	153	96	67	86	61	67	100
1964	12,954	6.7	6,110	4,506	1,604	298	93	145	95	67	88	68	68	97
1965	12,363	6.4	5,610	4,128	1,482	298	93	141	95	69	89	73	69	96
1966	11,595	5.9	5,214	3,854	1,360	294	92	128	94	71	90	83	70	96
1967	10,875	5.5	4,903	3,650	1,253	306	93	124	97	73	90	80	76	97
1968	10,454	5.2	4,749	3,535	1,213	300	92	125	95	76	90	68	75	97
1969	10,307	5.1	4,596	3,419	1,176	290	93	123	94	78	92	73	84	93
1970	9,712	4.7	4,523	3,348	1,175	293	93	119	94	78	92	76	87	90
1971	9,425	4.5	4,436	3,275	1,161	305	93	118	96	79	90	80	87	87
1972	9,610	4.6	4,373	3,228	1,146	294	91	117	94	79	89	85	81	85
1973	9,472	4.5	4,337	3,169	1,168	321	92	117	98	81	90	94	71	91
1974	9,264	4.3	4,389	3,075	1,314	328	97	115	99	85	86	99	87	97
1975	8,864	4.1	4,331	3,021	1,310	336	96	114	98	89	101	91	86	94
1976	8,253	3.8	4,363	2,992	1,371	337	97	111	99	91	113	100	84	99
1977	[8] 6,194	[8] 2.8	4,143	2,852	1,291	345	96	107	99	94	119	98	77	100
1978	[8] 6,501	[8] 2.9	3,937	2,680	1,256	338	101	107	98	96	125	108	91	118
1979	[8] 6,241	[8] 2.8	3,765	2,495	1,270	348	104	107	99	99	113	118	97	127
1980	[8] 6,051	[8] 2.7	3,699	2,401	1,298	352	106	108	101	102	110	131	102	116
1981	[8] 5,850	[8] 2.5	[9] 3,582	[9] 2,324	[9] 1,258	366	103	105	101	102	106	122	98	111
1982	[8] 5,628	[8] 2.4	[9] 3,466	[9] 2,248	[9] 1,218	362	100	100	100	100	100	100	100	100
1983	[8] 5,787	[8] 2.5	[9] 3,349	[9] 2,171	[9] 1,178	306	96	95	92	95	97	93	99	107
1984	5,754	2.4	[9] 3,233	[9] 2,095	[9] 1,138	348	98	97	97	91	100	106	101	108
1985	5,355	2.2	3,116	2,018	1,098	342	95	89	97	86	90	101	106	99
1986	5,226	2.2	2,912	1,873	1,039	325	92	87	94	80	84	111	105	89
1987	4,986	2.1	2,897	1,846	1,051	302	89	84	91	74	93	100	101	92
1988	4,951	2.1	2,954	1,967	1,037	297	87	86	90	70	93	90	98	90
1989	4,801	2.0	2,863	1,935	928	318	87	82	91	67	91	93	99	96
1990	4,591	1.9	2,891	2,000	892	322	89	87	90	65	90	90	105	97
1991	4,632	1.9	2,877	1,968	910	318	89	88	89	63	89	94	104	100
1992			2,810	1,944	866	319								
1993			2,800	1,942	857	308								
1994 [p]			2,767	1,925	842	321								

[1] Farm population as defined by Department of Agriculture and Department of Commerce, i.e., civilian population living on farms in rural areas, regardless of occupation. See also footnote 8. Series discontinued in 1992.

[2] Total population of United States including Armed Forces overseas, as of July 1.

[3] Includes persons doing farmwork on all farms. These data, published by the Department of Agriculture, differ from those on agricultural employment by the Department of Labor (see Table B-33) because of differences in the method of approach, in concepts of employment, and in time of month for which the data are collected.

[4] Prior to 1982 this category was termed "family workers" and did not include nonfamily unpaid workers.

[5] Acreage harvested plus acreages in fruits, tree nuts, and farm gardens.

[6] Fertilizer, lime, and pesticides.

[7] Nonfarm constant dollar value of feed, seed, and livestock purchases.

[8] Based on new definition of a farm. Under old definition of a farm, farm population (in thousands and as percent of total population) for 1977, 1978, 1979, 1980, 1981, 1982, and 1983 is 7,806 and 3.6; 8,005 and 3.6; 7,553 and 3.4; 7,241 and 3.2; 7,014 and 3.1; 6,880 and 3.0; 7,029 and 3.0, respectively.

[9] Basis for farm employment series was discontinued for 1981 through 1984. Employment is estimated for these years.

Note.—Population includes Alaska and Hawaii beginning 1960.

Sources: Department of Agriculture and Department of Commerce (Bureau of the Census).

TABLE B–101.—*Indexes of prices received and prices paid by farmers, 1975–94*

[1990–92 = 100, except as noted]

Year or month	Prices received by farmers			Prices paid by farmers												Addendum: Average farm real estate value per acre (dollars)[3]
	All farm products	Crops	Livestock and products	All commodities, services, interest, taxes, and wage rates[1]	Production items										Wage rates	
					Total[2]	Feed	Livestock and poultry	Fertilizer	Agricultural chemicals	Fuels	Farm machinery	Farm services	Rent		
1975	73	88	62	47	55	83	39	87	72	40	38	48		44	340
1976	75	87	64	50	59	83	47	74	78	43	43	52		48	397
1977	73	83	64	53	61	82	48	72	71	46	47	57		51	474
1978	83	89	78	58	67	80	65	72	66	48	51	60		55	531
1979	94	98	90	66	76	89	88	77	67	61	56	66		60	628
1980	98	107	89	75	85	98	85	96	71	86	63	81		65	737
1981	100	111	89	82	92	110	80	104	77	98	70	89		70	819
1982	94	98	90	86	94	99	78	105	83	97	76	96		74	823
1983	98	108	88	86	93	107	76	100	87	94	81	82		76	788
1984	101	111	91	89	94	112	73	103	90	93	85	86		77	801
1985	91	98	86	86	91	95	74	98	90	93	85	85		78	713
1986	87	87	88	85	86	88	73	90	89	76	83	83		81	640
1987	89	86	91	87	87	83	85	86	87	76	85	84		85	599
1988	99	104	93	91	90	104	91	94	89	77	89	85		87	632
1989	104	109	100	96	95	110	93	99	93	83	94	91		95	661
1990	104	103	105	99	99	103	102	97	95	100	96	97	96	96	668
1991	100	101	99	100	100	98	102	103	101	104	100	99	100	100	681
1992	98	101	97	101	101	99	96	100	103	96	104	104	104	105	684
1993	101	102	100	103	103	99	104	97	107	92	106	109	100	108	699
1994	100	105	95	106	106	105	95	106	112	84	110	112	108	111	744
1993: Jan	97	96	98	103	102	99	103	98	104	90	105	109	100	111	699
Feb	98	97	99												
Mar	99	97	101												
Apr	104	107	102	104	104	100	107	95	109	96	107	108	100	110	
May	103	103	103												
June	101	99	102												
July	101	102	100	103	103	97	104	98	108	92	106	109	100	105	
Aug	102	104	100												
Sept	102	104	100												
Oct	101	103	99	104	104	102	103	95	108	89	107	109	100	108	
Nov	102	106	98												
Dec	103	108	97												
1994: Jan	105	110	98	106	106	109	100	100	110	75	109	112	108	113	744
Feb	104	110	100												
Mar	105	109	101												
Apr	102	106	100	107	108	109	100	104	112	90	114	112	108	111	
May	101	107	97												
June	100	108	94												
July	97	101	93	106	105	104	91	109	113	83	109	111	108	107	
Aug	97	101	94												
Sept	97	102	91												
Oct	95	99	90	106	105	98	87	111	114	87	108	113	108	112	
Nov	95	100	90												
Dec	99	106	90												

[1] Includes items used for family living, not shown separately.

[2] Includes other production items not shown separately.

[3] Average for 48 States. Annual data are: March 1 for 1975, February 1 for 1976–81, April 1 for 1982–85, February 1 for 1986–89, and January 1 for 1990–94.

Note—New series on a 1990–92 base published on January 31, 1995. Data prior to 1975 are not available.

Source: Department of Agriculture.

TABLE B-102.—*U.S. exports and imports of agricultural commodities, 1940–94*

[Billions of dollars]

Year	Exports							Imports					Agri-cultural trade balance
	Total [1]	Feed grains	Food grains [2]	Oil-seeds and products	Cotton	Tobacco	Animals and products	Total [1]	Crops, fruits, and vegetables [3]	Animals and products	Coffee	Cocoa beans and products	
1940	0.5	(⁴)	(⁴)	(⁴)	0.2	(⁴)	0.1	1.3	(⁴)	0.2	0.1	(⁴)	−0.8
1941	.7	(⁴)	0.1	(⁴)	.1	0.1	.3	1.7	0.1	.3	.2	(⁴)	−1.0
1942	1.2	(⁴)	(⁴)	(⁴)	.1	.1	.8	1.3	(⁴)	.5	.2	(⁴)	−.1
1943	2.1	(⁴)	.1	0.1	.2	.2	1.2	1.5	.1	.4	.3	(⁴)	.6
1944	2.1	(⁴)	.1	.1	.1	.1	1.3	1.8	.1	.3	.3	(⁴)	.3
1945	2.3	(⁴)	.4	(⁴)	.3	.2	.9	1.7	.1	.4	.3	(⁴)	.5
1946	3.1	0.1	.7	(⁴)	.5	.4	.9	2.3	.2	.4	.5	0.1	.8
1947	4.0	.4	1.4	.1	.4	.3	.7	2.8	.1	.4	.6	.2	1.2
1948	3.5	.1	1.5	.2	.5	.2	.5	3.1	.2	.6	.7	.2	.3
1949	3.6	.3	1.1	.3	.9	.3	.4	2.9	.2	.4	.8	.1	.7
1950	2.9	.2	.6	.2	1.0	.3	.3	4.0	.2	.7	1.1	.2	−1.1
1951	4.0	.3	1.1	.3	1.1	.3	.5	5.2	.2	1.1	1.4	.2	−1.1
1952	3.4	.3	1.1	.2	.9	.2	.3	4.5	.2	.7	1.4	.2	−1.1
1953	2.8	.3	.7	.2	.5	.3	.4	4.2	.2	.6	1.5	.2	−1.3
1954	3.1	.2	.5	.3	.8	.3	.5	4.0	.2	.5	1.5	.3	−.9
1955	3.2	.3	.6	.4	.5	.4	.6	4.0	.2	.5	1.4	.2	−.8
1956	4.2	.4	1.0	.5	.7	.3	.7	4.0	.2	.4	1.4	.2	.2
1957	4.5	.3	1.0	.5	1.0	.4	.7	4.0	.2	.5	1.4	.2	.6
1958	3.9	.5	.8	.4	.7	.4	.5	3.9	.2	.7	1.2	.2	(⁴)
1959	4.0	.6	.9	.6	.4	.3	.6	4.1	.2	.8	1.1	.2	−.1
1960	4.8	.5	1.2	.6	1.0	.4	.6	3.8	.2	.6	1.0	.2	1.0
1961	5.0	.5	1.4	.6	.9	.4	.6	3.7	.2	.7	1.0	.2	1.3
1962	5.0	.8	1.3	.7	.5	.4	.6	3.9	.2	.9	1.0	.2	1.2
1963	5.6	.8	1.5	.8	.6	.4	.7	4.0	.3	.9	1.0	.2	1.6
1964	6.3	.9	1.7	1.0	.7	.4	.8	4.1	.3	.8	1.2	.2	2.3
1965	6.2	1.1	1.4	1.2	.5	.4	.8	4.1	.3	.9	1.1	.1	2.1
1966	6.9	1.3	1.8	1.2	.4	.5	.7	4.5	.4	1.2	1.1	.1	2.4
1967	6.4	1.1	1.5	1.3	.5	.5	.7	4.5	.4	1.1	1.0	.2	1.9
1968	6.3	.9	1.4	1.3	.5	.5	.7	5.0	.5	1.3	1.2	.2	1.3
1969	6.0	.9	1.2	1.3	.3	.6	.8	5.0	.5	1.4	.9	.2	1.1
1970	7.3	1.1	1.4	1.9	.4	.5	.9	5.8	.5	1.6	1.2	.3	1.5
1971	7.7	1.0	1.3	2.2	.6	.5	1.0	5.8	.6	1.5	1.2	.2	1.9
1972	9.4	1.5	1.8	2.4	.5	.7	1.1	6.5	.7	1.8	1.3	.2	2.9
1973	17.7	3.5	4.7	4.3	.9	.7	1.6	8.4	.8	2.6	1.7	.3	9.3
1974	21.9	4.6	5.4	5.7	1.3	.8	1.8	10.2	.8	2.2	1.6	.5	11.7
1975	21.9	5.2	6.2	4.5	1.0	.9	1.7	9.3	.8	1.8	1.7	.5	12.6
1976	23.0	6.0	4.7	5.1	1.0	.9	2.4	11.0	.9	2.3	2.9	.6	12.0
1977	23.6	4.9	3.6	6.6	1.5	1.1	2.7	13.4	1.2	2.3	4.2	1.0	10.2
1978	29.4	5.9	5.5	8.2	1.7	1.4	3.0	14.8	1.5	3.1	4.0	1.4	14.6
1979	34.7	7.7	6.3	8.9	2.2	1.2	3.8	16.7	1.7	3.9	4.2	1.2	18.0
1980	41.2	9.8	7.9	9.4	2.9	1.3	3.8	17.4	1.7	3.8	4.2	.9	23.8
1981	43.3	9.4	9.6	9.6	2.3	1.5	4.2	16.9	2.0	3.5	2.9	.9	26.4
1982	36.6	6.4	7.9	9.1	2.0	1.5	3.9	15.3	2.3	3.7	2.9	.7	21.3
1983	36.1	7.3	7.4	8.7	1.8	1.5	3.8	16.5	2.3	3.8	2.8	.8	19.6
1984	37.8	8.1	7.5	8.4	2.4	1.5	4.2	19.3	3.1	4.1	3.3	1.1	18.5
1985	29.0	6.0	4.5	5.8	1.6	1.5	4.1	20.0	3.5	4.2	3.3	1.4	9.1
1986	26.2	3.1	3.8	6.5	.8	1.2	4.5	21.5	3.6	4.5	4.6	1.1	4.7
1987	28.7	3.8	3.8	6.4	1.6	1.1	5.2	20.4	3.6	4.9	2.9	1.2	8.3
1988	37.1	5.9	5.9	7.7	2.0	1.3	6.4	21.0	3.8	5.2	2.5	1.0	16.1
1989	39.9	7.7	7.1	6.3	2.3	1.3	6.4	21.7	4.2	5.1	2.4	1.0	18.2
1990	39.4	7.0	4.8	5.7	2.8	1.4	6.7	22.8	4.9	5.6	1.9	1.1	16.6
1991	39.2	5.7	4.2	6.4	2.5	1.4	7.0	22.7	4.8	5.5	1.9	1.1	16.5
1992	42.9	5.7	5.4	7.2	2.0	1.7	7.9	24.6	4.9	5.7	1.7	1.1	18.3
1993	42.6	5.0	5.6	7.3	1.5	1.3	7.9	25.0	5.0	5.9	1.5	1.1	17.6
Jan–Nov:													
1993	38.5	4.5	5.1	6.5	1.4	1.2	7.2	22.6	4.5	5.4	1.4	.9	15.9
1994	40.7	4.1	4.7	6.2	2.3	1.2	8.3	24.4	4.9	5.3	2.2	.9	16.3

[1] Total includes items not shown separately.
[2] Rice, wheat, and wheat flour.
[3] Includes nuts, fruits, and vegetable preparations.
[4] Less than $50 million.

Note.—Data derived from official estimates released by the Bureau of the Census, Department of Commerce. Agricultural commodities are defined as (1) nonmarine food products and (2) other products of agriculture which have not passed through complex processes of manufacture. Export value, at U.S. port of exportation, is based on the selling price and includes inland freight, insurance, and other charges to the port. Import value, defined generally as the market value in the foreign country, excludes import duties, ocean freight, and marine insurance.

Source: Department of Agriculture.

TABLE B–103.—*Farm business balance sheet, 1950–93*

[Billions of dollars]

End of year	Assets								Claims			
	Total assets	Physical assets					Financial assets		Total claims	Real estate debt [5]	Non-real estate debt [6]	Propri-etors' equity
		Real estate	Nonreal estate				Invest-ments in cooper-atives	Other [4]				
			Live-stock and poul-try [1]	Machin-ery and motor vehicles	Crops [2]	Pur-chased in-puts [3]						
1950	121.6	75.4	17.1	12.3	7.1	....	2.7	7.0	121.6	5.2	5.7	110.7
1951	136.1	83.8	19.5	14.3	8.2	....	2.9	7.3	136.1	5.7	6.9	123.7
1952	133.0	85.1	14.8	15.0	7.9	....	3.2	7.1	133.0	6.2	7.1	119.7
1953	128.7	84.3	11.7	15.6	6.8	....	3.3	7.0	128.7	6.6	6.3	115.7
1954	132.6	87.8	11.2	15.7	7.5	....	3.5	6.9	132.6	7.1	6.7	118.9
1955	137.0	93.0	10.6	16.3	6.5	....	3.7	6.9	137.0	7.8	7.3	121.9
1956	145.7	100.3	11.0	16.9	6.8	....	4.0	6.7	145.7	8.5	7.4	129.8
1957	154.5	106.4	13.9	17.0	6.4	....	4.2	6.6	154.5	9.0	8.2	137.3
1958	168.7	114.6	17.7	18.1	6.9	....	4.5	6.9	168.7	9.7	9.4	149.7
1959	173.0	121.2	15.2	19.3	6.2	....	4.8	6.2	173.0	10.6	10.7	151.7
1960	174.2	123.3	15.6	19.1	6.2	....	4.2	5.8	174.2	11.3	11.1	151.7
1961	181.4	129.1	16.4	19.3	6.3	....	4.5	5.9	181.4	12.3	11.8	157.3
1962	188.7	134.6	17.3	19.9	6.3	....	4.6	5.9	188.7	13.5	13.2	162.0
1963	196.5	142.4	15.9	20.4	7.2	....	5.0	5.7	196.5	15.0	14.6	166.9
1964	204.0	150.5	14.4	21.2	6.8	....	5.2	5.8	204.0	16.9	15.3	171.8
1965	220.6	161.5	17.6	22.4	7.7	....	5.4	6.0	220.6	18.9	16.9	184.8
1966	233.8	171.2	19.0	24.1	7.9	....	5.7	6.0	233.8	20.7	18.5	194.6
1967	245.8	180.9	18.8	26.3	7.7	....	5.8	6.1	245.8	22.6	19.6	203.6
1968	257.0	189.4	20.2	27.7	7.2	....	6.1	6.3	257.0	24.7	19.2	213.0
1969	267.6	195.3	22.8	28.6	8.1	....	6.4	6.4	267.6	26.4	20.0	221.2
1970	278.7	202.4	23.7	30.4	8.5	....	7.2	6.5	278.7	27.5	21.2	229.9
1971	301.5	217.6	27.3	32.4	9.7	....	7.9	6.7	301.5	29.3	24.0	248.3
1972	339.7	243.0	33.7	34.6	12.7	....	8.7	6.9	339.7	32.0	26.7	281.0
1973	418.3	298.3	42.4	39.7	21.1	....	9.7	7.1	418.3	36.1	31.6	350.6
1974 [7]	449.1	335.6	24.6	48.5	22.5	....	11.2	6.9	449.1	40.8	35.1	373.3
1975	510.7	383.6	29.4	57.4	20.5	....	13.0	6.9	510.7	45.3	39.7	425.7
1976	590.7	456.5	29.0	63.3	20.6	....	14.3	6.9	590.7	50.5	45.6	494.6
1977	651.5	509.3	31.9	69.3	20.4	....	13.5	7.0	651.5	58.4	52.4	540.6
1978	767.3	601.8	50.1	68.5	23.8	....	16.1	7.1	767.3	66.7	60.7	639.9
1979	898.1	706.1	61.4	75.4	29.9	....	18.1	7.3	898.1	79.7	71.8	746.6
1980	983.2	782.8	60.6	80.3	32.7	....	19.3	7.4	983.2	89.7	77.1	816.4
1981	982.3	785.6	53.5	85.5	29.5	....	20.6	7.6	982.3	98.8	83.6	799.9
1982	944.5	750.0	53.0	86.0	25.8	....	21.9	7.8	944.5	101.8	87.0	755.7
1983	943.3	753.4	49.5	85.8	23.6	....	22.8	8.1	943.3	103.2	87.9	752.2
1984	857.0	661.8	49.5	85.0	26.1	2.0	24.3	8.3	857.0	106.7	87.1	663.3
1985	772.7	586.2	46.3	82.9	22.9	1.2	24.3	9.0	772.7	100.1	77.5	595.1
1986	724.4	542.3	47.8	81.5	16.3	2.1	24.4	10.0	724.4	90.4	66.6	567.5
1987	772.6	578.9	58.0	80.0	17.5	3.2	25.3	9.9	772.6	82.4	62.0	628.2
1988	801.1	595.5	62.2	81.2	23.3	3.5	25.1	10.3	801.1	77.6	61.7	661.7
1989	829.7	615.7	66.2	85.1	23.4	2.6	26.3	10.5	829.7	75.4	61.9	692.4
1990	848.3	628.2	70.9	85.4	22.8	2.8	27.5	10.9	848.3	74.1	63.2	710.9
1991	842.4	623.2	68.1	85.8	22.0	2.7	28.7	11.8	842.4	74.5	64.3	703.6
1992	860.8	633.1	71.0	85.6	24.1	3.9	29.4	13.6	860.8	75.0	63.6	722.2
1993	888.0	656.3	72.8	85.2	23.4	4.2	30.8	15.3	888.0	76.0	65.9	746.1

[1] Excludes commercial broilers; excludes horses and mules beginning 1959; excludes turkeys beginning 1986.
[2] Non-Commodity Credit Corporation (CCC) crops held on farms plus value above loan rate for crops held under CCC.
[3] Includes fertilizer, chemicals, fuels, parts, feed, seed, and other supplies.
[4] Currency and demand deposits.
[5] Includes CCC storage and drying facilities loans.
[6] Does not include CCC crop loans.
[7] Beginning 1974, data are for farms included in the new farm definition, that is, places with sales of $1,000 or more annually.

Note.—Data exclude operator households.
Beginning 1959, data include Alaska and Hawaii.

Source: Department of Agriculture.

TABLE B-104.—*International investment position of the United States at year-end, 1985-93*

[Billions of dollars]

Type of investment	1985	1986	1987	1988	1989	1990	1991	1992	1993
NET INTERNATIONAL INVESTMENT POSITION OF THE UNITED STATES:									
With direct investment at current cost.............	125.3	34.6	−22.8	−144.8	−251.4	−251.4	−349.5	−507.9	−555.7
With direct investment at market value.............	128.5	125.1	58.1	.9	−91.8	−224.1	−368.7	−590.0	−507.7
U.S. ASSETS ABROAD:									
With direct investment at current cost.............	1,296.4	1,468.8	1,625.4	1,773.0	1,979.0	2,066.9	2,137.0	2,149.6	2,370.4
With direct investment at market value.............	1,288.3	1,566.4	1,709.0	1,935.9	2,236.7	2,165.7	2,300.2	2,267.3	2,647.4
U.S. official reserve assets	117.9	139.9	162.4	144.2	168.7	174.7	159.2	147.4	164.9
Gold [1]	85.8	102.4	127.6	107.4	105.2	102.4	92.6	87.2	102.6
Special drawing rights	7.3	8.4	10.3	9.6	10.0	11.0	11.2	8.5	9.0
Reserve position in the International Monetary Fund..	11.9	11.7	11.3	9.7	9.0	9.1	9.5	11.8	11.8
Foreign currencies	12.9	17.3	13.1	17.4	44.6	52.2	45.9	40.0	41.5
U.S. Government assets other than official reserves.	87.8	89.6	88.9	86.1	84.5	82.0	79.0	80.6	80.9
U.S. credits and other long-term assets.............	85.8	88.7	88.1	85.4	83.9	81.4	77.4	79.0	79.0
Repayable in dollars	84.1	87.1	86.5	83.9	82.4	80.0	76.2	77.9	78.0
Other..	1.7	1.6	1.6	1.5	1.5	1.3	1.2	1.1	1.0
U.S. foreign currency holdings and U.S. short-term assets..	1.9	.9	.8	.7	.6	.6	1.6	1.6	1.9
U.S. private assets:									
With direct investment at current cost.............	1,090.7	1,239.3	1,374.1	1,542.7	1,725.8	1,810.2	1,898.8	1,921.5	2,124.6
With direct investment at market value.............	1,082.6	1,336.9	1,457.7	1,705.6	1,983.5	1,909.1	2,061.9	2,039.2	2,401.6
Direct investment abroad:									
At current cost......................................	387.2	421.2	493.3	515.7	560.0	620.5	650.6	668.2	716.2
At market value.....................................	379.1	518.7	577.0	678.6	817.8	719.4	813.8	785.9	993.2
Foreign securities..	114.3	143.4	154.0	176.0	217.6	228.7	301.5	331.4	518.5
Bonds...	73.3	80.4	84.3	90.0	97.8	118.7	142.7	153.4	220.8
Corporate stocks	41.0	63.0	69.6	86.0	119.9	110.0	158.8	178.1	297.7
U.S. claims on unaffiliated foreigners reported by U.S. nonbanking concerns...............	141.9	167.4	177.4	197.8	234.3	265.3	256.3	253.9	254.5
U.S. claims reported by U.S. banks, not included elsewhere.......................................	447.4	507.3	549.5	653.2	713.8	695.7	690.4	668.0	635.5
FOREIGN ASSETS IN THE UNITED STATES:									
With direct investment at current cost.............	1,171.1	1,434.2	1,648.2	1,917.8	2,230.4	2,318.3	2,486.5	2,657.5	2,926.2
With direct investment at market value.............	1,159.8	1,441.3	1,650.9	1,935.0	2,328.5	2,389.8	2,668.9	2,857.3	3,155.1
Foreign official assets in the United States.............	202.5	241.2	283.1	322.0	341.9	375.3	401.5	442.9	516.9
U.S. Government securities	145.1	178.9	220.5	260.9	263.7	295.0	315.9	335.7	388.5
U.S. Treasury securities	138.4	173.3	213.7	253.0	257.3	287.9	307.1	323.0	370.9
Other..	6.6	5.6	6.8	8.0	6.4	7.1	8.8	12.7	17.6
Other U.S. Government liabilities	15.8	18.0	15.7	15.2	15.4	17.2	18.4	21.0	22.7
U.S. liabilities reported by U.S. banks, not included elsewhere.......................................	26.7	27.9	31.8	31.5	36.5	39.9	38.4	55.0	69.6
Other foreign official assets	14.9	16.4	15.0	14.4	26.3	23.2	28.7	31.3	36.1
Other foreign assets in the United States:									
With direct investment at current cost.............	968.6	1,193.0	1,365.1	1,595.7	1,888.5	1.943.0	2,085.0	2,214.6	2,409.3
With direct investment at market value.............	957.3	1,200.1	1,367.9	1,612.9	1,986.6	2,014.4	2,267.4	2,414.4	2,638.2
Direct investment in the United States:									
At current cost......................................	231.3	265.8	313.5	374.3	436.6	468.1	491.9	497.1	516.7
At market value.....................................	220.0	273.0	316.2	391.5	534.7	539.6	674.2	696.8	745.6
U.S. Treasury securities	88.0	96.1	82.6	100.9	166.5	162.4	189.5	224.8	254.1
U.S. securities other than U.S. Treasury securities...	207.9	309.8	341.7	392.3	482.9	467.4	559.2	621.0	733.2
Corporate and other bonds	82.3	140.9	166.1	191.3	231.7	245.7	287.3	320.8	393.2
Corporate stocks	125.6	168.9	175.6	201.0	251.2	221.7	271.9	300.2	340.0
U.S. liabilities to unaffiliated foreigners reported by U.S. nonbanking concerns..............	87.0	90.7	110.2	144.5	167.1	213.4	208.9	220.7	233.3
U.S. liabilities reported by U.S. banks, not included elsewhere.......................................	354.5	430.6	517.2	583.7	635.5	631.6	635.6	651.0	672.0

[1] Valued at market price.

Note.—For details regarding these data, see *Survey of Current Business*, June 1991, June 1992, June 1993, and June 1994.

Source: Department of Commerce, Bureau of Economic Analysis.

[Millions of dollars; quarterly data seasonally adjusted, except as noted. Credits (+), debits (−)]

Year or quarter	Merchandise [1] [2]			Services			Balance on goods and services	Investment income			Unilateral transfers, net [4]	Balance on current account
	Exports	Imports	Net	Net military transactions [3] [4]	Net travel and transportation receipts	Other services, net		Receipts on U.S. assets abroad	Payments on foreign assets in U.S.	Net		
1946	11,764	−5,067	6,697	−424	733	310	7,316	772	−212	560	−2,991	4,885
1947	16,097	−5,973	10,124	−358	946	145	10,857	1,102	−245	857	−2,722	8,992
1948	13,265	−7,557	5,708	−351	374	175	5,906	1,921	−437	1,484	−4,973	2,417
1949	12,213	−6,874	5,339	−410	230	208	5,367	1,831	−476	1,355	−5,849	873
1950	10,203	−9,081	1,122	−56	−120	242	1,188	2,068	−559	1,509	−4,537	−1,840
1951	14,243	−11,176	3,067	169	298	254	3,788	2,633	−583	2,050	−4,954	884
1952	13,449	−10,838	2,611	528	83	309	3,531	2,751	−555	2,196	−5,113	614
1953	12,412	−10,975	1,437	1,753	−238	307	3,259	2,736	−624	2,112	−6,657	−1,286
1954	12,929	−10,353	2,576	902	−269	305	3,514	2,929	−582	2,347	−5,642	219
1955	14,424	−11,527	2,897	−113	−297	299	2,786	3,406	−676	2,730	−5,086	430
1956	17,556	−12,803	4,753	−221	−361	447	4,618	3,837	−735	3,102	−4,990	2,730
1957	19,562	−13,291	6,271	−423	−189	482	6,141	4,180	−796	3,384	−4,763	4,762
1958	16,414	−12,952	3,462	−849	−633	486	2,466	3,790	−825	2,965	−4,647	784
1959	16,458	−15,310	1,148	−831	−821	573	69	4,132	−1,061	3,071	−4,422	−1,282
1960	19,650	−14,758	4,892	−1,057	−964	639	3,508	4,616	−1,238	3,379	−4,062	2,824
1961	20,108	−14,537	5,571	−1,131	−978	732	4,195	4,999	−1,245	3,755	−4,127	3,822
1962	20,781	−16,260	4,521	−912	−1,152	912	3,370	5,618	−1,324	4,294	−4,277	3,387
1963	22,272	−17,048	5,224	−742	−1,309	1,036	4,210	6,157	−1,560	4,596	−4,392	4,414
1964	25,501	−18,700	6,801	−794	−1,146	1,161	6,022	6,824	−1,783	5,041	−4,240	6,823
1965	26,461	−21,510	4,951	−487	−1,280	1,480	4,664	7,437	−2,088	5,350	−4,583	5,431
1966	29,310	−25,493	3,817	−1,043	−1,331	1,497	2,940	7,528	−2,481	5,047	−4,955	3,031
1967	30,666	−26,866	3,800	−1,187	−1,750	1,742	2,604	8,021	−2,747	5,274	−5,294	2,583
1968	33,626	−32,991	635	−596	−1,548	1,759	250	9,367	−3,378	5,990	−5,629	611
1969	36,414	−35,807	607	−718	−1,763	1,964	91	10,913	−4,869	6,044	−5,735	399
1970	42,469	−39,866	2,603	−641	−2,038	2,330	2,254	11,748	−5,515	6,233	−6,156	2,331
1971	43,319	−45,579	−2,260	653	−2,345	2,649	−1,303	12,707	−5,435	7,272	−7,402	−1,433
1972	49,381	−55,797	−6,416	1,072	−3,063	2,965	−5,443	14,765	−6,572	8,192	−8,544	−5,795
1973	71,410	−70,499	911	740	−3,158	3,406	1,900	21,808	−9,655	12,153	−6,913	7,140
1974	98,306	−103,811	−5,505	165	−3,184	4,231	−4,292	27,587	−12,084	15,503	[5] −9,249	1,962
1975	107,088	−98,185	8,903	1,461	−2,812	4,854	12,404	25,351	−12,564	12,787	−7,075	18,116
1976	114,745	−124,228	−9,483	931	−2,558	5,027	−6,082	29,375	−13,311	16,063	−5,686	4,295
1977	120,816	−151,907	−31,091	1,731	−3,565	5,680	−27,246	32,354	−14,217	18,137	−5,226	−14,335
1978	142,075	−176,002	−33,927	857	−3,573	6,879	−29,763	42,088	−21,680	20,408	−5,788	−15,143
1979	184,439	−212,007	−27,568	−1,313	−2,935	7,251	−24,565	63,834	−32,961	30,873	−6,593	−285
1980	224,250	−249,750	−25,500	−1,822	−997	8,912	−19,407	72,606	−42,532	30,073	−8,349	2,317
1981	237,044	−265,067	−28,023	−844	144	12,552	−16,172	86,529	−53,626	32,903	−11,702	5,030
1982	211,157	−247,642	−36,485	112	−992	13,209	−24,156	86,200	−56,412	29,788	−17,075	−11,443
1983	201,799	−268,901	−67,102	−563	−4,227	14,095	−57,796	84,778	−53,700	31,078	−17,741	−44,460
1984	219,926	−332,418	−112,492	−2,547	−8,438	14,277	−109,200	104,075	−74,036	30,038	−20,612	−99,773
1985	215,915	−338,088	−122,173	−4,390	−9,798	14,266	−122,095	92,760	−73,087	19,673	−22,950	−125,372
1986	223,344	−368,425	−145,081	−5,181	−7,382	18,855	−138,789	90,858	−79,095	11,763	−24,176	−151,201
1987	250,208	−409,765	−159,557	−3,844	−6,481	17,900	−151,981	99,239	−91,302	7,937	−23,052	−167,097
1988	320,230	−447,189	−126,959	−6,315	−1,511	19,961	−114,824	127,414	−115,806	11,607	−24,977	−128,194
1989	362,116	−477,365	−115,249	−6,726	5,071	26,558	−90,345	152,517	−138,858	13,659	−26,134	−102,820
1990	389,303	−498,336	−109,033	−7,567	8,978	28,811	−78,810	160,300	−139,574	20,725	−33,663	−91,748
1991	416,913	−490,981	−74,068	−5,485	17,957	33,124	−28,472	136,914	−122,081	14,833	6,687	−6,952
1992	440,361	−536,458	−96,097	−3,034	20,885	37,862	−40,384	114,449	−109,909	4,540	−32,042	−67,886
1993	456,866	−589,441	−132,575	−763	20,840	36,773	−75,725	113,856	−109,910	3,946	−32,117	−103,896
1992:												
I	108,268	−126,333	−18,065	−559	5,311	9,435	−3,877	30,192	−27,755	2,437	−6,917	−8,357
II	108,803	−133,139	−24,336	−673	5,433	9,202	−10,375	30,236	−28,624	1,612	−7,776	−16,539
III	109,546	−136,906	−27,360	−525	5,138	9,960	−12,787	27,864	−26,644	1,220	−7,040	−18,607
IV	113,744	−140,080	−26,336	−1,277	5,005	9,262	−13,346	26,158	−26,887	−729	−10,308	−24,383
1993:												
I	111,664	−140,855	−29,191	−105	5,307	9,567	−14,422	27,727	−25,872	1,855	−7,283	−19,850
II	113,787	−147,514	−33,727	−128	5,565	9,221	−19,070	28,801	−28,133	668	−7,200	−25,602
III	111,736	−148,224	−36,488	−87	5,230	9,087	−22,258	28,513	−26,498	2,015	−7,613	−27,856
IV	119,679	−152,848	−33,169	−444	4,740	8,897	−19,976	28,816	−29,406	−590	−10,021	−30,587
1994:												
I	118,018	−154,980	−36,962	−337	4,098	8,874	−24,328	29,888	−30,699	−811	−7,178	−32,317
II	122,683	−164,315	−41,632	177	5,344	9,465	−26,646	31,878	−34,687	−2,809	−8,451	−37,906
III[*p*]	127,817	−172,450	−44,633	376	4,843	9,903	−29,511	35,399	−39,347	−3,948	−8,263	−41,722

[1] Excludes military.
[2] Adjusted from Census data for differences in valuation, coverage, and timing.
[3] Quarterly data are not seasonally adjusted.
[4] Includes transfers of goods and services under U.S. military grant programs.

See next page for continuation of table.

[Millions of dollars; quarterly data seasonally adjusted, except as noted]

| Year or quarter | U.S. assets abroad, net [increase/capital outflow (−)] | | | | Foreign assets in the U.S., net [increase/capital inflow (+)] | | | Allocations of special drawing rights (SDRs) | Statistical discrepancy | |
	Total	U.S. official reserve assets [3][6]	Other U.S. Government assets	U.S. private assets	Total	Foreign official assets [3]	Other foreign assets		Total (sum of the items with sign reversed)	Of which: Seasonal adjustment discrepancy
1946		−623								
1947		−3,315								
1948		−1,736								
1949		−266								
1950		1,758								
1951		−33								
1952		−415								
1953		1,256								
1954		480								
1955		182								
1956		−869								
1957		−1,165								
1958		2,292								
1959		1,035								
1960	−4,099	2,145	−1,100	−5,144	2,294	1,473	821		−1,019	
1961	−5,538	607	−910	−5,235	2,705	765	1,939		−989	
1962	−4,174	1,535	−1,085	−4,623	1,911	1,270	641		−1,124	
1963	−7,270	378	−1,662	−5,986	3,217	1,986	1,231		−360	
1964	−9,560	171	−1,680	−8,050	3,643	1,660	1,983		−907	
1965	−5,716	1,225	−1,605	−5,336	742	134	607		−457	
1966	−7,321	570	−1,543	−6,347	3,661	−672	4,333		629	
1967	−9,757	53	−2,423	−7,386	7,379	3,451	3,928		−205	
1968	−10,977	−870	−2,274	−7,833	9,928	−774	10,703		438	
1969	−11,585	−1,179	−2,200	−8,206	12,702	−1,301	14,002		−1,516	
1970	−9,337	2,481	−1,589	−10,229	6,359	6,908	−550	867	−219	
1971	−12,475	2,349	−1,884	−12,940	22,970	26,879	−3,909	717	−9,779	
1972	−14,497	−4	−1,568	−12,925	21,461	10,475	10,986	710	−1,879	
1973	−22,874	158	−2,644	−20,388	18,388	6,026	12,362		−2,654	
1974	−34,745	−1,467	[5] 366	−33,643	34,241	10,546	23,696		−1,458	
1975	−39,703	−849	−3,474	−35,380	15,670	7,027	8,643		5,917	
1976	−51,269	−2,558	−4,214	−44,498	36,518	17,693	18,826		10,455	
1977	−34,785	−375	−3,693	−30,717	51,319	36,816	14,503		−2,199	
1978	−61,130	732	−4,660	−57,202	64,036	33,678	30,358		12,236	
1979	−66,054	−1,133	−3,746	−61,176	38,752	−13,665	52,416	1,139	26,449	
1980	−86,967	−8,155	−5,162	−73,651	58,112	15,497	42,615	1,152	25,386	
1981	−114,147	−5,175	−5,097	−103,875	83,032	4,960	78,072	1,093	24,992	
1982	−122,335	−4,965	−6,131	−111,239	92,418	3,593	88,826		41,359	
1983	−58,735	−1,196	−5,006	−52,533	83,380	5,845	77,534		19,815	
1984	−34,917	−3,131	−5,489	−26,298	113,932	3,140	110,792		20,758	
1985	−39,225	−3,858	−2,821	−32,547	141,183	−1,119	142,301		23,415	
1986	−104,818	312	−2,022	−103,109	226,111	35,648	190,463		29,908	
1987	−71,443	9,149	1,006	−81,597	242,983	45,387	197,596		−4,443	
1988	−99,360	−3,912	2,967	−98,414	240,265	39,758	200,507		−12,712	
1989	−168,744	−25,293	1,259	−144,710	218,490	8,503	209,987		53,075	
1990	−70,363	−2,158	2,307	−70,512	122,192	33,910	88,282		39,919	
1991	−51,512	5,763	2,900	−60,175	98,134	17,199	80,935		−39,670	
1992	−61,510	3,901	−1,652	−63,759	146,504	40,858	105,646		−17,108	
1993	−147,898	−1,379	−306	−146,213	230,698	71,681	159,017		21,096	
1992:										
I	−7,726	−1,057	−269	−6,400	26,116	21,016	5,100		−10,033	4,818
II	−13,586	1,464	−289	−14,761	47,874	20,897	26,977		−17,749	592
III	−10,806	1,952	−394	−12,364	29,935	−7,417	37,352		−522	−6,375
IV	−29,395	1,542	−701	−30,236	42,581	6,363	36,218		11,197	966
1993:										
I	−12,659	−983	488	−12,164	16,772	10,968	5,804		15,737	6,105
II	−35,966	822	−281	−36,507	51,829	17,492	34,337		9,739	435
III	−35,651	−545	−192	−34,915	71,934	19,259	52,675		−8,427	−6,643
IV	−63,622	−673	−321	−62,628	90,162	23,962	66,200		4,047	103
1994:										
I	−48,236	−59	490	−48,667	95,078	11,530	83,548		−14,525	5,810
II	−7,031	3,537	462	−11,030	49,257	8,925	40,332		−4,320	639
III [p]	−20,394	−165	−118	−20,111	67,439	17,496	49,943		−5,323	−6,919

[5] Includes extraordinary U.S. Government transactions with India.
[6] Consists of gold, special drawing rights, foreign currencies, and the U.S. reserve position in the International Monetary Fund (IMF).
Source: Department of Commerce, Bureau of Economic Analysis.

TABLE B-106.—*U.S. merchandise exports and imports by principal end-use category, 1965-94*

[Billions of dollars; quarterly data seasonally adjusted]

Year or quarter	Exports							Imports						
		Agricultural products	Nonagricultural products						Petroleum and products	Nonpetroleum products				
	Total		Total	Industrial supplies and materials	Capital goods except automotive	Automotive	Other	Total		Total	Industrial supplies and materials	Capital goods except automotive	Automotive	Other
1965	26.5	6.3	20.2	7.6	8.1	1.9	2.6	21.5	2.0	19.5	9.1	1.5	0.9	8.0
1966	29.3	6.9	22.4	8.2	8.9	2.4	2.9	25.5	2.1	23.4	10.2	2.2	1.8	9.2
1967	30.7	6.5	24.2	8.5	9.9	2.8	3.0	26.9	2.1	24.8	10.0	2.5	2.4	9.9
1968	33.6	6.3	27.3	9.6	11.1	3.5	3.2	33.0	2.4	30.6	12.0	2.8	4.0	11.8
1969	36.4	6.1	30.3	10.3	12.4	3.9	3.7	35.8	2.6	33.2	11.8	3.4	4.9	13.0
1970	42.5	7.4	35.1	12.3	14.7	3.9	4.3	39.9	2.9	36.9	12.4	4.0	5.5	15.0
1971	43.3	7.8	35.5	10.9	15.4	4.7	4.5	45.6	3.7	41.9	13.8	4.3	7.4	16.4
1972	49.4	9.5	39.9	11.9	16.9	5.5	5.6	55.8	4.7	51.1	16.3	5.9	8.7	20.2
1973	71.4	18.0	53.4	17.0	22.0	6.9	7.6	70.5	8.4	62.1	19.6	8.3	10.3	23.9
1974	98.3	22.4	75.9	26.3	30.9	8.6	10.0	103.8	26.6	77.2	27.8	9.8	12.0	27.5
1975	107.1	22.2	84.8	26.8	36.6	10.6	10.8	98.2	27.0	71.2	24.0	10.2	11.7	25.3
1976	114.7	23.4	91.4	28.4	39.1	12.1	11.7	124.2	34.6	89.7	29.8	12.3	16.2	31.4
1977	120.8	24.3	96.5	29.8	39.8	13.4	13.5	151.9	45.0	106.9	35.7	14.0	18.6	38.6
1978 [1]	142.1	29.9	112.2	34.2	47.5	15.2	15.3	176.0	42.6	133.4	40.7	19.3	25.0	48.4
1979	184.4	35.5	149.0	52.2	60.2	17.9	18.7	212.0	60.4	151.6	47.5	24.6	26.6	52.8
1980	224.3	42.0	182.2	65.1	76.3	17.4	23.4	249.8	79.5	170.2	53.0	31.6	28.3	57.4
1981	237.0	44.1	193.0	63.6	84.2	19.7	25.5	265.1	78.4	186.7	56.1	37.1	31.0	62.4
1982	211.2	37.3	173.9	57.7	76.5	17.2	22.4	247.6	62.0	185.7	48.6	38.4	34.3	64.3
1983	201.8	37.1	164.7	52.7	71.7	18.5	21.8	268.9	55.1	213.8	53.7	43.7	43.0	73.3
1984	219.9	38.4	181.5	56.8	77.0	22.4	25.3	332.4	58.1	274.4	66.1	60.4	56.5	91.4
1985	215.9	29.6	186.3	54.8	79.3	24.9	27.2	338.1	51.4	286.7	62.6	61.3	64.9	97.9
1986	223.3	27.2	196.2	59.4	82.8	25.1	28.9	368.4	34.3	334.1	69.9	72.0	78.1	114.2
1987	250.2	29.8	220.4	63.7	92.7	27.6	36.4	409.8	42.9	366.8	70.8	85.1	85.2	125.7
1988	320.2	38.8	281.4	82.6	119.1	33.4	46.3	447.2	39.6	407.6	83.1	102.2	87.9	134.4
1989	362.1	42.2	319.9	91.9	139.6	34.9	53.5	477.4	50.9	426.4	84.2	112.5	87.4	142.4
1990	389.3	40.2	349.1	97.1	153.3	36.5	62.3	498.3	62.3	436.0	82.5	116.0	88.5	149.0
1991	416.9	40.1	376.8	101.7	166.5	40.0	68.6	491.0	51.7	439.2	81.2	120.8	85.7	151.5
1992	440.4	44.1	396.3	101.7	176.1	47.0	71.5	536.5	51.6	484.9	89.0	134.3	91.8	169.8
1993	456.9	43.7	413.2	105.0	182.2	52.4	73.5	589.4	51.5	538.0	101.0	152.4	102.4	182.2
1992: I	108.3	10.9	97.4	24.9	44.1	10.7	17.7	126.3	10.5	115.9	21.2	31.5	22.4	40.8
II	108.8	10.7	98.1	25.3	43.7	11.6	17.4	133.1	13.1	120.0	22.2	32.9	22.7	42.2
III	109.5	11.1	98.5	25.5	43.0	12.1	17.9	136.9	14.3	122.6	22.2	34.4	23.1	42.9
IV	113.7	11.4	102.3	26.0	45.2	12.6	18.6	140.1	13.7	126.4	23.4	35.5	23.6	43.8
1993: I	111.7	10.9	100.7	25.7	44.2	12.9	17.9	140.9	12.8	128.1	23.5	35.7	25.2	43.8
II	113.8	10.9	102.9	25.9	45.8	13.2	17.9	147.5	14.3	133.2	25.0	37.6	25.4	45.2
III	111.7	10.5	101.2	26.0	44.1	12.6	18.5	148.2	12.5	135.7	26.0	38.2	25.4	46.1
IV	119.7	11.3	108.3	27.4	48.1	13.7	19.1	152.8	11.9	141.0	26.5	40.8	26.5	47.2
1994: I	118.0	10.9	107.1	26.4	48.7	13.6	18.4	155.0	10.4	144.6	27.6	42.6	27.0	47.4
II	122.7	11.0	111.7	27.0	51.1	14.0	19.7	164.3	12.8	151.5	27.8	44.7	29.1	49.8
III	127.8	11.7	116.2	29.1	51.9	14.5	20.7	172.5	15.2	157.3	28.5	47.0	30.9	50.9

[1] End-use categories beginning 1978 are not strictly comparable with data for earlier periods. See *Survey of Current Business*, June 1988.

Note.—Data are on an international transactions basis and exclude military.

In June 1990, end-use categories for merchandise exports were redefined to include reexports; beginning with data for 1978, reexports (exports of foreign merchandise) are assigned to detailed end-use categories in the same manner as exports of domestic merchandise.

Source: Department of Commerce, Bureau of Economic Analysis.

[Billions of dollars]

Item	1985	1986	1987	1988	1989	1990	1991	1992	1993	1994 first 3 quarters at annual rate [1]
Exports	215.9	223.3	250.2	320.2	362.1	389.3	416.9	440.4	456.9	491.4
Industrial countries	140.5	150.3	165.6	207.3	234.2	253.8	261.3	265.1	270.7	289.0
Canada	55.4	56.5	62.0	74.3	81.1	83.5	85.9	91.4	101.2	112.0
Japan	22.1	26.4	27.6	37.2	43.9	47.8	47.2	46.9	46.7	51.7
Western Europe [2]	56.0	60.4	68.6	86.4	98.4	111.4	116.8	114.5	111.3	112.4
Australia, New Zealand, and South Africa	7.0	7.1	7.4	9.4	10.9	11.2	11.4	12.4	11.5	12.9
Australia	5.1	5.1	5.3	6.8	8.1	8.3	8.3	8.7	8.1	9.4
Other countries, except Eastern Europe	71.9	71.0	82.3	109.1	122.2	130.6	150.4	169.5	179.8	197.0
OPEC [2]	11.4	10.4	10.7	13.8	13.3	13.4	18.4	20.7	18.7	16.6
Other [3]	60.5	60.6	71.6	95.3	108.9	117.2	132.0	148.8	161.1	180.4
Eastern Europe	3.2	2.1	2.3	3.8	5.5	4.3	4.8	5.6	6.2	5.4
International organizations and unallocated	.2	....	....	.1	.2	.6	.4	.1	2	.0
Imports	338.1	368.4	409.8	447.2	477.4	498.3	491.0	536.5	589.4	655.7
Industrial countries	219.0	245.4	259.7	283.2	292.5	299.9	294.3	316.3	347.8	382.5
Canada	70.2	69.7	73.6	84.6	89.9	93.1	93.0	100.9	113.3	127.7
Japan	65.7	80.8	84.6	89.8	93.5	90.4	92.3	97.4	107.2	117.1
Western Europe	77.5	89.0	96.1	102.6	102.4	109.2	102.0	111.4	120.9	131.0
Australia, New Zealand, and South Africa	5.6	5.9	5.4	6.2	6.6	7.3	7.0	6.6	6.4	6.7
Australia	2.7	2.6	3.0	3.5	3.9	4.4	4.1	3.7	3.3	3.2
Other countries, except Eastern Europe	117.3	121.1	148.2	161.8	182.8	196.1	194.9	218.2	238.1	267.9
OPEC [2]	22.8	18.9	24.4	23.0	30.7	38.2	33.4	33.7	32.6	31.1
Other [3]	94.5	102.2	123.8	138.8	152.1	157.9	161.5	184.5	205.4	236.7
Eastern Europe	1.8	2.0	1.9	2.2	2.1	2.3	1.8	2.0	3.5	5.3
International organizations and unallocated	....	....	....	....	....	....	....	....	....	....
Balance (excess of exports +)	−122.2	−145.1	−159.6	−127.0	−115.2	−109.0	−74.1	−96.1	−132.6	−164.3
Industrial countries	−78.4	−95.1	−94.1	−75.9	−58.3	−46.1	−33.0	−51.2	−77.2	−93.5
Canada	−14.8	−13.2	−11.6	−10.3	−8.9	−9.6	−7.1	−9.5	−12.1	−15.6
Japan	−43.5	−54.4	−56.9	−52.6	−49.7	−42.6	−45.0	−50.5	−60.5	−65.4
Western Europe [2]	−21.4	−28.6	−27.5	−16.2	−4.0	2.2	14.8	3.1	−9.7	−18.6
Australia, New Zealand, and South Africa	1.4	1.1	2.0	3.2	4.2	3.9	4.4	5.8	5.2	6.2
Australia	2.4	2.5	2.3	3.3	4.2	3.9	4.2	5.0	4.8	6.3
Other countries, except Eastern Europe	−45.3	−50.1	−65.8	−52.7	−60.6	−65.6	−44.5	−48.7	−58.3	−70.9
OPEC [2]	−11.4	−8.5	−13.7	−9.2	−17.4	−24.8	−15.0	−13.0	−14.0	−14.5
Other [3]	−33.9	−41.6	−52.1	−43.5	−43.2	−40.7	−29.5	−35.7	−44.3	−56.4
Eastern Europe [2]	1.4	.1	.3	1.6	3.5	2.1	3.0	3.7	2.7	.1
International organizations and unallocated	.2	....	....	.1	.2	.6	.4	.1	.2	.0

[1] Preliminary; seasonally adjusted.

[2] The former German Democratic Republic (East Germany) included in Western Europe beginning fourth quarter 1990 and in Eastern Europe prior to that time.

[3] Organization of Petroleum Exporting Countries, consisting of Algeria, Ecuador (through 1992), Gabon, Indonesia, Iran, Iraq, Kuwait, Libya, Nigeria, Qatar, Saudi Arabia, United Arab Emirates, and Venezuela.

[4] Latin America, other Western Hemisphere, and other countries in Asia and Africa, less members of OPEC.

Note.—Data are on an international transactions basis and exclude military.

Source: Department of Commerce, Bureau of Economic Analysis.

TABLE B-108.—*U.S. international trade in goods on balance of payments (BOP) and Census basis, and trade in services on BOP basis, 1974–94*

[Billions of dollars; monthly data seasonally adjusted]

Year or month	Goods: Exports (f.a.s. value) [1][2]							Goods: Imports (customs value, except as noted) [5]							Services (BOP basis)	
	Total, BOP basis [3]	Census basis (by end-use category)						Total, BOP basis	Census basis (by end-use category)						Exports	Imports
		Total, Census basis [3][4]	Foods, feeds, and beverages	Industrial supplies and materials	Capital goods except automotive	Automotive vehicles, parts, and engines	Consumer goods (nonfood) except automotive		Total, Census basis [4]	Foods, feeds, and beverages	Industrial supplies and materials	Capital goods except automotive	Automotive vehicles, parts, and engines	Consumer goods (nonfood) except automotive		
	F.a.s. value [2]							F.a.s. value [2]								
1974	98.3	99.4						103.8	103.3						22.6	21.4
1975	107.1	108.9						98.2	99.3						25.5	22.0
1976	114.7	116.8						124.2	124.6						28.0	24.6
1977	120.8	123.2						151.9	151.5						31.5	27.6
1978	142.1	145.8						176.0	176.1						36.4	32.2
1979	184.4	186.4						212.0	210.3						39.7	36.7
1980	224.3	225.6						249.8	245.3						47.6	41.5
								Customs value								
1981	237.0	238.7						265.1	261.0						57.4	45.5
1982	211.2	216.4	31.3	61.7	72.7	15.7	14.3	247.6	244.0	17.1	112.0	35.4	33.3	39.7	64.1	51.7
1983	201.8	205.6	30.9	56.7	67.2	16.8	13.4	268.9	258.0	18.2	107.0	40.9	44.9	44.9	64.2	54.9
1984	219.9	224.0	31.5	61.7	72.0	20.6	13.3	332.4 [6]	330.7	21.0	123.7	59.8	53.5	60.0	71.0	67.7
1985	215.9 [7]	218.8	24.0	58.5	73.9	22.9	12.6	338.1 [6]	336.5	21.9	113.9	65.1	66.8	68.3	72.9	72.8
1986	223.3 [7]	227.2	22.3	57.3	75.8	21.7	14.2	368.4	365.4	24.4	101.3	71.8	78.2	79.4	86.1	79.8
1987	250.2	254.1	24.3	66.7	86.2	24.6	17.7	409.8	406.2	24.8	111.0	84.5	85.2	88.7	97.8	90.2
1988	320.2	322.4	32.3	85.1	109.2	29.3	23.1	447.2	441.0	24.8	118.3	101.4	87.7	95.9	110.0	97.9
1989	362.1	363.8	37.2	99.3	138.8	34.8	36.4	477.4	473.2	25.1	132.3	113.3	86.1	102.9	126.8	101.9
1990	389.3	393.6	35.1	104.4	152.7	37.4	43.3	498.3	495.3	26.6	143.2	116.4	87.3	105.7	147.2	117.0
1991	416.9	421.7	35.7	109.7	166.7	40.0	45.9	491.0	488.5	26.5	131.6	120.7	85.7	108.0	163.2	117.6
1992	440.4	448.2	40.3	109.1	175.9	47.0	51.4	536.5	532.7	27.5	138.6	134.3	91.8	122.7	176.6	120.9
1993	456.9	465.1	40.6	111.8	181.7	52.4	54.7	589.4	580.7	27.9	145.6	152.4	102.4	134.0	184.8	128.0
1993: Jan	36.7	37.4	3.3	9.4	14.3	4.1	4.3	46.1	45.6	2.3	11.7	11.6	8.1	10.5	14.8	10.2
Feb	36.4	37.0	3.4	8.7	14.2	4.4	4.4	45.0	44.9	2.2	11.0	11.8	8.3	10.3	15.5	10.1
Mar	38.6	39.1	3.5	9.3	15.5	4.4	4.5	49.7	48.9	2.4	12.5	12.3	8.8	11.3	15.3	10.5
Apr	37.9	38.6	3.5	9.2	15.2	4.4	4.4	49.2	48.5	2.2	12.7	12.4	8.6	11.1	15.5	10.6
May	38.6	39.3	3.4	9.6	15.3	4.5	4.6	48.6	47.8	2.3	12.4	12.3	8.2	10.9	15.4	10.4
June	37.3	37.9	3.2	8.8	15.3	4.3	4.4	49.7	49.3	2.3	12.8	12.9	8.6	11.2	15.4	10.6
July	36.5	37.2	3.2	9.2	14.2	4.1	4.5	48.8	48.0	2.3	12.2	12.8	8.0	11.2	15.6	10.7
Aug	37.4	38.1	3.1	9.0	15.1	4.2	4.6	49.0	48.2	2.3	11.8	12.5	8.6	11.5	15.4	10.6
Sept	37.9	38.6	3.4	9.5	14.7	4.3	4.7	50.4	49.2	2.4	12.2	12.9	8.7	11.7	15.7	11.1
Oct	39.4	40.0	3.5	9.9	15.5	4.5	4.6	51.9	50.8	2.6	12.5	13.6	8.9	11.7	15.1	11.1
Nov	39.4	40.1	3.5	9.6	15.5	4.7	4.9	50.9	50.0	2.3	12.3	13.3	8.9	11.5	15.1	11.1
Dec	41.0	41.7	3.7	9.6	16.9	4.5	4.7	50.1	49.4	2.3	11.5	13.9	8.7	11.3	15.8	11.2
1994: Jan	38.5	39.2	3.3	9.0	16.0	4.4	4.5	50.5	50.1	2.4	11.7	14.1	8.7	11.6	15.1	11.0
Feb	37.4	38.1	3.2	8.7	15.3	4.4	4.5	51.0	50.2	2.4	11.9	14.0	8.8	11.5	15.4	11.5
Mar	42.1	42.8	3.4	10.6	17.3	4.8	4.9	53.5	52.4	2.5	12.7	14.5	9.5	11.3	16.3	11.8
Apr	40.4	41.1	3.1	9.6	16.7	4.7	4.7	53.7	53.1	2.5	12.8	14.7	9.5	11.8	15.6	10.8
May	40.3	41.1	3.3	9.9	16.6	4.5	4.8	54.5	54.0	2.5	13.2	14.9	9.5	12.1	16.0	10.9
June	42.0	42.8	3.1	9.8	17.7	4.7	5.1	56.0	55.8	2.6	14.0	15.1	10.2	12.1	16.3	11.1
July	40.1	41.0	3.1	10.3	16.3	4.3	4.9	56.1	55.8	2.6	14.4	15.2	9.9	12.0	16.2	11.2
Aug	44.1	45.1	3.7	10.7	17.7	5.2	5.3	58.2	57.9	2.7	14.7	15.3	11.1	12.5	16.2	11.4
Sept	43.6	44.4	3.7	10.3	17.8	5.0	5.2	58.0	57.8	2.7	14.3	16.5	9.9	12.6	16.5	11.4
Oct	43.4	44.3	3.9	10.6	16.9	5.0	5.4	58.4	58.2	2.7	14.0	16.6	10.2	12.8	16.5	11.5
Nov	44.5	45.3	4.0	10.7	18.0	4.9	5.5	60.1	59.8	2.6	14.6	17.0	10.8	13.0	16.6	11.6

[1] Department of Defense shipments of grant-aid military supplies and equipment under the Military Assistance Program are excluded from total exports through 1985 and included beginning 1986.

[2] F.a.s. (free alongside ship) value basis at U.S. port of exportation for exports and at foreign port of exportation for imports.

[3] Includes undocumented exports to Canada through 1988. Beginning 1989, undocumented exports to Canada are included in the appropriate end-use category.

[4] Total includes "other" exports or imports, not shown separately.

[5] Total arrivals of imported goods other than intransit shipments.

[6] Total includes revisions not reflected in detail.

[7] Total exports are on a revised statistical month basis; end-use categories are on a statistical month basis.

Note.—Goods on a Census basis are adjusted to a BOP basis by the Bureau of Economic Analysis, in line with concepts and definitions used to prepare international and national accounts. The adjustments are necessary to supplement coverage of Census data, to eliminate duplication of transactions recorded elsewhere in international accounts, and to value transactions according to a standard definition.

Data include trade of the U.S. Virgin Islands.

Source: Department of Commerce (Bureau of the Census and Bureau of Economic Analysis).

TABLE B-109.—*International reserves, selected years, 1952–94*

[Millions of SDRs; end of period]

Area and country	1952	1962	1972	1982	1991	1992	1993	1994 Oct	1994 Nov
All countries................................	49,388	62,851	146,658	361,209	704,511	725,661	790,112	833,157	841,816
Industrial countries [1]...................	39,280	53,502	113,362	214,025	428,438	424,229	440,423	458,354	460,688
United States...........................	24,714	17,220	12,112	29,918	55,769	52,995	54,558	54,374	52,373
Canada	1,944	2,561	5,572	3,439	11,816	8,662	9,299	10,098	9,261
Australia.................................	920	1,168	5,656	6,053	11,837	8,429	8,359	7,952	7,983
Japan.....................................	1,101	2,021	16,916	22,001	51,224	52,937	72,577	84,192	86,777
New Zealand............................	183	251	767	577	2,062	2,239	2,430	2,355	....
Austria...................................	116	1,081	2,505	5,544	7,924	9,703	11,288	12,648	12,481
Belgium..................................	1,133	1,753	3,564	4,757	9,573	10,914	9,187	10,812	10,314
Denmark.................................	150	256	787	2,111	5,234	8,090	7,557	6,323	6,251
Finland...................................	132	237	664	1,420	5,389	3,862	4,009	7,529	7,414
France	686	4,049	9,224	17,850	24,735	22,522	19,354	19,721	20,008
Germany.................................	960	6,958	21,908	43,909	47,375	69,489	59,856	60,637	....
Greece...................................	94	287	950	916	3,747	3,606	5,792	9,158	10,039
Iceland...................................	8	32	78	133	316	364	312	244	225
Ireland...................................	318	359	1,038	2,390	4,026	2,514	4,326	4,397	4,275
Italy......................................	722	4,068	5,605	15,108	36,365	22,438	22,387	21,136	20,307
Netherlands.............................	953	1,943	4,407	10,723	13,980	17,492	24,046	25,068	24,871
Norway	164	304	1,220	6,273	9,292	8,725	14,327	13,246	13,857
Portugal.................................	603	680	2,129	1,179	14,977	14,474	12,094	11,345	....
Spain.....................................	134	1,045	4,618	7,450	46,562	33,640	30,429	29,134	29,132
Sweden..................................	504	802	1,453	3,397	13,028	16,667	14,081	15,925	15,810
Switzerland.............................	1,667	2,919	6,961	16,930	23,191	27,100	26,674	23,900	25,053
United Kingdom	1,956	3,308	5,201	11,904	29,948	27,300	27,420		
Developing countries: Total [2]	9,648	9,349	33,295	147,184	276,074	301,432	349,689	374,803	381,127
By area:									
Africa....................................	1,786	2,110	3,962	7,737	14,633	12,899	13,944	14,612	14,408
Asia [2]	3,793	2,772	8,129	44,490	157,533	164,435	191,673	218,738	222,349
Europe...................................	269	381	2,680	5,359	15,823	15,171	17,176	17,965	18,623
Middle East	1,183	1,805	9,436	64,039	41,777	44,151	47,355	45,519	45,839
Western Hemisphere..................	2,616	2,282	9,089	25,563	46,308	64,776	79,542	77,969	79,909
Memo:									
Oil-exporting countries	1,699	2,030	9,956	67,108	48,883	46,144	46,532	42,171	42,785
Non-oil developing countries [2]	7,949	7,319	23,339	80,076	227,191	255,288	303,157	332,632	338,342

[1] Includes data for Luxembourg.
[2] Includes data for Taiwan Province of China.

Note.—International reserves is comprised of monetary authorities' holdings of gold (at SDR 35 per ounce), special drawing rights (SDRs), reserve positions in the International Monetary Fund, and foreign exchange. Data exclude U.S.S.R., other Eastern European countries, and Cuba (after 1960).

U.S. dollars per SDR (end of period) are: 1952 and 1962—1.00000; 1972—1.08571; 1982—1.10311; 1991—1.43043; 1992—1.37500; 1993—1.37356; October 1994—1.48454; and November 1994—1.45674.

Source: International Monetary Fund, *International Financial Statistics.*

Year or quarter	United States	Canada	Japan	European Union [1]	France	Germany [2]	Italy	United Kingdom
	Industrial production (1987=100) [3]							
1969	63.5	59.9	48.3	69.6	69	70.9	64.2	78.5
1970	61.4	59.0	55.0	73.1	72	75.5	68.3	78.9
1971	62.2	62.3	56.5	74.7	77	77.0	68.0	78.5
1972	68.3	67.8	59.6	78.0	81	79.9	70.8	79.9
1973	73.8	75.8	69.0	83.7	87	85.0	77.7	87.0
1974	72.7	77.3	66.3	84.3	90	84.8	81.2	85.4
1975	66.3	71.6	59.3	78.7	83	79.6	73.7	80.8
1976	72.4	76.5	65.9	84.5	90	86.8	82.9	83.4
1977	78.2	79.0	68.6	86.6	92	88.0	83.8	87.6
1978	82.6	81.8	73.0	89.0	94	90.4	85.4	90.1
1979	85.7	85.7	78.2	93.1	99	94.7	91.1	93.6
1980	84.1	82.8	81.8	92.8	98.9	95.0	96.2	87.0
1981	85.7	84.5	82.6	91.1	98.3	93.2	94.7	84.2
1982	81.9	76.2	83.0	89.9	97.3	90.3	91.7	85.8
1983	84.9	81.2	85.5	90.8	96.5	90.9	88.9	88.9
1984	92.8	91.0	93.5	92.8	97.1	93.5	91.8	89.0
1985	94.4	96.1	96.9	95.8	97.2	97.7	92.9	93.9
1986	95.3	95.4	96.7	98.0	98.0	99.6	96.2	96.2
1987	100.0	100.0	100.0	100.0	100.0	100.0	100.0	100.0
1988	104.4	105.3	109.4	104.2	104.6	103.9	105.9	104.8
1989	106.0	105.2	115.7	108.2	108.9	108.8	109.2	107.0
1990	106.0	101.7	120.6	110.4	111.0	114.5	109.4	106.7
1991	104.3	97.5	122.9	110.3	111.0	117.9	108.4	102.5
1992	107.6	98.4	115.8	109.3	109.7	115.6	108.2	102.0
1993	112.0	103.2	111.0	105.6	105.6	107.2	105.4	104.5
1994 [P]	118.1							
1993: I	111.1	101.8	113.1	105.1	106.0	107.3	105.6	103.1
II	111.3	102.7	111.8	104.9	105.4	106.8	104.3	103.6
III	112.2	103.6	110.5	105.2	106.0	107.3	104.3	105.0
IV	113.7	104.6	108.3	106.1	105.0	107.1	104.5	106.3
1994: I	115.7	105.4	110.0	106.7	105.9	107.0	104.7	107.5
II	117.4	108.8	110.7	110.0	109.0	110.4	109.5	109.8
III	118.8	111.2	113.5	112.1	111.0	111.7	113.6	111.2
IV [P]	120.4							
	Consumer prices (1982-84=100)							
1969	36.7	34.0	35.8	25.3	27.4	51.0	16.6	20.4
1970	38.8	35.1	38.5	26.6	28.7	52.9	16.8	21.8
1971	40.5	36.1	40.9	28.3	30.3	55.6	17.6	23.8
1972	41.8	37.9	42.9	30.1	32.2	58.7	18.7	25.5
1973	44.4	40.7	47.9	32.7	34.5	62.8	20.6	27.9
1974	49.3	45.2	59.0	37.4	39.3	67.2	24.6	32.3
1975	53.8	50.1	65.9	42.8	43.9	71.2	28.8	40.2
1976	56.9	53.8	72.2	47.9	48.1	74.2	33.6	46.8
1977	60.6	58.1	78.1	53.8	52.7	76.9	40.1	54.2
1978	65.2	63.3	81.4	58.7	57.5	79.0	45.1	58.7
1979	72.6	69.1	84.4	65.1	63.6	82.3	52.1	66.6
1980	82.4	76.1	91.0	74.0	72.3	86.8	63.5	78.5
1981	90.9	85.6	95.3	83.2	82.0	92.2	75.3	87.9
1982	96.5	94.9	98.0	92.2	91.6	97.0	87.7	95.4
1983	99.6	100.4	99.8	100.2	100.5	100.3	100.8	99.8
1984	103.9	104.8	102.1	107.4	107.9	102.7	111.5	104.8
1985	107.6	108.9	104.1	114.0	114.2	104.8	121.1	111.1
1986	109.6	113.4	104.8	118.2	117.2	104.7	128.5	114.9
1987	113.6	118.4	104.9	122.2	120.9	104.9	134.4	119.7
1988	118.3	123.2	105.7	126.7	124.2	106.3	141.1	125.6
1989	124.0	129.3	108.0	133.3	128.6	109.2	150.4	135.4
1990	130.7	135.5	111.4	140.8	133.0	112.1	159.5	148.2
1991	136.2	143.1	115.0	148.0	137.2	116.0	169.8	156.9
1992	140.3	145.2	116.9	154.3	140.6	120.6	178.8	162.7
1993	144.5	147.9	118.5	159.4	143.5	125.6	186.3	165.3
1994	148.2	148.2	119.3		145.8	129.4	193.6	169.3
1993: I	143.1	147.2	117.4	157.5	142.5	124.2	183.5	162.9
II	144.2	147.5	118.5	159.2	143.4	125.5	185.5	165.6
III	144.8	148.1	119.1	160.1	143.7	126.0	187.2	166.0
IV	145.8	148.8	118.7	161.2	144.3	126.6	189.2	166.6
1994: I	146.7	148.0	118.9	162.6	144.9	128.4	191.2	166.8
II	147.6	147.5	119.4	164.2	145.8	129.3	192.8	169.8
III	148.9	148.3	119.1	164.9	146.0	129.7	194.2	169.9
IV	149.6	148.8	119.7		146.7	130.1	196.5	171.0

[1] Consists of Belgium-Luxembourg, Denmark, France, Greece, Iceland, Italy, Netherlands, United Kingdom, Germany, Portugal, and Spain. Industrial production includes data for Greece beginning 1981; data for Portugal and Spain are included beginning 1982.
[2] Data are for West Germany only.
[3] All data exclude construction. Quarterly data are seasonally adjusted.

Sources: National sources as reported by Department of Commerce (International Trade Administration, Office of Trade and Economic Analysis), Department of Labor (Bureau of Labor Statistics), and Board of Governors of the Federal Reserve System.

TABLE B–111.—*Civilian unemployment rate, and hourly compensation, major industrial countries, 1969–94*

[Quarterly data seasonally adjusted]

Year or quarter	United States	Canada	Japan	France	Germany [1]	Italy	United Kingdom
	Civilian unemployment rate (percent) [2]						
1969	3.5	4.4	1.1	2.3	0.6	3.5	3.1
1970	4.9	5.7	1.2	2.5	.5	3.2	3.1
1971	5.9	6.2	1.3	2.8	.6	3.3	3.9
1972	5.6	6.2	1.4	2.9	.7	3.8	4.2
1973	4.9	5.5	1.3	2.8	.7	3.7	3.2
1974	5.6	5.3	1.4	2.9	1.6	3.1	3.1
1975	8.5	6.9	1.9	4.2	3.4	3.4	4.6
1976	7.7	7.1	2.0	4.6	3.4	3.9	5.9
1977	7.1	8.1	2.0	5.2	3.4	4.1	6.4
1978	6.1	8.3	2.3	5.4	3.3	4.1	6.3
1979	5.8	7.4	2.1	6.1	. 2.9	4.4	5.4
1980	7.1	7.5	2.0	6.5	2.8	4.4	7.0
1981	7.6	7.5	2.2	7.6	4.0	4.9	10.5
1982	9.7	11.0	2.4	8.3	5.6	5.4	11.3
1983	9.6	11.8	2.7	8.6	[3] 6.9	5.9	11.8
1984	7.5	11.2	2.8	10.0	7.1	5.9	11.8
1985	7.2	10.5	2.6	10.5	7.2	6.0	11.2
1986	7.0	9.5	2.8	10.6	6.6	[3] 7.5	11.2
1987	6.2	8.8	2.9	10.8	6.3	7.9	10.3
1988	5.5	7.8	2.5	10.3	6.3	7.9	8.6
1989	5.3	7.5	2.3	9.6	5.7	7.8	7.3
1990	5.5	8.1	2.1	9.1	5.0	7.0	6.9
1991	6.7	10.3	2.1	9.6	ᴾ4.3	[3] 6.9	8.8
1992	7.4	11.3	2.2	10.4	ᴾ4.6	ᴾ7.3	10.0
1993	6.8	11.2	2.5	11.8	ᴾ5.8	[3] ᴾ10.5	ᴾ10.4
1994	[3] 6.1	10.3				11.6	ᴾ9.5
1993: I	7.0	11.0	2.3	11.3	5.3	9.3	10.6
II	7.0	11.4	2.4	11.7	5.6	10.8	10.4
III	6.7	11.4	2.6	12.0	5.9	10.6	10.5
IV	6.5	11.1	2.8	12.3	6.2	11.2	10.1
1994: I	[3] 6.6	11.0	2.8	12.3	6.4	11.2	9.9
II	6.2	10.7	2.8	12.4	6.5	11.9	9.7
III	6.0	10.2	3.0	12.4	6.5	11.4	9.5
IV	5.6	9.7				12.0	9.0
	Manufacturing hourly compensation in U.S. dollars (1982=100) [4]						
1969		30.4	14.6	20.5	18.1	20.6	17.4
1970		33.9	17.4	21.6	22.9	25.1	20.1
1971		37.7	20.7	24.4	27.0	29.4	23.7
1972		41.3	27.3	29.4	32.5	34.9	28.3
1973		44.3	37.4	38.4	44.2	41.2	31.6
1974		52.2	45.6	42.1	51.6	48.1	36.1
1975		57.3	52.1	58.2	59.7	60.5	45.8
1976		67.7	56.2	59.9	62.9	59.0	43.1
1977	62.8	69.5	68.6	66.1	74.5	65.7	46.9
1978	67.9	69.8	94.0	81.4	92.8	78.8	60.0
1979	74.4	74.8	95.5	97.5	109.1	97.4	78.7
1980	83.3	83.0	98.3	113.3	119.3	111.1	104.4
1981	91.5	93.1	107.6	101.8	102.2	100.9	105.1
1982	100.0	100.0	100.0	100.0	100.0	100.0	100.0
1983	102.7	106.2	107.7	95.3	99.9	104.3	92.9
1984	106.0	105.9	111.0	90.2	93.9	103.5	88.2
1985	111.3	105.6	115.0	95.0	96.0	107.0	93.8
1986	115.8	107.8	171.2	128.4	135.6	142.7	112.3
1987	118.4	116.3	204.2	153.4	171.4	173.3	136.9
1988	123.1	130.9	234.4	160.6	182.1	179.3	156.0
1989	127.9	141.2	231.2	158.1	178.4	187.0	162.8
1990	134.7	151.3	237.5	195.1	222.2	238.1	183.3
1991	141.9	163.4	270.6	196.3	230.5	254.3	201.8
1992	147.9	161.5	300.5	216.6	256.7	274.4	218.1
1993	152.8	152.1	352.2	209.5	259.6	230.5	195.4

[1] Data are for West Germany only.

[2] Civilian unemployment rates, approximating U.S. concepts. Quarterly data for France and Germany should be viewed as less precise indicators of unemployment under U.S. concepts than the annual data.

[3] There are breaks in the series for Germany (1983), Italy (1986, 1991, and 1993), and United States (1994). Based on the prior series, the rate for Germany was 7.2 percent in 1983, and the rate for Italy was 6.3 percent in 1986 and 6.6 in 1991. The break in 1993 raised Italy's rate by approximately 1.1 percentage points. For details on break in series in 1994 for United States, see footnote 5, Table B–33.

[4] Hourly compensation in manufacturing, U.S. dollar basis. Data relate to all employed persons (wage and salary earners and the self-employed) in the United States and Canada, and to all employees (wage and salary earners) in the other countries. For France and United Kingdom, compensation adjusted to include changes in employment taxes that are not compensation to employees, but are labor costs to employers.

Source: Department of Labor, Bureau of Labor Statistics.

[Currency units per U.S. dollar, except as noted]

Period	Belgium (franc)	Canada (dollar)	France (franc)	Germany (mark)	Italy (lira)	Japan (yen)
March 1973	39.408	0.9967	4.5156	2.8132	568.17	261.90
1969	50.142	1.0769	5.1999	3.9251	627.32	358.36
1970	49.656	1.0444	5.5288	3.6465	627.12	358.16
1971	48.598	1.0099	5.5100	3.4830	618.34	347.79
1972	44.020	.9907	5.0444	3.1886	583.70	303.13
1973	38.955	1.0002	4.4535	2.6715	582.41	271.31
1974	38.959	.9780	4.8107	2.5868	650.81	291.84
1975	36.800	1.0175	4.2877	2.4614	653.10	296.78
1976	38.609	.9863	4.7825	2.5185	833.58	296.45
1977	35.849	1.0633	4.9161	2.3236	882.78	268.62
1978	31.495	1.1405	4.5091	2.0097	849.13	210.39
1979	29.342	1.1713	4.2567	1.8343	831.11	219.02
1980	29.238	1.1693	4.2251	1.8175	856.21	226.63
1981	37.195	1.1990	5.4397	2.2632	1138.58	220.63
1982	45.781	1.2344	6.5794	2.4281	1354.00	249.06
1983	51.123	1.2325	7.6204	2.5539	1519.32	237.55
1984	57.752	1.2952	8.7356	2.8455	1756.11	237.46
1985	59.337	1.3659	8.9800	2.9420	1908.88	238.47
1986	44.664	1.3896	6.9257	2.1705	1491.16	168.35
1987	37.358	1.3259	6.0122	1.7981	1297.03	144.60
1988	36.785	1.2306	5.9595	1.7570	1302.39	128.17
1989	39.409	1.1842	6.3802	1.8808	1372.28	138.07
1990	33.424	1.1668	5.4467	1.6166	1198.27	145.00
1991	34.195	1.1460	5.6468	1.6610	1241.28	134.59
1992	32.148	1.2085	5.2935	1.5618	1232.17	126.78
1993	34.581	1.2902	5.6669	1.6545	1573.41	111.08
1994	33.424	1.3664	5.5459	1.6216	1611.49	102.18
1993: I	33.686	1.2608	5.5463	1.6349	1547.37	120.67
II	33.311	1.2703	5.4635	1.6198	1506.55	110.05
III	35.447	1.3039	5.8180	1.6776	1586.56	105.65
IV	35.857	1.3251	5.8368	1.6851	1653.17	108.35
1994: I	35.573	1.3425	5.8551	1.7213	1683.14	107.51
II	34.189	1.3825	5.6812	1.6601	1604.10	103.24
III	32.145	1.3717	5.3428	1.5604	1570.58	99.09
IV	31.778	1.3684	5.3026	1.5440	1589.34	98.88

Period	Netherlands (guilder)	Sweden (krona)	Switzerland (franc)	United Kingdom (pound) [1]	Multilateral trade-weighted value of the U.S. dollar (March 1973=100)	
					Nominal	Real [2]
March 1973	2.8714	4.4294	3.2171	2.4724	100.0	100.0
1969	3.6240	5.1701	4.3131	2.3901	122.4	
1970	3.6166	5.1862	4.3106	2.3959	121.1	
1971	3.4953	5.1051	4.1171	2.4442	117.8	
1972	3.2098	4.7571	3.8186	2.5034	109.1	
1973	2.7946	4.3619	3.1688	2.4525	99.1	98.9
1974	2.6879	4.4387	2.9805	2.3403	101.4	99.4
1975	2.5293	4.1531	2.5839	2.2217	98.5	94.0
1976	2.6449	4.3580	2.5002	1.8048	105.7	97.6
1977	2.4548	4.4802	2.4065	1.7449	103.4	93.4
1978	2.1643	4.5207	1.7907	1.9184	92.4	84.4
1979	2.0073	4.2893	1.6644	2.1224	88.1	83.2
1980	1.9875	4.2310	1.6772	2.3246	87.4	84.9
1981	2.4999	5.0660	1.9675	2.0243	103.4	101.0
1982	2.6719	6.2839	2.0327	1.7480	116.6	111.8
1983	2.8544	7.6718	2.1007	1.5159	125.3	117.4
1984	3.2085	8.2708	2.3500	1.3368	138.2	128.9
1985	3.3185	8.6032	2.4552	1.2974	143.0	132.5
1986	2.4485	7.1273	1.7979	1.4677	112.2	103.7
1987	2.0264	6.3469	1.4918	1.6398	96.9	90.9
1988	1.9778	6.1370	1.4643	1.7813	92.7	88.2
1989	2.1219	6.4559	1.6369	1.6382	98.6	94.4
1990	1.8215	5.9231	1.3901	1.7841	89.1	86.0
1991	1.8720	6.0521	1.4356	1.7674	89.8	86.5
1992	1.7587	5.8258	1.4064	1.7663	86.6	83.5
1993	1.8585	7.7956	1.4781	1.5016	93.2	90.0
1994	1.8190	7.7161	1.3667	1.5319	91.3	88.6
1993: I	1.8387	7.5299	1.5063	1.4769	93.3	90.1
II	1.8180	7.4130	1.4628	1.5331	90.9	87.7
III	1.8861	8.0151	1.4768	1.5037	93.7	90.3
IV	1.8907	8.2185	1.4676	1.4914	94.9	91.7
1994: I	1.9311	8.0029	1.4512	1.4881	95.5	92.5
II	1.8632	7.7999	1.4073	1.5046	92.9	89.9
III	1.7510	7.6716	1.3106	1.5515	88.8	86.4
IV	1.7302	7.3822	1.2970	1.5843	88.0	85.8

[1] Value is U.S. dollars per pound.
[2] Adjusted by changes in consumer prices.
Source: Board of Governors of the Federal Reserve System.

402

TABLE B-113.—*Growth rates in real gross domestic product, 1976-94*

[Percent change at annual rate]

Area and country	1976-85	1986	1987	1988	1989	1990	1991	1992	1993	1994[1]
World	3.4	3.6	4.0	4.7	3.4	2.2	0.9	1.7	2.3	3.1
Industrial countries	2.8	2.9	3.2	4.4	3.3	2.4	.8	1.5	1.3	2.7
United States	2.9	2.9	3.1	3.9	2.5	1.2	−.6	2.3	3.1	3.7
Canada	3.4	3.3	4.2	5.0	2.4	−.2	−1.8	.6	2.2	4.1
Japan	4.2	2.6	4.1	6.2	4.7	4.8	4.3	1.1	.1	.9
European Union	2.3	2.9	2.9	4.3	3.5	3.0	1.2	1.1	−.3	2.1
France	2.3	2.5	2.3	4.4	4.3	2.5	.8	1.2	−1.0	1.9
Germany[2]	2.2	2.3	1.5	3.7	3.6	5.7	2.9	2.2	−1.1	2.3
Italy	3.1	2.9	3.1	4.1	2.9	2.1	1.2	.7	−.7	1.5
United Kingdom[3]	1.9	4.3	4.8	5.0	2.2	.4	−2.0	−.5	2.0	3.3
Developing countries	4.5	4.8	5.7	5.3	4.2	3.8	4.5	5.9	6.1	5.6
Africa	2.4	2.4	1.4	3.9	3.6	1.9	1.4	.2	1.0	3.3
Asia	6.4	6.7	8.0	9.2	5.7	5.8	6.2	8.2	8.5	8.0
Middle East and Europe	3.5	2.5	6.0	.3	3.7	4.0	1.9	7.0	4.8	1.4
Western Hemisphere	3.3	4.1	3.3	1.0	1.6	.3	3.4	2.5	3.4	2.8
Countries in transition[4]	3.7	3.6	2.8	4.3	2.2	−3.5	−11.8	−15.5	−9.0	−8.3
Central and eastern Europe							−11.5	−11.7	−5.7	−5.4
Russia							−13.0	−19.0	−12.0	−12.0

[1] All figures are forecasts. For United States, preliminary estimates by the Department of Commerce show that real GDP grew at a 4.0 percent annual rate in 1994.
[2] Through 1990 data are for West Germany only.
[3] Average of expenditure, income, and output estimates of GDP at market prices.
[4] For most countries included in the group, total output is measured by real net material product (NMP) or by NMP-based estimates of GDP.

Sources: Department of Commerce (Bureau of Economic Analysis) and International Monetary Fund.

TABLE B–114.—*National wealth, 1946–93*

[Billions of dollars]

End of year	Total net worth [1]	Private net worth [2]							Government net financial assets		
		Total	Tangible wealth [3]			Financial wealth			Total [7]	Federal	State and local
			Total [4]	Owner-occupied real estate	Consumer durables	Total [5]	Corporate equity [6]	Noncorporate equity			
1946	536.0	757.3	220.1	149.6	53.2	537.2	102.6	201.0	−221.3	−221.6	−0.6
1947	626.2	833.2	260.7	175.5	65.1	572.5	100.2	236.9	−207.0	−207.4	−.5
1948	676.1	874.5	294.7	197.1	76.3	579.8	99.0	246.0	−198.4	−198.8	−.7
1949	708.6	910.8	323.5	214.7	86.6	587.3	108.1	244.9	−202.2	−202.4	−.9
1950	818.6	1,016.5	373.1	239.7	108.2	643.4	132.0	276.5	−197.9	−195.1	−3.9
1951	919.4	1,112.8	419.1	266.8	124.4	693.7	154.6	296.3	−193.4	−189.7	−5.0
1952	955.4	1,167.8	455.2	291.6	134.0	712.6	156.4	298.7	−212.4	−203.2	−10.5
1953	980.4	1,205.2	486.3	312.6	143.0	718.9	150.3	300.9	−224.8	−212.1	−14.0
1954	1,077.3	1,311.2	514.4	335.4	147.1	796.8	219.1	302.3	−233.9	−217.5	−17.9
1955	1,185.5	1,420.2	557.9	364.8	157.3	862.3	268.5	310.3	−234.7	−215.1	−21.1
1956	1,280.6	1,512.5	603.2	391.9	171.9	909.3	288.6	324.3	−231.9	−209.4	−24.1
1957	1,299.3	1,533.0	634.3	416.3	176.2	898.7	254.3	333.3	−233.7	−206.7	−28.7
1958	1,448.2	1,697.1	664.1	438.8	182.0	1,033.0	358.2	344.7	−248.9	−216.5	−34.2
1959	1,519.6	1,775.9	699.1	464.4	189.0	1,076.8	385.6	346.2	−256.3	−219.4	−38.6
1960	1,563.2	1,820.4	730.0	488.2	193.7	1,090.4	381.4	347.3	−257.2	−217.0	−41.9
1961	1,718.0	1,984.9	761.2	512.5	196.8	1,223.7	488.2	353.3	−266.9	−223.1	−45.7
1962	1,703.5	1,978.1	794.5	535.9	202.3	1,183.6	423.3	360.4	−274.6	−227.8	−48.8
1963	1,842.0	2,121.3	833.0	559.2	212.8	1,288.3	497.5	367.8	−279.3	−229.9	−51.5
1964	1,997.2	2,283.9	874.9	584.6	223.7	1,409.0	572.5	381.1	−286.7	−233.8	−54.5
1965	2,170.4	2,461.3	919.2	609.6	236.1	1,542.1	650.5	402.9	−290.9	−235.7	−57.0
1966	2,228.0	2,526.0	991.8	651.9	258.5	1,534.2	582.2	427.6	−298.0	−239.0	−60.9
1967	2,503.5	2,814.3	1,059.4	688.2	283.2	1,754.9	725.1	446.9	−310.8	−247.0	−66.0
1968	2,841.6	3,165.2	1,182.0	768.7	314.2	1,983.2	864.8	486.5	−323.6	−255.5	−70.5
1969	2,872.6	3,197.3	1,282.8	826.7	343.7	1,914.5	628.9	519.6	−324.7	−249.2	−78.2
1970	3,003.7	3,348.6	1,363.9	867.4	372.4	1,984.7	612.9	544.8	−344.9	−260.7	−87.3
1971	3,315.7	3,690.6	1,478.1	945.7	393.7	2,212.5	699.0	594.5	−374.9	−282.3	−96.2
1972	3,747.2	4,137.2	1,667.7	1,085.5	424.7	2,469.5	774.2	671.8	−390.0	−298.9	−95.1
1973	3,919.1	4,309.7	1,887.8	1,234.9	470.5	2,421.9	574.9	794.8	−390.6	−305.2	−90.6
1974	4,078.9	4,481.5	2,146.8	1,395.2	544.2	2,334.7	364.7	877.4	−402.6	−316.2	−93.9
1975	4,626.6	5,109.0	2,391.1	1,572.1	595.7	2,717.9	487.9	961.5	−482.4	−392.9	−99.0
1976	5,314.8	5,857.4	2,683.8	1,790.4	652.8	3,173.6	690.3	1,072.8	−542.6	−452.9	−100.8
1977	5,782.6	6,366.8	3,088.3	2,094.7	725.5	3,278.5	591.9	1,204.0	−584.2	−507.7	−88.1
1978	6,620.7	7,236.3	3,601.3	2,478.2	815.2	3,635.0	600.2	1,413.0	−615.6	−545.3	−83.0
1979	7,749.4	8,379.3	4,178.7	2,897.2	924.4	4,200.6	729.4	1,656.1	−629.9	−566.5	−77.3
1980	8,975.6	9,666.1	4,703.0	3,289.4	1,014.3	4,963.1	979.5	1,892.0	−690.5	−626.7	−79.2
1981	9,566.4	10,341.7	5,096.5	3,572.6	1,086.2	5,245.2	886.5	2,057.8	−775.3	−702.8	−89.3
1982	10,134.3	11,054.9	5,358.5	3,758.4	1,133.7	5,696.4	962.0	2,060.4	−920.6	−848.3	−90.9
1983	10,854.8	11,955.8	5,672.8	3,983.9	1,193.8	6,283.0	1,115.5	2,109.7	−1,101.0	−1,041.7	−79.3
1984	11,409.6	12,683.2	6,160.0	4,349.4	1,281.5	6,523.2	1,057.1	2,095.3	−1,273.6	−1,223.9	−72.6
1985	12,466.7	13,938.4	6,603.2	4,650.1	1,391.1	7,335.2	1,402.7	2,134.4	−1,471.7	−1,429.8	−64.6
1986	13,471.6	15,178.3	7,100.4	4,978.2	1,527.5	8,077.9	1,716.9	2,199.3	−1,706.7	−1,663.7	−66.7
1987	14,274.0	16,176.7	7,656.1	5,368.9	1,659.5	8,520.6	1,735.5	2,306.0	−1,902.7	−1,845.4	−83.1
1988	15,182.7	17,274.3	8,102.8	5,619.6	1,808.4	9,171.5	1,883.8	2,423.3	−2,091.6	−2,037.8	−83.2
1989	16,712.8	19,014.2	8,708.6	6,058.5	1,929.6	10,305.6	2,263.1	2,582.4	−2,301.4	−2,212.9	−121.7
1990	16,529.9	19,058.8	8,774.7	6,015.9	2,047.1	10,284.1	2,168.6	2,529.1	−2,528.9	−2,405.9	−160.1
1991	18,089.9	20,900.4	9,286.0	6,484.0	2,138.9	11,614.4	3,060.6	2,444.4	−2,810.5	−2,646.4	−204.6
1992	18,688.5	21,878.8	9,557.1	6,709.3	2,222.2	12,321.7	3,543.9	2,411.5	−3,190.3	−2,998.0	−239.4
1993	19,493.4	23,052.5	9,970.1	6,997.1	2,336.3	13,082.4	4,060.2	2,427.7	−3,559.1	−3,283.1	−330.9

[1] Sum of private net worth and government net financial assets.
[2] Referred to as household net worth in the *Balance Sheets.*
[3] Held by households and nonprofit organizations.
[4] Also includes nonprofit organizations' real estate and durable equipment.
[5] Also includes credit market instruments, life insurance and pension reserves, security credit, and miscellaneous assets, and is net of liabilities.
[6] Includes households and nonprofit organizations' direct (or through mutual funds) holdings of corporate equity. Equity held through pension and life insurance reserves is not included.
[7] Also includes government-sponsored enterprises and the Federal Reserve. Some tangible wealth is included for these agencies.

Note.—Data are from *Balance Sheets for the U.S. Economy, 1945–93,* September 1994, with updates for recent years from *Flow of Funds Accounts, Flows and Outstandings,* December 1994.
Data are measured at market value where available. For example, corporate equity and land are measured at market value, but bonds are measured at par value.

Source: Board of Governors of the Federal Reserve System.

TABLE B–115.—*National wealth in 1987 dollars, 1946–93*

[Billions of 1987 dollars]

End of year	Total net worth [1]	Private net worth [2]							Government net financial assets		
		Total	Tangible wealth [3]			Financial wealth			Total [7]	Federal	State and local
			Total [4]	Owner-occupied real estate	Consumer durables	Total [5]	Corporate equity [6]	Non-corporate equity			
1946	3,209.6	4,534.7	1,318.0	895.8	318.6	3,216.8	614.4	1,203.6	−1,325.1	−1,326.9	−3.6
1947	3,211.3	4,272.8	1,336.9	900.0	333.8	2,935.9	513.8	1,214.9	−1,061.5	−1,063.6	−2.6
1948	3,347.0	4,329.2	1,458.9	975.7	377.7	2,870.3	490.1	1,217.8	−982.2	−984.2	−3.5
1949	3,560.8	4,576.9	1,625.6	1,078.9	435.2	2,951.3	543.2	1,230.7	−1,016.1	−1,017.1	−4.5
1950	3,879.6	4,817.5	1,768.2	1,136.0	512.8	3,049.3	625.6	1,310.4	−937.9	−924.6	−18.5
1951	4,316.4	5,224.4	1,967.6	1,252.6	584.0	3,256.8	725.8	1,391.1	−908.0	−890.6	−23.5
1952	4,362.6	5,332.4	2,078.5	1,331.5	611.9	3,253.9	714.2	1,363.9	−969.9	−927.9	−47.9
1953	4,456.4	5,478.2	2,210.5	1,420.9	650.0	3,267.7	683.2	1,367.7	−1,021.8	−964.1	−63.6
1954	4,809.4	5,853.6	2,296.4	1,497.3	656.7	3,557.1	978.1	1,349.6	−1,044.2	−971.0	−79.9
1955	5,088.0	6,095.3	2,394.4	1,565.7	675.1	3,700.9	1,152.4	1,331.8	−1,007.3	−923.2	−90.6
1956	5,313.7	6,275.9	2,502.9	1,626.1	713.3	3,773.0	1,197.5	1,345.6	−962.2	−868.9	−100.0
1957	5,281.7	6,231.7	2,578.5	1,692.3	716.3	3,653.3	1,033.7	1,354.9	−950.0	−840.2	−116.7
1958	5,724.1	6,707.9	2,624.9	1,734.4	719.4	4,083.0	1,415.8	1,362.5	−983.8	−855.7	−135.2
1959	5,867.2	6,856.8	2,699.2	1,793.1	729.7	4,157.5	1,488.8	1,336.7	−989.6	−847.1	−149.0
1960	5,989.3	6,974.7	2,796.9	1,870.5	742.1	4,177.8	1,461.3	1,330.7	−985.4	−831.4	−160.5
1961	6,458.6	7,462.0	2,861.7	1,926.7	739.8	4,600.4	1,835.3	1,328.2	−1,003.4	−838.7	−171.8
1962	6,286.0	7,299.3	2,931.7	1,977.5	746.5	4,367.5	1,562.0	1,329.9	−1,013.3	−840.6	−180.1
1963	6,698.2	7,713.8	3,029.1	2,033.5	773.8	4,684.7	1,809.1	1,337.5	−1,015.6	−836.0	−187.3
1964	7,107.5	8,127.8	3,113.5	2,080.4	796.1	5,014.2	2,037.4	1,356.2	−1,020.3	−832.0	−194.0
1965	7,510.0	8,516.6	3,180.6	2,109.3	817.0	5,336.0	2,250.9	1,394.1	−1,006.6	−815.6	−197.2
1966	7,426.7	8,420.0	3,306.0	2,173.0	861.7	5,114.0	1,940.7	1,425.3	−993.3	−796.7	−203.0
1967	8,075.8	9,078.4	3,417.4	2,220.0	913.5	5,661.0	2,339.0	1,441.6	−1,002.6	−796.8	−212.9
1968	8,716.6	9,709.2	3,625.8	2,358.0	963.8	6,083.4	2,652.8	1,492.3	−992.6	−783.7	−216.3
1969	8,374.9	9,321.6	3,739.9	2,410.2	1,002.0	5,581.6	1,833.5	1,514.9	−946.6	−726.5	−228.0
1970	8,320.5	9,275.9	3,778.1	2,402.8	1,031.6	5,497.8	1,697.8	1,509.1	−955.4	−722.2	−241.8
1971	8,725.5	9,712.1	3,889.7	2,488.7	1,036.1	5,822.4	1,839.5	1,564.5	−986.6	−742.9	−253.2
1972	9,391.5	10,368.9	4,179.7	2,720.6	1,064.4	6,189.2	1,940.4	1,683.7	−977.4	−749.1	−238.3
1973	9,114.2	10,022.6	4,390.2	2,871.9	1,094.2	5,632.3	1,337.0	1,848.4	−908.4	−709.8	−210.7
1974	8,623.5	9,474.6	4,538.7	2,949.7	1,150.5	4,935.9	771.0	1,855.0	−851.2	−668.5	−198.5
1975	9,089.6	10,037.3	4,697.6	3,088.6	1,170.3	5,339.7	958.5	1,889.0	−947.7	−771.9	−194.5
1976	9,842.2	10,847.0	4,970.0	3,315.6	1,208.9	5,877.0	1,278.3	1,986.7	−1,004.8	−838.7	−186.7
1977	10,004.5	11,015.2	5,343.1	3,624.0	1,255.2	5,672.1	1,024.0	2,083.0	−1,010.7	−878.4	−152.4
1978	10,525.8	11,504.5	5,725.4	3,939.9	1,296.0	5,779.0	954.2	2,246.4	−978.7	−866.9	−132.0
1979	11,329.5	12,250.4	6,109.2	4,235.7	1,351.5	6,141.2	1,066.4	2,421.2	−920.9	−828.2	−113.0
1980	11,888.2	12,802.8	6,229.1	4,356.8	1,343.4	6,573.6	1,297.4	2,506.0	−914.6	−830.1	−104.9
1981	11,680.6	12,627.2	6,222.8	4,362.1	1,326.3	6,404.4	1,082.4	2,512.6	−946.6	−858.1	−109.0
1982	11,853.0	12,929.7	6,267.3	4,395.8	1,326.0	6,662.5	1,125.1	2,409.8	−1,076.7	−992.2	−106.3
1983	12,182.7	13,418.4	6,366.8	4,471.3	1,339.8	7,051.6	1,252.0	2,367.8	−1,235.7	−1,169.1	−89.0
1984	12,294.8	13,667.2	6,637.9	4,686.9	1,380.9	7,029.3	1,139.1	2,257.9	−1,372.4	−1,318.9	−78.2
1985	13,013.3	14,549.5	6,892.7	4,854.0	1,452.1	7,656.8	1,464.2	2,228.0	−1,536.2	−1,492.5	−67.4
1986	13,690.7	15,425.1	7,215.9	5,059.1	1,552.3	8,209.2	1,744.8	2,235.1	−1,734.5	−1,690.8	−67.8
1987	14,035.4	15,906.3	7,528.1	5,279.2	1,631.8	8,378.2	1,706.5	2,267.5	−1,870.9	−1,814.6	−81.7
1988	14,296.3	16,265.8	7,629.8	5,291.5	1,702.8	8,636.1	1,773.8	2,281.8	−1,969.5	−1,918.8	−78.3
1989	15,083.8	17,160.8	7,859.7	5,468.0	1,741.5	9,301.1	2,042.5	2,330.7	−2,077.1	−1,997.2	−109.8
1990	14,286.9	16,472.6	7,584.0	5,199.6	1,769.3	8,888.6	1,874.3	2,185.9	−2,185.7	−2,079.4	−138.4
1991	15,150.7	17,504.5	7,777.2	5,430.5	1,791.4	9,727.3	2,563.3	2,047.2	−2,353.9	−2,216.4	−171.4
1992	15,268.4	17,874.8	7,808.1	5,481.5	1,815.5	10,066.7	2,895.3	1,970.2	−2,606.5	−2,449.3	−195.6
1993	15,644.8	18,501.2	8,001.7	5,615.7	1,875.0	10,499.5	3,258.6	1,948.4	−2,856.4	−2,634.9	−265.6

[1] Sum of private net worth and government net financial assets.
[2] Referred to as household net worth in the *Balance Sheets.*
[3] Held by households and nonprofit organizations.
[4] Also includes nonprofit organizations' real estate and durable equipment.
[5] Also includes credit market instruments, life insurance and pension reserves, security credit, and miscellaneous assets, and is net of liabilities.
[6] Includes households and nonprofit organizations' direct (or through mutual funds) holdings of corporate equity. Equity held through pension and life insurance reserves is not included.
[7] Also includes government-sponsored enterprises and the Federal Reserve. Some tangible wealth is included for these agencies.

Note.—See Note, Table B–114.
Deflated by the GDP implicit price deflator. (The deflator was averaged for fourth quarter of year shown and first quarter of following year.)

Sources: Board of Governors of the Federal Reserve System and Department of Commerce, Bureau of Economic Analysis.

TABLE B-116.—*Historical series on gross domestic product and selected other NIPA series, 1929-59*

Year	GDP (current dollars)	Constant (1987) dollars					GDP implicit price deflator (1987=100)	Percent change from preceding period			Disposable personal income (1987 dollars)		Saving as percent of disposable personal income [1]	Population (thousands) [2]
		GDP	Personal consumption expenditures	Gross private domestic investment	Net exports of goods and services	Government purchases		GDP in current dollars	GDP in 1987 dollars	GDP implicit price deflator	Total (billions of dollars)	Per capita (dollars)		
1929	103.1	821.8	554.5	152.8	1.9	112.6	12.5				585.8	4,807	3.0	121,878
1930	90.4	748.9	520.0	107.2	−.3	122.0	12.1	−12.4	−8.9	−3.2	542.2	4,402	2.5	123,188
1931	75.8	691.3	501.0	67.2	−2.3	125.5	11.0	−16.2	−7.7	−9.1	519.7	4,186	2.1	124,149
1932	58.0	599.7	456.6	25.0	−2.4	120.5	9.7	−23.5	−13.3	−11.8	449.8	3,600	−3.1	124,949
1933	55.6	587.1	447.4	26.6	−3.0	116.1	9.5	−4.1	−2.1	−2.1	437.0	3,477	−3.9	125,690
1934	65.1	632.6	461.1	41.1	−1.0	131.4	10.3	17.1	7.7	8.4	462.0	3,652	−1.1	126,485
1935	72.3	681.3	487.6	65.2	−7.2	135.7	10.6	11.1	7.7	2.9	505.2	3,967	2.3	127,362
1936	82.7	777.9	534.4	89.9	−5.1	158.6	10.6	14.4	14.2	.0	565.9	4,415	4.4	128,181
1937	90.8	811.4	554.6	106.4	−1.9	152.2	11.2	9.8	4.3	5.7	585.5	4,540	4.0	128,961
1938	84.9	778.9	542.2	69.9	4.2	162.5	10.9	−6.5	−4.0	−2.7	547.6	4,213	−.3	129,969
1939	90.8	840.7	568.7	93.4	4.6	174.0	10.8	7.0	7.9	−.9	590.3	4,505	2.4	131,028
1940	100.0	906.0	595.2	121.8	8.2	180.7	11.0	10.2	7.8	1.9	627.2	4,747	3.8	132,122
1941	125.0	1,070.6	629.3	149.4	2.8	289.1	11.7	25.0	18.2	6.4	713.9	5,352	10.7	133,402
1942	158.5	1,284.9	628.7	81.4	−11.1	586.0	12.3	26.8	20.0	5.1	824.7	6,115	23.1	134,860
1943	192.4	1,540.5	647.3	53.5	−28.1	867.7	12.5	21.3	19.9	1.6	863.8	6,317	24.5	136,739
1944	211.0	1,670.0	671.2	59.8	−29.0	968.0	12.6	9.7	8.4	.8	901.8	6,516	25.0	138,397
1945	213.1	1,602.6	714.6	82.6	−23.9	829.4	13.3	1.0	−4.0	5.6	890.9	6,367	19.2	139,928
1946	211.9	1,272.1	779.1	195.5	26.5	271.0	16.7	−.6	−20.6	25.6	860.0	6,083	8.5	141,389
1947	234.3	1,252.8	793.3	198.8	41.9	218.8	18.7	10.6	−1.5	12.0	826.1	5,732	3.0	144,126
1948	260.3	1,300.0	813.0	229.8	16.6	240.6	20.0	11.1	3.8	7.0	872.9	5,953	5.8	146,631
1949	259.3	1,305.5	831.4	187.4	17.3	269.3	19.9	−.4	.4	−.5	874.5	5,862	3.7	149,188
1950	287.0	1,418.5	874.3	256.4	3.2	284.5	20.2	10.7	8.7	1.5	942.5	6,214	5.9	151,684
1951	331.6	1,558.4	894.7	255.6	11.1	397.0	21.3	15.5	9.9	5.4	978.2	6,340	7.3	154,287
1952	349.7	1,624.9	923.4	231.6	2.3	467.6	21.5	5.4	4.3	.9	1,009.7	6,433	7.2	156,954
1953	370.0	1,685.5	962.5	240.3	−7.1	489.8	22.0	5.8	3.7	2.3	1,053.5	6,603	7.0	159,565
1954	370.9	1,673.8	987.3	234.1	−2.3	454.7	22.2	.2	−.7	.9	1,071.5	6,598	6.2	162,391
1955	404.3	1,768.3	1,047.0	284.8	−5.2	441.7	22.9	9.0	5.6	3.2	1,130.8	6,842	5.7	165,275
1956	426.2	1,803.6	1,078.7	282.2	−1.2	444.0	23.6	5.4	2.0	3.1	1,185.2	7,046	7.1	168,221
1957	448.6	1,838.2	1,104.4	266.9	1.6	465.3	24.4	5.2	1.9	3.4	1,214.6	7,091	7.2	171,274
1958	454.7	1,829.1	1,122.2	245.7	−14.9	476.0	24.9	1.4	−.5	2.0	1,236.0	7,098	7.4	174,141
1959	494.2	1,928.8	1,178.9	296.4	−21.8	475.3	25.6	8.7	5.5	2.8	1,284.9	7,256	6.3	177,073

[1] Percents based on data in millions of dollars, current prices.
[2] Population of the United States including Armed Forces overseas; does not include data for Alaska and Hawaii.

Note.—Data for 1959 are shown to provide continuity with data for later years as shown in Tables B-1 through B-29.

Source: Department of Commerce, Bureau of Economic Analysis.

TABLE B–117.—*Selected per capita product and income series in current and 1987 dollars, 1959–94*

[Quarterly data at seasonally adjusted annual rates, except as noted]

Year or quarter	Current dollars							Constant (1987) dollars						Popula-tion (thou-sands) [1]
	Gross domes-tic prod-uct	Person-al income	Dispos-able person-al income	Personal consumption expenditures				Gross domes-tic prod-uct	Dispos-able person-al income	Personal consumption expenditures				
				Total	Dura-ble goods	Non-durable goods	Serv-ices			Total	Dura-ble goods	Non-durable goods	Serv-ices	
1959	2,791	2,209	1,958	1,796	242	838	716	10,892	7,256	6,658	646	2,928	3,083	177,073
1960	2,840	2,264	1,994	1,839	240	847	752	10,903	7,264	6,698	638	2,915	3,145	180,760
1961	2,894	2,321	2,048	1,869	228	857	784	11,014	7,382	6,740	595	2,926	3,218	183,742
1962	3,063	2,430	2,137	1,953	252	878	823	11,405	7,583	6,931	644	2,964	3,323	186,590
1963	3,186	2,516	2,210	2,030	273	895	861	11,704	7,718	7,089	688	2,977	3,423	189,300
1964	3,376	2,661	2,369	2,149	296	936	917	12,195	8,140	7,384	733	3,065	3,586	191,927
1965	3,616	2,845	2,527	2,287	327	987	974	12,712	8,508	7,703	803	3,173	3,726	194,347
1966	3,915	3,061	2,699	2,450	348	1,060	1,041	13,307	8,822	8,005	844	3,294	3,867	196,599
1967	4,097	3,253	2,861	2,562	355	1,091	1,116	13,510	9,114	8,163	841	3,316	4,006	198,752
1968	4,430	3,536	3,077	2,785	404	1,171	1,211	13,932	9,399	8,506	919	3,417	4,169	200,745
1969	4,733	3,816	3,274	2,978	425	1,244	1,308	14,171	9,606	8,737	941	3,469	4,327	202,736
1970	4,928	4,052	3,521	3,152	416	1,318	1,418	14,013	9,875	8,842	896	3,497	4,449	205,089
1971	5,283	4,302	3,779	3,372	468	1,364	1,540	14,232	10,111	9,022	970	3,494	4,558	207,692
1972	5,750	4,671	4,042	3,658	528	1,454	1,676	14,801	10,414	9,425	1,073	3,601	4,751	209,924
1973	6,368	5,184	4,521	4,002	585	1,602	1,814	15,422	11,013	9,752	1,164	3,670	4,917	211,939
1974	6,819	5,637	4,893	4,337	575	1,780	1,982	15,185	10,832	9,602	1,062	3,552	4,988	213,898
1975	7,343	6,053	5,329	4,745	622	1,926	2,197	14,917	10,906	9,711	1,050	3,552	5,110	215,981
1976	8,109	6,632	5,796	5,241	734	2,072	2,436	15,502	11,192	10,121	1,176	3,674	5,271	218,086
1977	8,961	7,269	6,316	5,772	829	2,226	2,717	16,039	11,406	10,425	1,271	3,722	5,433	220,289
1978	10,029	8,121	7,042	6,384	909	2,432	3,043	16,635	11,851	10,744	1,316	3,795	5,633	222,629
1979	11,055	9,032	7,787	7,035	952	2,725	3,359	16,867	12,039	10,876	1,284	3,833	5,760	225,106
1980	11,892	9,948	8,576	7,677	933	2,999	3,745	16,584	12,005	10,746	1,154	3,779	5,814	227,715
1981	13,177	11,021	9,455	8,375	994	3,236	4,146	16,710	12,156	10,770	1,150	3,774	5,845	229,989
1982	13,564	11,589	9,989	8,868	1,018	3,326	4,523	16,194	12,146	10,782	1,131	3,756	5,895	232,201
1983	14,531	12,216	10,642	9,634	1,173	3,490	4,971	16,672	12,349	11,179	1,270	3,842	6,066	234,326
1984	15,978	13,345	11,673	10,408	1,345	3,693	5,370	17,549	13,029	11,617	1,432	3,953	6,231	236,393
1985	16,933	14,170	12,339	11,184	1,480	3,855	5,849	17,944	13,258	12,015	1,552	4,019	6,444	238,510
1986	17,735	14,917	13,010	11,843	1,619	3,956	6,269	18,299	13,552	12,336	1,670	4,118	6,548	240,691
1987	18,694	15,655	13,545	12,568	1,662	4,163	6,742	18,694	13,545	12,568	1,662	4,163	6,742	242,860
1988	19,994	16,630	14,477	13,448	1,783	4,381	7,284	19,252	13,890	12,903	1,749	4,223	6,930	245,093
1989	21,224	17,706	15,307	14,241	1,857	4,647	7,737	19,556	14,005	13,029	1,781	4,251	6,997	247,397
1990	22,189	18,699	16,205	15,048	1,873	4,918	8,257	19,593	14,101	13,093	1,773	4,244	7,077	249,951
1991	22,656	19,234	16,766	15,444	1,807	4,978	8,659	19,263	14,003	12,899	1,683	4,146	7,069	252,688
1992	23,564	20,175	17,636	16,192	1,928	5,071	9,193	19,490	14,279	13,110	1,772	4,140	7,199	255,484
1993	24,559	20,810	18,153	16,951	2,083	5,185	9,683	19,879	14,341	13,391	1,897	4,176	7,318	258,290
1994 ᴾ	25,813	21,847	19,002	17,728	2,264	5,340	10,124	20,469	14,696	13,711	2,036	4,250	7,425	260,991

[1] Population of the United States including Armed Forces overseas; includes Alaska and Hawaii beginning 1960. Annual data are averages of quarterly data. Quarterly data are averages for the period.

Source: Department of Commerce (Bureau of Economic Analysis and Bureau of the Census).